The Complete Lyrics of

OSCAR HAMMERSTEIN II

ALFRED A. KNOPF   NEW YORK   2008

The Complete Lyrics of

OSCAR HAMMERSTEIN II

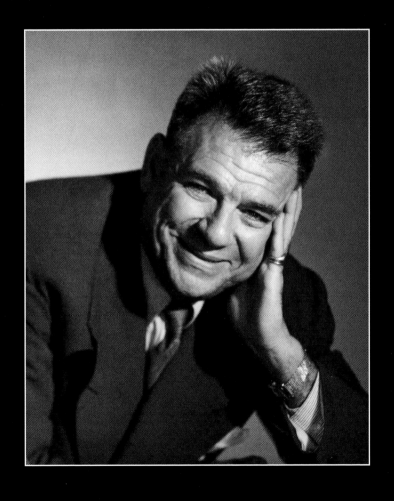

Edited by

AMY ASCH

For Rhoda and Roger Asch,
who raised me to love musicals

And for Robert Kimball,
who taught me how to research them

THIS IS A BORZOI BOOK PUBLISHED BY ALFRED A. KNOPF

Copyright © 2008 by Amy Asch and Hammerstein Properties LLC
Introduction copyright © 2008 by Ted Chapin
Foreword ("Random Reflections") © 2008 by Alice Hammerstein Mathias

To learn more about Oscar Hammerstein II please visit the official Web site of the Rodgers & Hammerstein Organization at
www.rnh.com

Library of Congress Cataloging-in-Publication Data
Hammerstein, Oscar, 1895–1960.
[Lyrics]
The complete lyrics of Oscar Hammerstein II / edited by Amy Asch.
p.   cm.
Includes index.
ISBN 978-0-375-41358-2
1. Musicals—Excerpts—Librettos.   2. Songs—Texts.   I. Asch, Amy.   II. Title.
ML49.H12H28 2008
782.14026'8—dc22
2008009549
Manufactured in China
FIRST EDITION

Contents

RANDOM REFLECTIONS

by Alice Hammerstein Mathias

Although many of these lyrics are written with music almost universally known, and many of us are proud to sing the songs with every lyric intact, how many of us are really aware of what some of the lines actually express besides fitting neatly with the music? I was once going on a train somewhere when it was raining. We were passing by a wheat field, and I thought of the line "the wavin' wheat can sure smell sweet when the wind comes right behind the rain," and it took me a few seconds to remember it was in the title song of *Oklahoma!* It seemed so real in this nowhere place.

And how many people have had the feeling of being "starry-eyed and vaguely discontented" or "gay, in a melancholy way" without remembering it came from "It Might as Well Be Spring"?

We remember "you are the promised kiss of springtime" from "All the Things You Are," but let's go a little further on to experience the idea that also "you are the breathless hush of evening that trembles on the brink of a lovely song." We may know those words, but do we really think about the idea of your kiss waiting so precariously for the lonely winter to pass? Will it still be waiting or would it have fallen off the "lovely song" by springtime?

After my father's salad days, mostly at college and shortly after, rhyming "love" and "above," "moon" and "June," as well as little chorus ditties that explain why "I'm the boy (girl) for you," he started writing lyrics and working with material that had more of a purpose, going into characterizations and giving them some depth of feeling. Besides doing research on the themes of the librettos he was working with, he started to take walks to get to know his characters and how they were to be portrayed and, what was probably the most important, to learn the colloquialisms of speech they would use in their period and locale. We don't know if they talked together, because we were not invited to accompany him.

Although he was not a social activist, my father was very aware of the conflict of cultures in the world. He exposed those conflicts in several of his shows (with the collaborative input of his composers). In *The King and I*, for instance, in *Flower Drum Song*, in *South Pacific*, the cultural divisions, many of which have to do with race, are represented to us not necessarily as a call to action, but certainly as a strong recognition of their existence. Even in *Oklahoma!* there are some passing remarks between the farmer and the cowman. As he says in *Pipe Dream*, "It takes all kinds of people to make up a world."

Some are offended by *Show Boat*, the musical produced with Jerome Kern in 1927. White people looked down on "colored people," using them for back-breaking work. So the show is often called *racist*. But I believe it to be the first protest show ever presented on the musical stage. The ever-present theme in "Ol' Man River" is in itself a protest by the "colored people" who want to leave the Mississippi and get away from the "white man boss." ("Don' look up an' don' look down. You don' dast make de white boss frown.") Yet they realize the futility of wishing for a better life. Life, like the river ("What does he care if de world's got troubles? What does he care if de land ain't free?") keeps rolling along.

Is this not a protest? A quiet one, perhaps, but one that we hope makes us think. And my father was more interested in the exposure of conflict than the preaching of it. As Carrie Pipperidge explains about her fiancé, in *Carousel*, "He don't say much, but what he says is awful pithy."

In his lyrics one finds recurrent themes of love that are expressed in unusual ways, i.e., the tongue-tied lover in "I've Told Ev'ry Little Star," "The Song Is You," and in the verse to "All the Things You Are." Then there are the "if" songs, "If I Loved You," "People Will Say We're in Love," "Make Believe." And there's the lover who comes at night only to disappear with the morning sun, as in "In the Heart of the Dark," and "All Through the Day."

Still a different expression of love is in "The Last Time I Saw Paris," originally written as a poem to express his emotion about the fall of Paris. "No matter how they change her, I'll remember her that way."

There is very young love ("Sixteen Going on Seventeen") and settled love ("An Ordinary Couple").

But one of the most beautiful expressions was that of old love, also first written as a poem, called "The Sweetest Sight That I Have Seen." Describing the picture

> I have seen a line of snow-white birds
> Drawn across an evening sky,

he will then give us more images of sensual beauty as well as those of poetic sound:

> I have heard church bells faintly echoing
> Over a distant hill.

But at the end he tells us:

> Here's the sweetest sight that I have seen—
> One old couple walking hand in hand.

Jerome Kern liked it so much that he set it to music. My father's wife Dorothy liked it so much that she made a sampler of it and framed it. I like it so much because it shows my father was a true poet who could write about everyday things and deeply though simply express them.

Yet he also had a way of transforming everyday phrases into playful ones. I remember doing a little research for him on *Carousel* at his request. Thus, I reported to him the sequence of making clams in New England. This was an intricate procedure, which was pronounced by New Englanders as "manna from heaven." He dutifully followed the process with his inimitable lyrics for "A Real Nice Clambake," translating the idea of manna from heaven to "fitten fer an angels', fitten fer an angels', fitten fer an angels' choir."

His positivity often resulted in using the word "dream" in his lyrics. In fact, he found it in so many songs that he decided he would avoid the word for his next show, which was *South Pacific*. But it appeared there in more songs than in any other show he had written lyrics for!

The song, "A Puzzlement," often infects the audience with humor regarding the dilemma of a king. But almost every verse is relevant to human nature.

There are times I almost think
I am not sure of what I absolutely know.
. . . .
Or am I right when I believe I may be wrong?

And particularly in today's world:

And it puzzle me to learn
That though a man may be in doubt of what he know,
Very quickly will he fight,
He'll fight to prove that what he does not know is so!

Life *is* a puzzlement, and though his day in the hills has come to an end, this cockeyed optimist, with his dreams of a hundred million miracles, has blessed his homeland forever.

Hammerstein at Highland Farm in 1944

Dorothy and Oscar Hammerstein in the 1950s

Rodgers and Hammerstein in front of the St. James Theatre in 1951

Introduction

If there is one towering figure in the history of the American musical theater, that person is Oscar Hammerstein II. For more than forty years he was a fully committed participant as vaudeville entertainments became musical comedies, operettas became musical plays, and everything merged into the art form known as the musical. He was a lyricist, librettist, director, dramatist, poet—and architect—of a genre that remains as popular today as it ever has been.

This book will show you only part of his talent. Writing lyrics was one of his many skills, and lyrics, by their very nature, are meant to be heard along with music. Reading them alone makes them something different. But as this Complete Lyrics series has illustrated, great lyrics can be appreciated on their own for the poetry they contain. They give us a wonderful window into the creative collaboration that musicals demand. However, it is important to consider the music that was composed to go with these words. With the familiar songs, we sing the music to ourselves. But with the unfamiliar ones, as we read, we can only guess the melody, rhythm, harmonies, tempo, and tonality of the accompaniment. Sometimes these lyrics came before the music; sometimes the music came first. And sometimes, when a collaboration was working at full tilt, lyrics and music were created at virtually the same time.

It is a daunting task under any circumstance to read through eight hundred lyrics and assess the career they represent. In the early 1920s, when Hammerstein was starting out, he worked almost exclusively with his mentor, the older Otto Harbach. They always took co-credit. Alas, they left no paper trail to explain who did what. As a result, it is almost impossible to ascertain which of these early lyrics Hammerstein actually wrote, fixed, edited, or had anything at all to do with. In the mid 1920s, he began to work solo and take his proper credit. By 1927 and *Show Boat*, evidence of an extraordinary talent began to emerge. During the next decade, his work continued to tend toward operetta, but it was a genre that was losing popular appeal. From that period, however, came some of his most beautiful lyrics in collaborations with Jerome Kern. Then, in the early 1940s, he teamed up with Richard Rodgers, in whom he found a fellow dramatist who matched his sense of theater perfectly.

Oscar Hammerstein II came from a family of theater people. Theater was in his blood: his grandfather and namesake built theaters and loved opera. Oscar I was a complicated man, whose entrepreneurial spirit had him inventing patents for the manufacture of cigars, selling those patents, and then putting that money toward buildings—first, apartment buildings and, later, theaters. He built ten theaters in New York City, of which two are still standing today: the New Victory on Forty-second Street

(originally the Republic Theatre) and the Hammerstein Ballroom on Thirty-fourth Street (originally the Manhattan Opera House, where he competed with the Metropolitan Opera—with a certain degree of success). Between Oscar I and II, there was a generation of theater managers and vaudeville presenters, including sons Arthur, who built a theater dedicated to his father (the Hammerstein, now the Ed Sullivan Theater), and Willie, who fathered the father of the musical.

Whereas Oscar I loved the structures in which theater took place, Oscar II was attracted to what happened onstage. Originally in pursuit of a law degree, he felt a kindred spirit with words. He began to work with words, both as a lyricist and as a playwright. His early work was influenced by what was au courant. Before long, he veered toward operettas. He told a story on himself about going to England to oversee the Drury Lane production of one of his operettas, *The Desert Song*, and hearing the opening male chorus "Feasting Song" enunciated with English precision. The traditional operetta opening choruses were ice-breakers, "to bellow while latecomers were seated," as biographer Hugh Fordin explained. Hammerstein was shocked to hear words that he had not paid much attention to, coming across the footlights with utmost clarity. He realized then the importance of each and every word.

The dramatist in Hammerstein loved theatrical storytelling. And unlike all the other lyricists who have been chronicled in this series—Cole Porter, Lorenz Hart, Ira Gershwin, Irving Berlin, and Frank Loesser—he wrote the librettos to most of the musicals for which he contributed the lyrics. Therefore, the scenes in which his lyrics are placed come from the same creative mind. But as Richard Rodgers stated in his preface to Hammerstein's 1949 collection of his work, titled *Lyrics*, "It should be immensely rewarding to examine [his lyrics] out of context if only to discover their indispensability to the context itself."

Part of the fun of this series is to chart the artistic development of the lyricist being chronicled. Another fascinating aspect is to watch collaboration at work. When we see early drafts of lyrics, and cut stanzas, and then see the finished product, all we can do is marvel. Although Hammerstein had a voice in these changes, chances are his wasn't the only voice. A recent example: As I write this, there is a new production of Rodgers & Hammerstein's *South Pacific* on Broadway. The artists who mounted the production examined all aspects of the original production with care, and asked many questions of us at the office. That, in turn, caused us to open every file drawer, look in every envelope, and generally comb through the material that we assumed simply documented the final product from 1949. But no—we found things like the original verse for "This Nearly Was Mine" and something that had been considered lost for over sixty years: the original song for Lt. Cable, titled "My Friend." Both of these new discoveries were cut, and clearly put aside. Are they bad? No, they are skillful. Is *South Pacific* better for not having them in the show? Absolutely. In the end, we must give Hammerstein the benefit of the doubt by considering, as definitive, the work that opened on Broadway. But the discarded material gives us another view of the creative process.

It is fun to find images and ideas that appear in the early years and reappear later on. From that we conclude that Hammerstein must have believed in and felt a connection to music, birds, love, nature, mountains, and, of course, dreams. You can chart those throughout this book, and you might take note of the entirely appropriate fact that the final word on the final curtain of his final show is "dream," when the Mother Abbess in *The Sound of Music* concludes a reprise of "Climb Ev'ry Mountain" as the von Trapp family walks off into a new world.

It is also important to remember that as a writer for the theater, Hammerstein always wrote for specific characters. Each one demanded a particular and appropriate vocabulary, and a particular sense of wisdom, sophistication, and humor. Hammerstein spoke of the spare and simple words that he wrote for the character of Joe in *Show Boat*, whose signature song, "Ol' Man River," has practically no rhymes. Then there is the country-girl humor of Carrie Pipperidge in *Carousel*, who is naturally capable of never taking herself too seriously as she describes "Mr. Snow," the man she has fallen in love with. Some characters sing with simple poetry—*Sweet Adeline*'s title character asks "Why was I born?" for example, while two in *The Sound of Music* share "favorite things" that make them feel good.

Hammerstein wrote with a variety of collaborators. He loved Jerome Kern but also worked in his early years with, among others, Sigmund Romberg, George Gershwin, Vincent Youmans, Richard Whiting, Herbert Stothart, and Arthur Schwartz. But as I read through these lyrics, something became clear to me: the teaming up of Oscar Hammerstein II and Richard Rodgers was not inevitable. For Rodgers, riding high on the wave of success with the Rodgers & Hart shows, to reach out to Oscar Hammerstein, whose output in the 1930s was inconsistent, looks more risky than it must have seemed after *Oklahoma!* opened. The two men, experienced in the field, worked in different styles. Joining forces involved its own risks— what if together they ended up being artistic oil and water? Luckily, in each other they found creative soulmates, collaborators who believed in the same theater and understood how together they could take it where it needed to go. The fact that during their sixteen years together they created five of the acknowledged classics of the American musical repertoire—*Oklahoma!*, *Carousel*, *South Pacific*, *The King and I*, and *The Sound of Music*—is pretty astonishing.

Robert Gottlieb has wanted to include Oscar Hammerstein II in this series from the very beginning. A fortuitous meeting in our offices got this project on track, and with it the blessing of Bill Hammerstein and his sister Alice Hammerstein Mathias. It was Gottlieb who assigned Amy Asch the task of assembling and editing this volume. Having assisted Robert Kimball on earlier volumes, she was ready, he felt, to take on the Herculean task of gathering and editing the lyrics for this book. She went digging in places few had ever dug before, and maintained a sense of equilibrium as she entered the world of inconsistent scripts (typed or published), inconsistent music (sheet music and vocal scores, musical manuscripts), and inconsistent lyrics (typed or handwritten on yellow pads). She found different drafts, different tenses, different characters, and different words for many songs. You might think the better known the song, the easier it would be to capture the lyrics in the form that Hammerstein was finally satisfied with. Not so. It is often the little words, even one letter of a little word, that makes the task harder. As an example, take the title song of *The Sound of Music*. On the original cast album, the lyric is sung "to laugh like a brook when it trips and falls over stones *in* its way," while the movie soundtrack has: "stones *on* its way." Which is correct? One letter, changing an "in" to an "on," may seem insignificant, and may even just be a typo. Both are valid, but the meaning is different—the stones are either in the way of the brook, or something the brook cascades over. For this one, we were in luck, since one early draft script has, in Hammerstein's own hand, a rewrite of four lines of the song stating, clearly, "stones in its way." But that is just one, and it's from a well-documented musical. There are, alas, many more that aren't as well documented. Amy has walked the line between academic scholarship and show business to make the best determinations possible.

One final observation. In 1931, Hammerstein's daughter Alice began to write poems. That Christmas, father gave daughter an Oxford Book of Verse, and with it, a letter: "Let me give you a little tip about reading poetry. It can be awfully dull—if you read it fast. Read it slowly, and when the meaning of a line is obscure, read it over, and try and find out what the poet had in mind. And don't read a lot at a time—don't read the book from cover to cover as you would a story. Pick it up once in a while and read one or two poems—and understand them as deeply as you can."

I would like to suggest that his words to Alice about poetry then are good words to apply to this book now.

—TED CHAPIN,
President, The Rodgers & Hammerstein Organization

Editor's Note

Oscar Hammerstein II, one of the great American writers of the twentieth century, was born in 1895 into a New York City theatrical family. His paternal grandfather, Oscar I, an emigrant from Hamburg, Germany, built several Manhattan theaters and produced operas and operettas. His father, Willie, was the manager of the Victoria Theatre, the most important variety house in the nation. His uncle Arthur, Willie's brother, was a successful producer of musical comedies. But Oscar—who took a keen interest in the acts at the Victoria and enjoyed the attention he'd get for reciting pieces or playing the piano—was slated to be a lawyer. After Willie's death in 1914, however, Hammerstein began supplementing his studies at Columbia University by writing and performing in campus dramatics. Even as he attended law school, he wrote and directed undergraduate shows. After a stint as an ineffectual process server, Hammerstein approached his uncle Arthur for a job. Oscar was preparing to marry and needed to increase his earnings. Despite having promised Willie that he'd keep Oscar out of show business, Arthur took his nephew on as an office boy / play reader / assistant stage manager. Arthur also teamed Oscar with veteran lyricist and librettist Otto Harbach, who became a lifelong influence and friend.

In the 1920s Hammerstein and Harbach had a string of successes, including *Wildflower, Rose-Marie, Sunny,* and *The Desert Song.* After working together on the frothy, star-driven *Sunny* (starring Marilyn Miller), Hammerstein and composer Jerome Kern wrote *Show Boat,* a serious musical drama with American themes based on Edna Ferber's best-selling novel. It changed the nature of the emerging art form. But except for *The New Moon* (1928) and *Music in the Air* (1932), the next fifteen years were discouraging. Hammerstein went back and forth to Hollywood (where the money was during the Depression), mostly without great results or satisfaction. His stage work in London and New York failed to please audiences or critics. "When a writer's in a slump like that," he later told Ed Sullivan, "he works just as hard as he ever did, and he likes what he's doing just as much as he ever did, but for some reason, nobody else likes what he's doing." Hammerstein credited his beloved wife Dorothy's belief in him for keeping him in balance. And amid the tremendous success of *Oklahoma!* and *Carmen Jones,* he alluded to those years, filling a customary "Seasons Greetings" advertisement in *Variety* with a list of his flops under the heading "I've done it before and I can do it again."

Hammerstein's triumphs of the 1940s and 1950s—*Oklahoma!,* *Carousel, South Pacific, The King and I,* and *The Sound of Music*—were all collaborations with composer Richard Rodgers. Rodgers had had great success in the 1920s, working exclusively with the brilliant lyricist Lorenz Hart. After some thin years in Hollywood, Rodgers and Hart returned to Broadway with such mid- and late-1930s hits as *Jumbo, On Your Toes, Babes in Arms, I Married an Angel,* and *The Boys from Syracuse,* and *Pal Joey* in 1940. But by the early 1940s, Hart's drinking had left him unable to continue working. Rodgers sought out Hammerstein and in that new partnership theater history was made. As critic Walter Kerr wrote in 1953, "No one working in the field of musical entertainment has been uninfluenced by the R&H vision. The face of musical comedy itself has changed beyond recognition."

In 1949 Hammerstein compiled seventy of his songs for an anthology called *Lyrics.* His opening essay is a wonderful introduction to his career and his craft, giving a detailed account of how a working lyricist thinks. (A posthumous second edition of *Lyrics*—expanded to 111 songs—has a foreword by Hammerstein's protégé Stephen Sondheim.) He explained, for example, that in the early stages of his career, the music often came first, and he would tailor his words to the rhythm and mood of the melody. He prided himself on his speed, sometimes writing one lyric on the train from his home in Great Neck, Long Island, into Manhattan, and writing another on the return trip. But the older he got, the harder it was to satisfy himself. A change in his working method during the Rodgers years may have added to the amount of time he needed. At his own request, Hammerstein began to write the lyrics first. Before a word was set to paper, however, R&H would discuss the show at length, mapping out the tone and the action and which aspects would be told in song, dance, or dialogue. As best as I can tell from the material I've seen, Hammerstein would often start by writing a lyric for early in the first act, then draft the entire libretto, and then tackle the remaining songs in plot order. In 1946, he told *The New York Times,* "Writing comes darned hard to me. I do most of it on our farm in Doylestown. There I have a room with one of those tall old-fashioned desks you used to see in shipping offices. It takes me a long time to get started, and even then the words come slowly. I keep walking up and down the room and when I get what I want I go over to the desk and write in longhand with a soft pencil. I often wonder how many miles an act I walk." Although he tried to schedule writing time each morning (and afternoons when possible), there never seemed to be quite enough time to finish. A 1953 letter to his uncle Arthur about *Me and Juliet* is typical: "I am moving ahead with my lyrics, but very slowly. Somehow or other, however, I know that when we open in Cleveland all the songs will be written. The one thing I do know is that they won't be written when we go into rehearsal, because they never are. I always have four or five songs left over to write while the company is rehearsing. Remember when we used to do shows together we very seldom had the second act written."

Between writing and maintaining his shows, Hammerstein devoted great amounts of time to other aspects of the business. In the spring of 1949, about two months after the opening of *South Pacific*, he wrote to Arthur, "I have been tied up with one crisis after another. I have been helping ASCAP try to negotiate a television deal with the networks, straightening out television troubles in the Authors League, and meeting with Dick to do what we could in the ticket situation here in New York. On top of all this, the courts have decided that the minimum basic agreement of The Dramatists Guild is in restraint of trade and there have been numerous emergency meetings on this issue. This week I have had to make two trips to Washington on ASCAP business, so now it is uncertain whether my future career will be as an author or a politician." Hammerstein also worked hard on behalf of the United World Federalists, who believed an international authority was the only way to prevent war. In his spare moments, he enjoyed tennis and swimming, bridge and chess.

There are 850 songs in this book, about a quarter of which have never before been published. In search of song titles and lyrics, I happily read through a few dozen boxes of Hammerstein's office files and examined the archival collections of his musical collaborators Kern, Rodgers, and Romberg (in the Music Division of the Library of Congress), Herbert Stothart (UCLA), and his lyric-writing partner and mentor Otto Harbach (New York Public Library for the Performing Arts). I reviewed as many drafts of each script and screenplay as I could find; I compared typed lyric sheets against published sheet music, published and unpublished scores, and composers' manuscripts. I watched films and listened to recordings. Additional sources are mentioned in individual chapters and in the acknowledgements.

The book begins with Hammerstein's first known lyric—written for a college musical in 1916—and proceeds chronologically through all of his stage and screen projects, with a chapter of undated material at the very end. Each chapter starts with details of the original production and information on revivals, films, and

recordings. Taking a cue from the *Catalog of the American Musical* (edited by Robert Kimball and Tommy Krasker), I have included a basic plot synopsis and a word or two about where the texts come from. Whenever possible, I've provided Hammerstein's own view of the show or the working experience, a theater critic's assessment of the show's strengths and weaknesses, or a discussion of how it broke the mold. Within each chapter the songs are arranged in the running order of the first Broadway production (or film release), followed by additions and then by lyrics that were cut as the show took shape. One difference from previous volumes is that I did not provide individual copyright registration dates, as these songs were most often registered in batches well after the date they were written.

Although a few lyrics turned up quite late in the editing process, there are about a hundred songs (mostly from the 1920s) that I was not able to find, and I've listed them in the head notes. There are also some stage projects that have left little or no trace. *Marco Polo*, also known as *Golden Bells*, a long-simmering project of Kern and Hammerstein's, was mentioned in letters, but I found no lyrics. I did not find any creative materials for the musical adaptation of *Pygmalion* that R&H contemplated in 1951, nor for *Tevye's Daughters*, which they had optioned in December 1949. (Later, Alan Jay Lerner and Frederick Loewe with director Moss Hart turned *Pygmalion* into *My Fair Lady*, and Sheldon Harnick, Joseph Stein, and Jerry Bock, with Jerome Robbins, turned Sholom Aleichem's stories into *Fiddler on the Roof*.) There is a detailed outline for a musical based on Elmer Rice's *Dream Girl*, to star Mary Martin, but again no lyrics.

Near the end of the introduction to his book, *Lyrics*, Hammerstein wrote, "I have not said nearly all I would like to say about lyrics and the plays for which I write them." By quoting from his letters, rough drafts, and interviews, I hope I have given the reader more of what he would have wanted to share. To conclude my preface to this complete volume, I echo the last lines of Hammerstein's introduction: "If I have been long-winded, please forgive me my extravagances and indulge my blind infatuation. I'm in love with a wonderful theatre."

—AMY ASCH

Chronology

1895

JULY 12   Oscar Greeley Clendenning Hammerstein born in Manhattan to William Hammerstein, a theater manager, and Alice (Nimmo) Hammerstein. They live in apartments in Harlem and the Upper West Side. His first school is P.S.9 on Eighty-first Street and West End Avenue.

1897

FEBRUARY   Birth of brother Reginald Kent Hammerstein, known as Reggie.

1902

JUNE 28   Birth of Richard Rodgers

1908

Hammerstein attends the Hamilton Institute on Eighty-first Street and Central Park West.

1910

AUGUST 20   Death of Hammerstein's mother, Alice. A year later William Hammerstein marries Anna "Mousie" Nimmo, his late wife's sister.

1912

SEPTEMBER   Oscar Hammerstein II enters Columbia University. He completes three years as an undergraduate and begins law school but leaves without a law degree.

1914

JUNE 10   Death of Hammerstein's father.

1915

APRIL 12–17   Hammerstein performs in the Columbia University varsity show *On Your Way*.

1916

APRIL 12–15   Hammerstein performs in the Columbia varsity show *The Peace Pirates*, which includes his first known song.

1917

FEBRUARY 6   Broadway opening of *You're in Love*, produced by Arthur Hammerstein, his paternal uncle. Hammerstein later becomes assistant stage manager.

MARCH 28–31   Hammerstein performs in the Columbia varsity show *Home, James*, which he wrote with Herman Axelrod. Richard Rodgers is introduced to Hammerstein after a matinee.

AUGUST 22   Hammerstein marries Myra Finn. They will live at 509 West 121st Street.

OCTOBER 9   Broadway opening of *Furs and Frills*. Act Two opens with Hammerstein's first professional lyric, "Make Yourselves at Home."

1918

MAY 2–3   Columbia University War Show, *Ten for Five*, written and directed by Hammerstein.

MAY   Hammerstein gets his final military classification as 2-A.

OCTOBER 4   Broadway opening of *Sometime*. Hammerstein is stage manager.

OCTOBER 26   Birth of son William Hammerstein.

1919

MARCH 24   Broadway opening of *Tumble In*. Hammerstein is stage manager.

MAY 21   New Haven tryout of Hammerstein's play, *The Light* (4 performances). It does not go to New York.

1920

JANUARY 5   Broadway opening of *Always You*, Hammerstein's first professional show as sole lyricist and librettist (66 performances).

AUGUST 17   Broadway opening of *Tickle Me* (207 performances).

NOVEMBER 17   Broadway opening of *Jimmie* (71 performances).

1921

MAY 17   Birth of daughter Alice Hammerstein.

NOVEMBER 8   Atlantic City opening of *Pop*, a comedy by Hammerstein and Frank Mandel. It does not go to New York.

1922

AUGUST 22   Broadway opening of *Daffy Dill* (71 performances).

OCTOBER 10   Broadway opening of *Queen o' Hearts* (40 performances).

1923

FEBRUARY 7   Broadway opening of *Wildflower* (477 performances)—Hammerstein's first show to run a full year on Broadway.

DECEMBER 24   Broadway opening of *Mary Jane McKane* (151 performances).

1924

JANUARY 14   Broadway opening of *Gypsy Jim*, a drama by Hammerstein and Milton Herbert Gropper (41 performances).

FEBRUARY 18   Broadway opening of *New Toys*, a comedy by Hammerstein and Milton Herbert Gropper (24 performances).

SEPTEMBER 2   Broadway opening of *Rose-Marie* (557 performances).

1925

MARCH 20   London opening of *Rose-Marie*.

SEPTEMBER 22   Broadway opening of *Sunny* (517 performances).

DECEMBER 30   Broadway opening of *Song of the Flame* (219 performances).

1926

OCTOBER 20   Broadway opening of *The Wild Rose* (61 performances).

NOVEMBER 17   Edna Ferber signs a contract giving Hammerstein and Jerome Kern "dramatico-musical rights" to her novel *Show Boat*.

NOVEMBER 30   Broadway opening of *The Desert Song* (417 performances).

1927

MARCH   On the S.S. *Olympic*, en route to England, Hammerstein meets Henry and Dorothy Blanchard Jacobson.

APRIL 7   London opening of *The Desert Song*.

NOVEMBER 15   World premiere of *Show Boat* in Washington, D.C. Tryout performances follow in Pittsburgh, Cleveland, and Philadelphia.

NOVEMBER 30   Broadway opening of *Golden Dawn* (184 performances).

DECEMBER 26   World premiere of *The New Moon* in Philadelphia. It does not go to Broadway.

DECEMBER 27   Broadway opening of *Show Boat* (572 performances).

1928

FEBRUARY   MGM releases a silent-movie version of *Rose-Marie*.

MAY 3   London opening of *Show Boat*. Rehearsals are supervised by Hammerstein and Kern.

SEPTEMBER 5   Broadway opening of *Good Boy*. Hammerstein is one of the show's three librettists (253 performances).

SEPTEMBER 19   Broadway opening of rewritten *The New Moon* (509 performances).

NOVEMBER 21   Broadway opening of *Rainbow* (29 performances).

1929

WINTER   Hammerstein and Dorothy Jacobson each file for divorce from their spouses.

APRIL 4   London opening of *The New Moon*. Hammerstein goes to Paris for a production of *The Desert Song*.

APRIL   Warner Bros. releases a screen version of *The Desert Song*.

MAY   Universal releases *Show Boat*, a silent film enhanced with an eighteen-minute "talkie" prologue of songs by the original cast.

MAY 14   Hammerstein marries Dorothy Blanchard Jacobson in Baltimore.

JUNE   Hammerstein and Sigmund Romberg sign a contract with Warner Bros./First National Pictures for four original screen musicals.

SEPTEMBER 31   Broadway opening of *Sweet Adeline* (234 performances).

FALL   Hammerstein, Dorothy, and her two-year-old daughter Susan move to Los Angeles. Her son, Henry, remains with his father.

1930

JANUARY   MGM releases a screen version of *New Moon*.

MARCH   Warner Bros. releases *Song of the West*, a screen version of *Rainbow*.

SPRING   The Hammersteins travel to Melbourne, where Oscar meets Dorothy's parents and siblings.

JUNE   Warner Bros. releases *Golden Dawn*.

NOVEMBER   Warner Bros. releases *Viennese Nights*. Warners buys out the Hammerstein-Romberg contract. The Hammersteins return to New York.

NOVEMBER   First National/Vitaphone releases a screen version of *Sunny*.

DECEMBER 22   Broadway opening of *Ballyhoo* (68 performances). Hammerstein wrote two lyrics and is credited with "supervision."

1931

WINTER   Hammerstein forges a business partnership with Laurence Schwab and Frank Mandel. Excepting one show a year for Arthur Hammerstein, Oscar is to "share in all their enterprises and write for nobody else."

FEBRUARY 18   Broadway opening of *The Gang's All Here* (23 performances). Hammerstein is one of three librettists and is codirector.

MARCH 23   Birth of son James Hammerstein.

JULY   Warner Bros. releases *Children of Dreams*.

SEPTEMBER 18   Broadway opening of *Free for All* (15 performances).

OCTOBER 27   Broadway opening of *East Wind* (23 performances).

1932

MAY–OCTOBER   *Show Boat* is revived on Broadway with Paul Robeson and most of the original cast (180 performances).

NOVEMBER 8   Broadway opening of *Music in the Air* (342 performances).

1933

MAY 19   London opening of *Music in the Air*, directed by Hammerstein and Kern.

SEPTEMBER 8   London opening of *Ball at the Savoy*, adapted and directed by Hammerstein.

1934

APRIL 9   London opening of *Three Sisters*, directed by Hammerstein and Kern.

JUNE   Hammerstein makes a one-year contract at MGM and moves to Los Angeles.

DECEMBER   Warner Bros. releases *Sweet Adeline* and Fox releases *Music in the Air*.

1935

JANUARY   MGM releases *The Night Is Young*.

JUNE   Hammerstein's contract with MGM is not renewed; he signs a nonexclusive agreement with Paramount.

DECEMBER 5   Broadway opening of *May Wine* (213 performances).

1936

WINTER   Hammerstein reports for work at Paramount, intending to make California his home, but does not find a suitable project.

FEBRUARY   MGM releases a screen version of *Rose-Marie*, starring Nelson Eddy and Jeanette MacDonald.

MARCH   Paramount releases *Give Us This Night*.

MAY   Universal releases a new screen version of *Show Boat* for which Hammerstein has written the screenplay and, with Kern, new songs.

SEPTEMBER   Hammerstein is chairman of the Hollywood Anti-Nazi League.

1937

MARCH   Paramount releases *Swing High, Swing Low*, for which Hammerstein is one of several screenwriters.

MARCH 21   Jerome Kern suffers a heart attack. The Hammersteins, in London when they get the news, immediately return to California.

SPRING/SUMMER   Hammerstein works at Columbia Pictures.

OCTOBER 24   Paramount releases *High, Wide, and Handsome*.

1938

JUNE 3–12 World premiere of *Gentlemen Unafraid* at the St. Louis Muny.

AUGUST 1–7 *Knights of Song*, a play about Gilbert and Sullivan being developed by Laurence Schwab and Hammerstein, is performed at the St. Louis Muny.

OCTOBER Columbia releases *The Lady Objects*.

OCTOBER 17 Broadway opening of *Knights of Song*, directed and coproduced by Hammerstein (16 performances).

NOVEMBER 4 MGM releases *The Great Waltz*.

NOVEMBER 15 Broadway opening of *Where Do We Go From Here?* produced by Hammerstein and Dwight Taylor (15 performances).

NOVEMBER 26 Broadway opening of *Glorious Morning*, a British drama directed and coproduced by Hammerstein (9 performances).

1939

MARCH RKO releases *The Story of Vernon and Irene Castle*, for which Hammerstein adapted Irene Castle's memoir.

MAY Hammerstein is elected to the ASCAP board and remains on it until his death.

NOVEMBER 17 Broadway opening of *Very Warm for May* (59 performances).

1940

MAY 12 *American Jubilee* opens at the New York World's Fair. It runs until October 2, with four performances a day.

JUNE Fall of Paris to the Nazis inspires Hammerstein to write "The Last Time I Saw Paris."

JULY MGM releases *The New Moon* starring Nelson Eddy and Jeanette MacDonald.

FALL The Hammersteins buy Highland Farm in Doylestown, Pennsylvania. It is Hammerstein's preferred home for the rest of his life.

1941

JUNE 5–15 World Premiere of *New Orleans* (renamed *Sunny River*) at the St. Louis Muny.

SUMMER Richard Rodgers approaches Oscar Hammerstein about future projects.

DECEMBER 4 Broadway opening of *Sunny River* (36 performances).

1942

WINTER/SPRING Hammerstein works on his adaptation of *Carmen*. He also works on finding a producer and cast for a revival of *Show Boat*.

JULY 22 The Theatre Guild announces that Rodgers, Hart, and Hammerstein will create a musical of *Green Grow the Lilacs*.

NOVEMBER Hammerstein turns down a two-year contract with MGM.

1943

MARCH 31 Broadway opening of *Oklahoma!* (2,212 performances).

APRIL Hammerstein joins the leadership of the Writers' War Board.

OCTOBER 15 *Oklahoma!* national tour begins in New Haven and runs (with a few summer layoffs) until 1954.

NOVEMBER 22 Death of Lorenz Hart. Hammerstein produces a tribute in February.

DECEMBER 2 Broadway opening of *Carmen Jones* (503 performances).

1944

APRIL/MAY Rodgers and Hammerstein are awarded a special Pulitzer Prize for *Oklahoma!*

JUNE Rodgers and Hammerstein send lyric sheets and demo records to Fox for the upcoming movie musical of *State Fair*. Hammerstein discusses a Marco Polo project with Jerome Kern.

OCTOBER 19 Broadway opening of the play *I Remember Mama*, produced by Rodgers and Hammerstein (713 performances).

1945

APRIL 1945 Broadway opening of *Carousel* (890 performances).

AUGUST Fox releases *State Fair*.

NOVEMBER 11 Death of Jerome Kern.

DECEMBER 3 Rehearsals for *Show Boat* begin under Hammerstein's direction.

1946

JANUARY 5 *Show Boat* revival opens (418 performances).

MAY Broadway opening of Irving Berlin's *Annie Get Your Gun*, produced by Rodgers and Hammerstein (1,147 performances).

JULY 1 *Oklahoma!* becomes the longest-running Broadway musical, a record it holds until July 1961.

OCTOBER 31 Broadway opening of the comedy *Happy Birthday*, produced by Rodgers and Hammerstein (563 performances).

1947

FEBRUARY 4 Broadway opening of the comedy *John Loves Mary*, produced by Rodgers and Hammerstein (423 performances).

APRIL 29 London opening of *Oklahoma!* at the Theater Royal, Drury Lane. The theater is continuously occupied by a Rodgers and Hammerstein musical for the next nine years.

OCTOBER Hammerstein is on the cover of *Time*. Articles run in the *Saturday Evening Post*, *The Saturday Review of Literature*, and *Life*.

OCTOBER 10 Broadway opening of *Allegro* (315 performances).

[NO DATE AVAILABLE] Hammerstein is president of the Authors League from 1947 to 1951.

1948

MAY 29 Broadway production of *Oklahoma!* closes after 2,212 performances.

SEPTEMBER A touring company of *Show Boat* performs at New York's City Center and embarks on a forty-five-city tour.

1949

APRIL 7 Broadway opening of *South Pacific* (1,925 performances).

SPRING The Hammersteins buy a townhouse in New York City at 10 East Sixty-third Street.

DECEMBER Hammerstein's anthology, *Lyrics*, is published.

DECEMBER 4 First performance of *The Myth That Threatens the World*, a theater piece explaining the goals of the United World Federalists, produced and directed by Hammerstein. The show is revised and repeated in a few major cities along the *South Pacific* national tour.

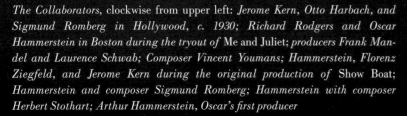

The Collaborators, clockwise from upper left: *Jerome Kern, Otto Harbach, and Sigmund Romberg in Hollywood, c. 1930; Richard Rodgers and Oscar Hammerstein in Boston during the tryout of* Me and Juliet; *producers Frank Mandel and Laurence Schwab; Composer Vincent Youmans; Hammerstein, Florenz Ziegfeld, and Jerome Kern during the original production of* Show Boat; *Hammerstein and composer Sigmund Romberg; Hammerstein with composer Herbert Stothart; Arthur Hammerstein, Oscar's first producer*

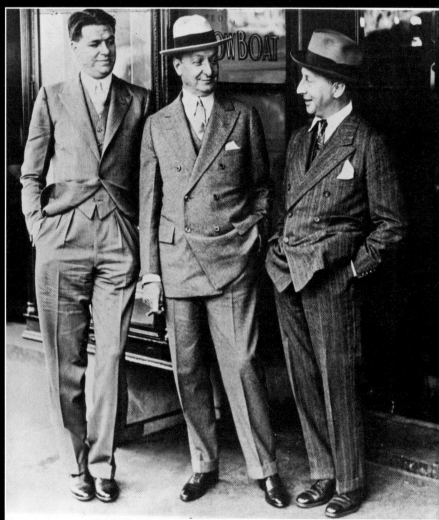

1950

JANUARY 17   Hammerstein is elected to the National Institute of Arts and Letters.

JANUARY 24   Broadway opening of *The Happy Time*, a play produced by Rodgers and Hammerstein (614 performances).

FEBRUARY 20   Boston opening of *The Heart of the Matter*, a play produced by Rodgers and Hammerstein. It plays in Boston through March 4 and does not reach New York.

APRIL   Hammerstein and Rodgers are among the founders of New Dramatists.

JUNE 7   London opening of *Carousel*.

OCTOBER 19   Broadway opening of *Burning Bright*, a play produced by Rodgers and Hammerstein (13 performances).

1951

MARCH 29   Broadway opening of *The King and I* (1,246 performances).

MAY 12   Hammerstein is profiled in *The New Yorker*.

JULY   MGM releases *Show Boat*.

AUGUST 11   *Business Week* magazine's cover story is "R & H Shows Are Pushing $8-Million."

SEPTEMBER 9 AND 16   Ed Sullivan broadcasts a two-part tribute to Hammerstein.

OCTOBER 8   Broadway opening of *Music in the Air* revival (56 performances).

NOVEMBER 1   London opening of *South Pacific*.

NOVEMBER 9   Death of Sigmund Romberg.

1953

MAY 23   Broadway opening of *Me and Juliet* (358 performances).

JUNE 15   Hammerstein narrates a two-hour television spectacular celebrating American culture from 1900 to the present and the fiftieth anniversary of the Ford Motor Company.

SUMMER   The U.S. State Department puts Hammerstein on a restricted passport because of concerns about alleged communist activity.

AUGUST 18   Harbach's eightieth birthday is celebrated with an ASCAP banquet at the Waldorf-Astoria. Hammerstein is master of ceremonies.

AUGUST 31–SEPTEMBER 6   New York City's Mayor Impellitteri declares "Rodgers & Hammerstein Week" on the occasion of four musicals running simultaneously: *South Pacific*, *The King and I*, and *Me and Juliet* on Broadway and *Oklahoma!* at City Center.

OCTOBER 8   London opening of *The King and I*.

CHRISTMAS   Hammerstein delivers a message to "captive peoples of Eastern Europe" on Radio Free Europe.

1954

MARCH 28   General Foods celebrates its twenty-fifth anniversary with a ninety-minute salute to Rodgers and Hammerstein that is carried on all four television networks.

APRIL 3   *Me and Juliet* closes on Broadway. For the first time in eleven years, there is no Rodgers and Hammerstein show on Broadway.

MAY   *Oklahoma!* tour closes in Philadelphia after more than a decade on the road.

MAY 14   Oscar and Dorothy's twenty-fifth wedding anniversary.

OCTOBER   Twentieth Century Fox releases a screen version of *Carmen Jones*.

SUMMER   The Hammersteins are in California and Arizona for the filming of *Oklahoma!*

DECEMBER   Hammerstein writes to a hundred prominent Americans, asking their opinion of the effect of Negro residents on housing values.

1955

SEPTEMBER   Richard Rodgers is diagnosed with cancer. He greets the company on the first day of *Pipe Dream* rehearsals and then has surgery. Part of his jaw is removed.

OCTOBER   Magna and Twentieth Century Fox release *Oklahoma!*

OCTOBER 12   Death of Arthur Hammerstein.

NOVEMBER 30   Broadway opening of *Pipe Dream* (246 performances).

1956

FEBRUARY   Twentieth Century Fox releases *Carousel*.

JUNE   Twentieth Century Fox releases *The King and I*.

FALL   The Hammersteins leave for Australia. They attend the summer Olympics in Melbourne.

1957

MARCH 31   *Cinderella* is broadcast on CBS, reaching more than 107 million U.S. viewers.

SUMMER   Hammerstein makes several trips to California and one to Hawaii for *South Pacific*.

1958

MARCH   Magna and Twentieth Century Fox release *South Pacific*.

MARCH 15   Hammerstein is a guest on TV's *The Mike Wallace Interview*.

JULY   Hammerstein has gall bladder surgery. During a four-week hospital stay, he works on lyrics for *Flower Drum Song*.

AUGUST 9   Death of Reggie Hammerstein.

DECEMBER 1   Broadway opening of *Flower Drum Song* (600 performances).

1959

APRIL 29   Hammerstein gives a major address for the United World Federalists in Boston.

SEPTEMBER 1   Rehearsals begin for *The Sound of Music*.

SEPTEMBER 19   Hammerstein has abdominal surgery for an ulcer, and cancer is found. His wife and Richard and Dorothy Rodgers are told it will be fatal, but Hammerstein is not told.

OCTOBER 15   Hammerstein begins writing "Edelweiss," his final song. A week later he sees *The Sound of Music* for the first time in Boston.

NOVEMBER 16   Broadway opening of *The Sound of Music* (1,443 performances).

1960

MARCH 24   London opening of *Flower Drum Song*, attended by Rodgers and Hammerstein and their wives.

SPRING/SUMMER   Hammerstein works on a television adaptation of *Allegro* and lyrics for the remake of *State Fair*.

AUGUST 23   Oscar Hammerstein II dies at age sixty-five on his farm in Doylestown, Pennsylvania.

Acknowledgments

This book and I owe a great debt of gratitude to many people and institutions. I am so glad to have this chance to publicly thank them. First there is Robert Kimball, who started the Complete Lyrics series twenty-five years ago. He modestly leads by example with his scholarship and his tireless devotion to the work of the great songwriters. He has been an Otto Harbach to me—graciously sharing his work with an interested youngster. Robert believed I was capable of doing a book and started me on this one.

Next, I must thank four people without whom I'd never have finished the book. I am so grateful to Ted Chapin of the Rodgers & Hammerstein Organization for smoothing my way at every turn and for his invaluable comments on the manuscript. He has been very generous with his time and knowledge. My editors at Knopf, Katherine Hourigan and Bob Gottlieb, patiently waited for the first draft. Kathy has guided me through each step of the editorial process. And Bob's great authority on all matters is matched only by his taste. Phil Birsh of *Playbill* noticed when I was floundering and handed me a life preserver.

I am grateful, too, to Alice Hammerstein Mathias—for writing about her father's work, and for the insights she has shared all along. I want to thank Hammerstein Executor and Trustee R. Andrew Boose for compiling the copyright information and obtaining the necessary permissions from the publishers of the lyrics.

The crack team at the Rodgers & Hammerstein Organization, under the leadership of Ted Chapin, has supported this book from beginning to end and from the mundane to the arcane. I thank Ted, Victoria Traube, Bert Fink, Bruce Pomahac, Maxyne Lang, Vince Scuderi, Cindy Boyle, Nicole Harman, Mike Hidalgo, Juliet Abbott, Nancy Di Turo, John Elmer, Kathy McCullough, Gina Scalia, Karen Smith, and Charlie Scatamacchia. Carol Cornicelli (photo archivist), Kara Darling (lyric reprints), and Robin Walton (legal affairs) have worked especially hard on what we call "CLOOH2."

My research in New York was done at the New York Public Library for the Performing Arts (Billy Rose Theatre Collection, the Music Division, and the Rodgers and Hammerstein Archives of Recorded Sound) and NYPL's Humanities and Social Sciences Library (Photographs and Permissions, Periodicals, and Microfilm); the Shubert Archive (Maryann Chach, Reagan Fletcher, and Sylvia Wang); Tams-Witmark Music Library (Sargent Aborn and Finn Byrhard); the Rodgers & Hammerstein Organization (Bruce Pomahac); the theater collection of the Museum of the City of New York (Marty Jacobs); the Paley Center for Media (formerly the Museum of Television and Radio) (Jane Klain); the Columbia University Archives and Columbia's Oral History Research Office. I spent several pleasurable weeks in the Music Division of the Library of Congress (Washington, D.C.) (Mark Horowitz and Betty Auman). In Los Angeles, I drew on the rich collections of the Institute of the American Musical (Miles Kreuger and Eric Davis); the University of Southern California's Cinema-Television Library (Ned Comstock) and Warner Bros. archive (Hayden Guest); the Academy of Motion Picture Arts and Science's Margaret Herrick Library (Barbara Hall); and UCLA's Performing Arts Special Collections (Tim Edwards). In London I did research in the Lord Chamberlain's Plays Collection at the British Library and at the Theatre Museum (Catherine Haill). Crucial information was found in the theater collection at the Philadelphia Free Library (Geraldine Duclow). Of all the librarians and archivists whose work has enhanced this book, I must make special mention of Mark Horowitz, Ned Comstock, and Barbara Hall for their extended efforts on my behalf.

Other mavens who kindly shared their special knowledge and collections are Katherine Axtell, Stephen Banfield, Geoffrey Block, Ken Bloom, Marilee Bradford, Tim Carter, James Curtis, Todd Decker, Nancy Kassak Diekmann, Eleanor Knowles Dugan, Bob Essman, Michael Feinstein, Hugh Fordin, Will Friedwald, Aaron Gandy, the late Mark Trent Goldberg, John Steele Gordon, Oscar Andy Hammerstein, William Harbach, Ed Harsh, David Jasen, David Lahm, David Leopold, Jeff Lunden, Ron Mandelbaum, Sandy Marrone, Louise Martzinek, Laurence Maslon, Jamie McGregor, Jeremy Megraw, Ruth Mueller-Maerki, Steve Nelson, Eleanor O'Connor, Laura Peters, Jeannie Poole, Jonathan Schwartz, Ben Sears and Brad Conner, Dave Stein, Jim Steinblatt, Laurie Stricks, Donald Stubblebine, Steven Suskin, Caroline Underwood, George Winters.

I am also grateful to historians I know only through their work: Richard Barrios, Gerald Bordman, Stephen Citron, William Everett, the late Stanley Green, Thomas Hischak, John McGlinn, Ethan Mordden, Richard Norton, Max Wilk. Four books were indispensable: *Lyrics* by Oscar Hammerstein (a 1949 anthology of 70 songs), *Getting to Know Him* by Hugh Fordin, *The Rodgers and Hammerstein Fact Book* (1980 edition) by Stanley Green, and *Berlin, Kern, Rodgers, Hart and Hammerstein: A Complete Song Catalogue* by Steven Suskin.

During the first years of research, three people voluntarily shouldered a tremendous amount of the typing, xeroxing, and filing that this project required. Diana J. Bertolini was such a natural that she earned a master's degree in library science well before this book reached manuscript stage. Chris Freeman, extraordinarily knowledgeable at a young age, carefully compared stage lyrics against screen versions. Marcail Briggs became my second pair of eyes and hands at the Lincoln Center library.

I thank the rest of the team at Knopf who have worked so hard and contributed so much to this book: Jessica Freeman-Slade, Kevin Bourke, Roméo Enriquez, Soonyoung Kwon, Caryn Burtt, Patrick Dillon, and Kathy Zuckerman.

I thank my coworkers at Playbill, Inc., especially Robert Viagas, Andrew Ku, David Gewirtzman, Jolie Schaffzin, Kenneth Jones, Terry Wilson, and Kesler Thibert.

And finally, I thank my dear friends and family for seven years of support and encouragement: Rhoda, Roger, Mark, Stephanie, Miller, Karl, and Mimi Asch; Jenn and Ken Birchby; Connie Chase; Lynn Christie; Suzanne DelGizzo and Tim McGraw; Mark Horowitz and Loie Clark; Eliza Lansdale; Peggy Kampmeier and Ed and Andrew Harsh; Anita M. Kramer; Sara Lesch; John MacNaughton; Nick Macrae; Norma Messing; Toby Moldave; Ben Moldave; Janet Pinkowitz; Sally Potashkin; Susan Soriano and Jonathan Ruttenberg; Adam Thorburn; Joanna West and Peter Hembrough; Wynelle Welch.

—AMY ASCH

Hammerstein wrote himself a leading comic role in Home, James. Above: *With Emile E. Gyss.* Below: *With Ormond V. Gould*

THE PEACE PIRATES (1916)

New York run: Hotel Astor; opened April 12, 1916; five performances. A musical comedy in two acts, presented by the Columbia University Players under the management of John Arthur Strang, class of '16. Book and lyrics by Herman J. Mankiewicz, '17. Music by Ray Perkins, '17. Additional music and lyrics by Walter Atkinson '15 and M. Wolff '15. Staged under the direction of Kenneth S. Webb '06. Orchestra under the direction of Roy Webb, '10.

Hammerstein, a member of the Law School graduating class of '18, had a major comedy role and danced in a spoof of the Ballet Russe. The *New York Tribune* said, "Honors of the evening were divided between Lorenz M. Hart, '17 and Oscar Hammerstein, 3rd [*sic*]."

SHAKESPEARE UP-TO-DATE

Music probably by Ray Perkins. Published in a limited edition piano-vocal score. Introduced by principals and ensemble.

Oscar Hammerstein II's first known lyric was a tercentenary tribute to the Bard (d. 1616).

VERSE 1

In my youthful college days
I read all of Shakespeare's plays
From *Henry VIII* to *Taming of the Shrew*.
I've seen almost ev'ry one
Of the plays that Shaw has done,
And can't find much resemblance in the two.
But strange to say I had an awful dream the other night.
I woke to see this weird unusual sight:

REFRAIN 1

Oh there was Romeo and Imogen parading around the room.
Lady Macbeth was getting married with Hamlet as the groom.
Then Juliet and Lear were playing cards
While Portia was keeping score.
Now this may all seem wrong to you
But I'm sure it would be true
If George Bernard Shaw had but written
Some of Bill Shakespeare's plays.

VERSE 2

Once a friend remarked to me,
How great would the profit be
To put some music to Bill Shakespeare's shows.
I have hunted all around,
There's a man that I have found
Could do the job as ev'rybody knows.
Just fancy George M. Cohan in a music comedy
For this is how his stunt would doubtless be:

REFRAIN 2

Henry VIII would wave a flag and sing "Hooray for the U.S.A."
Shylock would seek his pound of flesh in a patriotic way.
Then Cleopatra might be seen in tights
Or dancing with Romeo.
Now this may all seem wrong to you
But I'm sure it would be true
If George Cohan had ever produced
Some of Bill Shakespeare's plays.

HOME, JAMES (1917)

New York run: Hotel Astor, Grand Ballroom; opened March 28, 1917; 5 performances. A musical comedy in two acts, presented by the Columbia University Players under the management of Charles Steiner, class of '17. Book and lyrics by Herman A. Axelrod, '15, and Oscar Hammerstein II, '18L. Music by Robert K. Lippmann, '19. Additional music and lyrics by Kenneth S. Webb, '06; Roy Webb, '10; M. S. Wolff, '15; Robert A. Simon, '18; Frank Padwe, '16; Edgar Wolfe, '20; Cyril S. Laub, '18; and G. M. Watts, '17. Staged under the direction of Kenneth S. Webb. Orchestra under the direction of Roy Webb, '10. Orchestrations by Roy Webb.

Major roles: John D. Beals Jr., '17 (Gideon Guiness); Randolph M. Saville, '18 (Steve Guiness, his son); James D. Herbert, '19 (the Red Rose Girl); Phillip B. Leavitt, '18 (Marion Gay, Steve's sweetheart); Ormond V. Gould, '17 (Lucius Vodka, a mysterious personage); Oscar Hammerstein II, '18L (Armand Dubonnet, head waiter at Roget's); H. William Hanemann, '17 (Emma Guiness, Gideon's better 99/100); Louis C. Owens Jr., '20 (Vivienne, her daughter).

Except as detailed below, the lyrics were preserved in a lavish program-libretto and in a smaller pamphlet of lyrics. The program advertises a vocal score, but none of the music is known to survive. A song list published in the *Columbia Daily Spectator*, March 9, 1917, includes the title "What's This Old World Coming To?" by Axelrod, Hammerstein and Lippmann, to be performed in Act Two by the character Lucius Vodka; that song has not been found. This chapter does not include eight lyrics written by others.

Hammerstein played the leading comic role in the show, and after one of the matinees he received congratulations from fraternity brother Mortimer Rodgers and Rodgers' musical younger brother, Richard.

ACT ONE OPENING CHORUS

Lyric by Oscar Hammerstein II and Herman Axelrod. Introduced by the ensemble.

ENSEMBLE: People think we're bank directors
Just because we dine at Rector's.
But from eight o'clock till five,
We just have to keep alive
Behind a ribbon counter.
Every day when work is over,
We start out each one a rover,
Dancing till the break of day,
Trying hard to look blasé
In a careful, careless way.

GIRLS: We are ladies of the chorus.
Tired businessmen adore us.
We hate auto rides and pearls,
For we're just hard-working girls.
We are martyrs to the cause of art.

COMEDY GROUP: Our little group of serious thinkers
Always investigates and tinkers,
In our inimitable way
With the problems of the day.
Cubist art and verse that's free,
Surely are the things we
Find most interesting,
Oh, yes, we do.
We're the ones who set the craze
Dining in red-ink cafes
Until the lights go out.

ALL: Stick around, this is going to be some show.
We've seen all the rehearsals and we know.
Scenery quite disturbin'
Done by our own Urban.

2

The cast and the chorus are
    chock full of pep and go.
Every song has a tuneful melody,
Sparkling with originality.
As for the whole libretto and the
    lyricizing,
There's no use to start a-
    criticizing,
If you don't believe it, wait and
    see!

MARION

Lyric by Oscar Hammerstein II and Herman Axelrod. Introduced by Randolph M. Saville (Steve) and ensemble.

VERSE 1

Girlies by hundreds I've oft met before
And they've made no impression on me.
Those who were pretty had nobody home
And the bright ones were plain as could be.
Some girls were shy
But I passed them all by,
And I shunned all the wise dames too,
'Cause each little peach had her own little flaw;
But I'm glad I persisted
For I found there existed
The one and the only she!

REFRAIN

Marion, oh, won't you marry me?
You're the only girl I've found.
Marion, now please don't carry on,
For I'm hopelessly smitten
And weak as a kitten,
Whenever you're around.
All the rest are merely also-rans;
There's but one that I can see.
Won't you please stop your tarryin',
Dear little Marion,
And think of marryin' me?

VERSE 2

Where is the play of today that's completed
Without some love interest to blend?
Don't be so slow, dear,
You may as well know, dear,
You'll be in my arms at the end.
First you may dally,
But at the finale

I'll call you my blushing bride.
'Cause if you were not,
It would spoil all the plot.
And a good leading lady
Is never old-maidy,
So let's get the license now.

REPEAT REFRAIN

PLANKETY PLANK

Lyric by Oscar Hammerstein II and Herman Axelrod. Introduced by Randolph M. Saville (Steve), Phillip B. Leavitt* (Marion), and the Mandolin Club.

VERSE 1

A wee mandolin and a big guitar
Were thrown together by chance.
'Twas way downtown in a music store
They started their own romance.
The great big guitar told the mandolin
There was never an instrument cuter.
When he stole a kiss, she
Coyly told him that he
Was a suitor
Too ardent to suit her.

REFRAIN

"Plunkety-plunkety plunk, plunk?"
That's how he worded his plea.
"Planky-planky plankety, planky plank,"
She'd answer, "Not for me."
"See how you're pulling my heart strings?"
"Plankety, planky, plank."
Then at last his persistence
Broke down her resistance,
And so
'Tis said
They went
And wed,
And now they are both in tune.

---

* *Phil Leavitt, who played the "heroine" of* Home, James, *is best remembered for his role in introducing Richard Rodgers to Lorenz Hart. He also performed* "There's Always Room for One More," *the first song with words by Hammerstein and music by Rodgers.*

VERSE 2

The wee mandolin and the big guitar
Have learned how to harmonize.
He accompanies her every place she goes;
He knows he has won a prize.
He thrills as she trills in her rhythmic way
For indeed they are never quite quiet.
They have no cause to brood
O'er the high cost of food,
With their music and love for a diet.

REPEAT REFRAIN

POOR ARMAND

Lyric by Oscar Hammerstein II and Herman Axelrod. Introduced by Oscar Hammerstein II (Armand). The *New York Herald* called Hammerstein "funmaker in extraordinary as Armand Dubonnet, maître d'hôtel, who breaks into society as a supposed comte."

I

I was very young at the time,
The spring was in the air,
That is the season when a young man's fancy
Turns to thoughts that cause a lot of trouble.
She was a wispy, fairy-like thing,
Clad in her gossamer gingham.
Out into the country, we'd take long walks.
Oh—the bull! How I'd fling him.
But one fateful day, I proposed to her.
She coldly looked at me and said:
"Grande passion is out of fashion, my dear
    Armand.
It could never turn my head,
You are nice boy and I like you,
You are chivalrous—and all that sort of rot.
But we could never tie the lover's knot,
For we are lovers—not!"

II

Then I met another girl,
A ravishing vision of beauty!
She had that golden hair and deep blue eyes
That told of a nature
That was proud—though Swedish.
She was a cook in a beanery lunch,
And I was only a waiter.
But oh—the French pancakes that she could
    make!
How I loved her cooking!

But one day I looked through the kitchen door,
Behol' the sight that met my eye,
Sitting in my chair was a great big fat policeman.
Oh—I almost want to cry,
I break in the door
I say—"What does this mean?"
She—"Armand, no more French pancake for you."
This cop—he was Irish too,
And for him she make the Irish stew!

III

There was charming, chic 'Toinette,
She was my fourth or fifth affaire.
I thought she'd care,
But she became a barber's bride.
There was Julie—roguish Jou-Jou,
Sweet Marie and piquant Lulu,
Fluffy frou-frou swiftly flitting from my side.
I was always a girl's first love,
Never anybody's last.
Each said I was the first that ever kissed her,
But it mattered not what I did,
She decided very fast
That to me she would be
Just a sister.
Here's a letter from the last one:
"Dearest Armand,
I can't forget last night, just when you left me."
Oh, it was very nice.
"And how is my little papoose?"—
She always calls me that—
"And, Armand, dear, do you think
That my husband—?"!!!

HOME, JAMES

Lyric by Oscar Hammerstein II and Herman Axelrod. Introduced by Randolph M. Saville (Steve), Phillip B. Leavitt (Marion), Ormond V. Gould (Vodka), and ensemble.

VERSE 1

I want to be a star in moving pictures,
Like Mary, Charlie, Douglas, and the other
    fixtures.*

In the introduction to his anthology, Lyrics, *Hammerstein gave the opening lines as "I want to be a star in moving pictures/Like Chaplin, Pickford, Fairbanks, and the other fixtures" and commented: "Quite a rhyme! Like my two collaborators, I expected to make my living in another calling."*

I will sell my autograph
Written on my photograph.
My personality
Will make a hit for me,
And I'll be the talk of the town.

REFRAIN

You'll see me twinkle, twinkle, twinkle as a movie
    star
In glaring lights, from dizzy heights.
When once or twice you've seen
Me shine upon the screen,
I'll be riding round the city in my limousine.
And then I'll never, never, never go to bed until
The clock strikes one, two, three or four o'clock.
Then—"Home, James, drive me fast!"
That's the existence for me.

VERSE 2

I loved the dirty villain in the drama.
Poor dear Mathilda, he near killed her with a
    hammer.
He used to hiss, "Where is the child?"
But now his manner's meek and mild.
No more he'll villainize.
His aim with custard pies
Has made him Keystone Komedy King.

REPEAT REFRAIN

CARTOONS

Lyric by Oscar Hammerstein II and Herman Axelrod. Introduced by Phillip B. Leavitt (Marion), H. William Hanemann (Emma), Louis C. Owens Jr. (Vivienne), Ormond V. Gould (Vodka), John D. Beals Jr. (Gideon), Oscar Hammerstein II (Armand), and ensemble.

VERSE

Have you ever seen the pictures in the comic-
    section page?
Their buffoonery makes you chuckle—it's
    delightful badinage.
There's Mutt and Jeff, and Powerful Katinka,
And Briggs' when a feller needs a friend.
Aloysius! Sweep out padded cell three million
    ninety-nine,
You can name 'em without end.

REFRAIN

When pretty Polly and her pals
Gives a party for the boys and gals,
Mr. Baron Bean comes upon the scene, arriving in
    his limousine.
Then just as Abie Kabibble gets off his wheeze
Krazy Kat will nibble at the mouse's cheese,
And all the glooms will make way for the joys.
It will be a big night for us boys.
Won't you be excited, when you are invited
To the comic-section jubilee?

ACT ONE FINALE

Lyric by Oscar Hammerstein II and Herman Axelrod. Introduced by the company.

EMMA:	Just think of it, just think of it,
	The social fame we gain,
	We're right upon the brink of it—
ALL:	Just think of it, just think of it.
EMMA:	A French count true will visit me,
	His countess, too, our guest will be,
	Oh, how the neighbors' tongues will wag!
ALL:	Oh, how their tongues will wag!
ENSEMBLE:	The Guinesses are mixing with nobility galore,
	They never have consorted with gentility before.
	We don't know what to make of it;
	How could they have persuaded
	Such very famous guests?—and yet,
	It's evident that they did.
STEVE:	Marion, what can this mystery mean,
	Why take on this countess guise?
ENSEMBLE:	Marion, now please go on and tell us of the big sensation—
	Get a little pep and put us hep, and save your reputation.
	You'll make us furious;
	We are so curious—
	Won't you put us wise?
MARION:	Stevie, dear, I'll tell you later on,
	But you'll have to wait and see.
STEVE:	Oh, I wish you'd stop tarryin',
	Dear little Marion,
	And think of marryin' me.
ENSEMBLE:	Stevie, she's only parryin',
	Your little Marion
	Tries out her blarney on thee.

GIDEON: I wish you'd stop these social-
climbing con games.
EMMA: Come, Countie dear, the car is waiting.
Home, James!
GIDEON: [*spoken*] Home, James? So, at last I've
found you out!
[*sung*] I penetrate your puritanic poses,
So, you're the girl that flaunts the red,
red roses!
ENSEMBLE: Beautiful, beautiful red rose girl,
You've captured all our hearts.
If you'd let us bask in your smiles so
sweet,
We'd lay our fortunes at your feet.
We'd tenderly tender thee precious
things,
And give you riches rare.
You'd make us all forget our duty,
You're our pet, our beauty,
Cutie, you're all there!
EMMA: [*spoken*] Aren't they nice?
GIDEON: Of course, I shall divorce this awful
woman.
The marriage bond we'll surely have
to sever!
VIVIENNE: [*spoken*] Father, where are you going?
GIDEON: Home to get my other shirt and
collar,
And leave my house and home, and
her, forever!
Yes, forever.
VIVIENNE: Forever?
GIDEON: Almost forever.
ENSEMBLE: Go on and twinkle, twinkle, twinkle,
little movie star,
And you can sprinkle, sprinkle,
sprinkle money near and far.
Your salary's way up in the millions,
For you always fool the villyuns
In the movies!
EMMA: What's all this twinkle, twinkle,
twinkle moving-picture thing?
I don't know what you mean.
GIDEON: My dear, when you said "Home,
James,"
I was sure you were the queen of the
screen.
ENSEMBLE: Then where's our little star of moving
pictures
Like Mary, Charlie, Douglas and the
other fixtures?
There's something very wrong, we
fear,
Else she must be hiding here.
It strikes us oddest she
Should have such modesty,
When she's the talk of the town!
[*Crash.*]

What's that!
[*Crash.*]
What's that?
Sh! What was that terrible, weird
sound?
Sh! There's something doing around.
VODKA: Shush, shush yourself,
I'm the shusher in this show.
I can explain that—
I think I ought to know.
Sh, come around, sir.
Sh, don't you dare stir.
Hist, pst, list, not a whisper.
Once upon a time—
ALL: Yes, yes, yes.
MARION: There was a little girl—
ALL: Yes, yes, yes!
GIDEON: And she was very good—
ALL: Yes, yes, yes.
VODKA: And we thought she could—
ALL: Yes, yes, yes.
EMMA: Your story we're digesting,
It's very interesting.
MARION: Then—
ENSEMBLE: This suspense is quite unbearable,
Terrible.
VODKA: When—
ENSEMBLE: We're delirious,
Don't weary us,
It's serious!
GIDEON: She—
EMMA: Your ingenuities
Are given opportunities,
ENSEMBLE: But where are the unities?!
MARION: I fear they are suspicious.
GIDEON: They look as if they wish us—
ARMAND: In that region made famous by
Dante.
VODKA: 'Mid comforts very scanty.
A VOICE: Worthy people all, what's this fuss
about?
Your behavior isn't quite *au fait*.
There is nothing much for you to fuss
about,
So let us all prepare to go away.
You shall come with us to Guiness
Villa.
We shall start at once,
It won't take very long.
Just to make some peace,
Let us all join in a little song.
ALL: We want to twinkle, twinkle, twinkle,
little movie star,
And you can sprinkle, sprinkle,
sprinkle money near and far.
Your salary's way up in the millions,
For you always fool the villyuns
In the movies!

ANNIE MCGINNIS PAVLOVA

Lyric by Oscar Hammerstein II and Herman Axelrod. Introduced by H. William Hanemann (Emma) and chorus.

VERSE 1

Clancey was fond of a show,
From opera to movies he'd go.
On dancin' and prancin' Clancey was keen,
But the Ballet Russe he never had seen.
For five dollars a throw he decided to go
And he bought him a seat in the very first row.*
Annie came out. Clancey yelled, "Stop her!
She ain't no Roosian, for I knew her poppa!"

REFRAIN

Annie McGinnis Pavlova,
I'll stop you from puttin' one over,
'Twas in Hogan's back alley
You learned the bacchanale
And now you're the pride of the Ballet Russe.
They call you a zephyr, a fairy, an elf—
Put on your flannels, take care of yourself!
For the costume you're wearin's a shame to old
Erin,
Oh, Annie, you'd better go home.

VERSE 2

Clancey thought after the show
Around to the stage door he'd go.
As Annie came out he took off his hat
And asked her to come to a swell automat.
Before he could stop her, she dropped him a
copper.
He looked very shabby, she thought it was proper.
Then as she rolled around to the Ritz in her Rolls-
Royce,
He got up his Irish and yelled in a loud voice:
"Take this back, Annie, and save all your
dollars—
Your old man is still wearing celluloid collars."

REPEAT REFRAIN

---

* *The* Home, James *program-libretto offers two
additional lines following this one, along with a
variant ending:*
During one of the ballets, daring and risky,
There came on a maiden who danced very frisky.
Then Clancy arose in his seat and yelled, "Stop her!
She ain't no Russian, for I know her popper."

THE ETERNAL TRIANGLE

Lyric by Oscar Hammerstein II and Herman Axelrod. Introduced by Oscar Hammerstein II (Armand), John D. Beals Jr. (Gideon), and H. William Hanemann (Emma).

VERSE

It always starts with a cup of tea,
Then keeps on getting stronger.
The faithless wife keeps going wrong,
Until she can't go wronger.
Her lover is one of those dashing Romeos
Who struts as he strokes his six mustachios,
And there always is a husband who neglects his
    wifie dear,
And reduces her allowance to but fifty thou' a year.

REFRAIN

These are the problems of a poor young wife in a
    problem play,
Every author hands them to us in a different way.
Each young playwright wants to be a
Neat, eugenic Eugène Brieux,
Inspired by a vision.
Give them life, that's our decision.
Enough of the problem play.

ANOTHER HAWAIIAN SONG

Lyric by Oscar Hammerstein II and Herman Axelrod. Introduced by Ormand V. Gould (Lucius Vodka) and ensemble.

VERSE 1

They're all a-tryin'
Those songs Hawaiian today.
The new composers
Of musical shows are
Successful that way.
They find names in some geography,
Then they write Hawaiian songs like this:

REFRAIN

Oh, you beautiful Hawaiian belle
In your gown of shredded wheat,
You always look so neat.

From Anoloa to Li-li-wi
There's not a maiden so fair to see.
At Nakelele, your ukelele
Just wins my heart with its tone so sweet.
When you whisper "Halehakulu,"
Then I don't know what to do.
Waikiki, Anahola
Hula-hula, Coca-Cola,
That means I'm in love with you.

VERSE 2

They're all a-buyin'
Those things Hawaiian today.
No home's complete
Without a uke to beat—
They teach the babies to play.
No more words with the piano man,
No more trouble from the old installment plan.

REPEAT REFRAIN

FURS AND FRILLS

MAKE YOURSELVES AT HOME

This song was the Act Two opening for *Furs and Frills*, a musical presented by Arthur Hammerstein at the Casino Theatre, New York City, from October 9 through November 3, 1917. Book and lyrics by Edward Clark, based on his play *Coat Tales*. Music by Silvio Hein. Staged by Edward Clark. Orchestra directed by Herbert Stothart.

On September 23, 1917, using writing paper headed "Arthur Hammerstein's Productions, Inc.," Oscar Hammerstein explained to a family friend: "I have given up the study of law and entered the theatrical field, with my uncle's firm. I intend eventually to do some play writing, since that is the branch that appeals to me most, and for which I feel I have some talent." Arthur Hammerstein had asked his nephew not to write anything for a year, but the ban was short-lived. The novice's letter continued: "I have written some verses to the music of our new show, to be produced next month, and they have been accepted. It is really a very encouraging start."

Hammerstein included the following fragment in the introduction to his anthology, *Lyrics*. No additional material has been found.

Make yourselves at home,
'Neath our spacious dome.
Do just as you please
In twos or threes, if you'd rather—
But rest assured you'll be no bother.

TEN FOR FIVE (1918)

New York run: Gymnasium, Columbia University; May 2 and 3, 1918. A Musical Farce in two acts, presented by the 1918 Campus War Show Committee under the management of Walter Arthur Funcke, class of '18. Written and staged by Oscar Hammerstein II, '16. Music by Robert K. Lippmann, '19. Additional songs by H. William Hanemann, '17; Robert A. Simon, '19; and Marcus M. Wolff, '16.

Major roles: Harold J. Horan, '21 (Mrs. Thurlow, with society aspirations); Emil Gyss, '20 (Mr. Thurlow, only her husband); Herbert A. Rauchfuss, '20 (Emily Thurlow, a troublesome daughter); Percival E. Cowan, '19 (Helen Thurlow, another T.D.); Phillip B. Leavitt, '18 (Jack Jordan, a captain of finance); Richard West, '20 (Bob Barker, who is drawn into it); Max B. Cohen, '20 (Ivory); E. T. Clark, '21 (Caspar); and A. F. Richardson, '19 (Leftenant O'Shea).

Hammerstein abandoned Columbia Law School for marriage and a job with Arthur Hammerstein Productions, but stayed active in campus theatrics. *Ten for Five* was reviewed in the *Columbia Daily Spectator* by no less a personage than Professor George C. D. Odell, known for his *Annals of the New York Stage*. Odell praised "a libretto which has that almost unheard of thing, an intelligible plot," and "the brightness and snap of lines, the cleverness of the jingles, and the dash and 'go' of the dialogue."

No music is known to survive. Lyrics were published in the spring issue of *The Jester*, the campus humor magazine. *The Jester* preserves only refrains, but most songs would probably have had verses.

No lyrics have been found for the Act One finale, the Act Two opening chorus, or the Act Two finale. The editor suspects the "rousing Liberty song" mentioned in the *Spectator* was part of the Act Two finale.

OPENING CHORUS

Introduced by the ensemble and Harold J. Horan (Mrs. Thurlow).

ENSEMBLE: It's great to go weekending,
Your summer spending in fun.
Bring our host a box of candy,
And your duty is done.
You're bound to have a gay time,
The night and day time are one.
Come try some tennis, lady.
The glen is shady and cool.
And we'll all go off together
For a dip in the pool.
Just take a boat or motor along some heavenly road,
We can stop at an inn midst jazz and din,
And at night we'll get home with a load.

MRS. THURLOW: [*spoken*] Good morning, everybody. Having a good time?

BOYS: Fair and charming hostess gracious,
Your home is the acme of perfection.
Its halls so commodious and spacious
Can stand the test of critical inspection.
The grounds about your place
Abound in airy grace.
Your taste is *comme il faut*.
Extravagance so lavishing
Has made it all so ravishing.
No paradise
Is quite as nice
We know.

MRS. THURLOW: [*spoken*] I'm glad you're enjoying yourselves. Excuse me a moment. I have an audience with Her Majesty the cook.

1ST BOY: To tell you the truth, I don't think much of this place.

1ST GIRL: It's gawdy and garish and far too old for me.

2ND GIRL: And as for the hostess herself, well she's a queer case.

2ND BOY: Her spouse is a souse and he's always on a spree.

ENSEMBLE: Her spouse is a souse and he's always on a spree.
What she ever saw in that man is hard to see.

We don't like to talk, but to be quite frank,
They say that the lady's an awful crank.
However—we have to thank
Them graciously.

MRS. THURLOW: [*spoken*] Remember—dinner a half hour earlier this evening.

ENSEMBLE: The grounds about your place
Abound in airy grace.
Your taste is *comme il faut*.
Extravagance so lavishing
Has made it all so ravishing.
No paradise
Is quite as nice
We know.

THAT'S THE DOPE

Introduced by Percival E. Cowan (Helen), Herbert A. Rauchfuss (Emily), Richard West (Bob), and Phillip B. Leavitt (Jack).

ALL: Step right up and make believe you're not afraid.
That's the system, that's the dope.
Stand up straight and face the awful fusillade.

BOB: I think I'd better just send a letter.

ALL: Come on, pluck up your nerve.
Where's your vim and verve?
Show some speed with a spin on your old outcurve.

BOB: Suppose he speaks of money topics tiring?

ALL: Answer back and everything.
Make him think you've got the price to buy a ring.
And though you may receive a kick or two,
You mustn't let that bother you.
Don't stop to mope—
Keep right on hoping.
That's the dope!

HOW TO WIN A BOY

Introduced by Herbert A. Rauchfuss (Emily) and ensemble.

There is nothing like a loving sweetheart,
But to catch him is a rather neat art.

First he'll shy away;
Then he'll try to play.
Don't give in too early
Or you'll lose him, little girlie.
For you must be so dignified
And so exclusive.
Be elusive
And coy,
Just toy,
Until you make him thrill and tingle
So with joy
That he'll get sick of being single,
And you'll soon have another name.
If you play the game—
That's the only way to win a boy.

IF YOU DON'T GET CAUGHT

Introduced by Phillip B. Leavitt (Jack) and Richard West (Bob).

You start in very small
And then you begin to branch out.
It isn't hard at all
If only you know what you're about.
Read the lives of all the magnates—
See what old John D. has taught—
And it's a cinch that you
Can make a million, too,
If you don't get caught.

WHERE ARE MY CHILDREN?

Introduced by Harold J. Horan (Mrs. Thurlow) and ensemble.

Where are my children?
Where are my children?
Where are my little girls tonight?
I've learned of Broadway's glamours
From thrilling photo drammers;
They cause me no end of fright.
Any reckless chap
May set a wicked trap—
How can a mother know?
Even now my wayward lasses

May be sipping demitasses—
Where do my children go?

WHEN I DANCE WITH YOU

Sung and danced by Percival E. Cowan (Helen) and Phillip B. Leavitt (Jack). A second dance was performed by Max B. Cohen (Ivory) and E. T. Clark (Caspar).

My heart is always light when I dance with you,
The earth is heaven and the skies are blue.
There's a rhythm so sweet
In the swing of your feet.
You've a pep
In your step
That is hard to beat.
Your swaying fox trot drives away all care,
And when we waltz, you seem to float on air.
You've won a maiden's heart for fair
With your dancing.

I'LL ALWAYS THINK OF YOU

Introduced by Herbert A. Rauchfuss (Emily), Richard West (Bob), and ensemble.

When lovers say goodbye,
Two happy hearts are cut in twain.
But smiles are to save, dear;
Let's be brave, dear:
We'll be together again.
When lovers say goodbye,
Theirs is a sad and harsh adieu.
But wait for the day, dear,
While I'm away, dear,
I'll always think of you.

IN THE SOUTH SEA ISLES

Introduced by E. T. Clark (Caspar) and ensemble.

I'd like to live on an island
In the South Sea Isles,

Where drowsy sun-kissed breezes blow—
All the universe smiles.
They have no super income tax,
No fancy suits with belted backs,
It's great to live on an island
In the South Sea Isles.

BEANS

Introduced by A. F. Richardson (Leftenant O'Shea).

Don't mention beans!
We have them for breakfast and luncheon.
Don't mention beans!
For as sure as we're sinners,
Our dinners
Always find us munchin'
Big, baked, brown beans,
In the Army, the Navy, or Marines!
So remember what I've told yer—
Never try to serve a soldier
With your beans, beans, beans!

JAZZ

Introduced by E. T. Clark (Caspar).

Listen to the music
That is played so entrancing
By that big jazz band!
Thrills you through and through
Until you can't keep from dancing,
You must take a hand.
Skippin' with a pippin
On a glorious floor—
Hoppin', never stoppin'
Till they give you some more.
All the waiters rush around
In time to the melody;
Crowds surge at the door!
Tunes so rich and mellow
Seem to come from that fellow
With the saxophone.
When it comes to drumming
There's a man at the end
Who simply stands alone.

MISLEADING LEGENDS

Introduced by Herbert A. Rauchfuss (Emily) and Richard West (Bob).

I

EMILY: Once a pair of sweethearts wooed and won
    each other's love,
    In a most idealistic way.
    The boy's poetic passion seemed inspired
    from above,
    His history will live for aye.
    This youth was quite a model, for he never
    grew too bold;
    He was satisfied to touch her hand.
    And if anyone spoke lightly of his lady—
    so I'm told—
    He'd fight and kill the bravest in the land.
    If you'd be my true lover,
    Copy young Romeo.
    He'd die to get
    His Juliet,
    For he worshipped her so;
    And he'd never refuse her
    Whatever she bid—
BOB: Romeo was a mighty foolish kid!

II

BOB: 'Midst the blooming lotus of a bower in
    old Japan
    Dwelt a dainty Oriental maid.
    She tumbled for the sighing of a Yankee
    sailor man,
    And loved the game of hearts he played.
    But one fine day she saw him with a
    snappy blue-eyed queen,
    And it smashed the idol of her pride.
    Her little heart was bleeding, but she
    never made a scene.
    She made her bow and meekly stepped
    aside.
    Now the girl who loves me must
    Be like poor Butterfly.
    If I should see
    Another, she
    Must go off somewhere and die.
    Butterfly made no trouble,
    Butterfly said no word—
EMILY: But a fly is a very foolish bird!

THE SONG THAT GOES

Introduced by Percival E. Cowan (Helen), Herbert A. Rauchfuss (Emily), Richard West (Bob), and Phillip B. Leavitt (Jack).

Sing of boys and girls,
Sing of lips and curls,
Sing of moon, June, tune, spoon—
Any old rhyming,
Just so long as you can talk of youth and spring-
    timing.
Do this thing
À la Brice and King—
That's the song that goes
In musical comedy shows.

I SIMPLY CAN'T DO WITHOUT BOYS

Introduced by Harold J. Horan (Mrs. Thurlow) and ensemble.

VERSE

When I was a little girl, not so long ago,
I was known all round New York as
Dirty little tomboy Dorcas.
When I romped and played with boys, we
Used to have good times together.
Shouting, running, always noisy,
Outdoors in all kinds of weather.
And the sex they call the weaker
I detest unto this day—
Hypocrites! I'd rather be cour-
ageous. That is what I say:

REFRAIN

I simply can't do without boys, boys.
I'm crazy for male company.
I simply can't do without boys, boys—
You're all necessary to me.
To have a manly arm to lean upon
Is the sweetest of all joys.
I've a malady chronic,
And you are the tonic—
I must have the boys.

EARLY SONGS WITH RICHARD RODGERS

After meeting Richard Rodgers backstage at *Home, James* in 1917, Hammerstein wrote a few lyrics for his songs. The fledgling composer, then in high school, was providing music and some lyrics for amateur musicals presented by a group of slightly older boys called the Akron Club. Rodgers reused some of that material in subsequent shows at Columbia and the Institute of Musical Art. The program for the Akron Club's 1920 show *You'd Be Surprised* credits the words of "That Boy of Mine" to Hammerstein, but neither music nor lyrics are known to survive.

THERE'S ALWAYS ROOM FOR ONE MORE

Introduced by Phillip B. Leavitt (Robert Lorraine) and ensemble in *Upstage and Down* (Akron Club, 1919); reused in the score of *Fly with Me* (Columbia, 1920). Published in that show's vocal score, and recently reprinted in the songbook *Rodgers and Hammerstein Rediscovered*.

VERSE 1

BOY: You're sweet little things.
GIRLS: Oh, thank you, sir.
BOY: Petite little things.
GIRLS: Oh, thank you, sir.
BOY: The only things that make this world
            worthwhile.
        For money and fame—
GIRLS: Bring only woe.
BOY: It's an empty game—
GIRLS: Let's let it go.
BOY: There's naught to match a maid's
            bewitching smile.

REFRAIN 1

BOY: My heart is an airy castle filled with girls I
            adore;
        My brain is a cloud of memories of
            peaches galore.
        There was Jane and Molly, and Ruth and
            Sue,
        Camilla, Kit, and Patricia too.
        My heart is filled to the brim with you,
        But there's always room for one more.

VERSE 2

BOY: I've loved quite a lot—
GIRLS: We've heard it said.
BOY: But happy I'm not—
GIRLS: Why don't you wed?
BOY: A disappointed Romeo am I.
        My heaven is in the *Rubaiyat*—
GIRLS: By Omar Khayyam,
        We've heard of that.
BOY: For such a paradise I fain would try.

REFRAIN 2

BOY: A jug, and a loaf, a bough, a girl is all I
            implore;
        But my little list of loves increases daily a
            score.
        They would all imbibe any vineyard's
            brew;
        I'd have to purchase a bak'ry too.
        A forest of boughs wouldn't shelter you,
        For there's always room for one more.

WEAKNESSES

Alternate title: "A Weakness in My Family." Music does not survive. Introduced by Ralph Engelsman (Thaddeus Brownlow) in *Upstage and Down* (Akron Club, 1919); reused in *Fly with Me* (Columbia, 1920).

VERSE 1

Girlies are my mission,
Blonde, brunette, or titian,
My Spanish disposition makes me bold.
Almost any day,
Many times I'm led astray;
Any pretty pair of eyes can knock me cold.
But of course, you can't blame me,
It's a weakness in my family.

REFRAIN 1

Father had a fondness for the ladies,
And his papa before him was the same.
A filmy bit of fluff
Has always been enough
To fan the fatal flame.
All my uncles liked ankles so neat and trim;
A shapely little shoulder always got my brother
    Jim;
Ev'ry skirt is a signal of danger to me—
It's a weakness in my family.

VERSE 2

Mary, Meg, and Molly,
Doris, Dorcas, Dolly—
I could go on naming many more.
Most of them were stringing me,
Took delight in stinging me—
I don't trust any woman over four.
But you simply can't blame me,
It's an heirloom of my family tree.

REFRAIN 2

Father's father's father was a Mormon;
His family came from France when he was small;
His uncle came from Spain
With blood of Moorish strain—
He made the señoritas fall.
His granddad was Turkish, he led some life—
Each time he turned a corner he would bump into
    a wife.
Just imagine what they've handed over to me—
It's a weakness in my family.

VERSE 3

Look at old man Adam—
Little Eva had 'im
Buffaloed in forty different ways.
And the truth between us is
All the famous Venuses
Got away with murder in their days.
So, of course you can't blame me,
I'm justified by history.

REFRAIN 3

Tony had an awful crush on Cleo;
Another famous Roman was the same.
Soldier, saint, or sage,
Great men of every age
Were wild about some dame.
Napoleon fell for his Josephine;
Louis had Du Barry, and I've got my little queen;
It's hard to live with 'em; without 'em we're
    wrecks—
It's a weakness with the whole male sex.

CAN IT

Music does not survive. Introduced in *Upstage and Down* (Akron Club, 1919) by Phillip B. Leavitt (Robert Lorraine) and Blanche Stern (Louise).

ROBERT: Oh, I want to make love to you so badly.
LOUISE: You make love badly, dear. I'll say
            you do.
ROBERT: My feelings have run amuck!
LOUISE: Oh boy, then you're out of luck;
            If you want to propose, I'll listen—
            Only talk United States.
ROBERT: Remember the time I met you?
            You were falling on your skates.
LOUISE: Ain't this the darndest song you've ever
            heard?
ROBERT: Can I dare to hope that you'll consent to
            be my wife?
LOUISE: Can that mushy talk. Don't make me
            laugh, dear.
ROBERT: You could learn to like me.
LOUISE: You don't know the half, dear.
            I'm glad you asked me to be your partner
            for life.
ROBERT: Let's go. Let's go and seek a parson.
LOUISE: What could be sweeter love than that?
ROBERT: He will make us one who now are two.
LOUISE: And do you think that you will say
            You'll promise always to obey?
ROBERT: I'll tell the world that I do. Do you?

Three moments from Jimmie. *Top:* Frances White

Songs of 1920

ALWAYS YOU (1920)

Tryouts: Forest Theater, Providence, Rhode Island, week of November 27, 1919 (as *Joan of Arkansaw*); Majestic Theater, Boston, December 1, 1919 (as *Joan of Arkansaw*); Poli's Theater, Washington, D.C., December 29, 1919. New York run: Central Theatre, opened January 5, 1920; moved to Lyric Theatre January 26, 1920; closed February 28, 1920; 66 performances total. Music by Herbert P. Stothart. Book and lyrics by Oscar Hammerstein II. Presented by Arthur Hammerstein. Dances and ensembles by Robert Marks. Orchestra under the direction of Herbert P. Stothart. Settings by Julius Dove. Costumes by Paul Arlington, Inc.

Cast: Helen Ford (Toinette Fontaine), Walter Scanlan (Bruce Nash), Edouard Ciannelli (East Indian Peddler), Julia Kelety (Julie Fontaine), Russell Mack (Charlie Langford), Ralph C. Herz (Montmorency Jones), Bernard Gorcey (A Mysterious Conspirator), Anna Seymour (Joan Summers), Joseph Barton (Thomas), Emily Russ (Waitress), Cortez and Peggy (specialty dancers), and ensemble.

The story is set in Trouville in the summer of 1919. One year earlier, American soldier Bruce Nash had a romance with Toinette, a local girl. He has finally returned, but with a fiancée (Joan) in tow. Naturally, Toinette is devastated and avoids them. The audience soon learns that Bruce and Joan are not in love. In fact, an attraction is developing between Joan and Bruce's best friend, Charlie. Charlie travels with Monty, a comical valet who gets involved in the schemes of "A Mysterious Conspirator."

The main source for this chapter is the published sheet music. A draft of the script, with song descriptions but no lyrics, is preserved in the Oscar Hammerstein II Collection in the Music Division of the Library of Congress.

The songs "Let's Marry," "Act One Finale," "The Voice of Baghdad" and "Woman" have not been found. Two more songs, "Hayward's Harlem Hellions" and "Passing Through," are linked to this show by the *Rodgers and Hammerstein Fact Book*, but no material has been found and they may not be by Hammerstein and Stothart. Both songs are assigned to the character Joan; newspaper clippings from the post-Broadway tour credit them to Burton Green, husband and accompanist of Irene Franklin, who was then playing Joan.

In a 1953 letter, Hammerstein recalled:

I was working for my uncle as a stage manager and [a strike by] Actors' Equity stopped all shows that we were rehearsing here in the summer for the coming season, so I had some time on my hands. So did his musical conductor, Herbert Stothart. We sat down therefore and wrote a musical play. I read it to my uncle and Herb, the composer, sat on a sofa doubled up with laughter every time I came to what purported to be a joke. At the end of the session my uncle thought he had heard the funniest play ever written . . . No audience ever laughed as loud or harder than my collaborator did on the day we sold the play.

ALWAYS YOU

Published as an individual sheet. Introduced by Walter Scanlan (Bruce) and Helen Ford (Toinette). Those studying Hammerstein's development as a librettist may find his early stage directions of interest. Bruce has promised Toinette that "if he survives the war, he will come back to her. This leads into the theme song, 'Always [You].' The orchestra plays very softly through the dialogue immediately preceding the number. Bruce's speech blends right into the lyric of the verse."

VERSE

BRUCE: Now that fate has called me from your
    side,
    Dear little girl,
    Little girl of mine—
TOINETTE: Through the days of darkness I'll
    abide.
BRUCE*: Heart of my heart,
    I will wait and pine.
TOINETTE: Hope and the sun will shine through,
    dear,
    I'll think of you, always of you, dear.

REFRAIN

Always you,
Always you,
No one but you for my own.
Night and day,
Far away,
Longing for you alone
(So be brave, dear).
For time will fly,
By and by
We'll make our dreams come true—
Years may pass by,

---

* *The line assignments in the sheet music may be inaccurate: typically it is the woman who waits and pines for her lover's return. No character names are given for the refrain.*

Love cannot die,
It will be always you.

A WONDERFUL WAR

Published as an individual sheet as "Wonderful War." Introduced by Julia Kelety (Julie) and female ensemble.

VERSE

Rap-a-tap the tramp of feet.
Rap-a-tap tap down the street.
Rap-a-tap the brazen beat
Of the drums of war.
But the drums of war
Will be here no more,
And compared to what it was,
Our life's an awful bore.

REFRAIN

For we had oodles of heroes handsome.
Lieutenants and captains too.
When with a glance
You'd always land some,
What else could a poor girl do?
Blue Devils dashing and brave and tall, girls.
Sammies and Tommies galore.
Taking it all in all, girls,
It sure was a wonderful war.

I NEVER MISS

Published as an individual sheet. Introduced by Russell Mack (Charlie) and female ensemble.

VERSE 1

When I was but a stripling
I agreed with Mister Kipling
That the female was by far the deadlier sex.
Approached them with timidity,
Afraid of their frigidity—
They seemed incomprehensibly complex.
I learned what words in Cupid's dictionary meant,
But even that did not improve my rep.
Then I grew bold and started to experiment
And now I know that what they want is pep.

REFRAIN 1

I never miss, I never miss;
I've a system that is sure.
Ev'ry girlie seeks adventure,
Though her manner be demure.
I never try the mournful eye
Or a plea for just a kiss,
I just take it and they like it,
I never miss—
I never, never, never miss.

VERSE 2

I took a trip to Sweden,
Which you know is just an Eden,
Filled with beauties of the tall and stately type.
I chanced to meet a pretty one,
Her eyes were like the midnight sun,
Her hair was fair, her cheeks like apples ripe.
I told her I was captain in the navy an'
Some other lies—I write all my own stuff.
My copyrights include the Scandinavian.
In ev'ry country they like treatment rough.

REFRAIN 2

I never miss, I never miss.
So with confidence and ease
I embraced this pretty maiden
Without even saying please.
I stole a kiss, I stole a kiss;
Then she struck out with her fist.
She was young and strong and Swedish.
I'm glad she missed—
I'm awful, awful glad she missed.

SYNCOPATED HEART

Published as an individual sheet. Introduced by Helen
Ford (Toinette) and Russell Mack (Charlie).

VERSE 1

My poor heart is thumping, jumping—
Listen, can you hear?
How it flutters, stops and stutters—
Must be out of gear.
At other times my pulse is normal,
But when I know that he is near—

REFRAIN

I've got a syncopated heart
That beats in ragtime.
It will not regulate, you see.
A most seductive melody
Keeps jingling, ting-a-ling in me.
What can it be?
I've called upon physicians,
But
[spoken] No pill can cure. But still
[sung] A kiss from him will turn the trick,
That's my prescription;
He'd better hurry up and start,
Because this wicked little heart
Just wants to dance.
All the music of romance
Is in my syncopated heart,
My little syncopated heart.

VERSE 2

This peculiar palpitation
Takes your breath away;
Gives you such a queer sensation,
Makes you sad and gay.
And when at last you see him coming,
You never know just what to say.

REPEAT REFRAIN

SAME OLD PLACES

Published as an individual sheet. Introduced by Helen
Ford (Toinette) and Walter Scanlan (Bruce).

VERSE 1

BRUCE: I will take you back to a paradise—
TOINETTE: A lover's paradise I know.
BRUCE: To our secret haunt, you and I alone—
TOINETTE: Just you and I alone will go.
BRUCE: We'll sit upon the same old benches—
TOINETTE: Whisper same old talks—
BRUCE: Tread the same old by-paths in our
walks.

REFRAIN

Same old places, mem'ries so clear.
Same old places, landmarks so dear.
Same shelter'd bowers and corners where we
Would pass happy hours in youth's ecstasy.
Same old pouting, pert little fights,

Make-up kisses, wonderful nights.
Let's play the game just the same as before—
Same old sweethearts once more.

VERSE 2

BRUCE: I have been away for so long a time.
TOINETTE: It seemed a long, long time to me.
BRUCE: I just sat and waited in happiness.
TOINETTE: I fear'd that it could never be.
But when I used to visit
All the scenes we loved so well,
Each place had a joyful tale to tell:

REPEAT REFRAIN

SOME BIG SOMETHING

Published as an individual sheet. Introduced by Anna
Seymour (Joan).

VERSE 1

I cannot explain this queer emotion
For a man whom I have never seen.
When you've had it, then you'll know
Just exactly what I mean:

REFRAIN

Some big something
That just makes sport of
All your discretion and care.
Some big whispers,
A kind of sort of
"Come, you are mine, lady fair."
First you resist, then your heart starts to go;
Something has made all your senses glow.
You can't describe it, and yet you know
Whatever it is, it's there.

VERSE 2

On the desert sands you may encounter,
In a crowded city thoroughfare,
This big something comes to you,
Brings its magic message there:

REPEAT REFRAIN

POUSSE-CAFÉ

Alternate title: "My Pousse-Café." Published as an individual sheet. As Hammerstein biographer Stephen Citron points out, the French in this lyric is not always accurate. Introduced by Julia Kelety (Julie) and Ralph Herz (Montmorency).

VERSE 1

JULIE: Voulez-vous? Voulez-vous?
MONTMORENCY: What is it that you want me to do?
JULIE: Tra, la, la, la, la, la, la, la, la, la, la.
MONTMORENCY: I see you.
JULIE: Parlez-vous
I would like to sing your praise.
Steve, you'll get me
If you let me
Use my langue française.

REFRAIN 1

JULIE: You are such a dashing roué.
Monsieur, tu es chic and risqué.
You have so much savoir faire
about you
And a manner degagé,
Tu es sin nigaud et bourgeois,
Meet me ce soir,
Oh je t'aime!
En distant ma passion
I can only say
You are my pousse-café.

VERSE 2

MONTMORENCY: Ma chérie, ma chérie,
You seem to be attracted by me.
JULIE: Tra, la, la, la, la, la, la, la, la, la, la.
MONTMORENCY: Frenchie dear, listen here,
Tell me why I charm you so.
JULIE: It's a myst'ry, just a myst'ry
That I'll never know.

REFRAIN 2

JULIE: Can it be the graceful ennui
Of your bonne nuit?
Dites-moi, je pris.
Or perhaps it's something in your
ésprit?
Tu n'es que mon chimpanzee.
C'est peut-être vos yeux je crois,
dear,
Or that something
Je n'ai quoi, dear.

I cannot explain it
I can only say
You are my pousse-café.

I'LL SAY SO

Published as an individual sheet. Introduced by Russell Mack (Charlie) and Anna Seymour (Joan).

VERSE 1

CHARLIE: Will you be my sweet little wife,
Partner for life
Through care and strife?
Doesn't matter what I may do,
Can I depend on you?

REFRAIN 1

CHARLIE: I'll say so,
I'm for you while peaches grow, dear.
JOAN: Just say so,
And the two of us will go, dear.
CHARLIE: Round to the church with its funny
little aisle—
JOAN: We'll have a talk with the parson for a
while.
CHARLIE: Pretty wedding ring
And ev'ry little thing for you.
JOAN: Please say so,
For you know I'm crazy 'bout you.
Don't stray so,
I could never live without you;
I'll say so,
I'll promise I'll always be true.
CHARLIE: Expressing it briefly,
Little lady, I love you.

VERSE 2

CHARLIE: Will you be my cute little queen,
Sweet seventeen?
JOAN: Kid, use your bean.
Cancel all this poetry stuff,
I want to see the ring.

REFRAIN 2

CHARLIE: I'll say so.
You have got me on your staff, dear.
JOAN: I'll say so,
Really you don't know the half, dear.
I'm glad you asked me to be your little
wife.

CHARLIE: I'm here to state I belong to you for life.
JOAN: Am I idolized?
My dear, you'll be surprised to hear.
I'll say so,
You can bet your old fedora.
CHARLIE: Sweet cookie,
You have captured my angora,
I'll say so,
I'll utter, I'll tell the world true—
Expressing it briefly,
Little lady, I love you.

DON'T YOU REMEMBER*

Alternate title: "Lullaby." Published as an individual sheet. Introduced by Julia Kelety (Julie) and Helen Ford (Toinette). The line assignments in the sheet music may not be correct. Some sources say the song was cut before the New York opening.

VERSE

JULIE: Come dry your eyes;
There is nothing to fear—
TOINETTE: While you are here.
JULIE: Through nights of darkness
I'll always be near.
TOINETTE: My Julie, dear.
JULIE: Clear morning bells
Toll the coming of day.
TOINETTE: What do they say?
JULIE: Childhood phantom sorrow
Turns to joy tomorrow,
So brush those tears away.

REFRAIN

JULIE: Do you remember, my dear,
You used to tuck me up in sheets as
white as snow?
Your little mother stood near;
It doesn't seem to me so very long ago.
TOINETTE: I was afraid of the dark;
I used to hate to lose the candle's
gentle glow;
Then to our bundle of pink and pretty
baby—
BOTH: We would sing lullabies soft and low.

REPEAT REFRAIN

* Although the lyric itself asks "Do you remember?" the sheet music and copyright registration give the title as "Don't You Remember."

DRIFTING ON

Published with the *Joan of Arkansaw* sheet music cover as "Drifting" and with the *Always You* sheet music cover as "Drifting On." Introduced by Walter Scanlan (Bruce).

A scenario at the Library of Congress describes the song to be written. At the end of Act Two, Bruce is without a romantic partner. He "soliloquizes," and "all the different types of girls that have come in and out of his life glide across the stage during the song. Brief little episodes are enacted with some of them. After the number has taken its earned encores, Bruce returns to his chair and the stage is clear. The orchestra continues to play 'Drifting' very softly." Toinette enters and they reconcile.

VERSE 1

Memories of lost desire
Buzzing like a swarm of bees,
Mmm——Mmm——.
Each of them a burnt-out fire
Scattered by a vagrant breeze,
Mmm——Mmm——.

REFRAIN 1

Drifting, drifting, gliding swiftly
Over the sea of dreams,
Sweethearts, sweethearts without number,
Fair as the pale moonbeams.
Short and tall ones, large and small ones,
Visions of lost romance.
Some last but a single day;
Others come, longer stay;
One by one they drift away
And the world goes on.

VERSE 2

First there was a schoolgirl sweetheart,
Fluffy little seventeen,
Mmm——Mmm——.
Then I had a mild flirtation
With a pretty Red Cross queen,
Mmm——Mmm——.

REFRAIN 2

I was jilted by a widow
After a brief romance;
Then a fiery señorita
Led me a merry dance.
Sometimes I found love on horseback
Or in the briny sea;
Fell for a showgirl cute and smart,

Loved her art, had a speaking part;
Then a vampire gripped my heart . . .
And the world goes on.

A STRING OF GIRLS

Alternate title: "The Tired Business Man." Published as an individual sheet. Introduced by Anna Seymour (Joan), Russell Mack (Charlie), and female ensemble.

VERSE 1

It's a cinch to put across a show
If you try—'d ya ever try?
You can keep them laughing if you throw
Lots o' pie in the eye.
Pretty costumes and scenery—
These, of course, you must buy.

REFRAIN 1

Start with a little plot,
Cook it, but not too hot.
Throw in a heroine,
Maiden so simple and ingenuish.
Then let your tenor shine with his high C;
Write in a well-known joke,
Use all the old-time hoke,
For this is the surest plan
To entertain the tired business man.

VERSE 2

You've omitted one important thing.
Here's a hunch, here's a hunch.
Is it of the pretty girls you sing?
That's the bunch, that's the bunch.
It's the chorus that does the trick;
They're the crowd with the punch.

REFRAIN 2

Bring on a string of girls,
Each with her string of pearls.
Teach them some tricky twirls;
Dress them in costumes a trifle naughty.
Sing of a summer night under the stars;
Light up the yellow moon;
Write up a jazzy tune—
For this is the surest plan
To entertain the tired business man.

MISTERIOSO

Alternate title: "Mysterioso." Published as an individual sheet. Introduced by Bernard Gorcey (A Mysterious Conspirator), Ralph Herz (Montmorency Jones), and Joseph Barton (Thomas),* but dropped before the New York opening.

VERSE 1

COUNT: Conspirators we are,
A terrible three we are,
Oh——!
HUGO: With terrible anger we
Get very angry, we
Do——!

[*A man of few words,* ARMAND *pantomimes over music.*]

ALL THREE: We're perhaps as bad as any
crowd you know.

REFRAIN 1

COUNT AND HUGO: Misterioso!
COUNT: We are as vicious—
HUGO: As you could wish us.
COUNT AND HUGO: Misterioso!
COUNT: We keep the lid tight,
HUGO: We work at midnight.
COUNT: Just give us any old plot—
HUGO: We'll tie it up in a knot.

[ARMAND *pantomimes.*]

ALL THREE: That's what we'll do.
COUNT: Misterioso!
No crooks are keener
At misdemeanor.
HUGO: And we are oh so,
So very expert
At making necks hurt.
[*spoken*] If you want an enemy
disposed of quick, we'll
have him in the icebox by
the end of the week.
ALL THREE: We are a bold, bad crew
De-lid-dle-doo.

VERSE 2

COUNT: We're going to strike,
We don't care if you like it or
No——!

* *The published sheet assigns the lyrics to the characters "Count," "Hugo" and "Armand"; during the out-of-town tryouts, the gentlemen were renamed.*

HUGO: We're cranky and sweary
And quite Bolsheviki and
So——

[ARMAND *pantomimes*.]

ALL THREE: Lenin and Trotsky
They do notsky stand a show.

REFRAIN 2

COUNT AND HUGO: Misterioso!
COUNT: We want more wages.
HUGO: We want more wages.
COUNT AND HUGO: Misterioso!
HUGO: We're never quiet;
We love to riot.
COUNT: We'll tell the reason we strike.
HUGO: No, *he*'ll tell you just why we
strike.

[ARMAND *pantomimes*.]

ALL THREE: And that is why.
COUNT: Misterioso!
There's nothing grander
Than propagander.
HUGO: Misterioso!
We'll use our powers
For shorter hours.
[*Spoken*.] We'll commit for you
most any kind of crime, If
you will give us time and
one-half overtime.
ALL THREE: We are a bold, bad crew,
De-lid-dle-doo.

TICKLE ME (1920)

Tryouts: Stamford Theatre, Stamford Connecticut, August 2–3, 1920; Auditorium, Long Branch, New Jersey, August 4–7, 1920; Apollo Theatre, Atlantic City, New Jersey, August 9–14, 1920. New York run: Selwyn Theatre; opened August 17, 1920; closed February 12, 1921; 207 performances. A Musicgirl Comedy.* Produced under the personal direction of Arthur Hammerstein. Book and lyrics by Otto Harbach, Oscar

---

* *The typescript in the Harbach Collection is optimistically subtitled "A Musical Laugh in Two Hysterics and Ten Screams with a Book as Light as a Feather and a Score of Tickling Tunes."*

Hammerstein II, and Frank Mandel. Music by Herbert Stothart. Orchestra under direction of Herbert Stothart. Staged by William Collier. Dances and ensembles by Bert French. Scenic design by Joseph A. Physioc. Costume design by Charles LeMaire.

Cast: Frank Tinney (Frank Tinney), Louise Allen (Mary Fairbanks), Allen Kearns (Jack Barton), Victor Casmore (Marcel Poisson), Marguerite Zender (Alice West), Benjamin Mulvey (Customs Inspector), William Dorriani (Native Boatman), Olga & Mishka (specialty dancers), Frances Grant and Ted Wing (specialty dancers), Jack Heisler (Slave), Marcel Rousseau (the Tongra), Harry Pearce (Blah Blah), Tex Cooper (Keeper of the Sacred Horse), and ensemble.

The plot of *Tickle Me* had an American movie producer (Marcel Poisson) traveling with his stars (Jack Barton and Mary Fairbanks) to film the ceremony of the sacred bath on location in Tibet. Alice West is part of the movie unit and has been writing anonymous love letters to Jack. Frank Tinney, playing himself, impersonates a holy man and, when discovered, is sentenced to be tickled unto death.

Sources for this chapter include published sheet music and piano-vocal manuscripts in the Warner-Chappell Collection in the Music Division of the Library of Congress and in the Herbert Stothart Collection at UCLA. Typed libretti were found in the Frank Mandel Collection at UCLA and in the Otto Harbach Collection at the New York Public Library for the Performing Arts, which also contains contracts for the show.

Very little is known about the division of labor between Harbach, Hammerstein, and Mandel. In separate conversations Hammerstein and Harbach told historian Miles Kreuger that up to and including *Rose-Marie* (1924), Hammerstein did very little of the lyric writing. But Hammerstein apparently felt that *Tickle Me* was enough his work to be mentioned on Ed Sullivan's national television program and during an oral history interview at Columbia University. The third wordsmith on *Tickle Me*, Frank Mandel, is well known to theater historians as a producer and librettist, but not as a lyricist. Inside the published sheets, only Harbach and Hammerstein are credited for the words. But contracts state that Hammerstein, Harbach, and Mandel were co-authors of both book and lyrics, with equal billing and equal royalties.

Although the program and some reviews mention them, no lyrics have been found for "I Don't Laugh at Love Anymore," "Temptation," and "Broadway Swell and Bowery Bum." "Didja Ever See the Like" seems to be part of the Act Two finale. "Adagio" and "Valse du Salon" were probably instrumentals. The Warner-Chappell collection contains two lyricless manuscripts entitled "Bones" and "Opening Act 1."

SAFE IN THE ARMS OF BILL HART

Alternate titles: "Opening" and "Entrance of Girls." Lyric by Otto Harbach and Oscar Hammerstein II. Not published. Introduced by Victor Casmore (Marcel Poisson) and female ensemble (scenario writers).

GIRLS: Good morning, Mister Director,
You're looking quite well.
MARCEL: I'm feeling well. How are you?
GIRLS: Fine!
We hear you're looking for stories.
We have some to sell.
MARCEL: I'll give a thousand or two.
GIRLS: Sold!
MARCEL: First you must make your scenarios clear.
I want to know what I buy.
GIRLS: We'll tell you all, just be patient, old dear.
(Gee, he's a cranky old guy.)
Our work is happy and snappy and peppy and bright—
We know the tricks of our art.
And ev'ry reel always ends with the girlie held tight
[*Sigh*] Safe in the arms of Bill Hart!

Additional lyrics

In an early draft of the script, the song ends with these additional lines:

Here's one tells of a lover who lost his heart's delight.
Here's one tells of a maiden who almost . . . but not quite.
Here's one tells of hero fighting twenty-six Indians laid out.
Kiss—and fade out!

YOU'RE THE TYPE

Lyric by Otto Harbach and Oscar Hammerstein II. Not published. Introduced by Victor Casmore (Marcel) and female ensemble (actresses).

REFRAIN 1

MARCEL: You're the type.
You're the breezy, free and easy kind.

All the fellows will say you're a
    sport.
1ST GIRL: Attaboy!
MARCEL: You're the type
    That is never very far behind,
    And you've made quite a fortune in
    court.
2ND GIRL: Put that in writing.
MARCEL: I think I'm on to you.
    You never like them long,
    For you give them the air when
    they're short.
    But what's the diff'rence, girls?
    Just so long as you are beautiful,
    There's a lover for every sort.

REFRAIN 2

MARCEL: You're the type.
    In your eyes a thousand dangers
    lurk.
    You're the kind that is hard to
    avoid.
FRENCH GIRL: Ah, mon cher, tu est ravissant ce
    soir.
    Kees me!
MARCEL: You're the type
    That is never very fond of work.
    You are "Ritz" and you can't be
    annoyed.
TOUGH GIRL: Kin y'imagine the nerve of that
    dizzy blonde!
MARCEL: You're just the kind of girl
    To star upon the screen,
    If you just find the proper support.
    But what's the diff'rence, girls?
    Just so long as you are beautiful,
    There's a lover for every sort.

A PERFECT LOVER

Lyric by Otto Harbach and Oscar Hammerstein II. Not published. Introduced by Allen Kearns (Jack) and female ensemble.

VERSE

JACK: Take a little tip, girls,
    Make a little trip, girls.
    I've had enough.
    You've really gone too far.
GIRLS: We don't wanna trip,
    Oh, we don't wanna trip.
JACK: Oh, have a little pity,

Have a little pity.
It's pretty tough
To be a cinema star.
GIRLS: Not a bit o' pity,
    Not a bit o' pity.
JACK: Ev'rybody thinks I'm handsome, strong,
    and witty.
    Ev'rybody says* that I'm way over par!

REFRAIN

JACK: I'm a perfect lover,†
    Just a perfect lover,
    But I long to be free.
    All the girls are chasing and embracing—
    What a position for me!
    Now, too much is plenty;
    I have ten or twenty
    Little chickens running round me all the
    day.
    I like a little loving‡
    Just as much as anyone;
    But when it comes so easy,
    Then it isn't any fun!
    When a perfect lover
    Has to handle a mob,
    Love is a terrible job!

---

* *Another typescript has: "Advertisers say."*

† *Another typescript begins this way:*
    I'm a perfect lover,
    Just a perfect lover,
    And they're wild over me.
    My time is not my own;
    They won't leave me alone—
    I'm as wretched as a man can be.
    For too much is plenty . . .

‡ *Alternate ending for second refrain:*
    I think it's great to marry,
    To be home-loving is sublime.
    If I wed all of you
    I'd be home loving all the time.
    When a perfect lover
    Has to handle a mob,
    Love is a terrible job!

FINALETTO, ACT ONE, SCENE 1 including GLOBE TROT and BIG OLD WORLD

Lyric by Otto Harbach and Oscar Hammerstein II. Not published. Introduced by Allen Kearns (Jack), Louise Allen (Mary), Marguerite Zender (Alice), and female ensemble.

Globe Trot

VERSE 1

JACK: Come along, girls, we're going to cross the
    sea.
GIRLS: That's we!
MARY: Go and pack your old innovations for one
    big spree.
ALICE: Wonderful sights to view in desert
    sands—
GIRLS: My lands!
MARY: We would much, much rather hear some
    good jazz bands.

REFRAIN

JACK: Come and dance around the world
    with me.
GIRLS: Let's go!
JACK: Do the globe trot!
GIRLS: Do the globe trot!
MARY: Stop a little while in ev'ry port.
JACK: Do a little courting.
GIRLS: Let's go sporting.
JACK: We will learn a step—
GIRLS: Let's go!
JACK: —in ev'ry land where a flag is unfurled.
MARY: When we do the globe trot—
GIRLS: Just a little globe trot—
ALL: Round the world!

VERSE 2

ALICE: *Gulliver's Travels* once appealed to me.
GIRLS: Oh, gee!
    What a fine young Quaker this Alice
    turned out to be!
MARY: Baedeker's Guide won't help you on this
    tour—
GIRLS: That's sure!
ALICE: But for me this journey holds a magic
    lure.

REPEAT REFRAIN

17

Big Old World

ALICE: Big old world,
Wonder, wonder world,
How I long to learn a lot from you!
Myst'ries that appall—
Let me see them all.
Come I must, my wanderlust is calling.
Then by chance
I may meet romance,
Lurking in a bower built for two.
Be it out in Spain
Or down a lane
Of old Killarney,
Anywhere,
Yes, anywhere
Will do.

Encore

ALICE: Oh, big old world,
Wonder, wonder world!
Then by chance
I am apt to meet romance
Somewhere in this
Wonder, wonder world!
GIRLS: Come and dance around the world
with me—
A little bit of ev'rything we'll see,
All your troubles flee,
With the globe trot.
To the globe trot
We'll dance, prancing.
Come and do the globe trot
Round this great old world—
Some world!

THE SUN IS NIGH

Lyric by Otto Harbach and Oscar Hammerstein II. Not published. Introduced by William Dorriani (Native Boatman).

Sweet, sweet maid,
Another kiss from you, I pray.
Sweet maid
Hear what my heart would say:
For soon I join the Eastern moon in flight.
Love must await another wond'rous night!
Hold me, fold me,
Close in your arms.
Give me the paradise I'm eager for—
Just a precious sip of your charms, dear.
Velvet darkness melts in the sky.

Come, come—
The sun is nigh!

THEN LOVE BEGAN

Lyric by Otto Harbach and Oscar Hammerstein II. Not published. Introduced by Louise Allen (Mary) and Allen Kearns (Jack).

VERSE 1

Eve was wrought from one of Adam's ribs
One fine day,
So they say.
Soon she set her cap to nab his nibs—
Then love began.
Once a wistful shepherd watched his flock,
Heaved a sigh.
Maid passed by,
Wore a chic and modish bearskin frock—
Then love began.
Prince into his lady's boudoir crept,
Days of old,
Knighties bold!
Kissed her golden tresses while she slept—
Then love began.

REFRAIN

Cupid is a democratic sort of cuss;
He never cares who's who.
Whether you dress
As prince or pauper,
Nevertheless
He will
Present you with a mother-in-law.
Perhaps he'll wait,
But soon or late
He goes for us—
Hullabaloo to brew.
But while he is wandering to and fro,
Here is the riddle I want to know:
Why doesn't he pick on you?

VERSE 2

Tiny sunbeam tumbled from the skies,
Heaven knows.
Met a rose,
Kissed the dew of morning from her eyes—
Then love began.
Percival De Puyster Van De Vere
Chanced to go
To a show.

Girlie sang, "Come up and hold me, dear"—
Then love began.
Jimmy sought relief from care and toil,
Luna Park
For a lark,
Took along "an awful purty goil"—
Then love began.

REPEAT REFRAIN

PLAY A LITTLE HINDOO (LITTLE HINDOO MAN)

Lyric by Otto Harbach and Oscar Hammerstein II. Published as an individual sheet (verse and refrain only). The record is not consistent about who introduced this song. The following text comes from the Stothart piano-vocal score, which indicates the characters Tongra, Jack, and the female ensemble.

"Play a Little Hindoo" appears to have replaced the song "India Rubber" during the out-of-town tryouts. The songs share a verse, but the refrains differ in words and melody.

INTRODUCTION

TONGRA: Strew the magic sands
From the desert lands.
[*Spoken*] Oh mighty Vishnu, thou
propitious be! This sacred music, by
a lama strummed! Inspire prophecies
of silent peace! Buddha!
JACK: Boo!
TONGRA: Buddha!
GIRLS: Boo!

VERSE

JACK: Oh, Mister Fakir Man,
Oh, Mister Fakir Man,
You did a terrible thing.
Why did you maul it,
That what-you-may-call-it,
That wonderful, musical string?
Raggy with a rhythm like a summer
breeze,
Swings our knees,
'Scuse it, please!
Stretch your little rubber neck and see
us sway
In the American way.

REFRAIN

Come on and play a little Hindoo, man,
You little Hindostanee melody.
Play and keep it up all day.
Your music makes me sway
From the ankle to the knee,
[*Spoken*] And pretty nearly ev'ry other part of me.
[*Sung*] Ooh, you little Hindoo,
Do a little Hindoo
Blue as no other man can.
[*Spoken*] Ev'rything you strum is sweet and pretty
    sentimental. Wield a wicked thumb and beat a
    ditty Oriental.
[*Sung*] If you will play a little Hindoo Man!

CEREMONY OF THE SACRED BATH

Alternate titles: "Act One Finale," and "Tears of Love."
Lyric by Otto Harbach and Oscar Hammerstein II. Not
published. Introduced by an unidentified performer as
the White Lama, Marcel Rousseau (the Tongra), specialty dancers Frances Grant and Ted Wing and Olga &
Mishka, and ensemble.

This spectacular scene provoked rivers of descriptive
prose from the New York critics. An unsigned item in
the *World* gave these details: "Three foaming cascades of
soapsuds furnished a novel and striking finale. . . . The
soapsuds or bubbles flowed in apparently unending
streams from both sides of the stage, and from a flight of
steps in the centre. That they were real was evidenced by
the fact that the dancers making their entrance through
the foam emerged wet and glistening and aroused feelings of envy in the breasts of an August night audience." "Colgate's Octagon White Floating Soap" got a
special program credit.

TONGRA: To you who tears were shedding
    A healing balm I bring.
    For in their flood
    [*five syllables missing*] joy.

VERSE

WHITE LAMA: Love is full of phantom fears.
    In a vale of fancied sorrow
    Youth seeks romance in the wine of
        its tears.
    Love is full of phantom fears.
    Yesterday and then tomorrow
    'Twill be the same till the dawn of
        all years.

REFRAIN

WHITE LAMA: Tears of a lover's heart,
    Just for a while they smart.
    Buds cannot thrive alone on
        sunshine;
    Raindrops must play their part.
    Though doubt's jealous flame may
        burn,
    True love will always return.
    Grief of a maiden, with its sighing
        so forlorn,
    Fades like a shower on a fickle April
        morn.
    Rainbows come smiling from their
        home above,
    Through the tears of love.

Alternate opening

In the Harbach script, the finale begins with these lines.

TONGRA: Let the ceremony start!
    Maidens who tears for love hath shed,
    Bathe in the sacred fount of joy.
    The goddess will purge your love
        from sorrow.
    Oh holy lama, proceed with fitting
        song,
    A prelude to this miracle divine.

UNTIL YOU SAY GOODBYE

Alternate title: "You Never Know What a Kiss
Can Mean." Lyric by Otto Harbach and Oscar Hammer-
stein II. Published as an individual sheet. Introduced by
Allen Kearns (Jack) and Marguerite Zender (Alice).

VERSE

When love must bid adieu,
You're lonesome and blue,
But there's a sweet consolation:
The rapture of a tender kiss ere you part
Is engraved in your memory's heart.

REFRAIN

You never know what a kiss can mean
Until you say goodbye.
Words will not flow from a grief so keen,
And ev'ry speech is bound to end in just a sigh,
    love.
But there is a little way
Lips can feel each other say:

"I'll come back another day to my love!"
You never know what a kiss can mean
Until you say goodbye.

WE'VE GOT SOMETHING

Lyric by Otto Harbach and Oscar Hammerstein II. Published as an individual sheet. Introduced by Marietta
O'Brien and ensemble.

In an early draft of the script, this number was preceded by a conversation between the spirits of Comedy
and Tragedy, who have opposing interests in the story's
outcome. Tragedy insists the *Tickle Me* characters are in
such a tight spot that a happy ending is impossible.

COMEDY: I'll show you. I'm going to do a big girl
number right now.

TRAGEDY: But you have no excuse.

COMEDY: I don't need any. But it so happens that
this song fits right in with the story. Here's the
situation: The whole bunch is on the way home
now. Their steamer is three miles out of Frisco . . .
and they have so much booze aboard that they
can't drink it all. A lot of fellows have sailed out in
little boats to meet them, and the girls are going
to invite them to come up and help them drink
the supply before they cross the line. That's the
number.

VERSE 1

In these days of water, water ev'rywhere
Little drops of something else are very rare.
Come over, we've struck a mine.
Come over, across the line.

REFRAIN

We've got something
That you'd like to get,
Young man ahoy!
We've got something
That we'd like to bet
Would bring you joy.
Knock on the cellar door and wink an eye,
You'll get something that will make you spry.
We've got something
That you'd like to get—
Hop aboard, little boy.

VERSE 2

Why not come and try a little drink we serve.
Inspiration's waiting, fellows, where's your nerve?

We want you for company.
Come over, we'll have a spree.

REPEAT REFRAIN

TICKLE ME

Lyric by Otto Harbach and Oscar Hammerstein II. Published as an individual sheet. Introduced by Louise Allen (Mary) and ensemble.

VERSE

I'm susceptible,
So susceptible,
If you get what I mean.
Every little sensation causes me joy or vexation.
Don't deride it,
I try to hide it,
But there's a feeling I fear.
Gather around me, my children,
And you shall hear me:

REFRAIN

When but a teeny weeny kiddie,
I would kick and reel
When they'd tickle me.
I used to twist around and turn
And then I'd squirm and squeal:
"Please don't tickle me!
Spank me, tease me, I'll never yell.
Scare me, squeeze me, I'll never tell.
Anything but tickle!"
Well, of course, I was young at the time.
But now I'm older and I've gained a little dignity.
That's the reason why
Attempts to tickle couldn't even get a grin from me,
If you dared to try.
But there's a certain fellow, handsome and smart,
Seems to know that love is an art—
His kisses always tickle me around my heart,
And then I'm through before I start!

IF A WISH COULD MAKE IT SO

Lyric by Otto Harbach and Oscar Hammerstein II. Published as an individual sheet. It is not clear who intro-

duced this number. The program says Marguerite Zender (Alice), Allen Kearns (Jack), and ensemble. But several newspapers cited this song as a favorite because of the eight chorines who performed it.

VERSE

JACK: A little wish can oft work wonders
And that is why
ALICE: And that is why
We can correct Dame Fortune's blunders
JACK: If we but try.
If we but try.
ALICE: If there's anything you want,
Just keep awishing
And you'll surely get it by and by.

REFRAIN

ALICE: If a wish could make it so,
JACK: From dreams as light as air
I'd build a garden fair—
ALICE: Where a wand'ring heart could go—
JACK: And find awaiting there
A someone who could care.
ALICE: We'd be happy then, I know—
JACK: For I could go there, too,
And dearest, so could you.
BOTH: We could live and love forever,
If a wish could only make it so.

ACT TWO FINALE

Lyric by Otto Harbach and Oscar Hammerstein II. Not published. The scene is a concert aboard an ocean liner. Introduced by an unidentified performer (possibly Frank Tinney) as the Bengal Psychic and ensemble. The following text is taken from the Otto Harbach script, and since it reprises "Come Across," which was dropped, it may not be the final version.

PSYCHIC: I must have silence!
Cleanse your minds of all things worldly
And I will show you upon this glass
Visions of whatever you want to see.
Ephemeral reproductions of events
That were, are, or will be!
Wonder and gape and stare aghast,

For on this window I will show . . . the past!
GIRLS: When you have performed this miracle,
We'll applaud in manner lyrical.
PSYCHIC: Be it sad or be it pleasant,
Presently I'll show . . . the present!
GIRLS: It's a mighty good trick if you do it, Mister Hindoo.
It's very much more than any of us kin do.
PSYCHIC: And if 'twill add to my repute, you're
Then to see the dazzling . . . future!
GIRLS: Shoot, Professor. We won't refute yer!
PSYCHIC: [spoken] How far back in the past do you want to go?
GIRL: A hundred years.
PSYCHIC: A hundred years ago.
What would you like to see there?
ANOTHER GIRL: I—bub—b-b-b-b—I w-w-w—
Gee, y'make a girl nervous!
3RD GIRL: I want to see how they danced a hundred years ago.
PSYCHIC: Good! I will show you that picture on this window.
Now, if you will all move up closer,
The dance . . . a hundred years ago!

[OLGA is revealed in colonial costume, dancing a brief minuet.]

GIRLS: You've got to give him credit,
The little Hindoo's clever.
Didja ever see the like?
Didja ever, didja ever?
PSYCHIC: And now for the present.
Where shall our scene take place?
GIRL: Back in Thibet.
PSYCHIC: Whom do you want to see there?
GIRL: The executioner.
PSYCHIC: Very well.
I will show you what the executioner is doing
In far off Thibet
At this very instant.

[Picture: EXECUTIONER doubled up and rolling about in uncontrollable laughter.]

GIRL: What's the matter with him?

PSYCHIC: He can't forget the one about . . .
[*He tells an old joke.*]

GIRLS: He hasn't a thing up his sleeve;
He hasn't a wand to assist him.
We shout "Bravissimo!"
We'd like to kiss him—oh,
Could any woman resist him?

PSYCHIC: And now, ladies—what else?

GIRL: I'd like to see what Frank
Tinney is doing right now.

PSYCHIC: That will make an interesting
picture.

[*Picture:* TINNEY *in a cabin on the liner. A* BAD LAMA *enters and draws a knife.* TINNEY *escapes by diving out a porthole.*]

GIRLS: [*to the tune of "Come Across"*]
He's got it,
He's got it—
His gain, the lama's loss.
But he's fallen into the ocean—
Will he have to swim across?

PSYCHIC: He's safe! He's safe!

GIRLS: He's safe! He's safe!

PSYCHIC: [*spoken*] And now I will show you
what some of our friends
will be doing on this night
five years from now, when
the future is long ago.

[*Picture:* ALICE *seated by a fireplace;* JACK *on the floor beside her chair. When that scene is established, a second picture is revealed:* MARY *looking very angry.*]

OFFSTAGE TENOR: She's waited,
She's waited.
He left her after tea.
He went out to play poker,
But he must o' missed the joker,
For now it's a quarter past
three!

[TINNEY *enters and hands money over to* MARY.]

So you'll have to come across!

CUT AND UNUSED SONGS

COME ACROSS

Lyric by Otto Harbach and Oscar Hammerstein II. Published as an individual sheet but cut before the New York opening. This blackmailing song was a running joke, with Frank Tinney hounded by past girlfriends.

VERSE

ZAZA: I was young and an innocent girl
Till you came along one day.
Then you set all my senses awhirl
With your devilish, debonair way.
Your work was smooth, you little
rascal;
You knew just the thing to do.
And when we parted, you looked
in my eyes
And swore your love was true.

REFRAIN

ZAZA: I've waited,
I've waited;
Each day has seemed a year.
I remember those merry
Afternoons in January
When you used to call me
Your dear, ducky darling!
You promised,
You promised.
I trusted—to my loss.
But I've kept all your loving
letters,
So you'll have to come across!
Ah, ah, ah, ah!

Unpublished refrains

SCOTCH LASSIE: I've waited,
I've waited;
Each day has seemed a year.
We were tied by love's tether
That morn upon the heather
When you whispered softly,
"My dear heeland lassie."
You promised,
You promised.
And I trusted—to my loss.
But I've kept all your bonny
letters,

So you'll have to come across.
Ah, ah, ah, ah!

THIBET GIRL: Glib, gob, glub,
Flub, dub, bub,
Sammy sing-sing splishy splosh.
Gunga din din davi,
Rikki-tikki-tavi
Gangarene, oh golly, oh gosh!
Oh dum dum,
Oh bum rum.
Hunga one-lung linga loss
Jada jada de di de jada—
Which means
That you'll have to come across.
Ah, ah, ah, ah!

FAMOUS YOU AND SIMPLE ME

Lyric by Otto Harbach and Oscar Hammerstein II. Published as an individual sheet, but cut before the New York opening. Introduced by Allen Kearns (Jack), who comments on a fan letter as he reads it aloud.

VERSE

"Dearest friend: Your pardon if too bold I seem."
(She must be in her teens.)
"All the day with thoughts of you my fancies teem."
(I wonder what she means.)
"Though I know my hope has but a tiny gleam,
Still I keep on dreaming."

REFRAIN

"Simple me and famous you,
Can it ever be?
You, the radiant sun that lights the heavens blue;
I, a bird whose tiny wings will not pursue.
Though I'm never in your view,
You are all I see—
In my vision fair,
A pretty pair of lovers,
Famous you and simple me."

THE LOG OF THE SHIP

Lyric by Otto Harbach and Oscar Hammerstein II. Not published; cut before the New York opening. A travelogue introduced by Louise Allen (Mary) and female ensemble.

1.

We started out to cross the sea
Dressed up just like an ocean swell.
We tried to keep our dignity
And thought we kept it very well.

2.

The first day out we played at games;
The ones that played were those who could.
I do not like to mention names,
But some of us felt not so good.

3.

At somewhere north of longitude
And latitude, I just forget!—
We spied a mermaid in the nude.
We bet you envy us, we bet.

4.

The sight of land brought lots of smiles,
And though 'twas in the dead of night,
When we arrived at Sandwich Isles
We all got off to get a bite.

5.

And then we came to Yokohama—
That's a place in old Japan.
In tricky manner, quaint and calm, a
Geisha used a dainty fan.

6.

Then Hong Kong, China caught our eye.
How comfy were those coolies dressed!
They wore their little shirts Shang-high;
There's no use talking—"East is best."

7.

The hot Equator came our way—
Of that we'll tell you more anon.
We stayed down in our rooms all day
Without a stitch of clothing on.

8.

And that's as far as we have got,
A-sailing on our gallant ship.
We've told our story knot by knot—
You must agree we had some trip!

INDIAN RUBBER

Lyric by Otto Harbach and Oscar Hammerstein II. Published as an individual sheet (verse and refrain only), but appears to have been superseded by "Play a Little Hindoo." Performed by Harry Pearce (Blah Blah), Louise Allen (Mary), and female ensemble during the Stamford tryout.

INCANTATION

BLAH BLAH: Strew the magic sands
From the desert lands
And I will tell your fortunes, gentle
maids.
O, mighty Vishnu, thou propitious
be!
This sacred music, by a lama
strummed!
Inspire prophecies of silent peace!
Buddha!
GIRLS: Boo!
BLAH BLAH: Buddha!
GIRLS: Boo!

VERSE

MARY: Oh, Mister Fakir Man,
Oh, Mister Fakir Man,
You did a terrible thing.
Why did you maul it,
That what-you-may-call-it,
That wonderful, musical string?
Raggy with a rhythm like a summer
breeze,
Swings our knees,
'Scuse it, please!
Stretch your little rubber neck and
see us sway
In the American way.

REFRAIN

India* rubber!
Watch us dance.
India rubber!
Take a chance.
Play an Oriental blue
Beneath a big bamboo.
That music makes us bolder,
Won't stay put.
Got to shake a shoulder,
Kick a wicked foot.
Please don't blame us if we do

* "India" is pronounced in the British fashion, with only two syllables.

India rub-bub-bub beneath a
Bim-bam-boo!

JAZZ OBBLIGATO (COUNTERMELODY TO REFRAIN)

Bouncin' like a rubber,
Make a little dance.
Don't you cry or blubber—
Take a little chance.
A sentimental, gentle,
Temp'ramental, Oriental blue—
We said a blue,
A baby blue.
Oh, play a tune,
Just one,
Just for fun.
Son! We'd like to do the same for you.
India* rub-bub-bub beneath a
Bim-bam-boodle-oodle-oo!

HE DOESN'T WANT TO PLAY

Lyric by Otto Harbach and Oscar Hammerstein II. Not published. Apparently written for _Tickle Me_, but not used. A list of musical numbers in an early script assigns it to "Alice and Girls" before "Finaletto, Act One, Scene 1." A typed lyric sheet found in the _Daffy Dill_ materials in the Stothart Collection at UCLA is marked "Mary and Girls."

VERSE 1

I'm a child of dark misfortune—
Please, you mustn't laugh!
You who have young men to court you
Never ought to chaff
A miserable girl like me.
All my life I've hoped and longed for
Things that cannot be.
My love ignores my shy attentions;
His cold heart has small dimensions—
Ah, me! He's deaf to every plea.

REFRAIN

I have tried to catch his eye—
He never looked at me,
He doesn't notice me.
I have heaved my saddest sigh—
He never turned a hair,

* Here the word "India" takes three syllables.

He doesn't seem to care.
When with smiles I would allure,
He frowns and walks away
Without a thing to say.
I've supplied the words and music,
But he doesn't seem to want to play.

VERSE 2

But someday I'll turn the tables—
Please, you musn't grin!
I have read in Aesop's Fables
"Persevere and win,"
And persevere is what I'll do.
He'll regret his calm indifference
When he tries to woo.
I will tease, coquette, and languish
Just to cause him jealous anguish—
Ah, me! It sounds too good to be true.

JIMMIE (1920)

Tryouts: Woods' Theatre, Atlantic City, New Jersey, October 4, 1920; Playhouse, Wilmington, Delaware, October 8–9, 1920; Park Square Theatre, Boston, October 11–November 13, 1920. New York run: Apollo Theatre (inaugural presentation); opened November 17, 1920; closed January 15, 1921; 71 performances. A Musicomedy by Otto Harbach, Frank Mandel, and Oscar Hammerstein II. Music by Herbert Stothart. Presented by Arthur Hammerstein. Book staged by Oscar Eagle. Musical numbers staged by Bert French. Orchestra directed by Herbert Stothart. Scenic design by Joseph A. Physioc. Costume design by Henri Bendel, Inc.

Cast: Frances White (Jimmie), Ben Welch (Jacob Blum), Paul Porcasi (Vincenzo Carlotti), Dee Loretta (Madame Gambetti), Hattie Burks (Beatrice), Don Borroughs (Tom O'Brien), Harry Delf (Milton Blum), Howard Truesdell (Jerry O'Brien), Tom O'Hare (Watkins), Rita Owin (a Dancer), Irwin Rossa (a Violinist), Peter Mott (Peters), Raymond E. Oswald (Henri), Jack Heisler (Giuseppi), George Clifford (Antonio), Betty Marshall (Wanda Holmes), Mary Jane (Rose), Helen Neff (Henrietta), Tess Mayer (Blanche), and female ensemble.

Widower Jacob Blum intends to make dear little Jimmie, a singer at Carlotti's restaurant, his heir. He has even taught her the song he once wrote for his long-lost daughter. But Madame Gambetti tricks Blum into claiming her daughter Beatrice instead. Beatrice takes advantage of her new station, spending lavishly and neglecting her benefactor. After Jimmie becomes a cabaret star known as the Grey Kitten, she and her boyfriend Tom, a young lawyer, set things right.

Sources for this chapter include the published sheet music and typescripts in the Music Division of the Library of Congress and in the Otto Harbach Collection in the Billy Rose Theatre Division of the New York Public Library for the Performing Arts. Another script is in the Frank Mandel Collection at UCLA. The Harbach Collection at the NYPL also contains business correspondence for *Jimmie*. A medley of songs from *Jimmie* can be heard on the CD set *Broadway Through the Gramophone*, volume 4 (Pearl).

Again, as with *Tickle Me*, little is known about the division of labor between Harbach, Hammerstein, and Mandel, who by contract received equal billing and equal royalties.

In the introduction to *Lyrics*, Hammerstein described his early professional work with Harbach:

> From the very start our relationship was that of two collaborators on an equal footing, although he was twenty years older than I and had written many successes while I had been going to school and college. His generosity in dividing credits and royalties equally with me was the least of his favors. Much more important were the things he taught me about writing for the theatre. Otto is the best play analyst I have ever met. He is also a patient man and a born teacher . . . He taught me to think a long time before actually writing. He taught me most of the precepts I have stated in these notes. He taught me never to stop work on anything if you can think of some small improvement to make.

Lyrics for eleven songs cannot be found. The finales for Acts One and Three and Jimmie's Act Three "Fantasie" are described in the libretto in the New York Public Library for the Performing Arts Otto Harbach Collection. According to the Harbach script the second-act finale consisted of reprises. Cut during the out-of-town tryouts and now missing are: "Cabaret Girl," "Clothes," "Dig, Sister, Dig," "Tu Carissimo," "Tum-Tiddly-Tum-Tum," and "Up Is a Long, Long Climb." Also missing is Harry Delf's highly praised number "A Little Plate of Soup," which might not have been written by any of the show's collaborators: Delf's sister Juliette had been performing a similar soup number in vaudeville.

AN ARIA

Alternate title: "Trio." Lyric by Otto Harbach and Oscar Hammerstein II. Not published. Introduced by Paul Porcasi (Vincenzo Carlotti), Dee Loretta (Madame Gambetti), and Hattie Burks (Beatrice, who is practicing her singing offstage).

BEATRICE: [*offstage*] Ah, ah, ah—
MADAME GAMBETTI: Listen. Can't you hear Beatricia?
CARLOTTI: What? Can it be Beatricia?
BEATRICE: Ah, ah, ah—
CARLOTTI: Sweeter tone I never heard.
BEATRICE: Ah, ah, ah, ah, ah!
CARLOTTI: Magnifique! See, what did I tell you?
BEATRICE: Ah, ah, ah.
Tra la, la, la, la, la, la.
CARLOTTI: What a pretty voice is singing.
BEATRICE: From my heart there comes a-springing
Sad or glad emotions ringing.
CARLOTTI: Full of melody.
Such emotion!
BEATRICE: Ah, ah, ah, ah, ah, ah!
There is music so enthralling
When youth and life and love are calling,
Ever calling in a song of joy.

BABY DREAMS

Lyric by Otto Harbach and Oscar Hammerstein II. Published as an individual sheet. Introduced by Frances White (Jimmie), and favorably mentioned in almost every newspaper review.

VERSE

When the shadows are falling,
Melting sunshine away,
Sandman's drowsy voice is calling;
Weary little people must obey.

REFRAIN

Baby dreams are stories told
In a land that's never old.
Close those eyes, those wonder eyes,*
Sleep will bring a sweet surprise.
Funny clowns and princes gay†
Marching by in bright array.
Golden boats on silver streams.
Pretty baby dreams.

---

* *Libretto has "baby eyes."*

† *Alternate lines 5–6 from the libretto:*
    Night is dark, but mother's near
    Watching o'er her dreaming dear.

BELOW THE MACY-GIMBEL LINE

Lyric by Otto Harbach and Oscar Hammerstein II. Not published. Introduced by Mary Jane (Rose), Rita Owin (a Dancer) and female ensemble.

VERSE

Honey, I'm a-goin' to the south
Where the waffles melt in your mouth.
Down in Greenwich Village,
That's the place I want to be.
I'm gonna hop upon a subway train,
You'll never see me in Harlem again,
For I'm a-goin' home, no more to roam
From the folks I long to see.

REFRAIN

Down below the Macy-Gimbel, Macy-Gimbel Line,
Fine old southern people have their home—
No one ever uses soap or comb.
In the land of cotton stockings, bobbed-haired
    ladies shine—
Never see no mammies, sakes alive!
But there's an Uncle Joe to lend you five.
Though we have no levees there,
Our Levies treat us fine.
Worst families of old Virginia
Live down below the Macy-Gimbel line!

CUTE LITTLE TWO-BY-FOUR

Alternate title: "In a Two-by-Four." Lyric by Otto Harbach and Oscar Hammerstein II. Published as an individual sheet. Introduced by Don Borroughs (Tom) and Frances White (Jimmie).

VERSE

TOM: When we're married, then we'll have
        some fun
        In our palace for two.
        For when two are molded into one,
        Any palace will do.
JIMMIE: Just a piece o' ceiling and some walls,
        That's enough to shelter lovers true!

REFRAIN

JIMMIE: Nobody but you and me
        In our cute little two-by-four.

TOM: To ourselves we shall keep.
        We'll pretend we're asleep
        If we hear a knock on the door.
JIMMIE: We can rent two rooms and a kitchenette
        For five thousand or more!
TOM: Life will be so rosy—
JIMMIE: When we're comfy cozy—
BOTH: In our cute little two-by-four.

Unpublished refrain

Nobody but just we three
In our cute little two-by-four.
You'll awake from your sleep
When you hear just a peep,
For each peep turns into a roar.
And please be careful, dear,
Of the tacks on the floor
When you're feeding small daughter
Some barley water
In our cute little—

[Goes into "Baby Dreams," then returns to original song.]

Nobody but just we three
In our two-by-four.

ALL THAT I WANT

Lyric by Otto Harbach and Oscar Hammerstein II. Not published. Introduced by Harry Delf (Milton) and female ensemble.

VERSE

GIRLS: Try me, please.
        Don't you think one of us will do?
        Graceful ease—
        Don't these classic poses stagger you?
MILTON: Never mind that Grecian air;
        For aesthetics I don't care.
        I just want some snappy hoofer,
        Stylish, young, petite, and fair.

REFRAIN

MILTON: All that I want is
        Some cute little partner to twirl.
        All that I want is
        Some good little sort of a sport of a
            girl.
        If her feet are wary,
        Brains not necessary—

Just an I-don't-care-y,
Very light and airy girl.

CARLOTTI'S

Lyric by Otto Harbach and Oscar Hammerstein II. Not published. Introduced by Paul Porcasi (Vincenzo Carlotti), Harry Delf (Milton), Rita Owin (a Dancer) and female ensemble.

VERSE

O ladies fair, and gentlemen,
I thank you one and all—
Each one of you I try my best to please.
I serve to you a dinner
For a compensation small,
Most everything from noodle soup to cheese.
Yambo, yambo, all expense I bear.
Yambo, yambo, what the 'ell I care?

REFRAIN

Everybody's flocking down to old Carlotti's,
Where the meals are simply delish,
Where there is fun and bright good cheer
And some bohemian atmosphere—
Decorated prettily,
A bit of Italy
That found its way over here.
You can take your sweetheart and forget domestic
    strife,
Just the place to go if you don't want to meet the
    wife.*
All of this for just a dollar fifty—
You must admit that's not too dear.

JIMMIE

Lyric by Otto Harbach and Oscar Hammerstein II. Published as an individual sheet. Introduced by Frances White (Jimmie).

---

* Alternate lines 8–9:
    Twenty pretty chorus girls, all beautiful to view,
    They will sing and dance and do a lot of tricks for
        you.

VERSE 1

Peter Stuyvesant came from Holland
And ruled Manhattan a while.
Then the bally old Duke of York
Took the jolly old isle.
But today the town is owned by
Quite a different sort—
She's just a slip of a tomboy kid,
And they call her Jimmie for short.

REFRAIN

Jimmie, just Jimmie,
She's a chip of old New York.
Vagrant and whimmy,
A dear little bluffin' ragamuffin!
One smile from Jimmie
And a host of glooms depart.
There's a paradise
In those laughing eyes
Of Jimmie, just Jimmie—
She'll haunt your heart.

VERSE 2

I have tried to think of other things,
Some diversion to find.
But I'm sorry I must confess
I've a single-tracked mind.
My poor heart a hopeless prisoner
That will never be free—
The smiling face of a tomboy kid
Is all I ever can see.

SHE ALONE COULD UNDERSTAND

Lyric by Otto Harbach and Oscar Hammerstein II. Not published. Introduced by Hattie Burks (Beatrice).

VERSE

She was a peasant, demure as could be.
He was a swain, quite as bashful as she.
She used to smile as they'd pass on the street;
That's all that happened whenever they'd meet.
He used to play very pretty tunes on a fiddle,
But when she came he'd break off in the middle.
This put romance in a sad sort of way
Till inspiration o'ertook him one day.

REFRAIN

Of love he never told her,
For his lips were shy.
His arms had longed to fold her,
But they'd never dared to try.
His voice refused to ask her for her heart and
hand,
But soon he found a way:
A melody to play
That she alone could understand.

DON' YO' WANNA SEE THE MOON?

Alternate title: "Opening, Act Two." Lyric by Otto Harbach and Oscar Hammerstein II. Not published. Introduced by Hattie Burks (Beatrice), Irwin Rossa (a Violinist) and female ensemble.

Don' yo wanna see the moon?
Don' yo wanna see the moon,
Up in the sky most every night in June?
Night's the only time to spoon,
Night's the only time to spoon.
Come along, gal, and take a look
At the great big moon.

Honey gal o' mine,
I've been longing for to kiss you all the day.
Dis old party may be fine,
But I think just you and me is gwine away.

Don' yo wanna see the moon?
Don' yo wanna see the moon,
Up in the sky most every night in June,
July, September, October, and November?
Night's the only time to spoon,
Night's the only time to spoon.
Come along, gal, and take a look
At the great big beautiful moon.

IT ISN'T HARD TO DO

Lyric by Otto Harbach and Oscar Hammerstein II. Not published. Introduced by Harry Delf (Milton), Helen Neff (Henrietta), and female ensemble.

VERSE 1

MILTON: If you seek the road to fame, girls—
GIRLS: Help a little girl to get along.
MILTON: I'm the guy that wrote the game, girls.
GIRLS: Don't you think that that's a little
strong?
MILTON: Tell them all that you are wonderful,
Then you can't go wrong.

REFRAIN

MILTON: It isn't hard to do
When once you learn a trick or two.
Oh, you can put it over with a little
faking,
And Mister Public for a thrill is aching.
Barnum used to do it
With lots of bunk and ballyhoo.
They think you're dead when you are
quiet,
So make a noise and you're a riot.
And just remember that's your cue—
It isn't hard to do.

VERSE 2

GIRLS: Will you show us how to do it?
MILTON: Just a little trick will make it go.
GIRLS: There is really nothing to it.
MILTON: Here's a thing you see in every show:
Some sweet ambitious ballet girl
Does the flying zephyr whirl.

REPEAT REFRAIN

JUST A SMILE

Lyric by Otto Harbach and Oscar Hammerstein II. Not published. Introduced by Don Borroughs (Tom) and female ensemble.

VERSE

TOM: I'm dreaming of someone I adore.
GIRLS: He's been a-mooning in the clouds all day.
TOM: Someone I keep on wanting more and
more.
GIRLS: They're kind of hopeless when they talk
that way.
Wake up, let us cheer you!
He doesn't hear you.

REFRAIN

TOM: Jimmie, a dream beguiling,
Lovely vision your smile.
Just a smile, a smile from you,
And everything seems right.
Some laughing sunshine in that little grin
Travels straight to your heart with its
Winning, beaming, sweetly gleaming
Love surprise to twinkling eyes;
They make the world seem gay.
Hopes of the future are all wrapped up
In just a smile from you

REPEAT REFRAIN [*while girls sing patter*]

PATTER

GIRLS: Put that talk upon the shelf.
Cheer up, old Tom, be yourself,
And try to get that mind of yours
      arranged.
Pull yourself together, kid,
You're growing pale and thin
With that wild and raving craving
For that winning, beaming, sweetly
      gleaming.
Try to discover a love that's new.
Hopes of the future are all wound up
In just a smile from you.

RICKETY CRICKETY

Cut before the New York opening and then reinstated. Lyric by Otto Harbach and Oscar Hammerstein II. The published sheet has a second verse not in the Otto Harbach script. Introduced by Don Borroughs (Tom) and Frances White (Jimmie).

VERSE 1

Out in the West, when a groom took a bride
In the days of 'forty-nine,
They'd hop in a caravan and go for a ride,
In the days of 'forty-nine.
They'd spend a honeymoon in this quaint way,
Rumbling along in a ramshackle shay.

REFRAIN

Rickety crickety, lickety split,
And away they'd go.
Over the prairie rode Johnny and Mary.
He loved her so.
She was the breath of Maytime,

Calico maid of playtime.
Happy-go-lucky young hobbledehoy
In a wobbledy wagon of joy.

VERSE 2

Out in the West was a bold bandit maid
In the days of 'forty-nine.
She held up a wagon, ev'ryone was afraid
In the days of 'forty-nine.
She robbed the women, made 'em jump and
      start.
As for the men, well, she stole ev'ry heart!

REPEAT REFRAIN

THAT'S AS FAR AS I CAN GO

Alternate title: "Do Ra Me." Lyric by Otto Harbach and Oscar Hammerstein II. Published as an individual sheet. Introduced by Frances White (Jimmie).

VERSE 1

One, two, three, four—
Ah, ah, ah, ah, ah, ah, ah, ah, ah.
It makes me sore—
Ah, ah, ah, ah, ah, ah, ah, ah, ah.
I've tried to sing that silly song—
Gee, how I practice all day long!
Somehow I never get no further;
Sumpin' must be wrong!

REFRAIN

Do, re, me, fa, so far so good,
But that's all I know.
It makes no diff'rence how hard I try,
I cannot sing so very high,
And I'll let you in on a secret:
I can't sing low!
Do, re, me, fa, so far so good,
But that's as far as I can go.

VERSE 2

When I'm singing,
Something seems to get me in the throat.
Teacher wonders
Where I ever found that funny note.
I hit an F when I aim for a C.
What can this funny trouble be?

Maybe I've got a twisted tonsil,
That's what worries me.

REPEAT REFRAIN

Additional lyric from script

A certain someone
Who is not so very far away
Keeps on singing
All the day.
She will do some exercises queer
And then she'll spray her throat, the poor dear.

SOME PEOPLE MAKE ME SICK

Lyric by Otto Harbach and Oscar Hammerstein II. Not published. Introduced by Frances White (Jimmie).

VERSE 1

I just got a terrible licking,
And I didn't do nothing at all.
My whole blamed family picks on me;
I suppose it's because I'm so small.
Nothing I do seems right to them,
And nothing I say is so.
But who told them that they were so great?
That's what I'd like to know.

REFRAIN 1

Some people make me sick—
For instance, my big sister.
She puts on such airs when her boyfriend calls
And insists that I call him Mister.
He calls on her every night,
And he combs his hair so slick;
But whenever he leaves her,
His hair is all mussed—
Ah, some people make me sick.

VERSE 2

My cousin Maude is terribly jealous
And she's just as mean as can be.
She got so mad the other night
'Cause her beau was talking to me.
We was having a quiet little chat—
He was falling in love, I suppose—
When in comes Maude and she says to me,
"Ah, why don't you blow your nose?"
I was so humiliated.

REFRAIN 2

Some people make me sick.
Now can you imagine that jealous dame?
Why, she jumped at the chance
When that guy proposed,
Though he ain't got a cent to his name!
He says to her: "Will ya marry muh?
We'll do some light housekeeping."
Who wants to live in a lighthouse, huh?
Ah, some people make me sick.

I WISH'D I WAS A QUEEN

Lyric by Otto Harbach and Oscar Hammerstein II. Not published. Introduced by Frances White (Jimmie).

VERSE

Famous queens of history,
I read a book that tells about 'em all.
One of them I'd like to be,
But I fear that I was born too small.

REFRAIN 1

Gee, I wish'd I was a queen,
With a crown upon my bean.
I'd like to hold a golden sceptre in my hand;
Nurses and teachers, I'd kick every one of them
    off my land.
In my court I'd be so gay,
I could play in the mud all day.
No one to cross me, no one to boss me,
No one to make me keep clean.
That's why I wish'd I was a queen.

INTERLUDE

I guess I'm boss of my own palace.
Rise, Sir Walter, I knight thee a dub.
I like not the face of yon ka-nave;
Please take him out and shoot him—
Or better still, take him out in the desert
And feed him to the Sphinx!
James, is everything ready for the banquet
    tonight?
Is the poison ready? I'll fix the duke.

REFRAIN 2

Gee, I wish'd I was a queen,
Then my life would be serene.
No one to cross me, no one to boss me,
No one to make me keep clean.
That's why I wish'd I was a queen.

TOODLE-OODLE-UM

Lyric by Otto Harbach and Oscar Hammerstein II. Not published. Introduced by Frances White (Jimmie) and female ensemble.

VERSE

It's the biggest hit in the show,
Don't you love it?
It's a tune that's certain to go,
Don't you love it?
I just can't remember all the words precisely—
Words don't matter, my dear, you know.
Words are clouded deep in doubt—
What are all these songs about?

REFRAIN

This is all you ever hear:
Toodle-oodle-um, toodle-oodle-um.
Dimly ringing in your ear:
Toodle-oodle-um, toodle-oodle-um.
Girls don't have to sing, dance, or anything;
All they do is just appear:
Toodle-oodle-um, toodle-oodle-um.
Though their vocal cords are numb,
Still they dance and bravely hum,
And somehow they seem to put it over
With their toodle-oodle-um.

MING POO

Lyric by Otto Harbach and Oscar Hammerstein II. Published as an individual sheet. Introduced by Frances White (Jimmie).

VERSE

Ming Poo
Was a little Hong Kong girl.
Round her
Tiny finger all men twirl.
When the yellow moon shine on willow tree
She love pretty, they say.
Oh, she love in an Oriental
Sort of way:

REFRAIN

Ming Poo, she ver' bad girl,
Flirty all-ee time with men.
Ming Poo, she ver' glad girl,
Spend a many million yen.
Where she find this money no one knew—
I tink funny, don't you?
No?
Ming Poo, she ver' smart girl,
Had a little bag of tricks.
Ming knew ver' much more
Than all the other Chinese chicks.
In her little pagoda
What she do?
She mus' be clever Ming Poo.

OVERLEAF *Three moments from* Daffy Dill. *Bottom: The ensemble—"All of Captain Kidd's kids are flappers."*

Songs of 1921–1922

NO ONE WILL CARE

Music by Arthur Hammerstein. Published by Harms Incorporated in 1921. No show connection known.

VERSE

All that life could offer I have offered you,
But you thought my love was just a toy.
You have sold a treasure that was real and true,
For an empty bubble land of joy.

REFRAIN

I've gone away.
You laugh and say
You're glad that you are free.
From dreams that are false
You'll awake someday,
And then you'll think of me, you'll see.
There'll come the fall
That comes to all,
To all who can't play fair.
On the love you have squandered
Your heart will call—
But then no one will care.

DAFFY DILL (1922)

Tryout: Apollo Theatre, Atlantic City, August 14, 1922. New York run: Apollo Theatre; opened August 22, 1922 ; closed October 21, 1922; 71 performances. A Musicgirl Comedy. Produced under the personal direction of Arthur Hammerstein. Music by Herbert Stothart. Lyrics by Oscar Hammerstein II. Book by Guy Bolton and Oscar Hammerstein II. Staged by Julian Mitchell. Orchestra under the direction of Herbert Stothart. Scenic design by Clifford Pember. Costume design by Charles LeMaire.

Cast: Frank Tinney (Frank Tinney), Georgia O'Ramey (Gertie), Irene Olsen (Lucy Brown), Marion Sunshine (Estelle), Genevieve Markam (Teacher), Benjamin Mulvey (School Inspector), Harry Mayo (Dan Brown, Lucy's Father), Guy Robertson (Kenneth Hobson), Jacquelyn Hunter (Lucy's Grandmother in 1867), Lynne Berry (Lucy's Grandfather in 1867), Imogene Wilson (Lucy's Mother in 1899), Rollin Grimes Jr. (Harry Jones), Frances Grant, Mary Haun, Elizabeth Keene, margaret Keene, Frederick Renoff, Galdino Sedano, and Ted Wing (specialty dancers), and ensemble.

Sources for this chapter include the published sheet music and a typescript and music manuscripts in the Herbert Stothart Collection at UCLA.

No lyrics have been found for the "Adagio" and "Dance Pantomime" listed in the program; they were probably instrumentals. Also likely to have been dances are two "Fantasies": "Cinderella meets the Prince" and "At the stroke of twelve Cinderella runs away, leaving only a glass slipper." Frank Tinney's "Pianologue" was probably a semi-improvised specialty. Also lost are "Act One Finale," "Chinky Chink," and "Finale Ultimo." The lyric for "Doctor" was written by Kenneth Keith.

LET'S PLAY HOOKEY

Not published. Introduced by Marion Sunshine (Estelle), Genevieve Markham (Teacher), and ensemble.

VERSE 1

ESTELLE: Runnin' along a bank of
woodland
Is a little brook I know,
And you feel you're in a good
land
When you see its crystal flow.
Takin' a swim or maybe fishin'
You can hear its rippin' call.
And you can sit and get to
wishin'
That there was no school at all.

REFRAIN 1

ESTELLE: Let's play hookey!
We can have a lot of fun.
Children must play,
So let us stay away
From school
And break the rule
For just a day.
C'mon, play hookey!
If you're goody-goody
You're bound to be blue.

VERSE 2

TEACHER: [entering] Playing hookey?
I shall punish ev'ryone!
Now we shall see!
GIRLS AND BOYS: Teacher dear,
Don't be angry,
Teacher dear!
TEACHER: Taking a swim, or maybe fishing,
You could hear the school bell
call;
And you sat and got to wishing

That there were no school at all.
GIRLS AND BOYS: Spring breeze
Green trees
And we sat and got to wishin'
That there was no school at all.

REFRAIN 2

ALL: [to the audience] Let's play
hookey!
We can have a lot of fun.
Children must play
So let us stay away
From school
And break the rule
Just for a day.
C'mon, play hookey!
If you're goody-goody
You're bound to be blue!
So don't raise your eyes in
shocked surprise—
We're on to you.
We know that ev'ry once in a
while
You all play hookey too!

KINDERGARTEN BLUES

Not published. Introduced by Marion Sunshine (Estelle) and ensemble.

LEAD-IN

CHILDREN: [a capella] Good morning, merry
sunshine.
London Bridge is falling down.
ESTELLE: Kiddies used to sing their songs that
way,
But they've got advanced ideas today!

VERSE

ESTELLE: There is a bridge in London Town,
London Town, London Town!
And that old bridge is falling down,
Falling down, falling down, all aroun'!
Oh, fair lady, hear my plea!
Oh, sweet lady, take this key
And lock it up, wake it up, shake
it up,
Shake it up, shake it up!

REFRAIN

Oh, the farmer's in the dell,
The farmer's in the dell,
The farmer's in the dell.
High-O, Marjorie-O, by jingo,
The farmer's in the dell.
Oh, the farmer takes his wife,
The farmer takes his wife,
I said he takes his wife.
High-O, Marjorie-O, by jingo,
Big boy, get your wife!
Oh, the wife gets the child,
The wife gets the child,
Sweet momma, get your child!
High-O, Marjorie-O, by jingo,
Mammy, get your child.

PRINCE CHARMING

Published as an individual sheet. Introduced by Irene Olsen (Lucy).

VERSE

I'm the Ugly Duckling, Oliver Twist,
The Two Orphans, Cinderella,
All rolled into one.
I'm made for folks to rave and storm at;
Life uses me for just a doormat.
But hist'ry tells that girls like me,
Like Sally, and Irene,
All get a chance to have some fun.
They find a sweetheart, which is
Their first step from rags to riches—
And then their cares are done.
So I sit and wait all day
For a prince to come my way.

REFRAIN

When will I see my Prince Charming?
What will he be, my Prince Charming?
Will he be soldier, statesman, bold cavalier,
Or just a nice young millionaire dear?
I'm dreaming of you, Prince Charming,
If you will only come true.
Please, when you meet me,
Will you know I'm the girl?
My Prince, I'm waiting for you.

TWO LITTLE RUBY RINGS

Published as an individual sheet. Introduced by Irene Olsen (Lucy), Guy Robertson (Kenneth), and Harry Mayo (Dan).

VERSE

This one here belonged to Ma.
That one there was worn by Pa.
Little crimson rubies that mate so well
A pretty story tell.
Set in style a trifle old,
Just a simple band of gold—
These are all my fortune,
These jewels rare,
They make a loving pair.

REFRAIN

Two little ruby rings
Are all that I own,
Two little friends
When I'm alone.
Each little sparkle is a smile and a tear,
Teeming with mem'ries dear,
Thoughts that linger long,
Like a sweet old song.
One little heart
Can dream the dearest of things
With two little ruby rings.

MY BOY FRIEND

Published as an individual sheet. Introduced by Marion Sunshine (Estelle) and ensemble, then danced by Frances Grant and Ted Wing (specialty dancers).

VERSE

Wait until you meet him,
Wait until you meet him, girls!
Blue eyes and golden hair.
(So fair, he's there.)
All the others follow,
He's the one Apollo, girls!
He likes to hug and squeeze.
So I
Just try
To please.

REFRAIN

For he's my boyfriend,
Just as cute as he can be,
So young and handsome, big and strong.
(He is a daisy!)
I'm his coy friend,
I will make him marry me,
And if you don't believe me, you're wrong.
A very vampy little lady is this;
I can put a lot in a kiss.
Though demure I seem,
I know he's going to be my sweetie!
Soon my boyfriend
To the wedding chime will thrill.
He doesn't know it,
But he will!

I'M FRESH FROM THE COUNTRY

Not published. Introduced by Georgia O'Ramey (Gertie) and ensemble. The *Morning Telegraph* reported this song "went over with a bang."

VERSE 1

GERTIE: Laugh, and show your ignorance.
I know I ain't dressed like the rest of yer,
I may be a rube, but I'm bein' myself.
I don't care to copy the best of yer.
I've heard the city's just a snare
For country maidens young and fair.
But I think I can keep myself from harm
If I stick to the rules I learned on the farm.

REFRAIN 1

GERTIE: I'm fresh from the country,
And I don't care who knows it!
I'm rural, I'm rural,
I don't try to hide it!
My funny clothes disclose it.
ENSEMBLE: She's rural, she's rural.
GERTIE: And fer guys who get gay,
I have just this to say:
I got muscle from pushin' a plough.
And those that don't like the idea
Can just do the best thing they know how.

REFRAIN 2

GERTIE: I'm fresh from the country,
And I don't care who knows it!
I'm rustic, I'm rustic,
I don't try to hide it!
My funny clothes disclose it.
ENSEMBLE: She's rustic, she's rustic.
GERTIE: And a nice movie show is as far as I go
With a feller when I have a date.
And those that don't like the idea
Can do just what their fancies dictate!

VERSE 2

GERTIE: Men don't set no traps for you—
It's you girls who do all the capturin'.
You spend all your time in inventin'
new styles
And gowns that you know he'll find
rapture in.
You try to please him all you can.
You know it's clothes that makes the
man!
And you wear your skirts short
because you know
"Man wants but little here below."

REFRAIN 3

GERTIE: I'm fresh from the country,
And I don't care who knows it!
Provincial, provincial,
I don't try to hide it!
My funny clothes disclose it.
ENSEMBLE: Provincial, provincial.
GERTIE: I don't bob my curls
Like the swell city girls,
And when I sit down I don't show my
knees.
And those that don't like the idea
Can do most anything that they
please.

REFRAIN 4

GERTIE: I'm fresh from the country,
And I don't care who knows it!
I'm a hayseed, I'm a hayseed,
I don't try to hide it!
My funny clothes disclose it.
ENSEMBLE: She's a hayseed, she's a hayseed.
GERTIE: I don't sneeze and freeze
In your chiffon chemise,
I wear flannels—spring, winter, and fall.
And those that don't like the idea
Can just choose their own exit,
that's all.

I'LL BUILD A BUNGALOW

Published as an individual sheet. Introduced by Frank Tinney (Frank), Georgia O'Ramey (Gertie), Guy Robertson (Kenneth), and Irene Olsen (Lucy).

VERSE

Someday
We'll be looking for a little home.
Oh, someday
From the hustling, bustling town we'll roam,
And way far out on the countryside
I will take my little bride.

REFRAIN

HE: I'll build a bungalow
Big enough for me and my baby.
SHE: Baby.
HE: That means you.
I'll build a bungalow,
Just a tiny heaven for two;
And we'll keep the home fires a-burning
With love's own rapturous glow, and oh!
You'll be my own, I know,
When I build you a cute bungalow.

A COACHMAN'S HEART

Not published. Introduced by Frank Tinney (Frank) and Marion Sunshine (Estelle).

VERSE

"Oh, give me back my husband!"
The weeping widow cried
As from her carriage window
She stuck her head outside.
"Whoa there!" yelled the coachman
As he stopped his horses fleet,
And with these words consoled her
As he lighted from his seat:

REFRAIN

Driving down the avenue
In my horse and carriage,
Sometimes to a funeral,
Sometimes to a marriage.
Sound of laughter, sound of tears
Mix with the sound of my wheels—

Although I am only a coachman,
I know how a broken heart feels.

[*The script here instructs: "Second refrain yodel."*]

FAIR ENOUGH

Not published. Introduced by Guy Robertson (Kenneth), Rollin Grimes Jr. (Harry), Harry Mayo (Dan), Elizabeth and Margaret Keene (specialty dancers), and ensemble.

VERSE

For it's always fair weather
When good fellows get together
For a story and a toast.
And it's always fair ladies'
Pretty ears that burn like Hades
When good fellows start to roast.
Ev'ry father's son has been stung by a girl;
There are sirens ev'rywhere.
They're known far and wide as the fair sex,
But it's man who pays the fare.

REFRAIN

Fair enough, they're always fair enough
When they're far, far away;
But your idol of beauty rarest
Has dainty feet of clay.
In the sky of lovers' dreams you fly,
Until some other guy
Starts to call—
Then you find that the dearest and fairest
Is the most unfair of all!

MY LITTLE REDSKIN

Alternate title: "Opening, Act Two." Not published. Introduced by Elizabeth and Margaret Keene and Frances Grant (specialty dancers) and female ensemble. Sources disagree whether it was cut during the Broadway run or the tour and whether Marian Sunshine (Estelle) was one of the performers.

Miami,
Narragansett, Saratoga,
Long Beach,
Pawtucket, and Ticonderoga.
Pale hands and arms

Once were my charms,
But on the shore
The sun rays bore
And I am white no more.

My little Redskin,
My red skin,
My red skin,
My red skin,
How you burn-oo-hoo!
When I turn-oo-hoo!
Big Chief Sun-and-Water make his daughter so
    red, she's blue!
My little Redskin,
My red skin,
My red skin,
My red skin,
Oo-hoo-oo-hoo-hoo,
Yoo-hoo-oo-hoo-hoo
[war whoop]
Oh, I wonder what the Indians do?

Jar of cold cream,
Coconut oil and talcum powder too.
Yoo-hoo-hoo-hoo-hoo,
Yoo-hoo-hoo-hoo-hoo—
Oh, Comanche calls,
Even if Sioux Falls
I just can't stand Sitting Bull,
Canoe?

CAPTAIN KIDD'S KIDS

Not published. Introduced by Harry Mayo (Dan), Marion Sunshine (Estelle), Elizabeth and Margaret Keene (specialty dancers), and ensemble.

PATTER

GIRLS: You may think that we resemble
            Captain Applejack,
        But we come from sterner stock from
            generations back.
        We would have you know that our old
            man was Captain Kidd.
        We are digging for our share of all the
            Captain hid.

REFRAIN 1

All of Captain Kidd's kids are flappers:
Pirate flappers,
Sweetheart trappers.
We can dig the gold and garner the pelf

Better than Kidd the Captain himself.
With a smile, we tease you and fret you.
If we want you, we will get you.
You are lashed to the mast,
For we mash you to the last.
All of Captain Kidd's kids are flappers,
Ahoy!
Oh, boy!

INTERLUDE

SOLOIST: Like a bowl, the old bark a-rolling over
                the ocean blue
    GIRLS: Yo ho, ho, ho and a—

REFRAIN 2

    GIRLS: Flapper, Pirate flapper,
                Cute and dapper.
                Ah, the old sea pirate method was rough—
                Just you watch us doing our stuff!
  TENORS: Soft blue eyes
                And feminine lies
                Can beat any pirate crew.
    GIRLS: And for a brooch or a stole
                We would steal the ocean's roll.
                All of Captain Kidd's kids are pirates,
                Ahoy!
                Oh, boy!

CUT AND UNUSED SONGS

ONE FLOWER THAT BLOOMS FOR YOU

Published as an individual sheet, but cut before the New York opening. One Atlantic City reviewer called this waltz and its reprise "the prevailing air of the comedy." Introduced by Harry Mayo (Dan), Guy Robertson (Kenneth), and ensemble.

VERSE

Love is living somewhere.
Somewhere you will find love,
Waiting just for you to pass his way;
If you'll only come where
Love is never blind love,
Truth you shall see.
Come there with me,
Do not delay!

REFRAIN

Love is a flow'r that is planted in your heart;
Youth is the spring where each blossom plays a
    part.
Some are flirtations that live for but a day;
Some petals wither, their dust is blown away.
Somewhere's a garden where real romances grow;
Someday you'll find it and then your heart will
    know:
Sweet to discover a love forever true—
One flow'r that blooms alone for you.

Unpublished verse

Found in the Stothart Collection typescript, where the song is titled "Love Is a Flower."

        DAN: Just a little rain.
ENSEMBLE: Hear the tinkling teardrops clatter
                On her hanky, pitter patter.
        DAN: Soon the clouds are past.
ENSEMBLE: All the buds and flow'rs are shining,
                Kissed by rays of silver lining.
        DAN: Then the joy of sunlight
                Comes to love at last.

TARTAR

Published as an individual sheet, but dropped before the New York opening. Introduced by Georgia O'Ramey (Gertie) and ensemble.

VERSE 1

When Russia was Russia,
There lived a czarina
Named Cath'rine the Great,
Who longed for a mate.
She saw one and liked him
And served a subpoena
That summoned him to court
To make his report.
He was a bold Tartar man,
Son of an old Tartar clan.
It was Cath'rine's whim
To make love to him
On this informal plan:

REFRAIN 1

Tartar, Tar-tar-tar, Tartar.
Tartar, Tar-tar-tar, Tartar.
You are the way I like them, Papa—

Full of ginger and pepper,
And on the steppes you'd be some stepper.
Har! Har!—Har, har, har, har, har!
Be my czar, czar, czar, czar, czar!
Though I am Catherine* of Samovar,
I love you, my savage Tartar.

VERSE 2

Now Tartars are Tartars,
And this one was more so.
With ringing tambourine
He danced for the queen.
He leapt in the air and
He twisted his torso
And kicked a wicked heel,
Not very genteel.
Cath'rine's applause was intense,
She said, "This boy is immense!"
They had some tea,
But twixt you and me,
Her talk had no more sense than:

REFRAIN 2

Tartar, Tar-tar-tar, Tartar.
Tartar, Tar-tar-tar, Tartar.
You stick to ma† and you'll go far, far.
Though you're only a peasant,
Your company I find quite pleasant.
Har! Har!—har, har, har, har, har!
Be my czar, czar, czar, czar, czar!
Though I am Catherine of Samovar,
I love you, my savage Tartar.

VERSE 3

Now Cath'rine was Cath'rine,
A queen but romantic,
And game for any lark
In palace or park.
If clever, however
Eccentric the antic,
She liked to have her laugh—
You don't know the half!
She and Tartar night and day
Went to each gay cabaret.
She would drink with glee
Her vodka—vod cared she?—
And then she'd talk this way:

---

* In the refrain the name is always given three
  syllables; in the verse it's always contracted to two.

† Published sheet has "me"; copyist piano-vocal score
  in the Warner-Chappell Collection at the Library of
  Congress has "Ma."

REFRAIN 3

Tartar, Tar-tar-tar, Tartar.
Tartar, Tar-tar-tar, Tartar.
Princes and dukes have loved me, Tartar.
With these lobsters, my peasant,
A dash of tartar sauce is pleasant.
Har! Har!—Har, har, har, har, har!
You are the kitten's caviar.
Though I am Catherine of Samovar,
I love you, my savage Tartar.

YOU CAN'T LOSE ME

Published as an individual sheet, but cut before the New York opening. It was intended to be sung by a "Voice on the Radio."

VERSE

Take a look at me and you will see
A modern Romeo.
I can love you dearly pretty nearly
Any place you go.
Out in gloomy Russia, or sunny Italy,
You'll feel you're near me,
Dear, when you hear me,
Wherever you may be.

REFRAIN

For you're there and I'm here,
But what do I care?
Kisses sublime, dear,
I'll send through the air.
Love will go buzzing over the sea.*
With a little radio receiver
You can't lose me!

QUEEN O' HEARTS (1922)

Tryouts: Wieting Opera House, Syracuse, New York September 27, 1922; Toledo, September 29, 1922; Lafayette Theatre, Detroit, October 2, 1922. New York run: George M. Cohan Theatre; opened October 10, 1922;

---

* This line replaced the words:
  I'll find your wave length over the sea.

closed November 11, 1922; 40 performances. A Musical Comedy in Two Acts. Book by Frank Mandel and Oscar Hammerstein II. Music by Lewis E. Gensler and Dudley Wilkinson. Lyrics by Oscar Hammerstein II. Extra lyrics by Sydney Mitchell, Nora Bayes, Morrie Ryskind, Harry Richman, Cliff Friend, Bill Dugan, and Lou Davis. Additional music by Harry Richman, Cliff Friend, Bill Dugan, and Lou Davis. Presented by Max Spiegel. Staged by Ira Hards. Dances and ensembles arranged by David Bennett. Music direction by Gene Salzer. Scenic design by H. Robert Law Studios and Herbert Ward. Costume design by Cora MacGeachy and Schneider-Anderson.

Cast: Nora Bayes (Elizabeth Bennett), Max Hoffman Jr. (Tom), Norma Terriss [Terris] (Grace), Florence Morrison (Isabella Budd), Franker Woods (Ferdinand Budd), Gladys Dore (Miss Swanson), Georgie Brown (Alabama Smith), Harry Richman (Henry Rivers), Edna Hibbard (Myra, aka Mike), Dudley Wilkinson (Dudley), Lorin Raker (Alfred Armstrong), Arthur Uttry (William Amstrong), Sidney Brook (Policeman), Laura Alberta (Aunt Abigail), Eva Taylor (Georgia), Thomas Bradley (Butler), and female ensemble.

Elizabeth Bennett runs a matrimonial agency, although she herself is happily divorced. Her younger sister, Myra, known as "Mike," thinks of little but romance. Their situation is mirrored by two brothers who come to the office. Grumpy William Armstrong has little use for a wife, while his younger brother Alfred is highly susceptible.

Little material from this short-lived show is known to survive. The New York Public Library for the Performing Arts has the published sheet music and a typescript with first-act song lyrics and descriptions of other numbers to be written.

Neither music nor lyrics have been found for "Sizing Up the Girls," "My Busy Day," "Marriage C.O.D.," "System," "Finale, Act One," "My Highbrow Fling," and "Finale, Act Two." Also lost are the words and music for the following cut songs: "When You're Only Seventeen," "Just a Touch," "Stop, Look and Kiss 'em" and "Why Do You Keep Us Guessing?" This chapter does not include any of the songs by other writers.

DREAMING ALONE

Music by Dudley Wilkinson. Published as an individual sheet. Introduced by Arthur Uttry (William). An Act Two reprise may have had additional lyrics, but none have been found.

VERSE

Of the girls that I have met
I have never found one yet
Who is as ideal than [sic] girls that I can dream of.
With a picture in my mind
I can have most any kind,
Fair, dark, tall, or small—
No trouble at all.

REFRAIN

Dreaming alone,
Dreaming alone,
I find the sweetest romances.
The fairest of the fair
Are fashioned from the air.
With phantom darlings
I spoon under the moon,
Weaving my gay lover's fancies.
Mem'ries I own
When the visions have flown,
Dreaming, dreaming alone.

YOU NEED SOMEONE, SOMEONE NEEDS YOU

Music by Lewis E. Gensler. Published as an individual sheet. Introduced by Nora Bayes (Elizabeth) and Arthur Uttry (William). The sheet music assigns the first verse to "he" and the second verse to "she," but the character Elizabeth is a professional matchmaker, and William is a client. Possibly she sang the first verse and he sang the second.

VERSE 1

HE: Happiness must have a mate,
Experience has shown.
Life's a meatless bone
When you eat alone.
Ev'ryone must have someone,
A partner all his own.
In love's kingdom
Two must rule the throne.

REFRAIN

You need someone, someone needs you.
Someday there'll come one; then there'll be two,
Sharing ev'ry smile and tear,
Ev'ry hope and ev'ry fear,
Proving that love is true.
You need someone, someone needs you.
Look for a sweetheart, and when you do,
You'll be sure to find someone.

For somewhere beneath the sun,
Someone needs you.

VERSE 2

SHE: I can see just what you mean;
You plead a skillful case.
One is half of two
Any time or place.
If you want to kiss,
You need at least one other face.
A pair of deuces
Beats a single ace.

REPEAT REFRAIN

TOM-TOM

Music by Lewis E. Gensler. Published as an individual sheet. Introduced by Harry Richman (Henry) and female ensemble and danced by Georgie Brown (Alabama) and Eva Taylor (Georgia).

VERSE

Out in dark Africa lived a still darker man—
When I say "darker," I mean he was blacker than tan.
With an old tom-tom resting upon his knees,
He made the jungle jingle with melodies.
Then white composer came along,
Took a fancy to that rhythm;
Bought the music for a song
And took it back home with him.
And now all white folks stamp their feet
To that black man's tom-tom beat—
With his barbaric ways he
Has set us dancing crazy.

REFRAIN

Oh, tom-tom
Where did you come from?
From the Cannibal Isles?
Oh, tom-tom,
Tom-tom, tom-tom, tom-tom,
You make us dance miles and miles.
Most ev'ry lady and gent is
Non compos mentis
When they listen to you.
Oh, tom-tom, tom-tom, tom-tom,
Go back where you've come from
And we'll all go there too.

CUT AND UNUSED SONGS

DING DONG DING

Music by Lewis E. Gensler. Published as an individual sheet. Introduced by Lorin Raker (Alfred) and Edna Hibbard (Myra). *The Rodgers and Hammerstein Fact Book* lists this title and six others as dropped before the New York opening. It may have been replaced by "Marriage C.O.D."

VERSE 1

In ev'ry church throughout the land
There is a steeple tall.
In ev'ry steeple there's a bell,
So far away, so small.
In ev'ry note of that small bell
There can be joy for all.

REFRAIN

Ding dong ding, the church bells ring,
Summer, autumn, winter, spring.
Fellow woos, girl wears ring,
Rice and shoes, kind friends fling.
Bride and groom together cling,
Like two lovebirds on the wing.
Happy pair, queen and king,
Ding dong, ding dong, ding!

VERSE 2

Every girl has one fond hope:
Someday a bride to be.
She keeps a hope chest filled with things
That no one else may see.
I have one too, for who can tell?
Church bells may ring for me!

SOME FINE DAY

Composer has not been identified, and no music is known to survive. Dropped before the New York opening. It appears to have been replaced by "Dreaming Alone." Introduced by Arthur Uttry (William) and female ensemble.

VERSE

All men are created equal,
But women is superior.
When she sighs and gazes in your eyes,
She's thinking thoughts ulterior.
She has her own little motto,
This siren, clever and cute:
She stands for Life and Liberty
And the Happiness of Pursuit!
And, oh, how she'll pursue—
Some fine day she'll find you.

REFRAIN

Some fine day when the skies are clear
And all the birdies chant their tune,
And lovely lilacs lend romantic atmosphere
(A very dangerous thing in June,
July, or August),
You may try your best to escape the test
But in the end you're bound to pay.
Some pretty, bobbled-haired, bonehead baby
Will capture you
Some fine day!

EV'RY SILVER LINING HAS A CLOUD

Music by Lewis E. Gensler. Lyrics are from a rough piano-vocal manuscript found in the MCNY.

REFRAIN

Ev'ry silver lining has a cloud.
The song of glee is not for me.
When romance and fortune
Are cavorting my way
Hopes are high,
Then the sky
Starts to get gray
And the rain comes a pitter-patter.
All the jinxes flock around me in a crowd.
I try to look for the silver lining,
But I never seem to get beyond the cloud.

MISCELLANEOUS SONGS

I'VE CHANGED ALL MY IDEAS

This lyric is handwritten by Hammerstein in a notebook, now in the Hammerstein Collection at the Library of Congress, that is probably from 1922. No music is known to have been written. The subject matter suggests an association with Hammerstein's 1922 show *Queen o' Hearts*.

REFRAIN

I've changed all my ideas since I met you.
You made me change them.
You came along and set my [*illegible*] all askew,
I can't arrange them.
I used to think this talk of Cupid's glories
Was just an ad for *Snappy Stories*.
I never understood how hearts
Were led astray,
I never knew.
I never knew the pretty things two lips could say
And do.
I never cared for coy young misses,
I never longed for love and kisses,
But I've changed all [these? those?] ideas
Since I met you.

THE FIRST TIME

This lyric is handwritten by Hammerstein in a notebook that is probably from 1922. No music is known to have been written. No show connection is known.

REFRAIN

The first time you try it,
It's so hard to say.
You look, and you sigh it;
Caresses convey
A meaning that words always fail to impart,
A feeling so big that it [clogs?] up your heart.

Then Time, that magician,
Who changes things so,
Turns the breath of a thought
To a whisper so low—
As sweet and as soft as the coo of a dove
Your first shy confession of love.

ONE LITTLE WORD

This lyric is handwritten by Hammerstein in a notebook that is probably from 1922. No music is known to have been written. No show connection is known.

REFRAIN

One little word
And the whole world is new,
Opening gates to a joy undreamed.
One little glance
That is tender and true,
Spreading its light where a faint hope gleamed.
One little kiss
And a heaven is [born?]
As the sea bears its precious pearl.
One lover's heart
Hangs on one little word
From one little wonderful girl.

YOU WERE SO SWEET

This lyric is handwritten by Hammerstein in a notebook that is probably from 1922. No music is known to have been written. No show connection is known.

REFRAIN

You were so sweet
As you came o'er the hill,
Fresh as the dew in the morning.
Dear little maid in your calico neat,
You were so sweet.
There were only we two.
I kissed you, I kissed you,
What else would I do?

OVERLEAF *Edith Day and Guy Robertson embrace in a scene from* Wildflower.

Songs of 1923

WILDFLOWER (1923)

Tryouts: Grand Theatre, Wilkes-Barre, Pennsylvania, January 26–27, 1923; Auditorium, Baltimore, January 29–February 3, 1923. New York run: Casino Theatre; opened February 7, 1923; closed March 29, 1924; 477 performances. A Musical Play. Book and lyrics by Otto Harbach and Oscar Hammerstein II. Music by Herbert Stothart and Vincent Youmans. Book staged by Oscar Eagle. Dances and ensembles by David Bennett. Orchestrations by Robert Russell Bennett. Orchestra directed by Herbert Stothart. Scenic design by Frank E. Gates and Edward A. Morange. Costume design by Charles Le Maire. Entire production produced under personal supervision of Mr. Arthur Hammerstein.

Cast: Edith Day (Nina Benedetto), Guy Robertson (Guido), Esther Howard (Lucrezia La Roche), Jerome Daley (Luigi), Olin Howland (Gabrielle), Charles Judels (Gaston La Roche)*, Evelyn Cavanaugh (Bianca Benedetto), James Doyle (Count Alberto), Marion and Martinez Randall (specialty dancers), and ensemble.

Nina, a country cousin, will inherit a fortune if she can control her fiery temper for six months. Naturally, the other heirs try to provoke her. The conspirators include her city cousin Bianca, Bianca's fiancé Alberto, and Bianca's lawyer Gaston Larotta (who has loaned money to Alberto based on Bianca's expected inheritance). Guido, Nina's rustic boyfriend, fears that after she inherits, she may no longer want him. Her guardian Luigi has similar concerns. A comic subplot concerns the lawyer's bored wife, Lucrezia, who doggedly pursues Gabrielle, another of Nina's suitors.

A national tour began in Pittsburgh on March 31, 1924, and stopped in three other cities before ending on July 26, 1924. It resumed on September 6, 1924, and covered twelve more cities. A London production opened at the Shaftesbury Theatre on February 17, 1926, and ran for a total of 114 performances at a series of venues.

A substantial amount of material from *Wildflower* has survived, but there is no single definitive text. Several individual songs were published in 1923. A vocal score (lacking most of Act Three) was published in 1931. A script was published in 1937. Typescripts can be found in the Otto Harbach Collection in the Billy Rose Theatre Collection of the New York Public Library for the Performing Arts, at the Rodgers & Hammerstein Organization, the Tams-Witmark Music Library, and the Shubert Archive, all in New York City and in the Lord Chamberlain's Plays Collection in the British Library in London.

There are many textual differences between the

---

* In the London production, Gaston's surname was changed to Larotta—the name used in both the published score and the published script.

sources. For example, in the second line of the verse of "I Love You" the script and score have the words "making love," but the sheet music says "saying love." In the sixth line of the same verse, the script and score say, "It's always just the same"; the published sheet and a Tams-Witmark script say, "They're pretty much the same," and a script at the Shubert Archive says, "It's always much the same." There are three or four such variants in every song. The published score and script are this chapter's main sources. Where the score and script disagree, the score is preferred. When a typescript has additional verses or refrains, that material is included.

Very little is known about the division of labor between Harbach and Hammerstein. In separate conversations they told historian Miles Kreuger that up to and including *Rose-Marie* (1924), Hammerstein did very little of the lyric writing. However, contracts preserved in the Otto Harbach Collection at the New York Public Library for the Performing Arts identify Harbach and Hammerstein as coauthors of *Wildflower* and promise them equal royalties. In 1949, Hammerstein explained that his anthology, *Lyrics*, did not include songs from *Wildflower* (and several other well-known 1920s shows) because they were all "written in collaboration with Otto Harbach." Somewhat more is known about the division of musical labor on *Wildflower*. Drafts of the contract mention Youmans having separate credit for the songs "Bambalina," "Wildflower," and "I Love You," though the published sheets eventually bore both his and Stothart's names.

No lyrics have been found for three songs that were cut before the New York opening: "True Love Will Never Grow Cold," "Friends Who Understand," and "Everything Is All Right." The invaluable *Rodgers and Hammerstein Fact Book* lists three songs added to the London production after comedienne Maisie Gay stepped into the role of Lucrezia: "Spring Is Here," "If Your Name Had Been Larotta," and "The Como Camel Corps." Those lyrics have not been located, but were not likely to have been written by Harbach and Hammerstein. Gay's 1931 memoir says that she was hired to bring more laughter to *Wildflower* and does not mention the American songwriters at all.

Hammerstein remembered *Wildflower* as "a very big success and the first one of mine that ran for more than a year on Broadway." He also recalled that three days before the initial tryout in Wilkes-Barre, Youmans had still not supplied the verse to one of the songs. Hammerstein said that he appreciated the composer's perfectionism, but pointed out that "this gave his lyric writers, Otto Harbach and me, a very short time to set words, rehearse them and produce the number in time for the opening. It also gave the orchestrator very little time to make his arrangement. Nevertheless, Vincent just could not bat out something that was merely serviceable, even under the pressure of an imminent opening. I believe the originality of his verses show the loving care he put into them."

I LOVE YOU, I LOVE YOU, I LOVE YOU

Lyric by Otto Harbach and Oscar Hammerstein II. Herbert Stothart and Vincent Youmans are both credited for the music of this song, but it is by Youmans who reused the melody in the shows *Hit the Deck* and *Great Day*. Published as an individual sheet. Introduced by Gabrielle (Olin Howland) and girls.

VERSE

All this silly talk of ours,
Making love with books and flowers,
Take it from an expert that it's wrong.
For when you try to frame
A note to send your flame,
It's always just the same old sort of song.
There are no new words,
Just one or two words,
The tried-and-true words
We've heard so long:

REFRAIN

"I love you, I love you, I love you, I love you, I love
    you."
That's the gen'ral meaning of it all.
"Do write soon."
"Miss you so."
"Long to hug and kiss you so."
"Dearest, please forgive this hasty scrawl."
"Ev'ry day when you're away,
I don't know what to do."
"Do you ever think of me?"
"Darling, are you true?"
All these phrases merely say
The very same thing in a different way.
"I love you, I love you, I love you!"

SOME LIKE TO HUNT

Alternate title: "The Chase." Lyric by Otto Harbach and Oscar Hammerstein II. Music credited to Herbert Stothart and Vincent Youmans, but it is generally thought to be Stothart's work. Published in the vocal score. Introduced by Charles Judels (Gaston Larotta) and girls.

VERSE 1

LAROTTA: It is a merry, merry thing to hear the
          hunter's call.
GIRLS: There surely is a lot in what you say.
LAROTTA: To try to capture something is a thrill to
          nearly all.
GIRLS: What sort of capture will you make
          today?
LAROTTA: I let the other sportsmen go in search of
          boar or bear.*
          For sniping snipe, or trailing tripe, I
          really do not care!
          In my present state of happiness, I
          choose a different way.
          I seek my own peculiar kind of prey:
          [*yodel*] Allee-oho! Allee-oho! Allee-oh-
          oh-oh!

REFRAIN

For some like to hunt the wild elephunt,
The elk or caribou.†
Some like to trace the moose or the yak
Or stalk the kangaroo.
I will not run
With a big heavy gun
Where these animals like to lurk.
But just let me chase
A beautiful face
And then my heart is in my work.

VERSE 2‡

LAROTTA: When'er I go a-fishing, what successes I
          achieve!
GIRLS: You always fish for compliments, we've
          heard.
LAROTTA: I caught a whitebait, once, so large—
          you never would believe!
GIRLS: You're right, we don't believe a single
          word.
LAROTTA: But there's a form of angling that's
          much nicer, I affirm.

---

* *Alternate lines 5–6 in script at the Rodgers &
Hammerstein Organization:*
  I let the other hunters go a-hunting for a bear.
  At catching birds or shooting fish I really do not
  care.

† *Alternate lines 2–4 in script at the Rodgers &
Hammerstein Organization:*
  The lion or the gnu.
  Some like to shoot the one-eyed galoot,
  The flying kangaroo.

‡ *Verse 2 is found only in rental materials at the
Shubert Archive.*

You don't require to throw a fly or catch
  an early worm.
You merely cast an am'rous glance at
  some delightful miss,
And catch a rising flapper with a kiss!

REFRAIN

GIRLS: For some like to hunt the wild elephunt,
       The elk or caribou.
       Some like to trace the moose or the yak
       Or stalk the kangaroo.
       He will not run
       With a big heavy gun
       Where these animals like to lurk.
       But just let him chase
       A beautiful face
       And then his heart is in his work.

WILDFLOWER

Lyric by Otto Harbach and Oscar Hammerstein II.
Music credited to Herbert Stothart and Vincent Youmans, but is thought to be Youmans's work. Published
as an individual sheet. Introduced by Guy Robertson
(Guido) and male ensemble.

Vocal score version

VERSE

GUIDO: I call her wildflow'r.
  MEN: His little wildflow'r.
GUIDO: She's so capricious.
  MEN: Yet how delicious.
GUIDO: A blossom fragrant,
       That scents the vagrant air!
       The sunshine woos her,
       The rain bedews her
       With teardrops tender
       Or summer splendor.
       I'd feel less lonely
       If she would only care!

REFRAIN

GUIDO: Wildflow'r, I love you.
  MEN: His little wildflow'r, his little wildflow'r.
GUIDO: What else can I do?
  MEN: His little wildflow'r, his little wildflow'r.
GUIDO: When I see you swaying
       With a grace that's too entrancing,
       Then my heart is praying
       That you'll never cease from dancing.

Wildflow'r, tell me true.
  MEN: His little wildflow'r, his little wildflow'r.
GUIDO: If you only knew
  MEN: His little wildflow'r, his little wildflow'r.
GUIDO: How I dream about you,*
       And my heart is sad without you.
       Wildflow'r, I love you.

Sheet music version

VERSE

I call you wildflow'r,
My little wildflow'r.
For sweet and fragrant,
Perverse and vagrant,
You're ever dancing,
Oh, so entrancingly.
The sunshine haunts you,
The raindrop taunts you,
The zephyr woos you,
All things amuse you,
You're never lonely,
Forgetting only me.

REFRAIN

Wildflow'r, I love you.
My little wildflow'r, My little wildflow'r.
What else can I do?
My little wildflow'r, my little wildflow'r.
When I see you swaying,
While the breezes all caress you,
Then my heart is praying
That I too may hold and press you.
Wildflow'r, tell me true,
My little wildflow'r, my little wildflow'r.
If you only knew
My little wildflow'r, my little wildflow'r.
How I want the blisses
That the sun gets from your kisses,
Would you love me, too?

BAMBALINA

Lyric by Otto Harbach and Oscar Hammerstein II.
Music credited to Herbert Stothart and Vincent Youmans, but is thought to be Youmans's work. Published
as an individual sheet. Introduced by Edith Day (Nina)

---

* *Additional lyric for third refrain:*
  NINA: You can have the blisses
        That the sun gets from my kisses.
        Oh, I love you too.

and ensemble. A 1923 recording by Paul Whiteman and His Orchestra was one of the year's big hits.

VERSE 1

NINA: Wilt thou come with me to the fair?
Bambalina will be there.
ENSEMBLE: Who is Bambalina?
What sort of man is he?
NINA: He's a fiddler man by trade,
Both beloved by man and maid.
ENSEMBLE: Good for Bambalina,
Our fiddler he shall be!
NINA: He'll start in to fiddle
And stop in the middle
Of a dance as quick as a wink!
And there you are
In your sweetheart's arms,
Before you've time to think.
ENSEMBLE: It makes old Bambalina grin
To see the fix those girls are in.

REFRAIN

ENSEMBLE: When we're dancing at the fair,
We have to take the greatest care,
When good old Bambalina calls a stop.
That means I must stand still
In your arms and hold your hand still,
For we dare not dance or skip or kick
or hop.
When he calls a sudden stop
I get a good excuse to prop
My little head against my partner's
chest.
So you see the reason why,
Though other dances I may try,
I always like the Bambalina best.

VERSE 2 (ONLY IN PUBLISHED SHEET)

NINA: With his music soulfully sweet,
Bambalina stirs your feet.
ENSEMBLE: Here's to Bambalina,
He is the man for us.
NINA: Just like magic moves his bow,
Not too quick and not too slow.
ENSEMBLE: Clever Bambalina,
He doesn't cause a fuss!
NINA: He sets you all swaying in step with his
playing
Then he'll halt before you're aware.
You're caught quite tight in an
awkward plight,
And simply stand and stare!
Old Bambalina thinks it fun
To see the mischief he has done.

REPEAT REFRAIN

I'LL COLLABORATE WITH YOU

Lyric by Otto Harbach and Oscar Hammerstein II. Music credited to Herbert Stothart and Vincent Youmans. Not published, and no music is known to survive. Introduced by Esther Howard (Lucrezia, a bored wife) and Olin Howland (Gabrielle,* a would-be poet).

VERSE 1

LUCREZIA: If I worked with you, dear,
Wonders we could do, dear,
And we'd never be apart.
GABBY: Brazen woman, keep away from me,
I'm a modest man, as you can see.†
LUCREZIA: I would do my share, too.
Do you think it fair to
Stop me when I want to start?
If you do not care to
Cure my yearning heart's ache,
Won't you do it just for art's sake?

REFRAIN 1

LUCREZIA: I'll collaborate with you,
If you'll collaborate with me.
I know I can inspire
You with real emotion's fire.
To write romances, it's conceded,
Experience is all that's needed.
You can't describe a love affair
Till you've had one or two.
Just think how useful I can be,
When I collaborate with you.

VERSE 2

LUCREZIA: If I worked with you, dear,
Wonders you could do, dear.
You'd write something really smart!
GABBY: Brazen woman, keep away from me!
I'm a modest man, as you can see.
LUCREZIA: I would sit beside you
And my hand would guide you
On the royal road to art!
GABBY: Art may be a high road.
Love's a little byroad
Where a chap may lose his heart!

---

* *Gabrielle, also known as Gabby, is a man.*

† *A variant from the script at the Rodgers & Hammerstein Organization:*
I am full of animosity.

REFRAIN 2

LUCREZIA: I'll collaborate with you,
If you'll collaborate with me.
Just think how I'll inspire you,
With what ambition fire you!
GABBY: Really I don't need inspiring.
I should find it very tiring!
LUCREZIA: But when you write your first romance
You don't know what to do.
How useful I shall be, perchance,
If I collaborate with you!

REFRAIN 3

LUCREZIA: We'll write books about a sheik
With just the marvelous physique
That suits the weak women's fancies
In up-to-date romances!
GABBY: With the rough stuff he'll ensnare 'em
And conduct them to his harem!
LUCREZIA: A silent hero, brave and strong,
Who does as cavemen do.
We'll write "best-sellers" all day long
When I collaborate with you!

APRIL BLOSSOMS

Lyric by Otto Harbach and Oscar Hammerstein II. Music credited to Herbert Stothart and Vincent Youmans, but is generally thought to be Stothart's work. Published as an individual sheet. Introduced by Guy Robertson (Guido) and Edith Day (Nina).

Duet version from published vocal score

VERSE 1

GUIDO: You are mine at last,
All my doubt is past,
And the winter will not seem so drear.
NINA: Happy bride I'll be;
You'll be all to me,
When the first buds of springtime
appear.
GUIDO: When those buds arrive
How my heart will thrive!
Not a man alive—
NINA: No one as—
BOTH: —happy as I, dear.

REFRAIN

GUIDO: When April blossoms bloom, they'll
bloom for me!

When April blossoms bloom on this old
    tree!
NINA: We'll take the donkey cart
And on our journey start.
Just you and I, sweetheart, alone we'll be!
GUIDO: On yonder mountainside a home we'll share,
And love will surely guide our footsteps
    there.
BOTH: We'll own the skies so blue,*
All earth and heaven too.
When April blossoms,
April blossoms mean you.

VERSE 2

GUIDO: We will build a nest
On that mountain crest
Where in summer the nightingales sing.
NINA: And when winter's there,
'Neath the branches bare
We will wait for the coming of spring!
GUIDO: When the fragrant bow'rs
Are all filled with flow'rs
In that home of ours—
NINA: Our little home—
BOTH: —where love is king, dear.

REPEAT REFRAIN

Sheet music version

VERSE

You are mine at last,
All my doubt is past,
And the winter will not seem so drear.
You have promised me
My sweet bride to be,
When the first buds of springtime appear.
When those buds arrive,
Then my heart will thrive.
Not a man alive
Happy as I, dear.

REFRAIN

When April blossoms bloom,
They'll bloom for me.
The breath of spring's perfume
On ev'ry tree
Will tell me you are mine.
And ev'ry budding vine
Will be a tender sign of joy to be.

---

* *Variant lyric from a script at the Shubert Archive:*
    Where there's no place for gloom
    And only love has room
    With April blossoms,
    April blossoms abloom.

Those April blossoms gay will be my own.
The sun will light the day for me alone.
I'll own the skies so blue,
All earth and heaven, too.
When April blossoms,
April blossoms mean you!

ACT ONE FINALE

Lyric by Otto Harbach and Oscar Hammerstein II. Music credited to Herbert Stothart and Vincent Youmans, but is almost certainly Stothart's work. Published in the vocal score. Introduced by the company.

NINA AND GUIDO: Those April blossoms gay will
    be my own.
The sun will light the day for me
    alone.
I'll own the skies so blue,
All earth and heaven, too.
When April blossoms, April
    blossoms mean you.
GABBY: Come along.
Nina, we're ready to go.
NINA: Goodbye!
ENSEMBLE: Goodbye to you!
GUIDO: Goodbye.
LAROTTA: [*spoken to* BIANCA *and* ALBERTO]
    Don't worry. She has got to
    live with my wife for six
    months with-out losing her
    temper. It can't be done!
BIANCA
AND ALBERTO: [*sung*] We'd better trust
    the legal eagle*

---

* *Alternate lines from a script at the Shubert Archive:*
    We'd better trust our just adviser.
    I'm the lawyer to engage.
    There's not a man we know who's wiser.
    I'll surprise her in a rage.
    Yes, it's as sure as sure can be
    That he will shortly earn his fee,
    For a wise adviser, wise adviser is he.

Another alternate lyric from a script at the Rodgers &
Hammerstein Organization:
    We're going to trust the legal eagle.
    And I'm going to see you through.
    In all our knotty problems legal
    He will know just what to do.
    No matter what the case may be,
    He'll make the jury all agree,
    For a legal, legal, legal eagle is he.

LAROTTA: I'm the lawyer to engage.
BIANCA
AND ALBERTO: He will chase her like a beagle.
LAROTTA: I'll surprise her in a rage.
ALL PRESENT: Yes, it's as sure as sure can be
That he will shortly earn his fee,
For a legal beagle, legal eagle
    is he.
LAROTTA
AND GIRLS: Some like to hunt the wild
    elephunt,
The elk or caribou.
Some like to track the moose or
    the yak
Or stalk the kangaroo.
I [he] will not run with a big
    heavy gun
Where these animals like to lurk.
But just let me [him] chase a
    beautiful face
And then my [his] heart is in my
    [his] work.
NINA: [*offstage*] Ah, ah!
GUIDO: My little wild flow'r.
Wildflow'r, I love you.
NINA: [*very faintly from offstage*] Ah!

THE BEST DANCE I'VE HAD TONIGHT

Alternate title: "Opening Act Two." Lyric by Otto Harbach and Oscar Hammerstein II. Music credited to Herbert Stothart and Vincent Youmans. Not published, and no music is known to survive. Introduced by Evelyn Cavanaugh (Bianca) and ensemble.

From the London production forward, this song was replaced by "Come Let Us Dance Through the Night."

BOYS: [*to* LITTLE GIRLS] I must tell you
    that this is quite
The best dance I have had tonight.
[*turning to* BIG GIRLS] You're just in
    time for—a dance.
LITTLE GIRLS: That's what I call arrogance.
BIG GIRLS: Thank you, kindly.
We are waiting,
Waiting for romance.

[*They dance.*]

LITTLE GIRLS: And they'll tell them that is
The best dance they have had
    tonight.

BIANCA: Liars, liars, liars!
Tell me, pray,
Why all this frank display
Of angry passion?
GIRLS: It's because
We hate these social laws
And codes of fashion
That permit our beaux to
grieve us.
After they flatter,
They vanish and scatter,
And leave us.
BIANCA: If you cannot find a faithful man to
call your own, dears,
Take a chance and learn to do a
dance all you alone, dears.
I am sure you'll never mind it,
And I'm sure that you will find it
quite alright
And quite the best dance you have
had tonight.

COURSE I WILL

Lyric by Otto Harbach and Oscar Hammerstein II. Music credited to Herbert Stothart and Vincent Youmans, but is thought to be Youmans's work. Published in the vocal score. Introduced by Edith Day (Nina), James Doyle (Alberto), and Olin Howland (Gabrielle).

VERSE

ALBERTO: Will you say "yes" to every question
and suggestion
That I make to you?
NINA: I will.
No matter what the task,
Whatever you may care to ask,
I'll gladly grant.
I will.
ALBERTO: Will you say this to everyone, too?
NINA: It's lots of fun to agree with all.
ALBERTO: If you're so kind, then I am sure
You wouldn't mind if I should ask a
favor small?
NINA: Why, sir, I'm sure I shouldn't mind
at all,
I'd gladly grant a favor large or small.

REFRAIN 1

ALBERTO: When I make you my wife,
Will you support me all my life?

NINA: What do you say?
Course I will.
ALBERTO: And you'll obey in ev'ry way?
NINA: Forever and forever and a day,
'Deed I will.
ALBERTO: Give me your answer quite sincerely.
NINA: I'll tell you clearly that this is so.
ALBERTO: And when I hold you close like this,
And beg a kiss,
You will not answer "no."
NINA: Bet I will!

REFRAIN 2

GABRIELLE: I'd like to have a dance with you.
So will you do a step or two
With me?
NINA: Oui, Monsieur.
ALBERTO: But listen, Mr. Optimist,
I must insist she dances this
with me.
NINA: Si, Signor!
GABRIELLE: You're dealing with a desp'rate man,
sir!
NINA: I have a plan, sir, I think will do.
To settle this dispute,
Before it grows acute,
I'll dance with both of you.
Watch your step!

THE GIRL FROM CASIMO

Lyric by Otto Harbach and Oscar Hammerstein II. Music credited to Herbert Stothart and Vincent Youmans, but is generally thought to be Stothart's work. Published in the vocal score. Introduced by Guy Robertson (Guido) and ensemble.

For some 1940s productions the setting of the story was changed from Italy to Texas. Character names were Americanized, and throughout this lyric the word "Casimo" was replaced by "West Texas."

VERSE 1

GIRLS: Just what sort of place is Casimo?
Please tell us.
GUIDO: It's between a hill and a stream.
GIRLS: Oh my, we feel quite jealous!*
GUIDO: We've got a schoolhouse and bell.

---

* *A script at the Rodgers & Hammerstein Organization has:*
Oh please, go on and tell us.

A church with a steeple, as well.
But that isn't all Casimo can show.
GIRLS: What else, we'd like to know?

REFRAIN

GUIDO: You'll find something in Casimo
That cannot be found
All the world around,
Tho' you go to Paris, Rome,
And cities more renowned.
You will not find in Casimo
Any famous sights, cabarets at nights,*
But come there all the same,
And you'll be jolly glad you came,
When you've seen—
GIRLS: [*spoken*] Yes?
GUIDO: —My girl!

VERSE 2

GIRLS: Tell us of this girl in Casimo,
We pray you.
GUIDO: Can a lover speak of his dream?
GIRLS: Oh, yes. We'll not betray you.
GUIDO: So fair, so lovely is she,
There's nobody like her—
GIRLS: Maybe.
GUIDO: Nowhere upon earth her equal will find.
GIRLS: Perhaps.
Yet love is blind.

REPEAT REFRAIN

IF I TOLD YOU

Lyric by Otto Harbach and Oscar Hammerstein II. Music credited to Herbert Stothart and Vincent Youmans, but it is Youmans's work. Published as an individual sheet, but is not in the published vocal score. Introduced by Edith Day (Nina) and boys. A few weeks after the New York opening, the number was replaced by "You Can Never Blame a Girl for Dreaming."

Youmans used the tune again in *Lollipop* (1924), and, in 1928, Youmans and Hammerstein recycled the melody as "Virginia" in *Rainbow*.

---

* *A script at the Rodgers & Hammerstein Organization has:*
Any famous sights, bright or gay white lights.
But come there just the same
And you'll be mighty glad you came,
When you meet my girl.

VERSE

On her mouth he saw a kiss
And helped himself; you know that this
Was really most ungallant of the swain.
Flashing anger neath her brow,
She forced the lad to make a vow
That he would never speak of love again.
That was how it all befell,
And after that the tale is sad to tell.
Oh, precious words unspoken—
Each time he'd meet her,
This plea would greet her:

REFRAIN

If I could say what I feel in my heart
Wonderful things you would hear;
Were there a way all my thoughts to impart,
I could surprise you, my dear.
Flaming words of passion,
Sparkling fires would start;
You've never guessed
All that might be confessed
If I told you what is in my heart!

GOODBYE, LITTLE ROSEBUD

Lyric by Otto Harbach and Oscar Hammerstein II. Music credited to Herbert Stothart and Vincent Youmans, but is thought to be Stothart's work. Published as an individual sheet. Introduced by Guy Robertson (Guido).

VERSE 1

A clod, a simple clod of clay
Beneath a blushing wild rose lay.
He thought he held her fast.*
Till pluck'd by a roving swain
From out his life she passed
And left him to sigh in vain!

---

* A typed lyric sheet in the Otto Harbach Collection at the New York Public Library for the Performing Arts and a script at the Rodgers & Hammerstein Organization have:
   Nor gave me sign nor word,
   Till plucked by a passing swain,
   She thought it quite absurd
   On hearing this clod complain.

REFRAIN

Goodbye, little rosebud, goodbye.
Little friend, 'tis the end.
I thought you were blooming for me,
I was foolishly dreaming, I see.
For a clod that dares sigh*
At a rose blooming nigh,
Cannot hope for a tender reply.
For roses can see but the sky,
So goodbye, little rosebud, goodbye!

VERSE 2

The rosebud gazed at him with scorn;
She left that clod of clay forlorn!
Alas, he knew 'twere best
They never should meet again.
Yet still within his breast
Re-echoed that sad refrain:

REPEAT REFRAIN

ACT TWO FINALE

Lyric by Otto Harbach and Oscar Hammerstein II. Music credited to Herbert Stothart and Vincent Youmans. Published in the vocal score. Introduced by the company, except Guido, who has just left the stage.

NINA: Did he leave a note?
        Tell me what he wrote.
        Did he leave a word or message?
LAROTTA: [spoken]He told me to tell you that he was soon to be married to another girl in Casimo.
NINA: [sung] Nicolina!
         That explains it!
BIANCA: That's the girl he said,†
         She's the one he'll wed.
         That's so!
NINA: No, no!

---

* A typed lyric sheet in the Otto Harbach Collection at the New York Public Library for the Performing Arts and a script at the Rodgers & Hammerstein Organization have:
   For a clod that dare sigh
   At a rose blooming high,

† In the script at the Rodgers & Hammerstein Organization, these are Lucrezia's lines, and her last words are "back home" rather than "That's so!"

BIANCA: You've lost your young man, I declare!*
         What a painful humiliation to bear.
         He's jilted you—
LAROTTA: Now aren't you cross?
BIANCA: No great loss.
NINA: [furious] You—you—I—I—
GABBY: [spoken]: Nina, don't lose your temper. Only five seconds more—
LAROTTA: [spoken]: Get out of it!

[Clock strikes twelve.]

         Twelve o'clock! I'm cooked!

[Dialogue.]

NINA: [sung] I hate him, I hate him, I hate him, I hate him, I hate him!
         [spoken] Now go, everybody. I want to be alone! Go!
         [singing] Oh, Guido, Guido!
         Sweet April blossoms, we are all alone;
         He's gone away and left us all alone.
         I thought the day you came would be so happy, too
         Sweet April blossoms, April blossoms mean . . .
BIANCA: [spoken over music] What's this, Nina, another case of the poor little rich girl? It must be terrible to be jilted by one's sweetheart. Jilted! Come in, everybody, come in!
NINA: [sung] So you think it must be sad
         To lose a lover you adore?
         You want to know how it feels?
         It stabs like a knife!

[Dialogue over music. NINA accepts ALBERTO's previous offer of marriage.]

ENSEMBLE: Congratulations!
          They will make a perfect pair,
          Their happiness we're glad to share.
          And we will dance the Bambalina there!

---

* A variation from the script at the Rodgers & Hammerstein Organization:
   BIANCA: You've lost your young lover so fair
             What a painful humiliation to bear.
   LUCREZIA: He's jilted you—aren't you mad?
   BIANCA: It is too sad.

THE WORLD'S WORST WOMEN

Lyric by Otto Harbach and Oscar Hammerstein II. Music is credited to Herbert Stothart and Vincent Youmans, but is thought to be Stothart's work. Not published. Introduced by Esther Howard (Lucrezia) and Olin Howland (Gabby).

The *Baltimore Post* reported: "The comedy is clean and snappy. It is at its best in the third act where Miss Howard and Olin Howland have a song, 'The World's Worst Women,' that would stop any show. Salome never carried off the head of John the Baptist with more of an air than Miss Howard." Alexander Woollcott of the *New York Herald* was especially taken by the "Salome/Let go me" rhyme.

INTRODUCTION

GABBY: If you read the history you'll find that
women's lure*
Would tempt the male, but often fail
to mar his virtue pure.

LUCREZIA: That may be true but you will find that
these are in the minority†
The cases where the male was nailed
are in a vast majority.
One of the world's worst women I
want to be,‡
Just a girl like Helen of Troy.

GABBY: Be as bad as you like, but not with me.
Find another white-haired boy.

LUCREZIA: Helen's face wrecked a thousand
ships—

GABBY: And yours could do the same.

LUCREZIA: I'll be Helen, you be Paris,
And we'll lead a happy life.

GABBY: No, I will be just Joseph,
And you be Potiphar's wife.

---

* *Variant line:*
If you read history, you'll find that woman's lure.

† *Variant from two other scripts:* "in minority."

‡ *An alternate finish for the introduction:*
LUCREZIA: One of the world's worst women I want to be:
Cleopatra or Pompadour!
GABBY: Be as bad as you like, but not with me.
Find another paramour.
LUCREZIA: Salome was a vamp, 'tis said!
GABBY: I'll never lose *my* head!
LUCREZIA: You're so handsome!
Just like Samson! I'm Delilah to the life!
GABBY: No, I'm much more like Joseph,
And you're like Potiphar's wife.

I

LUCREZIA: Oh, Joe! Oh, Joe!
Don't go, don't go!

GABBY: Mrs. P., Mrs. P.,
Let me be, Mrs. P.!

LUCREZIA: Oh, Joe! Oh, Joe!
I want you so, so, so.

GABBY: So what, you got my goat.*

LUCREZIA: Come on and sow a wild oat.

GABBY: Mrs. P., I've got to go.
Mrs. P., I want my coat.

LUCREZIA: Come on and sow a wild oat.

GABBY: Mrs. P., your husband's coming.

LUCREZIA: No, Joe, the drums are drumming, the
bugles calling.

GABBY: Is there a war?

LUCREZIA: I made a war.

GABBY: What for?

LUCREZIA: So he would go.

GABBY: What for?

LUCREZIA: Oh, Joe, oh, Joe.

GABBY: Oh, no, no!

LUCREZIA: Oh, Joe.

GABBY: No.

LUCREZIA: Joe.

II

LUCREZIA: Oh, John! Oh, John!

GABBY: Miss Salome, you go on.

LUCREZIA: Oh, John! Oh, John!

GABBY: Miss Salome, you let go me.

LUCREZIA: I wanna be your gal.

GABBY: Go way, Salome, get over Sal.

LUCREZIA: I wanna love, I wanna kiss.

GABBY: Oh, Salome, you hardly know me.

LUCREZIA: I wanna head alive or dead.

GABBY: Oh, Salome.
Oh me, oh my.
Oh my, oh me.
Have a heart.

LUCREZIA: I'll get a head.

GABBY: Have a heart.

LUCREZIA: Get a head, poor John!
Poor John! Poor John, poor John!

III

LUCREZIA: Athenael, Athenael,
You look pale, Athenael.

GABBY: Thais, Thais,
Thais, Thais.

---

* *Variants:*
Sew what? You've got my coat!
and
Sew what? You get my goat.

LUCREZIA: Athenael, I'm female.

GABBY: Thais, Thais.

LUCREZIA: What's the matter, Athenael?
Don't you love me?

GABBY: Yes, yes.

LUCREZIA: Well, come and kiss me.

GABBY: No, no.

LUCREZIA: Well, what's the matter?

GABBY: Go, go!

LUCREZIA: But this is my house.

GABBY: I know.

LUCREZIA: What didja come for?
What didja come for?
What didja come for, Athenael?

GABBY: I come to save you, Thais.

LUCREZIA: That's an old one, Athenael.

GABBY: You're bad.
I must reform you.

LUCREZIA: You're cold.
I'd better warm you.

GABBY: Thais.

LUCREZIA: Athenael.

GABBY: Thais.

LUCREZIA: Athenael.

GABBY: Police!

LUCREZIA: Athenael.

GABBY: Police.

IV

LUCREZIA: Oh, Samson! Oh, Samson!

GABBY: Oh, Delilah! Oh, Delilah!

LUCREZIA: Oh, Samson, you're so strong,
You're so strong.

GABBY: What makes you think so?

LUCREZIA: Oh, Samson, oh, Samson,
The way you kiss me,
The way you treat me,
The way you beat me.
I love you, Sammy, 'cause you're so
strong.

GABBY: My hair is long, my hair is long,
That's the reason I'm so strong.

LUCREZIA: Strong for me.

GABBY: You've got me wrong.

LUCREZIA: A dirty dig, but I'll get even.

GABBY: I'll go to bed.

LUCREZIA: I'll get even.

GABBY: I'll rest my head,
I'll take a nap.

LUCREZIA: The poor sap.
I'll take my scissors, my pair of shears
And clip 'em clean above the ears.

[*Business.*]

GABBY: See what you've done?
I've lost my strength!

LUCREZIA: You've lost your strength?
GABBY: You'll have to suffer.
LUCREZIA: Well, so will you.
GABBY: It's the woman who has to pay.
LUCREZIA: I have toupee.
GABBY: You have to pay.
LUCREZIA: I have toupee.
GABBY: You have to pay.
LUCREZIA: I have toupee.

YOU CAN ALWAYS FIND ANOTHER PARTNER

Published as "I Can Always Find Another Partner." Lyric by Otto Harbach and Oscar Hammerstein II. Music credited to Herbert Stothart and Vincent Youmans, but is thought to be Youmans's work. Published as an individual sheet but does not appear in the subsequent published score and script. Introduced by Edith Day (Nina) and ensemble.

VERSE

NINA: Listen to me,
I'll give you good advice, girls.
GIRLS: Yes, yes.
Go on.
NINA: If ever you chance to choose a man,
Then you should lose a man,
You've lost nothing rare
And therefore do not care, for:

REFRAIN

You can always find another partner
When your partner's out of step with you.
If he leaves you, maybe you'll be lonely
Only for about a day or two.
If you find you can't be mates, girls,
You can cancel all your dates, girls.
He can run away with Mae or Flo;
You can carry on with John or Joe.
Any fellow's just as good as
Any other fellow at the loving game.
When you start to kiss, you close your eyes
And you will find they're pretty much the same.
If he tells you all is over,
Tell him he's no four-leaf clover.
You can always find another partner
Who will keep in step with you.

ADDED SONGS

COME LET US DANCE THROUGH THE NIGHT

Alternate title: "Opening, Act Two." Lyric by Otto Harbach and Oscar Hammerstein II. Music credited to Herbert Stothart and Vincent Youmans. Published in the vocal score. Added for the London production, replacing "The Best Dance I've Had Tonight." Introduced by Evelyn Drewe (Bianca) and ensemble.

VERSE 1

BIANCA: Come, let us dance through the night.
Dance till our cares take to flight.
All life's troubles
Burst like bubbles.
Joy redoubles
Dancing!
We'll turn the night into day,
Dancing our worries away
Till the morning
Light is dawning.
Whirling, twirling away.

REFRAIN

BIANCA: For there's music in our hearts
When we are dancing.
We swing and sway
And all is gay and bright.
And as we tread each happy measure
Life is fraught with pleasure,
Joy and delight.
Ah, the night was surely made
For love and laughter.
And though the day may bring us cares
and tears,
We'll not care
Whatsoe'er
May come after.
We will dance till the daylight appears.

VERSE 2

BIANCA: Daytime's a gay time, perchance.
Nighttime's the right time to dance.
When the shy light
Of the twilight
Starts all hearts
A-beating,
Love is aflame in each breath.
Who can be sad or depressed?
Bright eyes shining,

Hands entwining,
When all the world is at rest.

[BIANCA sings an obbligato while ensemble repeats refrain.]

YOU CAN NEVER BLAME A GIRL FOR DREAMING

Published as "You Never Can Blame a Girl for Dreaming." Lyric by Otto Harbach and Oscar Hammerstein II. Music credited to Herbert Stothart and Vincent Youmans. A few weeks after the Broadway opening this song replaced "If I Told You." Introduced by Edith Day (Nina) and boys.

VERSE 1

When I try to catch a moonbeam,
Somehow it will always melt away.
But in dreams alone
Bright moonbeams I own
Where my fancies stray.

REFRAIN

You can never blame a girl for dreaming,
You can never blame a star for gleaming.
Ev'ry little dreamer keeps a secret in her heart,
As ev'ry star must keep its light apart.
So let the little dreamer keep on scheming,
Making this old world seem bright and new.
You can never blame a girl for dreaming,
dreaming,
For she knows that maybe,
Some dream may someday be true!

VERSE 2 (FROM VOCAL SCORE)*

In that fairyland of fancies
Where each night a maiden's dreams are dear,
When the morning breaks,
And at dawn she wakes,
They must disappear!

REPEAT REFRAIN

* Alternate verse 2 from the published sheet:
Life at times is disappointing,
But I'll tell you how I alter this.
If reality
Is not pleasing me,
Dreams will bring me bliss.

HAMMERSTEIN'S NINE O'CLOCK REVUE

FLANNEL PETTICOAT GAL

Alternate title: "Flannel Petticoat Girl." Lyric by Oscar Hammerstein II and William Cary Duncan. Music by Vincent Youmans. This production number was first used in *Hammerstein's Nine O'Clock Revue*, supplementing material that Arthur Hammerstein had imported from London's Little Theatre. The revue opened October 4, 1923, at the Century Roof Theatre and closed after twelve performances. By October 25, the number was being used in the second act of *Plain Jane*, which was trying out in Wilkes-Barre, Pennsylvania, and would soon be renamed *Mary Jane McKane*. It was performed there by Hal Skelley (Joe), Kitty Kelly (Maggie), and a female ensemble to great acclaim: *Variety*'s Boston critic reported that the scene stopped the show for seven minutes. Sheet music was published with a *Mary Jane McKane* cover. In the published version, the lines of the verse are not divided between characters, and the lyric refers to "girls," plural, with "they" and "their" instead of "she" and "her."

VERSE

JOE: Oh, I wish I lived long, long ago
When a girl could cook and bake and
sew—
MAGGIE: When a girl had sense of modesty and
shame.
JOE: When she rolled her socks above the
knee—
MAGGIE: And she had no lacy lingerie—
JOE: In the day when ev'ry woman was a lady.

REFRAIN

Take me, take me back to the day
Of the flannel petticoat gal.
Simple, sweet, and pure was the way
Of the flannel petticoat gal.
No weak, slight thing,
Strong and hale and hearty—
Just the right thing
For a chowder party!
When you kissed her you didn't taste
Any paint upon her lips.
You could put your arm round a waist
In the days when hips was hips.
Those sweet mamas

Wore no crêpe-de-chine pajamas.
Take me, take me back to the day
Of the flannel petticoat gal.

I WONDER WHY THE GLOW WORM WINKS HIS EYE AT ME

Alternate title: "Glow Worm." Music by Herbert Stothart. Published as an individual sheet. Interpolated into Act Two of *Hammerstein's Nine O'Clock Revue*. Introduced by Colin Campbell, Irene Olsen, and female ensemble.

VERSE

PROFESSOR: Ladies!
Now the class will come to order.
Please study with me
Bugology.
GIRLS: Oh, what a cute professor!
PROFESSOR: Ladies!
Beetles, butterflies, and bumblebees.
SHE: Teacher, please, drop the bees.
I know a bug more puzzling.
PROFESSOR: [*spoken*] Puzzling?
SHE: He comes to see me ev'ry night—
It's a most unwelcome visit.
And I must ask you this question, sir.
PROFESSOR: Well, go ahead,
What is it?

REFRAIN

SHE: I wonder why the glow worm winks
his eye at me,
No matter where I chance to go he's
sure to be.
He's always blink-blink-blinking
With his little light.
He's always wink-wink-winking
When he's seeing things at night.
Whenever there's a caller sitting on
my porch,
He comes along and flicks his little
torch—
I almost hear him laugh aloud in sly
glow-worm glee,
And then he winks his eye at me.

MARY JANE McKANE (1923)

Earlier titles for the show: *Plain Jane* and *Mary Jane*. Tryouts: Irving Theatre, Wilkes-Barre, Pennsylvania, October 25–27, 1923; Auditorium, Baltimore, October 31–November 3, 1923; Shubert Theatre, Boston, November 5–24, 1923. New York run: Imperial Theatre (inaugural production); opened December 25, 1923; closed May 3, 1924; 151 performances. A New Musical Play. Presented by Arthur Hammerstein. Production supervised by Arthur Hammerstein. Book and lyrics by William Cary Duncan and Oscar Hammerstein II. Music by Herbert Stothart and Vincent Youmans. Book staged by Alonzo Price. Dances and ensembles by Sammy Lee. Orchestrations not credited. Orchestra directed by Herbert Stothart. Scenic design by Frank E. Gates and Edward A. Morange. Costume design by Charles Le Maire.

Cast: Mary Hay (Mary Jane McKane), Hal Skelley (Joe McGillicudy), Kitty Kelly (Maggie Murphy), Stanley Ridges (Andrew Dunn Jr.), Margaret and Elizabeth Keene, known as the Keene Twins (Cash and Carrie), Dallas Welford (Martin Frost), Laura De Cardi (Doris Dunn), Eva Clark (Louise Dryer), Louis Morrell (George Sherwin), James Heenan (Andrew Dunn Sr.), and ensemble.

Andy Dunn Jr. is not taken seriously at his father's toy company. When it comes time to hire a secretary for him, pretty girls are considered too distracting. Mary Jane flunks her first interview but returns in a drab disguise and gets the job. She falls in love with Andy, but he is pining for the pretty girl who once said "toodle-oo" to him.

The main source for this chapter is a piano-conductor score in the hand of Herbert Stothart, located now at the Tams-Witmark Music Library in New York City. Six songs were published individually. Typescripts survive at the Rodgers & Hammerstein Organization, the Shubert Archive, the Tams-Witmark Music Library, and in the collection of Aaron Gandy, an artistic advisor to the estate of Vincent Youmans. As with *Wildflower*, having so many sources to compare yields numerous small textual differences, such as "I have" in one typescript and "I've got" in another.

The extent of William Cary Duncan's contributions to the lyrics is not known.* In the program, all of *Mary*

---

* In the 1910s and '20s Duncan worked steadily as an adaptor, librettist, and lyricist, but, according to Kurt Gänzl's Encyclopedia never on a "truly top-drawer" show. In Mary Jane McKane's program and on the cover of the sheet music, Duncan's name precedes Hammerstein's, but on the first page of each published song Hammerstein's name comes first.

Jane McKane's melodies were credited jointly to Herbert Stothart and Vincent Youmans; but certain published sheets cite Youmans only.

THE RUMBLE OF THE SUBWAY

Alternate title: "Subway Chant." Lyric by Oscar Hammerstein II and William Cary Duncan. Music credited to Herbert Stothart and Vincent Youmans, but is probably Stothart's work. Not published. Introduced by the ensemble.

REFRAIN

ENSEMBLE: 'Mid the rattle, rattle, rattle of
the subway,
And the rumble, rumble
underneath the ground,
Herded like a lot o' cattle,
You can hear a lot o' prattle,
'Mid the rattle, rattle, rattle of
the subway.

PATTER 1

SHOP GIRL: [*spoken in rhythm over music*] 'N I
says to him, "That'll be about
all!"
STENOGRAPHER: 'N what'd he say?
SHOP GIRL: I gave him one look, then he
says to me, "What a little flat
tire you turned out to be!"

REPEAT REFRAIN

PATTER 2

MESSENGER BOY: I see where de Giants took a
game from de Cubs.
LAUNDRY BOY: Dem Cubs ain't nothin' but a
bunch of dubs!
BROKER: Baldwin closed at fifty-eight.
BANKER: The rails'll go higher if they
raise the freight.
MESSENGER BOY: D'ja hear what they said?
Sounds like a tip.
LAUNDRY BOY: I wasn't listenin'—
Look at that pip!
STENOGRAPHER: Don't say a woid.
This boob back here is givin' me
the eye.
Can you beat it?

REPEAT REFRAIN

[*Music slows as they "reach the station."*]

CONDUCTOR: All out—Glub, glub.
Next stop—Flub a dub.
Let 'em off. Let 'em off.

SPEED

Lyric by Oscar Hammerstein II and William Cary Duncan. Music credited to Herbert Stothart and Vincent Youmans, but is probably Stothart's work. Not published. Introduced by Hal Skelley (Joe) and Margaret and Elizabeth Keene (Cash, Carrie).

VERSE 1

JOE: Just tune in on what I've got to say.
Take my good advice or let it lay,
Do not be cross if I
Seem to philosophize
Here's my little sermon for today:

REFRAIN 1

JOE: Always keep moving, keep moving
along!
CASH
AND CARRIE: Yeah?
JOE: Never go slow and you'll never go
wrong!
CASH
AND CARRIE: Yeah?
JOE: Pepper and ginger and so forth—
Take those along when you go
forth.
This is the lowdown on how to
succeed:
Makes no difference what you do
As long as you have speed!
CASH
AND CARRIE: [*without enthusiasm*] Yeah?
JOE: Thanks.

VERSE 2

JOE: Ladies, you don't seem to get my
drift,
Your misunderstanding is a gift.
By all I say to you,
Can't I convey to you,
"Speed" is something "fast."
You get it? "Swift."

CASH
AND CARRIE: Yeah?

REFRAIN 2

JOE: Always keep moving, keep moving
along.
CASH
AND CARRIE: Huh?
JOE: Never go slow and you'll never go
wrong.
CASH
AND CARRIE: Oh!
JOE: Pepper and ginger and so forth—
Take those along when you go forth.
This is the lowdown on how to succeed:
Makes no difference what you do,
As long as you have speed.

[*Fast dance.*]

NOT IN BUSINESS HOURS

Lyric by Oscar Hammerstein II and William Cary Duncan. Music credited to Herbert Stothart and Vincent Youmans, but is probably Youmans's work. Not published. Introduced by Stanley Ridges (Andy), Eva Clark (Louise), and ensemble.

GIRLS: Wonder men who dare and do,
We are mighty proud of you.
BOYS: You're only girls,
But just the same,
With all modesty we must agree,
That you speak truly.
GIRLS: Haven't you an hour to spare?
Come forget your business care.
BOYS: Some other time, not now, my
dear,
For there's men's work to be
done right here.
LOUISE: [*to Andy*] I love you, dear.
I want you near.
No pow'r on earth can change
my heart,
So have no fear.
Ah, have no fear,
Ah, have no fear.
I want the whole wide earth
to know
I love you, dear.
ANDY: That can't be done in business
hours.

BOYS: It can't be done in business
    hours.
ANDY: This is not the place
    To waste your time in mooning.
BOYS: Crooning.
ANDY: Sappy sentimental talk
    In business hours
    Is taboo here.
BOYS: You hear!
ANDY: This is not the right time.
BOYS: Save it for the nighttime.
LOUISE: Can't you see I love you?
GIRLS: She loves you.
ANDY AND BOYS: But not in business hours.
LOUISE: There'll come a time
    When the stars are in the sky.
    There'll come a time
    When there's only you and I.
    When the sweet, rose-scented
    Breeze of night is singing,
    Bringing whispered thoughts.
    There'll come a time,
    Long-awaited, happy time,
    When you'll hold me, hold me.
    We'll be all alone, dear,
    All each other's own, dear,
    All the day together, together.
ANDY AND BOYS: But not in business hours!

STICK TO YOUR KNITTING

Lyric by Oscar Hammerstein II and William Cary Duncan. Music by Herbert Stothart. Published as an individual sheet, but this text from the score at Tams-Witmark. Introduced by Mary Hay (Jane), Hal Skelley (Joe), and boys.

VERSE 1

JANE: I'd knit and knit,
    Till it seemed like kingdom come.
    Just do my bit,
    Till my fingers were numb!
    How I used to wish that
    I could run away and play,
    But Uncle Abner used to say:*

REFRAIN

JANE: Just you stick to your knittin', dear,
    And the hours will run.

---

* *Published sheet has:*
    But Mother used to smile and say:

Just sit where you're sittin', dear,
And pretend it's fun.
Little fingers may ache,
But by and by comes chocolate cake.
And then a great big slice tastes twice
    as nice,
When you know your knittin's done.

VERSE 2

JANE: The boys I knew
    Used to whistle going by.
    And tease me too,
    And they said I was so shy.
BOYS: And they said that you were*
    Tied to mother's apron string.†
JOE: But Uncle Abner used to sing:†

REPEAT REFRAIN

MY BOY AND I

Lyric by Oscar Hammerstein II and William Cary Duncan. Music by Vincent Youmans.‡ Published as an individual sheet. Introduced by Eva Clark (Louise) and girls.

VERSE

When you're in love,
Of love you dream.
That's how the story old was told me.
When you're in love
Your fancies teem,
At least that's what I'm told.
Lost in sweet reverie's trances,
Weaving your tender romances,
I am in love and oh, I dream—
And when I dream, I meet a boy.

REFRAIN

My boy and I
Go hand in hand

---

* *Published sheet has:*
    Then they'd tell me I was

† *Published sheet has:*
    But Mother used to smile and sing.

‡ *Youmans subsequently changed the meter of the song from 3/4 time to 2/4 time, and Otto Harbach set the tune as the title song of* No, No Nanette.

Together as lovers ever do.
My boy and I
Have found a land
Together where hearts are ever true.
He'll hold me close and whisper low
The very things I want to know.
He'll sigh and say, "I love you so!"
No wonder I
Want to fly,
Fly to my boy.

YOU'RE NEVER TOO OLD TO LOVE

Lyric by Oscar Hammerstein II and William Cary Duncan. Music by Herbert Stothart and Vincent Youmans. Not published. Sung by Eva Clark (Louise) and the girls to Dallas Welford (Mr. Frost, the general manager).

    The song was added to the show a few months after the opening.

VERSE

LOUISE: Don't be so dignified, Daddy.
    Don't be so bashful and shy.
    You'd be a gay little laddie
    If you'd just try.
    I know, you fat little scamp, you,
    You know how.
    We've always been dying to vamp you
    So why not now?

REFRAIN

LOUISE: Sugar plum,
    Won't you come,
    Come to me?
    My little roly-poly papa be?
    What do you say we
    Rock-a-bye baby,
    By and by maybe
    On your knee.
    Leave the nest
    For a fling
    On the wing,
    You little roly-poly turtle dove.
    Cutie, you are growing old,
    But you are never too old to love!

REFRAIN 2 (PATTER VERSION)

GIRLS: Funny little sugar plum,
    How can you be so deaf and dumb
    When I am asking you to come to me?

Little roly-poly papa,
Come and be a sport and drop a
Little tiny bit of dignity.
If you'd only loosen up
How lovely it would be!
We could have a dandy time
With nobody to see!
We could do a rock-a-bye
Together, you and me—
Do a little rock-a-bye on Papa's little knee.
Leave the nest and have a fling
And fly around and ev'rything
As merry as a swallow on the wing.
Little roly-poly daddy
You could be as gay and gaddy
As a pretty turtle dove in spring.
Even if you're growing older,
That's the time for growing bolder,
That's the very time for making love.

TOODLE-OO

Lyric by Oscar Hammerstein II and William Cary Duncan. Music by Vincent Youmans. Published as an individual sheet. An additional verse was found at Tams-Witmark. Introduced by Mary Hay (Jane) and Stanley Ridges (Andy).

Unpublished verse

JANE: Our luck is zero,
I met my hero
And had to leave him flat.
ANDY: Just how d'you do goodbye, dear?
JANE: Just toodle-oo like that.
ANDY: It's like a hoo-doo.
JANE: I feel as you do.
ANDY: We're out of luck, that's plain.
JANE: But don't be moping.
Let's keep on hoping
BOTH: We'll meet sometime again.
JANE: And if we ever do some happy day
ANDY: We'd better practice what we're going
to say.

REFRAIN

JANE: Toodle-oo,
I'll be never weary, dearie,
Being true to you,
True as blue.
Toodle-oo,
Ev'ry day I'll send a tender
Thought or two to you,

Rush it through.
Toodle-oo,
Someone's going to find a kind of
Lovin' new to you.
You know who, too.
Toodle-oo,
My undying love is flying,
Honey, do to you,
Toodle-oo.

Published verses

VERSE 1

SHE: I guess it's silly,
Confess it's silly
To have to say goodbye.
But, oh, it sounds so lonesome,
It almost makes me cry.
I'm always tearful,
Just sort of fearful,
When happy days are past.
That goodbye spoken
When ties are broken
Maybe will be the last.
And so I say goodbye another way.
But this is what I'm thinking when I say:

REPEAT REFRAIN

VERSE 2

HE: Your information,
Your explanation,
They thrill me, I confess.
Maybe her goodbye message
Was just a sweet caress.
I'm going to dream so,
To make it seem so.
At least I'm going to try.
When dew is falling
I'll hear her calling,
That wonderful goodbye.
Until we meet again some happy day
I'll think of her and then I'll hear her say:

REPEAT REFRAIN

DOWN WHERE THE MORTGAGES GROW

Lyric by Oscar Hammerstein II and William Cary Duncan. Music credited to Herbert Stothart and Vincent

Youmans, but is probably Youmans's work. Not published. Introduced by Hal Skelley (Joe) and Kitty Kelly (Maggie).

VERSE 1

JOE: When we're sitting side by each
Spooning on the sandy beach,
MAGGIE: Where the lovesick lobsters gambol
And the clams in couples ramble,
JOE: When the catfish calls his mate,
Marriage seems a blissful state—
BOTH: But it's nothing to the fun it
Must be when you've gone and done it!

REFRAIN

MAGGIE: I'd like a house with an acre or so
with it.
JOE: One with a dear little mortgage to go
with it.
MAGGIE: We'd have a bee and some milkweed
to milk.
JOE: We'd keep a silkworm and we'd raise
our own silk.
BOTH: Just fancy!
MAGGIE: I'd like a lamb with some nice tender
chops in him.
JOE: I'd keep a toad and make beer from the
hops in him.
BOTH: Down in our dear little bungalow,
Down where the mortgages grow!
JOE: [spoken] 'Tis beautiful, Maggie! Again!
BOTH: Grow-oh-oh!
JOE: [spoken] We fear no one!
BOTH: Down where the mortgages grow!

VERSE 2

MAGGIE: Oh, what joy and wild delight
Being a suburbanite.
JOE: Where the bumblebees are singing
And the wild mosquitos stinging!
MAGGIE: Where the caterpillars fall
Gently from the bedroom wall.
JOE: Oh, what joy to be commuting
When the biscuit trees are fruiting!

REFRAIN 2

JOE: Won't it be nice to be sitting below a
tree?
MAGGIE: You'll get romantic and write me some
poetry.
JOE: [spoken] Poetry? Certainly!
[sung] Roses are red and the violets are
blue—
Garlic is strong and I'm garlic for you.

BOTH: Sweet cookie!

MAGGIE: We'll have an arbor all full of wisteria.

JOE: [*spoken*] Wisteria? Gee, that's a hard one. [*sung*] We'll have a swamp where we'll raise our malaria.

BOTH: Down in our dear little bungalow, Down where the mortgages grow-oh-oh-oh!

JOE: [*spoken*] 'Tis sweet, Maggie—continue!

BOTH: Grow-oh-oh-oh!

JOE: [*spoken*] Hold your bridge work, Maggie.

BOTH: Down where the mortgages grow!

TIME-CLOCK SLAVES

Alternate title: "Opening, Act Two." Lyric by Oscar Hammerstein II and William Cary Duncan. Music by Vincent Youmans. Not published. Introduced by Margaret Keene (Cash), Elizabeth Keene (Carrie), and the girls.

VERSE

CARRIE: Are we the kind to make a fuss Because our job's confining?

GIRLS: Like other girls, Like other girls.

CASH: Does ev'ry hour seem [ ]* to us And are we always whining?

GIRLS: Like other girls, Like other girls.

CASH AND CARRIE: Now do we hate to punch the clock And settle down to biz? Is work to us an awful shock? You bet your life it is!

[GIRLS *punch the clock in rhythm.*]

REFRAIN

GIRLS: Punching morning, noon, and night, We'd delight in smashing Your emphatic little, automatic little face, To teach you to behave. Someone made you just for spite. You deserve a thrashing. Hully gee, it's tough to be A time-clock slave.

* *The piano-vocal score is missing one syllable of text here.*

LAUGH IT OFF

Lyric by Oscar Hammerstein II and William Cary Duncan. Music by Herbert Stothart and Vincent Youmans. Not published. Introduced by Kitty Kelly (Maggie), Mary Hay (Mary Jane), and Stanley Ridges (Andy).

VERSE

MAGGIE: When life looks sad and gloomy, And wolves are at the door,

JANE: And nasty bill collectors Are crying out for more,

ANDY: When you're down on the ground, And getting kicked all around, Just grin and pretend that it's fun.

JANE: You can never see your shadow

ALL THREE: When you're looking at the sun.

REFRAIN

ALL THREE: Just laugh it off!

MAGGIE: And don't let on that you're losing.

ALL THREE: Just laugh it off!

ANDY: And make believe that it's amusing.

MAGGIE: When you are stuck, And down on your luck, Be ready to stand the gaff.

JANE: Plug right along, And don't admit they can beat you,

ANDY: Things will be bright.

MAGGIE: You'll come out alright.

ALL THREE: Just stand up and fight And laugh.

[*Dance.*]

JUST LOOK AROUND

Lyric by Oscar Hammerstein II and William Cary Duncan. Music by Herbert Stothart and Vincent Youmans. Not published. Introduced by Mary Hay (Mary Jane), Stanley Ridges (Andy), and the girls. According to Stanley Green's *Rodgers & Hammerstein Fact Book*, the number was added a few months after the show's New York opening.

VERSE

ANDY: I admit I'm tired of single freedom. With single freedom, I'm through.

JANE: Women are a nuisance, but you need 'em. The men all need 'em. You too.

ANDY: Someone sweet to cook for me, And make my breakfast right.

JANE: Someone sweet to look for you When you come home at night.

ANDY: But to find her— That's the burning question.

JANE: If you'll allow me just one suggestion.

REFRAIN 1

JANE: I know a girl Who is anxious to Darn your socks for you.

ANDY: I know a girl Whom I'd like to see Baking cake for me.

JANE: The girl in my mind is plain and small.

ANDY: The one I mean is beautiful and tall.

JANE: Not at all. Not the type. Not the kind for you, dear.

ANDY: I know a girl. She's a star on high, Shining in the sky. Too high for my poor love to bound.

JANE: Now what's the use o' lookin' up so high? Another may be standing by, If you just look around, Look around.

REFRAIN 2

JANE: I know a girl. And she's not a shirk, Not afraid to work.

ANDY: I know the kind. I have seen a few, And the work they do.

JANE: Now don't say that, 'cause it's not polite.

ANDY: Maybe it's not, but you'll admit it's right.

JANE: Not at all, Not at all. Not the one I speak of.

ANDY: I've come to think As I go along, That there's something wrong With every single girl I've found.

JANE: But if you'd make some single girl say
"yes,"
There'd be a single girl the less.
So you'd best look around,
Look around.

REFRAIN 3

[*Six girls enter.*]

ALL GIRLS: I know a girl.
1ST GIRL: She's a little scamp,
She's a baby vamp.
ALL GIRLS: I know a girl.
2ND GIRL: She has Titian hair,
And a baby stare.
ANDY: The girl in my mind is not like you.
ALL GIRLS: Oh, look around. Won't any of
us do?
JANE: Not at all,
Not at all.
Not the type for you, dear.
ALL GIRLS: I know a girl.
3RD GIRL: She's a blonde for fair,
Giddy, golden hair.
ALL GIRLS: Sought for but very seldom found.
4TH GIRL: I may not have their line of gab,
But I'm a riot in a taxicab.
ALL GIRLS: And she's here, so why look around?

THISTLEDOWN

Alternate title: "Opening, Act Three." Lyric by Oscar
Hammerstein II and William Cary Duncan. Music by
Herbert Stothart. Published as an individual sheet, with
a different verse than in the score. Introduced by Eva
Clark (Louise) and ensemble.

Production verse

VERSE

LOUISE: Thistledown, thistledown.
As you fly, thistledown,
Tell me, why do you never come to
me?
ENSEMBLE: Thistledown.
LOUISE: Won't you stop a while
And tell me where you wander?
Tell me now.
Ah—[*coloratura ad lib*]
Ah, tell me where you go?
Ah—

REFRAIN

LOUISE: Airy little bit of thistledown,
Wary little bit of thistledown.
Try and try to catch you as I may
You always go floating away.
Someday little bit of thistledown,
Someday I'll outwit you, thistledown.
As you fly on breezes speeding
Just by chance you'll fly unheeding
To my heart to be
My thistledown.

Published verse

VERSE

Thistledown, we all have met you—
Thistledown, thistledown.
Though we try, we can't forget you—
Thistledown, thistledown.
Tantalizing,
Hypnotizing,
Fickle as the breeze that blows in spring.
But though you float away so gayly that you
Seem to laugh and mock me as I sing.

MARY JANE MCKANE

Lyric by Oscar Hammerstein II and William Cary Duncan. Music by Vincent Youmans (who recycled the tune
in *Great Day*). Not published. Introduced by Mary Hay
(Mary Jane McKane) and male ensemble. When the
show's title changed during the out-of-town tryout, the
lyric that had been "Plain Jane" received a few hasty
patches.

VERSE

MARY JANE: [*to her ventriloquist doll*] What a pair of
misfit nitwits we turned out to be!
We're about as useful as the flu.
Dear little funny face,
We don't fit any place—
Not even in the race,
It's sad but true.
Mary Jane McKane,*
You're very plain, Jane.

---

* *In the "Plain Jane" version of the song this line and
the next are:*
Do you wonder why they call us "Plain Jane"?
Do you wonder why nobody cares?

No one seems to care a bit for you.
We can never stroll in Lovers' Lane,
Jane.
BOYS: Oh, yes you can, Jane.
And here's your man, Jane!

REFRAIN

BOYS: Jane McKane, Jane,*
I'll be your beau,
Can't refrain, Jane,
From saying so.
You're charming,
Disarming,
Just as you are.
A cutie
Patootie,
Way over par!
Jane, how came you
So fair to see?
I proclaim you
The kitten's knee.
You're just as sweet as sugarcane,
Jane,
And you're the main Jane for me!

CUT AND UNUSED SONGS

ALL FOR CHARITY

Lyric by Oscar Hammerstein II and William Cary Duncan. Music credited to Herbert Stothart and Vincent
Youmans, but probably Youmans's work. Not published.
Introduced in Act Two by Walter Tenney (Hooper) (a
character that appears to have been cut) and the ensemble. The Wilkes-Barre program and the scripts indicate
Joe, Doris, Louise, "Done," Cash, and Carrie were also
part of the number. Dropped before the Boston opening.

HOOPER: I'm willing to believe
It's better to give than receive.
I'll always help and do my share,
But you can't get me to a charity fair.
I'd take my whole bankroll and
Give it all to starving Poland,
If they'd only pass a law to bar
The society siren of the street bazaar!

---

* *In the "Plain Jane" version this line is:*
Plain Jane, Plain Jane,

GIRLS: We sell you chances,
Hold big dances,
All for charity.
We wave big banners,
Show bad manners,
All for charity!
BOYS: Ten bucks for one gardenia,
Just to help out poor Armenia.
GIRLS: We get away with murder
In the name of charity!
HOOPER: [*opening the fair dressed as Pagliacci*]
One moment, please!
Please pardon me,
Please pardon me.
One moment, please!
We welcome all
From near and far
To our bazaar.
We welcome all!
I must inform you,
I must inform you
The fair is on!
So come!
I invite you all!
One dollar . . .
GIRLS: Oh, won't you take us?
Boys, please take us
To this little show.
BOYS: Please don't make us,
Please don't make us.
We don't want to go.
We'll come out with light wads—
GIRLS: You're a lot of tightwads!
Boys, please take us?
BOYS: Course they make us—
GIRLS: Take us to the show.

COME ON AND PET ME

Lyric by Oscar Hammerstein II and William Cary Duncan. Music by Vincent Youmans. Published as an individual sheet. It is not clear which character would have sung it. With a new lyric by Irving Caesar, Youmans's tune later became "Sometimes I'm Happy."

VERSE

There's a girlfriend that I know.
Has a boyfriend who is slow.
When they're alone he is shy,
And she has to keep complaining:

REFRAIN

Come on and pet me,
Why don't you pet me?
Why don't you get me
To let you pet me?
You never ask me out for a spoon.
For all I know, there ain't any moon!
I'd like to bask in
Your fond caressin'.
You do the askin',
I'll do the yessin'.
Within your arms I'd stay for a year.
Come on and pet me, dear.
Do, dear!

OVERLEAF *Pearl Regay and the "Totem Tom-Tom" girls*

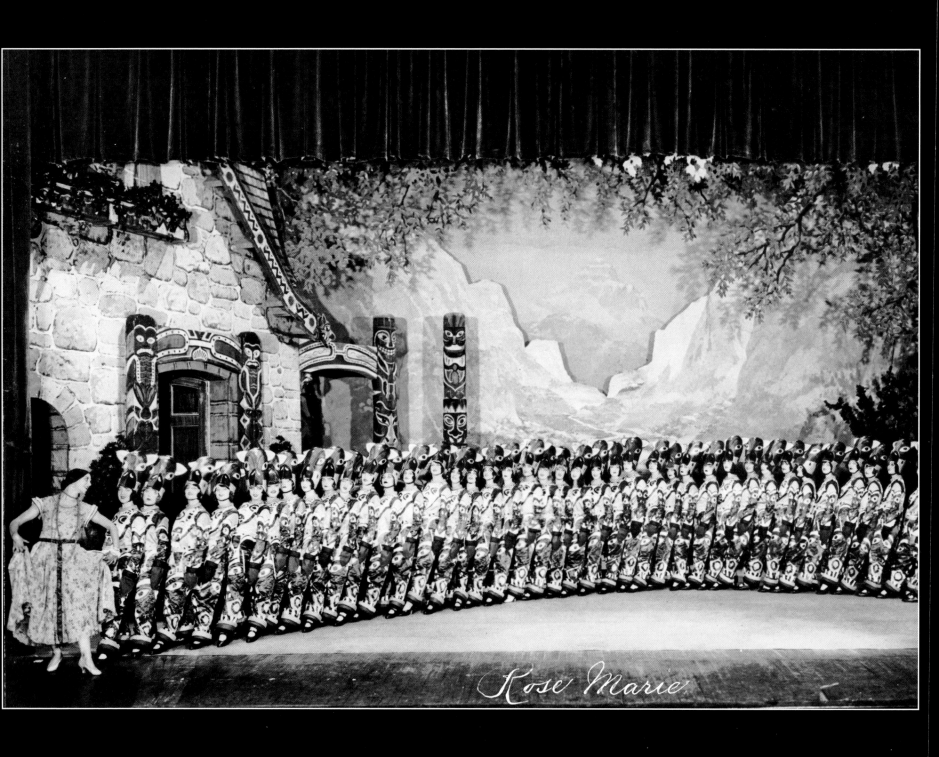

ROSE-MARIE | 1924

ROSE-MARIE (1924)

Tryouts: Apollo Theatre, Atlantic City, August 18–23, 1924; Auditorium, Long Branch, New Jersey. New York run: Imperial Theatre; opened on September 2, 1924; closed January 16, 1926; 557 performances. A Musical Play. Music by Rudolf Friml and Herbert Stothart. Book and lyrics by Otto Harbach and Oscar Hammerstein II. Production supervised by Arthur Hammerstein. Book staged by Paul Dickey. Dances arranged by David Bennett. Orchestrations by Robert Russell Bennett. Orchestra directed by Herbert Stothart. Settings designed by Frank E. Gates and Edward A. Morange. Gowns and costumes designed by Charles Le Maire.

Cast: Mary Ellis (Rose-Marie La Flamme), Dennis King (Jim Kenyon), William Kent (Hard-Boiled Herman), Arthur Deacon (Sergeant Malone), Dorothy Mackaye (Lady Jane), Arthur Ludwig (Black Eagle), Frank Greene (Edward Hawley), Edward Ciannelli (Emile La Flamme), Pearl Regay (Wanda), Lela Bliss (Ethel Brander), and ensemble.

In the Canadian Rockies, Rose-Marie La Flamme loves a miner named Jim Kenyon. She sings at a hotel run by Lady Jane, who juggles the romantic attentions of both Hard-Boiled Herman and Sergeant Malone of the Royal Canadian Mounties. Rose-Marie's brother Emile wants to ingratiate himself with the wealthy trapper Edward Hawley by arranging for him to marry Rose-Marie. Hawley has been having an affair with Wanda, wife of Black Eagle. When she kills her husband, Jim is framed for the murder. To forestall Jim's arrest, Rose-Marie sings him a prearranged signal to go away and she agrees to marry Hawley. Wedding plans progress. Just in the nick of time, Wanda confesses, and Rose-Marie and Jim are reunited.

A thirty-one-city national tour began on February 9, 1925, at Poli's Theatre, Washington, D.C. A second tour began on September 14, 1925, at the Shubert Theatre, Philadelphia, and visited nineteen cities. A third tour began on September 13, 1926, at the Opera House in Providence, Rhode Island, and visited twenty cities. A fourth tour began on September 29, 1926, at the Auditorium, Henderson, North Carolina, and visited twenty-four cities. A fifth tour began on November 8, 1926, at the Detroit Opera House and visited twenty-two cities. A sixth tour began on September 4, 1927, at the Hanna Theatre, Cleveland, and visited twenty-nine cities. A seventh tour began on September 3, 1928, at the Princess Theatre, Montreal, and visited twenty-one cities. Although it has not been revived on Broadway since the late 1920s, *Rose-Marie* was a staple in the light-opera repertoire for decades.

A London production starring Edith Day and Derek Oldham opened at the Theatre Royal, Drury Lane, on March 20, 1925. *Rose-Marie* was also presented in Paris (1927) and Berlin (1928).

Joan Crawford and James Murray starred in a silent 1928 MGM film directed and adapted by Lucien Hubbard; Jeanette MacDonald and Nelson Eddy starred in a 1936 MGM film directed by W. S. Van Dyke; Ann Blyth and Howard Keel starred in a 1954 MGM film produced and directed by Mervyn LeRoy. Hammerstein did not write any of the additional lyrics heard in these last two films.

The main source for this chapter is the published piano-vocal score. Eight songs were published as individual sheets. The New York Public Library for the Performing Arts has four typescripts, but even the one in the Otto Harbach Collection appears to date from 1927 or later (it mentions Charles Lindbergh). The Tams-Witmark Music Library in New York City has a prompt book and conductor's score. The Shubert Archive has a variety of scripts from the 1930s, 1940s, and 1950s, and piano-vocal scores in French and Spanish. The Oscar Hammerstein II Collection in the Music Division of the Library of Congress holds no creative materials from *Rose-Marie*. The Rudolf Friml Archive and the Herbert Stothart Archive, both at UCLA, have not been fully cataloged.

Programs from the earliest performances of *Rose-Marie* do not list musical numbers. Instead, the programs said:

> The musical numbers in this play are such an integral part of the action that we do not think we should list them as separate episodes. The songs which stand out, independent of their dramatic associations are "Rose-Marie," "Indian Love Call," "Totem Tom-Tom" and "Why Shouldn't We?" in the first act, and "The Door of My Dreams" in the second act.

That statement is of enormous interest to students of the development of musical theater as an art form—but, conversely, is an obstacle to those who would study *Rose-Marie* in particular, because usual lists of musical numbers are our best guide to what songs were added or cut as a show was polished.

Little is known about Harbach and Hammerstein's collaboration on this show. In separate conversations they told historian Miles Kreuger that Harbach wrote the lyrics to all the big songs in *Rose-Marie*. However, contracts show that Harbach and Hammerstein received joint credit in billing, and equal royalties for this show and their other collaborations. The composer of each number was specified in the published vocal score.

Beyond its commercial success, *Rose-Marie* is notable for its artistic aspirations. As the program note quoted above states, the authors believed the music was thoroughly integrated with the drama. In the early months of 1925, Hammerstein pointed out some of *Rose-Marie*'s intentions in an open letter to drama critics in cities to be visited by a touring company:

In a musical play we must paint thick outlines with a broad brush. There is no chance for sustained scenes. If they are not brilliantly written the audience merely sits back and waits for the number. If they are brilliantly written, drawing the audience into a mood for subtleties, the numbers are resented as blatant interruptions.

So the scenes between numbers must be as short as possible, and yet each one must make some definite point and mark a step of progress in the story. Hence, the ideal plot for a musical play is one which can be told largely in the number—a story which can be shown rather than talked about. Let the musician do your work for you and create the kind of plot which permits him to. The most tiresome type of musical play is the kind in which there is a definite cleavage between dialogue and lyrics—where the spoken words carry the story and the words that are sung come in as interpolated episodes of extraneous entertainment.

The construction of a musical play is a delicate job—a science rather than an art. The men engaged in this job—producers, authors, composers, performers and directors—are for the most part sincere and ambitious workers, and yet with all their combined skill in showmanship, their industry and co-operation, they frequently produce a work which seems wholly without merit. Why does this happen? For the same reason that a good high jumper often fails to clear the bar at six feet five. It is hard to jump six feet five, and it's hard to build a show that will be amusing to thousands of people of varied mental and emotional equipment.

All this to introduce a complaint which I wish to make. Since musical shows, good or bad, are constructed with painstaking attention to detail, great consumption of energy and carefully analyzed scientific principles of showmanship, it is unfair not to accord sincere and expert criticism to them.

Criticism of musical plays has degenerated to a formula—here is the drift of nine out of ten reviews:

"The manager has given his show a magnificent and costly production. But unfortunately he has chosen a frail libretto on which to lavish his expenditure. The plot is of the usual tedious variety. The score is a good deal better, containing several tunes that are decidely whistleable, if a trifle reminiscent. The comedy is pretty sad. We cannot help wishing that the manager had spent a little less on scenery and had used the money to buy one good joke."

This snappy formula was applied to a musical show some years ago, and continues to be used, almost word for word, and applied to shows of widely varying merits. It is just one thing to say when you can't think of anything else to say. . . .

When "Rose-Marie" opened this fall one fatigued and bewildered young man wrote half a column on what he wittily described as "the girl scout costumes" in Scene 1. He did not mention the fact that the play had several pioneer features: that it was a musical play with a melodrama plot; that the production combined modern whirlwind dancing with the old-time custom of having a cast of real singers; that the orchestra contained forty pieces—double the usual amount. Any man at all qualified to review a musical play should have noted these things.

PRELUDE AND OPENING CHORUS (VIVE LA CANADIENNE)

Lyric by Otto Harbach and Oscar Hammerstein II. Music by Herbert Stothart. Published in the vocal score. Introduced by the ensemble (visitors at Lady Jane's Hotel) and Edward Ciannelli (Emile La Flamme).

ENSEMBLE: Vive la Canadienne!
Vole, mon coeur, vole.
Vive la Canadienne,
Et ses jolis yeux doux!
Et ses jolis yeux doux,
doux, doux.
Et ses jolis yeux doux
Et ses jolis yeux doux,
doux, doux.
Et ses jolis yeux doux!
Vive la Canadienne!
Vole, mon coeur, vole.
Vive la Canadienne,
Et ses jolis yeux doux!

VOICES FROM THE
OFFSTAGE DANCE HALL: Sing fol-di-rol, fol-di
fol-di-rol,
Sing fol-di-rol, fol-di
fol-di-rol.

ENSEMBLE AND OFFSTAGE
DANCE HALL VOICES: Sing fol-di-rol, fol-di
fol-di-rol,
Sing fol-di-rol, fol-di
fol-di-rol.

EMILE: [offstage] Oh, Rose-Marie, where are you?
ENSEMBLE: There he goes again, He's calling her.

EMILE: [offstage] Oh, Rose-Marie, where are you?
ENSEMBLE: Ha, ha, ha, ha, Ha, ha, ha!
OFFSTAGE DANCE HALL
VOICES: Sing fol-di-rol,
Fol-di-rol-di-rol.
Sing fol-di-rol.
EMILE: [offstage, but getting closer] Rose-Marie!
ENSEMBLE: [mocking] Rose-Marie!

HARD-BOILED HERMAN

Lyric by Otto Harbach and Oscar Hammerstein II. Music by Herbert Stothart. Published as an individual sheet. Introduced by William Kent (Hard-Boiled Herman), Dorothy Mackaye (Lady Jane), and ensemble.

Miles Kreuger reports that in his conversations with Harbach and Hammerstein about their early collaborations, they both said that Hammerstein had written one outstanding line for this song—but neither could remember which line it was.

VERSE

HERMAN: When I get my gat I got them spellbound.
Don't get smart, or you'll be started hell bound!
Ask them if they know this loon
At the Marmaluke saloon—
Reckon you will hear this sort of tune:

REFRAIN 1

HERMAN: Hard-boiled Herman,
Hard-boiled Herman,
A gold-diggin', gun-totin', poker-playin' fool,
A big-hearted pal of the rough-and-ready school.
Foes of Herman die like vermin.
Them he likes, he loves,
'N them he hates, he kills!
Herman, the he-man,
Quick-to-disagree man,
Herman, the hellcat of the hills!

REFRAIN 2

JANE AND GIRLS: Hard-boiled Herman,
Hard-boiled Herman,

A gold-diggin', gun-totin', poker-playin' fool,
A big-hearted pal of the rough-and-ready school.
Quick at shootin'
You're darn tootin'
Them he likes he loves,
'N them he hates, he kills!
Herman, the he-man,
The quick-to-disagree man
Herman, the hellcat of the hills.
Likes no trimmin' on his women!
Likes 'em plain, but true.
JANE: Big boy, d'ye think I'll do?
HERMAN: Herman's just wild about,
Simply beguiled about,
Acts like a child about you.

ROSE-MARIE

Lyric by Otto Harbach and Oscar Hammerstein II. Music by Rudolf Friml. Published as an individual sheet, but verse two is only in the published vocal score. Introduced by Dennis King (Jim Kenyon) and Arthur Deagon (Sergeant Malone). Popular recordings were made by Paul Whiteman and His Orchestra, John McCormack, Slim Whitman, Howard Keel, and Nelson Eddy.

VERSE 1

JIM: Oh, sweet Rose-Marie,
It's easy to see
Why all who learn to know you love you.
You're gentle and kind,
Divinely designed,
As graceful as the pines above you.
There's an angel's breath beneath your sigh.
MALONE: There's a little devil in your eye.

REFRAIN

JIM: Oh, Rose-Marie, I love you.
I'm always dreaming of you.
No matter what I do I can't forget you;
Sometimes I wish that I had never met you!
And yet, if I should lose you,
'Twould mean my very life to me.
Of all the queens that ever lived I'd choose you
To rule me, my Rose-Marie.

VERSE 2

JIM: The song of the spring
Is heard when you sing,
And when you laugh the birds seem
    trilling.
But angry, oh my,
You'd think that the sky
With storms from the north is filling.
Then, when smiles have chased away
    your frown,
MALONE: Seems the sun itself is shining down.

REPEAT REFRAIN

THE MOUNTIES

Lyric by Otto Harbach and Oscar Hammerstein II. Music by Rudolf Friml and Herbert Stothart. Published as an individual sheet. Introduced by the male ensemble and Arthur Deagon (Sergeant Malone). Note: Hammerstein did not write the additional lyrics heard in the 1954 film.

REFRAIN

MOUNTIES: [offstage, a great distance away]
On through the hail,
Like a pack of angry wolves on the
    trail.
We are after you
Dead or alive.
We are out to get you
Dead or alive.
And we'll get you sure.
If you're the one,
Better run,
Better run away.
Son, you are done,
Throw your gun,
Throw your gun away.
Here come the Mounties,
To get the man they're after now!

INTERLUDE

MALONE: Far over the snow,
What are those voices?
MOUNTIES: [offstage] Over the snow.
MALONE: They sing as they go.
What do those voices?
MOUNTIES: [offstage] Sing as they go.
MALONE: Look out for the Mounties!
MOUNTIES: [offstage] For here come the Mounties!

MALONE: We come!
Somebody hide,
Somebody better hide!

REFRAIN

MALONE: On through the hail,
Like a pack of angry wolves on the
    trail.
MOUNTIES: We are after you.
MALONE: Dead or alive!
We are out to get you
Dead or alive.
MOUNTIES: And we'll get you sure.
MALONE: If you're the one,
Better run,
Better run away.
Son, you are done.
Throw your gun,
Throw your gun away.
Here come the Mounties,
To get the man they're after now!

LAK JEEM

Lyric by Otto Harbach and Oscar Hammerstein II. Music by Rudolf Friml. Published as an individual sheet. Introduced by Mary Ellis (Rose-Marie La Flamme) and the male ensemble. Curiously, this is the only song in the published score in which Rose-Marie's words have dialect spellings.

I

ROSE-MARIE: I know dat
No udder man I see lak Jeem.
BOYS: Who is Jeem?
ROSE-MARIE: I know dat
Ees lots of fun to be wid heem.
BOYS: [spoken] With Jeem?
ROSE-MARIE: Some tam he tease me for a while,
Den he mek a joke—Voila!—I
    smile.
Oh my, but he have a twinkly eye,
    dat Jeem.
Oh my, but how all de girls weel sigh
    for heem!
But let dem sigh, heigh ho,
Dey all better go.
He ees mine, I know.
He have told me so,
My Jeem.

INTERLUDE

BOYS: But would you take another man
    as good
As your Jeem?
ROSE-MARIE: [spoken] No, no, no!
[sung] Dere ees nobody else lak
    heem.
Lak ev'ry girl in all de worl'
I dream wan golden dream.
Ees my Jeem!

II

ROSE-MARIE: I know dat
Lak bird he sing a song,
My Jeem.
I know dat
No mountain lion strong as
    heem.
BOYS: [spoken] As Jeem?
ROSE-MARIE: But when it come to mek de love,
He can be so tender lak de dove.
Oh my, but he have a twinkly eye,
    dat Jeem.
Oh my, but how all de girls weel sigh
    for heem!
But let dem sigh, heigh ho,
Dey all better go.
He ees mine, I know.
He have told me so,
My Jeem.

INDIAN LOVE CALL

Lyric by Otto Harbach and Oscar Hammerstein II. Music by Rudolf Friml.* Published as an individual sheet. Introduced by Mary Ellis (Rose-Marie) and Dennis King (Jim).

An amusing, if probably apocryphal, story claims that during auditions for the London production, one girl warbled, "When I'm calling you, double-O, double-O."

Discographer Edward Foote Gardner ranks "Indian Love Call" as the sixth most popular song of 1925, with recordings by Paul Whiteman and the Leo Reisman Orchestra, among others. A 1937 Nelson Eddy–Jeannette MacDonald recording was a million-seller according to popular-song encyclopedist Robert Lissauer, who also points out a best-selling recording by Artie Shaw (Tony Pastor vocal) on the flip side of Shaw's

* Herbert Stothart claimed that he also worked on this song.

wildly popular rendition of Cole Porter's "Begin the Beguine." In 1952, "Indian Love Call" sold an additional million records with a vocal by country singer Slim Whitman.* "Indian Love Call" was also recorded by two pairs of opera stars: Anna Moffo and Sergio Franchi, and Robert Merrill and Roberta Peters.

INTRODUCTION

ROSE-MARIE: Oo-oo-oo!
JIM: Oo-oo-oo!

VERSE

ROSE-MARIE: So echoes of sweet love notes gently fall
Through the forest stillness,
As fond waiting Indian lovers call.
When the lone lagoon stirs in the spring,
Welcoming home some swanny white wing,
When the maiden moon, riding the sky
Gathers her star-eyed dream children nigh,
That is the time of the moon and the year
When love dreams to Indian maidens appear.
And this is the song that they hear:

REFRAIN

ROSE-MARIE: When I'm calling you-oo-oo, oo-oo-oo,
Will you answer too-oo-oo, oo-oo-oo?
That means I offer my love to you, to be your own.
If you refuse me I will be blue and waiting all alone.
But if when you hear my love call ringing clear,
And I hear your answering echo, so dear,
Then I will know our love will come true,
You'll belong to me,
I'll belong to you.

[Both repeat refrain.]

---

* Whitman's rendition was featured in the 1996 Tim Burton film Mars Attacks!, where it is found to be the best weapon against alien invaders.

Introduction to Scene 3

ROSE-MARIE: Now listen!
Oo-oo-oo, oo-oo-oo!
JIM: [offstage at great distance]
Oo-oo-oo, oo-oo-oo!
GIRLS AND BOYS: When through the valley
A voice is calling all alone,
Why does the answering echo
Sound so very baritone?

PRETTY THINGS

Lyric by Otto Harbach and Oscar Hammerstein II. Music by Rudolf Friml. Published in the vocal score. Introduced by Mary Ellis (Rose-Marie) and the female ensemble. Lela Bliss (Ethel Brander) led a reprise in Act Two; the words are the same.

VERSE

GIRLS: If a man should ask
The surest way of charming a maid,
He'd present a task
Not difficult but easy essayed.
ROSE-MARIE: He need not be ornamental
But he must be brave and gentle.
Muscle in his arm
To keep me safe from harm.

REFRAIN

GIRLS: Pretty things.
ROSE-MARIE: Where is the girl who can resist them?
GIRLS: Pretty things.
ROSE-MARIE: Unhappy the girlie who has missed them.
ALL: Gossamer laces, silk and satiny graces,
How they fill her with joy and thrill her,
GIRLS: Pretty things.
ROSE-MARIE: That show her charms and yet enfold them,
GIRLS: Pretty things.
ROSE-MARIE: To wear that man may not behold them.
ALL: Love comes enduringly
To her who alluringly
Can learn to wear
Life's pretty things.

WHY SHOULDN'T WE?

Lyric by Otto Harbach and Oscar Hammerstein II. Music by Herbert Stothart. Published as an individual sheet. Introduced by Dorothy Mackaye (Lady Jane) and William Kent (Hard-Boiled Herman).

VERSE 1

HERMAN: Sweetheart, sweetheart,
This is no season to be sad.
Buds of spring are sprouting,
Everything is ringing, shouting.
In your ear it
Brings a spirit
Gay and glad.

REFRAIN 1

HERMAN: The thing we call romance is in the air;
No matter where you look you find a pair.
Isn't it time to be heeding the call?
It seems a crime to be missing it all.
It makes me green with envy when I hear
Somebody call somebody else her "dear."
Everyone seems to be turning the trick,
Even the pollywogs down in the "crick."
Birds in the forest and fish in the sea
Are having their fun,
Why shouldn't we?

VERSE 2

JANE: Hoiman, Hoiman,
I know exactly what you mean.
It's a fact I recognize
That when the springtime brings the flies
It also makes us dizzy in the bean.

REFRAIN 2

JANE: The thing we call romance is in the air,
This is the time of year when every pair
Waxes poetic 'bout crickets and bees,
Feeling pathetic 'bout flowers and trees.
Out in the meadow green they take their lunch,
To gaze upon the scen'ry as they munch.
Watching a daffodil, full of caprice.
Eating a half o' dill pickle apiece.
Getting as cuckoo as cuckoo can be,

But having their fun.
Why shouldn't we?

TOTEM TOM-TOM

Lyric by Otto Harbach and Oscar Hammerstein II. Music by Rudolf Friml and Herbert Stothart. Published as an individual sheet. Introduced by Pearl Regay (Wanda) and the female ensemble. This spectacular number featured fifty girls dressed as totem poles, and received substantial attention in the press. The additional lyrics heard in the 1954 film are not by Hammerstein.

VERSE

WANDA: Long ago, there used to be
A tribe of Indian smarties
Throwing their parties here.
Long ago, you used to see
A wild young maiden in copper,
Dance with her popper dear.
In the shadow of the totem pole here,
In the shadow of this totem pole,
All night long they'd skip and prance,
Like birds on wing they would float-um;
Call it the Totem dance.

REFRAIN

WANDA: When my grandpa, Chief Chickeekotem,
Took Grandma out to a totem,
Totem tom-tom, totem tom-tom;
First they'd move their feet very blue like,
The drum would beat a tattoo like
Totem tom-tom, totem tom-tom.
Then, pretty soon each Injun
Was singein'
His throat with firewater gin-gin;
And faster, and faster
Round the totem they flew!
But, later on, all tired and sleepy,
They'd go back home to their teepee,
Totem tom-tom, totem tom-tom.

ACT ONE FINALE

Lyric by Otto Harbach and Oscar Hammerstein II. Music by Rudolf Friml and Herbert Stothart. Published in the vocal score. Introduced by Edward Ciannelli (Emile, Rose-Marie's brother), Mary Ellis (Rose-Marie),

Frank Greene (Hawley), William Kent (Hard-Boiled Herman), Arthur Deagon (Sergeant Malone), Lela Bliss (Ethel, Hawley's sister), and the men and women of the ensemble. Lady Jane is present but does not have a solo singing line.

EMILE: It's time to get ready.
Come, Rose-Marie,
You're going to Quebec
With Hawley and me.
ROSE-MARIE: I will not go,
I will not go!
EMILE: You'll do as I tell you.
ROSE-MARIE: I will not go,
I will not go!
EMILE: Maybe you'll be glad to
change your mind.
HAWLEY: You may change your mind.
ROSE-MARIE: Me change my mind?
No matter what will happen
I will never go.
EMILE AND HAWLEY: How can you?

[*Dialogue.*]

ROSE-MARIE: Lak ev'ry girl in all de worl'
I have one golden dream.

[*Mounties enter, with* HERMAN *as their prisoner.*]

GIRLS: They've got their man.
GIRLS AND MEN: They've got their man.
They've got their man!
HERMAN: [*spoken in rhythm*]
Hard-boiled Herman,
Hard-boiled Herman.
'Twas I killed Black Eagle
With my trusty Genevieve.
MALONE: [*spoken in rhythm*]
That you killed Black Eagle
Is a fact I can't believe.
To kill a man you've not the
nerve or sense,
But I'm thinkin' we'll be
holdin' you
For fun and evidence.
Take him away!
ENSEMBLE: [*spoken in rhythm*] Take him
away,
Take him away,
Take him away,
Take him away,
Take him away,
Take him away,
Take him away, him away!
MALONE: [*sung*] Is there anyone who
knows

The whereabouts of this Jim
Kenyon?

[*Dialogue.*]

ROSE-MARIE: When I'm calling you-oo-oo,
oo-oo-oo.
EMILE: [*to* HAWLEY] 'Tis an Indian
love song to you.
ENSEMBLE: She seems to love him true.
ROSE-MARIE: Will you answer true-oo-oo,
oo-oo-oo?
EMILE: 'Tis an Indian love song
So tender, sweet, and true.
MALONE: Tender, sweet, and true.
ENSEMBLE: She loves him tenderly and
true.

[*The next six stanzas are sung simultaneously.*]

ROSE-MARIE: It means I offer my love
to you,
To be your own.
If you refuse me I, I shall be
blue,
And waiting all alone, all
alone.
But if when you hear my
love call ringing clear
And you send your
answering echo so dear
Then I will know our love
It will come true!
You'll belong to me
I'll belong to you!
EMILE: Love she's offering,
She's offering to be
your own.
If you refuse
She'll wait alone, she will
wait alone.
Love's love call ringing clear.
Love call echoing clear.
So she will know, she will
know that her love
It will come true!
And she will belong to you.
HAWLEY: It means she offers her love
to me
To be my own.
If I should lose her, I shall
be blue
And waiting all alone,
waiting all alone.
Then I will know, that
our love
It will come true!
And I will belong to you!

ETHEL: She's offering to be your own.
If you refuse her, she'll be
blue
And waiting alone, don't
leave her alone.
Love call echoing, echoing
clear.
So she will know, she will
know that your love
It will come true!
She'll belong to you!
MALONE: Love she's offering,
Offering to be his own.
But she will
Never fool Malone.
Who can fool Malone?
Love call echoing clear.
So I will know, I will know
her love
It will come true!
She'll belong to you!
ENSEMBLE: For she's offering her love,
She's offering to be his own.
He'll not refuse her or
She'll be blue and alone,
alone.
Love's sweet call ringing clear.
Love call echoing, echoing
clear.
So she will know, she will
know that her love
It will come true!
You will see,
She'll belong to you!

ONLY A KISS

Lyric by Otto Harbach and Oscar Hammerstein II.
Music by Herbert Stothart. Published in the vocal score.
Introduced by Dorothy Mackaye (Jane), Arthur Deagon
(Sergeant Malone), and William Kent (Hard-boiled
Herman).

The *New York Sun* said this song "reduces to its ultimate absurdity the faded flower songs ordinarily sung in
the dumber part of the evening by Broadway's broken
lilies."

Only a kiss, only a kiss
That's what you laugh and say.
Two lips are true lips,
But few lips are true lips
You will find out someday.
Go have your fun,

Don't blame no one.
Don't mind the wrong you have done;
For a heart you have broke for your moment of
bliss.
And you call it only a kiss.

REFRAIN

JANE: Sorrow, joy, and passion—
All this a kiss may bring.
But out of ev'ry hundred kisses,
Ninety-nine don't mean a thing.
Sorrow, joy, and passion—
All this a kiss may bring.
But out of ev'ry hundred kisses,
Ninety-nine don't mean a thing.
MALONE: There's a gentle sort of kiss.
JANE: A sweet and tender kiss.
MALONE: A greeting of a mother and her son.
JANE: [spoken] Ah, my son. You're back!
HERMAN: [spoken] Where's he been?
[sung] There's a kiss that's most
polite.
A casual kiss: "Good night."
A greeting you could give to anyone.
[spoken] "Can I show you to the door?
That's all there are, there ain't no
more."
JANE: There's the movie kiss that's kind of
hot and scaldy,
À la Barbara La Marr, à Nita Naldi.

[JANE and MALONE demonstrate a movie kiss.]

HERMAN: There's another method, à la
Valentino
That will frequently inspire a trip to
Reno!

[HERMAN demonstrates a tango kiss with a passing
chorine.]

REFRAIN

ALL THREE: Sorrow, joy, and passion—
All this a kiss may bring.
But out of ev'ry hundred kisses,
Ninety-nine don't mean a thing.

ENCORE

HERMAN: There's the sanitary kiss,
The common cautious kiss
The greeting of a professor to his
love.
MALONE: There's a custom now I wish that they
would banish.

It's the kiss they give in op'ras that
are Spanish.
Señorita, Carmencita! Minneapolis
and St. Paul!

REPEAT REFRAIN

FINALETTO, ACT TWO, SCENE 1: I LOVE HIM

Alternate title: "Sextet." Lyric by Otto Harbach and
Oscar Hammerstein II. Music by Rudolf Friml. Published in the vocal score. Introduced by Mary Ellis
(Rose-Marie), Dennis King (Jim), Frank Greene (Hawley), Edward Ciannelli (Emile), Lela Bliss (Ethel Brander), and Pearl Regay (Wanda).

ROSE-MARIE: [to JIM, about HAWLEY]
I love him!
I love him!
I love him!
I love him!
JIM: So this is what I risked
my life to see!
Thank heav'n that I have
learned the truth at
last.
HAWLEY: It seems she's made
herself quite clear.
[spoken] Please go.
JIM: I'll go the way I went
before I met you;
Where men are beasts,
And woman all are bad.
'Twas she who made me
think
That other roads were
better.
But now in shame,
I've learned that
ev'rywhere
The ways of life are all
the same.
For men are beasts,
And woman all are bad.
ROSE-MARIE: Jim, it is not so!
JIM: All that I ask
Is that I may forget you.
ROSE-MARIE AND EMILE: Forget, forget!
ETHEL, WANDA, AND
HAWLEY: Forget you may,
You'll soon forget.

JIM: May my presence here
No longer fret you.

ROSE-MARIE, ETHEL
AND WANDA: No longer fret me.
May your love perish
Your love and yearning.

EMILE AND HAWLEY: No longer fret her.
Perish your love,
Your love and yearning.

ALL SIX: Naught but its ashes
Are burning, burning.

JIM: Days will come when
Memories beset you.

THE OTHER FIVE: Ah memories.
Ah, memories, bitter
memories.

JIM: Maybe they will hold a
thought of me
And help me realize

THE OTHER FIVE: Will help you to realize

JIM: What I've learned
From woman's eyes—

THE OTHER FIVE: What you are
In woman's eyes.

JIM: Love's inconstancy.

ALL SIX: I'll go.

MINUET OF THE MINUTE

Lyric by Otto Harbach and Oscar Hammerstein II.
Music by Herbert Stothart. Published in the vocal score.
Introduced by Mary Ellis (Rose-Marie) and William
Kent (Hard-Boiled Herman).

VERSE

ROSE-MARIE: Sedate and stately minuet
Did not afford a chance to pet.
They kept six inches apart;
No clinches could start.
Sedate and stately minuet.

REFRAIN

ROSE-MARIE: Quaint old-fashioned dance.
Ladies and gallants
Pointing toe and tapping so lightly
Thought that they were "on the go"
nightly.
Just to take her hand
That was simply grand!
Yet there was a way of wooing,
Doing that quaint old-fashioned
dance.

PATTER

HERMAN: The minuet*
Up to the minute
A girl you get
And then begin it.
There isn't time
For introduction.
There isn't time
For much instruction.
Just do anything that you feel like
Don't consider what it may be like,
Forget your brain
And gaily romp to
A careless strain
That sounds impromptu.
It seems insane
But do it anyhow.
Goodbye to the old gavotte and
lancers
The dance is different now!

*[The refrain and the patter are then sung
simultaneously.]*

DOOR OF HER DREAMS
(BRIDAL PROCESSION)

Lyric by Otto Harbach and Oscar Hammerstein II. Music
by Rudolf Friml. Published as an individual sheet. Introduced by the ensemble and Mary Ellis (Rose-Marie).

REFRAIN

ENSEMBLE: Now at last the door of her dreams
Is swinging wide.
There upon the threshold gleams
The happy bride.
Two lives must be blended,
Old ties must be ended;
For at last the door of her dreams
Is swinging wide.

---

* *Some scripts give* HERMAN *these additional lines to
start the patter:*
Put down your teacup filled with wine,
And put your cheek up close to mine!
We'll show them just how we sway
In the dances of today.
Put down your teacup filled with wine.
[Goes into the patter.]

INTERLUDE

ROSE-MARIE: Childhood days,
Go your ways,
With your romping games and plays.
Goodbye, girls,
With your swirls
Of fair, tossing, tangled curls.
Goodbye, maiden sigh,
Seeking rainbows in the sky.
And you boys,
You who have shared her joys,
Goodbye, goodbye.

REFRAIN

ENSEMBLE: Now at last the door of her dreams
Is swinging wide.
There upon the threshold gleams
The happy bride.

ROSE-MARIE: Two lives must be blended,
Old ties must be ended.

ENSEMBLE: For at last the door of her dreams
Is swinging wide.

BRIDAL FINALE

Lyric by Otto Harbach and Oscar Hammerstein II.
Music by Herbert Stothart. Published in the vocal score.
Introduced by Edward Ciannelli (Emile), Pearl Regay
(Wanda), Arthur Deagon (Sergeant Malone), Frank
Greene (Hawley), Mary Ellis (Rose-Marie), and ensemble.

EMILE: Come, Rose-Marie,
The happy groom is waiting.

ENSEMBLE: For you alone he's waiting,
Beneath the bow'r he's waiting.
In gay procession marching
We go to greet the pair!

WANDA: [*shrieking*] Wait, Rose-Marie!
Do not marry till you listen to me!
[*pointing at* HAWLEY] He came to my
house dat night!

MALONE: [*spoken*] You see!

WANDA: [*spoken in rhythm*] Dat's right.
I keel so I save da man I love!
Dat's right!

EMILE: [*spoken*] No!

ROSE-MARIE: [*spoken*] But yes, I see it clear as day!
[*sung*] My Jim!

ENSEMBLE: Now at last the door of her dreams.

ROSE-MARIE: I'm calling:
Oo-oo, oo-oo, oo-oo-oo-oo.

ENSEMBLE: [*over* ROSE-MARIE'*s call*] She is
calling to the man she loves,
Calling the man she loves!

FINALE ULTIMO

Lyric by Otto Harbach and Oscar Hammerstein II. Music by Rudolf Friml. Published in the vocal score. Introduced by Dennis King (Jim) and Mary Ellis (Rose-Marie).

JIM: Dear place,
Where once I thought the world my
own.
Dear place,
Where I'm living all alone.
I used to call her
From this very stone.
When I'm calling you-oo-oo,
oo-oo-oo!
ROSE-MARIE: [*in the far distance*] Oo-oo-oo,
oo-oo-oo!
JIM: [*spoken*] Just my own fancy making
fun of me.
ROSE-MARIE: [*nearer*] Oo-oo-oo, oo-oo-oo!

[*She enters, and they embrace.*]

ROSE-MARIE: You belong to me.
BOTH: I'll belong to you!

ADDED SONG

ONE-MAN WOMAN

Lyric by Otto Harbach and Oscar Hammerstein II. Music by Rudolf Friml and Herbert Stothart. Lyric published in the 1931 Samuel French libretto, but not included in the published vocal score. Introduced in the London production by Clarice Hardwicke (Lady Jane) and male ensemble.

The male names in the verse seem to come from Jane's cue line: "You could give me Ronald Colman, Jack Barrymore, and Ivor Novello all rolled into one—and I'd still want that good-for-nothin' heart-breakin' little lizard. [i.e., Herman]."

VERSE

JANE: Now, Johnny, please go 'way,
No, Ronny, not today—
Maurice, I'm busy—
That goes for you—
And as usual I must refuse you all.
Another love sublime
Is taking all my time.
There's only one that I can see,
He's a habit now with me.

REFRAIN 1

MEN: You're just a one-man woman.
JANE: A stay-at-home-and-waiting concentratin'
woman.

MEN: Have you a kiss for Tom or Jerry or Jim?
JANE: No! I'd be only thinking of him.
I've always known
He's not a handsome brute.
But he's my own,
And, gosh, he's awful cute.
MEN: You're just a one-man woman—
JANE: But I've been prying and trying
To learn if I can,
Is he a one-woman man?

REFRAIN 2

MEN: You're just a one-man woman—
A stay-at-home-and-waitin' concentratin'
woman.
Have you a kiss for Tom or Jerry or Jim?
She'd be only thinking of him.
She's always known
He's not a handsome brute,
But he's her own,
And, gosh, he's awful cute.
You're just a one-man woman
But she's been prying and trying
To learn if she can,
Is he a one-woman man?

Marilyn Miller as Sunny

Songs of 1925

SUNNY (1925)

Tryout: Forrest Theatre, Philadelphia, September 9–19, 1925. New York run: New Amsterdam Theatre; opened September 22, 1925; closed December 11, 1926; 517 performances. Produced by Charles Dillingham. Book and lyrics by Otto Harbach and Oscar Hammerstein II. Music by Jerome Kern. Staged by Hassard Short. Dances arranged by Julian Mitchell and Dave Bennett. Marilyn Miller's Hunt Ball dance arranged by Alexis Kosloff; Eight Marilyn Miller Cocktails' dances arranged by John Tiller; Marilyn Miller's dances with boys produced by Fred Astaire. Orchestrations by Robert Russell Bennett. Orchestra directed by Gustave Salzer. Settings and costumes designed by James Reynolds.

Cast: Marilyn Miller (Sunny Peters), Jack Donahue (Jim Deering), Paul Frawley (Tom Warren), Clifton Webb (Harold Harcourt Wendell-Wendell), Mary Hay ("Weenie" Winters), Joseph Cawthorn (Siegfried Peters), Esther Howard (Sue Warren), Elsa Peterson (Marcia Manners), Pert Kelton (Magnolia), George Olsen and His Orchestra, Charles Angelo (Bally Hoo), Elmer Brown (First Ship's Officer), Joan Clement (Millicent Smythe), Jeanne Fonda (Diana Miles), Helene Gardner (Mlle. Sadie), Louis Harrison (First Mate), Harry Spencer (Second Ship's Officer), and James Wilson (Ship's Captain). The ensemble included eight Marilyn Miller Cocktails: May Cornes, Nellie Douglas, Grace Holt, Lelia Riley, Iris Smith, Peggy Soden, Hilda Wynn Stanley, and Doris Wentworth and showgirls, dancing girls, and boys.

Sunny's plot was not one of Harbach and Hammerstein's carefully assembled structures. In fact, a week before rehearsals started, they hadn't finished the Act One finale and had written none of the second act. But the story was just an excuse for putting their star, dancer Marilyn Miller, into a variety of costumes and settings including a circus parade, an ocean liner, a wedding, and a fox hunt.

The title character is a British circus equestrienne who stows away on a New York–bound ocean liner in romantic pursuit of Tom, a visiting American she'd first met in 1918. Tom's affection for Sunny is obvious, but he now has an American fiancée, Marcia. Tom's best friend, Jim, is pledged to a British girl named Weenie, but Jim reluctantly agrees to marry Sunny in a shipboard ceremony so that she can disembark in America. They intend to divorce as soon as possible. Back in England, Weenie is consoled by Wendell, who would have liked to marry Sunny. By the time Weenie and Wendell arrive in the United States, Sunny's divorce is under way. Tom has yet to realize that Sunny is essential to his happiness, so during a fox hunt she stages a fall. In the Broadway production, Sunny and Tom are in each

other's arms for the final curtain, but for the London production, Sunny decides that she really loves Jim after all.

A London production, presented by Moss Empires Ltd. in conjunction with Lee Ephraim and Jack Buchanan, opened at the Hippodrome on October 7, 1926, and ran for 363 performances. It was directed by Charles Mast and starred Binnie Hale (Sunny), Jack Buchanan (Jim), Jack Hobbs (Tom), Elsie Randolph (Weenie), Claude Hulbert (Wendell), and Nancie Lovat (Marcia).

A screen version of *Sunny* was produced by Warner Bros./First National in 1930, directed by William A. Seiter and starring Marilyn Miller (Sunny), Lawrence Gray (Tom), Joe Donahue (Jim), Inez Courtney (Weenie), and Mackenzie Ward (Wendell). A second version was made by RKO Radio Pictures, in 1941, directed by Herbert Wilcox and starring Anna Neagle and Ray Bolger.

"D'Ye Love Me?" "Let's Say Good Night Till It's Morning," "Sunny," "Two Little Bluebirds," "When We Get Our Divorce," and "Who?" (as well as the non-Hammerstein songs "I've Looked for Trouble" and "I Might Grow Fond of You") were recorded in 1926 by members of the London cast. CD transfers of these can be heard on *Sunny, Show Boat, Lido Lady* (Pearl) and on *Sunny* (AEI), which also has two songs from the 1930 film, period recordings by George Olsen and His Orchestra and Cliff Edwards, and a 1950s radio adaptation of the show.

Several songs from *Sunny* were published as individual sheets, followed by a published vocal score and script. Other scripts are preserved at the Tams-Witmark Music Library, the Otto Harbach Collection in the New York Public Library for the Performing Arts, and the Lord Chamberlain's Plays Collection at the British Library. The Jerome Kern Collection in the Music Division of the Library of Congress has some typed lyric sheets and copyist scores. Even with so much material available, there is little documentation of the songs that were dropped during the out-of-town tryouts. No lyrics have been found for "Strolling, or What Have You," nor for the dropped songs "Tonsils" and "Two Total Losses."*

Comparing the sources yields myriad textual variants, even between the published versions. For example, in the song "D'Ye Love Me?," the third line of the refrain is either "Do you promise to love me alway" or "Do you promise to love me always." The published script, the published sheet, the Tams-Witmark prompt book, and a Harbach typescript show "always." But the published score and Binnie Hale's 1926 recording have

"alway." Although no source proved definitive, in most cases this chapter follows the published score.

Little is known about Harbach and Hammerstein's division of labor on the book and lyrics. All the lyrics are credited jointly to Otto Harbach and Oscar Hammerstein II.

In the New York production, Cliff Edwards (also known as "Ukelele Ike") had a specialty number during the second act, when he performed songs including "Just a Little Thing Called Rhythm" (music by Eddie Ward, lyrics by Chick Endor), "Paddlin' Madelin' Home" (by Harry Woods), "I'll Say Yes to You and You Say Yes to Me" (by Eddie Ward and Chick Endor), and "I'm Moving Away" (music and lyrics by Cliff Edwards and Irving Caesar). In Act Two, Scene 4, Pert Kelton performed "Magnolia in the Woods," about which little is known.

Hammerstein did not write the lyrics of the three songs added to the London production: "I've Looked for Trouble," "I Might Grow Fond of You," and "The Fox Has Left His Lair."

HERE WE ARE TOGETHER AGAIN (ACT ONE OPENING)

Lyric by Otto Harbach and Oscar Hammerstein II. Published in the vocal score. Introduced by Paul Frawley (Tom) and male ensemble.

Here we are together again,
All birds of a feather again.
We've traveled near,
We've traveled far,
We've done the world in under par—
Or nearly,
Nearly.
If you strike a city we missed,
And meet a girl we never have kissed,
Just kiss her once yourself for us,
And give her our regards,
And say we love her dearly.
We will say you love her dearly,
And still knew she'll be true.

---

* The song title has the same scan as the extant "Two Little Bluebirds," but a full score for "Two Total Losses" does not have the "Two Little Bluebirds" melody.

SUNNY

Lyric by Otto Harbach and Oscar Hammerstein II. Published as an individual sheet. Introduced by Paul Frawley (Tom) and the ensemble. Jerome Kern scholar Stephen Banfield points out that in the course of the show the title song is reprised six times.

VERSE

MEN: Here you come a-running
Back into my mem'ry's eye.
Little playmate, once my gay
    mate
In a day gone by.

TOM: Ragged dresses,
Tangled tresses
Flying o'er the hill.
Heaven bless us!
You've no less a
Share of Jack than Jill.
You funny little will-o-wispy,
Sassy little lispy Sunny.

MEN: [*sung over* TOM's *last two lines*]
That describes her to a T.
She is full of fun. He
Named the lady perfectly.
She is bright and sunny.

REFRAIN

TOM: Never comb your hair, Sunny!
Leave the breezes there, Sunny!
Let your stockings fall down,
For shocking the town
Is all that you do.

MEN: Do you ever lose your smile?

TOM: Smiling all the while, tomboy.

MEN: What a joyful tomboy.

TOM: Where'd you get your smile
    from, boy?

MEN: Only one like little Sunny.

TOM: Little Sunny girl,
Be my honey girl.
I'm for you.

CIRCUS CODA

MEN: [*beginning a countermelody*]
Circus is over
And they're coming in here.
Right over here the parade will
    pass us.
Stand by and cheer for Sunny!
Let Sunny see that we know
She is our only queen, oh.
What a surprise!

There'll be no end of her cries
Of glad surprises—

GIRLS: [*to "Sunny" melody*] Save your
    cheering for Sunny!
Save your cheering for Sunny!

MEN: [*to a rhythmic motif from "Sunny"*]
—In glad surprise.
Open wide those eyes,
Laughing, dancing eyes,
Tender, glancing eyes,
For the world to prize,
Love and idolize.

GIRLS: We can realize
Why they idolize.

GIRLS AND MEN: Such a little queen.
See her marching in,
Amid the din
That should be in
A gay and festive scene.
Oh, listen to the circus band.
Boom! Boom!
Trombone and flute and trumpet
    and
Boom! Boom!
With their drum
Let them come
For they're bringing someone.
Bring her near,
So we can cheer
The dearest queen of circus
    land!

[*to "Sunny" melody*] Smiling all
    the while, tomboy,
Where'd you get your smile
    from, boy?
Little Sunny girl,
Be my honey girl,
Do, do, do!

WHO?

Lyric by Otto Harbach and Oscar Hammerstein II. Published as an individual sheet. Introduced by Marilyn Miller (Sunny) and Paul Frawley (Tom) and reprised frequently. (See "The Chase" and "All These People I Have Wronged" for additional lyrics.) "Who?" became one of the most popular songs of 1926.

As Hugh Fordin points out in his biography of Hammerstein, Kern's melody was catchy, but right from the start it posed what seemed a hopeless problem for the lyric writer. Oscar stared in dismay at the first note, a B natural held for two and a quarter bars, or nine beats. What could fit that extraordinarily sustained note? He knew that it couldn't be a long, awkward word, because that would kill the song immediately. Nor could a phrase be used. It had to be a word which could be repeated again and again, progressing the song each time without becoming inane or monstrous because Jerry posed practically the same problem five times. Moreover, it had to be a word ending with an open vowel so that the singer could hold it for these long counts.

Oscar's answer was "who." Jerry credited this word with saving his tune . . . To the layman, Oscar's solution may seem an obvious one, and the fuss made over him for finding it just another example of theatrical exaggeration. But the professionals knew that even "why" would have killed the song because "why" sounded too nasal and whiny when a singer tried to hold it for nine beats; and that while "you" might have been passable, it would not have stood up under the five-time repetition.

Even this iconic song is plagued by textual variants. In the first verse alone, the published sheet and the published score differ in three places.

VERSE 1

TOM: When a man's in love with someone,
He must be indeed a dumb one
If her secret he cannot unmask.

SUNNY: Then when I'm in love with someone,
I will wait until there comes one
Boy who'll know the answer when I ask.

REFRAIN 1

SUNNY: Who stole my heart away?
Who makes me dream all day?
Dreams I know can never be true;
Seems as though I'll ever be blue.
Who means my happiness?
Who would I answer yes to?

TOM: Well, you ought to guess who.*

SUNNY: I can't tell you!

REFRAIN 2

TOM: Who stole your heart away?
Who makes you dream all day?
Dreams I know can never come true;
Seems as though you'll ever be blue.
Who means your happiness?

---

* *Some sources give this line and the next as:*
    TOM: Darned if I can guess who.
    SUNNY: No one but you.

Who would you answer yes to?
SUNNY: Well, you ought to guess who.
TOM: Darned if I know.

Sheet music verse

VERSE 2

TOM: Can't say that I'm sure that I know
What you're driving at.
SUNNY: Deny no
Further if you choose to feel that way.
MARCIA: Make your mind up, don't be shy. No
Game of "eenie, meenie, mino"
Can be played with ladies when they say:

INTO REFRAIN

Verse for Jim in the Act Two finale

JIM: When a man's in love with someone
He has got to overcome one
Obstacle that's always in the way.
Finding words to pop the question,
Gives him mental indigestion.
Possibly you'll get me when I say:

INTO REFRAIN

SO'S YOUR OLD MAN

Title in the Philadelphia program: "Heaven's Gift to the Girls." Lyric by Otto Harbach and Oscar Hammerstein II. Published in the vocal score. Introduced by Clifton Webb (Harold Harcourt Wendell-Wendell) and the Eight Marilyn Miller Cocktails.

VERSE

WENDELL: Ladies desist.
You really must excuse—
GIRLS: Won't you be my Romeo?
My heart is aching,
Oh me, oh my!
WENDELL: I get your gist,
But really must refuse.
GIRLS: If you're plighted to another,
Please at least be my big brother.
WENDELL: Ladies, I'm touched.
I know just how you feel.
So poignant an appeal
Would melt a heart of steel.

GIRLS: For all my part stay on the shelf.
This goofer simply hates himself.
WENDELL: I know just how you feel!

REFRAIN

WENDELL: I'm heaven's gift to the girls.
GIRLS: So's your old man.
WENDELL: Through the ages they have pleaded,
I am just the thing they needed,
Something far more precious than
pearls.
GIRLS: We don't blame you if you know it,
For when women love they show it.
WENDELL: I hear them croon in ecstasy.
To meet me is a treat.
I see them crane their necks to see
Me walking down the street.
GIRLS: But as for us we follow you,
You Belvedere Apollo. You
Are heaven's gift to the girls.
WENDELL: I am just a big Don Juan,*
And I'm wreaking wrack and ruin,
For I'm heaven's gift to the girls.
GIRLS: So's your old man.

LET'S SAY GOOD NIGHT TILL IT'S MORNING

Lyric by Otto Harbach and Oscar Hammerstein II. Published as an individual sheet at the time of the London production. Introduced by Mary Hay (Weenie) and Jack Donahue (Jim).

VERSE

WEENIE: Oh, must you really go?
I know I'll miss you so.
Why did you let me grow
So used to you?
JIM: It's hard to break away,
My arms to take away.
Say, can't you make a way
To follow too?
WEENIE: I'd simply gloat if that old boat
Should sail without you, dear.
Why don't you stay right here
And leave it flat?
JIM: I'll say good night
Until I hear the whistle blow.
And then I'll have to go

_____

* British pronunciation is "JEW-an."

Lickety-scat!
WEENIE: I've got a better suggestion than
that.

REFRAIN

WEENIE: Let's say good night till it's morning.
Somehow I hate you to go.
JIM: Although the hour is late,
You make it easy to wait.
Shadows are silently warning
Me to roam—
WEENIE: So, let's say good night till it's morning
And then you won't have to go home!

D'YE LOVE ME?

Lyric by Otto Harbach and Oscar Hammerstein II. Published as an individual sheet. Introduced by Marilyn Miller (Sunny) and ensemble.

Although this song did not have the longevity of "Who?," it was quite popular during *Sunny*'s run.

VERSE 1

SUNNY: When a man begins to angle,
And a heart he tries to entangle
He sings love's lullaby.
Like a sandman, while she's napping,
He'll begin his tender love-tapping.
Proving but a gay romancer
Unless these questions he can answer:

REFRAIN

SUNNY: D'ye love me?
D'ye mean it?
D'ye promise to love me alway?
Forever,
And ever?
And not for a week or a day?
For there are men
Who love now and then,
But they vanish when
They hear wedding bells playing.
So you must agree
It's going to be
Forever or *never* with me!

VERSE 2

SUNNY: On the other hand, it's maybe
She who'll start her "rock-a-bye baby,"
Lulling some heart to sleep.

Then while he is gently dozing
She'll see to it that he's proposing.
But he takes an awful chance, sir,
Unless these questions she will answer:

REFRAIN

MEN: D'ye love me?
GIRLS: Un-huh.
MEN: D'ye mean it?
GIRLS: Un-huh.
MEN: D'ye promise to love me alway?
Forever.
GIRLS: Un-huh.
MEN: And ever?
GIRLS: Un-huh.
MEN: And not for a week or a day?
For there are men
Who love now and then,
But they vanish when
They hear wedding bells playing.
So you must agree
It's going to be
Forever or *never* with me!

VERSE 3

SUNNY: If you are wise
You will take this suggestion
When first you fall in love.
Just shut your eyes
And remember this question.
Learn how to say it.
And sing it, and play it:

REFRAIN

GIRLS: D'ye love me?
MEN: Un-huh.
GIRLS: D'ye mean it?
MEN: Un-huh.
GIRLS: D'ye promise to love me alway?
Forever.
MEN: Un-huh.
GIRLS: And ever?
MEN: Un-huh.
GIRLS: And not for a week or a day?
For lots of men
May love you now and then,
But they all vanish when
They hear the wedding bells playing.
So you must agree
It's going to be
Forever or *never* with me!

THE WEDDING KNELL

Lyric by Otto Harbach and Oscar Hammerstein II. Published in the vocal score. Introduced by Paul Frawley (Tom), Jack Donahue (Jim), Marilyn Miller (Sunny), and the male ensemble.

MEN: Please pardon us
For butting in.
It is a sin.
We'll go,
If we're *de trop.*
TOM: You may bust in,
For you're just in
Time to hear the news.
MEN: [*spoken*] News?
SUNNY: [*sung*] Just ask him there,
Smiling Jim there,
Why he has the blues.
MEN: [*spoken*] Blues?
JIM: [*spoken*] Blues, nothing. I'm
happy as a, as a—well,
you'll understand how
happy I am when I tell you
I'm going to marry Sunny.
MEN: [*sung*] Sunny, are you really sure
You've chosen quite the best
of us?
Tell us how you're going to cure
The broken-hearted rest of us.
Think of all that we must
endure
When we shall hear those bells,
Wedding bells,
Ringing, ringing.
SUNNY: Don't you tell me you'll be blue
When you all hear the wedding
bells.
I thought ev'rybody knew
That they are sunshine-
shedding bells.
For it seems like dreams
coming true
When I hear wedding bells,
Wedding bells
Singing, singing.
MEN: That is well enough for you,
Because it's you who'll be the
bride.
What are we poor chaps to do
Who may not even see the
bride?
Mighty little sun shining
through,
When we shall see those bells,
Wedding bells,

Swinging, swinging.
SUNNY: Though you're talking through
your hat,
I think that I can follow you.
I am sorry, and all that,
But I can't marry all of you.
That's the way the old world
is run
You'll find the legalized limit
is one.
MEN: And none of us can be that one.
SUNNY: That is true, too.
MEN: Only too true!
Kick if you must
For it may not be just.
But for maiden or man
It's according to plan.
SUNNY: When the wedding bell is
pealing,
Tender love-tones seem to tell
Of golden sunshine stealing
Into each heart.
MEN: Into each heart.
SUNNY: Never to part.
MEN: Never to part.
SUNNY AND MEN: Yes, it's sunshine for the
bridegroom
As he hears his wedding bell.
For the other fellow,
It's dark as hell, oh,
It's his wedding knell!

[*The men repeat last 12 lines.*]

TWO LITTLE BLUEBIRDS

Lyric by Otto Harbach and Oscar Hammerstein II. Published as an individual sheet. Introduced by Clifton Webb (Wendell) and Mary Hay (Weenie).

VERSE

WENDELL: Look up in those branches.
Can't you see two little bluebirds?
Seems to me that few* birds
Ever looked so sad.
WEENIE: Maybe they've a story
That is just like yours and mine, dear.

---

* *The published script and a 1926 recording made by Claude Hulbert and Elsie Randolph use the word "no" rather than "few."*

There they sit and pine, dear,
For a love they've had.

REFRAIN

WENDELL: Two little bluebirds
Love two other bluebirds,
But those two untrue birds have flown.
WEENIE: High in the treetops
This lonely pair
Taking the air
Try not to care.
BOTH: Coo* to each other, like sister and
brother,
But somehow they seem all alone.
They miss the two birds
Who've been untrue.
That's why these bluebirds are blue.

ACT ONE FINALE

Alternate title: "Wedding Scene." Lyric by Otto Harbach and Oscar Hammerstein II. Published in the vocal
score. Introduced by ensemble (wedding guests) and
principals.

1ST GROUP OF GUESTS: Ev'ry guest is in the room,
On ev'ry face a knowin'
grin.
Not a sign o' bride or
groom
To step along to *Lohengrin*!
Don't say that I said so,
my dear,
But I consider it just a bit
queer.
2ND GROUP OF GUESTS: Wonder how she caught
the man?
She had no trouble
pleasin' him.
He was hardly worth the
plan.
I don't see what she sees
in him.
1ST GROUP OF GUESTS: Don't say that I said so, my
dear,
But I consider it just a bit
queer.
3RD GROUP OF GUESTS: Maybe he's the careless
kind

_____
* The published script and the 1926 recording use the
word "true," not "coo."

And clean forgot to get
her a
Wedding ring with which
to bind
Their promises, et cetera.
1ST AND 2ND GROUPS
OF GUESTS: Don't say that I said so,
my dear,
But I consider it just a
bit queer.
4TH GROUP OF GUESTS: Doesn't look as though
there'll be
A ceremony here today.
Maybe we are here to see
A marriage knot without
the "K."
1ST, 2ND, 3RD GROUPS
OF GUESTS: Don't say that I said so,
my dear,
But I consider it just a bit
queer.
ALL GUESTS: But, oh, my dear!
Observe who's here!
The kid, himself,
From off the shelf
Is drawing near!

[JIM enters.]

ALL GUESTS: You'll promise always to
be true,
Indeed there's nothing
else to do.
GIRLS: Oh, what a pretty
thought!
Oh, what a pretty
thought!
I don't know what there is
about a wedding
But I always want to cry,
cry, and cry.
I just want to cry.
MEN: But hush! Step aside—
Here comes the bride!
ALL GUESTS: The stern but kindly
captain of
The ship takes two hearts
rapt in love,
And makes those two
hearts one.
Two hearts are turned to
one.
We know it's not a witty
thing
To say, but love's a pretty
thing,
When all is said and done,
When all is said and done.

The captain gently lifts
her trembling hand,
And on her snow-white
finger slips a band—
We cannot help exclaiming,
"Ain't it grand!"
MARCIA: [singing over the ensemble]
Sue, you've won.
You've work'd your very
clever plan,
And Sunny is married to
another man.
'Twas a most effective
plan.
Now I know I'll keep him
for my own, my own,
All mine, all mine alone!
To marry me he will make
up his mind,
Though his love be blind.
CAPTAIN: [spoken] I now pronounce
you man and wife.
GUESTS: Dream a dream upon a
poppy petal,*
Poppies never fail to settle
Who your own true love
will surely be.
SUNNY: Romantic antics will be
taboo.
TOM: Bar all caresses too.
MARCIA: I hope he'll now forget
her love.
GIRLS: She dream'd a little
dream to find
That love is blind, love is
blind.
SUNNY: A most peculiar pair.
Young love is blind.
SUNNY,
MARCIA, TOM, AND JIM: We know this wedding is
all a blind.

[JIM reluctantly kisses SUNNY, his bride. Then she
passionately kisses TOM, the best man.]

MARCIA: She loves him,
She loves him after all!
GUESTS: It's only a kiss after
all!

_____
* These lines refer to a song that was dropped before
Broadway. The full lyric for "Dream a Dream" is at
the end of this section.

WE'RE GYMNASTIC (ACT TWO OPENING)

Alternate title: "Exercise Number." Lyric by Otto Harbach and Oscar Hammerstein II. Published in the vocal score. Introduced by Esther Howard (Tom's sister, Sue) and female ensemble.

GIRLS: We're gymnastic, we're
    gymnastic.
    We're disciples of physical
      culture and health.
    We are plastic and elastic,
    For a beautiful body is better than
      wealth.
SUE: Good morning.
GIRLS: Oh, Sue, dear,
    Tell us what to do, dear.
SUE: Heads up!
    Now inhale!
    Now inhale!
    Now inhale!
    Hold your breath till you have to
      let go,
    Then you slowly exhale and say,
      "Oh!"
GIRLS: Oh—oh—oh!
    We're gymnastic, we're
    gymnastic.
    We're disciples of physical
      culture and health.
    We are plastic and elastic,
    With a beauty more precious than
      wealth.
SUE: Let us take up our classical
    dancing.
    One, two, three, four!
SUE AND GIRLS: Supple and lithesome,
    Blithesome prancing.
    One, two, three, four!
SUE: I am a sylph, a sprite, an elf.
GIRLS: Be yourself.
    You don't look like an elf!
SUE AND GIRLS: But to look like an elf
    Each must try.
    So will I!
SUE: One, two, three, four!
    Day by day we lose a little bit,
    Lose a little bit, lose a little bit.
    One, two, three, four!
    For each meal we choose a little
      bit,
    Till we whittle it off.
SUE AND GIRLS: It is our duty, our beauty
    To keep while we may.

And on the Q.T., that duty
Is more work than play.
We keep on striving all day
To look our best at night.
So ev'ry day we do some punching
    after lunching.
Gliding and sliding and doing the
    dip
Until we've vanished and
    banished all signs of a hip.
SUE: A graceful torso may be more so
    If you dance it around.
ALL: That's what the beautifying
    Experts have found.

WHEN WE GET OUR DIVORCE

Lyric by Otto Harbach and Oscar Hammerstein II. Published as an individual sheet. Introduced by Marilyn Miller (Sunny) and Jack Donahue (Jim).

VERSE

SUNNY: Dearie, here we are waiting
    For one sweet day.
JIM: But we can't even budge,
    Till we hear from the judge,
    Who will say, "Go be gay.
    No more love and obey."
SUNNY: And, oh boy,
    What a joy
    To be free as the air.
JIM: And we won't have to care.

REFRAIN 1

JIM: When we get our divorce
    From the District Court,
    What a happy young pair we will be.
SUNNY: Won't life will be complete,
    When we get our sweet
    Interlocutory decree.
JIM: I will buy you a bunch of forget-me-nots
    And will dress myself up like a horse.
SUNNY: To the witness stand
    We'll go hand in hand.
    I won't care what you testify—
    I'll think it best, if I
    Know we can get our divorce.

REFRAIN 2

JIM: When we get our divorce
    From the District Court,
    What a happy young pair we will be.
    You can go your way,
    I can go my way.
SUNNY: That will be heaven for me.
JIM: I will buy you a cute little bungalow.
    But I'll never come near it, of course.
SUNNY: Still, if you are pressed
    There's an extra guest.
JIM: Then perhaps I'll get clubby
    With your second hubby
    And tell him about our divorce.

SUNSHINE

Lyric by Otto Harbach and Oscar Hammerstein II. Published as an individual sheet in 1925, but is not in the vocal score. Introduced by Dorothy Francis (Marcia) and the male ensemble.

Jerome Kern scholar Stephen Banfield points out that the melody was previously set as "Moon Love" in Kern's score for *The Beauty Prize* (London, 1923, lyric by George Grossmith and P. G. Wodehouse).

MEN: We wish that you would clarify
    The reason why a pair
    Should date
    To mate
    Right under the high noon's glare.
MARCIA: I don't see why you care if I
    Get married at high noon
    Instead of wedding underneath the
      moon.
MEN: Since moonlight is the right time
    For a pair to get engaged,
    Why is it not the right time
    For the parson to be paged
    And help to see the bridegroom safely
      caged?
MARCIA: Some may prefer the amorous glow
    Of the glimmering evening star.
    But as for me, my wedding won't be
    Where wav'ring shadows mar
    The gay sun's ray,
    The full light of the day.
MEN: You're right.
    No light can shimmer too bright
    To take your charm away.

REFRAIN

MARCIA: Sunshine,
The golden sunshine
My light of love shall be.
Shadows I'll keep in hiding,
As I go rainbow riding.
Sunshine
The golden sunshine
Is all I want to see.
Cold twilight is not my light,
The sunlight's the one light for me.

SUNSHINE [#2]

Lyric by Otto Harbach and Oscar Hammerstein II. This second "Sunshine" song was published in the vocal score. Introduced by Nancie Lovat (Marcia) and the male ensemble.

This tune is more cheerful, and its vocal line is higher than the first "Sunshine." Jerome Kern biographer Gerald Bordman identifies the refrain as the one previously set as "I Can't Forget Your Eyes" in *Oh, I Say!* (1913, lyric by Harry B. Smith). It would be used again as "In Araby with You" in *Criss-Cross* (1926, lyric by Otto Harbach and Oscar Hammerstein II).

VERSE

MEN: Why not have your wedding
At the evening hour?
Gentle moonbeams threading
Into the marriage bower.
MARCIA: You can find your new love
In the moonlight glow.
But when I've found my true love
I want the world to know.
So it seems more fun to be
Married when the sun can see.

REFRAIN

MARCIA: Sunshine, I invite you to my wedding.
Sunshine, with your lovelight shedding.
Sunshine, over aisle and altar spreading,
Come and kiss the bride-to-be.
Twilight I have found a very shy light.
My light is a golden high light.
Sunbeam, come and make me dream the
one dream
That brings happiness to me.

[MARCIA *repeats refrain while the men sing the obbligato.*]

OBBLIGATO

MEN: The sun is shining in the sky.
The silver lining has eclipsed the
cloud.
The bride and groom are passing by.
The bride and groom are looking very
proud.
We know you've married at the right
time,
Because you said you liked the bright
time.
Ah, ah!
Why should the sun do
What we all want to?
Of course, it's really up to you,
But we would much prefer to wed at
night.
For when the day's a lighter hue
We think publicity's a lover's blight.
If you can have your little sunbeam
Give me the spooning moon for you
To bring happiness to me.

ALL THESE PEOPLE I HAVE WRONGED

Alternate title: "Concerted Number." Lyric by Otto Harbach and Oscar Hammerstein II. Published in the vocal score. Introduced by Marilyn Miller (Sunny), Paul Frawley (Tom), Clifton Webb (Wendell), Jack Donahue (Jim) Mary Hay (Weenie), and ensemble.

SUNNY: [*apologizing to* JIM *and* WEENIE,
*using the verse melody for
"Who?"*] All these people I
have wronged, for
Just to win a prize I longed
for,
There was nothing that I would
not dare.
All the while that I've been
scheming,
It was only idle dreaming
For a man who doesn't seem to
care.
TOM: Who stole your heart away?
Who makes you dream all day?
Dreams, I know, can never come
true,
Seems as though you'll never
be blue.
Who means your happiness?

Who would you answer "yes"
to?
Darn'd if I can guess who.
SUNNY: No one but you.

[*As* TOM *takes in* SUNNY's *declaration, his fiancee enters, reminding* SUNNY *that she is to dance at their engagement party that evening. Then* WENDELL *enters and asks again if* SUNNY *will marry him. She sings to* WENDELL, *and when they begin dancing,* TOM *exits bewildered.*]

SUNNY
AND WENDELL: D'ye love me?
Un-huh!
D'ye mean it?
Un-huh!
D'ye promise to love me alway?
For ever?
Un-huh!
And ever?
Un-huh!
And not for a week or a day.
For lots of men may love you now
and then
But they all vanish when
They hear the wedding bells
playing,
So you must agree
It's going to be
Forever or never with me.

[SUNNY *and* WENDELL *dance off right.* JIM, WEENIE, *and ensemble enter from left and continue the song.*]

JIM: D'ye love me?
WEENIE: No, no.
JIM: D'ye mean it?
WEENIE: Uh, uh.
JIM: D'ye promise to love me
alway?
Forever?
WEENIE: Uh, uh.
JIM: And ever?
WEENIE: Uh, uh.
JIM: And not for a week or a day.
ENSEMBLE: For lots of men may love you
now and then
But they all vanish when
They hear the wedding bells
playing.
So you must agree
It's going to be
Forever or never with me.

Who stole your heart away?
Who makes you dream all day?

Dreams, we know, can never be
true,
Seems as though you'll ever be
blue.
Who means your happiness?
Who would you answer "yes" to?
Well, we ought to guess who—
No one but you.

[JIM *and* WEENIE *do a dance chorus of* "Who" *and all exeunt. Then* SUNNY, JIM, WENDELL, *and* WEENIE *return to dance to* "Who."* *When the principals leave the stage, the* ENSEMBLE *returns.*]

ENSEMBLE: Who stole my heart away?
Who makes me dream all day?
Dreams, I know, can never be
true,
Seems as though I'll ever be
blue.
Who means my happiness?
Who would I answer "yes" to?
Well, you ought to guess who—
No one but you.

THE CHASE

Lyric by Otto Harbach and Oscar Hammerstein II. Published in the vocal score. Introduced by the ensemble Paul Frawley (Tom), and Marilyn Miller (Sunny).

ENSEMBLE: The hounds have scented the fox's
trail,
The woodlands echo with bark and
wail.
The galloping hunters have caught the
sound,
Jumping at fences, they onward
bound.
Who's the girl that's madly
leading,
Dashing forward unheeding?

---

* *A souvenir program from the Broadway production noted: "When these four [Donahue, Miller, Hay, and Webb] dance and sing together in one scene of* Sunny *they constitute the highest salaried dancing quartet ever seen by any audience. Their combined salaries aggregate $9,200 a week. If anyone doubts this, Charles Dillingham is quite ready to show the salary list to prove it."*

She leaps at the wall,*
She laughs at Tom's mad call,
"Look out! Or you will fall!"
She tugs at the rein!
But all in vain.
Yet all the while she dares to wear a
smile.
Tom's still a length away.
Sunny's mount has run away!
Tom is gaining, and closer he crawls.
But no!
Sunny has missed, and she falls!
See how still she lies
As there beside her Tom is kneeling.
Now he starts to rise
And with a tenderness appealing
Carries her like a blossom rare.
Though not till now did red poppy
field
So white a flower yield.
GIRLS: There, like some lily fair
Dropped from paradise
Pale and white she lies—
TOM: [*entering, carrying* SUNNY] Please,
Sunny, open your eyes
And say you hear me, dear.
Close in my arms at last
Let me hold you fast.
Sunny dear, I love you.

[*Dialogue:* MARCIA *and* SUE *can't believe what they've just heard.*]

TOM: I don't care what I've done
For I've found only one
That I truly loved.
SUNNY: [*no longer pretending to be unconscious*]
Who?
ALL: [*spoken*] Sunny!
[*sung to* "Who" *melody*] You weren't
hurt at all!
You only staged the fall—
You have made fools of us all!

---

* *The published script and a Tams-Witmark prompt book have an alternate version of this and the next nine lines:*

See! She leaps at the towering wall,
Laughing only at Tom's mad call
Go easy there, Sunny, or you will fall!
Now see how she tugs at the tightened rein
Pulling for dear life but all in vain.
Yet all the while she dares to wear a smile,
For Tom still follows in blank dismay,
With ladies crying "A runaway!"
Now he is gaining and closer he crawls—

THE HUNT BALL

Alternate title: "Opening Chorus [Act Two, Scene Three]." Lyric by Otto Harbach and Oscar Hammerstein II. Published in the vocal score. Introduced by the ensemble.

At the Hunt Ball,
At the Hunt Ball
We will dance while romance
Sweet and mad'll
Fill the saddle.
At the Hunt Ball,
For the hunt call
Is the hunt thrall
Of fair ladies' chitter-chatter
As they gossip pitter-patter
At the Hunt Ball.
At the Hunt Ball
Foxes sly
Will be nigh
As they hover
Under cover
But we'll run them
Till we win them—*
For the wisest fox must fall
Who tempts the merry, mad Hunt Ball.

ADDED AND RESTORED SONGS

IT WON'T MEAN A THING

Alternate title: "Madrigalette." Lyric by Otto Harbach and Oscar Hammerstein II. Published in the vocal score. Dropped during *Sunny*'s out-of-town tryout, then restored in the London production.

SUNNY: I'll promise always to be true
And be a loving wife to you,
JIM: And I will do the same for you.
SUNNY AND JIM: But it won't mean a thing,
It won't mean anything.

---

* *The published script has* "Till we've run them." *A lyric sheet in the Otto Harbach Collection has* "Till we've won them."

SUNNY: I will wear your wedding band
And let folks think I think you're
grand.
But it won't mean a thing.
It won't mean anything.
TOM AND JIM: No matter what the other folks
may think,
We three will know.
It doesn't mean a thing.
JIM: I won't even buy the ring.
TOM: We'll have a great big wedding
cake,
With spice and ev'rything to
make it nice.
JIM: Oh, save some icing off the top
for me!
SUNNY: But it won't mean a thing!
It won't mean anything.
JIM: I have agreed to that before.
TOM: [to JIM] Or else I would not let
you wed this maid.
JIM: Made my promise to my Weenie
dear.
TOM: We neither of us need to be
afraid.
All's well now.
JIM: Frayed and frazzled is my
conscience now on.
SUNNY: Although I have to make a
marriage vow,
I promise that my promise to
be true,
Though made to him, is made
to you.
TOM: Vows, though made to him,
Are made for me.
Precisely, dear.
You put it nicely, dear.
SUNNY: I'll promise always to be true,
And be a loving wife to you,
But it won't mean a thing,
It won't mean anything.
TOM: She'll promise always to be
true,
And be a loving wife to you,
But it won't mean a thing,
It won't mean anything.
JIM: I'll promise always to be true,
To eat your biscuits and your
stew,
But it won't mean a thing,
It won't mean anything.

TOM: I think it's nice, we'll all agree.
The way the thing is going
pleases me!
JIM: As man and wife we'd not
agree.
And anyway, my Weenie waits
for me!
SUNNY: I think you'd be an awful pain
to me!
TOM: I think that I can depend on you
two.
SUNNY AND JIM: We'll see the whole thing
through!
TOM: You'll not obey or honor him or
love?
SUNNY: [to TOM] The least advance to
romance I'll shoo!
JIM: [to TOM] I'll be as hard to be had
as you.
TOM: Swear?
JIM: Swear?
ALL THREE: I do.

I WAS ALONE

Lyric by Otto Harbach and Oscar Hammerstein II. Published as an individual sheet. Written for the film *Sunny*, produced by First National Pictures in 1930. Introduced by Marilyn Miller (Sunny).

VERSE

Lover, can't you hear me?
You're passing oh so near me;
You'd see me, if you were not blind.
If you keep on going,
You'll go on never knowing
The secret I have on my mind.

REFRAIN

I was alone,
I worried alone,
I cried ev'ry night till three.
Wond'ring where love could be,
When it would come to me.
Then came one man
That I could crave for.
He's the one man
I'd be a slave for.
I've never told,
So he's never known
And that's why I'm all alone.

CUT AND UNUSED SONGS

DREAM A DREAM

Lyric by Otto Harbach and Oscar Hammerstein II. Published as an individual sheet, but cut before Broadway and not included in the vocal score. Introduced by Marilyn Miller (Sunny), Paul Frawley (Tom), and male ensemble early in Act One.

VERSE

SUNNY: Wherever poppies go,
There goes romance.
To see if this were so,
I watched my chance.
I stole up to your bed
And 'neath your sleeping head
I tucked this crimson red flower of
France.
And then I tiptoed away,
The while I whispered softly:

REFRAIN

SUNNY: Dream a dream upon a poppy petal.
Poppies never fail to settle
Who your own true love will surely be.
So dream a little dream,
But try to dream of me.

COUNTERMELODY

SUNNY: To think that he remembered me
Did not forget me,
Seemed a little glad he'd met me.
He came to sigh, "Hello," "Goodbye."
But I'll remember he
Remembered me.

[SUNNY *repeats the countermelody while* TOM *sings the refrain.*]

UNDER THE SKY

Alternate title: "Just You and I." Lyric by Otto Harbach and Oscar Hammerstein II. Dropped after the Philadelphia tryout. Would have been sung by Paul Frawley (Tom) and Dorothy Francis (Marcia) aboard the ocean liner in Act One.

This text is from a file of miscellaneous lyrics in the Otto Harbach Collection in the New York Public Library for the Performing Arts. Copyist piano-vocal scores and a full score in the hand of Robert Russell Bennett are in the Jerome Kern Collection at the Music Division of the Library of Congress. Also see "Rig Jig Jigging Away," which shares this song's opening lines.

VERSE

What a night, what a night,
For our two hearts
To prove they are true hearts.
Hand in hand
Here we stand,
On a good boat that is outward bound for home.
When the whistle shall blow,*
Out to sea we shall go.
Like a pair of night-born spirits we may roam
Beneath the moonlit dome
Of the star-spangled sky,
All alone, you and I.

REFRAIN

Dear, just you and I
Here under the sky.
While strains of the band
Waft to the land
One last goodbye.
We'll drive from our mind
Those left far behind.
Here under the sky
Dear, only you and I!

[TOM *stares at the flower that* SUNNY *had given him.*]

TOM: [*spoken*] "Drive from our mind." Sooner
said than done, I find.
[*catches himself and sings*]
Every leaving

---

* *Alternate lines from a copyist manuscript in the
Jerome Kern Collection:*
   Ev'ry care left behind,
   Perfect bliss we shall find.

Means someone grieving
For some must stay behind.
MARCIA: [*dropping the flower overboard*]
Each a dying ember,
Why should we remember?
It is best, you'll find
To forget them, for here
We're together, my dear.
Just you and I.
TOM: Here under the sky.
BOTH: While strains of the band
Waft to the land
One last goodbye.
We'll drive from our mind
Those left far behind.
Here under the sky,
Dear, only you and I!

RIG JIG JIGGING AWAY

Lyric by Otto Harbach and Oscar Hammerstein II. Not used. Found with miscellaneous lyric sheets in the Otto Harbach Collection in the New York Public Library for the Performing Arts. Would have been sung by Paul Frawley (Tom), Dorothy Francis (Marcia), and ensemble.

Stage directions explain: "When lights come up on next scene, it reveals the interior of a lounging room, full of ladies and gentlemen standing as though listening to the ship's whistle, which should not stop until the very end of the allegro motif. . . . At this moment Tom and Marcia enter."

VERSE

TOM AND MARCIA: What a night, what a night
For our two hearts
To prove they are true hearts.
Hand in hand
Here we stand,
On a good boat that is outward
bound for home.
ALL: For the whistle has blown,
And we've heard the wild
groan
Of the night wind wailing
through the rigging.
Under our feet
To rhythmical beat
The ship's propellers set us
jigging.

REFRAIN

Rig jig jigging away—
No renigging—for say,
Those propellers
Are two good "fellers"
Who keep on digging all day!
Once you start in to sway
To their rhythmical lay,
You'll keep jigging
A-rig-a-jig jigging
A-rig-a-jig jigging
A-rig-a-jig jigging
For aye!

[*Into an eccentric dance to the engine's rhythm.*]

ACT ONE OPENING CHORUS

Not published. Not used. Found in the Jerome Kern Collection at the Library of Congress, preceding "Here We Are Together Again" on typed sheets with lyrics for other Act One songs. No music for this song has been identified.

ENSEMBLE

Follow the gang
And hear the haranguing ballyhoo. We
Never tire of his talking, do we?
Telling of strong men,
Little men and long men,
Ladies tattooed, all black and bluey.
Just keep your eye on
Old Mr. Lion.
Roaring, roaring—
Monkeys jibbering of jungleland.
But, oh my gosh,
There's no lemon squash
As sour as a circus band.

SONG OF THE FLAME (1925)

Tryouts: Playhouse, Wilmington, Delaware, December 10–12, 1925; Academy of Music, Baltimore, December 14–19, 1925; Shubert Theatre, Philadelphia, December 21–26, 1925. New York run: 44th Street Theatre; opened December 30, 1925; closed July 10, 1926; 219 performances. A Romantic Opera. Presented by Arthur Hammerstein. Book and lyrics by Otto Harbach and Oscar Hammerstein II. Music by Herbert Stothart and George Gershwin. Book staged by Frank Reicher. Dances and ensemble pictures arranged by Jack Haskell. Orchestrations by [Robert] Russell Bennett. Orchestra directed by Herbert Stothart. Russian Art Choir directed by Alexander U. Fine. Scenery by Josef Urban. Costumes designed by Mark Mooring.

Cast: Tessa Kosta (Aniuta, "The Flame") Greek Evans (Konstantin Danilov), Dorothy MacKaye (Grusha), Hugh Cameron (Nicholas), Bernard Gorcey (Count Boris Kazanov), Ula Sharon (Nadya), Phoebe Brune (Natasha), Guy Robertson (Prince Volodya), Leonard St. Leo (a Dancer), Blanche Collins (Olga), Paul Wilson (Alexis), and Louise Dalberg (an Avenger), the singers of the Russian Art Choir, the dancers of the American Ballet, and ensemble.

It is 1917, a time of revolution, and many are inspired by a young woman known as the Flame. At the moment, however, she is recuperating in the country in the guise of a washerwoman, and despite her political beliefs finds herself falling in love with Prince Volodya, a local nobleman. For comedy we have earthy Grusha, who is involved with both Nicholas the chauffeur and Count Boris, his master. Konstantin is a menacing presence who works both sides of the struggle—encouraging the revolutionaries and fleecing the nobility in exchange for promised protection. A raid on the palace ends Act One. Act Two finds the principal characters in Paris two years later.

A national tour began on October 11, 1926, at Cleveland's Hanna Theatre and visited four additional cities.

A film version, directed by Alan Crosland, was released by First National in May 1930. The cast included Alexander Gray (Volodya), Bernice Claire (Aniuta), Alice Gentle (Natasha), Noah Beery (Konstantin), Bert Roach (Boris), and Inez Courtney (Grusha). Hammerstein did not write any of the new songs added to the film. A twenty-two-minute short film entitled The Flame Song and starring Gray and Claire was produced by Vitaphone in 1934.

The main sources for lyrics in this chapter are the piano-conductor score at the Tams-Witmark Music Library and the published sheets. There are typescripts at the Rodgers & Hammerstein Organization, in the Otto Harbach Collection at the New York Public Library for the Performing Arts, and in the Herbert Stothart Collec-

tion at UCLA (which also houses some music manuscripts). The Shubert Archive in New York has plentiful material for Song of the Flame, but the scripts and scores appear to be from a 1940s revision, with interpolations that cannot be definitively traced to Hammerstein.

Little is known about Harbach and Hammerstein's collaboration on the book and lyrics. A contract preserved in the Harbach Collection at the New York Public Library for the Performing Arts shows that Harbach and Hammerstein were to be billed as coauthors and that all four songwriters were to receive equal royalties. Credit for the musical work was more clearly divided, with Stothart or Gershwin getting sole credit on most of the published sheets.

This chapter does not include lyrics for the "Prelude" and "A Capella," which the Russian Art Choir sang to Russian texts. No lyric has been found for Act Two's "Going Home on New Year's Morning," which also was performed by the Russian Art Choir. The finaletti in Act One, Scene 3, and in Act Two, Scene 3, appear to be reprises. During the out-of-town tryout an Act Two trio for Grusha, Nicholas, and Boris called "You and You and Me" was replaced by "I Want Two Husbands" for the same characters, which was then replaced by a reprise of "Wander Away." Neither of the trios has survived.

In the spring of 1925 Hammerstein sent Harbach a long letter recapping ideas they had discussed for a show that would have a Russian flavor. After four pages he concluded,

It seems a shame to attack this poor little undeveloped plot in its infancy, but for the sake of helping it grow I'll point out three obvious faults.

First, we have no finish. Do you think there is one? I am anxious to have our next show go uphill in the second act, instead of downhill, which Rose-Marie assuredly does. And as soon as we leave colorful Russia and get to Long Island, I feel we're on the toboggan. On the other hand . . . I can not see a happy ending in leaving our hero and heroine in the unsettled Russia of today. There is this other possibility of maintaining Russian atmosphere with a scene in a place like The Russian Eagle in New York or any number of Russian cafes in Paris (all of which I am attending). But here you have your second act restaurant scene which is so often fallen back upon by lazy authors who want dancing teams to do their work.

Second, we have no comedy subplot or comedy characters, so far.

Third, I have an instinctive fear that we will never get a real good reason why Aniuta is in Judson's power when it comes to being admitted to the United States. This side of the story has a fakey feeling. And yet it would have to be our high spot, our main twist.

I merely submit these destructive comments to provoke thought and discussion and develop new values. I have not for a moment lost confidence in the general direction of our plans. . . .

Since seeing you, I have read no less than fifteen books on the Russian Revolution. I was thinking of starting our story there and then combining it with our present one, which would be tacked on later, the arrival at Ellis Island being somewhere along the middle of Act II.

There is undoubtedly great drama wound up in the revolution. Volodya could be one of the downtrodden peasants or workers, mistreated and tyrannized over by Aniuta's people, she alone treating him as if he were a human being. Then the revolution, and Volodya could be one of the leaders of the uprising. Aniuta is humiliated and enraged by a group of rough soldiers and peasants bursting into their palace, perhaps her bedroom and sacking the place, despoiling the treasures of her family home, and in their victorious lust going out of their way to insult the traditions which she reveres by instinct. And these are Volodya's people—and there is real conflict between the lovers. . . .*

As I describe these possibilities they feel rife with genuine drama. What was in my mind in objection to this kind of story was the fear of tampering with political and social problems which are as yet undecided and seem too serious to sing about. Yet, if we stick to the emotional side and keep our problems personal rather than general, we may be able to avoid committing ourselves politically.

FAR AWAY

Alternate title: "Prologue." Lyric by Otto Harbach and Oscar Hammerstein II. Music by George Gershwin and Herbert Stothart, based on a Russian folk song. Not published. Introduced by Greek Evans (Konstantin) and the Russian Art Choir.

Far away,
Too far away,
Birds of spring have flown.
Where is May,
Sweet, sunny May,
Bringing the singing

---

* This happens in the Act One finale of Song of the Flame, but the characters are reversed. Volodya is a prince and Aniuta the revolutionary.

Of voices with laughter ringing?
Blossoms gay,
Where do you stay?
Why am I left alone?
Far away,
Too far away,
Birds of the spring have flown.

SONG OF THE FLAME

Lyric by Otto Harbach and Oscar Hammerstein II. Music by George Gershwin and Herbert Stothart. Published as an individual sheet. Introduced by Tessa Kosta (Aniuta, also known as The Flame), Greek Evans (Konstantin), and the Russian Art Choir.

An early draft of the script contrasts this number with "Far Away": "Russia has had enough of wailing, she needs to learn a new song—of life, of courage and of freedom!" Recordings were made by Tessa Kosta, Vincent Lopez, the Ipana Troubadors, and the Victor Light Opera Co.

VERSE

Helpless children of the night
Groping blindly for the right,
The flame of hope is near!

REFRAIN

What's that light that is beckoning?
The Flame!
Through the night it is beckoning;
Come, come, come, come!
Take your new day of reckoning!
What new fire is enthralling you?
The Flame!
Soul of Russia is calling you!
On, on
Up the hill of hope and glory,
Follow, follow The Flame!

WOMAN'S WORK IS NEVER DONE

Lyric by Otto Harbach and Oscar Hammerstein II. Music by George Gershwin. Not published. Introduced by Dorothy Mackaye (Grusha) and ensemble.

MEN: Ladies fair, good morning, ladies.
GIRLS: We have no time to waste.
MEN: We beg your pardon. Pardon!
GRUSHA AND GIRLS: Early in the morning, drudging.
Ev'ry day, the same old way of drudging.
To the same canal we're trudging, trudging, trudging.
MEN: After all, what is there to it? Really quite an easy task for you, it
Seems to us a child could do it.
GIRLS: Woman's work is never done!

REFRAIN

GRUSHA AND GIRLS: Milk the cows and make a cup of coffee,
Take a basketful of wash and start the day.
Scrub, scrub all day long,
Scrub, scrub, same sweet song!
There's no letup from the time we get up
With the roosters and the dawning sun.
It's all day Monday
Right through Saturday;
All tired out by Sunday.
I know
Why no
Woman's work is ever done!

[*Women repeat refrain, while men sing countermelody.*]

COUNTERMELODY

MEN: Woman's work is never done
For they'll seize on any reason
To be shirking work for fun!
Each week's work
Should take but one day.
Milk the cows and make a cup of coffee,
And a woman's working day is done.

CODA

GIRLS: If you but knew the way
Women spend the day;
It's a terrible life.
Working for a husband,

Or a father or a brother,
Ev'ry day is dreary
And exactly like another.
For we cook, sew,
All the fun we know is when
We go to sleep in church on Sunday!

GREAT BIG BEAR

Lyric by Otto Harbach and Oscar Hammerstein II. Music by Herbert Stothart. Published as an individual sheet. Introduced by Dorothy Mackaye (Grusha).

VERSE

Great big bear,
Come along out of your lair.
Your little lamb,
That's what I am.
Waiting to play—
What do you say?
You're so strong—
I couldn't make you do wrong.
Why should you fear me?
Come and be near me,
That is where you belong.

REFRAIN

I wanna man,
I wanna man who's a
Great big bear.
I never can
Resist or refuse a
Great big bear.
I know that I like,
Know that I'd like to—
To be rudely kissed.
And if I chided,
I could be guided
By a great big fist.
I wanna be near,
I wanna be near my
Great big bear.
I wanna hug him,
Have him hug me for fair.
I'll be so happy,
When I have won one
Wonderful great big bear!

THE SIGNAL

Lyric by Otto Harbach and Oscar Hammerstein II. Music by George Gershwin. Published as an individual sheet. Introduced by Guy Robertson (Volodya), Dorothy Mackaye (Grusha), Tessa Kosta (Aniuta), and female ensemble.

VOLODYA: [offstage] Do you hear a sound like someone calling someone?
Do you wonder, dear, who can it be?
The one whose voice you're hearing now,
You very soon shall see.
GIRLS: We had better go,
I think we'd better go.
We are not wanted here,
It's plain to see.
We'll leave you to your lover, dear.
GRUSHA: Give him a kiss for me.
ANIUTA: I can hear a sound like someone calling someone,
And I wonder, dear, who can it be?
The one whose voice I'm hearing now,
That one I feign would see!

CODA FROM PIANO-CONDUCTOR SCORE

[ANIUTA continues her washing, pretending not to notice VOLODYA. To get her attention, he drops his handkerchief into the stream, and it floats down to her. He doffs his hat.]

VOLODYA: [spoken] My handkerchief, please.
ANIUTA: [spoken] This?
VOLODYA: [spoken] Yes, please.
ANIUTA: [spoken] I found it in the river, sir.
VOLODYA: [sung] I dropped it from the bridge.
ANIUTA: [sung] I washed it, sir.
VOLODYA: I thank you very kindly, miss.
ANIUTA: Washing's my profession, sir.
[spoken] Six kopeks, please.

COSSACK LOVE SONG

Alternate Title: "Don't Forget Me." Lyric by Otto Harbach and Oscar Hammerstein II. Music by Herbert Stothart and George Gershwin. Published as an individual sheet. Introduced by Tessa Kosta (Aniuta) and Guy Robertson (Volodya). A popular recording was made by the Ipana Troubadors.

VERSE

ANIUTA: When a Russian soldier bids his girl goodbye,
VOLODYA: He gives her a kiss,
Asking the miss
What promise he must pay her.
ANIUTA: Then the Russian soldier heaves a wistful sigh,
VOLODYA: He knows what she'll say.
And he'll obey,
ANIUTA: If she should ask this way:

REFRAIN

ANIUTA: Don't forget me,
Don't forget me.
Keep me in your heart and let me
Linger there no matter where you go.
VOLODYA: I'll be near you,
Always near you.
Think of me and I will hear you,
Though you're far away, I'll know.
ANIUTA: When you're all alone
And wondering if I am true
Don't forget the plans
That we have made, we two.
VOLODYA: Darling, don't forget that I am yearning,
Living just for your returning,
BOTH: Don't forget that I love you!

TARTAR

Lyric by Otto Harbach and Oscar Hammerstein II. Music by Herbert Stothart. Not published. Introduced by Greek Evans (Konstantin) and ensemble and danced by Phoebe Brune (Natasha).

This song is different than the "Tartar" number in *Daffy Dill*. A third "Tartar" song was found in the *Song of the Flame* materials at the Shubert Archive. Authorship of the Shubert version is not known; it may be by Rowland Leigh and Pierre DeReeder.

VERSE

KONSTANTIN: Maid of the East,
Reckless and wild,
Mad as a beast,
Sweet as a child.
ENSEMBLE: Castoff of some
Mongolian tribe of old.

REFRAIN

ENSEMBLE: Come do your Tartar dance.
KONSTANTIN: That Tartar dance
That makes your blood run cold.
ENSEMBLE: A stamping, whistling crowd
Will shout aloud
To make your feet more bold.

[NATASHA dances.]

ENCORE

ENSEMBLE: Ta, ta, ta, ta, ta, ta, ta, ta. [etc.]
A Tartar maid
Can make your pulse go up and down.
It makes your pulse
Go up and down to see a Tartar!

WANDER AWAY

Lyric by Otto Harbach and Oscar Hammerstein II. Music by Herbert Stothart. Published as an individual sheet. Introduced by Greek Evans (Konstantin) and Tessa Kosta (Aniuta).

Note: The published sheet reads as a sincere love song. But in the show, Aniuta does not return Konstantin's feelings and his words are menacing.

REFRAIN

KONSTANTIN: You may wander away,
Wander away from me.
You may go for a day,
Or for eternity.
I'll be waiting for you
Waiting for you, my all.
I'll be always waiting for you,
Waiting to hear you call!*

Unpublished interlude

KONSTANTIN: You may wander away,
Wander away from me.
You may go for a day
Or for eternity.
ANIUTA: Don't be so certain.
You may have to wait
For a long—,
Long time.

* For the reprise, the final line changes to:
Never to hear you call.

VERSE

KONSTANTIN: When you leave me, then I know
That all my joy must go with
you!
And a crimson sunset melts away
in blue.
But as sure as ev'ry sun
Will rise again to brighten the
sky,
You'll come back to me.
You'll come back to me,
That fond hope cannot die,
dear—

REPEAT REFRAIN

Unpublished countermelody

ANIUTA: [*over the first four lines of* KONSTANTIN'*s refrain*] "The Flame" is far away.
You cannot tell where she may be.
It may be that she may
Stay there, you see.
You'll be waiting for me,
Waiting for me to call.
You'll be waiting for me,
Waiting to hear me call.

VODKA

Lyric by Otto Harbach and Oscar Hammerstein II. Music by George Gershwin and Herbert Stothart. Published as an individual sheet. Introduced by Dorothy Mackaye (Grusha).

A favorite with cabaret performers, "Vodka" is one of the few songs from this score to have an independent life.

VERSE

Of all concoctions alcoholical,
I know but one that's diabolical.
I simply thrive on old Champagne,
And sparkling Burgundy.
Whiskey, Cointreau, Moselle, or Eau de Vie
Are just like tea,
But

REFRAIN

Vodka,
Don't give me vodka.
For when I take a little drink,
I forget to think,

What a little drink can do to me.
Vodka,
Don't give me vodka.
For when I take a little nip,
I begin to slip,
And I start romancing with
The man that I am dancing with.
For vodka
Makes me feel odd-ka.
I go and grab a six-foot-two—
Anyone will do
If he's only wise enough to see,
I'll not scream should he kiss me.
Couldn't if I would,
Wouldn't if I could.
Vodka,
You ruin me!

ACT ONE FINALE

Lyric by Otto Harbach and Oscar Hammerstein II. Music by George Gershwin and Herbert Stothart. Not published.

The scene is a bacchanal at the palace. Grusha has extolled "Vodka." Nadya has danced a bullfight ballet. Volodya interrupts them after "La Dance de Quo Vadis." The text that follows is from the piano-conductor score at Tams-Witmark.

VOLODYA: You dogs!
You pack of drunken libertines!
[*spoken*] No wonder the people of
Russia are sick of your rule.
[*sung*] I am your host
It is but right
[*spoken*] I bid you all goodnight!

[VOLODYA *covers a nearly naked girl with his coat and leads her into an (offstage) anteroom. The* TARTAR *follows and locks them in. Throughout the number,* VOLODYA *pounds on the door.*]

ENSEMBLE: La, la, la . . .
Vodka, bring on the vodka!
BORIS: [*entering with* GRUSHA]
What is this rapping?
What's the laughing for?
TARTAR: Volodya is napping.
Can't you hear him snore?
ENSEMBLE: Ha, ha, ha!
Ha, ha, ha!
GRUSHA: Boris, I'm frightened.
Please come over here.

BORIS: Don't worry, dear.
I'm near.
GRUSHA: Oh, Boris.
NICHOLAS: [*enters, sees them embracing*]
What do I see before me?
What do I see before me!
Now I understand
Your sly command
That I stay outside awaiting,
To be waiting in the car.
All the while I was awaiting—
BORIS: Well, I told you to be waiting.
NICHOLAS: You were hugging
And a-kissing.
GRUSHA: Maybe hugging.
Never kissing.
NICHOLAS: Oh, a kiss or two
From that 'n,
Or a kiss or two
From this 'n,
Never mattered much to Grusha.
Doesn't matter much to Grusha.
BORIS: Don't you listen to him, Grusha.
ENSEMBLE: Grusha, let us hope that few
shall
Know this Armageddon crucial.
But if he should quiz,
Say the fault is his,
That—

[*More offstage rapping on the door.*]

BORIS: What the hell is that?
ENSEMBLE: Ha, ha, ha, ha.
Ha-ha, ha-ha, ha-ha.
GRUSHA: Nicholas, don't be angry.
Nicholas, don't be angry!
NICHOLAS: Did you let him kiss you, Grusha?
I'm inclined to think you wouldn't
Dare to let him kiss you, Grusha.
With a man like that, you
couldn't!
BORIS: You can never tell about a
woman.
GRUSHA: If you can, you shouldn't.
BORIS: I have had quite enough now.
NICHOLAS: You have had quite enough
now?
Why, you stole my girl!
ENSEMBLE: [*to* GRUSHA] Are you this man's
girl?
GRUSHA: Well, I was his girl.
BORIS: How is she your girl?
She is my girl now.
What you gonna do about it?
ALL: What you gonna do about it
now?

You're a chicken-hearted
    fellow.
You are only fit to serve.

BORIS: You would like to come and get
    her
But you haven't got the nerve!

ENSEMBLE: Why not try to come and get
    her

BORIS: No, you haven't got the nerve!
Or you'd try to come and get
    her!

ALL: Why not try to come and get
    her,
If you have a little nerve.

GRUSHA: Nicky, show a little nerve!

ENSEMBLE: Poor unhappy Nicholas,
He's in an awful pickle as
He tries to make a breakaway
And take away the maid.
Sic 'em, Nicky, sic 'em.
Soak 'em, sock him, even kick
    him.
You are big enough to lick
    him
But we fear that you're afraid.
Coward!

NICHOLAS: [*shouting*] You! You! You! You!

[*A brawl ensues.* NICHOLAS *is overpowered.* BORIS *exults. He and other revelers begin a jeering rendition of the title song.*]

BORIS
AND REVELERS: What's that light that is
    beckoning?
Through the night it is
    beckoning.
Take your new day of
    reckoning.
Come, come, come, come,
    come!
Take your new day of
    reckoning.
What new fire is enthralling
    you
Soul of Russia is calling you.
On, on up the hill of hope and
    glory
Follow, follow—

[*Voices offstage, singing the same song, grow ever louder. The nobles begin to huddle together. The* TARTAR *shrieks in triumph. We hear the front door being battered in.* KONSTANTIN, *a mob, and eventually,* ANIUTA *enter.*]

ANIUTA: Stop!
Am I too late?

[*Dialogue:* ANIUTA *asks if* VOLODYA *is safe. The* TARTAR *unlocks the door and* VOLODYA *emerges with a scantily clad girl.* ANIUTA *is upset.* KONSTANTIN *reveals that* ANIUTA *is the Flame.* VOLODYA *thinks* ANIUTA *pretended to be in love with him in order to prepare this attack.*]

VOLODYA: Don't forget me,
Don't forget me.
Keep me in your heart and let me
Linger there no—

[*He breaks off.*]

ANIUTA: I'll forget you,
I'll forget you.
I'll not find it hard
    forgetting,
Forgetting I loved you.

ENSEMBLE: Forgetting she loved you.

MIDNIGHT BELLS

Lyric by Otto Harbach and Oscar Hammerstein II. Music by George Gershwin. Published as an individual sheet. Introduced by Tessa Kosta (Aniuta). Dropped soon after the New York opening.

VERSE

Ding, dong,
Ding, dong.
So you go, clanging away.
Ding, dong,
Ding, dong.
Pretty bells, what do you say?
Does your melody
Bring happiness to me?

REFRAIN

Ring on, beautiful midnight bells.
Ring on, weaving your mystic spells.
You sing a song of tomorrow,
And to yesterday's sorrow
You laugh and say goodbye.
You're happy and so am I.
Ring on, let me forget a while.
Ring on, let me but learn to smile
Oh, bells, ring in a New Year.
Bells, ring out a blue year.
Ring for me, beautiful bells.

REPEAT REFRAIN

CUT SONG

YOU ARE YOU

Lyric by Otto Harbach and Oscar Hammerstein II. Music by George Gershwin and Herbert Stothart. Published as an individual sheet. Dropped before the New York opening.

    In the Wilmington tryout this was sung in Act One by Aniuta and Volodya; it was probably replaced by "The Signal" and "Cossack Love Song."

VERSE

When you're in love,
What is the use
Trying to find out why?
I am in love,
Have no excuse,
All I can do is sigh.
My heart is mine no more,
And here's the only reason:

REFRAIN

You are you and that is why I love you.
You are you and I am only I,
And yet, from where you are
You deign to smile down on me.
Near my dear,
My only fear
Is that someday you'll frown on me.
It's just as though a golden star above you*
Had won away your heart and worry too.
It may but seem an idle dream
For me to love you,
But I am I and that is why you do.

---

* *A variant from the script in the Herbert Stothart Collection at UCLA:*
    If some bright star were shining far above you
    In loving her, I think you'd worry too.

MISCELLANEOUS SONG

I LOVE YOU, LEAH

Not published. No music is known to have been written.

After playing the title character in *Rose-Marie* for a year, Mary Ellis left the show. Contractually restrained from appearing in any other American musical, she took a major role in the Neighborhood Playhouse's December 1925 production of the Yiddish ghost story *The Dybbuk*. A program from *The Dybbuk* is preserved in the Oscar Hammerstein II collection in the Music Division of the Library of Congress, along with this lyric fragment.

I love you, Leah,
Dearest virgin flow'r,
My lonely nights with dreams of you are
    [pearled?].
Their echoes in your ear must ring,
The music in my soul must sing—
I love you, Leah,
As God loves the world.

OVERLEAF *Clockwise from bottom right: Sheet music from the original Broadway production, the 1929 film, the original London production, the 1943 film, and the 1953 film*

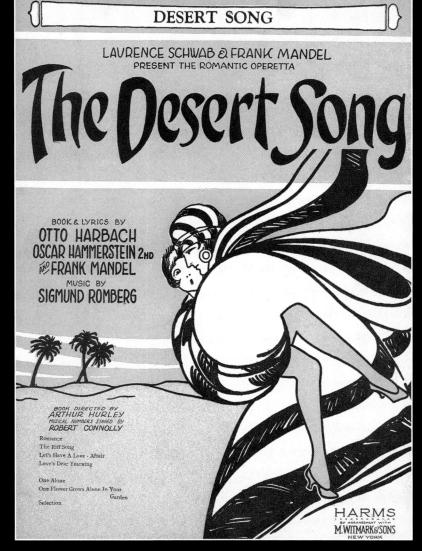

Songs of 1926–1927

THE WILD ROSE (1926)

Tryouts: Playhouse, Wilmington, Delaware, September 16–18, 1926; Forrest Theatre, Philadelphia, September 20–October 9, 1926. New York run: Martin Beck Theatre; opened October 20, 1926; closed December 11, 1926; 61 performances. A Musical Play. Presented by Arthur Hammerstein. Book and lyrics by Otto Harbach and Oscar Hammerstein II. Music by Rudolf Friml. Staged by William J. Wilson. Dances staged by Busby Berkeley. Orchestrations not credited. Orchestra under the direction of Herbert Stothart. Assistant musical director: Mario Agnolucci. Settings by Joseph Urban. Costumes designed by Mark Mooring.

Cast: William Collier (Gideon Holtz), Desiree Ellinger (Princess Elise), Joseph Santley ("Monty" Travers), Inez Courtney (Luella Holtz), Gus Shy ("Buddy" Haines), Nana Bryant (Countess Nita), Joseph Macaulay (Baron Frederick), Fuller Mellish (King Augustus III), George Djimos (Flower Vendor), Len Mence (General Hodenberg), Jerome Daley (Carl), Neil Stone (Peter), Dink Trout (Zeppo), the Pasquali Brothers (acrobats), the Randalls (dancers), and ensemble.

No script for *The Wild Rose* has been located, but newspaper clippings recount a plot along these lines: One night in a Monte Carlo casino, "Monty" Travers, a handsome and good-hearted American, meets a beautiful girl, who allows him to think she is the daughter of a tavern keeper although she is actually Princess Elise, heir to the throne of Borovina. Both are eager to continue the acquaintance and Monty's help becomes essential when malicious Baron Frederick attempts to take the throne and the princess by force. Comedy was provided by another visiting American, the millionaire oilman Gideon Holtz, who is taken up by Countess Nita, and may be the unwitting carrier of a bomb. Holtz's daughter Luella provides some modern pep and does snappy dances with Buddy Haines. The ensemble rounds out the evening's music and pageantry in scenes at the casino, a rose festival, and a coronation, and by portraying loyal subjects and unhappy revolutionaries.

Only five songs from *The Wild Rose* were published, and no other material has been found in the performing arts archives in New York or Washington, D.C. With luck, a score and libretto will surface when the two hundred boxes of Friml material at UCLA are cataloged. The missing numbers are "Riviera," "Lovely Lady" (added during the out-of-town tryouts, this lyric may have been solely Otto Harbach's work), "It Was Fate," "Lady of the Rose," "The Purple Rose," "The King Arises" (which may have been cut out of town), the opening of Act Two, Dramatico Musical Scene, "Won't You Come Across?" "The Coronation," and the finales of Acts One and Two. Also missing are songs dropped during the out-of-town tryouts: "I'm the Extra Man," "Entrance of Tommy," "How Can You Keep Your Mind on Business?" "Rumble, Rumble, Rumble," and "That's Why I Love You."

In an oral history taped a few months before his death in January 1963, Otto Harbach recalled that *The Wild Rose* (produced by Arthur Hammerstein) and *The Desert Song* (produced by Schwab and Mandel) were prepared simultaneously for fall 1926 openings. He and Hammerstein shared book-and-lyric credit on both shows, with Harbach in charge of *The Wild Rose* (a flop) and Hammerstein in charge of *The Desert Song* (a tremendous success). Harbach did not explain whether each worked on his own show from the outset, or they developed the stories together but wrote lyrics separately, or they worked together until *The Wild Rose* began its out-of-town tryouts while *The Desert Song* was in rehearsal in New York. (The transcript makes it clear that thirty-seven years later, Harbach was still bothered by the experience and felt he'd been slighted on *The Desert Song*'s opening night.) In any case, since "Brown Eyes" and "We'll Have a Kingdom" were added to *The Wild Rose* during the tryouts, they are probably Harbach's sole work, although they were copyrighted and published under both names. Neither appears in this chapter.

LOVE ME, DON'T YOU?

Lyric by Otto Harbach and Oscar Hammerstein II. Published as an individual sheet. Introduced by Nana Bryant (Countess Nita), William Collier (Gideon Holtz) and female ensemble.

The sheet music does not indicate which character sang which lines; the line assignments below are a conjecture based on Nita being a scheming countess and Holtz being a wealthy American oilman.

VERSE 1

NITA: You're so big and strong,
Is it wrong to be longing to be pressed tight
Right close against your best vest,
Lest any other one shall have the fun?
HOLTZ: Ah, ev'rything you say may be gay,
But you're playing with a red-hot volcano.
Better say no—
Take heed, dear.
NITA: But that's what I need, dear.

REFRAIN

NITA: Love me, don't you?
Then why won't you
Hurry and begin?
Make me happy,
But be snappy
Or you'll never win.
Don't be shy, dear;
Only try, dear.
Ask no questions;
I am open for suggestions.
After all, dear,
I can't fall, dear,
If you don't begin!

VERSE 2

NITA: Girls, I need your aid.
I'm afraid I have made an awful faux pas,
Ah, with this loving papa.
HOLTZ: Bah, what's a man to do with girls like you?
GIRLS: Ah, how can you resist being kissed?
You have missed a red-hot, we said, red-hotted.
HOLTZ: I will not trust
The girl well
Till I get my oil well.

REPEAT REFRAIN

WILD ROSE

Lyric by Otto Harbach and Oscar Hammerstein II. Published as an individual sheet. Introduced by Desiree Ellinger (Princess Elise), Joseph Macaulay (Baron Frederick), and male ensemble.

VERSE

One day a shepherd lad who met a maid,
Wanting his love to tell, was half afraid,
And so he gave his heart to her
Wrapped in a budding rose—
And that's the way we do today,
As ev'ry lover knows!

REFRAIN

This sweet wild rose you gave to me
Is pressed close to my heart.
And with it I'll remember thee,
If we shall ever part.
I may become a princess
Or a queen upon a throne,
But this wild rose will always be
The dearest thing I own.

ONE GOLDEN HOUR

Alternate title: "L'Heure d'or." Lyric by Otto Harbach and Oscar Hammerstein II. Published as an individual sheet. Introduced by Desiree Ellinger (Princess Elise) and Joseph Santley ("Monty" Travers).

The published sheet does not specify who sings what. This editor has suggested line assignments, based on Monty being an American and Princess Elise a European and a soprano. The French words with which Monty struggles are by J. B. Kantor and appear in full in the published sheet.

VERSE

ELISE: It's written plainly.
MONTY: I try but vainly
To read these words.
ELISE: I'll read it to you!
Now pay attention carefully to me
And you will know that—

REFRAIN

ELISE: Just one golden hour of happy madness.
Just one golden hour, a glimpse of
gladness.
Just once to feel all my soul and senses
reel,
Drowned in the blisses
I'd gather from love's burning kisses.
Just a little while for love dreams tender,
Filled with ecstasy of surrender—
For one such golden hour what would I
not do,
Could I but share it with you.

INTERLUDE

ELISE: Tra, la, la, la, la, [etc.]
MONTY: Won't you please say it in English?
ELISE: [continuing the obbligato] Tra, la, la, la, la
MONTY: "Toots mess pensees tooze mess revies
Sont alure door syeduce et breeve."
What's it mean, that word there?
Don't you think you are unfair?
ELISE: Ah—[cadenza]
MONTY: Wait, dear, you've not to go,
Tell me—I've got to know!

REPEAT REFRAIN

FRENCH REFRAIN

Toutes mes pensés, tous mes rêves
Sont à l'heure d'or si douce et brève.
Lorsque mon cœur plein de joie et de bonheur,

Je vais entendre
Ta confession troublante et tendre.
Oh! Cette heure de divine ivresse,
L'heure de baisers, de caresses,
L'heure que dans mes rêves je vis toujours
Avec toi, mon cher amour.

THE DESERT SONG (1926)

Tryouts (under the title *Lady Fair*): Playhouse, Wilmington, Delaware, October 21–23, 1926; Poli's Theatre, Washington, D.C., October 25–30, 1926; Shubert Theatre, New Haven, November 1–6, 1926; Shubert Theatre, Boston, November 8–27, 1926. New York run: Casino Theatre, November 30, 1926–October 8, 1927; moved to Century Theatre, October 10–31, 1927; moved to Imperial Theatre, November 2, 1927; closed January 7, 1928; total 471 performances. A New Operetta. Music by Sigmund Romberg. Book by Otto Harbach, Oscar Hammerstein II, and Frank Mandel. Lyrics by Otto Harbach and Oscar Hammerstein II. Presented by Laurence Schwab and Frank Mandel. Book directed by Arthur Hurley. Musical numbers staged by Robert Connolly. Orchestra directed by Oscar Bradley. Settings by Woodman Thompson. Modern costumes by Vyvyan Donner and Mark Mooring. French soldiers' and native costumes by Eaves.

Cast: Vivienne Segal (Margot Bonvalet), Robert Halliday (Pierre Birabeau),* Eddie Buzzell (Benjamin "Bennie" Kidd), Nellie Breen (Susan), William O'Neal (Sid El Kar, the Red Shadow's Lieutenant), Glen Dale (Captain Paul Fontaine), Pearl Regay (Azuri), Edmund Elton (General Birabeau, Governor of a French Moroccan Province), Lyle Evans (Ali Ben Ali), Margaret Irving (Clementina), O. J. Vanasse (Mindar), Earle Mitchell (Hassi), Albert Baron (Sergeant La Vergne), Charles Davis (Sergeant DuBassac), Elmira Lane (Ethel), Rachel May Clark (Neri), Charles Morgan (Hadji), and ensemble (French girls, soldiers' wives, ladies of the Brass Key, soldiers of the French Legion, members of Red Shadow's band.)

The story is set in the present (mid-1920s) at a French military outpost in Morocco that has been troubled by Riff raiders. Margot Bonvalet, a resident who is engaged to Captain Paul Fontaine, longs for an overpowering lover and soon attracts the romantic attentions of the Red Shadow, the Riffs' masked leader, who kidnaps her at the end of Act One. Very few characters know that the virile Red Shadow is the alter ego of Pierre

---

* *The Red Shadow does not appear in the program's cast of characters.*

Birabeau, the general's son, who is generally dismissed as bookish and feeble. Courtship and sex are a constant theme in the main and secondary plots. The General's ward, Susan, is pursuing a hapless reporter named Bennie, who later provokes the interest of an entire harem. The Red Shadow's friends Sid El Kar and Ali Ben Ali cannot understand his interest in only one woman. And Margot's fiancé has been involved with the native woman Azuri, who is not eager to let him go.

The first national tour began at the Hanna Theatre, Cleveland, on August 21, 1927, and visited fourteen cities, concluding in Indianapolis on December 29, 1928. A second tour started at the Majestic Theatre in Chicago on December 17, 1928, and played twenty cities through May 1929.

A London production, starring Edith Day (Margot) and Harry Welchman (Pierre/Red Shadow), opened at the Theatre Royal, Drury Lane, April 7, 1927, and ran for 432 performances.

Film adaptations were released in 1929 (Warner Bros.–Vitaphone, directed by Roy Del Ruth and starring Carlotta King and John Boles); 1943 (Warner Bros., directed by Robert Florey and starring Irene Manning and Dennis Morgan); and 1953 (Warner Bros., directed by H. Bruce Humberstone and starring Kathryn Grayson and Gordon MacRae). Hammerstein did not write the new material used in the 1943 film and reused in 1953. A television adaptation, produced by Max Liebman and starring Gale Sherwood and Nelson Eddy, aired on May 7, 1955 on NBC.

Recordings include the 1927 London cast (Pearl CD reissue); a 1944 studio cast featuring Kitty Carlisle and Wilbur Evans (Decca Broadway CD reissue); a 1960 studio cast featuring Mario Lanza and Judith Raskin (RCA Victor CD reissue); and a 1963 studio cast featuring Dorothy Kirsten and Gordon MacRae (EMI Angel CD reissue).

For decades a staple with light opera companies, *The Desert Song* did not return to Broadway until September 1973, when it lasted only 15 performances. It was more successful in a 1984 production at the Paper Mill Playhouse in Millburn, New Jersey, and in a 1987 production at the New York City Opera, which was revived in 1989 and 1992.

The main source for lyrics in this chapter is the published vocal score. Also consulted were the published script, and various typescripts: at the Rodgers & Hammerstein Organization (particularly one marked "Final Casino Theatre Version"); in the Otto Harbach Collection at the New York Public Library for the Performing Arts; at the Tams-Witmark Music Library in New York City; at the Shubert Archive in New York City; and in the Frank Mandel Collection at UCLA. The Romberg holograph piano-vocal score in the Music Division of the Library of Congress and vocal parts in the Warner-Chappell Collection there are the source for early versions of songs.

No lyrics have been found for "Women, Women,

Women," "Ali-Up," and "Not for Him," which out-of-town programs list as "principal themes" in Act Two. The title "Barber Song" appears on lists of Harbach and Hammerstein copyrights, but no lyric has been found.

Original programs list Harbach, Hammerstein, and Mandel as the co-authors of the book and do not give a separate lyric-writing credit. Contracts specify equal billing and equal royalties for these three authors and a smaller portion to Laurence Schwab. But in a June 1956 letter to author Elizabeth Rider Montgomery, who was compiling *The Story Behind Popular Songs*, Hammerstein explained: "*The Desert Song* started by my reading an account in the newspaper of the Riff trouble in Morocco. I gave it to Frank Mandel and Frank and I started to write the story, having evoked Romberg's enthusiasm to do the score. After we got him under way we then went to Otto and invited him into the collaboration. The three of us worked on the book and Otto Harbach and I collaborated on the lyrics."

In a 1954 article in *Variety* Hammerstein described one afternoon's collaboration:

Otto Harbach and I sat in his garden at Mamaroneck trying to write words to a melody by Sigmund Romberg. It was to be for *The Desert Song*. We were having trouble. We had a general idea of what the song was to be about, but a general idea is not good enough. A refrain of thirty-two bars lasts a little less or a little more than a minute. In that time you have to say something and say it clearly . . . We were in that not uncommon predicament in which two collaborators, trying to corner and capture a refrain, are themselves cornered. On such occasion the two collaborators seldom sit or stand together. There is always one seated and the other is standing or pacing. They take turns. The one who is standing may break the silence with a suggestion. The one who is sitting shakes his head. It gets to a point where neither has any confidence left. Each will preface a suggestion with: "This isn't it but it might be something like this—" Then he offers his feeble notion and breaks off in the middle—"No, it's lousy," he will say, taking the words out of his friend's mouth. It was at one of these discouraging moments when Otto said something wonderful: "You know, Oscar, we are not going to make this song, the song is here. It exists somewhere in the world. What we have to do is find it." The truth of this struck me with great force and I have never forgotten it. That afternoon we "found" the song we were looking for.

FEASTING SONG

Alternate title: "Opening, Act One." Lyric by Otto Harbach and Oscar Hammerstein II. Published in the vocal score. Introduced by William O'Neal (Sid El Kar) and male ensemble (the Riffs).

While this lyric does not appear in Hammerstein's anthology, *Lyrics*, he discussed it in the introductory essay:

I was not very careful about writing a subtle lyric. I knew that it was to be sung by a male chorus and that they would bellow it very loudly and indistinguishably. I wrote words that could be sung out comfortably for sound without any particular attention to shaded meanings. It turned out as I had anticipated. It was an effective opening from a musical standpoint, and nobody knew what the words were, and I didn't care . . . [In London, a year later,] to my dismay, I heard the English male chorus singing. They were clipping their consonants so sharply that every word could be understood! I felt like a cornered criminal.

SID: High on a hill is our stronghold,
Our shelt'ring cave.
RIFFS: Woe be to anyone who shall try to discover us.
Woe be to anyone who shall try to discover us.
SID: So, ho, then, you band of reckless men, Bold Morocco men.
RIFFS: Ho! Bold men of Morocco sand.
Bold band of reckless fellows of Morocco sand—
Ho! Ho!
SID: So pass the bowl and we'll drink it until we drink it up.
So pass the bowl and we'll drink it until we drain the cup!
RIFFS: As we are drinking, merrily drinking, Who would be thinking who we are?
As we are drinking, merrily drinking, Who would be thinking who we are?
RIFFS: Drink to the Caid,
Drink to the Caid,
To the leader of the band!
ALL: Drink on!

REPRISE

SID: Ho! Bold men of Morocco.
TENORS: Ho! Bold men of Morocco sand.
BASSES: Bold band of reckless fellows of Morocco sand!
SID: As we are drinking, merrily drinking,

Who would be thinking who we are?
As we are drinking, merrily drinking,
Who would be thinking who we are?
So pass the bowl and we'll drink it until we drink it up.
So pass the bowl and we'll drink it until we drain the cup.
RIFFS: As we are drinking, merrily drinking, Who would be thinking who we are?
As we are drinking, merrily drinking, Who would be thinking who we are?
TENORS: Drink to the Caid!
BASSES: Drink to the Caid,
To the leader of the band!
ALL: Drink on!

RIFF SONG (HO!)

Lyric by Otto Harbach and Oscar Hammerstein II. Published as an individual sheet. Introduced by Robert Halliday (Red Shadow), William O'Neal (Sid El Kar), and the male ensemble (the Riffs).

VERSE

RED SHADOW: Over the ground,
There comes a sound.
It is the drum, drum, drum of hoofbeats in the sand.
SID: Drumming on the sand.
RIFFS: Galloping horses in the sand.
RED SHADOW: Quiver with fear
If you are near.
It is the thunder of the "Shadow" and his band,
SID: His band will find you soon.
RIFFS: Red Shadow's band.
Fly away, for
All who plunder learn to understand.
RED SHADOW: To understand the cry of—

REFRAIN

RED SHADOW: Ho!
So we sing as we are riding.
SID AND RIFFS: Ho!
RED SHADOW: It's a time you'd best be hiding Low.
It means the Riffs are abroad.
Go!
Before you've bitten the sword.
BASSES: Go before the sword!
RED SHADOW,
SID, AND RIFFS: Ho!

RED SHADOW: That's the sound that comes to
warn you,
So
In the night or early morn you
Know
If you're the Red Shadow's foe,

RED SHADOW
AND SID: The Riffs will strike with a blow
That brings you woe!

ALL REPEAT REFRAIN

MARGOT

Lyric by Otto Harbach and Oscar Hammerstein II. Published in the vocal score. Introduced by Glen Dale (Paul) and male ensemble (French soldiers). Reprised, with slight adjustments to the lyric, by the female ensemble (soldiers' wives) during "All Hail the General."

Oh pretty maid of France,
My Margot.
A breath of sweet romance,
My Margot.
Her little roguish eye nearby
Can woo you,
Bring to you
The longing
To fly into the arms
Of Margot
And win the winsome smile
Of Margot.
My sweetest flight of fancy
Is when I can see
Margot of France!

I'LL BE A BUOYANT GAL

Alternate title: "Opening, Act One, Scene 2." Lyric by Otto Harbach and Oscar Hammerstein II. Published in the vocal score. Introduced by Nellie Breen (Susan) and Elmira Lane (Ethel).

VERSE

SUSAN: Has anybody seen my Bennie?*

_____

*The typescript marked "Final Casino Theatre
Version" gives the first line as:
I keep on looking for my Bennie.

I miss him so.
'Twas early in the morning
When he started forth to go.
ETHEL: The wife of ev'ry soldier
By fear and dread is harried—
SUSAN: But Bennie ain't no soldier
And we ain't even married.

REFRAIN

SUSAN: I hope of course to bring him lots of joy;
To be his wife, his sweetheart, and his pal.
I'll try my best to win that gallant boy,
And when I do, I'll be a buoyant gal.

WHY DID WE MARRY SOLDIERS?

Alternate title: "Opening Act One, Scene 3." Lyric by Otto Harbach and Oscar Hammerstein II. Published in the vocal score. Introduced by the female ensemble (French soldiers' wives).

Why did we marry soldiers?
Why did we leave our France
To live in old Morocco
The lives of maiden aunts?
Our men are always missing;
They're not around enough.
Just as we start our kissing,
The damn old Riffs get rough;
And then to quell this Riffian blight
Our hubbies heed the call to fight.
It seems a silly fuss;
For if they choose to spend a day
In fighting, why not let them stay
At home and fight with us?
Stay home and fight with us!
Life is dull and life is weary,
Life is hell without our men.
Hours lull, and days are dreary;
Nights are hell without,
Without men.
Ah, men,
Ah, men!

FRENCH MILITARY MARCHING SONG

Lyric by Otto Harbach and Oscar Hammerstein II. Published in the vocal score. Introduced by Vivienne Segal (Margot), female ensemble (girls dressed as soldiers and French girls), and male ensemble (French soldiers).

MARGOT: Oh, girls, girls, girls,
Here are cavaliers,
Handsome cavaliers!
SOLDIER GIRLS: [They wear men's uniforms and
march in formation.] Aren't
we fine?
MARGOT: We're men, men, men,
Fighters ev'ry one!
Ev'ry mother's son—
SOLDIER GIRLS: Look at our line!
FRENCH GIRLS: The soldiers are a sorry
lot.
Attracted by them we are
not.
MARGOT
AND SOLDIER GIRLS: We are not deceiving you.
Come, pretty maid,
Don't be afraid.
FRENCH GIRLS: A sorry lot of soldier men,
Not one can hold a rifle,
And their coats are large a
trifle—
They're heroes bold and
brave.
MARGOT: You must be believing—
We're heroes all bold and
brave.
SOLDIER GIRLS: You must not believe us, no!
SOLDIER GIRLS: They don't like our
uniforms.
MARGOT: They scoff at our uniforms.
Ha, ha. Aha!
FRENCH GIRLS: We can't help laughing—
Ha, ha, ha, ha, ha, ha!
SOLDIER GIRLS: Take care, take care.
ALL GIRLS: Girls, girls, girls,
Here are cavaliers!
Handsome cavaliers,
Aren't they [we] fine?
MARGOT: We're men, men, men,
Fighters ev'ry one—
And we can't be beaten
in the fighting line!
ALL GIRLS: [imitating bugle call]
Tra ra ra ra ra,
Tra ra ra ra,
Tra ra-ra ra ra ra!

MARGOT: Did you call for soldiers true?
For gallant fighting men of
France?
We are here to answer you,
So let the bugle blow advance!
Out we'll go to rout the foe,
For back at home there waits
perchance
A pretty, charming light
o' love,
An amourette we long to see,
Antoinette or sweet Marie!
That's why we love to fight—
To love the maids of France.

ALL GIRLS: Hark! We seem to hear
The sound of the soldiers
Drawing near.
Here they come at last.
Our day of doom is past.

[MEN *enter*.]

SOLDIERS: Here we are at last.
Our day of fighting is now
past.

MARGOT: Here they are at last.
Our day of gloom is past.

ALL: Here they [we] are at last
Our day of gloom [fight] is
past.
Ta ra, ta ra, ta ra!

MARGOT
AND SOLDIER GIRLS: Soldiers, when the battle is
over,
Let the bugle blow.

MARGOT
AND ALL GIRLS: Ta ta, ra ta, ra ta ta, ra ta,
Let the bugle blow.

SOLDIERS: Ta ra-ta ra ta,
Blow the bugle.
Ta ra-ta ra ta,
Home we go!
Ta ra ta ra ta.

ALL: Ta ra-ta ra ta,
Blow the bugle.
Ta ra-ta ra ta ra!

MARGOT
AND SOLDIERS: Did you call for soldiers true?
For gallant fighting men of
France?
We are here to answer you,
So let the bugle blow advance!
Out we'll go to rout the foe,
For back at home there waits
perchance—

ALL GIRLS: Soldiers, when the battle is
over,
Let the bugle blow.

Ta ta, ra ta, ra ta ta, ra ta,
Ra, ta-ra ta ra, ta,
Ra ta-ta ta,
Ra ta-ta ta,
Ra, ta, ta!
So let the bugle blow advance!
Soldiers, when the battle is
won,
Then let the bugle blow!
Ra ta ta ta,
Ra ta-ta ta ta,
Ra ta-ta ta ta ta.

ALL: A pretty, charming light
o' love,
An amourette we long to see,
Antoinette or sweet Marie!
That's why we love to fight—
To love the maids of France!

ROMANCE

Lyric by Otto Harbach and Oscar Hammerstein II. Published as an individual sheet. Introduced by Vivienne Segal (Margot) and female ensemble (French girls).

A note to singers: In his introduction to the published script of *Carmen Jones*, Hammerstein mentioned a special dislike of altered vowels "so that a lovely word like 'romance' becomes 'romonce'—no word at all."

MARGOT: Romance,
A playboy who is born each spring
To teach the nightingale to sing
A very pretty song:
"I love you."
Romance,
A legend on an old brocade;
A prince who tells a country maid:
"I love you."
Now where this whimsy comes from,
I don't know.
For when it comes it's just
About to go.
Romance,
A flower that will bloom awhile
With sunshine from a lover's smile
That lover's tears bedew.
Ah!

Yet, when I seek this beauty,
Flower of youth's first dawning,
I find a prosy workaday world
Stretching and yawning.
Love is locked up in cages

Kept for a poet's pages.
Life and adventure
Don't seem to be
Paying attention to me!

And so I dream
Of fair romance
And let my fancies
Weave pretty stories.
And though I know
They aren't so,
I like to go
Wand'ring
Amid their wistful glories.

My princes become what I would* them,
And they stay
For the breath of a sigh.
I open my arms to enfold them—
And they've gone,
Like a breeze rushing by.
Ah, this is a humdrum world,
But when I dream I set it dancing.

GIRLS: Her princes become what she would,
And then for a breath of a sigh.
She opens her arms to enfold—
Gone like a breeze rushing by,
Oh, rushing by.
Oh, what a world,
But when she dreams she sets it dancing.

MARGOT: When life is gray,
I have a way to keep it gay—
Passing the day
I dream of love.[†]

THEN YOU WILL KNOW

Lyric by Otto Harbach and Oscar Hammerstein II. Published in the vocal score. Introduced by Robert Halliday (Pierre), Vivienne Segal (Margot), and ensemble. The duet with its ensuing enesmble leads directly into "I Want a Kiss."

PIERRE: My passion is not to crash on
And woo a maiden in modern
fashion.

* *While the published score and script give the word "would," the Romberg holograph score and the published sheet say "mould."*

† *The published sheet and some typescripts end the song with this alternate wording:*
Passing the time of day romancing.

I like the ways of the Old World,
Days of a dear self-controlled
world.
I'd not give you mad embraces
To tear your laces
And make you frown, dear.
I'll kiss the hem of your gown,
dear.
Then you will know I love you.

MARGOT: It is very clear you've never been
a girl.
That's no way to win a girl.

PIERRE: Isn't there a dream that I can
realize?
One girl I can idealize?

MARGOT: Put her on a pedestal and she will
fall.
She is human after all.

PIERRE: All my love is gentle.
My appeal is mental.

MARGOT: She won't hear you* call.

PIERRE: My passion is not to crash on
And woo a maiden in modern
fashion.
I like the ways of the Old World,
Days of a dear self-controlled
world.

MARGOT: But I'm seeking mad embraces.
At courtly graces
I only frown, dear.

PIERRE: I'll kiss the hem of your gown,
dear.
Then you will know I love you.

MARGOT: That is why I can't love you,
dear.

[ENSEMBLE enters.]

MEN: Look at that sight, boys.
Do we see right, boys?
What a delight, boys!
Pierre is in love.

GIRLS AND MEN: Start the bells ringing,
Send the world singing,
Happy news bringing:
Pierre is in love.

MEN: Now, don't be hard on us for
butting in;
We did not mean to be so rude.

GIRLS: Pardon us for cutting in;
We wouldn't for the world
intrude.

MARGOT: Pierre is quite a noble knight,
But he is not the man for me.

---

* The vocal score has "hear you call," but other sources
have "hear your call."

MEN: Where's the sort you
Want to court you?
Who is he?

MARGOT: He must be a rough and ready
man.

MEN: Ready man.

MARGOT: Steady man.

MEN AND GIRLS: Not Pierre.

MARGOT: He must be a strong and heady
man.

MEN: Heady man.

MEN AND GIRLS: That can't be you, Pierre.

MARGOT: I must know that he can master
me.

MEN: What a girl!

MARGOT: What a man!
He must take me, shake me,
break me,
Make me know that I love a
man—
My man!

GIRLS: Who's the man?
He must take her, shake her,
break her,
Make her know that she loves a
man—
Her man!

MEN: Who's the man?
We would like to see him.
What a man—
Her man!

I WANT A KISS

Lyric by Otto Harbach and Oscar Hammerstein II. Published in the vocal score. Introduced by Glen Dale (Paul), Vivienne Segal (Margot), Robert Halliday (Pierre), and ensemble. The song directly follows "Then You Will Know."

PAUL: [entering] What's the noise?
What's the row?
Tell me, boys.
Tell me how
You started up this fearful fuss!

ENSEMBLE: Margot has been amusing us.

PAUL: Margot, I might have known.
What have you done, my own?

MARGOT: I was instructing good Pierre
How to win a lady fair.

PAUL: Pierre, you're not a Romeo—

BOYS: [to each other as PAUL sings] How to
win Margot.

PIERRE: Nor a gay Lothario.
Maybe it is better so.

ENSEMBLE: Oh me, oh my, oh,
Trouble is near, we know.

MARGOT: But till you try it
You never know.

PIERRE: Could you give lessons, dear,
Showing me how?

MARGOT: I will be glad to.

PAUL: We will be glad to.

MARGOT: Come, Paul, let's teach him now.

REFRAIN

PAUL: I want a kiss.
Give it to me—
You know I must have my way.
Love is like this.
Simple, you see.
Let poets say what they may, dear.

MARGOT: You want a kiss.
If you ask me,
What if my answer is
No, dear?
If I refuse,
Then you would lose—
Or would you take me so?

PAUL: You cannot say
No, dear.
If you refuse,
I will not lose—
I will just take you so!

PIERRE: [aside, simultaneous with MARGOT and
PAUL] Oh,
That I might show her that
I too know
How to take her so!

REPEAT REFRAIN

[All exit except PIERRE.]

CODA

PIERRE: If I could only
Hold you, in mad embracing,
Your pulses racing,
You'd not repel me.
Someday I might make you tell me,
Tell me that you love me too.

IT

Lyric by Otto Harbach and Oscar Hammerstein II. Published as an individual sheet. Introduced by Eddie Buzzell (Bennie), Nellie Breen (Susan), and female ensemble.

VERSE 1

BENNIE: There was a time when sex
        Seemed something most complex.
        Mister Freud then employed
        Words we never had heard of.
        He kept us on the string;
        We kept on wondering.
        But the seed of sin
        Now at last has been
        Found by Elinor Glyn.
        In one word
        She defines
        The indefinable thing.

REFRAIN 1

BENNIE: She calls it "It,"
        Just simply "It."
        That is the word
        They're using now
        For that improper fraction
        Of vague attraction
        That gets the action somehow.
        You've either got
        Or you have not
        That certain thing
        That makes 'em cling.
        So if the boys don't seem to fall for you,
        There's just no hope at all for you.
        Give up and quit.
        You'll never hit
        If you have not got "It."

VERSE 2

BENNIE: Joan has a magic lure.
        Jane has a way demure.
        Lou can pet you and get
        Anything she asks for.
        Fay rolls a wicked eye.
        Kay heaves a nifty sigh.
        Mabel shows her knee—
        That's the reason the
        Birds eye Mabel, you see.
SUSAN: Why do you
        Look at them
        And pay no attention to me?

REFRAIN 2

BENNIE: [as a girl walks past] Now, that's "It."
SUSAN: So that's "It."

BENNIE: That wasn't took
        From any book.
        See how her eyes get bolder?
        And look at that shoulder!—
SUSAN: I've got a shoulder.
BENNIE: Yes.
        You have two lips,
        But look at those.
        Look at those eyes,
        Look at those nose—
        Her personality just oozes out.
SUSAN: But what of me?
BENNIE: Your fuse is out.
        Give up and quit—
        You'll never hit.
SUSAN: I wish that I had "It."*

VERSE 2 (FROM BRITISH SHEET MUSIC)

It isn't charm of face
Nor little bits of lace.
Lipstick? No. That can go.
Means just painting the lily.
Somehow she's learnt a game
Making the sheiks go tame.
Girlfriends come around,
Say, "What's this you've found?
Beating us on our ground."
To reply
She may try
But can't quite give it a name.

Act Two reprise refrain

BENNIE: I didn't know
        What I know now:
        That when you kiss
        You are a wow!
        With that improper fraction
        Of vague attraction
        That gets the action—and how!
        I'm never thrilled
        To fingertips
        By baby words
        That leave your lips;
        But when those lips are closed,
        They can convey
        Things no nice girl ought to say.
        When they meet mine
        They make a hit—†
        And the result is "It."

---

* A third refrain followed, mostly dancing, but some
  typescripts give Bennie these lines:
    If I only had a needle so
    I could sew some wild oats.

† Alternate line from published script:
  They seem to fit—

THE DESERT SONG

Lyric by Otto Harbach and Oscar Hammerstein II. Published as an individual sheet. Introduced by Robert Halliday (Red Shadow) and Vivienne Segal (Margot).

Added to the score in Boston (the fourth tryout city), it replaced "Love's Dear Yearning" as the principal love theme. On November 20, 1926, Billboard reported: "Lady Fair to Be Retitled Desert Song for Broadway."

INTRODUCTION

MARGOT: [reprising "Romance"] I open my
            arms to enfold them—
            And they've gone,
            Like a breeze rushing by.
            When life is gray
            I have a way to keep it gay—
            Passing the time of day romancing!
RED SHADOW: Why waste your time *
            In vague romancing,
            When life itself is at your call?
            I come to you, my heart
            advancing—
            Oh, come to me and be my all!
            You turn away, and yet you tremble.
            My little bird has wings, I see.
            Come leave your cage and don't
            dissemble—
            If I but try, I'll make you fly
            with me.

VERSE

RED SHADOW: My desert is waiting—
            Dear, come there with me.
            I'm longing to teach you
            Love's sweet melody.
            I'll sing a dream song to you,
            Painting a picture for two:

REFRAIN

RED SHADOW: Blue heaven and you and I
            And sand kissing a moonlit sky,
            A desert breeze whisp'ring a
            lullaby,
            Only stars above you
            To see I love you:
            Oh, give me that night divine
            And let my arms in yours entwine!
            The desert song calling,
            Its voice enthralling,
            Will make you mine.

[RED SHADOW and MARGOT repeat the refrain.]

---

* This introductory stanza was retained from "Love's
  Dear Yearning," which "The Desert Song" replaced.

ACT ONE FINALE, including OH, LUCKY PAUL and MOROCCO DANCE OF MARRIAGE and SOFT AS A PIGEON and FRENCH MILITARY MARCHING SONG REPRISE and THE DESERT SONG REPRISE

Lyric by Otto Harbach and Oscar Hammerstein II. Published in the vocal score. Introduced by the company.

MARGOT: The wedding will be at nine o'clock.
We'll see you then.
PIERRE: [spoken] Oh, surely. I was just trying to
think what suit I ought to wear.

[PIERRE exits.]

PAUL: [spoken] Fool!

Oh, Lucky Paul

[Crowd enters. A girl gives flowers to MARGOT.]

GIRLS: Oh, lucky Paul,
Tell us all!
Is it really true?
May we but say, "Happy day
And good luck to you!"
PAUL: Thank you.
All we can find to say
Is "thank you."
MARGOT: You are so sweet, all of you.
BOTH: These flowers here mean
friendship dear.
MEN: Margot,
Our Paul will take a
precious cargo
To carry off to Paris.
MARGOT: I thank you all.
What am I to say?
PAUL: I love you, dear little bride-
to-be.
I love you, dear little bride-
to-be.
MEN AND GIRLS: Margot, you sweet, dear
little bride-to-be,
Margot, you sweet, dear
little bride-to-be.
MARGOT: It's hard to say goodbye to
all you dears.

I know that I'll miss you.
PAUL: Come to my side!
You'll be my bride—
PAUL AND MARGOT: Whether you [I] will it or
no, dear.
PAUL AND ENSEMBLE: If you [she] refuse,
I [He] will not lose.
PAUL: I will just take you so.
MARGOT: You'll have to take me so.

[MARGO exits.]

Morocco Dance of Marriage

AZURI: [spoken] Bridegroom, if you did
not have your bride, who
would you love the best?
PAUL: [sung] I'd choose you all.
MEN: He'd choose you all.*
MEN AND GIRLS: He'd like to have them [us] all
in his harem.
AZURI: [spoken] You must choose one.
PAUL: [sung] In that case, I'll choose
Azuri.
MEN AND GIRLS: Oh, what would Margot say
If she saw her bridegroom act
this way?
Now do your dancing, please,
Fair Azuri.
Charm, allure, and tease.
GIRLS: Now what comes next?
MEN: What is the game?
GIRLS: Let's see what's next.
MEN: Come play the game.

Soft as a Pigeon

[AZURI begins a seductive dance.]

SID: Soft as a pigeon lights upon the
sand,
Swift as a tiger she will grip his
hand.
Claws of a tiger sharp with fury,
So is the maid Azuri.
PAUL,
MEN, AND GIRLS: Soft as a pigeon lights upon the
sand,
Swift as a tiger she will grip my
[his] hand.
Oh, beware tiger's claw.
Bridegroom must beware of the
maid Azuri.
Ah!

----

* The published script says:
He'd take them all.

French Military Marching Song Reprise

[MARGOT returns to the stage. PAUL, soldiers, and ensemble exit while singing:]

GIRLS: Soldiers, when the battle is over
Let the bugle blow.
Ta ta, ra ta, ra ta ta, ra ta . . .
MEN: Out we'll go to rout the foe,
For back at home there waits perchance . . .

The Desert Song Reprise

[RED SHADOW and RIFFS enter and take BIRABEAU, SUSAN, and BENNY prisoner. MARGOT points a gun at the RED SHADOW.]

RED SHADOW: [recitative to RIFFS]
I have a command for you all:
If this lady should be brave enough
to kill me,
It is my order that you do not harm
her.
Let her go—
[spoken] unpunished, untouched.
You have heard my command.
[spoken to MARGOT] And you have
heard my command. There is
your pistol—
[sung to MARGOT] And here is my
heart.
RED SHADOW: Blue heaven and you and I
And sand kissing a moonlit sky,
A desert breeze whisp'ring a lullaby,
Only stars above you
To see I love you:
Oh, give me that night divine—
RED SHADOW
AND MARGOT: And let my arms in yours entwine!
The desert song calling,
Its voice enthralling,
Will make you mine!

MY LITTLE CASTAGNETTE

Alternate title: "Opening, Act Two." Lyric by Otto Harbach and Oscar Hammerstein II. Published in the vocal score. Introduced by Margaret Irving (Clementina) and female ensemble (Spanish girls in the palace of Ali Ben Ali).

CLEMENTINA
AND GIRLS: My little castagnette keep singing
(I love to sing to you),
My little castagnette keep bringing

(I love to sing to you)
The memory of Spain, my Spain.
Your clicking and clicking
Is tricking my brain
To make me sigh
For dancing beneath a Spanish sky.
Entrancing, my little castagnette
Never let me be forgetting my
    Spain!

SONG OF THE BRASS KEY

Lyric by Otto Harbach and Oscar Hammerstein II. Published in the vocal score. Introduced by Margaret Irving (Clementina), Lyle Evans (Ali Ben Ali), and female ensemble (harem girls).

VERSE

CLEMENTINA: On the streets of Spain
    Love lies at your feet.
    Love's adventure sweet—
GIRLS: Lives on the streets of Spain.
CLEMENTINA: Ladies beckon you
    With a little key.
    Follow and you'll see—
GIRLS: Just where they beckon you.
CLEMENTINA: So, if you see me slyly swinging
    my key,
    Soon I will see you shyly
      following me.
    I will bring to you
    All the joy I know.
    If you do not go,
CLEMENTINA
AND SOME GIRLS: Then I will sing to you.

REFRAIN 1

CLEMENTINA: There is a key, a key to my heart,
    If you can but find the door.
    Only for me, for me to impart,
    This secret of Loveland lore.
    There is a golden gateway
    That you can open straight'way.
    Just follow me
    And soon you will see
    One kiss is the key to more.
ALI: [spoken] When will these Western
    people be civilized?
    [sung] Women are slaves,
    Men have not realized.
GIRLS: So, we are only common slaves?
ALI: [spoken] Do keep them quiet.

GIRLS: We don't agree.
ALI: [spoken] This is too much.
GIRLS: You have only lived in caves.
    What could you see?
CLEMENTINA: Upon your hill you
    Can wait until you hear.
GIRLS: We tell you.

REFRAIN 2

CLEMENTINA
AND SOME GIRLS: There is a key, a key to my heart,
    If you can but find the door.
    Only for me, for me to impart,
    This secret of Loveland lore.
    There is a golden gateway
    That you can open straight'way.
    Just follow me
    And soon you will see
    One kiss is the key to more!
OTHER GIRLS: Open my heart, I am waiting.
    I will impart my dear secret.
    My golden gateway
    You'll open straight'way.
    Follow me, for a kiss is the key!

SPANISH DANCE

[RED SHADOW arrives with his prisoners MARGOT and SUSAN.*]

REPRISE

CLEMENTINA: Give him the key, the key to your
    heart
    And help him to find the door.
MARGOT: Never! Never!
    Sooner I die!
    [To RED SHADOW] I'll not submit
    to you!
CLEMENTINA: Tell him of Loveland's lore.
CLEMENTINA
AND GIRLS: There is a golden gateway
    That he will open straight'way.
MARGOT: Will you let me go?
CLEMENTINA
AND GIRLS: You know that he is ready to see
    That one kiss is the key to more!
MARGOT: Oh, I hate you, I hate you so!

---

* The Casino Theatre draft instructs: "Margot tugs at the grip of her captors, and stays on long enough to sing a high, dramatic obbligato to effect that she will never open her heart to him . . . She is dragged off on high note."

ONE GOOD BOY GONE WRONG

Title in the program: "One Good Man Gone Wrong." Lyric by Otto Harbach and Oscar Hammerstein II. Published in the vocal score. Introduced by Eddie Buzzell (Bennie), Margaret Irving (Clementina), and the female ensemble (harem girls).

BENNIE: Bold woman,
    Please unhand me!
    You do not understand me.
    I'm not the sort of man
    You seem to think I am.
    I'm not a gay homewrecker,
    I'm just a simple soul,
    Impervious to women, song, and
      drink I am.
CLEMENTINA: And are you sure you are?
BENNIE: Why, yes, I think I am.
CLEMENTINA: So very pure you are?
BENNIE: I'm on the brink, I am.
CLEMENTINA: Ah-ah-ah-ah-ah-ah-ah!
BENNIE: I'm in the sink, I am.
    Gosh, I might as well confess it—
    If I didn't, you would guess it.
    Women are the bane of my youth.
    Ev'ry one's a tiger cat with me.
    It's sad but certain
    That with women life can never be
      smooth;
    For they can trip you with tricks
      and
    Grip you like quicksand.
CLEMENTINA: Someday, dear, you will be mine.
BENNIE: Can't you see I don't want you?
CLEMENTINA: I'll be a constant nymph
    Or something sweet
    To him for whom I pine.*
BENNIE: [spoken] Why do I give in so easily?

REFRAIN 1

BENNIE: One good boy gone wrong,
    One good boy gone wrong.
    Youth must have its fling, so they
      say.

---

* Choral parts found in the Warner-Chappell Collection add here these lines for the female ensemble:
    Might as well give your consent,
    You know that you'll give in eventually.
    Might as well do it now.
    Tra la la la la . . .

Here's where I start flinging my
    youth away.
One more victim picked,
Once more sex has clicked.
One more saphead who's been
    tricked and trapped,
Just another boy gone wrong.

REFRAIN 2

GIRLS: One good boy gone wrong,
One good boy gone wrong.
Give him ten for trying his best
But he has failed just like all of the
    rest.
One more victim picked,
Once more sex has clicked.
One more saphead who's been
    tricked and trapped,
Just another boy gone wrong.

EASTERN AND WESTERN LOVE, including LET LOVE GO and ONE FLOWER GROWS ALONE IN YOUR GARDEN and ONE ALONE

Alternate title: "Concerted Number." Lyrics by Otto Harbach and Oscar Hammerstein II. This group of songs was published as an individual sheet. "One Alone" was also published alone in a simplified version. Introduced by Lyle Evans (Ali Ben Ali), William O'Neal (Sid El Kar), Robert Halliday (Red Shadow), and male ensemble.

The stage directions for this musical sequence explain:

Ali [a bass voice], in verse argues the Eastern theory of love: women are slaves, conveniences to men, not important enough for the slightest sacrifice, to be loved for an hour and then forgotten. Sid [highest tenor] and the men lend their vocal support to these ideas, as Red Shadow [baritone], seated on dais R., remains unimpressed and lost in his own thoughts. As Ali and men finish, there is a recitative interlude—"Romance" is playing beneath Pierre's dialogue, which answers the others. He then goes into song which describes the Western conception of love, and particularly his love for this girl, Margot.

Let Love Go

ALI: Let love come as some rare treasure
Lightly granted by Allah.
Let love go, and do not measure
Hours enchanted that can't return.
One woman you have once caressed—
MEN: When you once caressed—
ALI: Soon strikes you very like the rest.
MEN: Just like all the rest.
ALI: Her kiss is neither worst nor best.
MEN: There is only you, that is love's way.
There is only one way. Ah!
ALI: That is love's way.
So love will come as some rare treasure
Lightly granted by Allah.
Love will go, so take it while you may—
So take it while you may.

One Flower Grows Alone in Your Garden

SID: If one flow'r grows alone in your
    garden,
Its fragrant sweetness will soon pass
    away.
If one flow'r grows alone in your
    garden,
Soft petals blooming must wither
    someday.
Love's bowers should be
    overflowing
With sweet passion flowers of
    varied perfume;
So gather your precious collection—
A harem of blossoms,
Love's fire to consume.
Love's bowers should be overflowing
With passion flowers of varied
    perfume;
So gather a harem of blossoms,
Love's fire consuming—
So let it be known:
One love alone is not for men!
ALI: Let love come as some rare treasure
Lightly granted by Allah.
Let love go, but snatch its pleasure
And ere it fly, fly away.
SID: Snatch up all its joy
Before it starts to fly away.

RECITATIVE

ALI: [to RED SHADOW] Why are you
    silent, my friend?
SID: He is now dreaming of love!
RED SHADOW: I have heard all that you have been
    saying.
Yet I alone may love in my own way.

One Alone

In 1956 Hammerstein told Elizabeth Rider Montgomery that "One Alone" was one of several songs he and Harbach wrote by throwing out words and phrases to each other as they drove around near Harbach's home. It was twice a best seller in 1927, with recordings by Nat Shilkret and Donald Voorhees and their orchestras.

VERSE

RED SHADOW: Lonely as a desert breeze,
I may wander where I please;
Yet I keep on longing
Just to rest a while
Where a sweetheart's tender
    eyes
Take the place of sand and
    skies—
All the world forgotten
In one woman's smile.

REFRAIN

RED SHADOW: One alone
To be my own;
I alone
To know her caresses.
One to be
Eternally
The one my worshipping soul
    possesses.
At her call
I'd give my all,
All my life and all my love
    enduring.
This would be
A magic world to me—
If she were mine alone.

REPEAT REFRAIN [with choral arrangement]

SABRE SONG

Known as "Love Is a Two-Edged Sword" during out-of-town tryouts. Lyric by Otto Harbach and Oscar Hammerstein II. Published in the vocal score. Introduced by Vivienne Segal (Margot) and Robert Halliday (Red Shadow).

MARGOT: I find the simple life entrancing,
Gentle and calm and kind.

RED SHADOW: Didn't you say you liked
    romancing?
    Have you changed your mind?
MARGOT: To be changing her mind is a
    woman's way,
    As you well know.
    I only want Pierre,
    My sweet Pierre.
RED SHADOW: The mind of a woman changes,
    I well know.
    If you long for Pierre,
    That is fair.

[RED SHADOW *exits, saying he will bring* PIERRE *to her.*]

MARGOT: Why, I can take his sword here *
    And with one quick dart right
    through his heart
    Stab him as he mocks me!
    What sweet revenge for all his
    laughter!
    But what is there that halts me and
    stays my arm?
    Something is tearing my heart.
    Is it fate to love him whom I hate?

    There is his sabre there,
    So like the man.
    In brilliance shining fair,
    So like the man.
    Though I mean naught to him,
    Why do I sigh and give my thought
    to him?
    Please tell me why.

    Sabre bright and gleaming,
    Ever by his side,
    Dare I tell my dreaming,
    Dare my heart confide
    All my secret longing,
    Wishes that are thronging,
    Feelings that I vainly try to hide?
    When you're with your master,
    Promise not to tell
    That my heart beats faster
    Neath his magic spell;
    For if you should tell him
    What I'm dreaming of,
    He may call it love.

---

* *The published script begins this song with the words "Why can't I take." Some typescripts and the Warner-Chappell manuscripts have "Why can I take."*

ACT TWO, SCENE 3
FINALETTO

Lyric by Otto Harbach and Oscar Hammerstein II. The finaletto is largely underscoring of dialogue. The following lines of recitative then lead into a duet reprise of the title song. Introduced by Robert Halliday (Red Shadow) and Vivienne Segal (Margot).

RED SHADOW: You love me;
    Never mind how I know.
MARGOT: I'm afraid of you.
RED SHADOW: Blue heaven and you and I *etc.*

FAREWELL

Lyric by Otto Harbach and Oscar Hammerstein II. Published in the vocal score. Introduced by Robert Halliday (Red Shadow) and male ensemble (Riffs).

[*The orchestra plays "Let Love Go" and a melancholy version of the "Riff Song" as* RED SHADOW *says goodbye to each of his men.*]

RED SHADOW: So, it means the Riffs are abroad—
    Before you've bitten—
    [*He breaks off.*]
RIFFS: Mighty Mohammed, the king of
    man,
    Look down upon us and keep us
    from sin.
RED SHADOW: All alone
    To be my own;
    I alone
    To know her caresses,
    One to be
    Eternally
    The one my worshipping soul
    possesses.
    At her call
    I'd give my all,
    All my life and all my love
    enduring.
RIFFS: You'd give your all for your love.
RED SHADOW: This would be
    A magic world to me—
    If she were mine alone.
RIFFS: Good friend, we will pray for you.
    Goodbye!

ALL HAIL THE GENERAL

Alternate title: "Opening, Act Two, Scene 5." Lyric by Otto Harbach and Oscar Hammerstein II. Published in the vocal score. Introduced by Edmund Elton (General Birabeau), Glen Dale (Paul), Vivienne Segal (Margot), and female ensemble.

GIRLS: All hail to the Gen'ral,
    He is the hero of the day!
    All hail to the Gen'ral,
    He is the hero of the day!
GENERAL BIRABEAU: Now, ladies, please.
    The man whom I attacked last
    night
    Simply would not fight.
GIRLS: Dear, modest man,
    You won't deny
    You filled the flying Riffs with
    fright.

[PAUL *tells the* GENERAL *that* MARGOT *won't speak to him.*]

GIRLS: Ah, come and try to cheer
    Your Margot.
    For she is such a dear,
    Your Margot.
    Our highest flight of fancy
    Is when we can see
    Margot of France.

[MARGOT *enters.*]

PAUL: I want a kiss,
    Give it to me.
    You know I must have my
    way.
MARGOT: Please let me go.
GIRLS: Paul, don't you see?
    She is not happy today.

[*Dialogue.* PAUL *exits.*]

MARGOT: [*beginning in the middle of a phrase*] . . . kissing a
    moonlit sky,
    A desert breeze whisp'ring a
    lullaby,
    Only stars above you
    To see I love you—
GIRLS: Oh, give me that night
    divine,
    And let my arms in yours
    entwine!

MARGOT: The desert song calling,
Its voice enthralling—
MARGOT AND GIRLS: Will make you mine.

[MARGOT *bursts into tears.*]

Earlier version

GIRLS: Our troubles will end now—
We've overcome the Riff at last.
Brave soldiers we'll send now
To catch the Riff and tie him fast.
All credit go to one who stayed unafraid.
Where is the maid?
Where did she go?
We call for Margot.
Margot! Margot!

[MARGOT *enters.*]

We are here cheering you, lucky girl.
Quite a few envy you, lucky girl.
MARGOT: I am not a lucky girl;
I'm sad as I can be.
Please pardon me.
GIRLS: Modest maiden.
PAUL: I can't understand the girl.
She will not even talk to me.
BIRABEAU: Don't worry.
GIRLS: Once more you must land the girl—
You're losing out, it's plain to see.
ALL: But what of Birabeau, gallant hero?
It's time we cheered him this happy day.
A son of France, our conquering hero,
Sincerest honor we pay.
You made the fierce Red Shadow
surrender;
From single combat he ran away.
You are our bold and strong defender,
You are the man of the day.

CUT AND UNUSED SONGS

LET'S HAVE A LOVE AFFAIR

Lyric by Otto Harbach and Oscar Hammerstein II. Published as an individual sheet with both *Lady Fair* and *Desert Song* covers, but replaced soon after the show's Broadway opening by an Act Two reprise of "It." Introduced by Eddie Buzzell (Bennie) and Nellie Breen (Susan).

VERSE

BENNIE: Tell me why
Do we two
Wait so long?
SUSAN: What we try,
What we do,
Can't be wrong.
BENNIE: I love you,
And you say you love me.
But for some reason we
Made it a mystery.
SUSAN: Other girls,
Other boys
Play the game.
Lovers gay
Burn away
In Cupid's flame.
BENNIE: We have the right
To ignite like the rest.
Would it be a crime
If at this time
I should suggest—

REFRAIN

BENNIE: Let's have a love affair
And be a happy pair.
If you have time to spare,
Come on and take my dare.
SUSAN: I see no harm in you,
I may find charm in you.
And if I don't, then you
Will get the air.
BENNIE: You could be basking, dear,
In my caressing, dear.
You do the asking, dear;
I'll do the yessing, dear.
My home's a lonely lair;
I'm sick of solitaire.
BOTH: Let me invite you to a love affair.

LOVE'S DEAR YEARNING (DREAMING IN PARADISE)

Alternate title: "Riff Love Song." Lyric by Otto Harbach and Oscar Hammerstein II. Published with a *Lady Fair* cover under the titles "Dreaming in Paradise" and "Love's Dear Yearning," but cut before the Broadway opening. In Boston, the refrain of "Love's Dear Yearning" was replaced by a strain that became the operetta's new title, *The Desert Song*.

VERSE

PIERRE: Why waste your time
In vague romancing
When life itself is at your call?
I come to you,
My heart advancing,
Oh, come to me and be my all!
You turn away,
And yet you tremble;
My little bird has wings, I see.
Come, leave your cage,
And don't dissemble.
If I but try, I'll make you fly with me.

REFRAIN

PIERRE: Love's dear yearning
Shines in your tender eyes.
Love fires burning
Signals you can't disguise.
They have told me
Someday your arms will hold me
And enfold me,
Dreaming in Paradise!
MARGOT: Secret yearnings—
Dare I now look in his eyes?
Would he enfold me,
Hold me, enfold me,
Dreaming in Paradise?

FLAME OF LOVE DENYING

This song is not specifically listed in the New York program and does not appear in the published script or score. However, various scripts use this lyric to begin Act Two, Scene 3.

GIRLS: With scent of perfume rare,
entrancing,
Our little lady fair advancing
To meet her ardent love.
MARGOT: [*defiantly*] No love will he know.
There'll be no
Response to his love!
GIRLS: But what a shame, denying
And letting such a flame go dying!
GIRLS: The flame of love should be
Burning brave and free.
MARGOT: The flame of love may be
Glowing here in me,
But never for him!

CAPTIVE MAIDS OF WAR

This precursor to "My Little Castagnette" was found in the Romberg holograph piano-vocal score and in the Warner-Chappell collection, both at the Library of Congress.

SOME GIRLS: Captive maids of war,
Captive maids of war,
We have had exciting days—
Will there be more?
Maids of Spain,
We've come far away.
Though tomorrow
May bring us sorrow,
This is the day.
OTHER GIRLS: Still we will be gay,
Come then, come what may.
French, Spanish, or Riff,
What is the diff'rence?
All men have their way.
SOME GIRLS: Who is coming this way?
OTHER GIRLS: Ali is coming this way.
SOME GIRLS: What do you think he will say?
Is he deciding to slay?
OTHER GIRLS: Though he is nice in his way, they say,
Some way we'll pay.
SOME GIRLS: Oh, what a day for the maids of Spain!
We've come far away.
Though tomorrow
May bring us sorrow,
This is the day.
OTHER GIRLS: Come then, come what may.
French, Spanish, or Riff,
What is the diff'rence?
All men have their way.

GOLDEN DAWN (1927)

Tryouts: Shubert Playhouse, Wilmington, Delaware, September 22–24, 1927; Shubert Alvin Theatre, Pittsburgh, September 26–October 8, 1927; Detroit Opera House, October 10–22, 1927; Hanna Theatre, Cleveland, October 24–29, 1927; Shubert Theatre, Philadelphia, November 14–26, 1927. New York run: Hammerstein's Theatre (inaugural production); opened November 30, 1927; closed May 5, 1928; 184 performances. A Musical Drama. Produced by Arthur Hammerstein. Book and

lyrics by Otto Harbach and Oscar Hammerstein II. Music by Emmerich Kálmán and Herbert Stothart. Book staged by Reginald Hammerstein. Dances and ensembles staged by Dave Bennett. Musical direction by Herbert Stothart. Settings by Joseph Urban. Costumes by Mark Mooring.

Cast: Louise Hunter (Dawn), Paul Gregory (Steve Allen), Robert Chisholm (Shep Keyes), Marguerita Sylva (Mooda), Kumar Goshal (Hasmali), Gil Squires (Blink Jones), Olin Howland (Sir Alfred "Duke" Hammersley), Nydia d'Arnell (Johanna),* Reginald Pasch (Captain Eric), Carlo Benetti (Dago), Archie Leach [Cary Grant] (Anzac), Len Mence (Pigeon), Paula Ayers (Sister Hedwig), W. Messenger Bellis (Colonel Judson), Barbara Newberry (Ann Milford), Henry Pemberton (Dr. Milford), Robert Paton Gibbs (an Old Man of Africa), Jacques Cartier (Witch Dancer), Kohana (Dancing Girl), Hazel Drury (Mombassa Moll), and ensemble (German soldiers and English, American, and Italian prisoners; Native men, Askari guards and native women; nurses and sisters).

Several cultures interact in the 1917 East African jungle clearing where Mooda, a native woman, runs a canteen. Her patrons include German soldiers and rubber planters, and American and British men who became prisoners-of-war when hostilities erupted in Europe. Nearby are a church mission and a Red Cross infirmary. A romance has developed between Mooda's daughter Dawn and planter/prisoner Steve Allen, but Mooda strongly disapproves, because Dawn is expected to serve as a virgin priestess in the local religion. The other men warn Steve that he could never marry an African anyway. Also disapproving is the strong and violent native man known as Shep Keyes, who wants Dawn for himself. Subsidiary characters are the American "Blink" and the Englishman "Duke," two prisoners of war, who vie for the attentions of Johanna, a Red Cross nurse. The night before Dawn's initiation ceremony, Steve breaks away to be with her. But the lovers are parted at the end of Act One, when the prisoners are relocated.

The second act begins a few years later, during a terrible drought. Dawn has been sequestered the whole time. Johanna and Blink have married. The outpost is now under British command, in the person of Colonel Judson. Ann, a British girl, is expecting her fiancé to arrive; he is none other than the Duke. The natives believe their priestess has failed them and desperately ask the colonel for help from the white man's god. Steve arrives in time to see Dawn rushed by a frantic crowd. As she tries to make her way to safety in the mission, Shep grabs her. Mooda hits him over the head with a cross from the mission and reveals that Dawn is really the daughter of a white man. Dawn and Steve are reunited, and, finally, there is rain.

In some sources the name is Hannah.

A film version produced by Warner Bros.–Vitaphone Pictures, was released in July 1930. It was directed by Ray Enright and starred Vivienne Segal, Walter Woolf, and Noah Beery. Hammerstein did not write any of the new songs in the film.

The main source for this chapter is a piano-conductor score in Herbert Stothart's hand at the Tams-Witmark Music Library in New York City. Because the show's program does not provide a full song list, it was essential to study the script, drafts of which are preserved in the Oscar Hammerstein II Collection in the Music Division of the Library of Congress; in the Otto Harbach Collection in the New York Public Library for the Performing Arts; at Tams-Witmark; in the Stothart Collection at UCLA; and in the Warner Bros. archive at USC. No lyric has been found for "Belle of Mombassa."

Little is known about Harbach and Hammerstein's method of collaboration for this show, or about Kálmán and Stothart's, or how noted European operetta composer Robert Stolz became co-composer of the (not quite) title song.

Golden Dawn was the first show to play the new Hammerstein Theatre (now the Ed Sullivan Theatre), built by Arthur in tribute to his father, Oscar I. The leading female role was cast with a Metropolitan Opera soprano. The show's serious artistic intentions were further signaled by a note in the program: "The musical numbers are an integral part of the story as it evolves, and therefore are not listed as independent songs. The titles of the principal themes are: 'When I Crack My Whip,' 'We Two,' 'Here in the Dark,' 'My Bwanna,' 'Consolation,' 'Africa,' 'Dawn,' 'Jungle Shadows.'" The show's depiction of native African characters (and even Italians) was very much of its time.

OPENING: PLAY ON, PIPER

Lyric by Otto Harbach and Oscar Hammerstein II. Music by Emmerich Kálmán and Herbert Stothart. Not published. Introduced by Marguerita Sylva (Mooda, Dawn's mother), Kumar Goshal (Hasmali, the priest) and ensemble (natives). The actor playing the Piper was not credited in the program.*

ENSEMBLE: Play on, piper!
Keep on singing
While sacred gifts to Dawn we're bringing—

In the Wilmington tryout, the Piper was played by Jacques Cartier; in the Pittsburgh tryout, by Patrick Walshe. But the role is not even listed in the New York program.

Ah!

MEN: Go and say to the mother
We must speak of her daughter, Dawn.

ENSEMBLE: Mother Mooda,
Mother Mooda,
Songs we are singing
While we're bringing
Gifts for fairest Dawn.

MEN: Wedding songs we are singing,
Wedding gifts we are bringing.

MOODA: You say you're bringing your presents
for Dawn?

WOMEN: It's for your Dawn.

MOODA: All this?

ENSEMBLE: It's for Dawn.

MOODA: And this?

ENSEMBLE: Everything we've brought,
It is for Dawn.

MOODA: From you?

ENSEMBLE: Not from us.

MOODA: From you?

ENSEMBLE: Not from us.

MOODA: From you?

ENSEMBLE: Not from us.
The gifts we bring to you
Are from Mulunghu.
Gifts from Mulunghu, god of Africa!
Great god Mulunghu.
He comes to ask for Dawn,
For your Dawn.

MOODA: Dawn!*

HASMALI: From Mulunghu
I bring this word to you:
He loves your daughter, Dawn.
Your gentle Dawn
He would woo.

PIPER: To save a thousand souls
One soul I place apart:
A virgin. She shall be thabu!
No man shall touch her heart.

HASMALI: From Mulunghu
I bring those words to you:
With bad luck you'll be through
If Dawn will be thabu.

ALL: We [They] have chosen Dawn thabu,
We [They] have chosen Dawn thabu.
Our bad days are past,
Our good days will last,
For Dawn will marry
Our great god Mulunghu.
Our ancient god.

---

* In some scripts these lines follow:

MESSENGER: The holy man of the temple,
Hasmali, the servant of Mulunghu,
Brings a message from his sacred
master.

THE WHIP

Alternate title: "When I Crack My Whip." Lyric by Otto Harbach and Oscar Hammerstein II. Music by Emmerich Kálmán and Herbert Stothart. Published as an individual sheet. Introduced by Robert Chisholm (Shep Keyes). Recorded by Robert Chisholm (Brunswick); Noah Beery's rendition from the film soundtrack appeared on the Pearl Flapper CD *Why Ever Did They? Hollywood Stars at the Microphone.*

VERSE

Listen, little whip,
While yo' in my grip,
While I got an arm
Wid strength left to sling ya—
Yo' a friend to me,
You kin make me be
Way above de heads of frails when I sling ya.
I don't need no brains—
I kin hold de reins
Long as I have you to give dem pains.

REFRAIN

Dey hear me crack my whip
And dey crawl,
'Cause when I crack my whip,
Dat's my call.
Fo' in dis ole hell-hole down in Africa
I am de big boss man of dem all!
You must bow down to me,
White or black;
You got to bend yo' knee,
Break yo' back.
And when I wants a thing,
Den I gets dat thing,
Fo' in dis ole hell-hole
I'm de king!

AFRICA

Lyric by Otto Harbach and Oscar Hammerstein II. Music by Emmerich Kálmán and Herbert Stothart. Not published. Introduced by Reginald Pasch (Captain Eric), Paul Gregory (Steve Allen), Olin Howland (Sir Alfred "Duke" Hammersley), Gil Squires (Blink Jones), Carlo Benetti (Dago), and male ensemble (prisoners).

ERIC: What if you're defeated or victorious
Out in this glorious

Tropical land of sunny skies?
War, it isn't bad if you're in Africa,
Beautiful Africa,
Filled with a charm that mystifies.

MEN: Cap, we all agree with you—
Cap, we think you're right!

ERIC: Come and let us lift a glass to Africa,
Wonderful Africa—
Come, let us praise her with a song!

REFRAIN

MEN: We're for you, Africa,

ANZAC: One god-awful spot!

JIM: It's the worst bloomin' blot
That the earth ever got.

BUD: Where the sun, beatin' hot,
Keeps you dry an' drowsy.
Full o' frowsy flies!

MEN: Bugs!
The place is lousy!
Africa!

BLINK: All diamonds and gold.
You can read where it's told
On the maps of your old geography.

PIGEON: They say there are great spots in
Africa—

MEN: Where in the hell can they be?

STEVE: You can talk about this country—
It's the place I love to roam.

DUKE: You can roam about this country—
I will read about it at home.

MEN: Africa!

DUKE: Though the very most intriguing of all
after-dinner topics
Is a talk about the charm and
fascination of the tropics,
It's altogether different when you're in
the jungle thickness
And you meet a friendly tsetse fly who's
full of sleeping sickness—
Those are things I'd rather read about
at home!

MEN: Africa!

DUKE: When you're up a tree and realize no
cleverness or force'll
Keep a lioness from thinking you a most
enticing morsel,
You climb a little higher, and you think
that you have tricked her,
Till you meet a big, affectionate,
embracing boa constrictor—
Those are things I'd rather read about at
home!

MEN: Africa!

DUKE: Though it's hard to keep a pious
missionary a good believer

When mosquitos start to pump him with
   malaria and the fever.
If once I reach my native land, I never
   want to leave her,
For I'd rather read about those things at
   home!
MEN: You said it!
Home sweet home,
Wherever it be—
Take us back 'cross the sea.
BLINK: You said it!
America.
You guys like to sing
Like the birds on the wing
Of the "old country" thing.
But if I start to sing,
I will get the razz, Bo—
So I'll express the U.S. in the terms of
   jazzbo!

[He dances the second half of refrain.]

DAGO: Italy!
No place sweeter than
My old home in Milan!
That's the place where a man
Likes to sing all he can
In quartet or trio—
And if he's left alone, then it's sole mio!
"O, sole—"
MEN: That's enough of that!
DAGO: Italy mine,
Where the grapes bend the vine,
And the girls are as fine as can be!
I know a bambina back in Italy—
Italy, save her for me!

Additional lyrics from piano sketches

STEVE: When you leave the mystery of Africa,
Beautiful Africa,
Life will be humdrum, dull and tame.
Then you will no longer be adventurers,
Dashing adventurers—
Day after day will seem the same.
MEN: Steve, we don't agree with you—
Steve, we think you're wrong.
Furthermore, Steve,
You have your reasons why
You like this bloomin' god-forsaken place.
It's not the landscape or the seasons—
It's the smile upon a lady's face!
STEVE: What do you mean?
MEN: You know.
STEVE: Dawn?
MEN: You know.
STEVE: Maybe so.
Can you complain of darkest Africa

When Dawn's laughter calls the world to
   play?
MEN: We kind of thought you felt that way.

MY BWANNA

Lyric by Otto Harbach and Oscar Hammerstein II.
Music by Emmerich Kálmán and Herbert Stothart.
Published as an individual sheet. Introduced by Louise
Hunter (Dawn) and ensemble.

VERSE

DAWN: Someone maybe ask me question,
Why I'm glad or maybe why I'm sad.
I can always give the answer quick like
   fun,
Because there's only one.
Some day I am happy like a laughing
   boy
Playing with his spear, his newest toy.
Then the very thing that made me
   happy
Make me very mad and scrappy,
Till no more be happiness and joy.
It is fault of him I call my Bwanna.
ENSEMBLE: Tell us more about this wondrous
   Bwanna!

REFRAIN

DAWN: Who have brave and tender eyes?
My Bwanna!
Who be sensible and wise?
My Bwanna!
Not one single man alive can rule
   him;
Not one single girl alive can fool him.
Who be strongest of the strong?
My Bwanna!
Who be never in the wrong?
My Bwanna!
Who be chieftain always in my breast?
Who be the one that I must always
   love the best?
My Bwanna!

JOHANNA'S ENTRANCE and IT IS WAR

Lyric by Otto Harbach and Oscar Hammerstein II.
Music by Emmerich Kálmán and Herbert Stothart. Not
published. Introduced by Nydia d'Arnell (Johanna),
Louise Hunter (Dawn), and ensemble (nurses, soldiers).

Johanna's Entrance

NURSES: We have come to see our friend
   Fräulein Dawn.
SOLDIERS: Fräulein Dawn.
JOHANNA: *[to DAWN]* If you count to ten and close
   your eyes,
We'll give you a prize.
NURSES: It is something that you want,
   Fräulein Dawn.
SOLDIERS: Fräulein Dawn.
DAWN: Something nice to eat?
JOHANNA: No. Better guess again, dear.
DAWN: Shoes to hurt my feet?
JOHANNA: No. Better guess again, dear.
NURSES: Better close your eyes,
And you will get your prize!
JOHANNA: Eins, zwei, drei, vier, fünf,
   sechs, sieben, acht, neun, zehn!

[She presents a Red Cross apprentice uniform.]

DAWN: A Red Cross dress!
Mine.
JOHANNA: We need an assistant.
DAWN: Me?
JOHANNA: This is your uniform.
DAWN: Oh, Johanna!
JOHANNA: Here. Put it on.

It Is War

NURSES: You've become a nurse,
   Fräulein Dawn.
SOLDIERS: Fräulein Dawn.
JOHANNA AND NURSES: There are certain rules you
   must obey
Ev'ry single day,
So you might as well
   rehearse, Fräulein
   Dawn—
SOLDIERS: Fräulein Dawn.
JOHANNA AND NURSES: How to do your duty.
Wounded soldiers need
   some kissing on the
   QT—
For a noble deed, some
   sweet reward of beauty

JOHANNA, NURSES, AND
SOLDIERS:

Ought to come your way.

Watch your man with
tender eyes.
That is war, and you must
play the game.
On your arm his head
must lie.
That is war, and you are
not to blame.
If a kiss will reassure him,
And you think that it will
cure him,
Do your bit.
You'll have to make the
best of it.
It's only war!

WE TWO

Lyric by Otto Harbach and Oscar Hammerstein II.
Music by Emmerich Kálmán and Herbert Stothart.
Published as an individual sheet. Introduced by Nydia
d'Arnell (Johanna) and Olin Howland (Duke).

VERSE 1

JOHANNA: Though I'm interested in the thing
that you propose, sir,
Looking at it closer,
Sir, let me state:
If your offer of your life and love
includes your name, sir,
Then I will be game, sir,
To set the date.

REFRAIN 1

JOHANNA: Forever just we two,
A dream that we must see through.
If only you'll trust me to,
I'll make a good wife.
DUKE: Will you?
JOHANNA: If you would be with me,
Have breakfast and tea with me,
Sign up and agree with me
To make it for life;
If you want me to be
Exclusively yours,
Just guarantee to be
Exclusively mine.
And then, my pet, see to
Some church you can get me to—
Then we'll be all set, we two,
And that'll be fine.

VERSE 2

DUKE: As I understand it, you are willing to
be my girl,
Making my reply, girl—
Girl, let me state:
If it's your idea to make the contract
even firmer,
Darling, let me murmur:
I think it's great!

REFRAIN 2

DUKE: Forever just we two,
A dream that we must see through.
If only you'll trust me to,
I'll make you my wife.
JOHANNA: Will you?
DUKE: If you would be with me,
Have breakfast and tea with me,
Sign up and agree with me
To make it for life;
If you want me to be
Exclusively yours,
Just guarantee to be
Exclusively mine.
Just one step more—see to
A home with a doorkey too,
Another key for me too,
And that'll be fine.

DAWN

Lyric by Otto Harbach and Oscar Hammerstein II.
Music by Robert Stolz and Herbert Stothart. Published
as an individual sheet. Introduced by Paul Gregory
(Steve) and male ensemble.

VERSE

Early, when dawn of day is gleaming,
Pearly the morning dew lies dreaming,
Dreaming with me about a girl we know,
So sweet it seems dawn brought her
For her daughter.

REFRAIN

Dawn, that's the name we chose for you.
Dawn, ev'ry sunrise glows for you.
Daylight, it never breaks
Until my little Dawn awakes
To drive the dark of night away.
How you drive the night away—
Dawn, you were born to light my day!

Skies are more fair when they're reflected in your
eyes;
Ev'ry little thing about you
Makes me call you Dawn!

WHEN YOU'RE YOUNG

Lyric by Otto Harbach and Oscar Hammerstein II.
Music by Emmerich Kálmán and Herbert Stothart. Not
published. Introduced by Marguerita Sylva (Mooda).
Reprised by Mooda in Act Two.

Little girl, little girl,
You are all that I [illegible]
And I want you to know what I know.
For the right is the right,
And the wrong is the wrong,
And there's only one way
That you can go.
When you're young,
Then you love
And you fly
To the sky
With the man
That you think is a god.
Ah! then the man
That was god
Lets you go
And you fall
And you think
That there's no god at all.

LULLABY

Lyric by Otto Harbach and Oscar Hammerstein II.
Music by Emmerich Kálmán and Herbert Stothart. Not
published. Introduced by Marguerita Sylva (Mooda) and
Louise Hunter (Dawn).

DAWN: Mooda, Mooda,
I'll do what you say.
MOODA: Mooda loves you—
Let her show the way.
Ever since you baby girl,
Mooda watch and hope.

[Dialogue.]

MOODA AND DAWN: When you're dreaming, my
baby, baby,
Will you dream of me too?
For when Mother is dreaming,
baby,
All my dreams are of you.
All my dreams are for you.

I STAND BEFORE
THE MOON

Lyric by Otto Harbach and Oscar Hammerstein II.
Music by Emmerich Kálmán and Herbert Stothart. Not
published. Introduced by Louise Hunter (Dawn).

I stand before the moon,
Alone and unadorned,
And in his naked light
Bathe my soul tonight,
Cleanse my soul in the moon.
Tonight, I join a god
Beneath the moon.
I stand before the moon alone.

HERE IN THE DARK

Lyric by Otto Harbach and Oscar Hammerstein II.
Music by Emmerich Kálmán and Herbert Stothart.
Published as an individual sheet. Introduced by Paul
Gregory (Steve Allen) and Louise Hunter (Dawn).

UNPUBLISHED INTRODUCTION

DAWN: In the dark your eyes are shining so,
I'm afraid to listen to your voice.
STEVE: You are here.
I will not let you go, darling.
DAWN: Oh, Bwanna, I love you, darling.
STEVE: Dawn!
DAWN: Bwanna, I love you.
I love you!

VERSE

DAWN: If "despair is folly," Yasmin say,
I believe I ought to think that way.
When sometimes I start to worry,
I remember in a hurry
To be thankful for one happy day.

Happy day, when once I thrilled to hear
Pretty words from someone who was dear.

REFRAIN

STEVE: Here in the dark let the world melt away;
All that is left will be this place where we
can stay,
Only love and you and I
Neath a silent sky.
Let tomorrow die
With yesterday.
Here in the dark is a sweet place to be.
Here in your arms I'd while away eternity.
Here's the end of time and space—
There's no other place,
There's no other world,
When you're with me.

UNPUBLISHED CODA

STEVE: I am yours,
You are mine.
DAWN: Bwanna, that is true.
Other girls have their dreams,
I want my dream too.

ACT ONE FINALE, including
MULUNGHU THABU

Lyric by Otto Harbach and Oscar Hammerstein II.
Music by Emmerich Kálmán and Herbert Stothart. "Mulunghu Thabu" published as an individual
sheet. Introduced by Kumar Goshal (Hasmali), Louise
Hunter (Dawn), an unidentified player (Piper), and ensemble (natives).

PIPER: Where is the maid who will marry the
god,
Marry the great Mulunghu?
ENSEMBLE: Where is the maid who will marry the
god,
Marry the great Mulunghu?
HASMALI: All calm and still, she bows to your
will,
O Mulunghu!
ENSEMBLE: Waiting for you who will make her
thabu!
HASMALI: She's waiting now to make you her
vow,
O Mulunghu!
ENSEMBLE: Waiting for you who will make her
thabu!

HASMALI: Mulunghu, she waits for you.
PIPER: Who'll tell the maiden what she is
to do
When she becomes thabu?

REFRAIN

ENSEMBLE: "Mulunghu thabu,"
That means that you
Have given all your love to Mulunghu.
Jealous god above
Must have his love,
A maiden pure and tender as a dove;
When he wants to woo you, woo you,
woo you,
No man dare be lover to you, to you.
Be to Mulunghu forever true.
You are eternally thabu!
DAWN: To save a thousand souls
One soul I place apart.
A virgin I shall be.
[spoken] Oh, my people, I am
unworthy to marry the great god!
[sung] Mulunghu must know,
Mulunghu must know
To this heart of mine there comes a
blinding fear
To see his shining glory.

[Dialogue.]

ENSEMBLE: We have chosen you thabu,
Thabu, thabu.
DAWN: Thabu I've sworn to be.

CHANT SPIRITUAL:
MAKE IT BLACK

Alternate title: "Opening, Act Two." Lyric by Otto Harbach and Oscar Hammerstein II. Music by Emmerich
Kálmán and Herbert Stothart. Not published. Introduced by the ensemble (natives).

Look up,
Look up, up.
You look up,
We look up, up!
The sun is looking down with one big flaming eye.
The eye belong to some hot white face in the sky.
Make it black,
Make it black, black,
Make clouds black clouds.
Black, black, the heat,

Heat is like fire that runs through the land,
And his two slaves are sickness and death.
Drive him back.
Send him back, back!
The mothers cry out and beat their breast,
And the hearts of the fathers are heavy,
Heavy to see their dead chillun before them.

IT'S ALWAYS THE WAY

Alternate title: "Hannah's Lament." Lyric by Otto Harbach and Oscar Hammerstein II. Music by Emmerich
Kálmán and Herbert Stothart. Published as an individual sheet. Introduced by Nydia d'Arnell (Johanna).

VERSE

What does it matter?
It's all in the game,
The game where passions burn.
What does it matter?
All men are the same.
I guess we live and learn.

REFRAIN

It's always the way
That the man who will betray
Is the man you have foolishly trusted.
And though he may wed,
Flames of love are quickly dead
And the ring on your finger is rusted.
But the sweetheart who swore
That he'd always adore
And whose letters you've secretly dusted—
When he too forgets,
Leaves you only with regrets,
With the whole race of men you're disgusted.

CONSOLATION

Lyric by Otto Harbach and Oscar Hammerstein II.
Music by Emmerich Kálmán and Herbert Stothart.
Published as an individual sheet. Introduced by Barbara
Newberry (Ann) and Gil Squires (Blink).

VERSE 1

BLINK: Now that you see why I am blue,
You've got to agree that you could do

A lot
If you'd just be good to me.
ANN: What is the lot that I can do?
BLINK: The lot you can do is only to
Be not
Just a piece of wood to me.

REFRAIN

BLINK: I'll tell you what I need,
I need your consolation,
Just a touch of tender demonstration.
I need a little more than friendly
conversation.
What I need I cannot get by phone.
I need to feel that pressure upon my
lips
As they caress your own.
I'll tell you what I'll do to show
appreciation,
I'll let no one console me but you
alone!

VERSE 2*

ANN: Once in a while I get like you.
I try to smile, but no can do
And fun
Simply won't stay close to me.
BLINK: Then sympathy is what I crave,
And I get to be the willing slave
Of one
Who is not morose to me.

REPEAT REFRAIN

RAIN INVOCATION

Lyric by Otto Harbach and Oscar Hammerstein II. Music
by Emmerich Kálmán and Herbert Stothart. Not published. Introduced by Louise Hunter (Dawn), Robert
Chisholm (Shep Keyes), and ensemble (natives). Paul
Gregory (Steve), who has returned to the village just as
the ceremony begins, joins at the end of the number.

ENSEMBLE: Now, now Hasmali comes.
Listen to his words!
DAWN: Come near, oh, my people.
Come near, oh, my people,
And hear, oh, my people!

---

* *The lyric for verse 2 appears only in the published
sheet.*

SHEP KEYES: Now, before she prays send all
evil away!*
Let the tom-tom play louder,
And bring the sacred drum,
And bid the warrior dancer
come
And drive the devils all away!†
All evil he'll drive away—
Devils he'll drive away!
ENSEMBLE: Dabble a dooka, dooka!
DAWN: To you who rule the boundless
sky,‡
To you we raise our cry.
ENSEMBLE: O Mulunghu,
We pray to you:
Oh, send your people rain!
DAWN: And we must die
If you let us cry
In vain!
ENSEMBLE: Send us, oh, send us,
Oh, send us the rain!

[*Dialogue.*]

DAWN: Here in the dark, let the world
melt away;
All that is left will be a place
where we can stay.
Only love, you and I,
Neath a silent sky.
Let tomorrow die
With yesterday.
Here in the dark is a sweet place
to be.
Here in your arms I'd while away
eternity.
Here's the end of time and
space—
There's no other place,
There's no other world,
When you're with me.
STEVE: My words!
Why does she sing my song?
Can she mean it?
Dawn,
If she'd only comprehend me.
I'm in the dark

---

* *A typescript has:*
Now before we pray, drive all evil away.

† *A typescript has:*
And drive all evil away.

‡ *A typescript has:*
To you who rule the soundless sky,

For all eternity.
Just a word or two—
One would do!
What can I do?

NATIVE WOMEN: Great god Mulunghu!
She's been true to you,
O Mulunghu.
She is calling to our god!
O great god Mulunghu,
A faithful bride she's been to
you.
O Mulunghu,
Her wedding vow to you.
Mulunghu,
She's calling
Now to you,
O Mulunghu!

NATIVE MEN: Great god Mulunghu!
She's been true to you,
O Mulunghu.
She is calling to our god!
O Mulunghu,
She's been faithful and true.
True to you,
Mulunghu,
Through all eternity—
To her wedding vows
She has been true,
O Mulunghu!

SHEP: She is calling someone,
But quite in vain.
'Twas in the dark
That her love song re-echoed.
There in the dark,
She whiled away eternity.
'Tis the end of time and space,
No other place.
No place for me.

JUST TO TEST MY LOVE FOR YOU

Alternate title: "Be My Thabu." Lyric by Otto Harbach and Oscar Hammerstein II. Music by Emmerich Kálmán and Herbert Stothart. Not published. Introduced by Barbara Newberry (Ann), Gil Squires (Blink), Nydia d'Arnell (Johanna), and Olin Howland (Duke).

ANN: [*to* DUKE] Just to test my love for
you—
That is why I go with other boys.
How can you be sure I'm true

Until I have met some other boys?*

JOHANNA: [*to* BLINK] So you thought you could
deceive me!

BLINK: [*to* JOHANNA] Listen, dear, you must
believe me,
What I did was for the best—
I had to test my love for you.

DUKE: I'm just an old-fashioned sort of a man:
Don't believe in mingling the sexes.
Do not approve of the Freudian plan
Blaming it all on complexes!

JOHANNA: We'll take a tip from the African god—

BLINK: The one called Mulunghu!

JOHANNA: Each maid he takes in wedlock
He promptly makes—

ALL: Thabu!

DUKE: [*to* ANN] You be my thabu,
Be my thabu,
And keep those other boys away from
you!

JOHANNA: [*to* BLINK] When the girls like you,
Be nice to you,
Just shrink away and say
Thabu! Thabu!

DUKE: [*to* ANN] You must be a one-man
woman, damn me—
Don't you try to give me polygamy.

JOHANNA: [*to* BLINK] If you're what you say,
Decide today
To be or not to be—

ALL: Thabu!

JUNGLE SHADOWS

Lyric by Otto Harbach and Oscar Hammerstein II. Music by Emmerich Kálmán and Herbert Stothart. Not published.

The program note cites "Jungle Shadows" as a prominent musical theme and credits its performance to Hazel Drury (Mombassa Moll), but the script calls for Steve to sing it. Possibly the song was conflated with the missing "Belle of Mombassa," which immediately preceded it.

Jungle shadows falling
Like a leopard crawling.

* *A typescript gives* ANN *an alternate for lines 4–8:*
Until I can know some other boys?
Up to date I've tried a few, dear—
There's no mate for me like you, dear.
Let me flirt with all the rest,
It's just to test my love for you.

Black jaws open wide—
You better run and hide.
White man, when they've found you,
Black arms will surround you.
When they hold you so,
They never let you go.
You can fly away and go where
Jungle land seems nowhere,
And you laugh because you think that you're
free.
Jungle shadows crawling
Ever will be calling,
"White man, you'll come back to me!"

MISCELLANEOUS SONGS

IN ARABY WITH YOU

Lyric by Otto Harbach and Oscar Hammerstein II. Music by Jerome Kern. Published as an individual sheet. This song was interpolated into *Criss Cross* (opened Globe Theatre, October 12, 1926; book and lyrics by Harbach and Anne Caldwell; music by Kern). Introduced by Dorothy Francis (Yasmine) and female ensemble.

Kern biographer Gerald Bordman points out that the melody had been used twice before. Harry B. Smith set it as "I Can't Forget Your Eyes" for *Oh, I Say* (1913); and Hammerstein and Harbach used it as "Sunshine" in *Sunny*.

VERSE

Often I wonder whether
You, like myself, can see
Places we knew together
In distant Araby.
Saddle to saddle riding
Over the distant trail,
Secrets of love confiding;
Stars were turning pale.
Desert love is burning fire—
Could I have my one desire?

REFRAIN

I'd be with you very close beside me,
Waiting till the moon came spreading white
light,
Making all the desert night light,
Neath a silken tent of blue.

South breeze, blowing from the far-off South
    Seas;
Tom-toms beat a soft tattoo, too.
So tell me that my heart is mid the palm trees
There in Araby with you!

TRUE LOVE

Not published. No music has been identified for this
song. A typed lyric sheet was found inside a Hammerstein scrapbook from the mid-1920s.

VERSE

Once I had a silly notion
That I owed a man devotion—
'Twas all a mistake,
A bitter mistake.
Now I see the truth so clearly:
Only fools can love sincerely.
Were I to live my life again,
I'd never give my heart in vain.

REFRAIN

True love is a folly,
Full of melancholy—
Take the word of one who is wise.
Use love as a plaything,
Choose love as a gay thing—
Toy with joy but turn and go
Before you come to tears and woe.
Kind love is a fancy;
Blind love never can see—
Close your heart and open your eyes.
A new love that lives for only a day
Is sweeter than a true love that dies.

Top left: *Ava Gardner as Julie in the 1951 film*
Top right: *Julie swoons in the 1927 Broadway
production. Left to right, Rubber Face (Francis X.
Mahoney), Steve (Charles Ellis), Julie (Helen
Morgan), Magnolia (Norma Terris), Ellie (Eva
Puck), Captain Andy (Charles Winninger), and
Parthy (Edna May Oliver)*
Bottom: *In the 1936 film, Magnolia (Irene Dunne,
center) shows Joe (Paul Robeson, left), Queenie
(Hattie McDaniel), and Julie (Helen Morgan) how
she shuffles to the tune of "Can't Help Lovin' Dat
Man."*

SHOW BOAT | 1927

*Parthy (Edna May
Oliver, right of center
in striped gown) tries
to stop Gay and
Magnolia's wedding
(Howard Marsh and
Norma Terris, center).
Captain Andy (Charles
Winninger) is left of the
bridal couple. Between
Parthy and the pair are
Frank and Ellie (Sammy
White and Eva Puck).*

SHOW BOAT (1927)

Tryouts: National Theatre, Washington, D.C., November 15–19, 1927; Nixon Theatre, Pittsburgh, November 21–26, 1927; Ohio Theatre, Cleveland, November 28–December 3, 1927; Erlanger Theatre, Philadelphia, December 5–24, 1927. New York run: Ziegfeld Theatre; opened December 27, 1927; closed May 4, 1929; 572 performances. An All American Musical Comedy adapted from Edna Ferber's novel of the same name. Music by Jerome Kern. Book and lyrics by Oscar Hammerstein II. Produced by Florenz Ziegfeld. Dialogue staged by Zeke Colvan [and Oscar Hammerstein II uncredited]. Dances and ensembles arranged by Sammy Lee. Orchestrations by Robert Russell Bennett. Musical direction by Victor Baravalle. Scenery by Joseph Urban. Costumes by John Harkrider.

Cast: Norma Terris (Magnolia/Kim as a young woman), Howard Marsh (Gaylord Ravenal), Helen Morgan (Julie), Jules Bledsoe (Joe), Tess "Aunt Jemima" Gardella (Queenie), Charles Winninger (Cap'n Andy), Edna May Oliver (Parthy Ann Hawks), Eva Puck (Ellie), Sammy White (Frank), Alan Campbell (Windy), Charles Ellis (Steve), Bert Chapman (Pete/Old Sport), Francis X. Mahoney (Rubber Face), Thomas Gunn (Vallon), Jack Wynn (Faro Dealer/Jeb), Phil Sheridan (Gambler), Jack Daley (Jim), Dorothy Denese (La Belle Fatima), Annie Hart (Landlady), Estelle Floyd (Ethel), Annette Harding (Sister), Mildred Schewenke (Mother Superior), Eleanor Shaw (Kim as a child), Robert Faricey (Jake), Ted Daniels (Man with guitar), J. Lewis Johnson (Charlie), Tana Kamp (Lottie), Dagmar Oakland (Dolly), Laura Clairon (Old Lady on the Levee) and ensembles of black and white men and women.

This story begins "on the Levee at Natchez" in the late 1880s. Teenager Magnolia Hawks lives on the *Cotton Blossom*, a Mississippi River showboat run by her parents, ebullient Cap'n Andy and sour Parthy. Magnolia is a favorite of the white performers employed on the ship (Julie, Steve, Ellie, and Frank) and of the black servants, especially Queenie and Joe. Life-altering events take place during what should have been a routine docking. The troupe's leading lady, Julie, is revealed to be a mulatto, and she and her white husband, Steve, leave to escape punishment for the crime of miscegenation. Magnolia is promoted to leading lady. A new leading man presents himself in the form of Gaylord Ravenal, a handsome gambler looking for transport to the next city. The romances Magnolia and Ravenal perform each night mirror their growing love, and they marry. Soon after the birth of their daughter, Kim, Ravenal takes his young family to Chicago, where they live in fancy hotels or lowly boardinghouses according to the results of his gambling. Andy and Parthy visit during 1893 and attend the World's Columbian Exposition. But in 1904, when Ellie and Frank come to Chicago to headline at the Tro-

cadero, they find that Ravenal, bankrupt, has abandoned his wife and child. The seasoned performers arrange an audition for Magnolia. Unbeknownst to them, Julie, now an alcoholic, is the Trocadero's resident singer. When Julie spots Magnolia, she quits so that her young friend can have her job. The story jumps forward to 1927, with a grown-up Kim continuing the performing tradition started by her grandparents. Magnolia and Ravenal are finally reunited.

A national tour began on May 6, 1929, at the Colonial Theatre in Boston and stopped in nine cities, finishing at Ford's Theatre, Baltimore, in March 1930. Another major tour began October 20, 1947, at Hartford's Bushnell Auditorium; it visited thirteen cities before closing on June 26, 1948. Following further performances at New York's City Center in September 1948, the tour continued, visiting forty-five cities by April 30, 1949.

Major London productions have played at the Theatre Royal, Drury Lane (May 3, 1928–March 2, 1929); the Stoll Theatre (April 17–September 18, 1943, 264 performances); and the Adelphi Theatre (July 29, 1971–September 29, 1973).

Show Boat was first filmed by Universal Pictures in 1929 as a partial talkie directed by Harry A. Pollard, with performances by Helen Morgan, Jules Bledsoe, and Tess Gardella in a singing prologue. Universal gave *Show Boat* the full musical treatment in 1936, directed by James Whale and starring Irene Dunne (Magnolia), Allan Jones (Ravenal), Charles Winninger (Cap'n Andy), Paul Robeson (Joe), Helen Morgan (Julie), Helen Westley (Parthy), Sammy White (Frank), Queenie Smith (Ellie), and Hattie McDaniel (Queenie). MGM followed in 1951, a Technicolor production directed by George Sidney, starring Kathryn Grayson (Magnolia), Ava Gardner (Julie, dubbed by Annette Warren), Howard Keel (Ravenal), Joe E. Brown (Cap'n Andy), Agnes Moorehead (Parthy), William Warfield (Joe), and Marge and Gower Champion (Ellie and Frank). MGM's fictional biography of Jerome Kern, *Till The Clouds Roll By* (1946), includes scenes from *Show Boat* performed by Grayson (Magnolia), Lena Horne (Julie), and Tony Martin (Ravenal). A production at the Paper Mill Playhouse (Millburn, New Jersey) was aired by PBS's *Great Performances* in October 1989, starring Rebecca Baxter (Magnolia), Richard White (Ravenal), Shelly Burch (Julie), Eddie Bracken (Cap'n Andy), Marsha Bagwell (Parthy), P. L. Brown (Joe), Ellia English (Queenie), Lenora Nemetz (Ellie), and Lee Roy Reams (Frank).

There have been notable New York revivals at the Casino Theatre, May 19–October 22, 1932; at the Ziegfeld Theatre, January 5, 1946–January 4, 1947; at City Center, spring 1954, produced and directed by William Hammerstein; by the Music Theater of Lincoln Center in summer 1966, produced by Richard Rodgers; at the Uris Theatre, April 24–June 26, 1983, based on Houston Grand Opera's production; and at the Gershwin Theatre, October 2, 1994–January 5, 1997, pro-

duced by Garth Drabinsky, directed by Harold Prince, and choreographed by Susan Stroman, a staging first seen in Toronto the previous year.

Members of the 1928 London cast can be heard on a Pearl CD that also includes tracks from the London productions of *Sunny* and Rodgers and Hart's *Lido Lady*. Fuller versions of the score were recorded by the 1946 Broadway cast (Columbia/Sony); for the 1951 film soundtrack (MGM/Rhino-Turner); in a 1961 studio recording featuring John Raitt, Barbara Cook, William Warfield, and Anita Darian (Columbia/Sony); by the 1966 Lincoln Center cast, including Stephen Douglass, Cook, Warfield, and Constance Towers (RCA); by the 1971 London cast, including André Jobin, Lorna Dallas, and Cleo Laine as Julie; and by the 1994 Toronto cast, with Mark Jacoby, Rebecca Luker, and Lonette McKee (Quality Music). The complete 1927 score, along with every extant number ever written for *Show Boat*, was assembled by conductor John McGlinn in 1988, in a 3-CD set for EMI featuring Jerry Hadley, Frederica von Stade, and Teresa Stratas; the complete 1946 version was recorded by TER in 1993, using most of the cast of a 1989 co-production by England's Royal Shakespeare Company and Opera North.

The score of *Show Boat* interpolated two well-known songs by other writers: "After the Ball" by Charles K. Harris and "Goodbye My Lady Love" by Joseph E. Howard. Further interpolations were instrumentals.

This chapter draws from three published editions of the vocal score: T.B. Harms (New York, 1928); Chappell & Co. (London, 1928); and Harms (New York, 1946). Many of the songs have been also been published as individual sheets. The Music Division of the Library of Congress has *Show Boat* material in the Jerome Kern and Warner-Chappell collections. For information about material dropped before Broadway and added after Broadway, this chapter is beholden to the research done by John McGlinn for his recording and by Miles Kreuger for his book *Show Boat: The Story of a Classic American Musical* (Oxford, 1977) and his program notes for McGlinn's recording. Recently Katherine Axtell, Todd Decker, and Scott McMillin have made important contributions to *Show Boat* scholarship.

In addition to Miles Kreuger's book and the notes he and McGlinn wrote for the EMI recording, readers may be interested in the *Show Boat* chapters in Geoffrey Block's *Enchanted Evenings: The Broadway Musical from "Show Boat" to Sondheim* and Joseph P. Swain's *The Broadway Musical: A Critical and Musical Survey*. Also recommended are Gerald Bordman's *Jerome Kern: His Life and Music*, Stephen Banfield's *Jerome Kern*, and Ethan Mordden's *Make Believe: The Broadway Musical in the 1920s*.

Hammerstein and Kern worked together for most of a year before rehearsals began, then an exceptionally long time for developing a show. This one featured an unusual number of leading characters, multiple scenic locations, and the passage of decades. The world premiere lasted four hours. Almost an hour was trimmed immediately. Additional changes were made during the remaining five weeks of tryouts. Hammerstein made other changes for the 1928 London production and then reconsidered the content and the manner of unspooling the story for his 1936 screenplay, which included three new songs. He made further changes for the 1946 Broadway revival. Just weeks before his death in the summer of 1960, Hammerstein informed Kern's daughter Betty that producer Edwin Lester wanted

> to make a few changes in *Show Boat* for his Los Angeles and San Francisco production. He is building a great big boat that makes an entrance in the first scene, and this necessitated some changes in the opening chorus. I have assented to these. He also had a change in the very last scene . . . and I assented to this also. I did this with the complete confidence that you would also agree, because there is nothing in these changes that can hurt, and it does help Ed with his new and ambitious production.

There is no definitive text of *Show Boat*. This chapter reflects the running order at the time of the 1927 Broadway opening, followed by additions and then by dropped material. The version licensed by the Rodgers & Hammerstein Organization is based on the 1946 revival.

ACT ONE OPENING, including CAPTAIN ANDY'S BALLYHOO

Published in the vocal scores. Introduced by the black ensemble (stevedores and gals), the white ensemble (beaux and misses) and by Charles Winninger (Captain Andy).

The language and plot of *Show Boat* reflect the social conventions of the late nineteenth and early twentieth centuries. Certain words and the dialect spellings may jar or offend the modern reader, but Hammerstein also used dialect spellings for the white settlers in *Oklahoma!* and the New England folk in *Carousel*.

For the 1936 film the opening line, "Niggers all work on the Mississippi," was altered to "Darkies all work . . ." "Colored folks work . . ." was used in the 1946 stage revival and in Hammerstein's 1949 anthology, *Lyrics*. The 1946 Kern biopic, *Till The Clouds Roll By*, had Frank Sinatra singing "Here we all work . . ." The 1966 Lincoln Center production omitted the line entirely. John McGlinn's 1988 recording restored the original wording. Harold Prince's 1994 Broadway production used "colored folks." His director's note concludes:

Prior to *Show Boat*'s opening in Toronto in the autumn of 1993, a minority within the city's black community expressed concern about a revival of *Show Boat* on the basis of alleged racism. Throughout pre-production and rehearsal, I was committed to eliminate any inadvertent stereotype in the original material, dialogue which may seem "Uncle Tom" today. However, I was determined not to re-write history. The fact that during the 45-year period depicted in our musical there were lynchings, imprisonment and forced labor of the blacks in the U.S. is irrefutable. Indeed, the U.S. still cannot hold its head high with regard to racism.

The creators of *Show Boat* were men and women of moral stature, particularly Oscar Hammerstein II who time and time again (the subject of miscegenation was central to *South Pacific* 22 years later) took fierce aim at prejudice in our society. "You've Got to Be Carefully Taught" are *his* words. Once the production was premiered in Toronto, the protesters' allegations were proven to be unfounded and the protests ended.

I hope it is clear that *Show Boat*'s creators . . . share the deepest solidarity with those who have been victims of racism.

STEVEDORES:	Niggers all work on de Mississippi,
	Niggers all work while de white folks play.
	Loadin' up boats wid de bales of cotton,
	Gittin' no rest till de Judgment Day!
GALS:	Git yo'self a bran'-new gal,*
	A lovin' baby who's de apple of yo' eye.
	Coal-black Rose or high-brown Sal,
	Dey all kin cook de sparrergrass an' chicken pie.
STEVEDORES:	Hey! Git along, git along, Git along, git along!
	Hey! Git along, git along, Git along, git along, hey!
STEVEDORES AND GALS:	Niggers all work on de Mississippi,

---

* *The 1946 version changed lines 5–8 to:*
Drop dat bale and have some fun!
Dere's a lot o' lovin' on de levee fer you.
Y' work all day, y' git no fun.
We know sump'n better fer a feller to do!

	Niggers all work while de white folks play.
STEVEDORES:	Loadin' up boats wid de bales of cotton,
	Gittin' no rest till de Judgment Day.
STEVEDORES AND GALS:	Cotton blossom, cotton blossom,
	Love to see you growin' free.
	When dey pack you on de levee,
	You're a heavy load to me!
	Cotton blossom, cotton blossom,
	Love to see you growin' wild.
	On de levee, you're too heavy
	Fo' dis po' black child.

[*After a musical interlude, the white ensemble enters.*]

TOWN BEAUX:	What a pretty bevy!
	Ah, there—ah, there—
	The fairest of the fair!
	To Southern beauty ev'ry beau must bow.
MINCING MISSES:	How you love to flatter,
	You rogues, you rogues!
	Oh, goodness gracious, They're so flirtatious!
BEAUX:	Little women, don't be timorous.
	You will find acting thus Only makes a man more bold.
	These are not the days of old.
MISSES:	You naughty fellows seem to think you please us
	When you tease us so.
	You're a reckless lot, we know.
BEAUX:	See the show boat!
	That's old Captain Andy's *Cotton Blossom*.
	Will you go?
	Let me take you to the show!
GALS:	H'yah! Look live dere!
MISSES:	'Twill be delightful.
	But to rightfully accept, I have to make Mama
	Get permission from Papa!
STEVEDORES AND GALS:	H'yah! Look live dere!

MISSES AND BEAUX: Captain Andy has
          gathered a troupe
      In the greatest of
          drammers
      And jolly comedies.
      Stephen Baker,
      The handsomest leading
          man,
      And beautiful Julie
          LaVerne as well.

MISSES AND BEAUX: *Cotton Blossom,*
          Cotton Blossom
      Captain Andy's floating
          show!
      Thrills and laughter,
          concert after,
      Ev'rybody's sure to go!
      Cotton Blossom, Cotton
          Blossom,
      Captain Andy's floating
          show.
      Thrills and laughter,
          concert after,
      Get your girl and go.
      So get your girl and go!

STEVEDORES AND GALS: Cotton blossom, cotton
          blossom,
      Love to see you growin'
          free.
      When dey pack you on de
          levee,
      You're a heavy load to me!
      Cotton blossom, cotton
          blossom,
      Love to see you growin'
          wild.
      On de levee you're too
          heavy
      Fo' dis po' black child.
      So let dat whistle blow!

[*Dialogue.* ANDY *enters, leading a parade.*]

Captain Andy's Ballyhoo

MISSES: Captain Andy, Captain Andy,
      Here's your lemon cake and
          homemade candy,
      Quince preserve and apple
          brandy.
      Mama sends her best regards
          to you.

MISSES AND BEAUX: Captain Andy, Captain Andy
      We've been hearing all about
          your dandy show.
      Is this year's good as last year?*

---

* The 1946 score has "last year's."

      Won't you tell us what is new?

CAPTAIN ANDY: Look it* we got! Look it we got!
      How can we fail? How can we
          fail?
      You never seen a show like
          this before!
      We'll try to make the evening
          bright,
      An' if you come around
          tonight,
      Tomorrow night you'll come
          around for more!

MISSES AND BEAUX: Captain Andy! Captain Andy!
      You know how to make a show
          sound dandy!

CAPTAIN ANDY: Frank and Ellie, c'mon, let's
          show them
      Just a sample of your soft-
          shoe dance.

PARTHY: Captain Andy, Captain Andy!

CAPTAIN ANDY: Just a sample.

PARTHY: What a man! My land,
      He gives away his show for
          nothing!

CAPTAIN ANDY: Just a sample of the dance.

[*Dance.*]

MISSES AND BEAUX: *Cotton Blossom, Cotton*
          Blossom,
      Captain Andy's floating show.
      Thrills and laughter, concert
          after—
      Get your girl and go.

WHERE'S THE MATE FOR ME?

Published in the vocal scores. Introduced by Howard Marsh (Gaylord Ravenal).

Who cares if my boat goes upstream,
Or if the gale bids me go with the river's flow?
I drift along with my fancy—
Sometimes I thank my lucky stars my heart is
    free,
And other times I wonder, where's the mate
    for me?
The driftwood floating over the sea
Someday finds a sheltering lee,

---

* The 1946 score has "Look't."

So somewhere there surely must be
A harbor meant for me.
I drift along with my fancy;
Sometimes I thank my lucky stars my heart is
    free,
And other times I wonder, where's the mate for me?

MAKE BELIEVE

Published as an individual sheet and included in Hammerstein's anthology, *Lyrics.* Introduced by Howard Marsh (Gaylord Ravenal) and Norma Terris (Magnolia). Discographer Edward Foote Gardner ranks "Make Believe" as the 48th most popular song in 1928, with a memorable Paul Whiteman recording with vocals by Bing Crosby.

Hammerstein biographer Hugh Fordin reports that the lyric came about in an unusual way. After hearing Kern's melody, Hammerstein instantly thought of "Couldn't you? Couldn't I? Couldn't we?" for the middle section. He didn't consider the people who would sing it or the place in the plot; the tune just seemed to call for those words. The rest of the lyric was built around that single line. Hammerstein used this story to show how "inspiration" comes during work, not when you wait to be inspired.

REFRAIN 1

RAVENAL: Only make believe I love you,
      Only make believe that you love me.
      Others find peace of mind in
          pretending—
      Couldn't you? Couldn't I?
          Couldn't we?
      Make believe our lips are blending
      In a phantom kiss, or two, or three.
      Might as well make believe I love you,
      For, to tell the truth, I do.

INTERLUDE

RAVENAL: Your pardon, I pray.
      'Twas too much to say
      The words that betray my heart.

MAGNOLIA: We only pretend.
      You do not offend
      In playing a lover's part.
      The game of just supposing is the
          sweetest game I know.
      Our dreams are more romantic than
          the world we see.

RAVENAL: And if the things we dream about
          don't happen to be so,

That's just an unimportant
   technicality.
MAGNOLIA: Though the cold and brutal fact is
   You and I have never met,
   We need not mind convention's p's
      and q's.
   If we put our thoughts in practice,
   We can banish all regret,
   Imagining most anything we choose.

REFRAIN 2

MAGNOLIA: We could make believe I love you,
   We could make believe that you
      love me.
BOTH: Others find peace of mind in
      pretending—
   Couldn't you? Couldn't I?
      Couldn't we?
RAVENAL: Make believe our lips are blending
   In a phantom kiss, or two, or three.
BOTH: Might as well make believe I love
      you,
RAVENAL: For to tell the truth, I do.

Act Two reprise

Sung by Ravenal in farewell to his young daughter, Kim.
Introduced by Howard Marsh (Ravenal).

Only make believe I'm near you,
Only make believe that you're with me.
Girls and boys find it fun just pretending—
Couldn't you? Couldn't I? Couldn't we?

[*Dialogue.*]

Best of all, make believe I love you,
For, to tell the truth, I do.

OL' MAN RIVER

Published as an individual sheet and included in Hammerstein's anthology, *Lyrics*. Introduced by Jules Bledsoe (Joe) and black male ensemble.

Bill Hammerstein told historian Max Wilk that his father had conceived this song "as a sort of cord to hold together that whole sprawling story. Remember, no one up to that time had ever tried to spread such an expanse of epic drama, covering such a span of time, over the musical stage, and it had to be held together somehow. He felt that the one constant element was the river, and that's what he wrote about."

Hammerstein very deliberately crafted the lyric without much rhyme, later explaining:

"River," instead of being repeated in the second line, could have had a rhyme—"shiver," "quiver," etc. The next two lines could have rhymed with the first two, the "iver" sounds continuing, or they could have had two new words rhyming with each other. I do not believe that in this way I could have commanded the same attention and respect from a listener, nor would a singer be so likely to concentrate on the meaning of the words. There are, of course, compensations for lack of rhyme. I've already mentioned repetition. There is also the trick of matching up words. "Sumpin' " and "nuthin' " do not rhyme, but the two words are related. "He don' plant taters, He don' plant cotton": These two lines also match and complement each other to make up for the lack of a rhyme. Here is a song sung by a character who is a rugged and untutored philosopher. It is a song of resignation with a protest implied. Brilliant and frequent rhyming would diminish its importance.

Paul Robeson's performance brought the implied protest closer to the surface, and he began making unauthorized adjustments to the lyric. Asked in the late 1940s for a comment, Hammerstein said: "As the author of these words, I should like it known that I have no intention of changing them or permitting anyone else to change them. I further suggest that Paul write his own songs and leave mine alone."

Discographer Joel Whitman ranks "Ol' Man River" as number 37 among the 100 most recorded songs of 1890 through 1954. Robeson recorded it six times between 1928 and 1936. Other significant early records were made by Bing Crosby and Al Jolson. In *Stardust Melodies*, Will Friedwald discusses some fifty vocal and instrumental versions from the 1920s to the 1960s.

VERSE 1

JOE: Dere's an ol' man called de
      Mississippi;
   Dat's de ol' man dat I'd like to be!
   What does he care if de world's
      got troubles?
   What does he care if de land ain't
      free?

REFRAIN

JOE: Ol' Man River,
   Dat Ol' Man River,
   He mus' know sumpin'
   But don't say nuthin',
   He jes' keeps rollin',
   He keeps on rollin' along.
   He don' plant taters,

He don' plant cotton,
An' dem dat plants 'em
Is soon forgotten,
But Ol' Man River,
He jes' keeps rollin' along.
You an' me, we sweat an' strain,
Body all achin' an' racked wid
   pain—
"Tote dat barge!"
"Lif' dat bale!"
Git a little drunk
An' you land in jail . . .
Ah gits weary
An' sick of tryin';
Ah'm tired of livin'
An' skeered of dyin',
But Ol' Man River,
He jes' keeps rollin' along.

INTERLUDE

JOE: Niggers all work* on de
      Mississippi,
   Niggers all work while de white
      folks play.
   Pullin' dem boats from de dawn
      to sunset,
   Gittin' no rest till de Judgment
      Day!
COLORED MEN: Don' look up
   An' don' look down.
   You don' dast make
   De white boss frown.
   Bend your knees
   An' bow your head
   An' pull dat rope
   Until yo' dead.

VERSE 2

JOE: Let me go 'way from de
      Mississippi,
   Let me go 'way from de white man
      boss;
   Show me dat stream called de
      river Jordan,
   Dat's de ol' stream dat I long to
      cross.

REFRAIN 2

COLORED MEN: Ol' Man River,
   Dat Ol' Man River,
   He mus' know sumpin'
   But don't say nuthin'.
   He jes' keeps rollin',

---

* *Changed in 1946 to "Colored folks work."*

He keeps on rollin' along.

JOE: Long ol' river forever keeps
  rollin' on.

COLORED MEN: He don' plant taters,
  He don' plant cotton,
  An' dem dat plants 'em
  Is soon forgotten,
  But Ol' Man River,
  He jes' keeps rollin' along.

JOE: Long ol' river keeps hearin' dat
  song.
  You an' me, we sweat an' strain,
  Body all achin' an' racked wid
   pain—
  "Tote dat barge!"
  An' "Lif' dat bale!"
  Git a little drunk*
  An' you land in jail.

JOE AND MEN: Ah gits weary an' sick of tryin'.
  Ah'm tired of livin' an' skeered of
   dyin',
  But Ol' Man River, he jes' keeps
   rollin' along!

Act Two reprise

Introduced by Jules Bledsoe (Joe).

Ol' Man River,
Dat Ol' Man River,
He must know sumpin'
But don't say nuthin',
He jes' keeps rollin',
He keeps on rollin' along.
He don' plant taters,
He don' plant cotton,
An' dem dat plants 'em
Is soon forgotten.
But Ol' Man River,
He jes' keeps rollin' along.
New things come 'n' ol' things go
But all things look de same to Joe.
Folks git mad an' starts a war,†

---

* *The 1928 Harms piano-vocal score has:*
 We gits a little drunk
 An' we lands in jail.

† *These three lines vary in the 1936 film screenplay:*
 Folks git mad and start a war.
 Dey fight de war,
 Don't know what for.
and in the 1946 score:
 Wars go on an' some folks die.
 De res' ferget
 De reason why.

An' den git glad,
Don't know what for.
Ah keep laughin'
Instead of cryin'
Ah mus' keep livin'
Until ah'm dyin'
But Ol' Man River,
He jes' keeps rollin' along!

CAN'T HELP LOVIN' DAT MAN

Published as an individual sheet and included in Hammerstein's anthology, *Lyrics.* Introduced by Helen Morgan (Julie), Tess "Aunt Jemima" Gardella (Queenie), Norma Terris (Magnolia), Jules Bledsoe (Joe), and the black ensemble.

VERSE 1

JULIE: Oh, listen, sister,
  I love my mister man,
  And I can't tell yo' why.
  Dere ain't no reason
  Why I should love dat man—
  It mus' be sumpin' dat de
   angels done plan.

REFRAIN

JULIE: Fish got to swim, birds got
  to fly,
  I got to love one man till
   I die—
  Can't help lovin' dat man
   of mine.
  Tell me he's lazy, tell me he's
   slow,
  Tell me I'm crazy (maybe I
   know)—
  Can't help lovin' dat man of
   mine.
  When he goes away,
  Dat's a rainy day,
  And when he comes back, dat
   day is fine,
  De sun will shine!
  He kin come home as late as
   kin be,
  Home widout him ain't no
   home to me—
  Can't help lovin' dat man of
   mine.

VERSE 2

QUEENIE: Mah man is shif'less
  An' good fo' nuthin' too
  (He's mah man jes' de same).
  He's never near me
  When dere is work to do.

QUEENIE AND JOE: He's never roun' me [yo']
  when dere's workin' to do.

QUEENIE: De chimbley's smokin',
  De roof is leakin' in,
  But he don' seem to care.
  He kin be happy
  Wid jes' a sip of gin.

JOE: Why you all talk 'bout gin?

QUEENIE: Ah even loves him
  When his kisses got gin!

[*Women repeat refrain while men sing
countermelody.*]

1ST BARITONES: While de birds fly, till de
  world dies,
  I'll love dat gal of mine,
  Or else she ain't my gal!
  She's lazy and slow—crazy,
   I know.
  Can't help lovin' dat gal!
  She's jes' as crazy 'bout me!
  When I goes away, all de
   rainy day,
  An' when I comes back, dat
   day is fine.

2ND BARITONES: While de birds fly, till de
  world is dyin',
  I'll love dat gal of mine!
  Lazy and slow, crazy lovin'
   her so.
  Can't help lovin' dat gal!
  When I goes away, all de
   rainy day,
  An' when I comes back, dat
   day is fine.

JOE: While de birds fly up in
  de sky,
  My gal loves me!
  Dat's why she's true gal of
   mine!
  She may be lazy and slow
  As cold molasses, I know.
  Can't help lovin' dat gal
   of mine!
  When I goes away, dat's
   lovin',
  All the rainy day, dat's lovin',
  An' when I comes back, dat
   day is fine.

ALL: Yes, sister!

He [She] kin come home as
 late as kin be,
Home widout him [her] ain't
 no home to me.
Can't help lovin' dat man [gal]
 of mine!

LIFE UPON THE WICKED STAGE

Published as an individual sheet. Introduced by Eva Puck (Ellie) and white female ensemble.

In March 1927, Hammerstein met Dorothy Jacobson, who would become his second wife. She told biographer Hugh Fordin that soon after she recounted her own brief career as an actress, Hammerstein wrote this song for his new project, *Show Boat*.

VERSE

ELLIE: Why do stage-struck maidens clamor
 To be actin' in the drammer?
GIRLS: We've heard say
 You are gay
 Night and day.
ELLIE: [*spoken*] Oh, go 'way!
GIRLS: We drink water from a dipper—
 You drink champagne from a slipper.
ELLIE: Though it seems
 Cruel to bust
 All your dreams,
 Still, I must.
 Here's the truth, I tell you.

REFRAIN

ELLIE: Life upon the wicked stage
 Ain't ever what a girl supposes.
 Stage-door Johnnies aren't
 Raging over you with gems and roses.
 When you let a feller hold your hand
 (Which means an extra beer or
 sandwich),
 Ev'rybody whispers, "Ain't her life a
 whirl?"
 Though you're warned against a roué
 Ruining your reputation,
 I have played around
 The one-night trade around a great big
 nation.
 Wild old men who give you jewels and
 sables
 Only live in Aesop's Fables.

Life upon the wicked stage
Ain't nothin' for a girl.
GIRLS: Though we've listened to you moan and
 grieve,
 You must pardon us if we do not believe
 you.
 There is no doubt you're crazy about
 Your awful stage.
ELLIE: I admit it's fun to smear my face with
 paint,
 Causin' ev'ryone to think I'm what I
 ain't.
 And I like to play a demi-mondy role
 With soul!
 Ask the hero, does he like the way I lure
 When I play a hussy or a paramour?
 Yet, when once the curtain's down,
 My life is pure,
 And how I dread it!
GIRLS: Life upon the wicked stage
 Ain't ever what a girl supposes.
 Stage-door Johnnies aren't
 Raging over you with gems and roses.
ELLIE: If some gentleman would talk with
 reason,
 I would cancel all next season.
 Life upon the wicked stage
 Ain't nothin' for a girl.
GIRLS: You'd be back the season after!

[*They dance.*]*

TILL GOOD LUCK COMES MY WAY

Published in the 1928 American vocal score, but dropped from the 1946 production (and its vocal score). Introduced by Howard Marsh (Gaylord Ravenal) and white male ensemble (gamblers).

INTRODUCTION

RAVENAL: The man who ventures with chance
 Is the man who's adding the salt,
 romance,
 To a world that otherwise is dark
 and drear.

---

* *In 1946, the girls sang these lines at the end of the dance:*
 I got virtue, but it ain't been tested—
 No one's even interested!
 Life upon the wicked stage . . .

The sane conservative lot
Have their fate secure in a
 guarded spot
Of the world—
They're welcome to their drab
 career.
SOME MEN: It is all well enough to be grinning
 While your winnings grow.
OTHER MEN: It is easy to be grinning
 While your stack is growing.
ALL MEN: But when fortune reverses her
 spinning,
 Life is not a-glowing—
 That is why we like to see
 Someone who can be
 Unconcerned and free like you.
RAVENAL: If I am losing today,
 I will take my loss and I'll pay.
 For I know
 That in time my luck will turn—
 It's bound to turn.

REFRAIN

RAVENAL: Till good luck comes my way,
 I'll play along.
 While there's a game on the
 highway,
 I'll stray along,
 With just the turn of a wheel
 Or the flip of a card as my guide—
 I let fate decide
 If I walk or ride.
 Why sit alone with your sorrow
 And kill the day?
 There may be sunshine tomorrow
 To fill the day.
 While I've a heart and a brain
 And my ebony cane,
 I can borrow
 Until the day
 When good luck comes my way.
MEN: Never venture, never gain;
 Men of caution, it is plain—
RAVENAL: Never venture, never gain;
 Men of caution, it is plain,
 Live in vain.
MEN: Fortune will change
 Like an April day.
ALL: So I will wait
 Till good luck comes my way!

Unused introduction

Not published, but recorded by Jerry Hadley (Ravenal) and ensemble for John McGlinn. This lead-in, known as the "Waterfront Saloon Scene," was dropped before the 1927 Broadway opening.

RAVENAL: Fifty on red,
And that's my last.
I drift along with my fancy.
I lose today, but then,
Tomorrow luck may change.
MEN: He keeps on losing,
But tomorrow luck may change.

[*Dialogue.*]

MEN: Sir, you have our sympathy—
You're as game as you can be.
RAVENAL: Do not waste your sympathy,
Bad luck never worries me.
I know that fortune changes
Just like an April day.
MEN: A lad as brave as he
Deserves more good luck.
And should luck be false to him,
It would be strange to arrange things
that way.
RAVENAL: The man who ventures with
chance, [*etc.*]

I MIGHT FALL BACK
ON YOU

Published in the 1928 vocal score; dropped from the 1946 production; restored in the 1951 MGM film. Written during the 1927 tryout period and added in Philadelphia. Introduced by Sammy White (Frank) and Eva Puck (Ellie). Miles Kreuger points out that the refrain melody was first given to Magnolia, Andy, and Parthy during the Cleveland performances, with the title "Be Happy Too."

VERSE

FRANK: Little girl, you are safe with me,
I can protect what's mine.
I am a sturdy maple tree
And you're my clinging vine.
ELLIE: Woods are just full of maple trees,
Cedar and oak and pine.
Let me look them over, please,

And then I'll let you know
If you have a show.

REFRAIN

ELLIE: After I have looked around the world for
a mate,
Then, perhaps, I might fall back on you.
When I am convinced that there is no
better fate,
Then I might decide that you will do.
FRANK: I am just an average lad.
Though no gift to womanhood,
Some girls say I'm not so bad.
ELLIE: Others say you're not so good!
But if you are patient, dear, and willing
to wait,
There's a chance I might fall back on you.

C'MON, FOLKS
(QUEENIE'S BALLYHOO)

Published in the 1928 American vocal score; trimmed to just the opening stanza for the 1946 production. Introduced by Tess "Aunt Jemima" Gardella (Queenie) and the black ensemble.

QUEENIE: Hey, where yo' think yo' goin'?
Don't yo' know dis show is
startin' soon?
Hey, jes' a few seats left yere.
It's light inside, an' outside
dere's no moon.
What fo' you gals dress up dicty?
Where's yo' all goin'?
Tell dose stingy men o' yours
To step up here in line!
C'mon, folks, we's rarin' to go.
Is you or ain't you seein' this
show?
Get het up,
Dere'll be no letup here!
BLACK ENSEMBLE: Listen to that gal talk!
QUEENIE: You'll be excited all night,
Grippin' yo' man an' holdin'
him tight.
Two seats for twenty cents
Ain't so dear.
Story's 'bout a lady in love.
Loves her man but, heavens
above!
Dere's a villain bad as you
ever see.

BLACK ENSEMBLE: Um-um-um!
QUEENIE: White outside, but black in de
heart,
Swears dose two young lovers
to part.
He's de worstest scalawag dat
can be.
BLACK ENSEMBLE: Um-um-um!
QUEENIE: He tries to get her alone.
You hear dat little gal moan.
Ol' villain makin' her groan
Wid' woe!
BLACK ENSEMBLE: What does he do,
What does he do?
Tell us!
QUEENIE: He tries to choke her to death,
Den when she's almost out
o' her breath,
Somebody comes a-rappin' at
dat ol' door!
BLACK WOMEN: Open the door, oh Lord!
BLACK MEN: How does de rest of it go?
QUEENIE: Is yo' or ain't yo' dyin' to
know?
Step up an' buy yo' tickets
Fo' dis yere show!

YOU ARE LOVE

Published as an individual sheet; Hammerstein included the refrain in his anthology, *Lyrics.* Introduced by Howard Marsh (Ravenal) and Norma Terris (Magnolia).

VERSE

RAVENAL: Once a wand'ring ne'er-do-well,
Just a vagrant roving fellow,
I went my way.
Life was just a joke to tell.
Like a lonely Punchinello,
My role was gay,
But I knew the joke was aimless.
Time went on, I liked the game less.
For you see,
Somewhere lurked a spark divine
And I kept won'dring whether mine
Would come to me.
Then, my fortune turned and I
found you.
Here you are, with my arms around you.
You will never know what you've
meant to me.
MAGNOLIA: You're the prize that heaven has sent
to me.

RAVENAL: Here's a bright and beautiful world,
All new,
Wrapped up in you.

REFRAIN

RAVENAL: You are love,
Here in my arms
Where you belong.
And here you will stay;
I'll not let you away—
I want day after day
With you.
You are spring,
Bud of romance unfurled;
You taught me to see
One truth forever true:
You are love,
Wonder of all the world.
Where you go with me,
Heaven will always be.

MAGNOLIA: You are love,
Here in my arms
Where you belong.
And here you will stay;
I'll not let you away—
I want day after day
With you.
You are spring,
Bud of romance unfurled;
You taught me to see
One truth forever true—

BOTH: You are love,
Wonder of all the world.
Where you go with me,
Heaven will always be.

ACT ONE FINALE

Published in the vocal scores. Introduced by Norma Terris (Magnolia), the white ensemble, and the black ensemble. Captain Andy, Ravenal, and the rest of the troupe are present but have no individual vocal lines. Parthy enters the scene halfway through.

WHITE WOMEN: Oh, tell me, did you ever,
Did you ever hear of such a thing?

WHITE MEN: The leading man's about to give
The leading girl a wedding ring.

WHITE WOMEN: Her father has neglected none,
He's asked us all to see the fun.
And since we are invited to attend,
We are delighted to be there
When these united two are plighted to be one.

WHITE MEN: So now, you see, romance can start upon the stage.
Romance like theirs is not for ev'ryone.

WHITE ENSEMBLE: Captain Andy, Captain Andy!
My, but doesn't he look fine and dandy!
Now Magnolia's found her mate,
You know we're happy to congratulate you.

WHITE AND
BLACK ENSEMBLE: We thank you for inviting us
To see the wedding—it was friendly thus
To let us share your happy day
And see you give the bride away.

[*Dialogue.*]

WHITE ENSEMBLE: Happy the day
When the hand of a maid
Has been won by swift pursuing!
Happy the way
He has chosen to win her,
By bold and ardent wooing.
Theirs a lucky fate,*
To be romantic.
We can hardly wait
To see the frantic
Looks of the bridegroom
And quakes of the bride
Whom he takes,
Now or never,
And makes her forever
The one and the only one
Who will take care
That his life's not a lonely one
While she's the only one.

[MAGNOLIA *and* RAVENAL *enter.*]

———

* *The 1946 vocal score omits the lines "Theirs a lucky fate" through "Lovely bride-to-be."*

WHITE ENSEMBLE: Happy the bride!
May the greatest of happiness,
Health and wealth attend you,
Lovely bride-to-be.
We'd take pride to be
Wedded to anyone
Charming as you.

BLACK WOMEN: Miss Magnolia,
We always tol' ya
We knowed you'd find
Your man who'd be lovin'
you true!

MAGNOLIA: Can't I share some of my happiness,
Dear friends, with you?

WHITE AND
BLACK ENSEMBLE: Fish got to swim and birds got to fly,
I got to love one man till I die—
Can't help lovin' dat man of mine!
Tell me he's lazy, tell me he's slow.
Tell me I'm crazy (maybe I know)—
Can't help lovin' dat man of mine!

[*Dance break.*]

WHITE AND
BLACK ENSEMBLE: He kin come home as late as kin be,
Home widout him ain't no home to me—
Can't help lovin' dat man—

[PARTHY *bursts in.*]

PARTHY: [*spoken*] Stop them—he's a murderer!

[*Dialogue:* ANDY *defends* RAVENAL; *and* PARTHY *faints, allowing the wedding to proceed.*]

ALL:* Fish got to swim and birds got to fly,
I got to love one man till I die—
Can't help lovin' dat man of mine!

———

* *Variant ending from 1946 vocal score:*
MAGNOLIA: Can't stop me now, there's no use to try.
ALL: I've got to love my man till I die.
Can't help lovin' dat man of mine!

ACT TWO OPENING, including WHEN WE TELL THEM ABOUT IT ALL and DANDIES ON PARADE

Alternate title: "At the Fair." Published in the 1928 Harms and Chappell vocal scores; abridged in the 1946 vocal score ("Dandies on Parade" was cut entirely). Introduced by the white ensemble.

When We Tell Them About It All

ENSEMBLE: When we tell them about it all,
They're likely to doubt it all,
But why should we care
Just as long as we've been to the fair?
FIRST BARKER: Ho, ho!
Your kind attention bestow.
ENSEMBLE: Let's go near—
I can't hear.
Shall we go?
GIRLS: I don't know.
FIRST BARKER: The strongest little lady known to the world we'll show!
ENSEMBLE: He's talking through his hat, you bet,
I'm pretty sure of that.
FIRST BARKER: Come one and all,
Come up and feel the fist of her!
ENSEMBLE: Great Christopher!
FIRST BARKER: So just move along
And visit the Queen of the Strong!
Sixteen years of age!
ENSEMBLE: If Sandow felt her hand,
How he would stutter and mutter
And shiver and quiver with rage!
She's sixteen years of age.
SECOND BARKER: Hey, hey!
What have we here,
What have we here?
A marvelous display!
ENSEMBLE: Say, they're goin' to tell you
What they want to sell you now.
SECOND BARKER: The beauties picked from all the world
In super-fine array!
MEN: That's one show we must see!
GIRLS: Are you taking me?
FIRST BARKER: Get tickets this way.
SECOND BARKER: Just step up and pay!

FIRST BARKER: Just step this way!
Hey, right up this way!
Hey!
SECOND BARKER: Not much to pay for such display!
Come on this way!
BOTH BARKERS: And you will say in all Chicago
This is the best show!
GIRLS: We're in the face of a great temptation:
In such a place to attempt flirtation.
I don't really know.
MEN: Won't you let me take you in?
Do come! The show will soon begin—
Do let me take you in.
THIRD BARKER: Now for this special feature
I demand your strict attention.
Step closer, gentlemen—
You notice "ladies" I don't mention!
GIRLS: Goodness gracious me—
What ever can it be?
THIRD BARKER: My story's quickly told:
The world's sensation now behold!

[FATIMA dances.]

GIRLS: Hurry, hurry, let us run!
MEN: What for?
There's nothing wrong.
She's a princess,
From better folks than us, I guess.
GIRLS: You can stay, but I must run.
MEN: All right. You always spoil my fun.
ENSEMBLE: Belles and beaux,*
Dressed in the very latest style—
Here they come!
Goodness knows,
Aren't they swell?
Well, I should smile!
Look, dear! Look here!
Ain't they gorgeous?

---

* *Rewrite for the 1946 revival:*
Here they come,
Beautiful girls from near and far.
Here they are!
From Peru,
Timbuktu
And Zanzibar.
Europe,
Asia,
They'll amaze ya.

Dandies on Parade

ENSEMBLE: When the sports of gay Chicago
Pay a visit to the fair
(To the naughty midway),
You can tell ev'ry swell
By his dashing air.
They do credit to Chicago
With their clothes all tailor-made
(The latest on the midway).
All their country cousins gape and stare
When they see the dandies on parade.

WHY DO I LOVE YOU?

Published as an individual sheet; the refrain appears in Hammerstein's anthology, *Lyrics*. Added during the 1927 pre-Broadway tryouts, the song replaced "Be Happy Too" during the World's Fair sequence, and was reprised in place of "It's Getting Hotter in the North" at the end of Act Two. Introduced by Norma Terris (Magnolia), Howard Marsh (Ravenal), Charles Winninger (Captain Andy), Edna May Oliver (Parthy), and white ensemble.

Despite the out-of-town stress of making cuts and writing new material, Hammerstein took time to play a joke on his collaborator. In an undated statement, he recalled:

Jerome Kern detested songs which referred coyly to "Cupid" as the little schemer who brought lovers together. In the autumn of 1927 we were in Washington* with *Show Boat*. It had just opened there and we felt that we needed a new song for Act Two. He wrote the melody first. I took it up to my room and set words to it. It eventually became the very popular song "Why Do I Love You?" Before submitting the lyric to him, I wrote another one as a practical joke and sent it down to his room. This lyric is also set to the melody of "Why Do I Love You?" Eager as he always was to hear words written to his melody, he started gaily to play it and read my words, but a few bars later he brought his fists down on the keyboard in anger. Then, quickly realizing that I couldn't be serious about this, he burst into the kind of loud uncontrollable laughter for which I remember him. Below is the original copy of the lyric and

---

* *Various scholars place this change in Pittsburgh.*

110

the message I sent to him. He had it framed and kept it in his study for many years. His wife, Eva, gave it to me after he died.

Dear Jerry,

Here is a refrain for the Kim number. Before writing the verse I thot* I had better find out if you liked this idea.

Oscar

Cupid Knows the Way

Cupid knows the way
He's the naked boy
Who can make you prey
To love's own joy.
When he shoots his little arrow
He can thrill you to the marrow.
Hurry and depart
When you hear his name,
Once you feel his dart
You are his game.
Till you fall
Your heart he'll harrow—
Cupid always knows the way.

VERSE

MAGNOLIA: I'm walking on the air, dear.
For life is fair, dear, to lovers.
I'm in the seventh heaven
(There's more than seven,
My heart discovers).
RAVENAL: In this sweet, improbable and unreal world,
Finding you has given me my ideal world.

REFRAIN

MAGNOLIA: Why do I love you?
Why do you love me?
Why should there be two
Happy as we?
RAVENAL: Can you see
The why or wherefore
I should be the one you care for?
MAGNOLIA: You're a lucky boy;
I am lucky too.
BOTH: All our dreams of joy
Seem to come true.
Maybe that's because you love me.
Maybe that's why I love you.

* Hammerstein spelled "thought" this way in several letters.

ENSEMBLE REPEATS REFRAIN

INTERLUDE

RAVENAL: Darling, I have only just an hour to play.
MAGNOLIA: I am always lonely when you go away.
ENSEMBLE: Hours are not like years,
So dry your tears.
What a pair of love birds!
RAVENAL: My darling,
I'll come home as early as I can*
Meanwhile, be good and patient with your man.

ALL REPEAT REFRAIN

IN DAHOMEY

Published in the vocal scores. Introduced by the black ensemble (tribal villagers) and the white ensemble (fairgoers).

Historical note: More than one World's Fair included a model of an African village. According to Allen Woll's *Black Musical Theatre: From Coontown to Dreamgirls*, Bert Williams and George Walker donned feathers and loincloths to appear in San Francisco's 1893 Midwinter's Fair when the boat containing native West Africans was delayed. Ten years later they wrote, produced, and starred in *In Dahomey*, the first black musical on Broadway. Walker died young, but Williams later became a great star of the Ziegfeld Follies.

BLACK MEN: Dyunga doe, dyunga doe!
Dyunga hungy ung gunga,
Hungy ung gunga go!
Kyooga chek, kyooga chek,
Kyooga chek a chek uncha,
Chek a chek uncha chek!
BLACK WOMEN: Daringa doo!
Daringa dey da!
BLACK MEN: Daringa doo!
Daringa dey da!
BLACK WOMEN: Dyunga hungy ung gunga,
Hungy ung gunga go!
Dyunga hungy ung gunga,
Hungy ung gunga go!
BLACK WOMEN
AND MEN: Hoo go ga doo!

* These two lines use the same tune as "He kin come home as late as kin be/Home widout him ain't no home to me" from "Can't Help Lovin' Dat Man."

Hoo go ga doo!
Hoga hoga toogo togo togo to go doo!
WHITE ENSEMBLE: Don't let us stay here,
For though they may play here,
They are acting vicious—
They might get malicious.
And though I'm not fearful,
I'll not be a spearful,
So you'd better show me
The way from Dahomey!

[*They exit.*]

BLACK WOMEN
AND MEN: We're glad to see them go,*
We're glad to see those white folks go!
Dyunga doe, dyunga doe!
Dyunga hungy ung gunga,
Hungy ung gunga go!

REFRAIN

BLACK WOMEN
AND MEN: In Dahomey,
Where the Africans play.†
In Dahomey—
Gimme Avenue A.
Back in old New York,
Where your knife an' fork
Gently sink into juicy little chops
What's made of pork.‡
We are wild folks
When de Ballyhoos bawl,
But we're mild folks
When we're back in the Kraal.
'Cause our home (our little home),
Our home ain't in Dahomey at all!§
Oh, take me back today to Avenue A!

* The 1946 score substitutes:
We're glad to see them go,
We're glad to see those people go!
We've had enough of all this stuff.
We wish we'd never come here
To join a Dahomey show!

† The 1946 score has:
Let the Africans stay.

‡ The 1946 score has:
Of tender pork.

§ The 1946 score has:
Our home just ain't Dahomey at all.

BILL

Lyric by P. G. Wodehouse and Oscar Hammerstein II. Published as an individual sheet. Introduced by Helen Morgan (Julie).

The song was originally written by Kern and Wodehouse for the 1918 musical *Oh, Lady! Lady!* Another lyric, in which the object of affection was a dollar bill, was proffered by B. G. DeSylva for the 1920 musical *Zip Goes a Million*, which closed out of town. Later that same year, Kern once more attempted to find a home for the song, in *Sally*.

Hammerstein made adjustments to the beginning of each refrain, but characteristically downplayed his work on the song, writing in a 1946 program note: "I am particularly anxious to point out that the lyric for the song 'Bill' was written by P. G. Wodehouse. Although he had always been given credit in the program, it has frequently been assumed that since I wrote all the other lyrics for *Show Boat*, I also wrote this one, and I have had praise for it which belongs to another man."

VERSE 1

I used to dream that I would discover
The perfect lover someday.
I knew I'd recognize him
If ever he came round my way.
I always used to fancy then
He'd be one of the godlike kind of men
With a giant brain and a noble head,
Like the heroes bold in the books I've read.

REFRAIN 1

But along came Bill,
Who's not the type at all.
You'd meet him on the street
And never notice him.
His form and face,
His manly grace,
Is not the kind that you*
Would find in a statue.
And I can't explain,†
It's surely not his brain
That makes me thrill.
I love him because he's wonderful,
Because he's just old Bill.‡

---

* *The 1946 score has:*
Are not the kind that you

† *The 1946 score has:*
Oh I can't explain,

‡ *The 1946 score has:*
Because he's just my Bill.

VERSE 2

He can't play golf, or tennis, or polo,
Or sing a solo, or row.
He is not half as handsome
As dozens of men that I know.
He is not tall and straight and slim,
And he dresses far worse than Ted or Jim.
And I can't explain why he should be*
Just the one, one man in the world for me.

REFRAIN 2

He's just my Bill,
An ordinary boy.†
He hasn't got a thing that I can brag about.
And yet to be
Upon his knee,
So comfy and roomy,
Seems natural to me.
And I can't explain,
It's surely not his brain
That makes me thrill.
I love him because he's—
I don't know.
Because he's just my Bill.

Wodehouse's original opening lines

REFRAIN 1

But along came Bill,
Who's quite the opposite
Of all the men
In story books
In grace and looks.
I know that Apollo
Would beat him all hollow.
And I can't explain *etc.*

REFRAIN 2

He's just my Bill;
He has no gifts at all.
A motor car
He cannot steer.
And it seems clear,
Whenever he dances,
His partner takes chances.
Oh, I can't explain *etc.*

---

* *The 1946 score has:*
Oh I can't explain why he should be

† *The 1946 score has:*
An ordinary guy.

HEY, FELLAH

Published in the 1928 Harms vocal score, but not used in the 1928 London production or the 1946 revival. Introduced by Tess "Aunt Jemima" Gardella (Queenie) and the black ensemble.

VERSE

QUEENIE: When you yen for a gent,
Give him encouragement—
Only then will he come to stay.
You must declare yourself
Or you'll be on the shelf;
If you wait too long he'll get away.
Once you have picked your boy,
Waste no time in actin' coy:
Leave no room for doubt—
Step up and speak right out.

REFRAIN

QUEENIE: Hey, fellah!
I think you're swell.
I took a look an' then I fell.
Hey, fellah!
I've got to tell,
I can't deny what you know well:
I'm longin' to be baskin'
In your caressin'
Right now.
BLACK ENSEMBLE: Vodeodo, vodeodeo-dodo.
QUEENIE: And if you'll do the askin',
I'll do the yessin',
An' how!
BLACK ENSEMBLE: Vodeodo, vodeodo-dodo.
QUEENIE: Say, fellah!
I must admit
That I suspect that you've got it.
Hey, fellah!
I'm yours to take.
So give a girl an even break,*
And if you love her,
Tell her, tell her.
Hey, fellah!
Hey, hey!

REPEAT REFRAIN

---

* *Several typescripts have:*
So give a little girl a break,

ADDED SONGS

DANCE AWAY THE NIGHT

Published in the 1928 Chappell vocal score. Toward the end of Act Two, Kim, now grown to adulthood, has a number. In the original Broadway production, Norma Terris performed imitations in this spot. Kern and Hammerstein wrote "Dance Away the Night" for the London production, where it was introduced by Edith Day and the white ensemble. In 1946, "Dance Away" was replaced by "Nobody Else But Me."

VERSE

Music in the air
And a crowd on the floor,
Stepping to the beat of the band.
We can bury care
In a tune we adore,
In the sway of a gay wonderland.

REFRAIN

Dance away the night
And we can all be happy till the morning.
Dance away the night
And we can stick together till the dawn.
Blue will turn to gray,
And when the moon steals off without a warning,
You can turn and say
You're very glad you met us,
And then forget us.
But dance away the night
And we can all be happy till the morning.
Dance away the night
And we can stick together till the dawn.

PATTER

MEN: If you want to dance,
Here's one who's clever;
Have a cavalier with style and tone.
If you're on your toes
And kind o' follow where he goes,
You'll find a rhythm
That you feel you could do
With him forever.
Get the band to break into a foxtrot
Mean enough to make the trees and rocks trot.
Then you won't stay still,
You'll dance against your will,
And keep right on until the break of day!
You pray to stay to—

REPEAT REFRAIN

AH STILL SUITS ME

Published as an individual sheet with the title "I Still Suits Me." Written especially for the 1936 film. Introduced by Paul Robeson (Joe) and Hattie McDaniel (Queenie).

JOE: Keep on a-naggin'
'N bullyraggin'
'N criticizin'
'N call me pizin,*
Ah ain't apologizin', no siree.
No matter what you say, ah still suits me.
De rag yo're chewin'
Mus' be a ruin.
Keep right on knockin',
Keep right on mockin',
Mah rockin' chair ain't rockin', no siree!
No matter what you say, ah still suits me.

QUEENIE: Does you ever wash the dishes?
Does you do the things ah wishes?
Does you do dem?
No you don't.
Will you do dem?
No you won't.
When dere's any workin' to it
Ah'm de one dat's gotta do it.
When it's rainin' who's de feller
Uses up the whole umbreller?
Selfish as a man can be!

JOE: No matter what you say, ah still suits me.

QUEENIE: You don't make money.
JOE: Ah know dat, honey.
QUEENIE: Ah never see none.
JOE: Ain't gonna be none!
But dat don't worry me none, no siree.

QUEENIE: [spoken] Shif'less! Lifeless! No good!
JOE: No matter what you say, ah still suits me.
Ah may be no good,
No good fo' yo' good,
Ah may be lifeless,
But wid one *wife* less
My life would be mo' strifeless, yes siree!
No matter what you say, ah still suits me.

[Imitating QUEENIE.]

_____
* Meaning "poison."

"Does you ever wash de dishes?
Does you do de things ah wishes?
Does you do dem?
No you don't!
Will you do dem?
No you won't!"

QUEENIE: Always imitatin' me,
An' always aggravatin' me.
Den in spite of ev'rything,
In spite of all the grief you bring,
Expectin' me to love you true.

JOE: No matter what you say ah think you do.
QUEENIE: [spoken] Ah knows ah do!

GALLIVANTIN' AROUN'

Not published, but used in the 1936 Universal Pictures film, where it was performed in blackface by Irene Dunne (Magnolia). The number is part of Magnolia's nightly performance on the *Cotton Blossom*. In an early screenplay she introduces it as a lesson for young ladies whose men are standoffish. A jazzy reprise by Kim was planned for the latter part of the film, but the footage was cut and is now lost.

VERSE

Liza Matilda Hill
Visited friends in Louisville
Den came back home.
Her man was waitin' at her front door,
Jealous an' sore,
Axin' questions:
"Liza Matilda Hill,
What did you do in Louisville,
So far from home?"
She said, "Hon,
I had fun,
Here's all dat I done done."

REFRAIN

"Been gallivantin' aroun',
Jes' gallivantin' aroun'.
My feet been off'n de groun'.
Been gallivantin' aroun',
Been dancin' all night long,
Gittin' home to bed I don' know when.
Dere ain't no tellin'
All de times I fell in love an' out again.
Been gallivantin' aroun',
But now I reckon I'm through,
'Cause now I reckon I've foun'
It's more fun lovin' you."

GOT MY EYE ON YOU

Not published. Not used. An early attempt at the moment in the 1936 film that was filled by Magnolia singing "Gallivantin' Aroun'." At the time of John McGlinn's recording of *Show Boat* no music could be found, but it resurfaced in the papers of Betty Kern Miller following her death.

VERSE

My highfalutin lover,
Yo' heart is under cover.
Dat only makes me want you mo'.
You better make yo' mind up
Dat in de end I'll wind up
By findin' what I'm lookin' fo'.
'Twon't do no good to lock yo' do'!

REFRAIN

Got my eye on you,
Look out fo' me,
Look out fo' me.
Got my eye on you,
You better beware.
All de tea leaves in my teacup
Tell me love will sneak up
On you, befo' you know it's dere.
Got my eye on you,
Look out fo' me,
Look out fo' me.
No use tryin',
You cain't git away free.
Got my heart all set upon you,
I won't let up on you
Till you git yo' eye on me.

INTERLUDE

Does you remember?
I seemed to wantcha
De very day we met.
I had a feelin'
I'd always wantcha—
I got dat feelin' yet.

REPEAT REFRAIN*

---

* Kern's manuscript includes this instruction for the
repeat: "To be sung as if arranged by Cap'n Andy
for his troupe, not the Hall Johnson choir."

I HAVE THE ROOM ABOVE HER

Published as an individual sheet. Introduced in the 1936 film by Allan Jones (Ravenal) and Irene Dunne (Magnolia).

REFRAIN 1

RAVENAL: I have the room above her.
She doesn't know I love her.
How could she know I love her,
Sitting in her room below?
Sitting in her room below,
How could she dream how far a dream
could go?
Sometimes we meet.
She smiles, and, oh, her smile's divine.
It's such a treat to hear her say,
"Hasn't the weather been fine?"
I blush and stammer badly;
My heart is beating madly.
Then she goes into her room,
And I go sadly up to mine.

INTERLUDE

RAVENAL: A lover more impetuous than I
Would say his say or know the reason
why;
But when I get my chance,
I let my chance go by.

REFRAIN 2

RAVENAL: I have the room above her.
She doesn't know I love her.
How could she know I love her,
Sitting in her room below?
Sitting in her room below,
How could she dream how far a dream
could go?
MAGNOLIA: Sometimes we meet.
He smiles, and, oh, his smile's divine.
It's such a treat to hear him say,
"Hasn't the weather been fine?"
I blush and stammer badly;
My heart is beating madly.
Then he goes up to his room,
And I go sadly into mine.

Sheet music verse

She's tall, she's fair,
She's all that I desire.
Her eyes, her hair,

The kind I most admire.
A lover more impetuous than I
Would have his say or know the reason why;
But when I get my chance,
I let my chance go by.

NOBODY ELSE BUT ME

Published as an individual sheet in 1946, but not included in the 1946 vocal score. Introduced by Jan Clayton (Kim).

Miles Kreuger dates the writing of this number to a California trip Hammerstein made in mid-September 1945. It was the last Hammerstein-Kern composition to reach Broadway.

VERSE 1

GIRL: I was a shy, demure type,
Inhibited, insecure type of girl.
A pearl of no great price was I
Till a certain cutie called me "sweetie
pie."
Now I'm smug and snooty
And my nose is high!

REFRAIN 1

GIRL: I want to be no one but me—
I am in love with a lover
Who likes me the way I am!
I have my faults;
He likes my faults.
I'm not very bright;
He's not very bright.
He thinks I'm grand—
That's grand for me!
He may be wrong,
But if we get along,
What do we care, say we.
When he holds me close,
Close as we can be,
I tell the lad
That I'm grateful and I'm glad
That I'm nobody else but me!

VERSE 2

BOY: Once I was meek and fearful,
Unconfident and uncheerful, afraid.
I stayed within my little shell
Till a certain party told me I was swell.
Now I'm hail and hearty—
I have rung the bell!

BOY: I want to be no one but me—
I am in love with a lady
Who likes me the way I am!
I have my faults;
She likes my faults.
I'm not very bright;
She's not very bright.
She thinks I'm grand—
That's grand for me!
She may be wrong,*
But if we get along,
What do we care, say we!
Walking on the shore,
Swimming in the sea,
When I am with her,
I'm glad the boy who's with her
Is nobody else but me!

Alternate verse 1

I was a shy, demure type,
Inhibited, insecure type of maid.
I stayed within my little shell
Till a certain cutie told me I was swell.
Now I'm smug and snooty,
Confident as hell!

Alternate verse 2

In 1988, John McGlinn used the following as a second verse, leading into a dance. He did not record the verse and refrain the sheet music provides for a male singer.

ENSEMBLE: They are a modern couple—
They're sinuous, lithe, and supple,
And so
They know
The dance that is up to date!
KIM: We can do the Charleston
In the lightest way.
ENSEMBLE: Can they do the Charleston?
KIM: Boy oh boy! Hey, hey!

[*Dance.*]

---

* *On the McGlinn recording, when Kim repeats the refrain these line become:*
    I get a thrill
    Knowing he gets a thrill
    When I sit on his knee.

CUT AND UNUSED SONGS

I LOOKED DOWN AT HIM (PANTRY SCENE)

Not published. Magnolia's account of her first glimpse of Ravenal was dropped during the 1927 pre-Broadway tryout. It was sung by Frederica von Stade (Magnolia) and Teresa Stratas (Julie) for John McGlinn's recording. In *Make Believe*, a study of the Broadway musicals of the 1920s, Ethan Mordden identifies the melody as a reuse of the verse from Kern's 1913 song "If We Were on Our Honeymoon."

MAGNOLIA: I looked down at him
And he looked up at me.
No one spoke for a while.
I observed he was handsome,
'Twas easy to see,
That is why I decided to smile.
For fear he might go,
I just murmur'd "Hello,"
And he said, "How d'ye do?"
Then I lowered my eyes
And to my great surprise
I noticed a crack in his shoe!
And yet his clothes were so gorgeous;
He carried a cane in his hand.
He just seemed to look
Like he stepped from a book;
The way that he talked sounded
grand.
Don't laugh!
I know I'm in love with him truly.
JULIE: You dear,
Come tell the whole story to Julie.
MAGNOLIA: As we were talking a man appeared
And spoke to him mysteriously.
That was the end;
He left with his friend.
Parting that way seemed wrong!
JULIE: You haven't known him so long.
MAGNOLIA: But we pretended we met a hundred
years ago today.
That gave him a lovely excuse to look
in my eyes and say:
"Only make believe I love you,
Only make believe that you love me . . ."

[*Into refrain of "Make Believe."*]

THE CREOLE LOVE SONG

Not published. This love duet for Magnolia and Ravenal was one of the earliest lyrics to be written for *Show Boat*, but by the time rehearsals began, it had been superseded by "You Are Love." It was sung by Jerry Hadley (Ravenal) and Frederica von Stade (Magnolia) for John McGlinn's recording.

VERSE 1

RAVENAL: When a Creole wants to woo a
maid,
With a song he'll start.
If she be grateful for his love
serenade,
She'll pay him with her heart.
MAGNOLIA: Artful way of winning
Her whose heart is spinning,
Easy victim of—
BOTH: The Creole song of love.
RAVENAL: Forever true—
Let me sing it to you!

REFRAIN

RAVENAL: When you hear me whisper a yearning
sigh,
That means I'm wanting you.
And if you see a longing in my eye,
It's all from wanting you.
That sigh will go,
That yearning eye will glow,
When once you let me know
You love me too.
But if that joy should be denied us,
And years and miles divide us,
Remember I'm rememb'ring you and
wanting you.

VERSE 2

MAGNOLIA: Reckless maid is she who scorns to
fear
The Creole and his song.
For though she would repel the bold
cavalier
Her lips will yield ere long.
RAVENAL: Long as there's a chance of
Gaining such romance of
Swift adventure,
I will sing my song of love.
MAGNOLIA: 'Tis the same impatient love
I'm feeling too—
Let me sing it to you.

REFRAIN

MAGNOLIA: When you hear me whisper a yearning
sigh,
That means I'm wanting you.
And if you see a longing in my eye,
It's all from wanting you.
That sigh will go,
That yearning eye will glow,
When once you let me know
You love me too.
But if that joy should be denied us,
And years and miles divide us,
Remember I'm rememb'ring you and
wanting you.
BOTH: Good night—
Dream if you can.
RAVENAL: My wife!
MAGNOLIA: My man!

MIS'RY'S COMIN' AROUN'

Published in the 1928 American vocal score, despite being cut before the Broadway opening. Introduced by Tess "Aunt Jemima" Gardella (Queenie), Helen Morgan (Julie), and the black ensemble.

In the notes that accompany his *Show Boat* recording John McGlinn says, "This dark, brooding piece was deleted after only one performance in Washington, D.C. . . . Kern's affection for it must have been very high—not only did he salvage most of the music for use in the overture (not composed until well after the deletion of the song), but he also insisted that the number be published in the complete vocal score (issued in April 1928)."

The song, or at least the final stanza ("On my back in a hack") has been reinstated in various productions.

QUEENIE: Mis'ry's comin' aroun',
De mis'ry's comin' aroun'.
I knows it's comin' aroun',
Don't know to who.

QUEENIE AND
COLORED
WOMEN: Mis'ry's comin' aroun',
De mis'ry's comin' aroun'.
We knows it's comin' aroun',
Don't know to who.

[ENSEMBLE *hums under dialogue.*]

A WOMAN: Heaven keep dat devil away.

TWO WOMEN: Keep dat misery* far away.
TWO OTHER
WOMEN: An' if he is a-comin' today—
WOMEN
AND MEN: Heaven, don'cha let him stay!

[ENSEMBLE *hums under dialogue.*]

QUEENIE: Mis'ry's comin' aroun',
So if you done any wrong,
Den lif' yo' feet off de groun'
An' fly away.
MEN: If you done any wrong,
Jes' lif' yo' feet off de groun'
An' fly away,
An' fly away.

[ENSEMBLE *hums under dialogue.*]

QUEENIE: I know misery's near.
I don't know why it is here.
MEN: I only knows it's near.
QUEENIE: Don't know for who.
MEN: Don't know for who.
QUEENIE: Don't know for why.
MEN: I don't know for—
QUEENIE
AND MEN: Why dat misery's near.
A MAN: I knows misery done come here.
JULIE: When I dies, let me rest
With a dish on my breast.
Some give nickel, some give dime,
All dem folks is fren's o' mine.
QUEENIE,
JULIE, AND
WOMEN: On my back in a hack,
In a fo'ty-dollar hack.
No mo' gin, no mo' rum,
Oh, de misery's done come!
MEN: Upon my poor ol' back
Within a liv'ry hack.
With no mo' rum
Oh, de misery's done come!

YES MA'AM

Not published. Appears in early scripts as a number for Ellie and admiring white girls, but was replaced during rehearsals by "Life on the Wicked Stage." Sung by Paige

* *When the word "misery" is sung on two notes, as it is in the song's opening line, it is elided as "mis'ry." When the rhythm calls for three syllables, such as here, it is spelled "misery."*

O'Hara (Ellie) for John McGlinn's recording. McGlinn notes that the tune was reused as "Poor Wet Fish" (alternate title: "First Mate Martin") in Kern and Hammerstein's next show, *Sweet Adeline*.

GIRLS: Bet your hat
You're from the show boat!
Reckon that
Isn't a slow boat.
Stage life's giddy and gay.
We've heard actresses say
Some things out of the way, eh?
ELLIE: Yes, we sure do lead a bright life.
GIRLS: Quite a step from the polite life.
ELLIE: Lights and music and beautiful dresses
And men galore.
GIRLS: Nights assured of sweet caresses
When the hero politely confesses
His true love.
ELLIE: Yet, you can't forget it's just a play.
GIRLS: It is so thrilling to meet you.
ELLIE: Only too happy to treat you.
GIRLS: We'd just love your society—
Let us show you around.
ELLIE: What a shock to propriety,
Show an actress around!
GIRLS: We are just as swift as you are, dearie.
Few are swifter, I'll be bound!
Are we slow?
No, ma'am, we're not.
You don't yet know
Things that we forgot!
We're the life of the fairs and dances.
ELLIE: Devils on wheels with your flirting glances.
GIRLS: And we don't mind taking some chances.
Yes ma'am, we'll show you what's what!

I WOULD LIKE TO PLAY A LOVER'S PART (BOX-OFFICE SCENE)

Not published. Cut during the first tryout performances in 1927. Sung by Paige O'Hara (Ellie) and David Garrison (Frank) with ensemble for John McGlinn's recording. The men and girls of the white ensemble are admiring publicity photos of the *Cotton Blossom*'s leading romantic actors, Magnolia and Ravenal.

VERSE

MEN: Her face is fair to look upon;
She wins a heart with ev'ry smile.

And one could write a book upon
Her talent, rare and versatile.

GIRLS: No wonder we are thronging at
The gate for seats upon the aisle,
To sit and gaze with longing at
Our fav'rite leading juvenile.

MEN: We bet that she's in love with
him.

GIRLS: We bet that he's in love with her.

MEN: A stage career is seldom prim,
And such romances do occur.

GIRLS: Oh, why should she be havin' all
The kisses of this gorgeous man?
The actor Gaylord Ravenal
Should lead a life bohemian!

MEN: Magnolia Hawks, enchanted
name!
Your charm for me will never
cease.
I'll put your picture in a frame
And keep it on my mantelpiece.

MEN AND GIRLS: Would that I could be he [she]
Having her [him] play opposite
me!

REFRAIN

MEN AND GIRLS: How I would like to play a lover's
part
With the girl [man] I love with
all my heart!

GIRLS: The kissing scene would be
sublime—
We'd keep rehearsing all the
time!

MEN: To show my ardent fire
Would not require dramatic art.

GIRLS: Could I be his Ophelia for a day!

MEN: If I could be her Hamlet, what a
play!
There'd be no melancholy
Dane—
I'd make the role a jolly Dane.

MEN AND GIRLS: If I [he] could only play her [my]
lover's part.

INTERLUDE

ELLIE: Tickets on sale,
Better get 'em now!
Sellin' out fast,
Better get 'em now!

GIRLS: Tickets on sale,
Better get 'em now!
Sellin' out fast,
Better get 'em now!

[Business.]

GIRLS: Would that I could be she
Having him play opposite me,
Having him play opposite me.

FRANK: Misguided ladies, you will find
The haughty race of leading men
Are but a bane to womankind;
They're fickle and unheeding
men.
A heavy man is what you seek,
A wealthy clubman type like me,
A fellow with a wicked eye—
You're glad to meet me, so am I.

GIRLS: How I would like to play a lover's
part
With the man I love with all my
heart!
His clothes all fit him to the
quick;
His hair is shiny, soft and slick.

FRANK: It's always been my hobby
To look nobby, neat, and smart.

GIRLS: You're just the very fellow who
will do!

FRANK: May I presume that's meant for
me from you?

GIRLS: You zany in a checkered suit,
You silly oaf, you mad galoot,
You'd never do to play a lover's
part!

WORLD'S FAIR OPENING CHORUS

Not published. Not used. According to John McGlinn this was a waltz, but "as no choral material has survived, it proved impossible to match accurately the surviving lyric to the orchestral score." In a typescript at the New York Public Library, this lyric leads directly into the text eventually published as the "Act Two Opening."

FAIRGOERS: Quick—let's see!
That looks like something new to me.
What a fair!
Marvels not found anywhere.
We've all seen so much,
It's all such
Fun to see
Ev'rything at the fair.
They've so many things that are rare.
Did you feel
Dizzy up in the Ferris wheel?
Why, no!
My, no!

Now shall we go
Over
To the glorious Congress of Beauty?
Don't you think it is really our—

WOMEN: Duty
To see beauty
At the fair.

MEN: It is our duty
Not to miss one beauty.
There is no
Time to go
Ev'rywhere
At the fair.

TENORS: They display
An array
Bright and gay
Ev'ry single day.

BASSES: In a single day.

WOMEN: You must show me
The tribes of Dahomey.
We'll go
And see the show.

TENORS: Go through the
Walks to the
Place where we'll look at the
Show.
Wait 'til
We are telling
The folks back in Slateville.
We will certainly
Give them a—

BASSES: Thrill.
I guess it will.
They'll be wonderstruck,
Simply thunderstruck
Still.

WOMEN: Great
Thrill
It
Will.

[All begin to sing "When we tell them about it all . . ."]

BE HAPPY TOO

Alternate title: "Cheer Up." Not published. Not used. This lyric found in a typescript at the New York Public Library. According to John McGlinn, the surviving verse music was not sufficient for a restoration. Kern and Hammerstein had reused the refrain melody as "I Might Fall Back On You."

VERSE

MAGNOLIA: Why do you fret?
And worry and stew?
When life owes a debt of
pleasure to you.
ANDY: And there may be yet a
wild oat or two to sow!
PARTHY: Rubbish!
MAGNOLIA: Look at the sky.
Be thankful to see
The sun is on high, as bright
as can be.
ANDY: To cheer you and I—
PARTHY: You mean, "you and me."
ANDY: I know.
MAGNOLIA: You will keep youthful
features
If you will imitate nature's
creatures.
PARTHY: Tch.
MAGNOLIA: You'll find that there is no
death [sic] of happiness
fair.
ANDY: With worms in the earth
And birds in the air
Expressing their mirth
And bidding dull care to go.
PARTHY: Fiddlesticks!

REFRAIN

MAGNOLIA AND ANDY: When a little birdie sees a
sunshiny day,
Then that little birdie sings
a song.
When a little doggy waxes
merry and gay,
Then he wags his tail the
whole day long.
All contented roosters
crow—
Kittens purr and
glow-worms glow.
Out at sea we always know
Happy worms [sic] by their
blow.
If the birds and beasts and
mammals
Never are blue,
Don't you think you should
be happy too?

TROCADERO OPENING CHORUS

Not published, Not used in 1927. Sung by the Ambrosian Chorus for John McGlinn. McGlinn believes this ensemble opening for the Act Two New Year's Eve scene "never reached the stage (although it may have been rehearsed, as there are several copies of the music in existence)." The number was restored in the 1989 production at New Jersey's Paper Mill Playhouse, which was telecast as part of PBS's *Great Performances* series.

PARTY GUESTS AT
CHICAGO'S
TROCADERO
HOTEL: Let's make the new year
Far from a blue year.
No need to think,
Just sing and drink good cheer.
Drown all your sorrow,
Live for tomorrow,
Just drift along—
MEN: With wine and song.
PARTY GUESTS: Tonight no folly
Could be wrong,
So drink and be merry!
Here's where we bury all thought
of gloom.
We have no room for killjoys.
New Year, we greet you.
Let us entreat you
To bring good luck, good cheer,
good fortune
To those who welcome you as we
all do.
GIRLS: We have no room for thoughts of
gloom—
Send them to an eternal doom.
BASSES: For life keeps compelling us
And temptingly telling us
That youth can never last
As long as we'd like it to.
TENORS: So we're persuading you
To stop its evading you,
And let it not slip past.
Try to hold to it fast now.
GIRLS: Why should we remember
December?
The old year's done;
The happy new year has begun.
Just keep on dreaming and
scheming
To make your life a perfect
round
Of wonderful fun.

PARTY GUESTS: Why should anyone be blue?
Life is full of things to do.
Let's just be jolly in folly,
Supremely gay
To speed the old year away!
BASSES: New year's resolutions,
Dear old institutions—
Ere the dawn we make them,
In the morning break them.
Promises of virtue
Surely will not hurt you.
Whispering them discreetly,
Earnestly and sweetly.
GIRLS AND
TENORS: Just tonight the whole world's
bright
With sheer delight,
Bright with sheer delight!
PARTY GUESTIS: Let's make the new year
Far from a blue year.
Just drift along with wine
And song and laughter.
Shout, "Happy New Year,
Happy day!"

IT'S GETTIN' HOTTER IN THE NORTH

Not published. Not used, but recorded by Frederica von Stade (Kim) for John McGlinn. Miles Kreuger explains that this Act Two dance number for Magnolia's daughter, Kim (now a young adult), was intended to bring *Show Boat*'s story to the present day, when hot dances like the Charleston and the Black Bottom were all the rage. The music is a jazzed-up version of the piano exercises Magnolia did at the very beginning of the show. In the song's place in 1927, Norma Terris (who doubled as the adult Kim) performed celebrity impressions. For the 1928 London production, Kern and Hammerstein wrote "Dance Away the Night" as a replacement.

Now,
Up in the Northern land,
Wow,
They've started struttin' and
How!
Soon as they hear a band
Ev'ry man's daughter steps
To muddy-water steps.
It's gettin' hotter in the North ev'ry day.
It's not the temp'rature that's makin' it that
way—
It's 'cause they're dancin' all the time,

The dances of a warmer clime.
If you want lovin' gals you must learn to strut.
They leave you cold unless you do nothin' else
but.
Up on the levees of Broadway
It's gettin' hotter ev'ry day.
The levee shuffle of the South
Has traveled north by hoof and mouth
Makin' our feet slow down
Doin' those neat low-down
Twistin' and turnin' steps,
Blazin' and burnin' steps.
If you want lovin' gals you must learn to strut.
They leave you cold unless you do nothin' else
but.
Up on the levees of Broadway
It's gettin' hotter every day.

ME AN' MY BOSS

Not used, but Hammerstein included the lyric in his anthology, *Lyrics.* Written for Paul Robeson to sing in the 1928 London production, but withdrawn in favor of a reprise of "Ol' Man River." No music is known to survive.

Jes' look at me an' my boss,
Jes' look at me an' my boss!
We's both de same—
We ain't no diff'rent.
I go wherever he goes.
(Dey make me ride in "Jim Crows"—
Excep' for dat
We's both de same.)
Roast beef's his favorite dish;
I likes my taters an' fish—
Excep' for dat
We ain't no diff'rent.
We both git born;
We both grow old an' die,
Him an' I,
Me an' my boss.

OVERLEAF *Nelson Eddy and Jeanette MacDonald in the 1940 film of* The New Moon

RAINBOW | 1928
THE NEW MOON | 1928

RAINBOW (1928)

Tryouts: Chestnut Street Opera House, Philadelphia, October 29–November 10, 1928; Maryland Theatre, Baltimore, November 12–17, 1928. New York run: Gallo Opera House; opened November 21, 1928; closed December 15, 1928; 29 performances. A New Romantic Musical Play of California in the Days of '49. Presented by Philip Goodman. Book by Laurence Stallings and Oscar Hammerstein II. Music by Vincent Youmans. Lyrics by Oscar Hammerstein II. Book staged by Oscar Hammerstein II. Musical numbers staged by Busby Berkeley. Orchestrations by Max Steiner, with additional orchestrations by Paul Lannin and Oscar Radin. Orchestra under the direction of Max Steiner. Scenery designed and painted by Frank E. Gates and Edward A. Morange. Costumes designed by Charles Le Maire. Research and technical direction by Leighton K. Brill.

Cast: Louise Brown (Virginia Brown), Charles Ruggles ("Nasty" Howell), Allan Prior (Harry Stanton), Libby Holman (Lotta), Harland Dixon (Sergeant Major), Rupert Lucas (Major Davolo), Helen Lynd (Penny), Brian Donlevy (Captain Robert Singleton), Ned McGurn (Mess Sergeant), Henry Pemberton (Colonel Brown), Leo Mack (Corporal), Stewart Edwards (First Private), Leo Dugan (Second Private), Ward Arnold (Third Private), Randall Fryer (Rookie), Frank King (Bartender), Mary Carney (Señora Mendoza), Leo Nash (Peon), Charles Ralph (Servant), Valia Valentinova (Spanish Girl), May Barnes (Snow Ball), George Magis (Frenchie), Chester Bree (Mr. Jackson), Edward Nemo (Egg), Ralph Walker (Tough), Kitty Coleman (Kitty) and ensemble.

The story begins at Ft. Independence, Missouri, in 1848. Colonel Brown and his cavalry unit are planning to lead a wagon train of gold-prospectors to California. Among the travelers are "Nasty" the mule skinner and a well-mannered Sergeant Major who vie for the same woman, Penny. The colonel's lively daughter, Virginia, also has two suitors. Captain Singleton is a good man. Major Davolo has a long association with a "river belle" named Lotta, whom he intends to abandon in Missouri. Life has not been easy for Lotta. A few years earlier, while involved with Davolo, she was also courted by Captain Harry Stanton, who came to blows with Davolo over her honor. Davolo claimed the fight was unfair, and Stanton, who might have married Lotta, went AWOL to escape court martial. It is this same Stanton, now an experienced mountain guide, who arrives at the fort that night. He meets Virginia and is immediately smitten. He re-encounters Davolo; a fight begins; they struggle over a gun; and Davolo is killed. Stanton is put in the stockade and will most likely be hanged. But with help from his old friend Singleton and his new friend Nasty, Stanton escapes in the disguise of a sickly parson and joins the wagon train. Virginia is very attentive to the so-called parson, but when Stanton learns that she is his friend

Singleton's girl, he tries to avoid her. Another complication: Lotta has recognized him and wants him back. Stanton decides to let the wagon train and both women go on without him. But Virginia runs back to him, dressed in Lotta's red cape.

Act Two begins in Sacramento about a year later. Stanton and Virginia are married and run a gambling saloon, but Stanton feels he hasn't done right by her. When some of the old regiment appear and Virginia is delighted to see them, Stanton feels all the more keenly the stature he lost when he left the Army. It happens that Lotta is among the saloon's "hired songbirds" that evening. After Stanton picks a fight with Virginia, he leaves with Lotta. The next scene is six months later. Virginia is back with the regiment, and has sent Penny to find out how Stanton is. The answer is not good. Stanton is wounded, and he and Nasty have numerous enemies among the gamblers and gunslingers. Nasty is killed during the scene. Singleton advises Stanton to reenlist or to get out of town with Lotta. The final scene is at San Francisco's Presidio one year later. In a variation of the opening scene, Stanton arrives and sees Virginia. Apologies are exchanged and the curtain falls.

A 1930 Warner Bros. film adaptation was titled *Song of the West*. Directed by Ray Enright, it starred John Boles and Vivienne Segal. Hammerstein did not write any of the new songs added to the film. The film is considered lost.

The main source for this chapter is a piano-vocal score reconstructed by Youmans authority Aaron Gandy from music manuscripts and script material held by the Youmans family and at the Library of Congress. Four songs were published individually. Drafts of the script survive at the Library of Congress, at the Rodgers & Hammerstein Organization in New York City, at the Warner Bros. Archive at the University of Southern California, and in the private collection of Aaron Gandy.

Some material has not been found. The Act Two opening is missing. "A Faded Rose" was advertised as an individual sheet, but was cut before Broadway and apparently never published; the lyric is lost. "Forty-niner and His Clementine" was cut before New York and lost. The published song "Who Am I?" does not appear in this chapter because the lyric was written by Gus Kahn.

Rainbow was ambitious in its musical storytelling. Howard Barnes of the *New York Herald Tribune* noted, "The producer was well advised in calling his piece a musical play, rather than a musical comedy. . . . One is caught up in a trek across half a continent from a Missouri fort to the California of '49. . . . There is a killing in the first scene and another in the second act." Barnes also praised Youmans's "co-ordinated score." In the *Sun*, Richard Lockridge said, "It has music that you can get a voice into and voices for the singing. It has a story that begins at one end and goes through to the other—a story which is romantic but never flatly silly. It has lines that actors can speak without hiding their heads and

lyrics which actually make sense." But in 1959 Hammerstein reflected: "If the play had been as good as a great many people said it was, it would still be running in stock companies, and it would have run longer in New York. But it was a try, and I must say I always respect musical plays and other plays which try to break ground, even when they fail. We need that kind of failure very much, so that someone can come along and succeed with the same idea later on."

OPENING CHORUS: ON THE GOLDEN TRAIL

Not published. Introduced by an unidentified soloist, Rupert Lucas (Major Davolo), and ensemble. Reprised at the end of the show.

VERSE

SINGER: Gent around the lady*
And the lady don't go.
Gent around the lady
And the lady go slow.
Swing your partner
With a do-si-do—
Sashayyyy!
Gent around the lady
And the lady go slow.
Buck and wing around her;
Kiss her when you go.
Swing your partner
With a do-si-do—
Sashayyyy!

REFRAIN

ALL: Over the mountains and over the plain,†
On the golden trail.

---

* *An earlier version of the verse begins with these additional lines:*

SERGEANT: Stop and listen where you stand—
Go and take your partner's hand.
ENSEMBLE: Don't you tell us what to do!
We have waited long enough—for you.
MEN: Get started.
GIRLS: Teach us something new—
ALL: To do.

† *Sources vary in using singular or plural forms of the words "mountain," "valley," and "train."*

Why are we fighting the sun and
    the rain?
Gold is in the vale.
Ragged and dusty with sweat and
    pain,
But we will never fail—
Over the mountains and over the
    plain,
God will be watching the golden
    trail.

MAJOR DAVOLO: Wagon train leaving for the
    golden west—
Fill up with liquor and dance
    your best.

BOYS: There's gold in the valley and
    gold in the plain—

DAVOLO: So off to California in your wagon
    train.

MY MOTHER TOLD ME NOT TO TRUST A SOLDIER

Published as an individual sheet in 1930. Introduced by Harland Dixon (Sergeant Major) and Helen Lynd (Penny). Youmans had previously used the tune as "Draw Your Own Conclusion" in *Oh, Please!* (1926).

VERSE

SERGEANT MAJOR: Will you take a sergeant major
    With a chestnut steed?

PENNY: Sergeant Major, I'm afraid you're
    Not the man I need.
    I appreciate your offer kind,
    But there is another on my
    mind.

SERGEANT MAJOR: I am at a loss to understand
    your point of view.
    How can you reject the plea
    Of a man the likes of me?

PENNY: I've been warned against the
    Army blue!

REFRAIN 1

PENNY: My mother told me not to trust
    a soldier.
    A soldier's wife don't lead no
    life at all.
    Any night or day
    He can stay away
    And explain his absence by a
    bugle call.

And furthermore, my mother
    says a soldier
Will kiss me rough and hug me
    black and blue.

SERGEANT MAJOR: But I'm as gentle as a cat—
    I never hug a girl like that.

PENNY: Then why should I be wasting
    time on you?

Unpublished refrain 2

PENNY: My lover is a driver of a mule
    team.
    He drives a covered wagon
    cross the plain.
    On a starry night
    'Twill be my delight
    Just to sit beside him while he
    holds the rein.

SERGEANT MAJOR: Your lover may be fit to drive a
    mule team,
    Because you're so much hand-
    somer than he.
    So if you must be somebody's
    bride,
    I think you'd look your best
    beside
    A sergeant major on the type
    of me.

VIRGINIA

Not published, but uses the same melody as the published "If I Told You" from *Wildflower* (1923). Introduced by Louise Brown (Virginia Brown), Brian Donlevy (Captain Robert Singleton), and male ensemble.

REFRAIN

SINGLETON: "Be my Virginia—Virginia, be mine."
    Over and over again
    I give Virginia that heartbreaking
    line.
    But she is deaf to my pain.
    Standing neath her window,
    Singing off the key,
    Ev'ry star in the sky
    Hears me cry for Virginia,
    But Virginia only laughs at me.

INTERLUDE

BOYS: Miss Virginia, dear, why do you
    Let this lovesick mustang woo you?

You, who could have any who you
    choose?
If you want a Romeo, my
    Voice can warble—oh me, oh my.
    His voice only gives a girl the blues.

SINGLETON: Go away!

BOYS: The gall of you!

VIRGINIA: I wish you'd all go 'way—
    Yes, all of you.
    Love, love, that's all that I hear.

BOYS: And while we sigh here,
    You'd let us die here.

REPEAT REFRAIN

I WANT A MAN

Published as an individual sheet. Introduced by Libby Holman (Lotta). It has been reported that the tune was made to measure for Holman, who was called to Philadelphia to replace Francetta Malloy as Lotta. Youmans scholar Aaron Gandy points out that in 1926 the melody had been slated as an uptempo number for Dorothie Bigelow and male ensemble in the short-lived *Oh, Please!*

VERSE

When I was old enough for dances,
I believed romances lurked ev'rywhere.
That life was love I was persuaded;
With my hair in pigtails braided
I sought new love.
Now I still seek true love.

REFRAIN

I want a man,
A man I'll keep wanting until I die.
I want to find
The kind that keeps wanting the same as I.
Don't want a butterfly lover,
Stopping to pass the time.
If I am true to my lover,
He too
Has to
Be true.
Say it's a dream, say I'm a fool,
Tell me I don't belong;
Say it's a scheme that breaks the rule,
Tell me that I'm all wrong.
And yet,
There may
Come one

Someday—
Someone,
A man who will be a fool like me,
Loving the same as I.

STAR SOLILOQUY

Not published. Introduced by Allan Prior (Harry Stanton).

Star, you're the last one left in the sky.
Star, are you just as lonely as I?
Do you think we two might find a friend
Who would see us through
Our journey's end?
Far, far away though that one may be,
Star, light the way to someone for me.

I LIKE YOU AS YOU ARE

Published as an individual sheet. Introduced by Allan Prior (Harry Stanton). Reprise introduced by Louise Brown (Virginia) and Prior in Act One, Scene 5.

VERSE

STANTON: [*to* VIRGINIA] I guess you're not so glad
to know me, ma'am.
You've taken careful pains to show me,
ma'am,
My wit did not regale your
Evening and I'm a failure.
Pardon me, my mistake—
Something we all must make.
I did my best, a man can do no more.
Have I said things that you dislike
me for?
I'm far from perfect, that is true,
ma'am;
But I can say the same for you,
ma'am.

REFRAIN

STANTON: I could think of lots of things
That might improve you,
But I like you as you are, ma'am.
Though you have a heart of stone,
A man could move you
If he liked you as you are.

I should want to make you over just a
little;
I would not go very far, ma'am—
Just a change here and there, one or
two,
And I think I could make something
grand out of you.
I would like to see your eyes a little
bluer,
But they're all right as they are,
ma'am.
And the freckles on your nose,
They could be fewer,
But they're not enough to mar.
I'll admit that to me you look great,
But my friends all agree
I'm the worst judge of girls in the state.
I suppose that must be true,
And that's the reason why
I like you as you are.

REPRISE REFRAIN

VIRGINIA: You are not a good example of a
parson,
But I like you as you are.
STANTON: I've committed every crime excepting
arson.
VIRGINIA: But I like you as you are.
I should want to make you over just a
little;
I would not go very far—
Just a change here and there, one or two,
And I think I could make something
grand out of you.
STANTON: Would you like to have my eyes a little
bluer?
VIRGINIA: No, they're all right as they are.
STANTON: I have far too many faults;
They might be fewer.
VIRGINIA: Well, they're not enough to mar.
I'll admit that to me you look great.
STANTON: Then, my dear, I can see that you're
The worst judge of men in the state.
BOTH: I suppose that must be true,
And that's the reason why
I like you as you are.

THE ONE GIRL

Published as an individual sheet. Introduced by Allan Prior (Stanton) and male ensemble.
Added to Act One during the out-of-town tryouts, using the melody from the cut song "Sunrise." As Stan-

ton says in the script: "The best song I know is your own regimental song, because you can march to it, and at the same time be making love to your best girl as she waves to you from her window."

VERSE

When the troopers ride away along a trail,
When the sunny side of day begins to pale,
Then we like to sprawl about a fire aglow.
Then my dreams are all about a girl I know.
Laughing eyes, golden hair,
Tender arms, white and fair,
Lips that I press to my own.
When will I be riding home across the plain?
When will I be riding home to her again?

REFRAIN

The one girl that I love,
The one girl that loves me,
Waits until my troop comes over the trail.
The one girl that I love,
The one girl that loves me—
That's the prize I pray for,
That's what I go home to stay for.
When I say "Goodbye, love,"
The fair smile that I see
Cheers me on when I go out to the fight, boys.
And my heart is light, boys,
And I feel as strong as steel as long as
The one girl that I love will love me.

LET ME GIVE ALL MY LOVE TO THEE (HYMN)

Published as an individual sheet in 1930. Introduced by Louise Brown (Virginia), Libby Holman (Lotta), Allan Prior (Stanton) and ensemble. The scene is a prayer meeting, but Virginia and Stanton are singing directly to each other.

Let me give all my love to thee,
My love to thee,
My love to thee.
Then wilt thou give thy love to me,
Thy love to me,
Thy love to me.
If I know my soul is thine,
Even when I stray,
Guided by your light divine,
I will find my way.
Let me give all my love to thee,

My love to thee,
My love to thee.
Then wilt thou give thy love to me,
Thy love to me,
Thy love to me.

DIAMOND IN THE ROUGH

Not published. Introduced by Charles Ruggles ("Nasty" Howell) and Helen Lynd (Penny).

VERSE 1

NASTY: You think that I'm a nasty cuss,
A mean and low sarcastic cuss,
But underneath this flannel vest
There dwells an honest, hairy chest.
And underneath this hairy chest,
A tender, human heart may rest.

REFRAIN 1

NASTY: I'm just a diamond,
An unpolished diamond,
A diamond that gleams in the rough.
I like saloons at night
An' drinkin' hearty.
I always start a fight.
They say I'm the knife of every party.
I'll drink a snootful
And fill a galoot full
Of holes just to show I'm no bluff.
I never like to torture any victim.
So after I have shot him down and kicked
him,
If he's still in pain,
Then I shoot him again—
After all, I'm just a diamond in the rough.

VERSE 2

NASTY: When I was but a tiny tyke,
I had a nurse I didn't like.
I put some arsenic in her tea.
PENNY: You were as cute as you could be.
NASTY: My mother took me on her knee
And softly sighed and said to me:

REFRAIN 2

NASTY: "You're just a diamond,
An unpolished diamond,
A diamond that gleams in the rough."
The men I shoot and slay,
I always bury.

And every Easter day,
I plant a flower in the cemetery.
PENNY: You're just a playboy,
A big hearted gay boy,
But when you get mad you are tough.
NASTY: And if a gal don't give me what I sigh for,
She'll know what I have socked her in the
eye for.
I may break her arm,
But I don't mean no harm—
BOTH: After all, I'm [you're] just a diamond in
the rough.

WHO WANTS TO LOVE SPANISH LADIES?

Not published. Introduced by the ensemble.

WHORES: Who wants to love Spanish ladies?
If you would love Spanish ladies,
All that you need is a little gold.
If you get gold in the army,
Once a month doled in the army,
You'll get warm arms waiting to enfold.
So when you get your gold,
You come down here.
SOLDIERS: We come down here to buy a pretty
little lady.
WHORES: Soldier, down here.
SOLDIERS: When you have gold, it won't take long
To find a lady down here.
WHORES: We have to waste our time with miners
Till the soldiers come.
SOLDIERS: We're here.
WHORES: Somehow the world gets brighter
When we see the soldiers come
Down here.
SOLDIERS: With pockets full of gold—
Yes, we can offer gold, my dear.
WHORES: Now that you've mentioned that,
We'd like to ask you,
Who'll buy a nice Spanish lady?
WHORES: You can have this Spanish lady—
All that you need is a little gold.
When you get gold in the army,
Once a month doled in the army,
You'll get warm arms waiting to
enfold.
SOLDIERS: We'll buy a nice Spanish lady—
All that we need is a little gold.
When we get gold in the army,
Once a month doled in the army,
We'll get warm arms waiting to enfold.

I want a little señorita,
My one-night-only Carmencita.
WHORES: We will be faithful to you—
For that one night we'll be true.
SOLDIERS: Love—
WHORES: We want to love you.
SOLDIERS: Me—
WHORES: Be sweet as honey.
SOLDIERS: Dear.
WHORES: All we want of you—
SOLDIERS: What?
WHORES: Is plenty money.
SOLDIERS: We've been waiting.
WHORES: Red lips are waiting you,
Kisses awaiting you.
ALL: For one night of love
We're not too proud or unwilling.
Come join the crowd, make it
thrilling—
You'll be allowed anything you say.
Taking a chance is exciting;
Youth and romance are inviting.
On with the dance,
Let the music play.
Night shades are falling,
Romance is calling,
Love is enthralling
As we dance the night into day.
Ah!

HAY, STRAW

Published as an individual sheet. Introduced by Louise Brown (Virginia), Harland Dixon (Sergeant Major), and ensemble.

VERSE

SERGEANT MAJOR: When the boys come to the
awkward squad,
Keepin' in step is the thing.
Hay is tied to left feet,
Straw is tied to right feet.
VIRGINIA: When a girl's dumb and a bit
slipshod
Doing the reel or a fling,
Teach her to dance as the boys
in blue go
And she'll go where you go.

REFRAIN

BOTH: Hay, straw!
That's all a girl will have to know.
Hay! To have her left foot go—

124

Straw! And then her right.
Seesaw!
The principle is just the same,
Anyone can play the game.
Dancing through the night
With your partner,
There's no art nor
Science to the thing.
Keep your feet upon the beat
    and sing.
Hay, straw!
Just put your arm around your
    squaw—
Hay! And when she starts to
    thaw,
Straw! You've got her right!

PATTER [*sung in counterpoint as girls repeat refrain*]

SOLDIERS: Left an' right an' right an' left
He tells them all,
An' bright an' slight an' hefty
    belles
Are sure to know.
If they'll only murmur
Hay foot, straw foot, hay foot,
    straw foot!
It can be as simple as a little
    A-B-C,
A girl who has a little heel and
    toe
Has the brain to murmur
Hay foot, straw foot, hay foot,
    straw foot!

THE BRIDE WAS DRESSED IN WHITE

Published as an individual sheet. Introduced by Charles Ruggles ("Nasty" Howell).

VERSE 1

A miner met a girl in Sacramento.
The boy was handsome, and the girl was fair.
He kissed her in the moonlight—who can blame them?
For when it's moonlight, love is in the air.
He promised that he'd wed her in the springtime;
And this was only summer, so you see,
The girl would have to wait for wedding-ring time—

But what girl wouldn't wait for such as he?*
For he was an upright fellow,
And when springtime's voice was mellow,
He vowed that he'd make her an honest girl.
Ah—!

REFRAIN 1

The bride was dressed in white;
A spray of orange blossoms
Was dangling in a bouquet at her side.
The wedding bells were ringing,
And the choirboys were singing,
And the organ pealed to cheer the blushing bride.
The bridegroom didn't falter
When he led her to the altar
And he placed a ring upon her finger pink.
Then he gently kissed her head,
And these words he softly said:
"There never was a girl like Lizzie Glutz."

VERSE 2

Then heaven seemed to be in Sacramento,
Because they knew this was their wedding night.
He took her home and showed her to his mother,
And then he took a walk while they made friends.
When he returned, he found, to his amazement,
The blinds were drawn, no lights were burning gay.
The doctor met him at the door and murmured:
"My boy, your loving wife has passed away."†
He could hear his mother weeping,
And he saw his sweetheart sleeping;
He knew she must be with the angels now—
Ah—!

REFRAIN 2

The bride was dressed in white
Within an oaken casket
With shiny silver handles on the side.
The funeral bells were ringing,
And the choirboys were singing,
And the organ pealed to mourn the stricken bride.
The bridegroom didn't falter
As he walked up to the altar,
But he suddenly grew faint, and then he fell.

---

* *Several typed copies of the lyric add two lines here:*
    Now this part of my story I regret to tell,
    They loved each other not wisely, but too well.

† *Several typed copies of the lyric add two lines here:*
    How things like these occur is very hard to tell.
    Her heart was weak, and she was never very well.

He was dead, that's why he fell,
And his mother died as well.
He loved his bride when she was dressed in white.

Unpublished verse 3

So two more souls had gone to meet their maker;
In yonder graveyard three more bodies lie.

[PENNY *wails.* NASTY *stops singing and says "I'll skip to the nice part."*]

The bride of just one day had left a baby,
An infant scarcely more than one week old.
There's no one but an uncle to protect her,
And uncles as a rule are very cold.
But she ran around so merry,
Like a little laughing fairy,
Until her legs got mangled in the mill!*

CUT AND UNUSED SONGS

GET A HORSE, GET A MULE

This Act One trio was performed in Philadelphia but dropped before Broadway. A copyist piano-vocal score preserves a lyric for the verse, but only the final line of the refrain. Introduced by Helen Lynd (Penny), Charles Ruggles ("Nasty" Howell), and Harland Dixon (Sergeant Major).

VERSE

Some men give engagement rings
And some men give you pearls.
But there are lots of other things
That win the hearts of girls.
What?
I can't sing of stars above
Like poem-writing fools,
But if you'll take my honest love,
I'll throw in two fine mules.

---

* *Stage directions instruct that Penny's sobbing prevents Nasty from performing a fourth verse, wherein "the baby grows up and marries a bad man and then she has a baby and the baby gets took with the cholera, and in the chorus it says, 'The mother's dressed in black,' and so you know the baby's dead."*

REFRAIN (LAST LINE ONLY)

. . . What's a girl to do!

HOW TO WIN A MAN (PRIMPING NUMBER)

This song was used in the out-of-town tryouts. The lyric stanzas below were found in various sources; it is not known if all were in use at the same time. Introduced by Louise Brown (Virginia Brown), Helen Lynd (Penny), and female ensemble.

GIRLS: Along a covered-wagon trail,
You don't find fashions Parisienne.
But for Sunday meeting we must look
    our best.
I can't wait to see the minister—
The wagon train is in a stir
To meet him,
Greet him.
[*Three lines missing.*]

[*The girls ask* VIRGINIA *about the new preacher.*]

VIRGINIA: With a man so young and pious,
In religion we'll rejoice.
He will soothe and mollify us
With his tender voice.
When you hear this gentle preacher,
You will think the Bible grand.
GIRLS: Has this handsome Bible teacher
Ever tried to hold thy hand?

PENNY: Treat the man you love like dirt;
Let him see you kiss and flirt.
But if he should flirt instead,
Bounce a hammer off his head!
GIRLS: Just paint your face, don't come to
    blows.
She has the parson by the nose,
For she, you see, is painted like a rose.
PENNY: Take his money, spend it all.
Make him wriggle,
Make him crawl.
Ev'ry man was meant to squirm.
[*To* NASTY] Just like you, you little
    worm.
GIRLS: We are compelled to hide from men
    outside,
Who ought to, but can't, come in.
[GIRLS *hum for eight measures.*]
We make modesty a sentry,

To deny a man an entry
While we're primping, primping.
And for a man to see
Our lingerie
Is thought to be
Quite a sin.

If you wonder very often
Why you're under Cupid's ban,
Here's your blunder—not to soften
When you love a man.
You can make him love you blindly;
You can take him as you plan.
Don't forsake him, treat him kindly—
That is how to win a man.

Please go away and stay
Until we're dressed.
Girls need time to look their best.
[*Eight bars of humming*]
For you cannot place a bustle
If your hands are in a hustle—
That's not primping, that's skimping.
To place a beauty spot
Can take a lot of time,
And curls must be pressed.

VIRGINIA: My dear sisters,
If a girl is really clever
And would fascinate a man,
She must curl and powder ever;
She must use a fan.
She must see that all her features
Are what he, the foolish man,
Hopes to see, you silly creatures—
She must learn to use a fan.

I LOOK FOR LOVE

Advertised as an individual sheet, but apparently never published. Although there are similarities between this lyric and "I Want a Man," which replaced it, the melodies are very different. Introduced during the Philadelphia tryout by Francetta Malloy (the original Lotta).

REFRAIN

I look for love,
But love never looks for me.
I sit alone
And wonder where love can be.
Where is my man
Who'll search the world until at last he's found me?

Where is my man?
Where are those arms I long to feel around me?
Laugh if you want to;
Tell me I don't belong.
Maybe you're right,
And maybe my dream's all wrong.
Still I will dream
Of that one man that I never see.
I look for love—
Won't love ever look for me?

SUNRISE

Not published. Performed in Philadelphia but dropped before the New York opening. The melody was reused for "The One Girl." Introduced by Francetta Malloy (Lotta) and Allan Prior (Harry Stanton).

VERSE

Say, do you remember how we used to sing?
Maybe you remember how we used to sing
In the golden yesterdays beyond recall.
Through a crimson haze o' dreams I see it all.
Mem'ries like marching feet
Come to me down the street
'Mid the gray shadows that fall
While the boys go marching by,
A happy throng,
And they sing again the regimental song.

REFRAIN

The dawn breaks,
The sunrise is a flame in the sky,
And with sunrise you come over the hill.
My heart wakes at sunrise
And my hopes are up high
While we stroll together
Over fields of sage and heather.
You may go,
But I know
That my dreams
Cannot die.
When the morning sun comes up to remind me,
When I see a new sky,
A bright golden flame to change the blue sky,
I won't see the sunrise,
I'll see you.

THE NEW MOON (1928)

Tryouts: Chestnut Street Opera House, Philadelphia, December 26, 1927–January 7, 1928; closed without reaching Broadway.* Revised and reopened: Hanna Theatre, Cleveland, August 27, 1928–September 8, 1928; Shubert Alvin Theatre, Pittsburgh, September 10–15, 1928. New York run: Imperial Theatre, opened September 19, 1928; closed November 16, 1929; reopened Casino Theatre, November 18, 1929; closed December 14, 1929; 509 performances. A Musical Romance. Presented by Laurence Schwab and Frank Mandel. By Oscar Hammerstein II, Frank Mandel, and Laurence Schwab.† Music by Sigmund Romberg. Musical numbers staged by Bobby Connolly. Orchestrations by Emil Gerstenberger, Alfred Goodman, and (uncredited) Hans Spialek. Musical direction by Alfred Goodman. Settings by Donald Oenslager. Costumes by Charles Le Maire.

Cast: Evelyn Herbert (Marianne Beaunoir), Robert Halliday (Robert Misson), Gus Shy (Alexander), Marie Callahan (Julie), William O'Neal (Phillippe),‡ Pacie Ripple (Monsieur Beaunoir), Edward Nell Jr. (Captain Georges Duval), Lyle Evans (Besac), Earle Mitchell (Jacques), Esther Howard (Clotilde Lombaste), Frank Dobert (Doorman of the Tavern), Aleta Edwards (Flower Girl), Herman Belmonte (a Spaniard), Carola Taylor (a Dancer), Thomas Dale (Fouchette), Rosita and Ramon (Dancers), Lester Dorr (Captain Dejean), and ensemble.

The wealthy Beaunoir household of French New Orleans is agog when the great detective Ribaud arrives from Paris in pursuit of noble-born revolutionist Robert Misson, who is wanted for murder. The daughter of the house, Marianne, is attended by her maid, Julie, adored by the sailors who work for her father, and wooed by Captain Duval. New to the household are two bondservants, Robert and Alexander, who are really Misson and his servant in disguise. Robert has found local allies in Phillippe and other liberty-minded men, but instead of fleeing, he remains in order to court Marianne at a

---

* The 1927 cast included Jessie Royce Landis (Marianne), who was succeeded by Desiree Tabor (Marianne), William Wayne (Alexander), and Margaret Irving (Duchene). Robert Halliday, William O'Neal, Esther Howard, and Lyle Evans played the same roles in 1927 and 1928.

† The program does not separate book and lyrics credits. The uncredited direction of the book was also shared by Hammerstein, Mandel, and Schwab.

‡ The character named "Besac" in the original Broadway program is seen as "Besace" in certain other sources; similarly, the program has "Phillippe" while the vocal score has "Philippe."

---

masked ball. He is arrested by Ribaud and put on Beaunoir's ship, *New Moon*, to sail to Paris for sentencing. Before crossing the Atlantic, however, the ship has one stop to make. Marianne has promised to accompany a group of marriageable women destined for Martinique. But before they reach Martinique, the *New Moon* is overtaken by Phillippe and his men, who free Robert, arrest Ribaud, and establish a democratic community on a remote island. Robert and Marianne, still in love and still too proud to admit it, are married in word but not in deed. A year later, an enemy ship docks. Ribaud thinks he is vindicated, but the new arrivals explain that the king has been overthrown and the French are all free citizens. A subplot romantically links the servants Julie and Alexander—but Clotilde Lombaste, his first wife, is among the brides and wants him back

A London production, starring Evelyn Laye and Howett Worster, opened at the Theatre Royal, Drury Lane, on April 4, 1929, and ran for 147 performances.

For decades *The New Moon* was a staple at light opera companies. A production at the Paper Mill Playhouse in Millburn, New Jersey in April 1983 led to a subsequent staging by the New York City Opera in August 1986. New York City Center's Encores! series mounted a semistaged production in March 2003.

MGM released two film adaptations: the first in 1930 (directed by Jack Conway and starring Grace Moore and Lawrence Tibbett); and another in 1940 (directed by Robert L. Leonard and starring Jeanette MacDonald and Nelson Eddy). Both were liberally rewritten by hands other than Hammerstein's. In April 1989, the New York City Opera production, starring Leigh Munro and Richard White, was aired on the PBS series *Great Performances*.

Recordings by members of the original Broadway, Los Angeles, and Melbourne casts can be heard on the CD *The Ultimate Sigmund Romberg, Volume 2* (Pearl). Recordings made by members of the original London cast have been reissued on another Pearl CD, along with numbers from *The Desert Song* and Robert Stolz's *Blue Train*. A 1963 studio recording of highlights (EMI Angel) featured Dorothy Kirsten and Gordon MacRae; the 2003 Encores! production, with Christiane Noll and Rodney Gilfry, led to the most complete recording of the score to date (Ghostlight).

The main source for this chapter is the published vocal score. (Some slight differences between the American edition and the British edition are noted below.) The script was published as well. Additional script and score material for the 1928 version was reviewed at the Rodgers & Hammerstein Organization in New York City, the Music Division of the Library of Congress (Hammerstein and Romberg collections), the Tams-Witmark Music Library, and the Shubert Archive. The major sources for the 1927 version of the show are manuscripts in the Warner/Chappell Collection and Romberg's holograph piano-vocal score, both at the Library of Congress. A script for the 1927 version

has not been located, but as extensive passages were underscored, some dialogue survives in the piano-vocal material.

There is no evidence of how, or if, Schwab, Mandel, and Hammerstein collaborated on lyrics. It is generally thought that neither Schwab or Mandel wrote lyrics. It may be worth noting that Hammerstein included two *New Moon* selections in his anthology, *Lyrics*, without special credit to Schwab and Mandel, while he deliberately omitted lyrics from *The Desert Song* (which he identified as a collaboration with Otto Harbach).

No material has been found for three songs performed during the 1928 out-of-town tryouts, but dropped before New York: "A Love That Lasts," "The First Man I Kiss," and "Hot and Cold."

Several titles from the 1927 Philadelphia program are also missing: "Close Your Eyes and Love Me" for Julie, Alexander, and female ensembles in Act One (although we have a 1927 published song for Julie and Alexander called "When I Close My Eyes"); "I Love You," a solo for Robert at the end of Act Two; and "Women, Women, Women," which is believed to have turned into "Funny Little Sailor Men." The Act Two "Musical Scene" for Duval, Robert, Phillippe, and male ensemble may have been mostly underscoring; and "The Call of Home," for Robert, Besac, and ensemble might be the same as the Warner-Chappell "Finaletto, Act Two Scene 3," which mentions "home" several times. This chapter does not include a lyric in French titled "A l'Abordage," found in the Warner-Chappell piano-vocal material, which does not name the characters who would sing it or indicate its place in the score.

Hammerstein recalled the December 1927 Philadelphia tryout of *The New Moon* as:

a hopeless flop. I heard a couple coming out of the theatre, before the curtain was down one night, and the woman said to the man, "They can never fix this one if they work for the rest of their lives." We closed the show after two weeks in Philadelphia, and we wrote a new libretto keeping very little of the old one. We also wrote a new score. What was left of the original production was the scenery and costumes. We also gave it a new cast. We reopened the play in Cleveland eight months later, and then we played Pittsburgh and then brought it to New York, where it became one of the biggest operetta vehicles ever produced here. It has been playing on and off all over the world ever since.

ACT ONE OPENING

Published in the vocal score. Introduced by the ensemble.

GIRLS: Dainty wisp of thistledown,
On a summer evening
You'll be near some cavalier.
Dainty wisp of thistledown,
Vaguer than the mist,
Magic for maidens to wear,
When they're young and fair
And want to be kissed—
Delicate gossamer charm
Is made to be crushed in a lover's
arm.
MEN: Here do we introduce a faithful
servant of the King!*
GIRLS AND MEN: Here is the great Monsieur
Ribaud,
Who made all Paris ring!
GIRLS: Here in Louisiana
He'll be happy, we know!
GIRLS AND MEN: Here there's not a man alive
who'll not try to be Ribaud.

MARIANNE

Published as an individual sheet. Introduced by Robert
Halliday (Robert), Gus Shy (Alexander), and male
ensemble. An earlier and entirely different "Marianne"
is with the cut songs at the end of the chapter.

INTRODUCTION

ROBERT: I'll sing to my love and I'll tell her
The secret I keep in my heart.
ALEXANDER: If her father once overhears you,
They'll wheel you away in a cart.

---

* In 1927, Ribaud's entrance was instead the entrance
of a noble Parisienne:
ENSEMBLE: Here do we introduce no less than la
Duchesse Duchene.
Here, may you feel at home as in your
home upon the Seine.
DUCHENE: Here in Louisiana I'll be happy, I know.
ENSEMBLE: Dear, there's not a man alive who'll not try
to be your beau.

VERSE

ROBERT: Marianne is what they call you,
But there's no name describing all
you
Could mean to any lucky fellow.
Oh, lucky fellow,
Who will he be?
In your eye an elfin gleaming
Can make me lose myself in
dreaming
And hoping too
Someday you
May dream of me.

REFRAIN 1

ROBERT: Marianne, I want to love you.
I'll repeat it ev'ry day, dear.
Marianne, I want to love you.
It's a simple thing to say, dear.
Were there more praises to sing
And phrases to ring,
I'd sing them to you.
Let others doubt them who will,
But I would be still
Believing them true.
And though you may never love
me,
I will never cease to woo you.
Though you're flying high above
me,
I will try to fly up to you.
I know the worry and strife
That come with a wife,
But here is a man
Who'd gladly give up his life
To marry you, Marianne!

REFRAIN 2

SAILORS: Marianne, we want to love you.
We'll repeat it ev'ry day, dear.
Marianne, we want to love you.
It's a simple thing to say, dear.
ROBERT: Were there more praises to sing
And phrases to ring,
I'd sing them to you.
Let others doubt them who will,
But I would be still
Believing them true.
SAILORS: And though you may never love us,
We will never cease to woo you.
Though you're flying high above
us,
We will try to fly up to you.
ROBERT: I know the worry and strife
That come with a wife,

But here is a man*
Who'd gladly give up his life
To marry you, Marianne!

THE GIRL ON THE PROW

Published as an individual sheet. Introduced by Evelyn
Herbert (Marianne), Lyle Evans (Besac), and ensemble.

VERSE

MARIANNE: As a child, on an old sailor's
knee,
I would hear ev'ry tale of the sea,
And my eyes would open wide
To the thrill of each adventure.
With a breath of the salt in
the air
And a breeze from the sea in my
hair,
In my young imagination
I'd sail away.
GIRLS AND MEN: Cast away! Don't delay!
Little Marianne must sail today.
MEN: Living in her childhood fancies,
Childhood fancies . . .
Ev'ry sailor friend's romance
GIRLS: First in childhood fancies . . .
Lost romances.
GIRLS AND MEN: Far from home we can roam,
Cutting through the spray of
silver foam.
BESAC: Then from across the blue
We will return with you—
ENSEMBLE: Bringing back the same old
tales—
BESAC: That you'll swear are true.

[*Dialogue.*]

REFRAIN

MARIANNE: Let me be like the girl on the
prow,

---

*Alternate lines for the other singers and for
mini-reprise by Marianne:
SAILORS: But where is a man
Who wouldn't give up his life
To marry you, Marianne?
MARIANNE: I pity the man
Who gladly gives up his life
To marry a Marianne.

Riding high on the roll of the
    sea.
Like a queen on her throne in the
    bow,
O'er the world, sails unfurled,
My good ship will always have to
    follow me.
In the blast of a gale we'll be
    tossed,
And a mast or a sail may be lost.
Through the night, through the
    storm, we will plough
And the morning sun will shine
On the girl on the prow.

GIRLS AND MEN: You will bring good luck to our
    craft,
But no man would ever be aft.
They would spend their days
Only gazing at their beautiful
    figurehead.
MARIANNE: I'd feel proud to be riding there
With my chin held high in the
    air.
GIRLS AND MEN: Goddess of the blue
We want to be led by you.

REPEAT REFRAIN

VERSE 2 (FROM PUBLISHED SHEET)

I have seen you return ev'ry year
And I still feel a thrill when I hear
Any story of the sea
And a sailor's gay adventures.
With a breath of the salt in the air
And a breeze from the sea in my hair,
Once again imagination
Calls me away.

GORGEOUS ALEXANDER

Published in the vocal score. Introduced by Marie Callahan (Julie), Gus Shy (Alexander), and female ensemble.

VERSE

JULIE: This is the end.
My heart is broke,
It will not mend,
And that's no joke.
The man I love's a trifle-er,
A wolf who wears the clothing of a
    sheep!
ALEXANDER: Am I to blame

If women prize
My manly frame,
My sexy eyes?
She knew I was a trifle-er,
So I say: as she sows so shall she
    reap!
JULIE: If he begged upon his knee,
He could not make up with me.
Alexander, won't you come back?
Alexander, dear, I cannot live with
    out you!
ALEXANDER: No, my girl, my love is dead
After all the things you said.
JULIE: [*begging*] Alexander!
GIRLS: [*to* ALEXANDER] Reprimand her!
JULIE: Alexander!
GIRLS: Alexander!
We are ready
Now that you have lost your steady.

REFRAIN

JULIE: Gorgeous Alexander, give me all
    your love.
Why can't you be always true to me
    alone?
ALEXANDER: Selfish woman,
What can you be thinking of?
Heaven sent me for the good
Of a starving womanhood.
GIRLS: Gorgeous Alexander, you're too
    grand to be
Any single girl's exclusive property.
JULIE: Why do you philander
With these women, Alexander?
When I tell you in all candor
I'm the best.
GIRLS: Do not talk such slander
To our gorgeous Alexander!
ALEXANDER: How can I decide until I've tried the
    rest?

AN INTERRUPTED LOVE SONG

Published in the vocal score. Introduced by Edward Nell Jr. (Captain Georges Duval) and Evelyn Herbert (Marianne). Each time Duval begins to woo Marianne in song, Robert finds a reason to enter the room.

VERSE

DUVAL: I'm seeking the hand of a maiden
In my incompetent way.
With passion my poor heart is laden,
But I don't know what to say.
MARIANNE: I think you should sing her a love song
With words both tender and gay.
DUVAL: I'm not very good at a love song,
But your command I obey.

[*He goes to the spinet and improvises.*]

I love you, love you, love you, love you.
Da da, dee dee, da dum.
I love you, love you—
[*spoken*] No, that isn't very good.

[*He starts again.*]

REFRAIN

DUVAL: When I am here with you alone,
And you're alone with me, love,
A place with only you, my own,
Is just the place to be, love.
When your eyes divine
Look up into mine,
There's no sweeter sight I would see,
    love.

[ROBERT *enters and breaks the mood.* MARIANNE *encourages* DUVAL *to try again.*]

DUVAL: When I am here with you alone,
And you're alone with me, love,
A place with only you, my own,
Is just the place to be, love.
When your eyes divine
Look up into mine—

[ROBERT *enters with a snuff box, which makes* DUVAL *sneeze during his third attempt.*]

DUVAL: When I am here with you alone,
And you're alone with me, love,
A place with only you, my own,
Is just the place to be, love.
When your eyes divine—

[ROBERT *re-enters with servants bearing luggage,* DUVAL *gives up.*]

TAVERN SONG

Published in the vocal score. Introduced by Aleta Edwards (Flower Girl) and ensemble.

In *The Films of Jeanette MacDonald and Nelson Eddy*, Eleanor Knowles Dugan points out that the song "Stranger in Paree" in the 1940 film version of *New Moon* uses the "Take a flower" melody.

FLOWER GIRL: Red wine in your glasses,
Black night quickly passes.
Gray dawn may discover
Your dear lover
Pressed to your heart.
GIRLS AND MEN: Ah-ah-ah-ah.
FLOWER GIRL: Take a flower, fair flower.
Who'll take a girl with a flower?
I'll not part with my flower.
Buy it and you will buy me.
GIRLS AND MEN: Take a flower, fair flower.
Who'll take a girl with a flower?
I'll not part with my flower.
Buy it and you will buy me.
Ah-ah-ah-ah.

SOFTLY, AS IN A MORNING SUNRISE

Published as an individual sheet. Introduced by William O'Neal (Phillippe).

VERSE

Love came to me,
Gay and tender.
Love came to me,
Sweet surrender.
Love came to me
In bright romantic splendor.
Fickle was she,
Faithful never.
Fickle was she,
And clever.
So will it be
Forever, forever!

REFRAIN

Softly, as in a morning sunrise,
The light of love comes stealing
Into a newborn day.

Oh, flaming with all the glow of sunrise,
A burning kiss is sealing
The vow that all betray.
For the passions that thrill love
And lift you high to heaven
Are the passions that kill love
And let you fall to hell.
So ends the story.
Softly, as in an evening sunset,
The light that gave you glory
Will take it all away!

STOUTHEARTED MEN

Published as an individual sheet. Introduced by Robert Halliday (Robert), William O'Neal (Phillippe), and male ensemble.

REFRAIN

ROBERT: Give me some men who are
stouthearted men,
Who will fight for the right
they adore.
Start me with ten who are
stouthearted men
And I'll soon give you ten
thousand more.
Oh, shoulder to shoulder,
and bolder and bolder
They grow as they go to the
fore.
Then, there's nothing in the
world
Can halt or mar a plan
When stouthearted men
Can stick together man to
man.

VERSE

PHILLIPPE: You, who have dreams,
If you act, they will come
true.
To turn your dreams
To a fact, it's up to you!
ROBERT: If you have the soul and the
spirit,
Never fear it, you'll see it
through.
PHILLIPPE AND MEN: Hearts can inspire
Other hearts with their fire.
ROBERT: For the strong obey

When a strong man shows
them the way.

REPEAT REFRAIN

TANGO

Published in the vocal score. Introduced by the female ensemble; danced by Rosita and Ramon. The British and American editions of the vocal score have slightly different versions of the song.

American version

FIRST GIRL: Sweet Creole lady,
My Creole lady,
Whom Spain has given
To bless Louisiana,
Sweet Creole lady,
You've won my heart.
GIRLS: Fair Rosita,
When I see her dancing,
Then I'd like to dance too,
If I had the chance to.
Fair Rosita,
With her blue eyes glancing,
When she looks at me,
She is all I see.
If you ever meet a
Little señorita,
My Rosita,
You'll be just like me.

British version

GIRLS: Fair Maria,
When I see her dancing,
Then I'd like to dance too,
If I had the chance to.
MARIANNE: Fair Maria,
With her blue eyes glancing,
When she looks at you,
She is all you see.
GIRLS: If you ever meet a
Little señorita,
My Maria,
You'll be just like me.

ONE KISS

Published as an individual sheet. Introduced by Evelyn Herbert (Marianne) and female ensemble. Written during the 1928 out-of-town tryouts to replace a similar number titled "One Kiss Is Waiting for One Man." The earlier "One Kiss" can be found with the cut material at the end of this chapter.

VERSE

MARIANNE: In this year of seventeen ninety-two
Our conventions have been thrown all askew;
And I know I'm out of date
When I seek one mate,
One faithful lover true.
To be really in the fashion today
You must have a dozen beaux in your sway;
But somehow I don't believe in the modern plan,
I want to wait for just one man.

GIRLS: It's more fun to love 'em all,
Kiss 'em all, short and tall.

MARIANNE: I have another scheme;
It's my only dream.

REFRAIN

MARIANNE: One kiss, one man to save it for.
One love for him alone.
One word, one vow, and nothing more
To tell him I'm his own.
One magic night within his arms
With passion's flow'r* unfurled—
And all my life I'll love only one man
And no other man in the world.

INTERLUDE

GIRLS: You've been reading stories
Of romantic glories.
Are you growing sad
For your Galahad?

MARIANNE: Soon my knight may find me,
Softly steal behind me,

Put me on a horse
And carry me away.
Laugh all you like at me,
I'll find my man, you'll see.

REPEAT REFRAIN

LADIES OF THE JURY (THE TRIAL)

Published in the vocal score. Introduced by Gus Shy (Alexander), Marie Callahan (Julie), Esther Howard (Clotilde Lombaste), and female ensemble.

CLOTILDE: Too long this world has been obsessed by women such as you.
It's time a faithful wife put up a fight!

GIRLS: Right!

ALEXANDER: Now, what's the use of fighting?

CLOTILDE: Alexander, that will do!
I'm going to win you back this very night.

JULIE: Not tonight!

CLOTILDE: We must decide who owns the right and title to this man.
Let's argue calmly, without fuss or fury.

JULIE: I'm willing to discuss the case if you will state your plan.

CLOTILDE: We'll leave it to my girl friends as a jury.

JULIE: That isn't fair!

CLOTILDE: But that's the way we'll do it,
I'll not budge.

ALEXANDER: Don't worry, Julie.
Alexander's going to be the judge.
Order!
Here's a case
Wherein two lovesick girls
Lay claim to one fine man—
Ahem, that's me.

GIRLS: We'll decide which girl should get the prize.

ALEXANDER: And, ladies, what a prize that prize will be!

CLOTILDE: Dear judge and ladies of the jury,
I have one thing to suggest:
Why not take each of us by turn and give her a test?

JULIE: That will be rough on you,
For anything you'll do
I can do twice as well.

CLOTILDE: You lie like hell!

ALEXANDER: Order!

CLOTILDE: I can sing.

JULIE: I can dance.

ALEXANDER: You'll get your chance to sing and dance
To a tune* that's light and lilty.
But don't forget the law of France:
Until you prove you're innocent,
We assume that you are guilty.
Proceed!

[JULIE *dances.*]

CLOTILDE: [*to the "Marianne" tune*]
Alexander dear, I love you.
I'll repeat it ev'ry day, dear.
Alexander dear, I love you,
It's a simple thing to say, dear.

[*A juror faints.*]

ALEXANDER: I think we've seen sufficient evidence;
The case is fairly tried.
And both these dames are guilty—
That is what I decide.

GIRLS: But then, you poor dear judge,
You're left without a girl.

JULIE AND CLOTILDE: You have to take a girl!

ALEXANDER: I'll take the jury!

---

* Sources vary whether the wording is "passion's flow'r" or "passion flow'rs." The issue was discussed at the time of the 2004 Ghostlight recording, and with Alice Hammerstein Mathias's assent it was decided that the former was more singable.

---

* Both editions of the vocal score have the word "time" here, which seems like an error.

ACT ONE FINALE, including GENTLE AIRS, COURTLY MANNERS and WANTING YOU

Published in the vocal score. "Wanting You" published as an individual sheet. Introduced by the ensemble, Evelyn Herbert (Marianne), Robert Halliday (Robert). The characters of Alexander, Monsieur Beaunoir, and Ribaud are present but do not have solo singing lines.

Gentle Airs, Courtly Manners

GIRLS: Gentle airs, courtly manners
Grace the court of France.
These airs and these courtly
manners come from Paris.

MEN: [*overlapping the girls' lines*] This
could be the court of France.
That is why we ape the courtly
manners seen at old Versailles.

GIRLS: Do not cry for Versailles
While you're in Louisiana.
This is a royal dance!

MEN: Here is Louisiana now!
We know the new cotillion dance!

GIRLS: Oh, gentlemen,
No gentlemen
Act like this in a dance.

MEN: We fall in line,
We're all in line
Hoping to win a dance.

GIRLS AND MEN: Dance with Marianne
And know the bliss of her sweet
kiss.

[ROBERT *enters, masked.*]

GIRLS: Who is this young cavalier?
Who is he that ventures here
now?

MEN: Who is this cavalier now?

[*With* ALEXANDER'S *connivance,* ROBERT *draws the winning ticket. He asks* MARIANNE *for five minutes of conversation in addition to the dance and kiss that are his prize.*]

GIRLS AND MEN: If I were only sure such good
fortune could be mine,
I think I would rush up and seize
my prize divine.

Wanting You

VERSE

ROBERT: My heart is aching for someone,
And you are that someone.
You know the truth of my
story—
You must believe what you see.

MARIANNE: I, too, may someday love
someone.
From somewhere, there'll come
one,
One who will hear the same
story
That you're telling me.

REFRAIN

ROBERT: Wanting you,
Ev'ry day I am wanting you.
Ev'ry night I am longing to
Hold you close to my eager
breast.
Wanting love,
In that heaven I'm dreaming of,
Makes that heaven seem far
above
Any hope that I'll gain my
quest.
Dreams are vain,
But I cling to the merest chance
that you may hear me.
Dreams are vain,
For whenever I wake I never
find you near me.
Wanting you,
Nothing else in the world will
do.
In this world you are all that I
adore,
All I adore!

MARIANNE: Wanting you,
Ev'ry day I am wanting you
Ev'ry night I am longing to
Hold you close to my eager
breast.
Wanting love,
In that heaven I'm dreaming of,
Makes that heaven seem far
above
Any hope that I'll gain my
quest.

MARIANNE
AND ROBERT: Dreams are vain,
But I cling to the merest chance
that you may hear me.
Dreams are vain,
For whenever I wake I never
find you near me!

MARIANNE: Wanting you,
Nothing else in this world will
do.

MARIANNE
AND ROBERT: In this world you are all that I
adore!
All I adore! All I adore!
Dreams are vain,
But I know I'm awake at last
and you are near me.

[*They begin a slow waltz.*]

ENSEMBLE: So they dance
To the garden that breathes
romance.
They're beginning to climb the
heights of love.

[*Suddenly,* RIBAUD *arrests* ROBERT *and implies that* MARIANNE *had set* ROBERT *up for capture.*]

OFFSTAGE MEN: Give me some men who are
stouthearted men,
Who will fight for the right they
adore.
Start me with ten who are
stouthearted men
And I'll soon give you ten
thousand more.
Oh!

ROBERT: Dreams are vain:
But I clung to the merest
chance that you would hear
me.
Dreams are vain:
I've awakened to find that love
is nowhere near me.

[MARIANNE *announces she will join* DUVAL *on the ship that will deliver brides to Martinique and then bring* ROBERT *to judgment in Paris.*]

MARIANNE: One kiss, one man to save it for,
One love for him alone.
One word, one vow and nothing
more
To tell him I'm his own.

GIRLS AND MEN: One magic night within his
arms,
With passion's flow'r unfurled.

MARIANNE: And all my life I'll love only one
man—

MARIANNE, GIRLS,
AND MEN: And no other man in the world.

ACT TWO OPENING: CHANTY

Published in the vocal score. Introduced by Lyle Evans (Besac) and male ensemble.

BESAC: Yes, heave ho!
Round the capstan go.
Heave, men, with a will,
Tramp and tramp it still.
The anchor's off the ground
And we are outward bound.
BESAC AND MEN: Yo ho, heave ho!
Yo ho, heave ho!
Yo ho, heave ho!
Yo ho, heave ho!
So all together, now: ye ho!

1927 version

In 1927, the Act Two opening was called "Sailor Songs" or "Sea Chanties"—both plural. The number began as above and continued with the following:

BESAC: Away, haul away.
Come haul away together.
SAILORS: Away, haul away, haul away, yo.
BESAC: Away, haul away,
We'll haul away together.
SAILORS: Away, haul away,
Haul away, yo.
RED JACQUES: The maiden, oh,
The maiden, oh,
The sailor loves the maiden, oh,
So early in the morning,
The sailor loves the maiden, oh!
SAILORS: A maid that is young,
A maid that is fair,
A maid that is kind and pleasant,
oh,
So early in the morning,
The sailor loves the maiden, oh!
RED JACQUES: The maiden, oh,
The bottle, oh,
A pipe of good tobacco, oh,
So early in the morning,
The sailor loves all these,
Heigh ho.
SAILORS: A bottle of spirit,
A maiden fair,
A plug of good tobacco, oh,
So early in the morning,
These are the sailor's love,
Heigh ho.

FUNNY LITTLE SAILOR MEN

Published in the vocal score. Introduced by Lyle Evans (Besac), Esther Howard (Clotilde Lombaste), and ensemble.

In *The Films of Jeanette MacDonald and Nelson Eddy*, Eleanor Knowles Dugan points out that the melody from "Funny Little Sailor Men" was recycled as "Dance Your Cares Away" for the 1940 film.

VERSE

BESAC: I hates the sight of ev'rything
What calls herself a female,
For hell is what they always bring
To ev'ry happy free male.
MEN: No good can come of pettin' 'em
And lettin' 'em near to you.
BESAC: Oh, I hates a sex
What can make poor wrecks—
MEN: Out of any sailor crew!
BESAC: They find an unsuspecting man
And treat him kind and tender.
They scheme and plot, connive and
plan,
And force him to surrender.
MEN: They take his grog and bacon
And feed him on milk and tarts.
BESAC: Oh, I hates the sex,
With their swan-white necks
And their coal-black hearts!
GIRLS: How can you speak that way?
Such dreadful things to say!
You should not be afraid of us;
You know that women pay.
What could we ever do
To harm that mighty crew?
When ev'ry single maid of us
Is scared to death of you?
CLOTILDE: There is no need to hide away in
corners,
Like sheepish and gigantic young Jack
Horners.
BESAC: Oh, I hates the sex
To be on their decks*
Hangin' round our necks,
Just to hound and vex.
CLOTILDE: If our lips once touch—
GIRLS: You will find it won't hurt so much.

---

* *Both editions of the vocal score have "their decks," but some scripts have "these decks," which seems a better choice.*

REFRAIN

CLOTILDE: Oh, what are you afraid of,
What are you afraid of?
GIRLS: Funny little sailor boy.
CLOTILDE: Oh, what are you afraid of,
What are you afraid of?
What is making you so coy?
GIRLS: You say that we pursue you;*
We only lag behind.
We would never dare.
MEN: Hey, get over there!
GIRLS: How can you be so unkind?
CLOTILDE: We're really very harmless.
Is a sailor armless
When he has a girl to hug?
MEN: Please, run away and leave us,
You cannot deceive us
With a lot of love humbug.
Now smile and show your dimples,[†]
And all those teeth of pearl.
ALL: For a sailor's eyes can win sweet sighs
From this adoring girl.

LOVER, COME BACK TO ME

Published as an individual sheet, and the refrain appears in Hammerstein's anthology, *Lyrics*. Introduced by Evelyn Herbert (Marianne).

The song was immediately popular, with recordings by Paul Whitman and Rudy Vallee, among others. Discographer Joel Whitman ranks "Lover, Come Back to Me" as number twenty of the one hundred most-recorded songs of 1890–1954. Romberg scholar William Everett cites recordings by some of the biggest names in jazz, including Billie Holiday, Ella Fitzgerald, Louis Armstrong, Charlie Parker, Dizzy Gillespie, Art Tatum, Dave Brubeck, and John Coltrane.

VERSE

You went away, I let you.
We broke the ties that bind.
I wanted to forget you
And leave the past behind.
Still, the magic of the night I met you
Seems to stay forever in my mind.

---

* *Some scripts have:*
You say that you adore us.

[†] *Sources vary as to who sings the song's last four lines.*

REFRAIN

The sky was blue,
And, high above,
The moon was new,
And so was love.
This eager heart of mine was singing:
"Lover, where can you be?"
You came at last,
Love had its day.
That day is past,
You've gone away.
This aching heart of mine is singing:
"Lover, come back to me!"
Remem'bring ev'ry little thing you used to say and
    do,*
I'm so lonely!
Ev'ry road I walk along I've walked along with
    you.
No wonder I am lonely!
The sky is blue,
The night is cold.
The moon is new
But† love is old.
And while I'm waiting here
This heart of mine is singing:
"Lover, come back to me!"

LOVE IS QUITE A SIMPLE THING

Published in the vocal score. Introduced by Lyle Evans (Besac), Marie Callahan (Julie), Gus Shy (Alexander), and Esther Howard (Clotilde Lombaste).

VERSE 1

BESAC: Why do the poets throw us in
    confusion
    By sugar-coating love with false
    illusion?
JULIE: Why do we let romantic writers all
    conspire to cram us
    With fairy tales that make us seek
    one love alone serene?
ALEXANDER: Why not admit the fact that we are
    mostly poly-gamous?

———

* *Alternate wording from the published sheet:*
    When I remember every little thing you used to do.

† *In Hammerstein's anthology,* Lyrics, *this line begins
    with the word "And."*

CLOTILDE: And men are men, and girls are not,
    If you get what I mean.

REFRAIN

ALL FOUR: Love is quite a simple thing,
    And nothing so bewild'ring,
    No matter what the poets sing
    In words and phrases lyrical.
    Birds find bliss in ev'ry tree
    And fishes kiss beneath the sea.
    So when love comes to you and me,
    It really ain't no miracle.

VERSE 2

JULIE: They try to libel good Queen
    Isabella,
    Implying that Columbus was her
    fella.
CLOTILDE: It's true that just before he tried to
    cross the broad Atlantic,
    He came to see her now and then, to
    have a little chat.
BESAC: He taught her some geography.
ALEXANDER: But when she got romantic,
    He proved to her the earth was round
    And then he left her flat.

REPEAT REFRAIN

TRY HER OUT AT DANCES

Published as an individual sheet (verse and refrain). The introductory material is in the published vocal score under the title "Marriage Number." Introduced by Marie Callahan (Julie), Gus Shy (Alexander), and ensemble.

INTRODUCTION

GIRLS: Just one year ago we were
    mated,
    That is why today we are
    feted
    As a lot of happy brides
    and grooms.
MEN: You have honored and
    obeyed us,
    Good and faithful brides
    you have made us.
    We'll forget the times you
    have flayed us
    With the heavy handles of
    your brooms.

GIRLS: You made handsome
    young grooms.
    And now at last the first
    year's over.
    What a chance we all were
    taking
    When we gave our pledge.
    Standing here in fear and
    quaking,
    All our nerves on edge.
MEN: Has it been for worse or
    better?
GIRLS: So far it's been so-so!
MEN: Here comes Alexander,
    He's been married just as
    long.
    You are glad you're
    married,
    Are we right or are we
    wrong?
GIRLS: Has he made you happy,
    Julie?
MEN: Has she never been
    unruly?
GIRLS AND MEN: Tell us now and tell us
    truly
    How you get along.

VERSE

JULIE: Marriage is a gamble, that
    is trite but true.
GIRLS: The same for me and you.
    But what's a girl to do?
ALEXANDER: Just gamble,
    And the ones that beat the
    game are very few.
MEN: You cannot tell who'll be
    sweetest or brightest.*
ALEXANDER: You'll come out well† if
    you put her to my test.

REFRAIN

ALEXANDER: Try her out at dances,
    And if her step advances
    When you advance,
    The chance is:
    She'll be the girl!
MEN: What a way to pick them!‡
JULIE: But if when you're leading
    She trips along unheeding,

———

* *The published sheet has "sweetest and brightest."*

† *The published sheet has: "You'll know it well . . ."*

‡ *The published sheet has:*
    That's the stuff. Let's try it.

134

Slows down when you are
speeding,
Then free the girl.
MEN: Send her right away!
ALEXANDER: If you cannot blast her
Desire to be your master,
Disaster will pile upon
disaster!
JULIE: But if she should follow
The arm of her Apollo
And nestle in its hollow—
JULIE AND ALEXANDER: She'll be the girl!

REPEAT REFRAIN

NEVER FOR YOU

Published in the vocal score. Introduced by Robert Halliday (Robert) and Evelyn Herbert (Marianne).

ROBERT: As long as she is near,
Somehow my hope will not die.
MARIANNE: [entering] Monsieur, I have overheard,
My window's just above.
Your duty is very plain,
Don't shirk it for a hope that's vain.
Your people come first.
Give me up and let me go!
Our love is dead, you know.
For you destroyed it long ago, long
ago.
Once my heart was yours for the
asking.
I would have given all to you.
Once my heart was yours for the
asking,
But you tried to take it away
And now that heart has gone astray.
Love may return,
And start anew,
But never, never for you!

ACT TWO FINALE (CABIN SCENE)

Published in the vocal score. Introduced by Robert Halliday (Robert) and Evelyn Herbert (Marianne).

ROBERT: One kiss, one girl to save it for.
One love for her alone.
One word, one vow and nothing more
To tell her I'm her own.
MARIANNE: One magic night within his arms
With passion's flow'r unfurled.
BOTH: But all my life I'll love only one man
[girl]
And no other man [girl] in the
world.*
MARIANNE: Dreams are vain,
But I cling to the merest chance that
you may hear me.
BOTH: Dreams are vain,
For whenever I wake, I long to find
you near me.†

FINALE ULTIMO

Published in the vocal score. Introduced by Evelyn Herbert (Marianne) and ensemble.

GIRLS: [shouting in derision] The Princess herself!
GIRLS AND MEN: The Princess, the Princess!
ONE GIRL: How is Your Highness?
GIRLS AND MEN: (Ha, ha, ha, ha, ha!)
This morning?
(Ha, ha, ha, ha, ha!)

[Dialogue.]

MARIANNE: [spoken] Let the cowards and
poltroons desert him, but you
who have stout hearts rally, rally
[sung] Back to him.
See him through,
See him through!
Give me some men,
Who are stouthearted men,
Who will fight for the right they
adore . . .

[The others join the refrain.]

---

* The American vocal score has:
But I will try to love only one man [girl],
And no other man [girl] in the world.

† The American vocal score has:
For whenever I wake, I never find you near me.

CUT AND UNUSED SONGS

MUSICAL PANTOMIME

Not published. Used in the 1928 out-of-town tryout, but the song and the character were dropped before Broadway. Early in Act One, Duchesse Duchene shocks the ensemble with the latest gossip from Paris. Introduced by Olga Albani (Duchene), Edward Nell Jr. (Duval), Pacie Ripple (Beaunoir), and ensemble.

DUCHENE: You, who all believe the king can do no
wrong,
Meet the king, and you will not believe
it long.
DUVAL: That's the truth, I know.
It's a standing joke.
BEAUNOIR: This is quite a blow
To provincial folk.
DUCHENE: Listen to the gossip all around
Versailles
And you'll hear of more than ever
meets your eye.
DUVAL: Tell us what you hear.
BEAUNOIR: Not with servants near!
DUCHENE: I would love to shock your shell-pink
ear.

[BEAUNOIR leans in and then moves away, shocked.]

BEAUNOIR: No!
GIRLS: We should love some scandal of the
king.
MEN: No, you'd better come away.
GIRLS: Out with it!
And don't omit a thing.
MEN: What an awful thing to say!
DUCHENE: [illustrating] Here's the boudoir of
Madame Frou-Frou.
Here's a keyhole someone's looking
through.
GIRLS: Who?
DUCHENE: Louis!

[DUCHENE begins to pantomime undressing. She removes her shoes and unhooks her dress.]

GIRLS: There goes her dress.
ALL: Look out, Duchesse!

[DUCHENE pantomimes removing her stockings; unpins her hair. Then she goes to the other side of the pantomime door and impersonates the king at the keyhole.]

ALL: What's left now?

[DUCHENE *returns to the pantomime strip. Soon she is* "naked."]

GIRLS: You were right. We'd better go away.
MEN: It's beginning to be good.
GIRLS: She may go still further. Who can say?
MEN: We sincerely wish she would.
DUCHENE: [*pointing to the imaginary door and then to a window*] Louis knocked, and waited, then knocked more. Neath her window sang her troubadour.

[*What will she decide? She looks back and forth between the door and the window.*]

BEAUNOIR: Well?
GIRLS: What did she do?
ALL: What could she do?

[*She pantomimes the king offering jewels. She throws a kiss out the window and opens the door with a curtsey.*]

MEN: Oh, woman!
ALL: The king was in the parlor, and the troubadour outside.
DUCHENE: The troubadour sang on with such a sweet inspiring song That they did not stay in the parlor very long.
ALL: T-t-t-t-t-t-t-t-t-t-t.

ONE KISS IS WAITING FOR ONE MAN

Published as an individual sheet, but this song and its reprises were replaced during the 1928 tryouts by the similarly titled "One Kiss." Introduced by Evelyn Herbert (Marianne), Edward Nell Jr. (Duval), and ensemble.

VERSE

MARIANNE: You may like to taste a stolen sweet, But a stolen kiss is incomplete.
DUVAL: It might seem complete to me.
GIRLS: We agree.
ENSEMBLE: We agree.
MARIANNE: My true lover will not have to steal— My kiss will match his zeal.
DUVAL: Lucky man who knows Two red lips like those.

ENSEMBLE: Two lips like a rose Should not wait long to bloom.
MARIANNE: These lips wait and pray That he'll come my way.
ENSEMBLE: And then that rose will bloom.

REFRAIN

MARIANNE: One kiss is waiting for one man, One man alone will own my heart. I want to give him all the love that I can give, First, and last, and always. One kiss is waiting for one man, Kept guarded like a flower tender— I'll keep it safe till I surrender All to one man alone.

KISS WALTZ

A third waltz with a lyric about "one kiss" was found in the Romberg holograph piano-vocal score in the Music Division of the Library of Congress.

MARIANNE: I have one kiss I keep for only one man. I'm saving up for my own All of the love that I own. I have one heart I'll give to only one man. So I am waiting, patiently waiting, For the day I find my man. And if I'm lonely, It will be only Till I can find my man.
GIRLS: Dear, why do you dream all day With romance at your door? Should a bud that blooms in May Waste away her springtime?
MARIANNE: Better let me go my way; I'm enjoying my springtime.
GIRLS: Will your Galahad fly And land with a sigh Out of the sky?
MARIANNE: Maybe I'll wait and lose my romance. Still I will wait; It's worth the chance.

MARIANNE AND GIRLS: I have one kiss I keep for only one man. I'm saving up for my own All of the love that I own. I have one heart I'll give to only one man. So I am waiting, patiently waiting, For the day I find my man. And if I'm lonely, It will be only Till I can find my man.

LIAR

Published in 1928 as an individual sheet, but dropped during the out-of-town tryouts. This Act One tirade addressed to Alexander was superseded by "Ladies of the Jury (The Trial)." Introduced by Esther Howard (Clotilde) and female ensemble.

VERSE

GIRLS: Look upon this woman's face and weep, And her story you will quickly tell!
CLOTILDE: All my nights have been deprived of sleep; All my days have been a living hell.
GIRLS: And the reason is a reptile man, Whom she trusted with a maiden's trust.
CLOTILDE: For the happy home we used to plan Has turned out to be an awful bust!
GIRLS: And are you the fiend in human form Who has left this poor girl flat?
CLOTILDE: Did you? Or not?
GIRLS: What do you say to that?

REFRAIN

GIRLS: Liar! Why d'ye want to fool a girl? Liar! Trying to ridicule a girl!
CLOTILDE: Boo-hoo! You-oo Traded a promise for a kiss.
GIRLS: Son of a gun, you'll pay for this! Why are People like you allowed to live? Liar! Scum o' the earth, we'll make you give! Give up! Liar!

Come through!
Settle with her or we'll settle with you!
Shut up!

AWAKE, MY LAD

Not published. Dropped during the 1928 out-of-town tryouts. Introduced in Act Two after "Love Is Quite a Simple Thing" by William O'Neal (Phillippe), Lyle Evans (Besac), Evelyn Herbert (Marianne), and male ensemble.

PHILLIPPE: Awake, my lad,
And look all about you!
Love's waiting just round
the corner.
Don't quake, my lad!
If one girl should flout you,
Just take your pick from
the rest.
They wait in the north,
south, east, and west.
BESAC AND MEN: They wait in the east and
west, north and south,
Your cup of desire they're
ready to fill.
PHILLIPPE: We all find the woods are
full of sweet pretty
maidens,
One just as fair as another.
BESAC AND MEN: The woods are full of
maidens, to take or leave.
PHILLIPPE: Believe the one that you
choose
Always best!
BESAC AND MEN: Do not grieve and wail with
woe
If one should want to be
wandering away.
Let her leave, and let her go,
And fill her place
With another face today.
PHILLIPPE AND BESAC: And if loving one makes
you blue,
You can get your fun loving
two.
It's the only thing to do—
That is what we're telling
you.
MEN: Be true and they'll forget,
And you will weep alone—
That is what we're all
telling you.

MARIANNE: They are right in telling
you.
Always wake, my lad! And
look all about you.
Love's waiting just round
the corner.
PHILLIPPE,
BESAC, AND MEN: The woods are full of
young, eager maidens
now.
MARIANNE: The woods are full of
young, eager maidens.
Do not bother with one—
ALL: Just love all.
Just love all.

I'M JUST A SENTIMENTAL FOOL

Published as an individual sheet in 1928, but dropped during the out-of-town tryouts. Sung in Act Two by Robert Halliday (Robert) and male ensemble, and immediately reprised by Evelyn Herbert (Marianne).

VERSE

ROBERT: Love has brought me naught but pain,
Love has passed me by.
Still I keep my faith in vain,
And you wonder why.
I'll lose all, beyond a doubt,
In the game I play.
Do not try to help me out—
Let me go my way.

REFRAIN

ROBERT: The world is filled with pretty eyes
That might look into mine,
And lips that hold a precious prize—
A word, a kiss divine.
But love makes man a gentle fool,
No lips nor eyes I hear or see—
I am just a sentimental fool,
Who thinks there's one girl alone for
me.

[ROBERT, PHILLIPPE, BESAC *and men repeat refrain.*
They exit singing some of "Awake, My Lad."]

MARIANNE: The world is filled with deep blue eyes
That might look into mine,
Lips that hold a precious prize—

A word, a kiss divine.
Love makes a girl a gentle fool,
No lips nor eyes I hear or see—
I am just a sentimental fool,
Who thinks there's one man alone for
me.

ACT ONE OPENING SEQUENCE (1927 VERSION), including BACK AT THE COURT OF FRANCE and CARNIVAL ENSEMBLE and IN A LITTLE FRENCH CAFÉ and THE VOICE IN THE DARK and 'NEATH A NEW MOON

Not published. Used only in 1927. Introduced by Margaret Irving (Duchene), Marie Callahan (Julie), Desiree Tabor (Marianne/Zeforstas), Robert Halliday (Robert), and ensemble.

Back at the Court of France

Note: The 1927 program lists a song called "Paris" as part of the Act One Opening. It seems likely that "Paris" is an alternate title for "Back at the Court of France." It is definitely not the same song as the non-Hammerstein addition to the 1940 film variously known as "Paree," "I Was a Stranger in Paris," and "The Way They Do It in Paree."

DUCHENE: I can tell you truly
They are most unruly.
There is nothing they won't
do.
I'd not have confessed it,
But since you have guessed
it,
All that you have heard is
true.
JULIE: Won't you tell us more about
them?
GIRLS: We should love to know.
JULIE: Are you lonesome here with
out them?
GIRLS: I imagine so.
DUCHENE: After court life I admit
This does seem rather slow.
In the brilliant court of
France
On s'amuse so gaily.

DUCHENE,
JULIE, AND GIRLS: Why can't we
Be just as free?
DUCHENE: Many folks would look
askance
At the things they do.
One lady even said "Damn!"
GIRLS: Oh, how could she dare?
JULIE: And what do they wear?
DUCHENE: Gowns of the naughtiest sort.
For ever at court
No one seems to care.
GIRLS: Daren't we ever be just as
fancy free
Though we are not in Paris?*
JULIE: Très méchantes!
Si charmantes!
Elles sont ravissantes.
GIRLS: Back at the court of France.
DUCHENE AND JULIE: In the brilliant court of
France
On s'amuse so gaily,
Why can't we
Be just as free?
Many folks would look
askance
At the things they wear.
Even the ladies say "Damn."
You just have to stare
At things that they wear,
Gowns of ev'ry fanciful sort
Back home in the court of
the King of France!
GIRLS: Ladies of court are so gay.
They're sure to have spent
every day.
Why couldn't we
Only be
Half as free?
Seems to me,
We ought to see
All the fun.
Ev'ryone else has!
They don't care what people
say.
Perhaps they are right in a
way.
Their daring is most
amazing.
You have to stare and see
what they wear,
Gowns ev'rywhere—
Way back in the court of
France!

[Dialogue. Guests arrive for the masked ball.]

* Pronounced "Pa-ree."

Carnival Ensemble

GIRLS: Who can tell if you are belle or beau
Behind a masque and domino?
Laughing or serious,
Always mysterious,
Your whim pursue,
No one will know it's you!
Your domino
Will hide you so
No one will know,
No one will know it's you
Till you all unmask at the ball!
MEN: Who can tell if you are belle or beau
Behind a masque or flowing domino?
If you are serious
You will but scary us.
So you may be mad and gay
No one can say it's really you!
In your domino,
Nobody can recognize you.
Who can tell if you are belle or beau?
So we advise you to accept this cue,
Play your part and fool us all
Till we unmask you at the ball!

[Dialogue: Where is Marianne? She has a surprise for you.]

ENSEMBLE: How will she surprise us?
Please don't tantalize us—
We'd prefer to know!

[Dialogue: MARIANNE has invited the notorious dancer ZEFORSTAS.]

ENSEMBLE: Zeforstas we're waiting to see.
How truly enchanting you'll be!
TRIO OF MEN: Fair siren of Spain,
All men may try in vain
To flee her charms.
ENSEMBLE: Hearts are a prey to her.
TRIO OF MEN: But there is no way;
They cannot help but sway
Into her arms.
ENSEMBLE: Men always say to her—
TRIO OF MEN: Softest of smiles,
Surest of wiles—
ALL: Has this maid of Spain.

[Dialogue: CAPTAIN D'AUBIGNY, MARIANNE's fiancé, says ZEFORSTAS's visit is improper.]

ENSEMBLE: We all want to see her, you know.
And no law forbids you to go.
MEN: From the Café des Femmes Nues
There comes a star tonight.

ENSEMBLE: Come, you must put your swords
away.
This is no time to fight.

[ZEFORSTAS enters. It is MARIANNE in disguise.]

ZEFORSTAS: This is indeed an honor
I have long waited for.
ENSEMBLE: We're thrilled to see the great
Zeforstas,
Whom all the men adore.

In a Little French Café

ZEFORSTAS: Do you desire a sweet
and gentle
Ballad that is
sentimental?
ENSEMBLE: We aren't in the mood
to cry, and see
If you can sing us
something spicy.
ZEFORSTAS: I know a song that's
thrilling—
That is, if you're
willing.
ENSEMBLE: Surely you will let us
hear it,
Now that you have
come so very, very
near it.
ZEFORSTAS: All the verse is chatter,
And the chorus doesn't
[matter?]*
ENSEMBLE: Has the song no
meaning?
ZEFORSTAS: I will tell you how it
goes.

REFRAIN

ZEFORSTAS: In a little French café
There's a little lady
Whom the men refer
to as
"La bien aimée."
ENSEMBLE: The sweet one!
ZEFORSTAS: This is all she has to
say,
"La, la, la, la, la, la, la,
la, la, la, la, la, la—
Monsieur, voyez!"
ENSEMBLE: Petite one!
ZEFORSTAS: Then in her enchanting
way,

* The manuscript lacks text for two syllables.

138

Making ev'rybody fall
for her
And call for her
"La chère bébé"—

ENSEMBLE: Coquette so charming,
She is disarming!

ZEFORSTAS: She sings in Spanish,
French, or Dutch.
Words don't matter
much.

ENSEMBLE: She merely glances
The while she dances.

ZEFORSTAS: She just says,
"La la la la l'amour."

ENSEMBLE: Yet her meaning is
clear, I'm sure.

ZEFORSTAS: Simply "la la la la la la
la la,"
And they understand
toujours!

ENSEMBLE: In a little French café
There's a little lady
Whom the men refer
to as
"La bien aimée"—
The sweet one.
This is all she has to
say,
"La la la la la la la la la
la la la la—
Monsieur, voyez!"
Petite one.

ZEFORSTAS: Then in her enchanting
way,
Making ev'rybody fall
for her
And call for her,
"La chère bébé"—

ENSEMBLE: Coquette so charming,
She is disarming.

ZEFORSTAS: Spanish, French, or
Dutch

ZEFORSTAS AND ENSEMBLE: Words don't matter
much.

ENSEMBLE: She merely glances
The while she dances.
She just sings
"La la la la l'amour."

ZEFORSTAS AND ENSEMBLE: Yet her meaning is
clear, I'm sure—
Simply "la la la la
la la,"
And they know that
means l'amour!

[MARIANNE removes her mask. All are surprised.]

ENSEMBLE: Marianne, Marianne,
Marianne—
Coquette so charming,
She is disarming.
She sings in Spanish,
French, or Dutch—
Words don't matter
much.
She merely glances
The while she dances.

MARIANNE AND ENSEMBLE: She just says,
"La la la la l'amour,"
Yet her meaning is
clear, I'm sure.
Simply "la la la la
la la,"
And they know that
means l'amour!

[Dialogue: MARIANNE teases D'AUBIGNY that she has another love interest.]

The Voice in the Dark

MARIANNE: When the pale moon
Shimmered brightly,
Lover of mine
Ventured nightly.
Ladders of rope preparing,
Courageous and daring,
A pirate was he.
He who sought me.
Over the sea
He had brought me
Jewels and silks and chests of gold
From an isle of buried treasure.

GIRLS: We know that you are teasing—
Please stop your fooling and tell the
truth.
We must discover
Who is your lover.

MARIANNE: There isn't much for [me to tell]*

ENSEMBLE: Then surely you can tell it well.

MARIANNE: It was at night,
I was sleeping.
Up to my room,
Softly creeping,
Came a bold man and wooed me.
He madly pursued me,
So after I tried to resist him,
Finally I up and kissed him.
[Two measures of text missing.]
When I am alone,
My lover unknown
Caresses my dreams with a song;
His voice in the dark

_____
* Three syllables are missing from the manuscript.

Has lighted the spark
That I have kept smothered so long.
The veil of the night
Always hides him from sight,
Lending mystery to my adventure.
And could he but guess
All I might confess,
I think he would no longer hide from
me.

'Neath a New Moon

ROBERT: [offstage] Good luck will bless
The dreams of success
That you long for 'neath a new
moon.
Chances are bright
All things will be right,
If you start them 'neath a new
moon.

ENSEMBLE: It is true,
She really has a lover
Who woos her with a song.

ROBERT: Good luck will bless
The dreams of success
That you long for 'neath a new
moon.
Chances are bright
All things will be right,
If you start them 'neath a new
moon.

[CROWD rushes to window, MARIANNE intervenes.]

MARIANNE: Wait!
You'll break the magic spell.
You see my
[three measures of text
missing] voice!
So, perhaps you can believe in my
love.
When I am alone
My lover unknown
Caresses my dreams with a song.

ENSEMBLE: His voice in the dark
Has lighted the spark
That you have kept smothered so
long.

MARIANNE: The veil of the night
Always hides him from sight,
Lending mystery to my
adventure.

MARIANNE
AND ENSEMBLE: And could he but guess,
All you might confess,
I think he would no longer hide
from you.

ONE DAY

Not published. Used only in 1927. The lyric for this Act One duet for Duchene and Robert (who were lovers before he fled France) was found in the Romberg holograph sketchbook at the Library of Congress. Introduced by Margaret Irving (Duchene) and Robert Halliday (Robert).

VERSE

DUCHENE: I remember ev'rything you used to say.
I remember when you bellowed "No!"
    that way.
You'd be hard to manage and
    unpleasant
Only for the present;
Easy to handle another day.

ROBERT: You speak of quite another man you
    used to know.
Many things can happen in a year or so.

DUCHENE: You will always be the same to me
No matter what you do.
Oh, let me be the same to you!

REFRAIN

DUCHENE: One day your lips were mine, dear!
One day, one night divine, dear.
For each tender hour
While sweet romance unfurled,
Within our lover's bow'r
We thought we owned the world.
One day had quickly flown, dear.
Next day I was alone, dear!
Dreaming my dream that someday, in
    some way,
I might adore you just one day more!

WHEN I CLOSE MY EYES

This Act One duet for Alexander and Julie was published as an individual sheet in 1927, but not retained for the 1928 production. Introduced by William Wayne (Alexander) and Marie Callahan (Julie).

VERSE

ALEXANDER: A good imagination
Is just a gift divine.
There is no compensation
That I would take for mine.
So I can pass the time with

Most any girl at all,
And make believe that I'm with
The fairest of them all.

JULIE: There is no truth in
The things we see.

ALEXANDER: If you are too thin
Or stout for me,
My little method can make you be—

BOTH: The one I've always longed for.

REFRAIN

ALEXANDER: Oh, when I close my eyes and love
    you—

JULIE: Oh, I just close my eyes and love
    you—

ALEXANDER: So I can make a vision of you,
Rare to see—

JULIE: And fair to me.

ALEXANDER: Oh, when you're nestled in my arms,
It's lots of fun
To think of Venus and the Helen girl
Rolled into one

JULIE: Your eyes are just the shade of blue
I always want them to be.

ALEXANDER: No lips are like the rosy two
That you are offering me.
From head to toe,
I can make my ideal girl.

BOTH: Tho' you're an ordinary real girl,
Oh, you're a dream
When I close my eyes.

ACT ONE FINALE (1927 VERSION)

Not published. Used only in 1927. Introduced by Desiree Tabor (Marianne), William Wayne (Alexander), Robert Halliday (Robert), and ensemble.

GIRLS AND MEN: What a night of pleasure, of
    delight full measure.
We've a right to treasure Beauty's
    powers.
Strains of music, dancing, lights,
    and flowers
Make these the sweetest,
    completest of all life's hours.
There's a thrill to new things,
We've the will to do things,
Life can still add few things
To our dowers.
We're all excited

Since we've been invited
To attend the cotillion now.

GIRLS: This is an aristocratic dance—

MEN: Just a new dance.

GIRLS: Being done in all the courts of
    France.

MEN: From the courts of France.

GIRLS: Surely you could tell that at a
    glance.

MEN: What a bright dance!

GIRLS: I enjoy the element of chance.

MEN: Just the right dance.

GIRLS: It is fun to see—

MEN: Waiting to see—

GIRLS: Who your partner'll be.

MEN: Who she will be.

GIRLS AND MEN: What a night of pleasure, of
    delight full measure!
We've a right to treasure Beauty's
    powers.
We're all excited,
Since we've been invited
To attend the cotillion now.

MEN: Give me the number that you gave
    to someone very sweet.

GIRLS: But don't you dare to misbehave!
It isn't fair to cheat.

MEN: They're all as lovely as can be,
I'm ready to confess.

GIRLS AND MEN: I wonder who will dance with me.
I wish that I could guess.

GIRLS: I vow I'll not refuse whomever
    fate shall choose.

MARIANNE: There is an air of romance
Lending a charm to the dance.

ENSEMBLE: Mystery's thrill is enduring;
Lovers unknown are alluring.

MARIANNE: Song of a bird in his flight,
Lost in the dark of the night.

ENSEMBLE: Dreams of a day
That is still far away—

MARIANNE
AND ENSEMBLE: Fill us with strange delight.

[The lottery begins.]

GIRLS: What will he get?
Let's make a bet!
He will draw number four.

ALEXANDER: [shouting] Sixteen!

ENSEMBLE: Here's where lovers part.
Your choice is not that of your
    heart.

MEN: Draw number one.
Hush, ev'ryone,
D'Aubigny should draw one.

ALEXANDER: [shouting] Thirteen!

ENSEMBLE: Goodness me!
How will my luck be?
Who's the man who'll win
Marianne?

ROBERT: [masked] Will fortune be kindly to
me?

ALEXANDER: [shouting] Number one!

MARIANNE: Be at your ease, sir.
Since luck decrees, sir,
I am your partner for this dance.

ROBERT: My pride is great, miss.
It is my fate, miss,
To have been favored.

ENSEMBLE: Why this delaying?
The music's playing
And we are eager for the dance.

MARIANNE: Why are you waiting, hesitating
To lose one moment of romance?

ROBERT
AND MARIANNE: Hesitating to lose one moment of
romance.

ENSEMBLE: Don't lose one moment of
romance.

ENSEMBLE: It's so amusing!
Let's not be losing
A single moment of romance.
So with the partner of Fate's
choosing
We'll go within and join the
dance!

[MARIANNE asks ROBERT to cede his prize. She wants
to be alone.]

ROBERT: This hour it seems
As though my dreams
Have all come true.

MARIANNE: Please leave me, sir.
Believe me, sir,
I want you to.

ROBERT: I'm sorry I intrude.
Please forgive me if I do.

MARIANNE: Please, do not think me rude—
To tell the truth, you do.

ROBERT: Are you perchance thinking of
your bond servant?
Oh, sell him and be done with
him!

MARIANNE: I will. Will you buy him?

ROBERT: I?

MARIANNE: You name your own price.

ROBERT: No, that's impossible.

MARIANNE: You think he's unruly?
Why, thrash him!

[The next four lines are spoken.]

ROBERT: I'm afraid I could not do that.

MARIANNE: Why not?

ROBERT: It would hurt me too much.

MARIANNE: Who are you? You seem so
sympathetic, so tender-
hearted.

ROBERT: [sung] I'm one whom you
Have listened to
Before tonight.

MARIANNE: I can't recall
Your voice at all.
Sir, are you right?

ROBERT: Dear lady,
If I tell you,
Our whole romance will end.

[Pause.]

Good luck will bless
The dreams of success
That you long for neath a new
moon.

MARIANNE: Take off your mask
And let me see your face!

[Dialogue.]

ROBERT: There is a legend old
All ancient sailors hold.
If you seek wealth and gold
And fortune's boon—

MARIANNE: When you head out to sea,
Wait for the sky to be—

BOTH: Lighted invitingly
By the new moon.

ROBERT: Good luck will bless
The dreams of success
That you long for neath a new
moon.
Chances are bright
All things will be right
When you start them neath a new
moon.
So if you'd start
To offer your heart
To the girl who comes once in a
blue moon—

BOTH: You'll never miss,
If you steal that first kiss
With a new moon above.

[Again MARIANNE orders ROBERT to remove his mask.
When he does she is incensed. A crowd gathers as she
orders that ROBERT be whipped, and even administers
one lash herself. Eventually they drag him offstage to
be locked up. BEAUNOIR invites his guests to resume
dancing.]

ENSEMBLE: There's a thrill to new things,
We've the will to do things,
Life can still add few things
To our dowers
We're all excited,
Since we've been invited—

[Word comes that ROBERT has escaped. A sailor song
is heard from offstage.* MEN exit to track down the
escapee. WOMEN are sent upstairs. MARIANNE lingers.]

MARIANNE: The veil of the night always hides
him from sight,
Lending mystery to my
adventure.

ROBERT: [suddenly entering] Good luck will
bless
The dreams of success
That you long for neath a new
moon.
But if you start
To offer your heart
To the girl who comes once in a
blue moon—

BOTH: You'll never win
If you steal that first kiss
With a new moon!
Ah!

INTRODUCTION TO TRY HER OUT AT DANCES (1927 VERSION)

Not published. Used only in 1927. Introduced by the
ensemble.

GIRLS: Here's the day we've all been
awaiting,
Now there is no further debating:
You and I will soon be bride and
groom.

MEN: Here's an end to all your playing;
From today you'll start obeying,
From today there'll be no
delaying—
You must learn to cook and wield
a broom.

GIRLS: We're going to our doom!
I hope you never want to scold
me.

* No lyrics are given.

In your arms you'll gently fold
    me,
Saying I'm dear.
I'll remember all you told me
While we waited here.
MEN: You will be my loving wife.
GIRLS: And you my loving husband.
MEN: Wait until you see
How cross and cranky I can be.
When we disagree,
You'll start to wish that you were
    free.
GIRLS: There's a chance we all are
    taking.
MEN: That's why bride and groom are
    quaking.
GIRLS AND MEN: Lest from dreams we'll be
    awaking
Only gloom to see.

[*Continues with verse and refrain of "Try Her Out at Dances."*]

MARRIAGE HYMN

Not published. Used only in 1927. This prayer followed "Try Her Out at Dances." Introduced by Desiree Tabor (Marianne), Marie Callahan (Julie), Robert Halliday (Robert), William Wayne (Alexander), William O'Neal (Phillippe), and ensemble.

MARIANNE, JULIE, GIRLS: God in Heaven,
We patiently beg of
    Thee
Help and guidance in
    our wedded life.

MARIANNE, JULIE, ROBERT,
ALEXANDER, ENSEMBLE: Help us all to be
    steadfast in loyalty
And with all our hearts
    to keep from strife.

[PHILLIPPE *performs the marriage ceremony.*]

PHILLIPPE: Dear Father above
    them,
Please guide them and
    love them.
We bless them in Thy
    name.
May they live in lasting
    love and peace.

MARIANNE (1927 VERSION)

Published as an individual sheet. This earlier and entirely different "Marianne" is not listed in the 1927 program. If it was used, its place in the running order is not known. However, the sheet music, and the reprises in the 1927 Finale Ultimo and the Act Two Finaletto, suggest that it was the major love theme at some stage of the writing process.

VERSE

ROBERT: Long after you're away,
Memories of you will stay behind.
And there may come a day
When a thought of me may cross your
    mind.
And that is why, before you go,
There's just one thing I'd have you
    know:

REFRAIN

ROBERT: I've never told you, Marianne,
A hope that filled my breast.
Someday to hold you, Marianne,
Caress and be caressed.
Since love is such a gentle fool,
You can't account for what he'll do.
So forgive a sentimental fool
Who dares to hope you could love him
    too.

ACT TWO FINALE
(1927 VERSION)

Not published. Used only in 1927. Introduced by Robert Halliday (Robert) and Evelyn Herbert (Marianne).

ROBERT: I never told you, Marianne,
A hope that filled my breast—
Someday to hold you, Marianne,
Caress and be caressed.
MARIANNE: Since love is such a gentle fool,
You can't account for what he'll do.
BOTH: So forgive a sentimental fool
Who dares to hope you could love
    him too.

YOU LIE

Not published. Not listed in the 1927 Philadelphia program, but a piano-vocal score was found with the 1927 *New Moon* material in the Warner/Chappell Collection at the Library of Congress. Intended for Besac, Clotilde, and male ensemble.

VERSE

BESAC: [*very downcast*] I've sailed
    across ev'ry ocean
Just searching for you,
And with a husband's
    devotion
All mournful and blue.
BASSES: [*almost crying*] Poor
    fellow!
How he must have
    suffered.
TENORS: [*almost sobbing*] Yes,
    suffered.
BASSES: The pain that he's gone
    through!
TENORS: It's terrible.
Come, monsieur, your
    story.
BASSES: Oh, tell us, please!
ALL MEN: We would listen too!
BESAC: I started out in a sailboat.
CLOTILDE: Sailboat?
BESAC: No, it was a rowboat.
No, I guess I swam.
CLOTILDE: Across the sea?
BESAC: Well, at any rate,
Here I am.

REFRAIN

BESAC: Just listen to me and I'll
    explain.
CLOTILDE: You lie, you lie, you lie!
BESAC: The day that I lost you in
    the rain—
CLOTILDE: You lie, you lie, you lie!
BESAC: I turned around and you
    had fled,
And why and where you
    had not said.
CLOTILDE: You lie, you lie, you lie,
    you lie!
TENORS AND CLOTILDE: You lie, you lie, you lie!
BESAC: Wait,
You're the one who ran
    away.
CLOTILDE: You lie!
BESAC: I don't.

CLOTILDE: You do.

BESAC: Will you give me a chance to say—

CLOTILDE: You lie!

BESAC: I don't.

CLOTILDE: You do.

BESAC: D'ye want to keep this up all day?

ALL MEN: It's pretty hard on you!

CLOTILDE: You lie, you lie, you lie, you lie!

BESAC: I don't, I don't, I don't, I don't!

CLOTILDE AND MEN: You lie!

BESAC: I don't.

CLOTILDE AND MEN: You lie!

BESAC: I don't.

CLOTILDE AND TENORS: You lie, you lie!

BESAC: I don't!

CLOTILDE AND TENORS: You lie, you lie!

BESAC: I don't!

CLOTILDE AND TENORS: You lie!

BESAC: I don't

CLOTILDE: You lie!

BESAC: I don't!

CLOTILDE: You do!

FINALETTO, ACT TWO, SCENE 3 (1927 VERSION)

Not published. Music and lyric survive in the Romberg holograph piano-vocal score, and in Warner-Chappell manuscripts dated 1927. Perhaps this is the missing "The Call of Home" which preceded the Finale.

BESAC: When you've skimmed the breeze
Of the seven seas,
There's a feeling you will understand.
You will find no joy like the cry "Ahoy!"
To the gray mist of your native land.
One land, your land,

Forever, whatever the flag unfurled.

BESAC AND MEN: One home, your home,
Only one place in all the world!

PHILLIPPE: The home calls to ev'ryone.
There's duty that must be done.
That home will be a barren place
If you return in disgrace.
We've all been sincere and real,
True comrades with one ideal.
We can't betray
The man who's led our way.

MEN: We've been true and loyal comrades,
But we are longing to go,
All to be home,
To stay at home now!

BESAC: We have faced the breeze of the seven seas,
And we've lived like some barbaric band.
Now it's time to live, while we've wealth to give,
For contentment in our native land.
One land, our land,
Forever wherever the flag unfurled.

BESAC, MEN, AND GIRLS: One land, our land.
And so for home!

PHILLIPPE: So your leader you'd betray for home?!

MEN: [*subdued*] Robert, our leader!

ROBERT: I'll accept your decision.
I'll hide till you all depart from here.

PHILLIPPE: You'll remain alone behind?

ROBERT: Yes!

PHILLIPPE: [*spoken*] I will stay too!

ROBERT: [*spoken*] Phillippe, don't be a fool.
[*sung*] That is a useless sacrifice!
I don't want you to stay.

MEN: But you're alone.

PHILLIPPE: We've fought our fight together,
So let us lose together!

MEN: One friend is faithful.

ONE BOY: [*shouting*] The French are landing!
They are waiting for our surrender.

[MARIANNE *enters.*]

BESAC: [*spoken*] Robert, we'll give you ten minutes to hide. We'll hold the French back that long— after that, if they find you—

ROBERT: Before we dissolve this state of ours,
I want ev'ryone to bear witness:
This moment our laws are still in force,
The French have not yet won possession.
Phillippe, go up to the pulpit rock.
Marianne, give me your hand!

[*At* ROBERT's *request,* PHILLIPPE *formally dissolves* ROBERT *and* MARIANNE's *marriage. They exchange a few awkward words.*]

REFRAIN

ROBERT: I've never told you, Marianne,
A hope that filled my breast—
Someday to hold you, Marianne,
Caress and be caressed.
Since love is such a gentle fool,
You can't account for what he'll do.
So forgive a sentimental fool
Who dares to hope you could love him too.

ALL REPEAT REFRAIN*

---

* *Lyrics are adjusted to suit the characters. Robert sings: "I've never told you." Marianne sings: "You never told me." Ensemble sings: "He never told you, etc."*

OVERLEAF *Stage and screen Adelines: Helen Morgan (left),* Irene Dunne *(right)*

SWEET ADELINE (1929)

Tryouts: Apollo Theatre, Atlantic City, August 19–24, 1929; Shubert Theatre, Newark, August 26–31; 1929. New York run: Hammerstein's Theatre; opened September 3, 1929; closed March 22, 1930; 234 performances. A Musical Romance of the Gay Nineties. Produced by Arthur Hammerstein. Music by Jerome Kern. Book and lyrics by Oscar Hammerstein II. Dances and ensembles staged by Danny Dare. Book staged by Reginald Hammerstein. Orchestrations by Robert Russell Bennett. Musical direction by Gustave Salzer. Stage settings designed by Gates and Morange. Costumes designed by Charles Lemaire.

Cast: Helen Morgan (Addie), John D. Seymour (Sid Barnett), Violet Carlson (Dot), Charles Butterworth (Ruppert Day), Robert C. Fischer (Emil Schmidt), Caryl Bergman (Nellie), Max Hoffmann Jr. (Tom Martin), Robert Chisholm (James Day), Irene Franklin (Lulu Ward), Robert Emmett Keane (Dan Ward), Jack Gray (Doctor), Tom Thompson (Orderly), Ben Wells (Colonel), Gustave Salzer (Gus), Len Mence (Sam Herzig), Tom Rider (Eddie), Thomas Chadwick (the Sultan), George Djimos (the Jester), Helen Ault (Maizie O'Rourke), George Raymond (August), Pauline Gorin (Lena), William Sheppard (Head Carpenter/Gabe Case), Joe Reilly (Props), Louis Leo (On the Ladder), Borrah Levinson (George), Jackson Fairchild (Young Blood), Martin Sheppard (Colonel), Harry Esmond (Old Sport), George Magis (Doc), Jim Thornton (Jim Thornton), Jerry Jarnagin (Mr. Gilhooley), Sally Bates (Hester Van Doren Day), Peter Bender (Willie Day), Gertrude Clave, Polly Fisher, Frances Flanigan, Laura Mutch, Josephine Rice, Mabel Thilbault (George Smith's Girl Band), and ensemble.

This "musical romance of the gay '90s" is the story of Addie Schmidt, who waits tables in her father's beer garden, but dreams of singing on a big stage. Her opportunity comes by chance—she is at the theater to scold a man who's been flirting with her sister Nellie—and she swiftly becomes the toast of New York. Her romantic life takes a similar upturn, going from an unrequited crush on Tom Martin (who prefers Nellie) to a proposal from socialite Jim Day. But Jim decides that he cannot marry an actress, and Addie leaves New York, returning only to help her theatrical friends with a new show. Among the theater folk are Sid, a songwriter; Lulu, an aging small-time leading lady; and Dan, Lulu's husband and business manager. A dress rehearsal of Lulu and Dan's show is a set piece in Act One. Interwoven with Addie's story is the comical courtship of Dot, who leads the band at the beer garden, and Ruppert Day (Jim's brother), who becomes a backer of Dan and Lulu's show.

Ruppert, Jim, and Tom all spend part of the first act in Cuba, where the Spanish-American War is being fought.

A national tour began at the Colonial Theatre, Boston, on September 8, 1930, and ended at the Erlanger Theatre, Philadelphia, on January 24, 1931.

A film version was produced by Warner Bros. and released in December 1934. Directed by Mervyn LeRoy, it starred Irene Dunne and Donald Woods.

Six songs from *Sweet Adeline* were published. The Tams-Witmark Music Library has an unpublished script and a piano-conductor score (which sometimes disagree). This chapter relies heavily on the research done for a concert production by New York City Center's Encores! series in February 1997. Despite efforts made for Encores! (and for a 1977 production at the Goodspeed Opera House in East Haddam, Connecticut), two lyrics have not been located. "Winter in Central Park" was an ensemble number at the beginning of Act Two. "Take Me for a Honeymoon Ride" (one manuscript is titled "Take Me for a Bicycle Ride") was a comedy number for Dot and Ruppert toward the end of Act Two. Another song, "I'm Dreaming," for Addie and Jim in Act Two, was cut after the Atlantic City opening and has not been located.

This chapter does not include lyrics for "My Husband's First Wife," "Indestructible Kate," and "She's Doing It All for Baby," all written by vaudeville star Irene Franklin, who played the role of Lulu. Another interpolation was "Just a Little Bit of String (The Fishhook Number)," from The Circus Girl (1897), music by Lionel Monckton and lyric by Harry Greenbank and Adrian Ross.

PLAY US A POLKA, DOT

Not published. Introduced by Violet Carson (Dot) and ensemble.

VERSE

All night I stand here and blow
Upon an old piccolo
While all the other girls are dancing,
Gay and free,
Getting thrills that never come to me.
I'm a girl men hear but never see,
For this is all they ever say from ten to three:

REFRAIN

Play us a polka, Dot—
Gotta play a polka, Dot!
Play a waltz, and play it sweet and low.
"Play" is all they say to Dot.

How can any dance be gay to Dot?
Not a chance for me to get a beau.
On a bright
Summer night
Under the moon,
All the boys say to me:
Whoops! Another tune!
Play us a polka, Dot!*
Gotta have another polka, Dot!
On with the dance, you piccolo!

'TWAS NOT SO LONG AGO (ES WAR SCHON DAMALS SO)

Published as an individual sheet, with English and German lyrics and a full choral arrangement. Introduced by Helen Morgan (Addie) and ensemble. The song was meant to resemble an old German folk song.

VERSE

Though new young blossoms are born each May,
They burst their buds in the same old way.
So love that's true is a story told
As ever new in a world that's old.

REFRAIN

'Twas not so long ago
That Pa was Mother's beau.
And though their styles and fads
Have gone like old sachet,
The things Pa said to Ma,†
The things Ma said to Pa,
Were quite the same as all the things
That lovers say today.

VERSE

In grünen Wald ist es schön zu sein.
Die Sonne strahlt und der Mai Kehrt ein.

---

* *Alternate final three lines for a repeat of the refrain:*
   How can I ever kiss
   While my lips are always glued to this?
   Gosh, how I hate the piccolo!

† *Alternate lines 5–8 for second refrain:*
   The way that Pa kissed Ma,
   The way that Ma kissed Pa,
   Is one thing that will never be
   Improved upon today.

Mit frischer Lust steht das Herz bereit
Die Liebe blüht in der Frühlingszeit.

REFRAIN

Es war schon damals so.
Vor hundert tausend Jahr
Zur schonen Sommerzeit,
Ein Knab' warleicht und froh.
Mit einmal fiels ihm ein
Er möcht beliebet sein,
Es war schon so, Schon immer so,
Es war schon damals so!

HERE AM I

Published as an individual sheet. Introduced by Helen Morgan (Addie) and Violet Carson (Dot).

VERSE

ADDIE: I won't know my fate until he finds me.
I will wait until he finds me
And gently reminds me
That I am his girl
And he is my man—
Just like in a play.
DOT: Do you think he'll ever know?
Supposing he should never know
You're waiting.
ADDIE: I'll be like a fly
And hover nearby,
Just patiently waiting
Till he turns my way;
Then I'll say:

REFRAIN

ADDIE: Here am I,
Here I'll stay
Till you notice me,
In your path,
In your way,
And if you look, you're bound to see.
If you could only like me,
How I'd love you!
I'm very lonely; maybe you're lonely too.
Here is love,
Here am I—
Please don't pass us by.

FIRST MATE MARTIN

Alternate title: "Tom's Entrance." Introduced by Max Hoffman Jr. (Tom Martin), Charles Butterworth (Ruppert Day), and ensemble. Some of the music for this number had been used previously in "Yes, Ma'am," a song dropped from *Show Boat*.

MEN: First Mate Tom W. Martin,
The great Tom W. Martin!
TOM: I have nothing to say.
Thank you for the bouquet.
What's a fellow to say now?
GIRLS: First Mate Tom W. Martin!
MEN: When are you going to start in?
Tell all about the rescue out at
sea.
That wonderful deed
That has made you a hero!
GIRLS: Telling every little detail
Of your rescue brave—
Tell us how
You were a hero.
TOM: [*pointing to* RUPPERT] I saw him
jump in the ocean;
I was choked up with emotion.
My face was pale, and my lips
were blue.
My heart with agony thumped!
MEN AND GIRLS: All the credit is due to you.
RUPPERT: *I'm* the fellow that jumped.
MEN AND GIRLS: From that point we know the
way:
You rescued Ruppert Day!
He jumped right down into the
spray,
And you could hear the fellow
yelp—
It was a dying cry for help.
Presently you jumped
And rescued Ruppert Day,
Pulling the poor wet fish
Out of the ocean!

SPRING IS HERE

The program subtitles this number "Buffo Duo." Not published. Introduced by Violet Carson (Dot) and Charles Butterworth (Ruppert Day).

VERSE 1

DOT: When crocuses are blooming
And birds are busy pluming,
I'm blooming and pluming
Just like the buds and birds.
When rams are asking ewe lambs
To promise to be true lambs,
And cattle start to prattle
Of love among the herds,
Then I feel too wonderful for words.

REFRAIN 1

DOT: Something gets alive in me
Urging me, driving me—
When the spring is here I get that way.
Like the sap that's in the tree,
All the sap snaps in me—
When the spring is here I get that way.
What is this vivacity
That comes each year to storm us?
Why is my capacity
For kissing so enormous?
It's because the spring is here,
Spring is here,
Spring is here—
Every time it comes I get that way.

VERSE 2

RUPPERT: The pussy willows purring
May start my pulse a-stirring,
But I cure that stirring
In quite a novel way.
I have a friend named Cyril,
And when we're feeling virile,
We get out and play out
A round of fast croquet—
That just sort of sets us for the day.

REFRAIN 2

DOT: Ain't that thing alive in you,
Urging you, driving you?
When the spring is here ain't you that
way?
Like the sap that's in the tree,
All the sap snaps in me—
When the spring is here ain't you that
way?
RUPPERT: Goodness, what vitality!
You ought to rise above it.
This is immorality—
Oh, the pity of it.
DOT: It's because the spring is here,
Spring is here,
Spring is here—

Every time the spring is here I get that
way.

OUT OF THE BLUE

Published as an individual sheet. Introduced by Robert
Chisholm (James "Jim" Day), Max Hoffmann Jr. (Tom
Martin), Violet Carson (Dot), Caryl Bergman (Nellie),
and ensemble.

When the song begins, Jim and Tom are servicemen
in Cuba, reading and writing letters. According to Hammerstein's stage directions: "More boys enter and the
song develops into a male chorus number, well harmo-
nized. This, however, should be a lively march to contrast with another male harmony in Act Two. Tom and
boys pick up refrain. Sing to dim out—only cigarette
lights remain. Blackout. Almost immediately, like an
answer in the dark, the girls' chorus sing the same
refrain. Curtain rises on Scene 3, discovering girls finishing refrain."

VERSE 1

JIM: Writing letters over here.
MEN: In Cuba.
JIM: Sending letters over there.
MEN: From Cuba.
JIM: I am hoping you will care enough, my
    dear,
    To let me hear
    A word from you.
TOM: You don't know just how it seems
    Just how much a fellow dreams.
JIM: You know I dream of you.
TOM: You don't have to write in reams—
    A line will do.
JIM: You'd make my hope run high
    With a note from a clear blue sky.

REFRAIN 1

JIM: Send me just one word
    Out of the blue,
    Like a gliding bird
    Out of the blue.
    Let it fly and bear the good news
    Straight to me
    And straight from you.
MEN: I love you,
    I love you.
JIM: While I'm far away,
    Sad as can be,
    Now's the time to say
    You will love me.
    Send the word,

Like sunlight shining through!
One word from you—
Out of the blue.

MEN: Send me just one word
    Out of the blue,
    Like a gliding bird
    Out of the blue.
    Let it fly and bear the good news
    Straight to me
    And straight from you:
    I love you,
    I love you.
    While I'm far away,
    Sad as can be,
    Now's the time to say
    You will love me.
    Send the word,
    Like sunlight shining through!
    One word from you—
    Out of the blue.

Postman, hurry with my mail—
Don't delay a single second.
Start with a hop and a skip and a jump.
You can try, try to fly through the sky,
Fly over land, and
Swift as a bird
Bring the word on to me over sea
From where she's waiting for me.
Quick as a flash,
With a dash for a pen,
I will then
Send the answer
She already must know.

INTERLUDE

GIRLS: Send me just one word
    Out of the blue.
    Just one word from you,
    Not two—
    One word from you.
ALTOS: Just one word from you,
    Not two—
    One word from you
    Out of the blue.

VERSE 2

A GIRL: Will your letter be addressed to Cuba?
NELLIE: I am writing to the best in Cuba.
DOT: I am writing to the best,
    For need I say
    The man I love
    Is Ruppert Day.
GIRLS: Ev'rybody has a boy
    In Cuba.

Getting letters we enjoy
From Cuba.
How much can a girl believe them
When they say,
"Send me just one word"?

REFRAIN 2

GIRLS: Out of the blue,
    Like a gliding bird
    Out of the blue,
    Let it fly and bear the good news
    Straight to me
    And straight from you.
    While I'm far away,
    Sad as can be,
    Now's the time to say
    You will love me—
    Send the word,
    Like sunlight shining through!
TENORS: Postman, hurry with my mail.
BASSES: Don't delay a single second.
MEN: Start with a hop and a skip and a jump.*
    Fly through the sky and over land,
    Swift as a bird
    Bring the word on to me over sea
    From where she's waiting for me.
    Quick as a flash,
    With a dash for a pen,
    I will then
    Send the answer
    She already must know.
GIRLS: Postman, hurry with my mail—
    Don't delay a single second.
    Bring me the word that is long overdue.
    Over the wide ocean blue
    Send the word,
    Like sunlight shining through—
    One word from you, out of the blue.

NAUGHTY, NAUGHTY BOY

Not published. Introduced by Irene Franklin (Lulu) and
chorus girls. Marked "After the manner of 1898."

VERSE

Someone I know
Isn't a shy fellow—
He's making eyes at me.
Fly away, you butterfly fellow—

---

* This stanza is a condensation of overlapping vocal
  lines.

Please leave me be.
Why do you tease me so?
Why do you squeeze me so?
Naughty, naughty boy,
My heart goes pit-a-pat,
I don't know where I'm at,
Naughty, naughty boy.

REFRAIN

I am like a tiny rosebud on the vine,
Honey mine.
You are my bumblebee
Who's always bringing me joy.
On Sunday afternoons
When you come round to spoon,
You're so spick-and-span
I can't resist you
Although I do all that I can.
But when you grow bold and try to steal a kiss
Just like this [kiss noise],
You're not a naughty boy—
You're just a terrible man.

ORIENTAL MOON

Not published. Kern had previously used the tune as "Oriental Dreams" in *The Cabaret Girl* (London, 1921). Introduced by Thomas Chadwick (the Sultan) and George Djimos (the Jester). This song and "Molly O'Donahue" are from Lulu and Dan's show, which we see in rehearsal.

VERSE

When the lights are low
In the eastern sky,
When the night draws nigh,
Hours sweet roll by.
Then a rajah bold
Meets a maiden fair.
There's perfume in the air
And moonbeams in her hair.
Ya, ho . . . oh.
Ya, ho . . . oh.

REFRAIN

Oriental moon,
Crimson glow on high,
Like a pale balloon
Burning in the sky,
Oriental moon,
Light the blue lagoon—

While soft voices croon,
Love will never die!

MOLLY O'DONAHUE

Not published. Kern had previously used the tune as "All You Need Is a Girl" in *Sitting Pretty* (1924). Introduced by Helen Ault (Maizie O'Rourke) and female ensemble.

VERSE

Patrick Michael Shamus O'Brien
Could never stop sighin'
For sweet Molly O'.
Ev'ry mornin' up with the sparrow,
And out like an arrow
Just leavin' a bow,
Off to her house by the spring,
He'd whisk to her window and sing:

REFRAIN

It's good mornin' to you,
Molly O'Donahue.
It's yourself that I'm askin' to go
For a bit of a walk,
And it's me that will smile if you do.
There's a sun in the sky—
There'll be one in my eye
If you'll say that you'll go,
Molly, oh,
Molly O'Donahue.

WHY WAS I BORN?

Published as an individual sheet, and the refrain appears in Hammerstein's anthology, *Lyrics*. Introduced by Helen Morgan (Addie).

Sid Barnett, the orchestra leader, has asked Addie to try a song he's written, boasting that "if this song is properly sung, it'll put your show over, no matter how bad the rest of the show is." Helen Morgan and Libby Holman both made best-selling recordings of it in 1930.

VERSE

Spending these lonesome evenings
With nothing to do
But to live in dreams that I make up

All by myself,
I'm dreaming that you're beside me.
I picture the prettiest stories,
Only to wake up
All by myself.
What is the good of me by myself?

REFRAIN

Why was I born?
Why am I living?
What do I get?
What am I giving?
Why do I want a thing I daren't hope for?
What can I hope for?
I wish I knew!
Why did I try
To draw you near me?
Why do I cry?
You never hear me.
I'm a poor fool,
But what can I do?
Why was I born
To love you?

ADELINE BELMONT

Not published. Not listed separately in the program, the song leads directly into "The Sun About to Rise." Introduced by a few men of the ensemble.

To the toast of giddy New York,
To the belle of Manhattan Island so gay,
May we greet you and entreat you
For a tiny smile today,
Just a tiny smile today?
Adeline the Belmont,
The lady gay—
There's a light within her eyes
Shining like a sun about to rise.

THE SUN ABOUT TO RISE

Published as an individual sheet. Introduced by John D. Seymour (Sid), Helen Morgan (Addie), and Robert Chisholm (Jim).

REFRAIN

When you see the sun about to rise,
Then you know the hope of morning skies,
And a new day's laughter
Comes following after
A night of downhearted sighs.
Maybe you will meet your love today;
Maybe you will know her right away
By a light within her eyes,
Shining like a sun about to rise.

VERSE

You all have had your nights out
And hung around cafés
Until they've put the lights out
And sent you on your ways.
You walk into the morning,
The air is damp and cool,
You know that you're a fool,
There's no one else to blame,
You are sick of the game—
Till all at once the sky is brightened
With a soft, pale flame;
The dark of the night is fading,
A pink glow invading the gray—
It is day!

REPEAT REFRAIN

SOME GIRL IS ON YOUR MIND

Not published. Introduced by Jim Thornton (Thornton), Robert Chisholm (Jim), Max Hoffman Jr. (Tom), John D. Seymour (Sid), Helen Morgan (Addie), and male ensemble. This extended sequence can be heard on the CD *Broadway Showstoppers* (EMI Angel), conducted by John McGlinn.

THORNTON: Pretty Jennie Lee,
Please come back to me—
I am waiting all alone.
You know I yearn*

---

* The prompt book at Tams-Witmark gives this text instead of lines 4–6 and omits line 9:
　　Though we had a fight
　　Just the other night,
　　Must you have a heart of stone?
　　How I long to kiss you,
　　How I long to spoon!*

For your return—
Come back and be my own.
Jennie, how I miss you—
When I see a moon,
How I long to kiss and spoon!
Please come back and be
Just the girl for me,
Pretty little Jennie Lee.
Please come back and be
Just the girl for me,
Pretty little Jennie Lee.

JIM: Have one on me.
Drink hearty, sir.
I understand just how you feel.*

THORNTON: I don't mind if I do.

JIM: I think you need a pal
To tell your troubles to.
Why are you so gloomy
When the other boys are having fun?
Why do you get blue
And want to run away from ev'ryone?
Some girl is on your mind,
Some girl is on your mind.

TOM: Why does ev'ry sailor
Who goes out upon the seven seas
Sigh to see a whaler
That is passing on a homeward breeze?

JIM AND TOM: A girl is on his mind,
Some girl is on his mind.

JIM: Though all the fellows around here
May say their sorrows are drowned here.†
There isn't one who could be found here
If some girl would be kind.

JIM AND ENSEMBLE: I am no exception to the rule.
I wouldn't try to fool you.
There's someone on my mind,
Some girl is on my mind.

SID: Have one on me, and drink hearty.
We're in the same boat, all of us.

MEN: Half the time
When you fall,

---

* Variant line:
　　Here's to your girl, let's drink to her.

† Variant line:
　　May say their trouble is drowned here.

The very girl you want
Won't fall for you at all
And that is why—

SID: Why you're always moody
When the other boys are having fun—
Why you get blue
And want to run away from ev'ryone?

THORNTON: Pretty Jennie Lee,
Please come back to me—
I am waiting here alone.
We had a fight
The other night—
She has a heart of stone.

MEN: Some girl is on your mind,
Some girl is on your mind.

SID: Why should I be haunted by
A voice that's never meant for me?

ADDIE: Why do I try
To draw you near me?

MEN: Her voice may come to you
And you will hear her say
Words never meant for you—
Your fancies run that way.

SID: Why should I imagine that
Her heart is always calling me?

ADDIE: Why do I cry?
You never hear me.

MEN: Her voice may come to you
And you will hear her say
Words never meant for you—
Your fancies run that way.

MEN: Some girl is on your mind,
Some girl is on your mind.

JIM, SID, AND TOM: Though all the fellows around here
May say their sorrows are drowned here,
There isn't one who could be found here
If some girl would be kind.

JIM: I am no exception to the rule.
I wouldn't try to fool you—
There's someone on my mind,
Some girl is on my mind.

ADDIE: I'm very lonely—
Maybe you're lonely too.

MEN: Her voice may come to you—
Your fancies run that way—
You hear her out of the blue!
There's someone on your mind,
Some girl is on your mind.

DON'T EVER LEAVE ME

Published as an individual sheet. Introduced by Helen Morgan (Addie) and Robert Chisholm (Jim).

This lyric was written on July 4, 1929, while newlyweds Oscar and Dorothy Hammerstein were staying with the Kerns on their yacht *Show Boat*. It is dedicated to Dorothy.

Musical-theater historian Michael Feinstein warns of an error in the sheet music that has been perpetuated since the first recordings: the published verse ends "I am no one,/Just part of two." It should be "I am not one."

VERSE 1

ADDIE: I was created for one man alone;
He wasn't easy to find.
Now that I've found him, I wonder just how
I could have lived
Right up to now.
Now I am something completed by you.
I am not one,
Just part of two.

REFRAIN

ADDIE: Don't ever leave me—
Now that you're here,
Here is where you belong.
Ev'rything seems so right when you're near;
When you're away it's all wrong.
I'm so dependent—
When I need comfort,
I always run to you.
Don't ever leave me,
'Cause if you do,
I'll have no one to run to.

VERSE 2

JIM: All that you say that you feel about me
Is how I feel about you.
While you were seeking the one man you love,
I sought one girl,
One all my own.
We found each other and both of us know
Heaven is here—
Don't let it go.

REPEAT REFRAIN

ACT TWO FINALE

Not published. Introduced by Helen Morgan (Addie) and either Robert Chisholm (Jim) or John D. Seymour (Sid).

The surviving materials give conflicting endings. The Tams-Witmark piano-conductor score follows Addie's lines with "Don't Ever Leave Me" but doesn't identify the singer. In the Tams prompt book and a script at the Shubert Archive, Jim responds to Addie's stanzas with "Don't Ever Leave Me," but Addie doesn't acknowledge him and he walks away (ending 1 below). In another script at the Shubert Archive, it is Sid who approaches Addie, and they embrace while she sings "Don't Ever Leave Me" (ending 2 below).

ADDIE: [*reading from a script of* DAN *and* LULU's *new show*] The scene is in a garden;
The season is spring.
The trees are all in blossom;
From their branches hangs a swing.
Enter from the left side and cross to the right;
You look around and in your eye
There gleams a hopeful light.
A young man enters from the other side;
His manner seems preoccupied

Ending 1

JIM: A girl is on his mind,
A girl is on his mind.
ADDIE: [*no longer reading*] Mind you're not forgetting
The last scene you played.
Remember how he went away
Just when he should have stayed.
When a love has once passed you by,
It's best to let it die.
JIM: Don't ever leave me—
Now that you're here,
Here is where you belong [*etc.*]

Ending 2

SID: A girl is on his mind,
A girl is on his mind.
ADDIE: [*looking up, and then back at the script*] Mind you're not forgetting
The primness that's due
A maiden who is gently bred,
Demure and sweet as you.
You don't dare to look in his eye,
But let him hear you sigh:

[*During a short instrumental interlude,* SID *comes to her and takes her gently in his arms.* ADDIE *looks up and sings:*]

Don't ever leave me *etc.*

CUT AND UNUSED SONG

I'VE GOT A NEW IDEA

Not published. Cut after the Atlantic City tryout. It appears in the Tams-Witmark piano-conductor score as "#26, Duettino Act 2, Scene 1." Introduced by Max Hoffmann Jr. (Tom) and Caryl Bergman (Nellie).

VERSE

TOM: [*pretending he's addressing his father*] You must realize life is serious, Father.
We have worries that wear and weary us, Father.
There comes a time when youth must have its fling—
Adventure comes to birdies on the wing.
What I mean to say, I'm so keen to say, Father,
I'm about to do one original thing.

REFRAIN 1

TOM: I'm going to marry a wonderful girl.
I've got a new idea:
I want to marry a girl.
I'm going to build her a wonderful home.
Is that a new idea?
I want to build her a home,
A cute verandah and a front door—
Could she command a man to give more?
I'm going to love her
And even be true.
I've got a new idea
I think I want to be true.

PATTER

NELLIE: [*pretending to be* TOM's *father*] Listen to your daddy, son.
Lean upon your daddy, son.
You are in the clutches of a hussy.
Has she hair that's blond and fuzzy?
Have you met her father?

Does he not sell lager beer?
TOM: What's a little lager beer?
Wait until you see my dear.
Wait until you look into her eye,
And then you'll know just why
I'm going to marry a wonderful girl.

REFRAIN 2

NELLIE: You've got a new idea:
You want to marry a girl.
TOM: I'm going to build her a wonderful home.
NELLIE: Is that a new idea?
You want to build her a home,
A cute verandah and a front door—
TOM: Could she command a man to give more?
NELLIE: I'm going to love him
And even be true.
BOTH: Don't you think we're kind of clever
To have had an idea so terribly new!

ADDED SONG

WE WERE SO YOUNG

Published as an individual sheet. Written for the 1934 film version of *Sweet Adeline*. Introduced by Irene Dunne (Addie).

VERSE

At the high-school cotillion
There were dance cards to fill,
And I met the one boy in a million
And his name was Bill.
Bill, you were a shy boy,
But you were my boy,
And the high-school cotillion
Was my first big thrill.

REFRAIN

We were so young; the time was an evening in May.
I wore the pale pink organdie you thought so gay.
Life was a thing of eager spring and moonlight,
And I was a girl and you were a boy from over the
  way.
We were so young; the heavens were smiling above.
I let you keep my handkerchief; I kept your glove.
Life was a thing of eager spring and moonlight,
And I was a girl and you were a boy and we were in
  love.

OVERLEAF *Rehearsing the music for* Viennese Nights: *Vivienne Segal (right) sits on the piano being played by Sigmund Romberg. Director Alan Crosland and Hammerstein have their backs to the camera.*

151

Songs of 1930

VIENNESE NIGHTS (1930)

A film produced by Warner Bros. and Vitaphone under the personal supervision of J. L. Warner. Released November 26, 1930. Screenplay and lyrics by Oscar Hammerstein II. Music by Sigmund Romberg. Directed by Alan Crosland. Dances directed by Jack Haskell. Musical direction by Louis Silvers. Cinematography by James Van Trees. Art direction by Max Parker. Edited by Hal McLaren and Frank Good.

Cast: Vivienne Segal (Elsa Hofner), Alexander Gray (Otto Stirner/his grandson Larry), Jean Hersholt (Herr Hofner), Walter Pidgeon (Franz von Renner), Louise Fazenda (Gretl Kruger), Alice Day (Barbara, Elsa's granddaughter), Bert Roach (Gus Sascher), Philipp Lothar Mayring (Baron von Renner), June Purcell (Mary), Milt Douglas (Bill Jones), Virginia Sale (Emma Stirner), Freddie Burke Frederick (Otto Stirner Jr.), Dorothy Hammerstein (Socialite), Bela Lugosi (Count von Ratz), Ullrich Haupt (Hugo), Isabelle Keith (Franz's Rejected Girlfriend), Russ Powell (Herr Schultz), Mary Treen (Shocked Woman on Street), Paul Weigel (Man in Vienna Opera Box).

The story is told in three parts. In Vienna in 1879 childhood friends compete for the same girl. Franz is a baron's son, and now an Army officer. Otto is a commoner with a gift for music, so he plays in the Army band. Otto has two dreams: to write a great symphony and to marry Elsa. Prospects are good, as Elsa returns his love and the main theme of the symphony is already written, with words known only to the pair ("I Bring a Love Song"). But one night when Otto and his friend Gus take Elsa out on the town, Franz takes a liking to her. Unfortunately for Otto, Elsa's father takes a liking to Franz. In despair, Otto gets so drunk that he brings a prostitute into the café where Franz and Elsa are dining. And so Elsa decides to marry Franz. For part two, the story leaps forward to 1890 in New York City. Otto has a shrewish wife who hates music, a loveable son, and a job in a theater orchestra. One night, during a routine performance of an operetta about fishermen, Otto recognizes Elsa and Franz in the audience. Elsa returns the next night and she and Otto realize they still love each other. She considers leaving her husband, but decides not to take Otto away from his son. For part three, the story returns to Vienna, but it is now 1930 and Elsa is a grandmother. She goes to a concert of symphonic music composed by her granddaughter's American beau, Larry, and is stunned to hear "her" theme, played in the lush orchestration it always deserved. Otto's dream has been achieved by his grandson Larry.

The main source for this chapter is a piano-vocal score published by Harms, just as if *Viennese Nights* had been a stage musical. The Warner-Chappell Collection in the Music Division of the Library of Congress includes a cut song for Gus and Otto, "If You Want to Kiss a Girl." There are also two volumes of piano-vocal scores and lead sheets (one with holograph material) in the Romberg Collection at the Library of Congress. The Warner Bros. Archive at the University of Southern California has draft screenplays and synopses as well as internal memoranda about contracts, casting, and production. The film itself has been preserved and restored by UCLA's film and television archive, but the editor of this book has seen only a damaged copy.

Special mention must be made of two secondary sources. "The Film Operettas of Sigmund Romberg," a master's thesis by John Koegel (California State University, Los Angeles, 1984), and *A Song in the Dark: The Birth of the Musical Film* by Richard Barrios (Oxford, 1995), an indispensible guide to screen musicals between 1926 and 1934.

Although Hammerstein would later dismiss his Hollywood efforts, he did enjoy the work on his first original movie.* In March 1930, he informed his New York lawyer:

> Neither by phone, nor mail, nor wire have I properly expressed to you the extent of the good feeling and cooperation which featured our first picture. It is impossible to say whether it will be a popular success but it was surely a success in the taking. There is no question but that we have made a big hit with everyone, from the assistant prop boy up through Crosland, [general manager of production William] Koenig, Zanuck and Warner. It is also equally certain that they have made a hit with me.
>
> About ten days ago, Koenig sounded me out on how I would feel about supervising all the musical productions of both First National and Warners when they move the whole business over to the First National lot.

Hammerstein was noncomittal, but already calculating:

> whether they would pay enough money to claim all my time for a full year that is, in the form of a salary. I would hesitate to relinquish the gambling chance of making more than any set sum that it would be necessarily confined to, and I am most anxious, in fact, determined, to keep my identity as an author. I would always have time to write at least one original work of my own every year, in addition to what ever administrative duties such a job would entail.

---

* *There already had been silent screen adaptations of* Rose Marie *and* Show Boat *and early talkies based on* Sunny, Song of the Flame, The Desert Song, Golden Dawn, *and* New Moon.

OVERTURE

Published in vocal score. Introduced by the ensemble (grape pickers on the Renner estate).

GIRLS: Wake up, oh, wake up
And bless the day,
Bless the day.
Harvest is over,
The grapes are off the vine.
Fill the cart, fill the cart
And off we'll go to the fair.
Fill the cart, fill the cart
And off we'll go to the fair.
Wake up, oh, wake up,
And bless the day,
Bless the day.
Harvest is over,
The grapes are off the vine,
Off the vine,
Fresh and fine,
Eager to be crushed for wine.
Grapes are fine
On the vine,
But give me mine in the wine.

GIRLS: Joy liveth in ev'ry vine;
'Tis tomorrow's wine awaiting you.
Joy liveth in ev'ry vine;
'Tis tomorrow's wine.
MEN: Off the vine, fresh and fine,
Eager to be crushed for wine.
Grapes are fine on the vine;
'Tis tomorrow's wine.

GIRLS: Climb up, my stout-hearted lad,
Climb to the skies.
For ev'ry stout-hearted lad
There waits a prize:
He wins a kiss from a maid,
Choose whom he may,
She will be his love always.
Oh, would I were she whom he chooses today!

GIRLS: Gus has done it!
Gustave has done it,
Gustave has won it!
Now, whom shall he kiss?
MEN: Gustave has won,
Gustave has won!
Who'll be the one he chooses to kiss?

OPENING

Alternate titles: "Yessus, Yessus" and "Oli, Oli, Oli." Published in the vocal score. As appropriate for happy revelers, the text means roughly: "Oh my God, we are merry today. Let's start the singing now."

Yessus, Yessus,
Lustig sa ma heut',
Alles breit und weit;
Ja, da gibts a Freud'!
Yessus, Yessus
Jetzt geht's amal los,
Sing mal feste los.

[*Yodeling.*]

Oli, Oli Oli, Oli,
Lustig sa ma heut',
Alles breit und weit;
Ja, da gibt's a Freud'!

[*Yodeling.*]

Oli, Oli Oli, Oli,
Jetzt geht's amal los,
Sing mal feste los.

YOU WILL REMEMBER VIENNA

Published as an individual sheet. Introduced by Alexander Gray (Otto), Walter Pidgeon (Franz), and Bert Roach (Gus).

VERSE

A place for life to ebb and flow,
A place for love to live and glow,
Vienna is her name,
A fairyland of fame.
When once you've heard her laughter gay,
You weep when you are torn away.
A thousand mem'ries call you back
For one more day.

REFRAIN

As the years roll on,
After youth has gone,
You will remember Vienna.
Nights that were happy

And hearts that were free,
All joined in singing a sweet melody.
When your race is run,
Whether lost or won,
You will remember Vienna.
You will recall evenings in May,*
Sweethearts who came
And vanished away.
Whence did they come?
Where did they go?
Vienna will never let you know.

GOODBYE, MY LOVE

Published in the vocal score. Stage directions explain that this "popular waltz song" is sung with "raucous banality by a good-natured, somewhat drunken crowd."

Darling, must you go?
I will miss you so,
In the morning and the afternoon,
In the nights when lights are low.
Though I know you'll be
Far across the sea,
I won't sigh, love,
I won't cry, love,
If you'll think of me.

Goodbye, my love,
Goodbye, my love—
I hate to see you go.
Come back, my love,
Come back, my love—
I'm waiting here, you know.
Goodbye, my love,
Goodbye, my love—
I hate to see you go.
But stay a day, a month, a year,
I'll wait for my lover here.

---

* *Earlier ending of refrain:*
   You will recall one night in May,
   One girl who came
   And vanished away.
   Still in your dreams,
   Clinging to you,
   You'll wonder if she'll remember too.

REGIMENTAL MARCH

Published in the vocal score. Introduced by Walter Pidgeon (Franz), and ensemble (officers, and other patrons of a café).

We're sons of sons of a regimental crew,
Who fought for kings
And did the things
That we are here to do.
And our sons' grandsons will join the army, too—
And they will be
The same as we,
Until their days are through.
And so on, so on, so on, forevermore—
Most ev'ry name
Will be the same
Within this army corps.
We'll drink the same old wine with the same ones
And may the girls we meet not be tame ones!
But if the girls we meet should happen to be tame ones,
Let's make them wilder than they were before.
May all the beer we drink be the best beer
(For we're the boys who know how to test beer),
And may our swords be bright,
Our backs as stiff as starch
As we walk through Vienna to our regimental march.

PRATER ENSEMBLE

Published in the vocal score. Introduced by Walter Pidgeon (Franz), Vivienne Segal (Elsa), and ensemble.

OFFICER A: Sweet young thing.
OFFICER B: Much too young to love.
OFFICER C: Old enough to learn.
OFFICER D: Could be taught.
OFFICER B: Sweet young things are the dang'rous kind.
     When you catch them, you are caught!
FRANZ: Gentlemen, will you pardon me?
     There is a friend I have to see!*
TENORS: We're on to you—
     We've seen her, too.
FRANZ: She may be good.
TENORS: Cheer up, my lad!

---

* *The holograph score has:*
   There is a friend whom I must see.

OFFICERS: Don't be downhearted,
She may be bad!

ENSEMBLE: Tonight we lift our glasses high
To crown Vienna's queen.

GIRLS: She's doing very well for one
Who's only seventeen.

MEN: Let's not forget
This night we met
When we are old and gray.

ELSA: Let's remember always
All the joy of these days—

ENSEMBLE: When we were young and gay.

[*Leads into another reprise of "You Will Remember Vienna."*]

HERE WE ARE

Published in the vocal score and as an individual sheet. Introduced by Walter Pidgeon (Franz), Vivienne Segal (Elsa), ensemble (officers, students, girls). When it is reprised in the 1930s section of the film, it is characterized as an old folk song.

INTRODUCTION

FRANZ: Fräulein, I wish I were a Gypsy.

ELSA: What good would that do, pray?

FRANZ: Gypsies are real,
Say what they feel.
Therefore I would say:

VERSE

FRANZ: I love you,
I love you.
If I were a Gypsy that is all I'd sing.
I'd woo you,
And to you
Life would be a simple thing.

OFFICERS: We take life too seriously,
Treating love mysteriously.

ELSA: But if we were Gypsies,
This is all we'd sing:
I love you,
I love you,
Isn't life a simple thing?

REFRAIN

FRANZ: Here we are,
Here are we!
I'm with you, and you're with me.
Don't we make a happy pair?

Here's a moon
In the sky;
You like moons and so do I—
Don't we make a happy pair?
Here we are together
With that moon up in the sky;
I could do without that moon,
But without you I'd die!
That's why we are here,
Here are we,
I love you and you love me—
Don't we make a happy pair?

WHEN YOU HAVE NO MAN TO LOVE

Published in the vocal score. Introduced by Louise Fazenda (Gretl), Vivienne Segal (Elsa), and female ensemble. In one script this is labeled "No. 10 Comedy Song."

GRETL: When you have no man to love,
Life is very weary,

GIRLS: Life is very weary.

GRETL: You are like an extra glove
Looking for a hand to hold.

ELSA: But when you've a man to love,
Life is very diff'rent,

GIRLS: Life is very diff'rent.

GRETL: All of the woes you had before
Are multiplied a thousandfold.

GIRLS: He will kiss you in the nighttime*
And be cross to you all day.

GRETL: If you cook him stew,
He'll yell at you
And push his plate away.

GIRLS: Soon you'll wish you had a husband who
Is more ideal to you.

GRETL: When you start to look around for one
And get to know a few—

ELSA: Will you find a perfect lover
Who's a perfect husband too?

GRETL: You will not!

GIRLS: You will not!

GRETL: You will not!

GIRLS: You will not!

*An earlier version of girls' lines:
First you wake up in the morning
And you get the morning mail.
Where's his letter?
There's no letter,
So you start to weep and wail.

GRETL: So you spend your life in trying
To improve the one you've got.

ALL: When you have no man to love,
Life is very weary,
Life is very weary.

GRETL: You are like an extra glove
Looking for a hand to hold.

ELSA: I have found a man to love;
He is very diff'rent.

GIRLS: All of them are diff'rent.

ELSA: I cannot wait until tomorrow,
When I see the man I love.

GIRLS: Dear, you must wait until tomorrow;
Then you'll see the man you love.

I BRING A LOVE SONG (LIEBESLIED)

Published as an individual sheet, with adjustments allowing for its performance as a solo. The piano-vocal score supplies words in English and in German. The melody, written by aspiring composer Otto, is the musical motif for his love of Elsa. Introduced by Alexander Gray (Otto) and Vivienne Segal (Elsa).

VERSE

OTTO: I've been trying hard to find a way
Of telling you just how I feel.
Now, at last, that I've designed a way,
My dearest hope I would reveal.

ELSA: I am all attention, dear.

OTTO: Dear, keep your attention here.
Look at me.

ELSA: Dear, what would you say to me?

OTTO: I bring a gift for you.

ELSA: And how I'm longing to
Know what that gift may be.

REFRAIN

OTTO: I bring a love song,
Only a love song,
Shy as a day in spring.
Trying to tell you all that it knows,
All that a heart dare not speak,
Songs may sing.

ELSA: Born in the moonlight,
Fed by caresses,
Our song should never die.

OTTO: Keep it caressed, dear,
Hold it always to your breast, dear.
Don't let our love song die!

Solo verse

I've been trying hard to find a way
Of telling you just how I feel.
Now, at last, that I've designed a way,
My dearest hope I would reveal.
From the music in my heart,
My pen has set apart
A symphony of sighs
To make it known to you
How far my dreams pursue,
How high my fond hopes rise.

JA, JA, JA! (YES, YES, YES!)

Published as an individual sheet with text in English and German. Appears in the vocal score with German text only. John Koegel, in his 1984 thesis on Romberg's screen musicals, noted that this title does not appear on the May 22, 1930, cue sheet; nor was the song present in the videotape viewed by the editor. The published music does not indicate who would have sung it.

VERSE

While I wash, I dream of my lover true,
But no lover true dreams of me.
I know ev'ry stitch that a man may wear,
But what I wear, none seems to care.
Tell me why I can never get close
To a shirt that is filled by a man?

REFRAIN

Am I not a comely miss?
Answer no or yes!
(Ja, ja, ja!)
Wouldn't I be nice to kiss?
Don't you like my form?
(Ja, ja, ja!)
I agree with you
That I'm a prize for a lover—
Tell me, then,
Why none will discover
All the charms that seem to be
So plain to you and me?
Am I cross-eyed, old and lame?
Am I knock-kneed too?
(Nein, nein, nein!)
If you had no other girls,
Don't you think I'd do?
Yet my days are spent in endless toiling,
Washing, rinsing, drying, boiling

Collars that I should be soiling
With my wild embrace.

PART ONE FINALE

Published in the vocal score. The film is divided into three parts; this is the entire finale of the first part. In the videotape seen by the editor, the number was danced but not sung.

GIRLS AND MEN: Pretty Gypsy, pretty little Gypsy,
Do the czardas with me.
Pretty Gypsy, pretty little Gypsy,
Do your kisses come free?
GIRLS: If you like to whirl around,
I'll whirl you all the faster;
Whirl a Gypsy girl around
And you will court disaster.
MEN: If you whirl the faster,
Then you will court disaster.

[First section repeats.]

BASSES: Dance, Gypsy, dance a czardas.
GIRLS: Play while we dance the
czardas,
While we dance the czardas, play.
Dance the czardas,
Dance your cares away.
Ah!
MEN: Madly, madly, dance the
czardas,
Come and madly dance the
czardas.
Come and dance the czardas,
Dance your cares away.
Ah!
GIRLS AND MEN: How can you have care and
trouble
When there is a czardas to dance
away?

[Dialogue.]

OTTO: As the years roll on, after youth
has gone
You will remember Vienna.

[Dialogue.]

GIRLS AND MEN: Here we are,
Here are we!

I'm with you and you're with
me—
Don't we make a happy pair?
Here's a moon
In the sky;
You like moons and so do I—
Don't we make a happy pair?
FRANZ AND ELSA: Here we are together
With that moon up in the sky.
OTTO: I could do without that moon,
But without you, I'd die.
[singing his love theme]
Born in the moonlight
Fed by caresses,
Our song should never die.
Keep it caressed, dear,
Hold it always to your breast,
dear,
Don't let our love song die!

PART TWO OPENING (WAITING)

Published in the vocal score. Introduced by June Purcell (Mary), Milt Douglas (Bill Jones) and ensemble.

The second part of the film finds Otto employed as a violinist in a theater, where this song and "I'm Lonely" are selections from the operetta being performed.

GIRLS AND FISHERMEN: Waiting, we're always
waiting
Until our men come home
from sea to see
How faithful fisherwives
can be.
We're waiting, for love
we're waiting,
And while our men are all
away at sea,
We fret and worry.
Winds blow, and
dark'ning clouds grow,
But may their sails be
strong so they can
hurry
Back to those who fret and
worry!
Look, girls!
Our men are home now.
And there is old Bill Jones
Hurrying home now.
GIRLS: You've been shipwrecked,
Praise be you're alive!

GIRLS AND TENORS: Saved from shipwreck!
Bill's still alive!

MARY: You were wrecked with my
John.
Did you save him, too?
What's become of my
John—
Wasn't he with you?

BILL JONES: I'm bringing you bad
news,
Mary, dear.
I'm bringing you sad
news—
John's not here.
John died like a hero,
Strong and brave.
Stood he by his good ship
as it
Bowed to the storm and
wave.

MARY: Then it is goodbye, John.
I will weep for you;
You'll be always my John,
Till my days are through.

BILL JONES, GIRLS, MEN: Down, down by the
waters,
She'll walk alone.
Weep, weep for your lover,
dear,
For he will be always your
own.

Early version of the opening chorus

Working, we're always working.
There's not a single little finger
That can linger for a moment while
We're working and never shirking.
We have to weave our nets;
To leave our nets would be neglectful.
Our men are stern and dour men,
And they'd be sour men
If they came home and found
That we had been neglectful maidens,
Young fisher maidens.

I'M LONELY

Published as an individual sheet. Introduced by June Purcell (Mary).

"I'm Lonely" is the climax of an operetta sequence that begins with "Waiting." A planned reprise by Elsa appears not to have been used in the final cut.

VERSE

In the hush of nighttime, gazing at the sky,
Dreaming of a thousand things,
Lost in magic silence,
My romance and I
Flew away on golden wings.
Gone are all those nights he spent with me,
But their faded mem'ry clings.

REFRAIN

When I hear the night wind sighing,
I'm lonely, so lonely.
Is it for the moon I'm crying?
I'm lonely, so lonely.
Is it for a kiss forgotten
The night wind is sighing?
Is it for a kiss remembered
My poor heart is crying?
Is it for the man I want in my arms
Here in the moonlight?
If he isn't here, what good are my arms?
What good is moonlight?
Living in a world of laughter,
My poor heart is crying.
When I hear the night wind sighing,
I'm lonely for my love.

CUT AND UNUSED SONG

IF YOU WANT TO KISS A GIRL

Alternate title: "Musical Scene #5, Gus and Otto." Not published and not seen in the film. The number called for a lot of underscored pantomime but had no real refrain.

GUS: If you want to kiss a girl,
I can tell you how it's done;
You can only play the game one way.
You must take 'em by surprise,
That's the only way they're won—
And you'd better start to learn today.
Now suppose that you're a girl
And you're sitting on a bed
And I come into the room like this—

[*Puts his hand under* OTTO's *chin and speaks ardently.*]

"Oh, my darling, I have traveled such a
long way
Just to find you."

[OTTO *pushes* GUS *away.*]

That's the wrong way.
There's one system that I use—
If you try it, you can't lose.
And this is how the thing is done.

OTTO: But suppose she tells you she can do
without you.
'N' if you kiss her, she will clout you!

BALLYHOO (1930)

Oscar Hammerstein II is credited with "Supervision" of this vehicle for W. C. Fields—which opened on December 22, 1930, and closed on February 21, 1931, at Hammerstein's Theatre in New York City—and with the lyrics for two songs. The show's overall book and lyrics are credited to Harry Ruskin and Leighton K. Brill, with music by Louis Alter. Arthur Hammerstein produced, and Reginald Hammerstein directed the book. Both of Oscar's songs were published as individual sheets, as were five songs credited to Ruskin, Brill, and Alter ("If I Were You," "Throw It Out the Window," "How I Could Go for You," "That Tired Feeling," and "Blow Hot, Blow Cold"). Not published and not located were the openings and closings of each act and "Good Girls Love Bad Men."

Musical-theater historian Miles Kreuger is skeptical about Brill's creative contributions to the show, and points out that he has no other lyrics registered with ASCAP. Brill was best known as Oscar Hammerstein II's associate, who gave copious feedback on scripts in progress, researched local color for various stories, and handled preliminary casting interviews. Kreuger posits that after one too many rewrites by W. C. Fields, Hammerstein substituted Brill's name for his own. The editor has not been able to find evidence one way or the other.

However, Hammerstein was clearly bothered by reviews that described the tunes as "reminiscent." On December 23, he wrote somewhat testily to Brooks Atkinson of the *Times*, Gilbert Gabriel of the *Evening Sun*, and Alison Smith of the *World* asking them to explain just what they meant. The letter to Atkinson concluded: "Knowing that your criticisms are never carelessly written, I am sure you will be able to tell what earlier tunes are recalled to you by those in *Ballyhoo*. Will you take the trouble to make me a list of these songs? Choosing melodies is an important part of my work and I do not like to think I am getting a tin ear."

Atkinson's response was not found in Hammerstein's correspondence, but Hammerstein's next letter was more cordial:

> Thank you very much for your letter. I don't agree with any part of it, but that is beside the point. I have a vaguely pleasant feeling of coming closer to a critical mind—a type of mind which, God knows, seems pathetically far away on mornings after my opening nights. When I can get rid of the tenacious cold that has kept me in bed all week, I should like to have lunch with you some day and find out what you like in the musical play. Please forgive me for being so in earnest about such a trivial subject, but somebody ought to be.

I'M ONE OF GOD'S CHILDREN (WHO HASN'T GOT WINGS)

Words by Oscar Hammerstein II and Harry Ruskin. Music by Louis Alter. Published as an individual sheet. Introduced by Janet Reade (Goldie La Marr).

Hammerstein biographer Hugh Fordin reports that this song was written in Baltimore to lift a dull spot in the second act. Louis Alter worked all day and evening until he'd come up with a torchy melody, with strange chords and a syncopated beat. Hammerstein received the unusual melody at 11:30 p.m. and supplied a finished verse and chorus by 7 a.m. Several New York critics cited the number for Janet Reade's enthusiastic performance and the audience's enthusiastic response. Libby Holman's recording was a big seller in 1931; Judy Holliday recorded the song in 1958.

VERSE

What did I do?
Why do fellows leave me alone,
Leave me with a heart like a stone?
Ain't I got what I used to own?

What did I do?
No one comes to see me no more,
No one ever knocks on my door—
What on earth am I living for?

REFRAIN

When I got no man to mess me around,
I'm a lonesome weed that grows in the ground—
I'm one of God's children who hasn't got wings.
When the bats fly low and night's in the sky
And there's no one home but just me and I,
I'm one of God's children who hasn't got wings.
I just want a sweet accommodatin' man to have a
    sip o' gin with.
Then we'd have some lovin' 'cause the gin would
    just be somethin' to begin with.
But I got no man to mess me around;
I'm a poor lost mare a-pawin' the ground—
I'm one of God's children who hasn't got wings.

Male version

VERSE

What did I do?
Why do all girls leave me alone,
Leave me with a heart like a stone?
Tell me why my bluebird has flown—
What did I do?
No one wants to see me no more,
Got no one to knock on their door—
What on earth am I living for?

REFRAIN

When I got no gal to mess me around,
I'm a lonesome weed that grows in the ground—
I'm one of God's children who hasn't got wings.
When the bats fly low and night's in the sky
And there's no one home but just me and I,
I'm one of God's children who hasn't got wings.
I just want a sweet accommodatin' gal that I can
    pass the time with.
In my flat a cat and a canary are the only gals that
    I'm with.

'Cause I got no gal to mess me around,
I'm a poor lost steed a-pawin' the ground—
I'm one of God's children who hasn't got wings.

NO WONDER I'M BLUE

Words by Oscar Hammerstein II. Music by Louis Alter. Published as an individual sheet. Introduced by Grace Hayes (Flora Fay).

VERSE

What's the trouble with me?
The trouble with me is plain as day:
I'm in need of a mate,
In need of a mate who'll come to stay.
In my shy possession
There lurks a feeling
That needs expression;
But not having the gift,
I'm fated to drift my lonely way.

REFRAIN

No wonder I'm blue.
A doe with no stag, that's me.
A bud with no bee,
No wonder I'm blue.
When love comes along,
My heart's in my mouth, that's true,
And when it goes wrong,
My heart's in my shoe!
For deep inside me there's a mad but sweetly
    gentle fool,
Urging me to be a sentimental fool.
A room with no view,
A girl with no boy, that's me;
A sky with no sea,
No wonder I'm blue.

Sheet music mementos of two disappointments

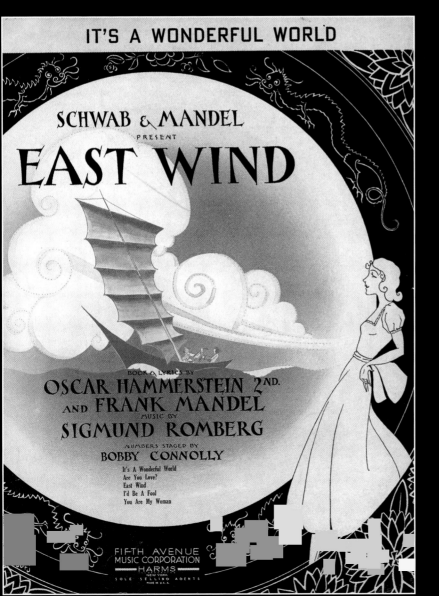

CHILDREN OF DREAMS (1931)

A film produced by Warner Bros. and Vitaphone. Released July 18, 1931. Screenplay and lyrics by Oscar Hammerstein II. Music by Sigmund Romberg. Directed by Alan Crosland. Musical direction by Louis Silvers. Edited by Harold McLernon. Cinematography by James Van Trees. Art direction by Max Parker.

Cast: Margaret Schilling (Molly Standing), Paul Gregory (Tommy Melville), Tom Patricola (Gus Schultz), Marion Byron (Gertie McNulty), Bruce Winston (Hubert Standing), Alison Skipworth (Sarah Standing), Charles Winninger (Dr. Joe Thompson), John Rutherford (Gerald Winter), Almeda Fowler (Mrs. Winter), Luis Alberni (Signor Boccabadotti), Paul Porcasi (Benoni), Ivan Simpson (Squizzy Murphy), Lenen Holtz (Concert Manager), Milton Douglas (Boyo-Prince), John Ince (Buckner), Robert Elliott (Thomas Melville Sr.), May Boley (Marie), John Lytel (Jarman), Wallace McDonald (Johnson).

Tommy and Gus are cheerful young rovers who meet up with their sweethearts Molly and Gertie at a campground for migrant fruit pickers. Molly, who gives such pleasure with her songs, has promised to marry Tommy. One evening, while driving near the campground, wealthy Mrs. Winter hears Molly and offers musical training in Europe. The offer couldn't come at a better time. Molly's father, a known drunk, seems to have disappeared with the payroll for the entire camp. The only thing for Molly to do is accept Mrs. Winter's offer and the money that comes with it. She promises to return in two years, but Tommy is devastated. The film follows Molly to Rome where she is tutored by Signore Boccabadotti and squired by Mrs. Winter's handsome son Jerry. In short order she makes her Metropolitan Opera debut. Tommy is there, but as he feared, he doesn't fit into her new life. The story flashes forward two years. Molly is engaged to Jerry and about to start a world tour, but she is unhappy. Kindly Dr. Joe diagnoses her problem. The best thing would be a quiet life with Tommy. She'll have to give up singing, except at home.

The primary source for this chapter is the piano-vocal score published by Harms. The Warner Bros. Archive at the University of Southern California has a "final screenplay" from July 1930. The Academy of Motion Picture Arts and Sciences' Margaret Herrick Library has another screenplay and some musical manuscripts. The film itself is considered lost.

The editor is not aware of any material that did not appear in the vocal score. However, certain numbers are not included in this chapter. For instance, the finale of part one consists of reprises of the "Fruit Pickers' Song" and "Sleeping Beauty"; the opening of part two is scales and vocalises; and the "Tango d'Amour" is instrumental.

FRUIT PICKERS' SONG

Published in the piano-vocal score. Introduced by the ensemble.

FRUIT PICKERS: We'll comb the trees,
As busy as bumblebees,
And like the bees,
We'll hum a song
Till sundown.
Hello, hello.
Tomorrow's another day.
Ripe apples to pick,
Ripe apples to cart away.
MEN: Roughnecks, good men and
sinners,
Stretch your big, lazy bones.
Outcast crew,
There is work to do
In the orchard,
Work to do!
WOMEN: Up and work for your dinners,
Sweat and laugh under the sun.
MEN: Son of a gun.
WOMEN: Laugh in the sun!
ALL: Hello, hello!
And what'll we do today?
The same as we've done,
The same as we'll do tomorrow.
We'll work and work
And do as the bosses say.
Ripe apples to pick,
Ripe apples to cart away.
We'll comb the trees,
As busy as bumblebees,
And like the bees,
We'll hum a song
Till sundown.
Hello, hello!
Tomorrow's another day.
Ripe apples to pick,
Ripe apples to cart away.

OH, COULDN'T I LOVE THAT GIRL

Published in the piano-vocal score. Introduced by Paul Gregory (Tommy), uncredited man (Beppo), Tom Patricola (Gus), and ensemble.

TOMMY: [driving up in a jalopy with
GUS] Oh, couldn't I love
that girl,
Oh, couldn't I love that girl,
Oh, couldn't I love that girl,
If that girl could o' loved
me!
BEPPO: Oh, couldn't you drive a
horse—*
BEPPO AND FRUIT
PICKERS: Oh, couldn't you drive a
horse,
Oh, couldn't you drive a
horse,
If you had a horse to drive!
GUS: Are you glad that Tommy's
back again?
TOMMY: Are you glad that Gus is
back again?
FRUIT PICKERS: We are glad you're back
again,
But please don't stay too
long!
TOMMY: Oh, couldn't I love that
girl—
TOMMY AND GUS: Oh, couldn't I love that girl,
Oh, couldn't I love that girl,
If that girl could o' loved
me!
FRUIT PICKERS: Are you glad the boys are
back again?
MOLLIE AND GERTIE: We are glad the boys are
back again!
TOMMY AND GUS: We are glad we're back
again.
FRUIT PICKERS: But please don't stay too
long.

---

*Published score has horse, but the "final screenplay" in the Warner Bros. Archive at USC has car for this line and the following three.

HERR PROFESSOR SCHNIGGLEFRITZ

Published in the piano-vocal score, but not listed in the table of contents. Introduced by Tom Patricola (Gus) and ensemble.

GUS: Herr Professor
Schnigglefritz,
Schnigglefritz,
Schnigglefritz,
Kissed the girls and gave
them fits,
With his big moustache.
This moustache won
ev'ry girl in town,
All but one who sneered.

GUS AND FRUIT PICKERS: She wouldn't say "yessir,"
So now the Professor
Has started growing a
beard.
She wouldn't say "yessir,"
So now the Professor
Has started growing a
beard.

CHILDREN OF DREAMS

Published in the piano-vocal score. Introduced by Margaret Schilling (Molly) and ensemble.

MEN: There's comfort in the fire's glow.

WOMEN: When all the cares of daylight go
away,

MEN: Away go the cares of a—

ALL: —restless day.

MEN: So stretch your legs and lie at
ease.

FRUIT PICKERS: And say whatever you may please
to say,
Anything you may please to say.

DANCERS: On a platform built right over the
ground
You can dance right under the
moon.
Like the horses on a merry-go-
round,
You go round in time to a tune.
When the dance they play is a
love song
(Just a song, so romantic, ah!)

And you feel the spell of its
romance,
In the magic charms of each
other's arms
You forget it's just a dance.

SOLO BARITONE: Bright stars above,
Are you shining on my
homeland?
Can you take a message there?
Tell them I am well.
I miss them all!
Ask them if they're missing me,
Back in my homeland,
Bright stars above.

MOLLY: [*to a group of children*] We live
and hope for things,
Children of dreams.
Our fancies fly on wings,
Children of dreams.
One wants her bonnet blue,
One cries for drums,
One seeks her lover true
Who never comes.
Perhaps the chances are
We won't succeed,
But hope's romances are
The things we need.
And while the teasing light
Of fortune gleams,
Don't let's give up the fight,
Children of dreams.

ROLLING HOME AFTER DARK

Published in the piano-vocal score, but not listed in the table of contents. Introduced by Ivan Simpson (Squizzy), Bruce Winston (Hubert Standing), and ensemble.

SQUIZZY: Rolling homeward after dark,
Raise your voices with the lark.
Men who drink are men who sing,
And that's a very good thing.

CROWD: Rolling homeward,
Tra, la, la, la, la, la.
Raise your voices,
Tra, la, la, la, la, la.
Men who drink are men who sing,
And that's a very good thing.

CHILDREN: Oh, Mister Standing's drunk again,
Oh, Mister Standing's drunk again!

SQUIZZY: Oh, Mister Standing's drunk again,
And so is Squizzy too!

CROWD: Rolling homeward,
Tra, la, la, la, la, la.
Raise your voices,
Tra, la, la, la, la, la.
Men who drink are men who sing,
And that's a very good thing.

SLEEPING BEAUTY

Published in the piano-vocal score. Introduced by Paul Gregory (Tommy), Margaret Schilling (Molly), and ensemble.

VERSE 1

FRUIT PICKERS: Hmm, hmm [*humming*]
See, my lady's eyes are closing.
Hmm, hmm [*humming*]
Now my pretty lady's dozing.

REFRAIN 1

TOMMY: Dream on, my beauty,
My sleeping beauty,
Dream while I watch over you—
Your hair on your pillow,
Like soft leaves of willow,
Caressing the snow of your
shoulders.
My sleeping beauty,
I'm keeping duty—
Dream on while I worship you.
Though I'm awake, dear,
Though I'm wide awake, dear,
I am dreaming too.

VERSE 2

MOLLY: Gentle voice, as I fall asleep
I begin to dream I'm near you.
Lullaby, singing me to sleep,
Through the hush of night I hear
you.

REFRAIN 2

FRUIT PICKERS: Dream on, my beauty,
My sleeping beauty,
Dream while I watch over you—
Your hair on your pillow,
Like soft leaves of willow,

Caressing the snow of your
   shoulders.
My sleeping beauty,
I'm keeping duty—
Dream on while I worship you.
TOMMY: Though I'm awake, dear,
Though I'm wide awake, dear,
I am dreaming too.

IF I HAD A GIRL (I'D BE HAPPY)

Published in the piano-vocal score. Introduced by Margaret Schilling (Molly) and Paul Gregory (Tommy).

INTRODUCTION

MOLLY: [*spoken in rhythm*] She really wants a man
   to think that she's the whole world;
   She really wants a man to tell her she's
   the whole world.
TOMMY: [*sung*] That's what I thought.
I've figured out
[*spoken in rhythm*] Successful business-
   men can't do that.
It takes a man like me
Who has no other int'rest.
My own* career would be
To make my woman happy.
[*sung*] I'd work right here
Out in the orchards.
MOLLY: [*sung*] Perhaps that is the best way after
   all.

VERSE

TOMMY: Put me on the open road,
Let me grin and bear my load.
Youth is mine and I'll succeed;
There is just one thing in life I need.

REFRAIN

TOMMY: I have the sun
And the world for my fun,
And if I had a girl I'd be happy.
Fair is the day
And my health is okay,
And if I had a girl I'd be happy.
Birds are singing to the blossoms near
   them—

* *Final screenplay says:*
   My one

I want someone to help me hear them.
I own a share
In the earth and the air,
And if I owned a girl I'd be happy.
MOLLY: Birds are singing to the blossoms near
   them—
TOMMY: I want someone to help me hear them.
BOTH: I own a share in the earth and the air,
And if I owned a girl [boy] I'd be happy.

THAT RARE ROMANCE

Published in the piano-vocal score. Introduced by Margaret Schilling (Molly) and ensemble.

FRUIT PICKERS: Seek love,
Look ev'rywhere for her.
Find love,
And always adore her.
What good is your life to you
With no one to give it to?
MOLLY: So keep love
When once you have found her.
Hold tight
With both arms around her.
Don't leave her,
Don't take any chance;
Hold on to that rare romance.
FRUIT PICKERS: Maybe you'll find her at morning,
High on the crest of a hill.
Maybe she'll wait by some garden
   gate,*
'Mid rose and daffodil.
MOLLY: Maybe you'll find her by moon-
   light,
Sweet in the dew-laden air.
FRUIT PICKERS: Maybe she walks in a shady lane;
Maybe she rides on a subway train.
Once in a lifetime she'll call,†
And when she calls, be there.
MOLLY: Be there to fill her arms.
FRUIT PICKERS: Be there to fill her arms, oh!
MOLLY: Seek love,
Look ev'rywhere for her.
Find love,
And always adore her.
What good is your life to you
With no one to give it to?

* *Final screenplay has:*
   Maybe she'll wait behind a white gate.

† *Final screenplay has:*
   Once in a life she will call.

MOLLY AND
FRUIT PICKERS: So keep love
When once you have found her.
Hold tight
With both arms around her.
Don't leave her,
Don't take any chance,
Hold on to that rare romance.

YES, SIR

Alternate title: "Bungalow for Two." Published in the piano-vocal score. Introduced by Tom Patricola (Gus) and Marion Byron (Gertie). He is giving a tour of his one-room motor home.

VERSE

GUS: Lady, my love is all for you,
So take it if you care.
GERTIE: You're so dutiful,
I'm so beautiful—
This must be an affair.
GUS: I have something to ask you, dear.
GERTIE: Have a loan o' my shell-pink ear.
GUS: Would you like to come with me
And see a bungalow?
GERTIE: That is most improper,
But I'd kind o' like to go.

REFRAIN

GUS: Bungalow.
GERTIE: Yes, sir!
GUS: Just for two.
GERTIE: Yes, sir!
GUS: New idea, bungalow only for two.
Dining room.
GERTIE: Yes, sir!
GUS: Sitting room.
GERTIE: Yes, sir!
GUS: Kitchen and pantry and knitting room,
And two twin folding beds
For two weary, sleepy heads.
GERTIE: I understand, sir!
GUS: Ent'ring this wonderland, a
Doorway and a cute veranda.
Bungalow.
GERTIE: Yes, sir!
GUS: Just for two.
GERTIE: Yes, sir!
GUS: Just for two.
And can you
Guess who?

A SCENE FROM *ANTONIA*

Published in the piano-vocal score. Except for Margaret Schilling (Molly), the performers have not been identified.

Molly is playing the title role in a new opera. In this sequence, the Baron (lead baritone) and his noblemen (basses) confront a Robin Hood–style Robber Chief (lead tenor) and his band of robbers (tenors) in a forest. The Baron demands the return of his kidnapped sister, Antonia, and challenges the Chief to single combat. When the Baron kills the Chief, we learn that Antonia loved him and had been a willing captive.

NOBLES: Hold! Move not!
Move not a head, men!
Move no hand or foot, or
   dead men be!
Would ye dead men be?

ROBBERS: Shout not so!
We will obey you,
For dead men we'll not be.

WOMEN: You have to do what
   you're told, men.
If you are bold, men,
You dead men are.
Ah!

ROBBER CHIEF: What would you have us
   do, sir?
Now what seek ye to do,
   sir?

BARON: Give me an answer true,
   sir—

NOBLES: Hark ye now.
Now speaks he.

BARON: Where is my sweet
   Antonia?

ROBBER CHIEF: Your sweet sister Antonia
Will stay here by my side,
   till I die!

WOMEN: Now bring out his sweet
   Antonia,
Sweet Antonia,
Else ye have to die!

BARON: Bring out my sweet
   Antonia here,
Else ye die,
And die by my hand!

ROBBERS: So brave and bold, our
   chief will die!

NOBLES: Ah, you will die,
And die by my hand!

CHIEF, ROBBERS, AND
SOME CAPTIVE WOMEN: But would ye dare
Fight me [him] fair?
Fight if ye can, sir.

OTHER CAPTIVE WOMEN: Would he fight fair?
In faith he can, sir.

BARON: Rogue!
Do I dare?
By my beard I think I can,
   sir.

NOBLES: By all our faith
He can, sir.

CHIEF AND ROBBERS: Draw your gleaming
   sword.
My [his] stout staff will—

BARON,
NOBLES, AND WOMEN: His broad sword and you
Will meet soon and—

ALL: —give you answer!

CHIEF: Shall we start twenty-two
   feet apart?

WOMEN: Stand far apart now.

BARON: Start wherever you want
   to start, now.

ROBBERS AND NOBLES: [*humming*] Ah—!

WOMEN: Shhh—

[*The duel begins.*]

BARON: Guard well your heart now.

CHIEF: Guard well your head
   against my blow.

BARON: Guard well your heart now.
Strike if you can,
For once I strike you,
Then you die.

ROBBER: 'Tis I who'll see that you
   die.
My heart is stout and
   strong.

BARON: Guard your heart,
'Twill not breathe much
   longer.

[*The* ROBBER CHIEF *knocks the* BARON's *sword from his hand.*]

ROBBERS: Oh, he's unarmed,
But unharmed.
Bravely done!

NOBLES: What!
He's unharmed,
Bravely done!

CHIEF: [*giving the* BARON *back his weapon*] I kill no man
   without sword.

BARON: Your death will honor my
   sword.

[*The* BARON's *thrust pierces the* CHIEF's *heart.*]

WOMEN,
ROBBERS, NOBLES: He had won!
He has lost!
It has cost all,
All that he thought to keep,
All his life and love
Forever.

CHIEF: Once may I see fair
   Antonia?

BARON: Now I have won back
   Antonia!

[ANTONIA *enters.*]

ANTONIA: [*spoken in rhythm*] Brave
   brother, you fought for
   me, not knowing the
   pain you brought me.
Gone is my life. Gone
   is my world.

ARIA

ANTONIA: Leave me not alone,
Leave me not alone.
Take not all I love,
The only love I've ever
   known.
If you smile no more,
Then no more smile I.

MEN: You smile no more,
No more smile I.

WOMEN: As you smile, then so
   smile I.
If you're sad, then I'm
   sad.
If you're sad, then I smile
   never more.

ANTONIA: No more does the moon
   arise
To see the day of summer
   die
If you speak no more.

MEN: No moon sees a day of
   summer die.

BARON,
SOME WOMEN, NOBLES: Pray, will you speak no
   more.

ANTONIA,
BARON, OTHER
WOMEN, ROBBERS: Sunshine lights the sky no
   more.

ALL: No more live I.
Leave me not alone,
Leave me not alone.
Take me, let me go
   wherever you go,

For if you go from the
    world to die,
No more live I.
Ah!

ANTONIA: Do these eyes no longer
    see me?
Can these hands no longer
    feel?

WOMEN: Do those eyes not see?

ANTONIA: Arms that were strong
No longer crush me.

MEN AND WOMEN: Arms that were once
    strong,
Strong arms no more.

ANTONIA: You die,
So drops the sun from the
    breast of the sky.

MEN AND WOMEN: Sun drops from the sky.

ANTONIA: So go, go I.
Goodbye, my love,
    goodbye!

MEN AND WOMEN: Go I.

FREE FOR ALL (1931)

Tryouts: Colonial Theatre, Boston, August 10–22, 1931; Garrick Theatre, Philadelphia, August 24, 1931. New York run: Manhattan Theatre (formerly the Hammerstein Theatre, now the Ed Sullivan): opened September 8, 1931; closed September 19, 1931; fifteen performances. A musical comedy. Presented by Laurence Schwab and Frank Mandel. Written by Oscar Hammerstein II and Laurence Schwab.* Music by Richard A. Whiting. Staged by Oscar Hammerstein II. Numbers staged by Bobby Connolly. Ben Goodman's Recording Orchestra conducted by John McManus. Settings by Donald Oenslager. Costume design by Kiviette.

Cast: Jack Haley (Stephen Potter Jr.), David Hutcheson (Joe Butler), Thelma Tipson (Gracie Maynard), Vera Marsh (Anita Allen), Peter Higgins (Michael Byrne), Tamara (Marishka Tarasov), Don Tomkins (Andy Bradford), Dorris Groday (Joan Sumner), Lilian Bond (Marie Sinnot), Peter Lang (Tom, a butler), Edward Emery (Stephen Potter Sr.), Dorothy Knapp (Miss Gibbs), Philip Lord (Dr. Raymond Allen, a psychoanalyst), Charles Althoff (Mr. Vergil Murgatroyd), Jeanette Loff (Mrs. Ida Jones), Seth Arnold (Sheriff Pete Weber), Gus Howard (a miner), Clair Kramer (a miner), John Donahue (a miner),

---

* *The program does not offer separate credits for book and lyrics.*

G. Pat Collins (Terence Canavan, a mine foreman), Harry Shannon (Jim Allison), Grace Johnston (Silver Dollar Kate), Dorothea James (a divorcée), Olive Bayes (a divorcée), Julia Chandler (a divorcée), Al Downing (Digger Watkins), Robert Randall (a reporter), Rae Powell (a nurse), E. Saulpaugh (Preston), and Edward Walters (a judge).

Being a wealthy man's son and a goofy amateur magician has not prevented Steven Potter Jr. from getting friendly with the student communists at Stanford. The kids are planning a trip to Russia, and he wants to tag along. Potter Sr.'s first reaction is to send Steve to a psychiatrist. Then he makes a counteroffer: he'll provide land for a commune if they'll stay closer to home. And so Steve, Joe, Gracie, Marie, Joan, Andy, Michael, and Marishka head off to an abandoned copper mine in Nevada. Anita has no interest in communism, but comes along to keep Marie away from Steve. The locals don't take kindly to single men and women living together, even in separate bunk houses, so marriages are arranged with mostly unhappy results. Despite comic mishaps, their summer of labor yields two of Nevada's principal exports: silver from the mine and divorces for all.

Free for All is one of the least documented shows in this volume. Six songs were published. Typescripts at the New York Public Library for the Performing Arts and in the Music Division of the Library of Congress map out the plot and the location of the songs in the story, but contain no lyrics. Some unpublished lyrics were found in the Saul Paugh (stage manager) typescript in the Theater Collection at the Museum of the City of New York and in a heavily annotated typescript at USC's Cinema-Television Library. A box of *Free for All* full scores and orchestra parts at Tams-Witmark Music Library in New York City yielded some additional lyrics as well as piano-vocal scores for a few melodies that were believed to have been lost. Still missing are songs cut before the New York opening: "Ain't Everything Grand," "Russian Song," "Men and Women Are Awful" (probably replaced by "Nevada Moonlight"), and "How I React to You."

Free for All lasted only fifteen performances. But John Byram's comments in the *New York Times* document Hammerstein's continuing exploration of what a musical could be:

> *Free for All* [is] a comedy with music rather than a musical comedy. That there is a difference was made clear several times during the evening, and there were those who left the theatre in the opinion that musical comedy, for all the unimaginative artificiality of its formula, is sometimes not so bad, after all.
>
> For here is a show that endeavors occasionally to the point of actual strain, to avoid the cliches that abound in its field. There is no chorus, and therefore no stage full of young women expend-

ing their youth and beauty on the monotonous stomping of precision dancing. The lovers are not torn apart in the customary fashion at the end of the first act. And the leading man and comedian are one, he being the personable Jack Haley, who is almost handsome enough for a juvenile and almost funny enough for a first division comedian. There are other innovations, all of them, in intent at least, designed to let some fresh air into the stuffy chambers where musical shows are conceived.

> So far, so good. Musical comedy, however, is among the many fields where intentions do not entirely suffice when accomplishment is wanting. Although much of *Free for All* is funny, and although it is tuneful when it should be tuneful, and is handsomely and expertly produced, it has not found effective substitutes for the conventions, trite though they may be, which it so blithely disregards.

I LOVE HIM, THE RAT

Not published. Introduced by Vera Marsh (Anita) and David Hutcheson (Joe). The typescript at USC indicated there would be two refrains about Anita's unrequited affection for Steve, but provided only this verse.

ANITA: I'm a woman and I'm in love,
Heaven looked down on me.
I've gone goofy over a man,
I'm no longer free.

JIM: Don't go into a torch song, kid,
Or this poor old heart will break.

FREE FOR ALL

Not published. Leadsheet, full score and parts located at Tams-Witmark. Introduced by Peter Higgins (Michael) and ensemble. A draft of the libretto had this song cue:

MARISHKA: Look, comrades, what Michael wrote last
    night.

MARIE: Why, this may be our battle hymn.

Onward, onward, into the light we go.
Into the world that we make free for all.
Forward, forward, into the fight we go,
Right we go.

Crashing through the breadline
With our Red Line.
Down with the captains of industry,
Every son of the rich must fall!
Onward, onward, into the light we go.
The world is free for all.

YOU'RE ONLY THE GIRL NEXT DOOR

Published as an individual sheet. Introduced by Jack Haley (Steve) and Vera Marsh (Anita).

VERSE 1

STEVE: Your house was right next to my house,
My folks and your folks were friends.
You and I grew up together,
And that's how the story ends.
I could feel romantic
For a strange and mysterious Venus,
But I knew you when your stockings had holes
And that's what stands between us.

REFRAIN 1

STEVE: You've got looks
And you've got the brains, too.
And your eyes
Are a beautiful blue.
I could go
Simply nuts about you,
But you're only the girl next door.
You've got boys
Falling under your spell.
You've got charm
And they think that you're swell.
So do I
But I know you so well,
You're only the girl next door.

PATTER 1

STEVE: When we were kids, you'd ask me to scratch
The skeeter bites on your knees.
We've gone bobsledding down a hill,
And I've seen your little BVDs.
Now strong men beg for your kisses divine,
Poets say that your lips are like wine.
I knew that when I hadn't turned nine—
You're only the girl next door!

VERSE 2

ANITA: I've helped you solve every problem.
I've been your friend and ally.
When you wore your first tuxedo
I had to tie your tie.
Now you take me for granted—
In your life I am only a habit.
STEVE: Our families said we were certain to wed
And that alone would crab it.

REFRAIN 2

STEVE: You've got looks
And you've got the brains, too.
And your eyes
Are a beautiful blue.
Just one thing
Is the matter with you.
ANITA: I'm only the girl next door.
STEVE: You've got boys
Falling under your spell.
You've got charm
And they think that you're swell.
So do I,
But I know you so well.
ANITA: I'm only the girl next door.

PATTER 2

STEVE: When we were kids, I licked Jimmy Smith
And all of your other beaux.
When I caught cold, you caught it, too,
And I used to blow your little nose.
Now strong men beg for your kisses divine.
I kissed you when I hadn't turned nine.
You said, "Thanks, dear, the pleasure is mine."
You're only the girl next door.

LIVING IN SIN

Not published. Piano-vocal score located at Tams-Witmark. Introduced by Dorris Groday (Joan), David Hutcheson (Joe), Don Tomkins (Andy), and Thelma Tipson (Gracie).

VERSE 1

JOAN: Ev'ry novel that you read
Tells you just how much you need
Some big red-hot romance to season your life.

JOE: You begin to feel alarm
If you aren't doing harm
To some young woman who is not your own wife.
ANDY: Newspaper articles are heart int'rest tales,
GRACIE: Whole pages giving hints in living in sin!

REFRAIN 1

ALL FOUR: Living in sin—
GRACIE: That is what they're taking up
In a world that is eager for thrills that are new.
ALL FOUR: Living in sin—
JOE: There's a charm in waking up
In a cute little hideaway,
Tucked in and tied away.
JOAN: [*wistfully*] Hanging chintz in ev'ry window with a view.
GRACIE: [*also wistfully*] And enjoying life as no nice folks ever do.
JOE: Not for me, darling.
GRACIE: Not for me, darling.
JOE: You're a liar!
GRACIE: You're a liar, too!

VERSE 2

JOAN: Your idea is not so new,
We're a jump ahead of you.
Loving illicitly went out with Mah Jong.
ANDY: Ev'ry time you had a yen
For a pretty little wren,
Dozens of house detectives rang a brass gong.
JOAN: But things are better now for people in love.
They are no longer harried— they get married!

REFRAIN 2

ALL FOUR: Living in sin—
ANDY: With the one you're wedded to.
JOAN: That's the latest, most daring of all modern fads!
ALL FOUR: Living in sin—
What can we be headed to?
GRACIE: And our poor children, what of them?
JOE: There'll be a lot of them!
ANDY: On the night boats travel's very nearly ceased,
JOE: And the number of Smiths in hotels has decreased.

GRACIE AND JOAN: [*"in Duncan Sisters harmony"*]
Single girls now lead lonely
    lives—
All the men they love are
    cheating with their wives!

JUST EIGHTEEN

Not published. Leadsheet, full score, and orchestra parts located at Tams-Witmark. Introduced by Dorris Groday (Joan) and Don Tomkins (Andy).

VERSE 1

JOAN: Seems but yesterday,
    I was young and gay.
    Now I am sophisticated, jaded, and blasé!
    All my indiscreet behavior
    Gets in Sunday's rotogravure.
    I'm so tired of it all,
    The world is such a small town, a fall town.

REFRAIN 1

JOAN: I'm just eighteen
    And I have had my fill of life.
    I have loved
    And I've known ev'ry thrill of life.
    I've cruised on showboats and come home
      a wreck*
    From spending nights in rowboats on old
      "B" Deck.
    I have known Parisienne sensations.
    I have seen the famous House of Nations!
    I've sown my oats
    And now there's nothing left to do
    But marry some good boy like you.

VERSE 2

ANDY: You think I'm a boy.
    Just a pretty toy.
    Something nice to occupy an idle hour of
      joy.
    That's a thought you ought to banish,
    All my mistresses were Spanish!
    I cavorted with bacchantes
    Long before you got your first panties!

---

* Discarded couplet:
  I know my Palm Beach, speakeasies, and jails.
  And I have had my dance with the Prince of Wales.

REFRAIN 2

ANDY: I'm twenty-one,
    My career has been electric.
    I have loved
    And I know ev'ry neck trick.
JOAN: I've bathed in bathtubs filled up with
      champagne.
ANDY: When I run out of hashish, I try cocaine.
    I've rehearsed with Dietrich in a talker.
JOAN: I have gone to lunch with Jimmy Walker.
BOTH: I've sown my oats
    And now there's nothing left to do
    But marry some good boy [girl] like you.

NOT THAT I CARE

Published as an individual sheet. Introduced by Jack Haley (Steve) and Vera Marsh (Anita). Several reviewers liked this number. Percy Hammond wrote in the *Herald Tribune:* "Among the songs that set the first nighters swaying was a tempting ditty entitled, 'Not That I Care,' sung, one suspects, first by Mr. Haley and Miss Vera Marsh and later by Tamara, a grimly exotic beauty, and Peter Higgins, a barytone of skill and reputation."*

VERSE 1

STEVE: Congratulate me on one thing,
    I left you flat before you fooled me.
    I did that big hit-and-run thing.
    Some lucky instinct must have ruled me.
    You didn't even save a place in your heart
    That tender mem'ries could be kept in;
    You cleaned the place right out and made
      a fresh start,
    And soon another fellow stepped in.

REFRAIN 1

STEVE: Not that I care,
    Why should I care what you may do?
    Now that we're through, ev'rything's
      swell.
    Not that I care
    If a new boy dances with you,
    And does my old steps—and perhaps
      quite as well.

---

* *Hammond's reference to a reprise by the characters Marishka and Michael may solve the question of what song they performed (with the three "Divorcées") in Act Two, Scene 1, but no additional lyric has been found.*

Not that I care,
Why should I care who you go for?
Let someone else get his good-night kiss at
    your door;
But after he goes, don't you dream of me
    anymore!
Not that I care, why should I care?

VERSE 2

ANITA: You're like a dog in the manger,
    Except that dogs are faithful always.
    You should have known there was
      danger
    In playing 'round too many hallways.
    To eat your cake and keep it may be
      sublime,
    But if you like the part with spicing,
    You've got to work on just one cake at a
      time,
    Or all you'll get will be the icing.

REFRAIN 2

ANITA: Not that I care,
    Why should I care what you may do?
    Now that we're through, ev'rything's
      swell.
    Not that I care
    If a new girl dances with you,
    And does my old steps—though perhaps
      not so well.
    Not that I care,
    Why should I care what you think right?
STEVE: Make a big date with your white-haired
      boy ev'ry night.
    Keep right on that way, and there'll be one
      hell of a fight!
    Not that I care, why should I care?

Unpublished reprise refrain

According to an early libretto, later in the same scene "Anita bawls him out in blank verse to melody of 'Not That I Care' second half. The burthen of her tirade is: Do you know what you are? You're just a blank. No guts. Glad my husband isn't a chicken-livered man without any gumption! Not that I care!"

ANITA: Not that I care
    If your new girl walks over you.
    I said we were through. You're a fish!
    Not that I care
    Why should I care?
    Be as chicken-hearted as you want to be.
    Once I thought you might amount to
      something

But you haven't got the courage or the
gumption of a flea.
Once I looked upon you as my hero
But now—you—you don't mean a damn
thing to me!

[*She bursts into tears and exits.*]

STEVE: [*weakly*] Not that I care. Why should I
care?

SLUMBER SONG
(GOOD NIGHT)

Published as an individual sheet. Introduced by Peter
Higgins (Michael) and Tamara (Marishka).

VERSE

Ev'ry day I spend with you,
Ev'ry day I end with you,
Cries for one day more.
On a night like this, you
Are lovely when I kiss you
And leave you at your door.

REFRAIN

Good night.
Time to go to your bed, dear,
And I'll go to mine.
Sleep tight
In your own little bed, dear,
And I'll sleep in mine.
Moonbeams stealing down through the willow,
Will kiss you as they shine;
While I lie awake on my pillow
And wish those kisses were mine.

WHEN YOUR BOY
BECOMES A MAN

Published as an individual sheet. Introduced by Grace
Johnston (Silver Dollar Kate) and Vera Marsh (Anita).
Several reviews mention that Johnston's performance
stopped the show.

VERSE

He's young, he plays with the other boys—
Then his mother sees him throwing away his toys.
She knows, she knows that her work is through—
And she turns him over to you.
You take your boy,
As women have since time began,
And make your boy a man.
He fights, he wins, and you swell with pride—
With a conqu'ring hero resting by your side.

REFRAIN

He's sweet, and he's yours,
And you love as a woman can.
And you thrill to know
That he loves you so,
When your boy becomes a man.
He hopes and he dreams,
And he tells you his ev'ry plan;
You pretend to hear,
But you're thinking: "Dear
Little boy, you're now a man!"
He may go down to the sea in ships,
And leave you alone;
But he'll come back with eager lips
Pressed to your own.
You cry, you're so glad,
For you love as a woman can;
And the kid you knew
Is a king to you,
When your boy becomes a man.

TONIGHT

Published as an individual sheet. Introduced by Peter
Higgins (Michael) and Tamara (Marishka).

VERSE

A cricket sighs in the warm night breeze,
And all the world seems young,
Teeming with melodies
Left unsung.

REFRAIN

Tonight,
There is stardust in your hair,
And enchantment ev'rywhere
Tonight.
Tonight,
We are in a silver beam;
I don't have to sleep to dream

Tonight.
Someday, ev'ry star may fade from the blue,
Someday, we may part as some lovers do.
But tonight,
Heart upon my heart you lie.
Tonight,
I belong to you.

REPEAT REFRAIN

NEVADA MOONLIGHT

Not published. Instrumental parts survive. Introduced
by David Hutcheson (Joe), Thelma Tipson (Gracie), and
ensemble.

In a largely positive review of the show, *Billboard*'s
Eugene Burr called this number a "hilarious piece . . . a
splendid take-off on the usual popular ditty which if it
becomes popular itself will be taken seriously by the
Great Crooners."

VERSE 1

JOE: [*in a burlesque tragic mood*] Love came to
me in old Nevada
Blooming like a new-blown rose.
But flowers fade in old Nevada
And love's like any flower, goodness
knows!

REFRAIN

JOE: Nevada moonlight,
Remember me
And the girl 'neath the old elm tree.
Nevada moonlight,
She's gone away
And with her all my dreams went astray.
I used to dream we'd have a home
To make our hearts rejoice.
Then, I thought we'd hear
A lisping baby voice—
I've got no baby,
There's only me
And the moon, and the old elm tree!

[*Dialogue.*]

VERSE 2

GRACIE: I've learned my lesson in Nevada
And its message sadly clings.
Don't leave your lover in Nevada

Or you'll feel simply lousy when he
    sings.

REPEAT REFRAIN

PATTER

[ ]*: You'll find a moon in old Kentucky,
    And a moon in Tennessee,
    And a moon that shines on old New
      Mexico.
    But one moon lingers in my
      memoree—
    It isn't in the state of Georgia,
    Or the state of Illinois.
    It's a moon in old Nevada
    And I've loved it since a boy.
    It's the moon my dear old mother gave
      to me.

REPEAT REFRAIN

VERSE 3

MICHAEL: There is a courthouse in Nevada,
    Shun it as you would a blight.
    Or you'll leave someone in Nevada
    Whose voice will haunt you nearly
      every night.

FINAL REFRAIN

ALL: Nevada moonlight,
    Remember me
    And the girl 'neath the old elm tree.
    Nevada moonlight,
    She's gone away
    And with her all my dreams went astray.
    I used to dream we'd have a home
    To make our hearts rejoice.
    Then I thought we'd hear
    A lisping baby voice—
    You've got five babies!
    You might get another three
    With a moon and an old elm tree.

---

* The singer is not identified in the only known copy of
the patter.*

CUT AND UNUSED SONGS

WHEREVER YOU ARE I'M LOOKING AT YOU

Not published and not listed in the New York program.*
Leadsheet, full score, and orchestra parts are located at
Tams-Witmark. A typed lyric sheet assigns the song to
the character Michael.

VERSE

Though you don't know I'm alive, dear,
I know ev'ry move you make.
I know you like tea at five, dear,
And your fav'rite kind of cake.
I haunt the places where you go, dear,
Gaze at you night and day.
When I see you at a show, dear,
I never see the play.

REFRAIN

Wherever you are
I'm looking at you,
I'm looking at you.
Wherever you are
I can pick you out in any throng,
Doesn't take me long to find you.
Wherever you go
I follow you there
And park alongside of your car
In hopes you'll see and recognize me—
The fellow who's looking at you
Wherever you are.

PSYCHOANALYZE ME

Not published. Dropped before the New York opening. A
piano-vocal manuscript, a full score, and orchestra parts
are preserved at Tams-Witmark. In Act One, Scene 2,

---

* In fact, the New York program does not list any solo
for Michael. The lyric was found with the Museum
of the City of New York's typescript, on a page
simply numbered "3." (Pages 1, 2, or 4 have not been
identified.) Stage directions instruct: "Both girls
look up at Michael adoringly."*

Steve, while visiting Anita's psychoanalyst father, is mis-
taken for a doctor.

VERSE 1

MRS. JONES: The women of my family are all high-
    strung
    And full of suppressed desire.
    The first time Grandma kissed a man,
    She caused the Chicago fire!
    Although her fam'ly doctor knew
      biology
    And dabbled in pills and cuts—
    They hadn't yet discovered
      psychology
    So Grandma just went nuts!
STEVE: [playing along] Gone are those dark
    and dreary days
    When emotions were incurable.
    Science has now found charming
      ways
    Of making life and love endurable.

REFRAIN 1

MRS. JONES: Psychoanalyze me, Doc.
    Show me all you know.
    Set my inhibitions free,
    Set them free!
    Tell my why my milk-white skin
    Turns a crimson glow
    Ev'ry time you look at me—
    Look at me!
    Is my libido a trifle complex?
    (Down at the Lido you'd notice my
      sex.)
    Psychoanalyze me, Doc.
    Read me through and through.
    Don't you think the whole darn thing
    Could be cured by you?

VERSE 2

STEVE: We used to have diphtheria and
    barbers' itch,
    Lumbago and housemaids' knee.
    But now they're called neuroses
      which
    Began at the age of three.
    We used to think it pretty when two
      lovers clung
    And hung on each others' necks.
    But that has been disposed of by
      Freud and Jung
    As so much Oedipus Rex.
MRS. JONES: [intensely] How can there be a doubt
    of love

When it weaves its mystic spell with
    you?
Why am I never out of love?

STEVE: Your endocrines are raising hell with
    you!

REFRAIN 2

MRS. JONES: Psychoanalyze me, Doc.
    Ask me something queer.
STEVE: At the seashore do you burn?
MRS. JONES: Do I burn!
STEVE: Do you dream of cold champagne
    After drinking beer?
    In the nighttime do you yearn?
MRS. JONES: Do I—
STEVE: [spoken] Don't tell me. I get it.
    [sung] When your dreams gnaw at
      and urge to be kissed [sic]
    Chew an old straw hat and try to
      resist.
    Then if you should lose control
    And you're getting worse—
MRS. JONES: Yes?
STEVE: Take your phone and call me up.
MRS. JONES: Yes?
STEVE: And I'll send a nurse.

[Pantomime dance.]

REFRAIN 3

STEVE: I have diagnosed with care
    Your subconscious mind.
    I have found there's lots to learn.
MRS. JONES: Lots to learn, Doctor?
STEVE: In a crisis you are there,
    Never left behind.
    In a real tight pinch, you're stern.
MRS. JONES: Pinch my stern, Doctor?
STEVE: [spoken] Let it go, let the whole thing
      go.
MRS. JONES: [putting his hand on her heart] Doctor,
    oh, Doctor,
    Just feel my poor pulse.
    Feel my heart beating.
    You must get results.
STEVE: I do!
    Have you got an old straw hat?
    I would like a chew.
    You're [sic] make any analyst
    Just as bad as you.

OPEN YOUR EYES

Published as an individual sheet, but dropped before the New York opening. Introduced by Vera Marsh (Anita) and Jack Haley (Steve). An early libretto describes the number to be written: "He says, 'Open up your eyes and look around you. Open your arms and take the whole world in.' She says, 'Open up your eyes and look at just me. Open up your arms and just hold me, etc., etc.' In her verse and refrain, her more natural and elemental argument triumphs for the moment, and he kisses her."

VERSE 1*

STEVE: Marriage is something you can try
    When you are old and gray.
    Never take a wife,
    Until you've taken your fun before!
    Beautiful girls await your eye,
    From Holland to Bombay;
    And the more you meet,
    The more you'll want to be meeting
      more.

REFRAIN 1

STEVE: Open your eyes,
    And what do you see?
    Hot Havana! Gay Paree!
    What do you say?
    Open your eyes!
    Open your arms
    And what do you do?
    Hold the Follies close to you.
    What do you say?
    Open your arms!
    You can go to Honolulu
    And meet up with a peach.
    You can take her through a breaker
    As you go for the beach.
ANITA: Go for the beach.
STEVE: Open your mind
    And get in the know;
    See the world and spend your dough!†
    Don't miss a thing—
    Open your eyes!

VERSE 2

ANITA: Loving adventure as you do,
    Will you let me suggest

---

* The published sheet puts Anita's verse and chorus
  before Steve's.

† Another source has:
  See the world, take fun in tow.

There are pretty things to see,
    And not very far away.
    Lots of excitement waits for you,
    If you stay in the west;
    You can save yourself a trip
    And never go near Bombay.

REFRAIN 2

ANITA: Open your eyes,
    And what do you see?
    Here's romance dressed up as me!
    What do you say?
    Open your eyes!
    Open your arms
    And what do you do?
    Let me move in close to you.
    What do you say?
    Open your arms!
    I have had my eagle eye on you
    For over a year,
    And your love call, I am now all
    Of a twitter to hear.
STEVE: Twitter to hear.
ANITA: Open your heart
    And what do you feel?
    Don't you wish this dream were real?
    Maybe it is,
    Open your eyes!

THE CAREFREE MINERS

Not used. Not published. No music known to survive. An early libretto instructs:

All get set to enjoy a good lively song. Michael sings a short refrain which is gay. Then he goes into verse which starts a sad story. He repeats refrain and gets them to join in, which they do with relief. Then the second verse is sadder. Even the happy refrain now sounds sad in light of its associations. They try to join in but their efforts end in several sniffles. Steve enters during number very bright. They shush him. He stands and listens and at the finish he's crying too.

VERSE 1

Honest John MacDougall was a plumber
But somehow he could never find employment.
He had a wife and several little mouths to feed
But they had little food and no enjoyment.
Then gold was discovered in California!
Fortune beckoned from the river's rock.

MacDougall got himself a prairie schooner
And set out with his sturdy little flock.
Beside him rode his wife, whose name was
    Hester,
They had a little girl, whose name was Joy,
They had a little dog, whose name was Rover,
And Isaac was their young four-year-old boy.
The trip was a hard one—
But they were brave and strong.
And when misfortune came their way
They always sang this song:

REFRAIN

Oh, we are the carefree miners,
The jolly Forty-Niners.
We laugh at our troubles,
For troubles are bubbles,
When you are carefree like us.

VERSE 2

Driving through the sagebrush and the cactus*
Occasionally they would ford a river
But one day little Joy fell off the wagon seat;
Her tiny body started floating downstream.
But look! Only a hundred feet beyond her
They could see a roaring waterfall.
If Joy fell o'er that precipice of water
There'd hardly be a chance for her at all.
Then Hester leaped and cried, "I'll save my
    daughter."
She swum and swum to race the rushing flow.
But little Joy went over ere she reached her;
Then Hester joined her on the rocks below.
Poor John looked at Isaac
And said, "My boy, be strong.
We may have lost our dear ones,
But we still have our song."

REPEAT REFRAIN

IF THAT ISN'T LOVE, WHAT IS?

Not published. Not used. This title was not seen in the extant scripts or programs, but a typed lyric sheet, as well as leadsheet, full score, and instrument parts, was found at Tams-Witmark.

---

* It is odd that the first six lines have no rhymes, but
    there is no other version to check.

STEVE: I like an ice cream soda,
        You like a sloe gin fizz.
        When you're with me, you have soda free.
        If that isn't love, what is?
        I like my funny stories.
        When I take you to dine
        I pay my half and throw in a laugh.
        If that isn't love, what is?
        Many's the time you talk of marriage,
        Trying to put me on the skids.
        What would I get from that there
            marriage?
        What would I get?
        I'd get nine or ten kids!
        I'll take an ice cream soda.
        You keep your sloe gin fizz.
        I'll buy you toys
        For your girls and boys.
        If that isn't love, what is?

EAST WIND (1931)

Tryouts: Pittsburgh, Nixon Theatre, October 5–10, 1931; Cleveland, October 13–17, 1931; Baltimore, October 19–25, 1931. New York run: Manhattan Theatre; opened October 27, 1931; closed November 14, 1931; twenty-three performances. A musical play. Presented by Laurence Schwab and Frank Mandel. Written by Oscar Hammerstein II and Frank Mandel.* Music by Sigmund Romberg. Staged by Oscar Hammerstein II. Musical numbers staged by Bobby Connolly. Orchestrations by Hans Spialek. Musical direction by Oscar Bradley. Settings by Donald Oenslager. Costume design by Charles Le Maire.

Cast: Charlotte Lansing (Claudette Fortier), William Williams (Rene Beauvais), J. Harold Murray (Captain Paul Beauvais), Vera Marsh (Marie Martel), Joe Penner (Victor Cliquot), Ahi (Tsoi Tsing), Greek Evans (Monsieur Granier), Vance Elliott (Jacques), Betty Junod (Gabrielle), Francis Markey (Julie), Rose Mullen (Claire), Sherry Pelham (Mimi), Dennie Moore (Lorraine Fortier), Thomas Chadwick (Captain Dejan), I. Anchong (Taxi Driver), Gus Howard (A Tourist), Jules Epailly (Pierre Fortier), Ivan Izmailov (King of Luang-Prabang), Y. Y. Hsu (The King's Interpreter), J. C. Donsu (Hop Sing), Gladstone Waldrip (Captain Gervais), [Robert Emmet] Bobby Dolan (Pianist), Marjorie Dille (A Maid), O. J. Vanasse (The Stage Manager), Emile Ladoux (The Compere), Lorraine and Leatrice Pearl (The McNulty Sisters), Alex Yakovleff (King in ballet), Aron Tomaroff (Prince in ballet), George Chap-

---

* No specific credit is given for the lyrics. Most
    historians believe Hammerstein wrote them alone.

pel (Dr. Duval). The large ensemble of singers, dancers, and "international gypsies" portrayed schoolgirls, barkers, entertainers, and fairgoers; officers, congais, and tourists, Hindu and Chinese potentates and retainers; Parisians; and waterfront characters in Marseilles.

Six songs (and one dropped number) were published as individual sheets. The Romberg Collection in the Music Division of the Library of Congress contains a holograph piano-vocal score with inserted dialogue (possibly the rehearsal version of the script). Additional music manuscripts are in the Music Division's Warner-Chappell Collection. Another score is in the Tams-Witmark Music Library in New York City. Scripts survive at Tams-Witmark, the Shubert Archive, the New York Public Library for the Performing Arts, and the Frank Mandel Collection at UCLA.

Various drafts of the script call for a hearty rendition of "All Is Well in Singapore" in Act Two, Scene 2, but neither words nor music was located. There is no singing in Act Two's Indochina Ballet.

Hammerstein had very high hopes for *East Wind*. Writing on opening night to a Melbourne acquaintance, he explained:

In the last eight months I have written and produced two musical comedies for the stage and they have taken up every minute of my time. The first of these [*Free for All*] was a failure, but the second looks like a very solid success. It is another operetta written in collaboration with Romberg and seems to have a great deal of the richness of *Desert Song* both as to music and its melodramatic plot, although, of course, the stories have no resemblance to each other. I should be very much surprised if it doesn't reach Australia within the next year. It is called *East Wind*. Watch for it!

But most newspaper critics found little to praise. John Mason Brown's review in the *New York Post* carried the subheads "A book which makes O'Neill's trilogy seem simple" and "A completely negative evening."* Robert Garland's report in the *Telegram* concluded "Even if it were good it would be too old fashioned."

---

* Although Brown loathed the show, his plot synopsis
    was not exaggerated:

It jumps from France to Indochina and back again just when it is beginning to make some kind of atmospheric use of its Oriental setting. It tells a tale of two brothers—one a dashing officer (Mr. Murray) and the other a weakling dope fiend (Mr. Williams, believe it or not)—who are both in love with the same blonde maiden (Charlotte Lansing). Nor does this intra-mural triangle with its Cyrano touches, suffice to keep the story moving. To it are

The show was a financial disappointment as well as an artistic one. (Between *Free for All* and *East Wind*, Hammerstein lost $80,000 of a $100,000 contract buy-out from Warner Bros.) Soon after the opening, Hammerstein grumbled to his ex-wife:

After breaking box office records, not to mention the backs of salaaming critics, on the road, *East Wind* has opened in New York, and is a flop. There are sundry and complicated explanations, but the only important significance is the break-down of a musical-play formula on which I used to make a lot of money. What new device is destined to take its place I don't know, and for the moment I don't intend to find out.

Rather than continue living on his capital—"now a shrunken nugget"—he said that he intended to give up the theater, move to France, and write a novel.

ACT ONE OPENING

Not published. Introduced by the ensemble. The scene is a village fair near Marseilles.

SINGING GIRL: Let us climb up and over the hill.
We'll chase the sun over the hill.
We may learn where it hides,
Over the hill.
JEWELER: Over here, Mesdames,
Messieurs.
Gold rings and necklaces,
Pretty bibelots.
Just the thing
For your sweetheart to buy.
FORTUNE TELLER: Your fortune told by your palm.
Only two francs.

added a Chinese dancer (Ahi), who leads Mr. Williams astray; a flower boat scene on the river front at Saigon; comic by-play in which an ordinary gray elephant is sold as a sacred white one; a subplot in which Chinese waiters threaten to murder the comedian; a cabaret scene in Paris; an effectively melodramatic backstage scene when an IndoChinese ballet is in progress; and a finale in a Marseilles wine shop in which the heroine has taken to brandy and the temporarily blinded Mr. Murray is at last persuaded to claim her as his own when the words of a reassuring chorus remind him that "cows are in the clover."

And I'll tell your past
And your future, too.
BAKER: Rolls and brioches all hot.
The freshest and finest
Patisseries money can buy.
FAIRGOERS: What a lot of different things,
Buns and fortunes, cakes and
rings.
GIRLS: Let's go in that tent.
MEN: The money I've spent.
FAIRGOERS: We've spent all the money
We'd saved for the rent.
Here's some wine to buy today,
Burgundy and old Tokay.
GIRLS: Come, look over there.
MEN: Why not over there?
FAIRGOERS: There's something for all at the fair.

[*A Punch and Judy puppet show is in progress.*]

JUDY: You take that, you blackguard,
you scoundrel, you thief.
You ruffian, you rascal, I'll give
you grief.
PUNCH: But take it easy, Judy,
Or I'll take it hard.
JUDY: All right then, take it now.
SPECTATORS: Poor Punch will get it now.
PUNCH: But now we'll tell a different
story.
SPECTATORS: He'll hit her on the head.
He'll beat her till she's dead.
JEWELER: Over here, Mesdames, Messieurs.
Gold rings and necklaces,
Pretty bibelots.
A gem to catch your lady's eye
And just the thing for a
sweetheart to buy.
FORTUNE TELLER: I tell your future and past by
your palm.
Let me examine your palm.
And if you do not believe in
palmistry,
I'll tell it by
The stars in the sky.
BAKER: Freshest patisseries,
Finest confiseries
For you to try.
Why not have a try?
Rolls and brioches all hot.
The freshest and finest
patisseries,
Money can buy.
SINGING GIRL: Let us climb up and over the
hill,
We'll chase the sun over the
hill.

We may learn where it hides,
Over the hill.
PUNCH: [*to the puppet* POLLY] Pretty
Polly, I love you so.
I will never leave you, no, no.
Had I all the wives of King Sol,
I'd kill all the lot
But I'd keep my own Pol.
BARKER: Let me introduce you to the
L'Oiseaux family,
Playing plays by Racine,
Corneille, and Molière.
This one is Papa,
And this one here is Maman,
Celimene, Lisette, and the boy
Robert.
SPECTATORS: But where is petite Grisette,
André, and Pierre?
BARKER: We will have a very pretty song
and dance now,
From their daughter Mimi and
their daughter Claire.
SPECTATORS: Bravo! Wonderful!
Let's hear the song!

IT'S A WONDERFUL WORLD

Published as an individual sheet. Introduced by Rose Mullen (Claire), Sherry Pelham (Mimi), and ensemble.* Reprised by Charlotte Lansing (Claudette Fortier) and Greek Evans (Monsieur Granier, her schoolteacher and guardian).

MIMI: Have you ever heard a cowbell
ringing?
Have you heard it?
ALL: Yes, we've heard it.
MIMI: Have you ever heard a bluebird
singing?
Have you heard him?
ALL: Yes, we've heard him.
MIMI: Have you taken off your socks
and waded,
In a brook that friendly trees
have shaded?
ALL: Yes, we have, and we are all
persuaded
Life is gay!

---

* *The sheet music assigns this song to the nonexistent character "Roberta." That may be a misprint for "Robert," the boy soprano who led this number in some drafts of the script.*

MIMI: Have you heard the bluebird
    sing?
    He will tell you just one thing.

REFRAIN

MIMI: It's a wonderful world when you
    fall in love with it.
    It's a wonderful world.
    It's a wonderful life when you're
    hand in glove with it.
    It's a wonderful world.
    When you hope and you dream
    And your dreams come true,
    And the dreams you love fall in
    love with you,
    Then you're glad to be, proud
    to be
    Just allowed to be
    In this wonderful world!

INTERLUDE

GIRLS: Take a look around you.
    Look around and see.
MEN: Sheep are in the meadow.
    Birds are in the tree.
GIRLS: Cows are in the clover,
    Just where they belong.
MEN AND GIRLS: So the world can't be all wrong.
    Morning sees the sun rise,
    Evening sees it set.
    These are things that never
    Failed to happen yet.
    We are here together,
    Just where we belong.
    So the world can't be all wrong!

REPEAT REFRAIN

MUSICAL INTERLUDE

Alternate title: "Boat Deck scene." Not published. Introduced by William Williams (Rene Beauvais), Charlotte Lansing (Claudette Fortier), Dennie Moore (Lorraine Fortier), and Vera Marsh (Marie Martel). This recitative consists of fragments of overlapping conversations. Lorraine and Marie are discussing marriage prospects in Saigon. Claudette and Rene stroll back and forth.

PART 1

RENE: [*to* CLAUDETTE] Now you can see the
    Southern Cross.
LORRAINE: [*to* MARIE] They're getting on, I
    think.
MARIE: [*to* LORRAINE] I know it.
CLAUDETTE: [*to* RENE] I never saw stars shine so
    brightly.

PART 2

LORRAINE: [*watching the strollers*] Hand in hand.
MARIE: Getting warm.
CLAUDETTE: [*to* RENE] . . . and you saved him?
RENE: Yes, just in time.
LORRAINE: Ain't love silly.
MARIE: Ain't it swell.
CLAUDETTE: They saw us.
RENE: Think so?

PART 3

LORRAINE: [*stating her fiancé's address*] Nine
    miles north on the Hangchow
    Road.
MARIE: Nine miles north on the Hangchow
    Road?
LORRAINE: Nine miles north on the Hangchow
    Road.
MARIE: Nine miles north on the Hangchow
    Road.

[*Exeunt.*]

PART 4

RENE: Nobody else is left on deck.
CLAUDETTE: We seem to be alone.
RENE: And this is our last night at sea.
CLAUDETTE: Where is the Southern Cross now?
RENE: [*leaning in to kiss her*] There is the
    Southern Cross now.

EAST WIND

Published as an individual sheet. Introduced by J. Harold Murray (Captain Paul Beauvais), soldiers, casino patrons, and dancing girls.

VERSE

PAUL: If you want good luck, you must
    gamble,
    You must gamble for your good
    luck.
    And if you'd love life, you must
    seek it,
    You must seek life if you'd love
    it.
    Out in the east here,
    Nearer the sunrise,
    Fortune may change here
    With ev'ry breeze,
    Ev'ry breeze.
MEN: Ev'ry breeze
    That is blowing here
    May be bringing you grief or
    cheer,
    May be things that you want or
    fear,
    May be riding ev'ry breeze.
PAUL: So may my fate ride with the east
    wind.
    With the east wind may my fate
    ride,
    Out in the tropics
    Under a burning sky.
MEN: Under a burning sky.
PAUL: Here's where I have chosen to
    cast my lot,
    To live and love and die!

REFRAIN

PAUL: East wind, what do you bring?
    I am waiting.
    Lift your quivering wing,
    Fly to me.
    Blow me men who can sing,
    Laughing girls, and yellow
    sunshine.
    Make me beggar or king.
    East wind, I wait for you.
GIRLS: You—oo
    Blow—ow
    Fill up ev'ry sail.
PAUL: Fill up ev'ry sail
    And blow.
GIRLS: Blow and
    Bring me the ship that
    Brings me the
    Lover I'm awaiting.
MEN: Blo—ow
    Bring my love to me,
    Bring the lover I'm awaiting.
PAUL: Bring me new love,
    False or true love.
    Take her
    When you go.

PAUL AND MEN: East wind,
What do you bring?
I am waiting.
Lift your quivering wing,
Fly to me.
Blow me men who can sing,
Laughing girls, and yellow
sunshine.
Make me beggar or king.
East wind,
I wait for you.
Out of the east
Bring me my love.

GIRLS: Eastern wind,
What do you bring?
Waiting alone,
Waiting here.
Lift your quivering wing.
Flying wing.
Fly on,
Fly on to me,
East wind.
Blow me
Men who can sing,
Laughing girls
With slanting almond eyes.
Make of me
Beggar or king.
East wind,
I wait for you-oo.
Out of the eastern sky
Bring me my love.

ENCORE

MEN: Sun sun sun sun
Heat heat heat heat
Rain rain rain rain
Sand sand sand sand
Girls girls girls girls
Love love love love
Leave leave leave leave
Home home home home
Back back back back
Sun sun girls girls
Love love heat heat
Rain rain sand sand
Make me beggar or king.
East wind
I wait for you.
Out of the east
Bring me my love.

I SAW YOUR EYES

Not published. Introduced by J. Harold Murray (Paul),
six officers, Charlotte Lansing (Claudette), and William
Williams (Rene).

PAUL: You may find it very
strange out here.
You may find it quite a
change out here,
But I hope that you will
like it.
OFFICERS: Introduce us if you
dare.
CLAUDETTE: I imagine that the days
are hot,
But I understand the
nights are not.
I am sure that I will
like it.
OFFICERS: [louder] Introduce us if
you dare!
PAUL: In tropic climes, as you
will learn,
At certain times you need
a drink.
A light Chablis, a mild
Sauterne . . .
FIRST OFFICER: Give us a drink!
CLAUDETTE: Er—just a lemon squash,
I think.
PAUL: Lemon squash.
Make it two.

[OFFICERS jeer.]

CLAUDETTE: This is very kind of you.
PAUL AND CLAUDETTE: It is nice to be here
In this tropic
atmosphere.
I'm glad that I am here.
1ST OFFICER: One cognac.
2ND OFFICER: One beer.
3RD OFFICER: Same here.
ALL OFFICERS: Let's do all we can do to
spoil
His game here!
CLAUDETTE: There is so much I want to
see:
A congai girl, a banyan
tree.
PAUL: I will do my best to show
you 'round,
You won't miss anything
with me.

CLAUDETTE: I want to know the natives,
too.
I find romance in all that's
new.
PAUL: And "romance" is just the
word,
Describing
What I'm finding in you.
CLAUDETTE: There is so much
I want to see.
A congai girl,
A banyan tree.
Ah! I'll see
And I want to know
The natives, too.
I find romance
In all that's new.
That is
Just the thing
I am trying to do!
PAUL: There is so much
For you to see.
A congai girl,
A banyan tree.
You will not
Miss anything with me.
I'll help you know
The natives, too.
You'll find romance
In all that's new.
My romance
Is in you.
OFFICERS: Must we sit and wait all day?
He will not invite us over
there,
So we'll go over anyway.
AN OFFICER: You go first.
ANOTHER OFFICER: But you come too.
OFFICERS: And romance is just the
word
That all of us
Are finding in you!
OFFICERS: Did you think you'd lose
us?
Mad'moiselle, excuse us.
PAUL: Meet Ma'mselle Claudette
Fortier.
She has just arrived today.
OFFICERS: Join us while you can,
dear,
He's a dang'rous man,
dear!
CLAUDETTE: I think he's charming.
PAUL: She thinks I'm charming.
OFFICERS: Poor young thing!
PAUL: She may be young, but
then

SHE'S quite a judge of
men.

CLAUDETTE: I saw your eyes, and I liked
your eyes.
Their look was tender and
kind.
That we would be the best
of friends
I soon made up my mind.

PAUL: I saw your eyes, and to
know those eyes
My heart was strongly
inclined.

CLAUDETTE: And so we start a
friendship true.

CLAUDETTE, PAUL,
AND OFFICERS: You like me [him],
I like you [He likes you].

CLAUDETTE: [continuing alone] When
you meet the man I
love,
You will like him too!

OFFICERS: [to PAUL] What an awful
disappointment
You turned out to be.
What a credit to the Army
You turned out to be.

PAUL: I've had girls with
sweethearts before.
That just makes me want
them the more.

OFFICERS: Spoken like a little soldier
and gallant Don Juan.
Tell the little lady you are
the pride of Saigon.

CLAUDETTE: Come and drink your nice
lemon squash.

[OFFICERS laugh.]

PAUL: Mad'moiselle, I thank
you.

CLAUDETTE: I know
How you love
A good lemon squash.

OFFICERS: Oh, gosh!
Drink up all your nice
lemon squash.
Lemon squash, lemon
squash.
Lemon squash!
Drink down your lemon
squash.
Juice of the lemon in
Not too much water.
Though it may be
feminine,
Why should you slaughter

Your gullet with cognac
And whiskey and wine?

[RENE *enters. In a brief exchange of dialogue we learn
that he and* PAUL *are brothers.* PAUL *and the officers
learn that* CLAUDETTE *is engaged to* RENE.]

PAUL: [spoken] Rene, you always
were a lucky kid.

CLAUDETTE: [sung] I'm lucky too.
I saw his eyes
And I loved his eyes,
Their look was gentle and
kind.

PAUL: That you would be the
best of friends
You soon made up your
mind.

CLAUDETTE: [to RENE] I love
Your eyes,
And I am inclined
To feel that we'll be always
true.
You love me,
I love you.
Now you've met my
darling,
Don't you like him too?

PAUL AND OFFICERS: You saw her eyes,
And to know her eyes
Your heart was strangely
Inclined.
You love him,
He loves you.
Now he's here
We must like him too.

RENE: I saw her eyes,
And to know her eyes
My heart was strangely
Inclined.
I love you,
Now you've met my
darling,
You must like her too.

CONGAI

Not published. Introduced by William Williams (Rene),
Ahi (Tsoi Tsing), dancing girls, and men in the Casino.
The first version was found in Romberg's handwritten
piano-vocal score and in an arrangement by Hans
Spialek. The alternate stanzas were found in scripts at

the New York Public Library for the Performing Arts
and at the Shubert Archive.

RENE: Funny little heathen,
With your slanting eye,
Bring me out an absinthe.
I'll stay for one drink, and then
goodbye.

[TSOI TSING *begins to dance.*]

BASS: Congai,*
When you are dancing
You are like a young fern swaying
in the wood.
Congai,
I can resist you, but
I see no reason why I should.

GIRL: Congai,
When you are dancing†
You're a wild plum tree with
blossoms on the bough.
Congai,
If you should let a blossom fall
Some man would catch it now.

THREE GIRLS: Congai,
When you are dancing
You're a wild plum tree with
blossoms on the bough.
Congai,
If you should let a blossom fall
Some man would catch it now.

TENORS: Frenchman, you're in Indochina
now.
You know your Indochina now.

ALL MEN: When Tsoi Tsing fascinates you
with her dance,
You know you're far away from
France.

GIRLS: The same thing happens to the
very best.
And you'll do the very same as
all the rest.
You may hold out a while

---

* *Alternate lines:*
Congai, you're like a willow tree,
A slender willow tree
With blossoms on the bow.
Give me a blossom now
My slender willow tree.

† *Alternate lines:*
Congai, I like to see you sway,
For when you sway that way,
I want to do it too.
I want to stay with you,
I want to sway that way.

But not for long.

MEN: For in the end all join the song
Of Congai!

MEN AND GIRLS: Congai,
When you are dancing
You are like a young fern swaying
in the wood.
Congai,
I can resist you, but
I see no reason why I should.
Congai,
When you are dancing
You are like a wild plum tree
with blossoms on the bough.
Congai,
If you should let a blossom fall,
Some man would catch it now!
Tsoi Tsing of Indochina,*
You cast a spell of romance.
Tsoi Tsing of Indochina,
There's nothing like you in
France.
Congai,
When you are dancing
You are like a young fern swaying
in the wood.
Congai,
I can resist you
But I see no reason why I should.
Dance, Tsoi Tsing of Indochina,
dance!
Congai,
Congai!

THESE TROPICS

Not published. Introduced by Vera Marsh (Marie) and
Joe Penner (Victor Cliquot), and encored by Dennie
Moore (Lorraine).

* *Alternate lines:*
Congai, I like to see you sway.
For when you sway that way,
I want to do it too.
I want to sway with you,
I want to sway that way.
Tsoi Tsing of Indochina,
You cast a spell of romance.
Tsoi Tsing of Indochina
There's nothing like you in France.
Congai, Congai,
Congai, Congai,
Congai!

VERSE 1

MARIE: Home in your armchair
You read of hot countries,
But little do you realize how hot they
are.
VIC: What they are.
MARIE: Plants here grow bigger
And birds overrun trees,
And ev'rything in nature
Is exaggerated.
VIC: All the force of life
Is warmed by equatorial flame,
So if you're not quite yourself—
The climate is to blame.

REFRAIN 1

MARIE: These tropics,
They get you
And there is no cure.
These tropics
Won't let you
Escape from their lure.
Emotions are brewing,
I feel them bursting forth.
Down south here I'm doing
The things I dreamt of in the north!
These flowers
Are luscious,
These palm trees are grand.
These moonlights
Were made to enthrall.
The slightest insistence
Can break down my resistance.
Oh, these tropics
They get you,
That's all!

VERSE 2

VIC: I know the feeling,
When sunshine gets in you.
The energy absorbed from these
actinic rays
Lasts for days.
MARIE: In ev'ry tendon
And in ev'ry sinew
You feel your strength
And so at length
You yearn to use it.
VIC: Ev'ry noon you take siesta,
Resting all the day.
MARIE: So, of course, when night comes
'round
You're all pepped up to play.

REFRAIN 2

VIC: These tropics,
They get you,
And there is no cure.
These tropics
Won't let you
Escape from their lure.
You gaze at the coral,
You lie on burning sands.
The heat is immoral
And puts ideas into your glands.
Temptation
Was born here,
And boys will be boys.
And you can't
Be blamed if you fall.
Your brain and your muscles
Are slaves to red corpuscles.
In these tropics
They get you,
That's all!

ENCORE REFRAIN

LORRAINE: These tropics,
They've got me.
I'm under their spell.
They give me
A feeling
Of "Oh, what the hell!"
I've wasted enough time
In being circumspect.
I'm out for a rough time;
I'll take my chance of being wrecked.
They say that
The women
Die younger down here.
The men love
With ardor so hot,
Our lifetime diminish,
But what a way to finish!
Oh, these tropics!
They've got me.
Why not?

WEDDING SCENE

Not published. Introduced by Jules Epailly (Pierre
Fortier, Claudette's father), Charlotte Lansing (Claudette,
the bride), William Williams (Rene Beauvais, the groom),
J. Harold Murray (Paul Beauvais, the best man) and
assorted well-wishers. Tsoi Tsing (Rene's mistress) is present, but does not sing.

GIRLS: With a bride from
    Normandy,
    Normandy,
    Lucky is the bridegroom,
    Lucky is the bridegroom.

GIRLS AND MEN: Each of us would like to be,
    Like to be,
    Lucky as the bridegroom,
    Happy as the bride.

GIRLS: Ah—
    Come along,
    Now kiss the bride.

RENE AND ENSEMBLE: It's a wonderful world when
    you fall in love with it,
    It's a wonderful world.
    It's a wonderful life when
    you're hand in glove with
    it,
    It's a wonderful world!

RENE: When you hope and you
    dream
    And your dreams come
    true.
    And the dreams you love
    fall in love with you.

RENE AND ENSEMBLE: Then you're glad to be,
    proud to be
    Just allowed to be
    In this wonderful world!

PIERRE: My little daughter.
    What a beautiful bride, eh?
    [to CLAUDETTE] Are you
    happy?
    And tired too, eh?

CLAUDETTE: My friends—
ALL: Claudette.
CLAUDETTE: Good night.
ALL: Good night.
CLAUDETTE: Give all the girls some
    wedding cake
    To sleep upon this happy
    night.
PIERRE: My little angel.
PAUL: [to himself] She is an angel.
MEN: Good night, Rene, best of
    luck.
PAUL: [to RENE] And your brother,
    too
    Hopes your luck will keep
    up with you.
CLAUDETTE: [at stairs] Again.
ALL: Again.
CLAUDETTE: Good night.
ALL: Good night.
    We're going to keep this
    wedding cake
    To sleep upon, this happy
    night.

[PIERRE *motions for* CLAUDETTE *to give the best man a kiss.* TSOI TSING *approaches* RENE, *but he waves her away.*]

PIERRE: [*seeing* RENE's *worried look*]
    Look, he's jealous.
    The young husband is
    jealous—ha, ha.

[CLAUDETTE *throws the bouquet. The ensemble exits singing.*]

GIRLS: Sweet dreams,
    Claudette.
MEN: Claudette,
    Sweet dreams.
ALL: Good night, Claudette,
    Sweet dreams.

ARE YOU LOVE?

Published as an individual sheet. Introduced by Charlotte Lansing (Claudette Fortier) and William Williams (Rene Beauvais). As soon as this duet ends, Claudette steps back into her bedroom and Rene exits offstage toward Tsoi Tsing.

VERSE

CLAUDETTE: Have you come to me at last
    With your kiss to bind me fast?
    Have I left a lonely past behind me?
RENE: Are you romance,
    My one big chance?
BOTH: Are you romance come to find me?

REFRAIN

CLAUDETTE: Are you love?
    Are you the dream I've waited for?
    Are you my brave and shining knight
    With the right to take me?
RENE: Are you mine?
    Then I am yours forevermore.
    Ev'rything I do
    Will be done for you;
    You can make or break me.
CLAUDETTE: Are my arms
    The arms you want around you now?
    Then let them hold you here.
    While I have you near
    Heaven won't forsake me.
BOTH: Are you love?

    Then come and prove that you are
    mine alone.
    Take me now,
    Keep me for your own.

YOU ARE MY WOMAN

Published as an individual sheet. Introduced by J. Harold Murray (Paul). It is the wedding night, and Rene has temporarily abandoned his bride. When she calls for Rene, his brother, Paul, who secretly loves her, sings this response without showing himself.

REFRAIN

You are my woman.
You are beauty,
You are joy.
I am your lover,
No force can change me
Nor time destroy.
You are my mate,
But fate may alter her plan
And by some foolish blunder
We may be torn asunder.
Still you will be my woman,
I will be your man.

MINNIE, THERE'S NOTHING LIKE LOVE

Not published. Introduced by Joe Penner (Victor Cliquot).

VERSE

Minnie, you're only an elephant,
But elephants never forget.
So remember what I'm telling you:
Love is the world's best bet.
Someday you'll meet a he-elephant,
And you'll feel the hand of fate
Urging and compelling you
To run to your chosen mate.

REFRAIN

The birds will sing in the heavens blue
And your heart will be singing, too,
When your mate comes to call on you.

Minnie, there's nothing like love.
You'll flap your ears and wag your tail
And seek your big protecting male
And share with him your dinner pail.
Minnie, there's nothing like love.
He'll take you walking in the woods,
And life will seem so sweet.
To show his strength, he'll root up trees
And lay them at your feet.
Then one spring night 'neath a moonlit sky,
When your blood pressure's way up high
You'll see a light come in his eye*
Minnie . . .

[*Elephant trumpet sound.*]

. . . You said it!

EMBRACE ME and ACT ONE FINALE

Alternate title: "Your Two Soft Arms Embrace Me." Not published. Introduced by William Williams (Rene), native girls, gamblers, and a fortune teller. The refrain appeared in the first edition of Hammerstein's anthology, *Lyrics.*

VERSE

RENE: The long river sings in a
    droning sigh.
GIRLS: Lie here, lie and eat the
    lotus.
RENE: And white herons soar in
    the moonlit sky.
GIRL: Lie here, lie and eat the
    lotus.
RENE: I come to steal night,
    Our brief, unreal night.

REFRAIN

RENE: Your two soft arms
    embrace me,
    And you are mine to hold.
    The moon is on the river,
    And yellow sails are gold.
    Our lives like clouds are
    flying,

---

* *Some versions say:*
   You'll see a strange look in his eye

    And men with hopes are
    dying,
    But two soft arms embrace
    me,
    And you are mine to hold.
    The moon is on the river,
    And yellow sails are gold.
FOUR GIRLS OFFSTAGE: Far across the water glows
    the lantern of a sampan.
    May my voice be borne on
    gentle breezes to that
    sampan.
    For there sleeps a dreaming
    boy.
    On his boat he's dreaming
    And his brow is pale as
    snow beneath the
    starlight's gleaming.
    May my voice be borne on
    gentle breezes to that
    sampan.
    Would my heart the
    breezes bore as well.
FORTUNE TELLER: Long green leaves of
    willow,
    Sunflower seeds I brew.
    May my seven-flavored cup
    Bring luck to you.
    Green jade of China
    Bring us good fortune.
    If we have tears of sorrow
    Melt them away tomorrow
    Like slender raindrops
    That die in sunshine.
    If we have tears of sorrow
    Melt them away.

[MARIE *and* CLAUDETTE *arrive with* PAUL, *in search of* VICTOR. PAUL *sets soldiers to emptying the small boats that are used for gambling, drugs, and sex.* CLAUDETTE's *father and a native woman emerge from one of the flower boats.* RENE *and* TSOI TSING *enter in each other's arms. Bitterly disappointed,* CLAUDETTE *reprises the "Wonderful World" and "Are You Love" motifs last heard during the wedding.*]

CLAUDETTE: When you hope and you
    dream
    And your dreams come
    true,
    And the dreams you love
    Fall in love with you.
    Then you're glad to be,
    Proud to be,
    Just allowed to be
    In this wonderful . . .

PAUL: [*spoken*] Claudette, I don't
    know if I could make
    you any happier, but I'd
    like to try.
CLAUDETTE: [*looking at* RENE] Are you
    love?
    Are you the dream I've
    waited for?
    Are you my brave and
    shining knight
    With the right to take me?
PAUL: [*to* CLAUDETTE] Are you
    mine?
    Then I am yours forever-
    more.
    Everything I do will be
    done for you.
    You can make or break me.
CLAUDETTE: [*moving toward* RENE *as she sings*] Are my arms the
    arms you want around
    you now?
TSOI TSING: [*defiantly*] He has my arms.
CLAUDETTE: [*spoken*] Rene, if you want
    to smoke opium, if you
    want to live on the
    waterfront with a
    woman, do it! But I'll be
    the woman! Not you,
    Miss Congai. Me.
    [*singing a last appeal to* RENE] Are you love?
    Then come and prove that
    you are mine alone.
    Take me now, keep me for
    your own.

[RENE *staggers to* CLAUDETTE, *and they exit together.*]

PAUL AND ENSEMBLE: Make me
    Beggar or king
    East wind
    I wait for you.
    Out of the east
    Bring me my love.

THE AMERICANS ARE COMING

Not published. Introduced by Vera Marsh (Marie) and girls. This number is part of the floor show in a Parisian café.

VERSE 1

MARIE: The boats are steaming out of
New York harbor,
The tugs are giving them their
final shove.
And every boat is laden down
with suckers,
All bound to see the Paris that
they love.
So learn to speak your English
weez an accent
And geev zem everysing zat zey
expect.
And gigolos brush up on that old
tango
And see that every wealthy dame
is wrecked.

REFRAIN 1

MARIE: The Americans are coming!
Take them for a buggy ride.
The Americans are coming!
And they must be satisfied!
Turn those Yankee dollars
Into the francs of France.
Empty all their pockets
And kick them in the ponts.

INTERLUDE

GIRLS: La la la—
La la la—
La la la la la la la.
MARIE: Show 'em life,
Show 'em art,
And the tomb of Bonaparte.
Sell 'em shoes,
Sell 'em hats,
Sell 'em ermine made from cats.
GIRLS: La la la—
La la la—
La la la la la la la.

VERSE 2

MARIE: Come gather up your chiffon and
your satin
And sew it up in sizes large and
small.
And when you give them dresses
they look fat in
Just smile and say, "Madame look
very small."
Surround each one and rave about
her beauty
And shower her with
compliments galore.

And when she's bought the
dresses that she's wanted,
Then talk her into buying twenty
more.

INTERLUDE

GIRLS: La la la—
La la la—
La la la la la la la.
Oui, Madame,
Step zees vay,
You are jus' in time today.
LADY: I want to buy some dresses.

VERSE 3

MARIE: [spoken over first two lines of verse]
Collette. Mimi. Adrienne. Yvonne.
ALL SHOPGIRLS: Oh! Madame! Quelle forme. Quelle
figure!
MARIE: [sung] We sink you'll find zis little
sing amusing,
And if you don't perhaps your
husband might.
We do not like zat perfume you
are using,
Here's one we make ourselves,
"La Wedding Night."
Put this on, Madame.

INTERLUDE

GIRLS: La la la—
La la la—
La la la la la la la.
La la la—
La la la—
La la la la la la la.

VERSE 4

MARIE: [spoken] Ah, Madame! But Madame
must have a leetle dress. Queek
queek, Celeste—something
very special. Madame, a leetle
dress we call "Romance"—Do
you like it?
PEARL: Will I look like that?
MARIE: Oui—certainment.
GIRLS: Certainment.
PEARL: Then I'll take it.
MARIE: She takes the dress—hurrah!

REFRAIN 2

MARIE: The Americans are coming,
Take them for a buggy ride.

We have made you what you are
today,
We hope you're satisfied.
LADY: Do you think it fits me?
MARIE: It fits you like a tent.
Will you take it with you,
Or will you have it sent?
Ten francs for the flowers,
A thousand for the stem.
Tell your friends to come here
And we'll do the same to them.

INTERLUDE

GIRLS: Trés jolie—
Trés jolie—
You are chic as you can be.
Oo la la—
Oo la la—
You will fascinate Papa.
Quelle figure!
Et quelle forme!
Oo la la la la la la.
MARIE: Many sanks,
Many sanks,
For your fifty sousand francs.

REFRAIN 3

ALL: The Americans are coming!
Take them for a buggy ride.
The Americans are coming!
And they must be satisfied!
MARIE: They bring money with 'em,
We always get it all.
We Gauls have not got rhythm
But, boy, have we got gall!

I'D BE A FOOL

Published as an individual sheet. Introduced by Charlotte Lansing (Claudette), who supports herself and
Rene by singing in a café.

VERSE

Don't tell me I'm crazy;
I know, I know.
My ideas are hazy;
I know, I know.
My heart has always ruled my brain—
I've been romantic.
Am I glad or sorry I've been romantic?
I only know—

REFRAIN

I'd be a fool to fall in love again,
A fool to even think of love again.
Though the start is bright as a May day,
And your heart is right in its heyday,
At the end that heart is dull with pain.
If love should ever sing to me again
I would know the raven dressed up as a dove.
And if it tried to woo me
Then I know just what would happen to me.
I'd be a fool again—
A fool—
I'd fall in love!

FINALETTO, ACT TWO, SCENE 1: I'M DRUNK AND I'M GLAD and YOU ARE MY WOMAN (REPRISE)

Not published. Introduced by Greek Evans (M. Granier, Claudette's former teacher), men who have been out on the town, and J. Harold Murray (Paul). Paul has asked Claudette to return to Saigon with him. Granier encourages the match.

GRANIER AND MEN: I'm drunk and I am glad.
What's the use of being sad?
What's the use of being sad
When a drink can make you glad.
Fill 'em up again,
Fill 'em up again!
GRANIER: We live and love and learn a little
Following the way of youth.
We play with fire and burn a little
Then at last we learn one truth:
PAUL: Man only lives* for one love
And you are my one love.
This I know and this I feel,
This one thing is real.

REFRAIN

PAUL: You are my woman,
You are beauty,

*Alternate wording in some versions:
   Men only live for one love

You are joy.
I am your lover,
No force can change me
Nor time destroy.
You are my mate,
But fate may alter her plan
And by some foolish blunder
We may be torn asunder.
Still you will be my woman,
I will be your man.

REGARDEZ-MOI

Alternate title: "Song of the Comedians." Not published. Introduced by Lorraine and Leatrice Pearl (The McNulty Sisters), who are performers on a bill that includes Tsoi Tsing's fatal "Indochina Ballet."

Regardez, regardez!
Qu'est-ce que c'est, ma mère?
S'il vous plait, si tu sais,
Dites-moi
Qu'est-ce que c'est, ma mère?

Est-ce qu'elle une femme
On est-ce qu'il un monsieur?
O maman, o maman,
Dites-moi,
Qu'est-ce que c'est, ma mère?

WHEN YOU ARE YOUNG

Published as an individual sheet. Introduced by Greek Evans (M. Granier) and J. Harold Murray (Paul).

VERSE

GRANIER: Tender longings all remind you
Of a joy you've left behind you.
She won't come again to find you,
You must seek her now.
PAUL: Fortune gives no second chances
To the men who've spurned romances.
GRANIER: There's a prize you still can win.
You must seek her now.
PAUL: How and where could I begin?
GRANIER: There's a prize you still can win.
You must seek her now.

REFRAIN

GRANIER: Love while your heart is young.
Youth's a song, and it must be sung.
In your springtime years life will open all her doors,
The world is yours.
Dream while your heart is young.
Hang your hopes on the highest rung.
Go and fight for love—win the girl that you adore.
That's what you are living for
When you are young.

ACT TWO, SCENE 5 OPENING

Not published. Introduced by the ensemble, Charlotte Lansing (Claudette), Joe Penner (Vic), and Vera Marsh (Marie). Some time has passed. Tsoi Tsing and Rene are dead. Paul, although blind, has been searching for his lost love. Lorraine runs a seedy wine cellar in Marseille, where Claudette works as a waitress when she is sober. She has aged terribly. As the curtain rises, an impromptu sextet is singing earnestly.

SIX DRUNKEN SAILORS: Happy Christmas,
Christmas is a happy time
Ev'rybody loves his neighbor,
Ev'rybody should.
Happy Christmas,
Happy songs in jolly rhyme.
Is it any wonder ev'rybody feels so good?
Snow is on the windowpanes
And winds are blowing
But the fire is cozy
And the bowl is flowing.
Happy Christmas
Christmas is . . .
CLAUDETTE: [oblivious] I'd be a fool to fall in love again.
A fool to even think of love again.
Though the start is bright as a May day
And your heart . . .
I wouldn't know the raven dressed up as a dove.

I know just what would
   happen.
I'd be a fool again.
A fool.
I'd fall in love.

VIC AND MARIE: [*entering*] I'm drunk and
   I'm glad.
What's the use of being sad?
What's the use of being sad,
When a drink can make
   you glad.

FINALE

Not published. Introduced by the company.

PAUL: You are my woman.
You are beauty,
You are joy.
I am your lover.
No force can change me.

GRANIER: Take a look around you,
Look around and see.
Sheep are in the meadow,
Birds are in the tree.
Cows are in the clover,
Just where they belong.
So the world can't be all
   wrong.

GRANIER AND MEN: Morning sees the sun rise.
Evening sees it set.
These are things that never
Failed to happen yet.
We are here together,
Just where we belong.
So the world can't be all
   wrong.

CLAUDETTE, GRANIER,
   AND ENSEMBLE: It's a wonderful world when
   you fall in love with it.
It's a wonderful world.
It's a wonderful life when
   you're hand in glove with it.
It's a wonderful world.
When you hope and you
   dream
And your dreams come true,
And the dreams you love fall
   in love with you—

PAUL: You'll always be my woman.
I will be your man.

[*Entire company reprises "It's a Wonderful World."*]

CUT AND UNUSED SONGS

A MAN OF MY TYPE

Alternate title: "Don't Trust a Man of My Type." Not published, but the refrain appears in Hammerstein's anthology, *Lyrics*. Introduced by J. Harold Murray (Paul), men, and girls.

In early and transitional drafts, this song opens Act One, Scene 3. But it is not listed in the New York program.

VERSE

PAUL: Men in the Army are a bad lot,
We're a bad lot in the Army.
If you're a mother with a
   daughter,
Keep your daughter from the
   Army.
Keep her from captains,
Keep her from majors,
Colonels, and generals.
They're all the same,
All the same.

MEN: Captains and majors too.
They're all the same
If your heart is warm, lady,
Go for a uniform, lady.
We'll take your love by storm,
   lady,
If your heart is warm.

PAUL: If you want madness in the
   moonlight,
In the moonlight we'll find
   madness.
But if you ask me
If I'll be always true—

MEN: You will be always true.

PAUL: Then I will not make any vows,
   my dear,
But I'll be frank with you.

REFRAIN

PAUL: Don't trust a man of my type.
A man like me can mean no good
   to a girl.
A gay deceiver, a butterfly type
Without a good redeeming trait.
Don't trust a man of my type
Or you will soon regret your fate.

Each pretty face I see suggests a
   story in it.
I am weak, and I glory in it.
Now I've warned you,
How about a date?

INTERLUDE

GIRLS: No girl wants a man who is too
   good.
Bad men are the kind who can do
   good.
Give us libertines or give us
   death!
I've always found that
Loving a man who's harmless
Isn't any fun!

MEN AND GIRLS: You want to be wooed and won,
So if they're rude, don't run.

PAUL: If prim and pure you'd be,
Then keep away from me.

REFRAIN

PAUL AND MEN: Don't trust a man of my type.
A man like me can mean no good
   to a girl.
A gay deceiver, a butterfly type
Without a good redeeming trait.
Don't trust a man of my type.
Or you will soon regret your fate.

GIRLS: [*countermelody*] Out of our way,
   we hate big sissies.
Men of today are great big
   sissies.
Give us libertines or give us
   death.
Your warning has not frightened
   us unduly,
When do you begin to get
   unruly?
Truly we would like to know:
How bad are you?
We want to know.

PAUL: In terms of maidens' broken
   hearts
I measure loving.
I'm licentious, wild, and
   pleasure-loving.
Now I've warned you,
How about a date?

GIRLS: We want a date.

MEN: Would you like to make a date?

YOUNG MAN IN LOVE

Published as an individual sheet, but replaced by "Are You Love?" before the New York opening. Introduced by Charlotte Lansing (Claudette Fortier), William Williams (Rene Beauvais), and J. Harold Murray (Paul Beauvais).

VERSE

CLAUDETTE: When my young man and I
Gaze at an evening sky—
CLAUDETTE AND RENE: Then my young man [girl]
and I
Long for romance.
CLAUDETTE: When nights like this come
'round,
With me he will be found.
BOTH: When nights like this come
'round
Then comes our chance.

REFRAIN

CLAUDETTE: Young man in love,
There's moonlight above
And your best girl wants to
see you.
Spring's in the air,
With kisses to spare,
And your best girl wants to
see you.
Saturn and Mars,
The planets and stars,
Will look down and all
wish they could be you.
BOTH: Young man in love,
You have heaven above,
And a girl all your own.

[RENE *exits. When* CLAUDETTE *repeats the refrain,*
PAUL *sings the duet part.*]

NOT "THE VOLGA BOATMAN"

Not published. Not used. This cabaret entertainment from Act Two, Scene 1, was replaced by "The Americans Are Coming."

VERSE

BARITONE: There's a dark-eyed maiden
by a frozen river
Waiting for the spring to
turn the white to blue.
FOUR GIRLS: There's a dark-eyed maiden
by a frozen river
Waiting for the spring to
turn the white to blue.
SOLO GIRL: When the naked trees are
green,
When the mountain crest is
seen,
When the streams are high
with rain,
Love drifts back to her
again.
FOUR GIRLS AND MAN: When the streams are high
with rain,
Love drifts back to her
again.
MAN: We may sing of Russian
rivers—
GIRLS: But although we do—
MAN: There is one song we shall
not sing.
FOUR GIRLS: This we promise you.

REFRAIN

GIRLS: We're not going to sing
"The Volga Boatman,"
"Volga Boatman."
Tra-la-la,
Tra-la-la.
We're not going to sing
"The Volga Boatman."
You can shoot us if we do.
ONE GIRL: We're not going to bend like
this—

[*They bend.*]

Jerk our backs and groan
like this—

[*They jerk.*]

ALL: Ugh!
GIRL: We're not going to sing that
song,
That has bothered you so
long.
FOUR GIRLS AND MAN: We're not going to sing
"The Volga Boatman,"
"Volga Boatman."
Tra-la-la,
Tra-la-la.
We're not going to sing
"The Volga Boatman,"
You can shoot us if we do.
Hi!

VOULEZ-VOUS

Not published. Not used. A Romberg leadsheet at the Library of Congress with lyrics in Hammerstein's hand is marked "Opening Act Two, Scene 1. Marie and Stage Band."

MARIE: Voulez-vous?
That's what they say in France.
Voulez-vous?
That's all they know.
Voulez-vous—
If once you visit France
You're sure to learn before you go:
GUESTS: Voulez-vous?
MARIE: You mad Americans.
GUESTS: Voulez-vous?
MARIE: And English too.
You're very bold to ask me if I will.
But if I say I will,
Then voulez-vous?

BEARDED STRANGER

Not published. Not used. This lyric for Marie and dancing girls was found in the *East Wind* piano-conductor score at Tams-Witmark. The marking "No. 13" puts it in the same slot occupied by "The Americans Are Coming" and other sketches.

VERSE

MARIE: When I started out for la belle Paree,
My dear old mother said to me:
There are [*illegible*—snares?] and pitfalls
in the street
And you must be careful whom you meet.
You're an age just right for a certain type
Who'll feed you champagne with your
tripe.
When you're walking along the Champs
Élysées,
Have a care when they look your way.

REFRAIN

MARIE: Keep away from
Ev'ry bearded stranger.
Ev'ry bearded stranger brings you danger.
With his curly whiskers he is handsome;
He is debonair, bohemian, and some.
But his only object is to land some
Pretty little girl and make her his.
When he's making love to you, ma cherie,
Tu es ravissante.

GIRLS: Cherie, tu es ravissante.

MARIE: It's time to get away.

GIRLS: But if you [*illegible*] to love that bearded
stranger—

MARIE: There is only one way out of danger.
You must try to marry that there stranger.

GIRLS: Then of course the stranger won't be
strange.

TU COMPRENDS L'AMOUR

Not published. Not used. The Romberg holograph piano-vocal score in the Music Division of the Library of Congress includes this fragment to be performed table-side (by a Russian character and strolling musicians), while Marie explains to Papa Gouli why she and Claudette work in the café.

Quand je dit "je t'aime,"
Tu me comprends.
Car ce n'est que l'amour
Que tu comprends.
Mais, ma mad'moiselle
Tu es jeune et belle
Tu ne doit pas rien connaître
Quand je connais vos levres.
Tu comprends l'amour.

Hammerstein and Jerome Kern wrote and directed
Music in the Air.

MUSIC IN THE AIR | 1932

MUSIC IN THE AIR (1932)

Tryout: Garrick Theatre, Philadelphia, October 17–November 5, 1932. New York run: Alvin Theatre, opened November 8, 1932; closed March 13, 1933; reopened at the Forty-fourth Street Theatre, March 31, 1933; closed September 16, 1933; total 342 performances. A Musical Adventure in Two Acts. Presented by Peggy Frears (and A. C. Blumenthal). Music by Jerome Kern. Book and lyrics by Oscar Hammerstein II. Staged by Oscar Hammerstein II and Jerome Kern. Orchestrations by Robert Russell Bennett. Orchestra conducted by Victor Baravalle. Scenery by Joseph Urban. Costumes designed by John W. Harkrider.

Cast: Al Shean (Dr. Walther Lessing, the music teacher), Walter Slezak (Karl Reder, the schoolmaster), Katherine Carrington (Sieglinde Lessing, Walther's daughter), Tullio Carminati (Bruno Mahler, the playwright), Natalie Hall (Frieda Hatzfeld, the star), Nicholas Joy (Ernst Weber, the music publisher), Harry Mestayer (Uppmann, the orchestra leader), Dorothy Johnson (Marthe, secretary to Ernst), Reinald Werrenrath (Cornelius, a bird breeder), Gabrielle Guelpli (Mrs. Pflugfelder), Robert Williamson (Pfugfelder, the hotel proprietor), Mary McQuade (Tila), Marty Semon (Burgomaster), Robert Rhodes (Town Crier), Clifford Heckinger (Heinrich), Paul Donah (Father Joch), George Bell (Apothecary), Lydia Van Gilder (Frau Schreimann), Charles Belin (Herman), Edward Hayes (Hans, the goatherd), Mlle. Desha (Hulde), Carrie Weller (Stout Mother), Carl Edem (Stout Father), George Dieter (Their Son), George Ludwig (Waiter), Alfred Russ (Zoo Attendant), Laura (The Bear), H. Pallenberg (Bear Trainer), Alexis Obolensky (Herr Direktor Kirschner), Ivy Scott (Frau Direktor Kirschner), Kathleen Edwards (Sophie), Frank Dobert (Assistant Stage Manager), Marjorie Main (Anna), Carl Spiegel (Baum), William Torpey (Gusterl), Georg Gerhardi (Tobacconist), Paul Janvert (Doctor), Claire Cole (Frau Lena Baum), and ensemble.

Among the villagers in rustic Edendorf, Germany, are music teacher Dr. Walther Lessing and his daughter Sieglinde. Lessing has written a song with the handsome young schoolmaster Karl Reder, and decides to bring it to his old friend Ernst Weber, a music publisher in Munich. Karl must come along, since he is the lyricist. And Sieglinde will see the city for the first time. When the three reach Weber's office, they find librettist Bruno Mahler acting out scenes from his operetta-in-progress. Also in the office are Frieda Hatzfeld, a prima donna who is sometimes Bruno's lover; Uppmann, the orchestra leader; and Marthe, Weber's secretary. Bruno and Frieda take an almost predatory interest in the young newcomers, and spend the next few days showing them the city's delights and making each other jealous. When

Frieda storms off, Bruno decides to cast Sieglinde as leading lady. She has a nice face and a nice voice, but her lack of experience threatens the entire production. In the nick of time Frieda returns and makes up with Bruno. Sieglinde and Karl take a little longer to reconcile, but the entire village insists on a happy ending.

A London production opened at His Majesty's Theatre, May 19, 1933 (275 performances). Starring Eve Lister (Sieglinde), Bruce Carfax (Karl), Mary Ellis (Frieda), Arthur Margetson (Bruno), and Horace Hodges (Walther). Directed by Hammerstein and Kern.

Music in the Air was filmed by Fox in 1934, directed by Joe May and starring Gloria Swanson (Frieda), John Boles (Bruno), June Lang (Sieglinde), Betty Hiestand (singing voice of Sieglinde), Douglass Montgomery (Karl), James O'Brien (singing voice of Karl), and Al Shean (Walther). The screenplay was written by Howard I. Young and Billy Wilder.

Rodgers and Hammerstein produced a Broadway revival which opened at the Ziegfeld Theatre on October 8, 1951, and closed on November 24, 1951. It starred Jane Pickens (Frieda), Dennis King (Bruno), Lillian Murphy (Sieglinde), Mitchell Gregg (Karl), and Charles Winninger (Walther). Conrad Nagel played Ernst Weber, the music publisher, and Julie Kelety, who had performed in Hammerstein's first professional musical, *Always You* (1920), had a minor role.

AEI's *Music in the Air* CD features a 1952 radio production, along with three bonus tracks from the 1933 London production. Sepia's *Music in the Air* features Jane Pickens, from the 1951 revival cast.

The main source for this chapter is the 1933 published vocal score. Some piano-vocal material is in the Jerome Kern Collection in the Music Division of the Library of Congress. There are typed lyrics and scripts at the Rodgers & Hammerstein Organization. No preliminary drafts of the script were located.

There is a confusing array of names for the dramatic and musical elements of *Music in the Air*. The published vocal score provides two sets. Its "Synopsis of Scenes" gives each scene a musical name, thus Act Two, Scene 1, at the zoo is dubbed "Sonata"; Act Two, Scene 2, in Frieda's hotel suite is "Nocturne"; etc. The vocal score's table of contents has a more detailed list of musical numbers, but does not specifically identify each song's verse and refrain. About half of the entries in the table of contents are not singing moments.

Some songs are introduced as fragments and not heard in full until later in the story. There are a number of fragmentary reprises in addition to the full-length reprises. For ease of reading, this chapter contains one full version of each song and omits the fragments and reprises.

In a newspaper article shortly before the 1951 revival, Hammerstein explained why the show was his "very special darling":

I had the beginning of a story, the general background being a music publisher's office. I talked

it over with Jerome Kern. With his customary shrewdness he suggested that I move the publisher from the blare of New York's Tin Pan Alley to the more mellow and romantic atmosphere of Europe (it was more mellow and romantic then, anyway). A few weeks later and for a year thereafter I found myself involved with a group of people I loved very dearly. My story dealt with the convergence of two contrasting groups of characters—a father and a daughter, and the daughter's young man, who came down from the mountains and suddenly found themselves caught up and whirled through a cyclonic month of adventures with some passionate and irrational people of the theatre. I sympathized with the mountain people, and understood the theatre people very well, and they combined to provide sweet refuge for me after my two recent failures and my unfortunate excursion to Hollywood. There they were, waiting for me in my study every morning, and joyfully I went to meet them, composing their dialogue and lyrics with loving care, and describing their behavior with stage directions that were unsparing in detail. They got Jerry too, and together we chortled and cooed over our handiwork with a kind of sentimentality that frequently jeopardizes the success of a venture.

We did, however, manage to maintain a kind of balance. We knew very well that we were not writing a powerful drama, nor a luscious operetta, nor a swiftly paced musical comedy. We knew that the plot was neither sturdy nor original, and that it would depend almost entirely on the affectionate details with which we were lavishly endowing it. We were finding new ways to use music in the telling of the story of *Music in the Air*. Jerry was weaving music through nearly all the scenes, and in some instances I was writing rhythmic dialogue to be recited to the music rather than sung. When we actually came to spots for songs, we asked for no operatic license for their introduction. All the songs were to be introduced as alleged folk songs or refrains from a play that one of the characters was writing. We decided to make no bid for encores, and indeed no singer was to be permitted to direct his efforts toward the audience for this purpose. They were to sing to each other, and attention was never to be concentrated exclusively on the performance of a song. In mapping out the staging of the musical numbers we conceived distractions on the part of the other characters, so that life would not seem to stop every time the orchestra stuck up a refrain, and a singer would sing it. These defiances of conventional musical comedy direction tickled us, and we became so protective of our conceptions that we decided to stage the play ourselves.

For a man who needed a hit as badly as I did at

the time, these were reckless goings-on. But I was having too good a time to be deterred by the nudgings of theatrical prudence. *Music in the Air* opened at the Alvin Theatre, New York, November 8, 1932, and became an immediate success.

MELODIES OF MAY

Music by Beethoven (Op. 2., No. 3); choral arrangement by Jerome Kern. Introduced by Katherine Carrington (Sieglinde) and ensemble (Edendorf Choral Society), this anthem segues immediately into "I've Told Ev'ry Little Star."

SINGERS: Melodies of May,
Melodies of May
And sunbeams in the blue
Light up the road to you.
Melodies of May
Cheer me on my way.
Here I come,
Here I come,
I'm on my way.
SIEGLINDE: My love, I come to you.
SINGERS: To play the songs of May,
Cheer me on my way.
TENORS: I walk through fields of daisies,
I walk through forest mazes,
I walk on air to meet you.
I'll soon be there to greet you.
With springtime whispers
mingling
To set our pulses tingling.
BASSES: A thousand whispers mingling
To set our pulses tingling.
Hear! The crickets in the rushes.
Hear! The meadowlarks and
thrushes.
Hear! A breeze in cedars calling—
Hear! To flaky blossoms falling.
Oh, how I long to say it,
Why do I never say it?
WOMEN: Springtime whispers
Bid me tell you.
SINGERS: Though I have told the flowers
What keeps my heart aflutter.
I sit with you for hours
And I can only stutter.
With my heart aflutter
I can only stutter.
I know I'll never tell you,
I can never tell you, dear.

SOME WOMEN: [*in rhythmic contrast to the group*]
But I never, never tell you
Cannot tell you.

I'VE TOLD EV'RY LITTLE STAR

Published as an individual sheet, and the refrain appears in Hammerstein's anthology, *Lyrics*. Introduced by Walter Slezak (Karl), Katherine Carrington (Sieglinde), and the ensemble (Edendorf Choral Society). A 1933 rendition by Mary Ellis (who played Frieda) can be heard on the CDs *Oscar Hammerstein, The Legacy: The Operettas* (Pearl) and *The Song Is . . . Jerome Kern* (ASV). It reached a new audience in the spring of 1961 when Linda Scott's recording climbed to number 3 on Billboard's Hot 100 chart.

In the play, Walther Lessing has composed a song based on a bird's melody. Karl, the schoolmaster, has added some words, and they hope it can be published in Munich. The number also functions as a typically indirect Act One love theme for Sieglinde and Karl.

Evidently Kern was himself inspired by a bird's trill (accounts vary whether this happened in Bronxville or Nantucket). Hammerstein recalled: " 'I've Told Ev'ry Little Star' proved to be a stubborn tune, and for a while that summer, resisted my efforts to set words to it. There were times during those hot August days when I wished the finch had kept his big mouth shut."

VERSE

I make up things to say
On my way to you.
On my way to you
I find things to say.
I can write poems too
When you're far away.
When you're far away
I write poems too.
But when you are near
My throat goes dry.*
When you are near,
I only sigh—
Oh dear.

REFRAIN

I've told ev'ry little star
Just how sweet I think you are.

_____

* *The published sheet says:*
My lips go dry.

Why haven't I told you?
I've told ripples in a brook,
Made my heart an open book.
Why haven't I told you?
Friends ask me, am I in love?
I always answer "Yes."
Might as well confess.
If I don't they guess.
Maybe you may know it too—
Oh, my darling, if you do,
Why haven't you told me?

PRAYER

Published in the vocal score. Introduced by Walter Slezak (Karl), Katherine Carrington (Sieglinde), and ensemble (Edendorf Walking Club).

Our journey may be long,
Thy strength will keep us strong.
And in the dark of night,
If one stray heart should roam,
Hold up thy shining light
And guide us safely home.
Amen.

THERE'S A HILL BEYOND A HILL

Alternate title: "Edendorf Walking Club Song." Published as an individual sheet and included in Hammerstein's anthology, *Lyrics*. Introduced by the ensemble (Edendorf Walking Club).

VERSE

The world can be a wonderful world
When the thrill of adventure comes.
If you don't like that kind of thing,
Stay home and twiddle your thumbs.
A day can be a wonderful day
When you're out on the open road.
There is no road too long to walk,
If you can sing to pass the time.
There is no road too long to walk,
No mountain peak too high to climb!
To climb the highest mountain,
To ford the deepest river,
Will make you feel the zest of life.

Come on and get the best of life,
Come on, the best of life is further on—

REFRAIN

There's a hill beyond a hill,
Beyond a hill, beyond a hill.
If your limbs are young and strong,
You must follow along.
There's a dream beyond a dream,
Beyond a dream, beyond a dream.
If your heart is young and gay,
Follow along our way.
There's a hill beyond a hill,
Beyond a hill, beyond a hill.
If your limbs are young and strong,
Follow along, follow along.
There's a dream beyond a dream,
Beyond a dream, beyond a dream.
If your heart is light and gay,
Follow along our way.
If you are young and strong,
Put your pack on your back
And come walking along.

INTERLUDE

Hurry, ev'ryone,
We want to catch up to the sun.
The sun won't wait, so hurry on!
Mountain climbers all
Obey the mountain climber's call.
The sun won't wait, so hurry on!
Hold your heads up high
And let the world go skimming by,
The sun won't wait, so hurry on!
The restful glades may be enthralling you
And though the clear, cool streams are calling you,
Forget them all,
Forget them all and hurry on!
There's time enough to bathe in streams
Tomorrow is another day.
The more we walk, the more it seems
The sun is brighter far away,
Beyond, on, on, on.

REPEAT REFRAIN [LINES 1–8]
REPEAT VERSE [LINES 1–8]

AT STONY BROOK, including WHEN YOU'RE YOUNG and AND LOVE WAS BORN

Published in the vocal score. Introduced by Katherine Carrington (Sieglinde) Walter Slezak (Karl), and Reinald Werrenrath (Cornelius). The dialogue in this scene is metrically accompanied by the music. Stage directions paint Cornelius as "a man who will walk along a mountain path just like this, singing just like this, through eternity . . . On discovering Karl and Sieglinde, he favors them with the most friendly of smiles and continues singing happily as if he knows some cryptic solution for all the world's ills, but prefers to keep it a secret just a while longer."

Lawrence Tibbett's 1932 rendition of "And Love Was Born" can be heard on the CD *Oscar Hammerstein, The Legacy: The Operettas* (Pearl).

SIEGLINDE: Did you find them pretty?
KARL: I don't understand.
SIEGLINDE: The actresses in Munich.
Were they very grand?
KARL: Well-ll, I wouldn't say that they were
so grand.
SIEGLINDE: So?—But attractive—
KARL: Yes, they're attractive—
[*catching her look*] Not *so* attractive.
SIEGLINDE: No?
KARL: [*boldly*] Not like Sieglinde!
SIEGLINDE: [*surprised*] Oh!
KARL: Not one Sieglinde there!
SIEGLINDE: Karl, when you wrote that poem
to my father's song,
Did it take you long?
KARL: When I wrote it I was inspired
By something beautiful that I
desired.

[*Both become bashful and silent.*]

When You're Young

CORNELIUS: [*offstage*] When you're young,
When you're young,
Life's a song that must be sung.
When you're old,
Life's a story to be told,
When you're old.

[*Spoken in counter meter to* CORNELIUS' *waltz theme.*]

SIEGLINDE: It's Cornelius with birds in a cage.
KARL: He breeds them, I guess.
Then he sells them in Munich.
SIEGLINDE: They look like nightingales.
KARL: I'm taking a bird from the mountains
to Munich, too.
But she is not for sale.
SIEGLINDE: Why, Karl—
KARL: I'm glad we stayed behind the rest,
It's good to be alone with you.
The sun is lower in the west.
We're all alone, just we two . . .
Look out, he's just around the bend.
I'll put on my other shoe.

And Love Was Born

Published as an individual sheet and included in Hammerstein's anthology, *Lyrics*.

CORNELIUS: A warm spring night was stirred by a
breeze,
And love was born.
A moon in flight was caught in the
trees,
And love was born.
A lark sang out,
And through the mist
There came a sigh upon a sigh,
And two young lips were gently
kissed,
And two young hearts learned to
fly . . .
A shepherd boy awoke from a doze
And blew his horn.
The sun came up and smiled on a
rose
And love was born.
Tra la la la.

EXCERPTS FROM *TINGLE-TANGLE*, including LETTER SONG and I'M ALONE, and I AM SO EAGER

In the office of music publisher Ernst Weber, librettist Bruno Mahler and leading lady Frieda Hatzfeld narrate and perform scenes from Bruno's new operetta. Uppmann (the orchestra leader) accompanies them on the piano. The audience consists of Ernst, Walther Lessing, Sieglinde, Karl and Marthe (Ernst's secretary).

There is cross-talk throughout,* with Frieda particularly playing up to Karl, and Bruno playing to Sieglinde.

Letter Song

Published in the vocal score. Introduced by Tullio Carminati (Bruno Mahler). The song is for the leading man, Emil, a French soldier whose regiment will soon pass through the town where his girl lives.

BRUNO: [as EMIL, and as narrator] "Give me
    some paper
    And lend me a pen."
    A fellow says:
    "Paper right here."
    Another fellow says:
    "Here is your pen."
    Thank you.
    "I have a letter
    I must write today."
    And they say:
    "Bet it is a girl."
    "It is a girl.
    It's not a secret.
    Furthermore, you may
    Hear what I'm going to say."
    He sits down to write.
    The men surround him,
    And look over his shoulder.
    "I'm coming home to get a look,
    I'm coming home to get a smile,
    I'm coming home . . .
WALTHER: [talking over the music] What's the name
    of this song?
ERNST: "I'm Coming Home"!
BRUNO: [continuing as EMIL] . . . to get a kiss
    From you.
    I'm coming home to hear a word,
    A word that I have often heard,
    An old sound that will now sound new.
    Through rain and sun we're walking on,
    When day is done we're walking on.
    But I am one who's walking on the air.
    Because I know I'm coming home.
    I'm coming home, I'm coming home
    Because I know my little girl is there."
    And then the curtain comes down
    At the end of this scene.

* Not all of the spoken lines are reproduced here.

I'm Alone

Alternate title: Arietta. Published as an individual sheet. Introduced by Natalie Hall (Frieda Hatzfeld, playing the role of Emil's girl Marie) and Tullio Carminati (Bruno, playing the role of Emil).

MARIE: I'm alone,
    And the night is all my own—
    To dream of love,
    To love my dreams,
    To lose them all in shadows.
    I'm alone, wondering where
        you may be.
    And wishing, dear, that you
        were here,
    To be alone with me.
EMIL: I'm coming home to get a
        look,
    I'm coming home to get a
        smile,
    I'm coming home to get a
        kiss.
FRIEDA: [narrating] She turns and sees
        her lover there.
MARIE: Can this be a waking dream?
    Can such joy be?
    Are you Emil?
    Stay here my own,
    Stay here alone with me.

[Dialogue.]

ERNST AND BRUNO: [as soldiers] Make way, make
        way for the grenadiers,
    The soldiers of the king,
    Who fight to die,
    And live to sing.
    Tra la, tra la.
MARIE: Emil, Emil!
EMIL: Come out, Marie.
    My cute,
    [correcting himself]
    My sweet Marie.

[Dialogue.]

I Am So Eager

Published as an individual sheet. Introduced by Natalie Hall (Frieda, playing the role of Marie) and Tullio Carminati (Bruno, playing the role of Emil). This number will be Tingle-Tangle's big waltz.

EMIL: I am so eager,
    You are so sweet.

We're so in love
    That life seems complete.
MARIE: Night is so silent.
    Spring's in the air,
    And there is stardust aglow in
        your hair.
EMIL: Time is so short, so swift,
    Each moment is dear.
MARIE: Dear,
    Ev'ry moment you're here
    Must be spent in my arms.
EMIL: Arms,
    Arms that wait for lips to
    Blend in a kiss.
MARIE: Kisses
    So tender and shy—
EMIL: Shyly
    Surrendering.
    I am so eager.
BOTH: You are so sweet.
    We're so in love
    That life seems complete.
    Life can't be wrong,
    Love is beautiful and right,
    That is why we must belong to
        each other tonight!

[Dialogue.]

ERNST: [narrating] All the other
        prisoners plead for Marie.
    Imagine a chorus of forty
        voices plugging the song hit!
MARIE AND AN
OFFSTAGE CHOIR: I am so eager,
    You are so sweet.
    We're so in love that
    Life seems complete.
    Life can't be wrong.
    Love is beautiful and right,
    That is why we must belong to
        each other tonight.

[They all sit, exhausted.]

PLAY ON

Published in the vocal score. Introduced by Dorothy Johnson (Marthe, secretary to the music publisher). This is a fragment of a song that Ernst, Walther, and Marthe knew when they were young.

Play on, sweet music of springtime's young
    dream.
Forever and ever, play on.
Play on, sweet music of springtime's young
    dream.
Play long after springtime has gone . . .

ZOO SCENE

Published in the vocal score. Introduced by Katherine Carrington (Sieglinde), Tullio Carminati (Bruno), Reinald Werrenrath (Cornelius), and members of the ensemble.

Stage directions explain: "The following speeches are synchronized in counter meter to melodies played by the orchestra. It is partly rhyme, partly blank verse, partly prose, read without too much cadence and without any apparent consciousness on the part of the performers that it is anything but prose."

SIEGLINDE: I'm fascinated by that eagle.
BRUNO: Doesn't he look stern and regal.
    He could lift you right up in the air!
SIEGLINDE: Can he lift up that pelican?
BRUNO: Most certainly!
A BOY: The hell he can!
SIEGLINDE: [laughing] I thought he'd take your
    head right off.
BRUNO: [cutting her off] Let's have some
    coffee.
    Hsst! Waiter! Come here!
WAITER: Some nice light wine?
BRUNO: [to SIEGLINDE] Some light wine?
SIEGLINDE: Just coffee, please.
BRUNO: And some cake?
SIEGLINDE: Yes, some cake.
BRUNO: [to WAITER] Bring two coffees and
    some cake.
CORNELIUS: Good afternoon.
SIEGLINDE: Good afternoon.
CORNELIUS: Where's the boy?
SIEGLINDE: You mean Karl?
CORNELIUS: Yes, of course I mean your Karl.
    Er, whenever you see him, please tell
    him for me
    Not to stay here in Munich too long.
    For people so used to the mountains
    as we,
    The air here in Munich is wrong.

[Looking at BRUNO.]

For folk of the country this food is
    too rich.
The food that we thrive on is simple
    and plain.
Our strength is that very simplicity
Which a city can never attain.
For people like Karl and like you and
    like me
The life here in Munich is wrong.
See all of the sights, but whatever
    you do,
Don't stay here in Munich too
    long.
Good day.
SIEGLINDE: Good day.
CORNELIUS: [singing]: Tra-la, la-la, la-la.
BRUNO: Who's that?
SIEGLINDE: An old man we met on the way.
CORNELIUS: [singing] Tra-la, la-la, la-la.
SIEGLINDE: He is all the time laughing and
    singing.
BRUNO: A very depressing old man.
SIEGLINDE: Depressing?
BRUNO: Rich food in Munich, and looking
    at me!
    I don't agree!
    I tell you the opposite.
    I say stay here in Munich forever.

ONE MORE DANCE

Published as an individual sheet. Introduced by Tullio Carminati (Bruno).

Bruno tells Sieglinde that the man in his play "Loves a sweet young girl, and he daren't hope she loves him. And today I've learned how he feels. I could hear him sing an appeal, humble, pathetic in its futility."

INTRODUCTION

SIEGLINDE: You've been humming that all
    afternoon.
BRUNO: [spoken in rhythm] That's a new waltz
    I've been writing, Sieglinde.
    Pardon me, dear, if I work while I
    play. Sometimes the words come
    so naturally, Sieglinde.
SIEGLINDE: That's why you've been humming,
    All through the day!
BRUNO: I have a part in my new operetta,
    A man about my age and wicked
    like me.

REFRAIN

BRUNO: One more dance
    In the arms of love.
    With sad eyes of autumn I'm looking
    at spring.
    Asking the pretty thing
    Just one more favor.

    One more glance
    From that shy white dove
    One more night, if you will.
    One more flight, one more thrill,
    One more dance with love.

CODA

BRUNO: [spoken over the music] Those are the
    words I have written, Sieglinde.
    And the poor creature who sings it
    is I, filled with desire but too
    worshipful to touch you or tell you
    how much you have made my
    heart fly.
SIEGLINDE: Look at the swing.
BRUNO: What of it, Sieglinde?
SIEGLINDE: That makes me feel I am just six years
    old.
    Come give me a push!

EPISODE OF THE SWING

Published in the vocal score. Introduced by Natalie Hall (Frieda), Katherine Carrington (Sieglinde), Walter Slezak (Karl), and Tullio Carminati (Bruno). They speak in rhythm over the music.

FRIEDA: Why, Bruno, what are you doing
    here? Good afternoon, my dear.
    Imagine the four of us meeting
    here.
SIEGLINDE: Karl!
KARL: Sieglinde, Sieglinde!
SIEGLINDE: How ever did you know you would
    find us here?
KARL: I didn't know, we didn't know.
SIEGLINDE: Father said he was tired, so Herr
    Mahler brought me to the zoo.
    Karl, just look at your collar.
KARL: It's hot, I've been out in the sun all
    the day. Ach! What a busy day!
    I've seen ev'rything in Munich.
BRUNO: What made you pick the zoo?

FRIEDA: Ha, ha, ha! That's what I'd like to ask
you.
KARL: We've been out on the lake.
SIEGLINDE: We've had coffee and cake.
BRUNO: Won't you join us?
SIEGLINDE: Yes, join us, please do.

NIGHT FLIES BY

Published in the vocal score. Introduced by Natalie Hall (Frieda).

This is an alternate lyric for the "One More Dance" tune Bruno has just sung to Sieglinde. Frieda explains: "I'm an innocent little girl, you see—in the play. And I'm waiting for my sweetheart on a balcony. And I sing a kind of vocal soliloquy." After Frieda demonstrates a portion of the "Night Flies By" lyric, Bruno joins her, loudly singing his newer lyric. The script instructs: "They sing these tender words of love in the manner of two bulldogs, glaring at each other the while."

FRIEDA: Night flies by,
You fly too,
Your love is like starlight that fades with
the day.
Why can't you ever stay?
Why can't I hold you?
Night flies by,
Dawn breaks through!
I awake and I'm lonely,
My lover is only a dream of you.

WHEN THE SPRING IS IN THE AIR

Alternate title: "Bedroom Scene." Published as an individual sheet and included in Hammerstein's anthology, *Lyrics*. Introduced by offstage revellers heard through the hotel bedroom window and taken up inside by Katherine Carrington (Sieglinde), Al Shean (Walther), Tullio Carminati (Bruno), and Ivy Scott (Lilli Kirschner).

VERSE FROM SHEET MUSIC

I'm at a critical stage now,
I'm at a wonderful age now,
Eager as I can be.

Ready to leave my cage now.
I'm the ingenuous sort of
Kind of a girl they make sport of.
All that I can hear and see
Can make exciting impressions on me.

REFRAIN

When the spring is in the air
I want my fill of the spring.
With all the thrill of the spring
I want to dance.
When I see a happy pair
I want to fall right in love
And get my own portion of
Romance.
When I hear a pretty song
I want to sing like a bird.
I want to learn ev'ry word
And ev'ry rhyme.
I'm susceptible and foolish and young.
But I have a damn good time.

INTERLUDE

I want to live a little bit,
Take a little bit,
Give a little bit.
Just let me live a little bit—
I can do no harm.

REPEAT REFRAIN

IN EGERN ON THE TEGERN SEE

Published as an individual sheet and included in Hammerstein's anthology, *Lyrics*. Introduced by Ivy Scott (Lilli Kirschner, a retired actress). The song is one of her old numbers.

In Egern on the Tegern See
Where we have our home,
We watch the sunset fade away
And melt in the gloam.
And then my man and I,
Beneath a starlit sky,
Look out across the water,
The calm, contented water.
When lights along the shore go out
My man looks my way,
Then we let one light more go out
And end one more day.

And while soft breezes bless us
And moonbeams caress us,
We dream in Egern on the Tegern See.

THE SONG IS YOU

Published as an individual sheet and included in Hammerstein's anthology, *Lyrics*. Introduced by Tullio Carminati (Bruno), who sings it to Sieglinde as if she has just inspired the words. The audience later learns that he's been using this song as an aid to seduction for years.

As a sincere love song, the song achieved a certain popularity with recordings by Eddy Duchin, Jack Kenny, Tommy Dorsey, and Frank Sinatra.

I hear music when I look at you,
A beautiful theme of ev'ry dream I ever knew.
Down deep in my heart
I hear it play,
I feel it start,
Then melt away.
I hear music when I touch your hand,
A beautiful melody from some enchanted land.
Down deep in my heart
I hear it say:
Is this the day?
I alone
Have heard this lovely strain,
I alone
Have heard this glad refrain.
Must it be
Forever inside of me?
Why can't I let it go
Why can't I let you know?
Why can't I let you know the song my heart would
sing—
That beautiful rhapsody of love and youth and
spring?
The music is sweet,
The words are true,
The song is you.

WE BELONG TOGETHER

Alternate titles: "Finale," "The Village of Edendorf." Published as an individual sheet. Introduced by the ensemble (assorted Edendorf villagers and children as they go about their day), Reinald Werrenrath (Cornelius), Walter Slezak (Karl), and Katherine Carrington (Sieglinde).

We belong together,
We're happy together
And life is a song.
When we are together
We know we are where we belong.
We belong together,
Like birds of a feather
Together we thrive,
Little caring whether
The rest of the world is alive.
All alone I'm only a half,
Like a joke without any laugh.
We belong together,
We're happy together
And life is a song.
When we are together
We know we are where we belong.

CUT AND UNUSED SONG

GOOD GIRL

Not published. Little is known about this number, which exists in a copyist piano-vocal manuscript and a typed lyric sheet in the Oscar Hammerstein II Collection in the Music Division of the Library of Congress. An association with *Music in the Air* is presumed because of the name Sieglinde, but the words seem out of character for the naive country girl. The lyric was also submitted to the Production Code Administration on June 5, 1942, as song #3991 for the screen version of *Very Warm for May*.

SIEGLINDE: Good girl!
BOYS: That's a good girl.
SIEGLINDE: I pat my head and say,
"Good girl."
BOYS: That's a good girl.
SIEGLINDE: You did a job today.
Couldn't hold my fellow.
BOYS: Why should you want to hold him?
SIEGLINDE: So I up and told the fellow,
"Goodbye."
BOYS: We're glad you told him goodbye.
(Good riddance!)
SIEGLINDE: Good girl.
BOYS: That's a good girl.
SIEGLINDE: Now I am ready for those wolves.
Who hang around my door.
BOYS: That's a good girl.
SIEGLINDE: To all who may be concerned,
My heart's no longer interned.
BOYS: We all welcome the turning.
We are concerned where you're
concerned.
Now that you're free . . .
SIEGLINDE: I'm free.
And I am furthermore
A very good girl!
BOYS: Don't you be
Too good a girl.

Top: *Natalie Hall and Maurice Evans*
Bottom: *Oskar Denes (center) surrounded by girls at the titular ball*

BALL AT THE SAVOY (1933)

No tryout. London: Theatre Royal, Drury Lane; opened September 8, 1933; closed January 13, 1934; 148 performances. An operetta in three acts. Music by Paul Ábráham. Book (and lyrics) by Alfred Grünwald and Fritz Löhner-Beda. English version adapted and produced by Oscar Hammerstein II. Staged by Reginald K. Hammerstein. Dances and ensembles arranged by Jack Donohue. Orchestra directed by Charles Prentice. Scenery designed by Joseph and Phil Harker. Costumes by Motley.

Cast: Maurice Evans (Aristide, Le Marquis de Faublas), Natalie Hall (Madeleine, his wife), Oskar Denes (Mustapha Bei, attaché at the Turkish Embassy), Rosy Barsony (Kathi Mihazy, Madeleine's cousin), Joan Marion (Nina, a dancer), Dick Francis (Archibald, butler to Le Marquis), Barry Mackay (Celestin Fromant, a young lawyer), Tom Scott (Pomerol, head waiter at the Savoy), Rita Nugent (Bebe, Madeleine's maid), Brenda Clether, Shelagh Patrick, Bruce Seton, and John Huson (guests at the de Faublases' house), Basil Neale (Albert, a dressmaker), Pamela Dawn (Lena, of Berlin, an ex-wife of Mustapha Bei), Kate Cavil (Angela, of Paris, an ex-wife of Mustapha Bei), Eileen Clifton (Lucia, of Rome, an ex-wife of Mustapha Bei), Valerie Tuck (Lola, of Rio de Janeiro, an ex-wife of Mustapha Bei), Bobby Huby (Bess, of London, an ex-wife of Mustapha Bei), Valerie Hobson (Gracie, of Manchester, an ex-wife of Mustapha Bei), Leo Britt (Ernest Benuet, a friend of Celestin Fromant), Barry Sherwood (Gardener), and ensemble (guests in the Faublas home, guests at the ball, dancers, waiters, pages, mannequins, and so on).

Returning to society after a year-long honeymoon, Aristide and Madeleine, Marquis and Marquise de Faublas, reaffirm that they will be true to each other. But that very day Aristide is summoned to the infamous ball at the Savoy by Nina, a former mistress to whom he once promised "an hour of his life." Aristide and his close friend Mustapha concoct a cover story, but Madeleine is immediately suspicious and attends the ball herself, disguised in a risqué dress and a veil. Seeing her husband and Nina go to a private dining room, Madeleine turns her charms on Celestin, a clean-cut young lawyer looking for a romantic adventure, and they take the room next door. When she returns to the ballroom, she unmasks and announces that she has been unfaithful. Aristide doesn't know whether to believe her or not, but the next morning popular opinion is firmly with Madeleine and her form of revenge. For contrast is the coupling of Mustapha and Kathi. They are instantly and easily attracted to each other, although Mustapha is very surprised to learn that Kathi has a second identity as jazz composer José Pasodoble. She offers Mustapha a marriage contract that gives each of them the right to see other people, but he is willing to concede his freedom in order to have her exclusively.

Oskar Dénes and Rosy Barsony recorded their numbers—"All I Want Is a Home," "[On the] Bosphorus," "I Always Keep My Girl Out Late," "I'll Show You Off," "Oh Why, Oh Why, Oh Why," and "Up and Down"—for Columbia, with the Drury Lane Theatre Orchestra conducted by Charles Prentice.

A "Vocal Gems" folio was published with nine songs, six of which were also released as individual sheets. The published German-language piano-vocal score provides the melodies for the others. The Hammerstein Collection in the Music Division of the Library of Congress includes two typescripts: one dated July 14, 1933; the other one, possibly a translator's work, with annotations by Hammerstein. The Lord Chamberlain's Play Collection at the British Library has a typescript dated July 13, 1933.

The Drury Lane program lists the opening of Act One as a number performed by the ensemble. The editor has not found English lyrics for this moment. Between "I Always Keep My Girl Out Late" and the Act Two Finale, the German-language piano-conductor score gives Madeleine two songs: "No. 13 Lied (Madeleine mit Herren) 'Ich küss genau so gut wie Tangolita!' Tango," followed by "No. 13A Reminiszenz 'Toujours l'amour' also Überleitungsmusik zum zweiten Bild (Madeleine, Celestin)." The editor has not found English lyrics for either of these. The Drury Lane programs list a reprise of "I Live for Love" instead.

In the mid-1950s, when details were being collected for the first *Rodgers and Hammerstein Fact Book*, Hammerstein said that *Ball at the Savoy* "opened cold in London. When it closed it was even colder." The operetta had had two successful years in Berlin, but Hitler's election made the Jewish composer, librettists, and prima donna unemployable. The Drury Lane production was lavish—there were almost twenty tons of scenery—but it could not compensate for some innate problems. The *Evening Standard* asked, "Why were two of the principal characters [Barsony and Dénes], who have some difficulty in speaking English at all, given swift and tongue-twisting patter songs in that language? Why did a husband fail to recognize his pretty wife at the ball merely because she was wearing a mask and an ugly dress?"

THE MOON WILL RIDE AWAY

Original title: "Es träumt Venezia." Not published in English. Introduced by ensemble (offstage serenaders), Natalie Hall (Madeleine), and Maurice Evans (Aristide).

The moon will ride away,
The stars will fade with day,
But I'll remember
You were in my arms tonight.
The moon will ride away,
With the golden glow of dawning day,
But I'll remember
You were mine tonight.

THIS LOVELY DREAM

Original title: "Bist du mir treu, von Herzen treu?" Not published in English. Introduced by Natalie Hall (Madeleine) and Maurice Evans (Aristide). Also see Madeleine's reprise in the Act Two Finale.

MADELEINE: This lovely dream
    Let's make it last,
    This lovely dream
    Let's hold it fast.
    Love is no plaything
    To take or leave alone.
    Love is a gay thing to own.
ARISTIDE: Let's make it last.
    Let's plan and scheme
    To hold it fast,
    This lovely dream.
MADELEINE: If it's old-fashioned
    To stay forever true—
BOTH: I'll be old-fashioned with you.

LE MARQUIS DE FAUBLAS

Original title: "Sevilla." Not published in English. Introduced by Dick Francis (Archibald, the butler) and ensemble.

VERSE

ARCHIBALD: The girls
Couldn't ever resist him.
They up and they kissed him
As soon as could be.
They loved the Marquis.

ENSEMBLE: Monsieur le Marquis.

ARCHIBALD: But he
Had the soul of a Pan, as
Inconstant a man as
You ever would see.
That was the Marquis!

ENSEMBLE: Monsieur le Marquis.

REFRAIN 1

ARCHIBALD: In love his ways would never waver,
Le Marquis de Faublas!
When once he'd won a lady's favor
Le Marquis would go blah!
Blasé and bored with his successes
Until he scented new caresses
Then—
You should have seen Monsieur le
Marquis,
Le Marquis de Faublas!

REFRAIN 2

ARCHIBALD: In love his ways would never waver,
Le Marquis de Faublas.
When once he'd won a lady's favor
Le Marquis would go blah!
Does he look bored with his successes
And looking out for new caresses?
No!
Good luck and welcome to le Marquis
And Marquise de Faublas.

I THINK I'M IN LOVE WITH MY WIFE

Original title: "Ich hab' einen Mann, der mich liebt!"
Not published in English. Introduced by Maurice Evans
(Aristide) and Natalie Hall (Madeleine).

REFRAIN 1

ARISTIDE: I think I'm in love with my wife,
I think I've been captured for life.
My friends say Delilah has cut off
my hair,
I let them laugh. What do I care?

I once was a lad of renown,
A heart-breaking man about town,
I loved many women—
I think I still do—
For now all my women are you.

REFRAIN 2

MADELEINE: Oh please stay in love with your wife,
And please be the love of her life.

[*There is dialogue over the music for lines 3–6.*]

As long as I know
You are faithful and true,
Then I'll be all women to you.

ON THE BOSPHORUS

Original title: "Am Bosporus." Published in the Vocal
Gems folio. Introduced by Oskar Denes (Mustapha Bei)
and female ensemble.

GIRLS: Halla, halla, haj!
Halla, halla, haj!
Halla, halla, halla, halla, halla, halla,
haj!

VERSE 1

MUSTAPHA: My dear papa, a Pasha was he,
And he has left his mark upon me.
For his wild romantic antics, he was
famous in France.
He made love to debutantes and
debutantes' aunts!
But now and then a girl would refuse,
And dear Papa, who hated to lose,
Used to fret and fume about the
Western women and say,
"Oh, take me back to Turkey, and I'll
never go away!"

REFRAIN 1

MUSTAPHA: My home is on the Bosphorus.
I like it on the Bosphorus
Because I am a man.
My life upon the Bosphorus
Is pleasant on the Bosphorus
Because I am a man!
The women never argue
And they always treat me well.
And any time I want a kiss,

I merely ring a bell.
The little darlings know they must
Do ev'rything to please me, just
Because I am a man!

VERSE 2

MUSTAPHA: My dear papa could not understand
Why girls in France were so in
demand.
It disgusted him to see that men were
willing to pay
For a thing that really should be given
away!
He said, "Why can't these men be
embraced
Without the talk and the time that
they waste?
Treating women as an equal is a thing
overdone,
When you spoil your women you are
spoiling all your fun!"

REFRAIN 2

MUSTAPHA: My home is on the Bosporus.
I like it on the Bosporus
Because I am a man.
My life up on the Bosporus
Is pleasant on the Bosporus
Because I am a man!
The women never argue
And they always treat me well.
And any time I want a kiss,
I merely ring a bell.
And if I chance to feel that way,
I ring a dozen bells a day!
You see, I'm quite a man.

REFRAIN 3

MUSTAPHA: Halla, halla, halla haj!
Halla haj! Halla haj!
Father said that men should lead their
lives
Halla, haj!
Halla, halla, halla haj!
Halla, halla, halla haj!
Father married eighty-seven wives.
They tucked him in his blanket,
And they fed him from a cup.
And one would sing him off to sleep
And one would wake him up.
Oh, halla, halla, halla haj!
Halla, halla, halla haj!
Father was a man!

UP AND DOWN

Published in the Vocal Gems folio. Introduced by Rosy Barsony (Kathi) and male ensemble. In the German original, this new dance craze was called "Känguruh."

VERSE

I saw him only for a fleeting moment,*
And then I understood what vertigo meant.
I was as dizzy as a spinning spool,
Giddy as a girl at school.
This morning seemed the same as other mornings,
My heart was unattached, my life was free.
Then came a perfect stranger,
And with this perfect stranger,
This strange effect on me.

REFRAIN

Up and down
My heart has started thumping,
Jumping up and down.
Up and down,
I'm not responsible
For acting like a clown.
I don't know if I am hot or cold.
The one sensation that I feel
Fills me up with more than I can hold.
I don't know what it is,
But what it does
Is keep me jumping up and down.
I know a thrill that I have never known before.
Up and down,
And now I know it,
I would like to know some more!
Just because I've seen a certain man
I want to tell the stars above
Feel my heart,
Feel my heart
Jumping up and down for love.

---

* The published verse starts with this variation of
lines 1–5:
    I saw him standing there so graceful and tall.
    He didn't move his lips but I heard him call.
    I grew as giddy as a girl at school,
    Dizzy as a spinning spool!
    Before today I never though I could fall,

I DREAMED WHAT A GIRL LIKES TO DREAM OF (MADELEINE'S SOLILOQUY)

Original title: "Was hat eine Frau von der Treue?" Not published in English. Introduced by Natalie Hall (Madeleine).

REFRAIN

I dreamed what a girl likes to dream of.
I wanted my husband to be
A lover and friend
Who would stick to the end,
Whose life was all bound up with me.
No matter what girls like to dream of
Their dreams, like their men, are untrue.
Your soul you would give for
Just one man to live for.
You'd give—but what good does that do?

VERSE

And now that it's done,
What can I do?
Sit here and plot out my revenge?
That sounds like a thin consolation,
And yet I must get revenge!

REPEAT REFRAIN

I'LL SHOW YOU OFF

Title in German original: "Oh, Mister Brown!" Published as an individual sheet. Introduced by Oskar Denes (Mustapha), Rosy Barsony (Kathi), and male ensemble.

VERSE 1

MUSTAPHA: When we step
On the floor
Ev'rybody will adore
My little partner.
KATHI: That's right!
In your grip,
Strong and firm,
Give me breath enough to murmur,
"What a partner."
MUSTAPHA: That's right!
With our heads held up high.
KATHI: And a bored expression in the eye.

MUSTAPHA: I'll be glad.
KATHI: I'll be proud.
MUSTAPHA: I'll be proud to be
Allowed to be your partner.
KATHI: That's right!

REFRAIN

MUSTAPHA: I'll show you off
To all of the boys.
KATHI: I'll show you off
To all of the girls.
MUSTAPHA: When we are dancing,
The fellows in the band
Will stand up and sing:
BOTH: "Oh, ain't they glorious, ain't they
grand!"
KATHI: The girls will say,
"Oh, look at that boy!"
MUSTAPHA: The boys will say,
"Oh, look at that girl!"
KATHI: But we'll keep dancing
As if we didn't care.
MUSTAPHA: Just showing off—
BOTH: And walking on air!

VERSE 2

MUSTAPHA: Let them stare,
Let them glance
Let them think I'm romancing
With my partner.
KATHI: Hot dog!
And to show
You're the best,
You'll be sticking out your chest
To touch your partner.
MUSTAPHA: Hot dog!
KATHI: When they give us the prize
MUSTAPHA: We will raise our supercilious eyes.
KATHI: What a bore!
MUSTAPHA: What a fag!
KATHI: What a fag!
BOTH: Oh, what a gag
To be your partner!
Oh, boy!

REPEAT REFRAIN

ACT ONE FINALE, including THE NIGHT IS YOUNG

German-language piano-vocal score lists: "#9 Finale 1 mit der Nummer 'Heut' möcht' ich einmal Schampus trinken!' " and "#9A Zwischenaktsmusik, 'Ich hab' einen Mann, der mich liebt!' " Not published in English. Introduced by Dick Francis (Archibald), Maurice Evans (Aristide), Oskar Denes (Mustapha), and male ensemble; Natalie Hall (Madeleine), Basil Neale (Monsieur Albert, a dressmaker), and female ensemble.

ARCHIBALD: There is a ball at the Savoy.
Girls ev'rywhere,
Tender and fair.
Shoulders that are young
And bare.
Youth is short,
And it comes once only.
Live life now,
When you're old, you're lonely.

[*Dialogue.*]

MUSTAPHA: Right!
ARCHIBALD: Right!
ARISTIDE: Right!
MUSTAPHA: Come on!
ARISTIDE: Right!
I'll be gay now while I can,
I will show you who's a man!
[*spoken*] But, Madeleine. She wouldn't understand.
MUSTAPHA: Any man is entitled to
One night!
ARCHIBALD: That's right!
ARISTIDE: That's right!
ARCHIBALD: Hat!
MUSTAPHA: Gloves!
ARISTIDE: Cane!
MUSTAPHA: [*shouting*] That's your old self!
ALL THREE: There is a ball
At the Savoy!

[*Dialogue.*]

The Night Is Young

ARISTIDE: The night is young,
And so is my heart.
Romance is in the air.
Another night
That bids me to start
Another love affair.

Though I may meet some sweet
adorable girl
Whose kisses seem the best,
I'll not be signed up,
I'll not make my mind up
Till I've tried all the rest.

[*The men exit.* MADELEINE *enters with her dressmaker and various maids and assistants.*]

MADELEINE: Swinging the hips,
Pursing the lips.
Thank you for your useful tips!
Too much rouge,
And a posture erotic;
Wild perfume
With a scent too exotic;
Sex revealing,
Naught concealing—
Then you've got
Mademoiselle Cocotte!
ALBERT: Right!
MANAGERESS: Right!
MADELEINE: Right!
I'll do what these cocottes do at the ball.
It's an instinct with us all.
I'm a woman
And I'll show I'm a woman
Tonight.
ALBERT: Right!
MANAGERESS: Right!
ALL: Right!
MADELEINE: Now, Monsieur le Marquis de Faublas,
I'll see you at the ball at the Savoy!

The night is young,
And so is my heart.
Romance is in the air,
Another night
That bids me to start
Another love affair.
Though I may meet some sweet
adorable man
Whose kisses seem the best,
I'll not be signed up,
I'll not make my mind up
Till I've tried all the rest.

A GIRL LIKE NINA

Original title: "#9C Auftritt (Tangolita mit Herren) 'Man nennt mich nur: La bella Tangolita.' " Published as an individual sheet. Introduced by the female ensemble (women at the ball) and danced by Brenda Clether (Nina).

GIRLS: No wonder we all want to be like Nina,
A girl like Nina
That men desire.
No wonder we all seek the key to Nina.
What has this Nina
That men admire?
This sex allure, how do the gods allot it?
Perhaps they had a surplus and she got it.
No wonder we all want to be like Nina,
A girl like Nina
That men desire.

VERSE (PUBLISHED SHEET ONLY)

She's not too tall
Nor yet too small;
She's just a medium girl
That no other girl thinks beautiful.
But in her eyes
Some power lies,
To make all good men be bad
And bad men be good and dutiful.

Unpublished Act Two reprise refrain for Madeleine

No wonder we all want to be like Nina,
A girl like Nina
That men desire.
It seems to me no trick to be like Nina;
To keep man eager
With mad desire.
For I can give them all that she can give them.
Love one and then another and outlive them!
In ev'ry woman there's a girl like Nina,
A girl like Nina
That men desire.

ALL I WANT IS A HOME

Original title: "Wenn wir Türken küssen." Published in the Vocal Gems folio. Introduced by Oskar Denes (Mustapha), his six ex-wives, and additional girls.

The July 1933 script instructs: "To be sung with the sentimental tenderness of a conventional 'Build a Little Love-Nest' type of song."

VERSE 1

MUSTAPHA: The simple life is what I like best,
I'm a bird who's fond of his nest.
I want a pipe and slippers, a book to
   read.
All I need is a rest.
I want to shun society's frills
In a home high up in the hills.
I want to live there happily and
   contented,
Growing daffodils.
High on the hills,
Growing daffodils.
With no one else but me and my wives,
We could lead such heavenly lives.

REFRAIN

MUSTAPHA: All I want is a home.
Just a dear little home
With a small harem for seven and no
   more!*
Just a tiny gray shack
With a porch at the back
And some rambler roses creeping
   'round the door.
Tripe and milk for lunch,
Ripe young prunes to munch.
And a room just for two,
Just for me and for you.
And sometimes for you and you and
   you and you and you!

VERSE 2

MUSTAPHA: At nine o'clock there'd be a levee
When the master started his day.
Like little bees you'd flutter and fly
   and buzz
'Round my breakfast tray.
One little woman darning my socks,
And another winding the clocks,
And still another one out in the garden
Picking hollyhocks and phlox.

---

* The July 1933 script says that to allow more girls on
stage during additional refrains, the words "and no
more" can be replaced by "maybe more." In case extra
lyrics were needed for dance refrains Hammerstein
instructed: "Sing one refrain as written, changing
only second half as follows:
   Some day there may be
   [à la Jolson] Some "Sonny Boys" upon my knee,
   And a daughter or two,
   Who'll look something like you,
   And ten or twelve who look like you and you and
      you!

Socks and clocks,
Phlox and hollyhocks.
And ev'ryone would come when I call
All for one and one for all!

REPEAT REFRAIN

I LIVE FOR LOVE

Original title: "Toujours l'amour." Published as an individual sheet. Introduced by Natalie Hall (Madeleine,
disguised as a vamp).

VERSE 1

If I am sought
Like any girl,
I can be bought
Like any girl.
So look at me,
Who wants to be the buyer?
I'll sell a smile
For something gay.
I'll sell a kiss
If you will pay.
I'll sell my heart—
But that will come much higher.

REFRAIN

I live for love,
For love is my living.
How much are you giving for me?
I'm tall and fair
And love is my living.
How much are you giving for me?
Shall this be the love of a moment?
Or shall I be faithful and true?
You'll never know,
For I'll never tell you
How much I am giving to you.

VERSE 2

I know my art
Like any girl.
I play my part
Like any girl.
I can be cold,
I can be warm and tender.
You want to dance?
I'll lift my skirt;
You want romance?
Well, I can flirt.

You want my heart?
I want complete surrender.

I ALWAYS KEEP MY GIRL OUT LATE IN THE NIGHT

Original title: "Es ist so schön, am Abend bummeln zu
geh'n!" Published as an individual sheet. Introduced by
Rosy Barsony (Kathi), Oskar Denes (Mustapha), and
ensemble.

VERSE 1

MUSTAPHA: I've studied feminine lore,
I've tried my best to explore,
And the only things that I've learned
   so far
Make me want to know more.
I've played with fire and been burned,
And here's a lesson I've learned:
Never ask a girl in the afternoon
Or you're sure to be spurned.

REFRAIN 1

MUSTAPHA: I always keep my girl out late in the
   night,
Late in the night,
Late in the night.
For when the moon and stars alone are
   alight
That is the time they fall.
I know that sunshine is their shy
   light,
And they're uncertain in the twilight,
But when I keep my girl out late in the
   night
She won't go home at all!

VERSE 2

KATHI: I think you're probably right,
It all depends on the light.
To a good and normally careful girl
Night is dynamite.
At lunches women just tease.
At teas they're mild as a breeze.
But as soon as ever the sun goes down
They get eager to please.

REFRAIN 2

KATHI: So always keep your girl out late in the
   night,

Late in the night,
Late in the night.
For when the moon and stars alone are
    alight,
That is the time they fall.
She may be bashful as a ninny
But after dark she gets "give-inny."
And if you keep your girl out late in
    the night
She won't go home at all!

PATTER REFRAIN

Though you may
Find a pretty little lady
Timid when it's sunny.
When it starts in getting shady
She will start in feeling funny.
She will start in feeling funny
Very shortly after seven.
And her heart, becoming warmer,
Will be warmer by eleven.
And the warmer she is getting
Then the more she'll want your
    petting.
And the more she'll want your petting
More's the petting she'll be getting.
She'll be getting all your petting
Yet regretting that she isn't getting
    more.
And when you feel her growing
    amorous
And actually clamorous
For something that is wonderful
And radiantly glamorous,
Don't hesitate, to hesitate is fatal,
For your mate'll want a quick and
    eager answer to her call.
And if you keep your girl out late in
    the night
She won't go home at all.

ACT TWO FINALE, including BALL AT THE SAVOY and OH WHY, OH WHY, OH WHY?

Original title "Finale II mit Duett 'Warum bin ich ver-liebt in dich?'" "Ball at the Savoy" and "Oh Why, Oh Why, Oh Why?" were both published as individual sheets. Introduced by the ensemble, Oskar Denes (Mustapha), and Rosy Barsony (Kathi). Madeleine enters at the end of the scene and sings reprises of "This Lovely Dream" and "I Dreamed What a Girl Likes to Dream of."

Ball at the Savoy

VERSE

ENSEMBLE: Lovely girls, all abloom like flowers,
    Sparkling eyes with enchanting
      powers.
    Young hearts beating;
    New loves meeting.
    Day has gone
    And the dance goes on!

REFRAIN

ENSEMBLE: There is a ball at the Savoy,
    Music and laughter will dance
      tonight.
    Drink up your wine and drown your
      care,
    There is adventure waiting
      ev'rywhere.
    There is a ball at the Savoy,
    There is a girl with her eyes alight;
    Yield to her spell,
    You might as well,
    What's a little kiss to you?
    You might as well,
    She'll never tell,
    What's a little kiss to you?

[MUSTAPHA *enters with his ex-wives.*]

MUSTAPHA: One, two, three, four, five, six ex-wives
    Gave me heaven,
    And soon there will be seven,
    I wish I were in my seventh heaven
      tonight.

[KATHI *is revealed to be the famous composer* JOSÉ PASADOBLE.]

KATHI: Glad to meet you all, Messieurs,
    Mesdames,
    I'm glad you've liked my little
      songs—
    José Pasadoble, here I am.
MUSTAPHA: You can't be Pasadoble!
    How can you be Pasadoble?
MUSTAPHA: [*into radio microphone*] How d'you do?
    New York and Budapest,
    Oh, how d'you do, hello!
ENSEMBLE: Hello.
KATHI: [*to* MUSTAPHA] How d'you do?
MUSTAPHA: So you are Pasadoble!
    [*plaintively*] How d'you do, hello!

ENSEMBLE: [*to* KATHI] Come and show 'em how
    you lead the band.
    Your little stick is in your hand.
    Show them how,
    Show them how,
    Show 'em how you lead a band!

[KATHI *leads the gathering in a reprise of "I'll Show You Off." Then she announces she is going to marry* MUSTAPHA.]

KATHI: This is our engagement kiss!
MUSTAPHA: One more kiss, please.
    But it doesn't seem fair
    To broadcast these
    All over the air.
ENSEMBLE: Just keep on kissing as if you didn't
    care,
    And we'll shove off,
    Just walking on air!

Oh Why, Oh Why, Oh Why?

VERSE 1

KATHI: You're not the type young girls adore
    In cinemas or in books.
    You couldn't win a medal for
    Your gallantry or your looks;
    Yet here I am and here I stay
    Just looking into your eyes,
    And wondering what
    You've possibly got
    That's making my temp'rature rise.

REFRAIN

KATHI: Oh why am I in love with you?
    In love with you,
    In love with you?
    Oh why am I in love with you?
    Oh why, oh why, oh why?
    Why do we kiss the way we do?
    The way we do,
    The way we do?
    Why do we kiss the way we do?
    Oh why, oh why, oh why?
    To the greatest minds of history
    The thing remains a mystery,
    But this one fact I know is true,
    It's good for me and good for you
    To love and kiss the way we do.
    So what's the difference why?

VERSE 2

MUSTAPHA: The type I seek is somewhat Greek,
    An Amazon, tall and svelte;

While your physique is small and
weak
And similar to a smelt.
Yet here I am and here I stay,
And nothing can make me go,
For something in you
Does something to me
And something must happen, I
know!

REPEAT REFRAIN

LAUGHING REFRAIN

Ha, ha, ha, ha, ha
Ha, ha, ha, ha, ha
Ha, ha, ha, ha, ha [etc.]

ENCORE REFRAIN

Oh why am I etcetera?
Etcetera,
Etcetera?
Oh why am I etcetera?
Pourquoi, pourquoi, pourquoi?
Warum bin ich verliebt in dich?
Verliebt in dich,
Verliebt in dich?
Warum bin ich verliebt in dich?
Warum, warum, warum?

[Tango music begins. MADELEINE enters, glaring at
NINA and ARISTIDE.]

MADELEINE: [parlando] How many thwarted wives
do you think
Suffer daily—and starve—
For revenge?
How many do you think deceive
their husbands secretly—
Just for—revenge?
What they do in secret I confess—
For the world to hear—
My husband has deceived me.
[singing] And now I have won my
revenge!

[Dialogue.]

MADELEINE: [mockingly] That lovely dream
It couldn't last.
That lovely dream
Has quickly passed.
Love is no plaything
To take or leave alone,
Love was a gay thing
To own.
It couldn't last,

No plot or scheme
Could hold it fast.
That lovely dream
It's too old-fashioned to be forever
true
So I'll be modern with you.

[ARISTIDE and NINA exit separately.]

MADELEINE: [overcome] And he was in love with
his wife,
And she was the love of his life.

[Continuing, quasi parlando.]

I dreamed what a girl likes to dream
of.
I wanted my husband to be
A lover and friend
Who would stick to the end,
Whose life was all bound up with
me.
No matter what girls like to dream
of,
Their dreams, like their men, are
untrue.
Your soul you would give for
Just one man to live for.
You'd give—but what good does that
do?

[Realizing the room has gone silent, she urges the
guests to resume their dance. The mood lightens until
she sings again.]

MADELEINE: You'll never know
For I'll never tell you,
How much I am giving to you!

IF IT'S GOOD ENOUGH FOR GENTLEMEN

Original title: "Kommen Sie mit mir nach Beludschis-
tan!" Not published in English. Introduced by the
ensemble.

Hail, hail!
Hail la Marquise!
Hail, hail!
Hail the woman who has freed us all!
If your gentleman likes to roam
Buy a gigolo for your home.
If it's good enough for gentlemen

It must be good enough for ladies too!

If it's good enough for gentlemen,
It must be good enough for ladies too.
If it's done by ev'ry gentleman,
Then why not let a lady do it too?
Men like a little change in loving,
Always looking for a thrill that's new.
If new thrills are good for gentlemen,
A lady ought to have a new thrill too!

CUT AND UNUSED SONG

BABY, WAIT TILL IT HAPPENS TO YOU

The published German-language piano-vocal score
includes an Act One duet for Madeleine and Daisy (renamed Kathi by Hammerstein) titled "Die erste Nacht
mit ihm allein." Programs from the Drury Lane Theater
do not list such a duet, nor was it mentioned in articles
about the show. But an English-language typescript
from July 1933 contains this lyric.

VERSE 1

MADELEINE: I'm very glad that I'm a wife,
I'm mad on married life,
I am!
KATHI: That's good!
But are you certain it would be
The kind of life for me?
MADELEINE: I am!
KATHI: That's good!
MADELEINE: You're just a baby at eighteen.
KATHI: In other words, I'm young and green.
MADELEINE: But when you do love
And find your true love,
You'll know exactly what I mean.

REFRAIN

MADELEINE: There'll come a day,
There'll come a boy.
KATHI: [spoken] Yes.
MADELEINE: There'll come a night—
KATHI: [spoken] Ooh!
MADELEINE: That's filled with joy.
Oh, baby,
Wait till it happens to you!

KATHI: [*spoken*] I hope it will.

MADELEINE: There'll come a dance
And at the close
He will propose
As man proposes.
Baby,
Wait till it happens to you!
What will you do?

KATHI: I'll look away, and then
I'll simply say, "Say when!"

MADELEINE: Then ev'ry day
You'll have your boy.
And ev'ry night
Will bring you joy.
Oh, baby,
Wait till it happens to you!

VERSE 2

MADELEINE: When first you feel his manly arms
It gives you vague alarms.

KATHI: Why vague?

MADELEINE: And on your happy wedding day
Those arms will come to stay.

KATHI: Not before?

MADELEINE: No!

KATHI: Sez you!

MADELEINE: There'll come a golden moment
    when
You'll feel an eager kiss and then . . .

KATHI: Yes?

MADELEINE: He'll hold you closer,
A little closer,
And then . . .
He'll kiss you once again.

OVERLEAF *Left to right, Stanley Holloway (with bowtie), Charlotte Greenwood, Esmond Knight, Victoria Hopper, Eliot Makeham, and Adele Dixon in the wedding scene*

THREE SISTERS | 1934

THREE SISTERS (1934)

London: Theatre Royal, Drury Lane; opened April 9, 1934; closed June 9, 1934; forty-five performances. A Musical Play in Three Acts. Produced by H. M. Tennent. Production staged by Oscar Hammerstein II and Jerome Kern. Book and lyrics by Oscar Hammerstein II. Music by Jerome Kern. Ensembles and dances arranged by Ralph Reader. Orchestrations by Robert Russell Bennett. Orchestra directed by Charles Prentice. Scenery and costumes designed by G. E. Calthrop.

Cast: Eliot Makeham (Will Barbour), Charlotte Greenwood (Tiny, his eldest daughter), Adele Dixon (Dorrie, his second daughter), Victoria Hopper (Mary, his youngest daughter), Dick Francis (Alf, his brother), Albert Burdon (George Purvis), Esmond Knight (Gypsy Hood), Stanley Holloway (Eustace Titherley), Leonard Thorn (Philip), Anthony Hankey (David Glainley), Richard Dolman (Sir John Marsden), Gladys Henson (Mrs. Titchmarsh), Clare Lindsay (Lady Marsden), Bruce Seton (Hugh Willoughby), Eileen Clifton (Zenida), and ensemble.

The Theatre Royal, Drury Lane, was known for lavish spectacles. Hammerstein and Kern chose to linger affectionately upon the rituals of English village life: a fair, a horse race, a wedding, a summer outing. The story begins in May 1914, when an itinerant photographer and his three daughters set up their cart near Epsom Downs. Practical Tiny is engaged to Eustace, a constable, and looking forward to a permanent home. Dorrie, who loves reading about aristocrats, meets two of them that night. And young Mary falls shatteringly in love with Gypsy, a fairground busker who loves her deeply but can't bear to be tied down. He abandons her on their wedding night. In Act Two the war has taken Dorrie and Tiny's men away as well, but only temporarily. Eustace and Gypsy unexpectedly meet up in France, where Gypsy's former busking partner George is rehearsing a show for the troops. On the home front, Tiny is troubled by gossip about Eustace being seen in the company of a lady (who turns out to be Dorrie). In France, Gypsy is tormented by an officer's memory of a special night with a photographer's girl (who also turns out to have been Dorrie). Learning the truth, Gypsy begs Mary's forgiveness and asks her to join him on his travels. An epilogue, set on the river Thames in August 1924, shows that all three couples and their children are "doing very well."

A few songs were recorded in 1934 by the original cast and orchestra. Those tracks can be heard on the Encore CD *Americans in London in the 1930's.* Stanley Holloway's renditions of "Keep Smiling" and "Hand in Hand" can also be heard on the Conifer CD *The Great Musicals Theatre Royal Drury Lane.*

Most of the lyrics in this chapter come from scripts at the Library of Congress (Hammerstein Collection), the Rodgers & Hammerstein Organization, and the British Library (Lord Chamberlain's Plays). Eight songs were published; some additional piano-vocal material is in the Jerome Kern Collection in the Music Division of the Library of Congress. No lyric has been found for Act Two's "Buffo Chorale: Welcome to the Bride." No music has been found for "Gaiety Chorus Girls" or the wedding sequence. Some scripts include "An Impression of the Derby," a montage of shouts by bookies and spectators. Various lines rhyme, but it is not clear how it would fit the music recorded as "Derby Day." In his 2006 study *Jerome Kern,* Stephen Banfield writes convincingly of *Three Sisters*'s unacknowledged significance in Kern and Hammerstein's careers,[*] but also explains that not enough musical material survives for an authoritative reconstruction.

ROLL ON, ROLLING ROAD

Published as an individual sheet. Introduced by Esmond Knight (Gypsy Hood) and Albert Burdon (George Purvis), who are buskers.

Roll on, rolling road,
Winding through the green,
Climbing over the hill.
Let me follow you
Through life's changing scene,
Go wherever you will.

VERSE

Take me through a city[†]
For a taste of brief adventure.
Then away and out we'll go again

---

[*] *Sophisticated use of music to tell the story, including thematic underscoring and a pre-*Oklahoma! *dream ballet; and an ambitious story that spans a decade and features "gambling, pre-marital sex, wedding day desertion, concert-party minstrelsy in and out of khaki and the leisure pursuits of the English masses."*

[†] *On a 1934 recording, Esmond Knight sings this variation of lines 1–5:*
Take me to a city
For a life of gay adventure.
Then away and out we'll go again
To the rolling countryside.
Take me to a wood

To the rolling countryside.
Take me through a wood
Where a lassie and her lad
Have decided to be good,
And are wishing they were bad.

Roll on, rolling road,
Winding through the green,
Climbing over the hill.
Let me follow you
Through life's changing scene.
Go wherever you will.

Unpublished verse for Act One, Scene 1

Take me to the Derby,
Where a hundred thousand punters
Make a hundred thousand different bets
And the bookies always win.
Take me to the Downs,
Where I see a happy pair.
With his arms around her waist,
They are standing over there.

NOW THAT I HAVE SPRINGTIME

Melody published in the British piano selection. Introduced by Esmond Knight (Gypsy) and Albert Burdon (George). See also: "There's a Joy That Steals Upon You."

GYPSY: Now that I have springtime,[*]
The springtime has me.
I want to be
Footloose and free.

---

[*]*One lyric sheet starts with this introductory stanza for Gypsy:*
Like a weather vane I sway.
My mood goes with the day.
When the winter comes I'll dreary be.
Ah, me,
Ah, me.
Now the winter's gone. It's May—
I'll point another way.
Old thrills will start again,
Churning my heart again.
New thrills await somewhere,
Playing with my fate somewhere.

GEORGE: That's because he's so irresponsible!

GYPSY: Now that birds are trilling
And filling each tree,
I sing
Because I feel their melody
Inside of me.

GEORGE: Don't believe a word he is telling you!

GYPSY: Now that I have springtime
And now that I have you
I sing . . .

GEORGE: [holding hat out for coins] De dee de le li
De dee de li de loo

GYPSY: Now that I have springtime
And now that I have you
I sing
Because it's what all lovers do.

ENSEMBLE: Oo-oo-oo
Lovers do.
Sing the springtime song they know,
Then on they go.

MY BEAUTIFUL CIRCUS GIRL

Alternate title: "Circus Queen." Melody published in the British piano selection. The characters in the show treat it as an old familiar song, equivalent to "After the Ball" or "Sweet Adeline." Introduced by Esmond Knight (Gypsy), Albert Burdon (George), Eliot Make-ham (Will Barbour), and ensemble.

VERSE

She cantered out on a snow-white horse
With bells a-tinkle and ribbons awhirl.
The queen of the ring was a tiny thing,
My beautiful circus girl.
And all the swells in their evening clothes
Would lift their monocles up to their eyes.
The queen of the ring had them on a string,
My beautiful circus girl.
But after the show I'd meet her
And say to my circus girl:

REFRAIN

Mary, come out with me,
Come out to dine.
I want to show you to the town.
I want them all to see
And know you're mine,
Dressed in your shiny spangled gown.

Hoop la! Little girl,
Hoop la! Little girl.

Round the ring you go
And we think you know
Why we love you so.
Hoop la! Little girl,
Hoop la! Little girl,
With your cheeks aglow.
Can you really wonder why
The fellows love you so?*

WHAT'S IN THE AIR TONIGHT?

Not published. Introduced by the ensemble (strolling couples), and repeated by Esmond Knight (Gypsy) and Victoria (Mary).

What's in the air tonight?
Why are the stars so bright?
Why is my heart inspired to start in flight?
What's in the air so new,
Making me want to do
Nothing at all but follow you?

Take me where you are going,
For I will go wherever you will take me.
Without a thought of whither or where you're
    leading me
I'll follow.
Over a field of clover
Or up a hill all silvery with dew,
I don't care where I am going
If I go with you.

What's in the air tonight?
Why are the stars so bright?
Why is my heart inspired to start in flight?
What's in the air so new,
Making me want to do
Nothing at all but follow you.

---

* Hammerstein wrote this lyric fragment on a sheet
headed "To 'Circus Girl' Air":
    Heigh-ho
    The breezes blow.
    The nightlark sings
    Heigh-ho.
    The moon is bright above
    Why, oh,
    Why do I say such foolish things
    Heigh-ho
    I think I am in love.

THERE'S A JOY THAT STEALS UPON YOU

Not published. Introduced by Victoria Hopper (Mary), Charlotte Greenwood (Tiny), Esmond Knight (Gypsy), and Albert Burdon (George). This quartet immediately follows a reprise of "Now That I Have Springtime."

There's a joy that steals upon you*
When you're unaware.
The night is fair,
The night is young,
Love is in the air.
There's a faintly stirring wildness in the mildness
    of the air.
Maybe it's the gentle drip of water by the mill
    side.
Maybe it's a filmy mist afloat upon a hillside.
Maybe only a firefly can make a sweet desire fly to
    you.
I want to sing,
I want to dance.
There's a joy that steals upon you,
Fills you with romance.
It makes you fall in love,
It makes you want to sing,
It makes you want to dance!

HAND IN HAND

Published as an individual sheet. Introduced by Stanley Holloway (Eustace Titherly).

Stanley Holloway's recording with the Drury Lane Theatre Orchestra can be heard on the CDs *Oscar Hammerstein, The Legacy: The Operettas* (Pearl) and on *The Great Musicals Theatre Royal Drury Lane* (Conifer).

VERSE

I have but one heart to give,
But that heart is true.
I, who have one life to live,
Give that life to you.
Though no fabled wealth have I,
Here's the earth and air.
Here's a love you cannot buy.
These I offer you, and only you, to share.

---

* This text is a condensation of the four characters'
  overlapping vocal lines.

Share the world with me,
We can live most anywhere.
Come and live with me.

REFRAIN

Hand in hand we'll walk together
When dawn is timidly fading.
Hand in hand we'll talk together
In twilight's delicate shading.
Other men alone adventure
And seek the stars above.
I will have my own adventure
If I have you to love.
We'll grow old and walk together
And smiles will sweeten our tears
While we gently talk together
Of bygone, beautiful years.

CODA

I have but one heart to give,
But that heart is true.
I, who have one life to live,
Give that life to you.

SOMEBODY WANTS TO GO TO SLEEP

Melody published in the British piano selection. Introduced by Charlotte Greenwood (Tiny).

Somebody wants to go to sleep
And I know who.
Somebody longs for slumber deep
And I know who.
Moonbeams that haunt the evening air
Will stoop to kiss her tousled hair,
And I'll meet them all,
For I'll be there
To kiss her too.

MARY'S DREAM

Not published. Introduced by Charlotte Greenwood (Tiny), Esmond Knight (Gypsy), Victoria Hopper (Mary), and female ensemble.

Hammerstein's stage directions instruct: "The spot fades out on Tiny and Mary and up on Gypsy, an ide-alised figure of Mary's dream. His guitar is silvered, his shirt is white silk with flowing sleeves. He is wearing tweed shorts like a small boy, with grey woollen stockings turned down below the knees . . . [Mary] is clad in a silken robe very like her white flannel nightgown, except that it has a white silk cord around the waist creating a sort of Grecian effect."

TINY: Somebody wants to go to sleep,
And I know who.
Somebody longs for slumber deep,
And I know who.
Moonbeams that haunt the evening air
Will stoop to kiss her tousled hair,
And I'll meet them all,
For I'll be there
To kiss her too.
GYPSY: Kiss her too,
I will kiss her too.
Now that I have springtime,
The springtime has me.
I want to be
Footloose and free.
MARY: My lover,
Come out of the shadow.
Come out of the shadow
And into my heart.
My lover,
I'm longing to give you,
I'm eager to give you,
The joy in my heart.
GIRLS: Gypsy, Gypsy, come with us,
Never let us down.
We're the ladies who depend on you.
We can sing and dance.
We can light the road to romance.
MARY: Where are you going?
GYPSY: You see, these ladies rather depend on me.
GIRLS: He can't let us down.
He's a theatrical figure.
You need your freedom,
Never lose your freedom.
You need your freedom,
Never lose your freedom.
Don't go with one girl,
Don't be tied to one girl.
Don't go with one girl,
Don't be tied to one girl.
She doesn't need you,
We're the ones who need you.
She doesn't need you,
We're the ones who need you.
GYPSY: [*spoken to* MARY *over the* GIRLS' *song*] Let me alone, can't you? I've got to go with all these ladies. I can't let it be known I'm tied to one girl.

MARY: [*spoken to* GYPSY] I let you say all those things this afternoon about going with other girls, and I didn't tell you what I really thought. I don't want you to have any other girls. I want you all to myself, just the way you want me.
[*to the* GIRLS] He doesn't need you. You don't know him. Nobody knows him but me. You all think he's a big strong man, but I know he's not. I know he's a little boy.
GYPSY: Ssh! You must never say that. No matter how well you know it, you must never say it.
MARY: But you like people to be truthful!
GYPSY: No more of that about my being a little boy. You'd better be afraid of me.
GIRLS: [*sung while* GYPSY *continues his speech*]
You've lost him,
You've lost him,
You've lost him,
You've lost him.
GYPSY: [*spoken*] I'm mean, and I treat women cruel, I do. I'll go with all these other girls if I like, and who's going to stop me?
MARY: [*sung*] I know that I'm your mate, dear,
Your mate I'll always be.
I know that soon or late, dear,
You will come back to me.
GIRLS: Why can't you see you've lost him?
You can't keep him,
You can't tame him.
He will take no wife to blame him.
He wants one and then another,
He wants none to be his mother.
He wants women free as air.
MARY: My lover,
Come out of the shadow.
Come out of the shadow
And into my heart.
GIRLS: [*over* MARY] You've lost him,
You've lost him.
GYPSY: All alone
And on my own,
I seek no woman's heart.
GIRLS: Your love is flying away.
Your lover
Is only a shadow,
A wandering shadow
Eluding your heart.
MARY: Only for a while,
Just a little while,
Come and put your head upon my breast.
Come into my arms.
In my tender arms,
You will find contentment and rest.

203

[GIRLS *laugh in derision.*]

GYPSY: [*spoken*] What the hell are you laughing at?
You mustn't laugh at her. She's—
she's—well, you mustn't laugh at her,
that's all. I'm tired.

MARY: [*spoken*] I know you are. Put your head
here a moment.
[*sung to* GYPSY] Somebody wants to go to
sleep,
And I know who.
Somebody longs for slumber deep,
And I know who.
Moonbeams that haunt the evening air,
Will stoop to kiss his tousled hair,
And I'll meet them all
For I'll be there.
To kiss him too.

YOU ARE DOING VERY WELL

Published as an individual sheet. Introduced by Charlotte Greenwood (Tiny) and Stanley Holloway (Eustace).

VERSE 1

TINY: Don't envy brilliant fellows.
Let them brag and blow like bellows.
Don't try to imitate the rest.
Just be an av'rage bloke,
And light your pipe
And have your smoke,
And stick to the job that you know best.
Let others say you are
Not very bright.
Just be the way you are,
You're all right.

REFRAIN 1

TINY: You are doing very well
If the woman you like likes you,
If she listens while you tell
All the wonderful things you do.
If you have your pint of beer
And a bit of a place to dwell,
You're as good a man as any
And you're doing very well.

VERSE 2

EUSTACE: All that you say is true,
But you need some advising too.
And now, dear, I think the time is ripe.

Don't mix with mad romantics,
For their wild eccentric antics
Are not becoming to your type.
Ladies much snappier
End on the shelf.
You'll be much happier
As yourself.

REFRAIN 2

EUSTACE: You are doing very well
If the feller you like likes you.
If he listens while you tell
The ridiculous things you do.
If you have your pot of tea,
And a bit of a place to dwell
You're a very lucky woman
And you're doing very well.

LONELY FEET

Published as an individual sheet. Introduced by Adele Dixon (Dorrie). Reused in the film version of *Sweet Adeline.*

Liza Minnelli brought the song to a new generation of listeners in her 1987 Carnegie Hall concerts and the live recording.

VERSE

Music is softly playing,
And girls in the arms of their boys
Join in the dances.
I would be dancing if I were there.
Timidly I am swaying.
The music has started me dreaming,
Wistfully dreaming,
Wistfully wishing I could be there.
I know all the steps
But they're no use, I fear,
Without a partner near.

REFRAIN

Lonely feet,
While others are gliding by
Here are my lonely feet
Waiting to dance.
Lonely waist,
Intended for arms to hold,
Lonely waist, unembraced,
Waits for a dance.
If I could find someone,
Some mother's awkward son,

Wouldn't we dance
And wouldn't I think him simply divine?
Oh, to meet
The thrill of a joy that's new,
Feeling two other feet
Stepping on mine.

Second refrain for male singer

In August 1934, Jerome Kern received a letter from the New York office of Harms music publishing regarding sales prospects for "Lonely Feet." To enhance its chances as a popular song, the letter writer, Henry, "respectfully recommends" cutting the last two lines of the verse ("I know all the steps . . .") and rewriting part of the refrain: "The first half is written in real 'pop' style, but after 'waits for a dance' it switches into a musical comedy spirit. If you can suggest to Oscar that he change this portion to continue the 'wail of the wallflower' in street language, I think we would have a sure fire selling hit. While he is giving this some thought, would you also ask him to write a male version so that we can get prominent men voices on the air to sing it as well as the ladies."

The sheet music for "Lonely Feet" issued in conjunction with the film of *Sweet Adeline* includes the entire verse, as above, and this second refrain.

Lonely feet,
While others are gliding by
Here are my lonely feet
Waiting to dance.
Lonely arms,
All eager to hold a waist,
Well embraced.
Lonely arms, wait for a dance.
If any girl would be
Willing to follow me,
Wouldn't I lead her,
Wouldn't I think her simply divine!
Oh, to feel
The thrill of a joy that's new
Feeling two other feet,
Stepping on mine.

WHAT GOOD ARE WORDS?

Published as an individual sheet. Introduced by Esmond Knight (Gypsy) and Victoria Hopper (Mary).

What good are words
When you can thrill me with a touch of your
hand?

What good are words,
When there are silences that both of us under-
stand?
What good are phrases
When arms that you love surround you?
What good are poems
When eloquent sighs are saying life has found
you?
What good are words
When, in the hush of night, I hear your heart beat
on mine?

A FUNNY OLD HOUSE

Published as a stand-alone song in 1945. Introduced by Stanley Holloway (Eustace), Victoria Hopper (Mary), Esmond Knight (Gypsy), and male sextet. In November 1944 Kern sent Hammerstein ". . . a new musical version of 'Funny Old House' in the form, as you will hear, of a sort of rondo taking us through sundry keys, but always coming back to the key for the 'little grey cat' on the repetition of the line and coming back to the original 'there's a funny old house' on the repetition of those words. The interlude or bridge between stanzas may be either hummed *bouche fermee,* or 'ah-ed,' and on the very high ones they are to be performed sotto voce, or even falsetto." The editor has not found a copy of the song as it was performed in 1934.

There's a funny old house
In a crooked old lane,
And a garden where zinnias grow.
There's a patch of green ground;
And in all the world around,
It's the greenest green ground I know.
Ah, ah.

There's a little gray cat
And a little brown dog,
And they're sittin' there side by side.
And it's proud that they'll be
When I bring you home with me,*
For they'll know that
I've won my bride.
Ah, ah.

When the crocuses bloom,
And a robin flies home

----

* *Alternate lyric for female singer:*
When it's home you're bringin' me
For they'll know that
You've won your bride.

Just ahead of the lark and thrush.
Then a vine that seemed dead will become a rosy
red,
And the funny old house will blush.
Ah, ah.

And the little gray cat
And the little brown dog
Will be knowin' it's springtime too;
And it's proud that they'll be
For the looks you're givin' me
And the looks that I'm givin' you.
Ah, ah.

There's a funny old house
In a crooked old lane,
And a garden where zinnias grow.
There's a patch of green ground;
And in all the world around,
It's the greenest green ground I know.
Ah, ah.

THE WEDDING

Not published. A medley of overlapping reprises intro-
duced by unidentified soloists at the church where Tiny is being married to Eustace and Mary to Gypsy. The script calls for two false starts of the number before the brides actually appear.

MEZZO-SOPRANO: You are doing very well
If the fellow you like likes you;
If he listens while you tell
All the wonderful things you do.
If you have your pot of tea
And a bit of a place to dwell,
You're a very lucky woman
And you're doing very well.
You are doing very well
If the woman you like likes you,
If she listens while you tell
All the wonderful things you do.
SECOND TENOR: Let me follow you
Through life's changing scene;
Go wherever you will.
BARITONE: We'll grow old and walk
together
And smiles will sweeten our
tears,
While we gently talk together
Of bygone, beautiful years.
If you have your pot of tea
And a bit of a place to dwell,

You're a very lucky couple
And you're doing very well.
THREE GIRLS: Somebody wants to go to sleep
And I know who.
You'll be a circus lady too.
You've won your lover,
We wish you well.

KEEP SMILING

Published as an individual sheet. Introduced by Stanley Holloway (Eustace).

Although Eustace has written this song, he some-
times fumbles for the words, and eventually starts singing parts of other songs.

Stanley Holloway's performance with the Drury Lane Theatre Orchestra, including some of the dialogue, can be heard on the CD *The Great Musicals The-
atre Royal Drury Lane* (Conifer).

VERSE 1

A child of only three
Sat on his father's knee.
The sun was shining brightly from above.
The child of three said, "Dad,
To have you I am glad.
But why do I not get a mother's love?"
At first the father coughed,
To hide the way he felt,
And then he said,
"My child, it's time you knew.
I have a tale to tell,
And I will tell it well,
But first I'd like to sing you this refrain."

REFRAIN

Keep smiling!
Remember you're a man.
Laugh away your care,
That's the only plan.
Keep smiling!
And always wear a grin.
That's the spirit that I think will sometimes win.

VERSE 2

I never shall forget
The day when first we met.
I asked her, and she said she would be mine.*

----

* *On the recording, Holloway sings:*
I asked her and she said that she'd be mine.

And then I took her home,
And showed her to my mother,
And then I took a walk while they made friends.

[*He pauses.*]

On the road to Mandalay
Where the flying fishes play*

[*Stops himself and tries again.*]

That summer we were wed
I kissed her on the head.
And then we lived happily
In a little red house
And had three children, then.
Her father died and I lost my job,
But then years later we got a cable from
    Mesopotamia
That they struck oil on my uncle's property
And we came into practically thirty thousand
    pounds.

REPEAT REFRAIN

I WON'T DANCE

Published as an individual sheet from *Three Sisters*, but better known in the revised version performed by Ginger Rogers and Fred Astaire in the film *Roberta*, where the song is credited to Kern, Hammerstein, Otto Harbach, Dorothy Fields, and Jimmy McHugh. Introduced by Adele Dixon (Dorrie), Richard Dolman (Sir John Marsden), and ensemble.

Three Sisters published version

VERSE

HE: When I seek the pleasure
    To tread a little measure with you, my dear,
    A little one-step or two, my dear,
    Your only answer is no.
SHE: Though my feet are more than ready,
    My brain is strong and far more† steady.
    My answer, therefore, is a definite no!

---

* *On the recording, Holloway sings:*
    Where the village smithy lay.

† *The sheet music's "far from steady" is probably an error. "Far more steady" appears in the typescripts.*

REFRAIN

SHE: I won't dance, don't ask me.
    I won't dance, don't ask me.
    I won't dance, don't ask me to.
    I'm fond of dancing, but I won't dance with
        you.
    When your arms enfold me.
    With your arms you hold me.
    You hold me so close and tight.
    I sort of like it but it gives me a fright;
    It's never harmed me, but who knows when
        it might?
    Dancing as an exercise may do good.
    I've no doubt it's doing quite a few good.
    Though I know your partners all call you
        good,
    For me you're too good,
    Too good to do good.
    So that's why
    I won't dance, don't ask me.
    I won't dance, don't tempt me.
    I won't dance, don't urge me to.
    I've got good reason why I won't dance with
        you.
    I'm fond of dancing, but I won't dance with
        you.

Three Sisters script version

BOYS: When I seek the pleasure
    To tread a little measure with you, my
        dear,
    A little one-step or two, my dear
    Your only answer is no.
GIRLS: Though my feet are more than ready
    My brain is strong and far more steady,
    My answer, therefore, is a definite no!
BOYS: Let your feet forget
    Your brain a bit.
    Try just one dance,
    Just for fun dance.

REFRAIN 1

DORRIE: I won't dance, don't ask me.
    I won't dance, don't ask me.
    I won't dance, don't ask me to.
    I'm fond of dancing, but I won't dance
        with you.
JOHN: But I do ask you to.
    You may have the pleasure
    To tread a little measure
    Within my arms.
DORRIE: When your arms enfold me,
    With your arms you hold me.
    You hold me so close and tight,
    I sort of like it, but it gives me a fright.

It's never harmed me, but who knows
    when it might?
JOHN: When you have the leisure
    We'll tread a little measure tonight.
DORRIE: Dancing as an exercise may do good,
    I've no doubt it's doing quite a few good;
    Though I know your partners all call you
        good,
    For me you're too good,
    Too good to do good.
    So that's why
    I won't dance, don't ask me.
    I won't dance, don't tempt me.
    I won't dance, don't urge me to.
    I've got good reason why I won't dance
        with you.
    I'm fond of dancing, but I won't dance
        with you.
JOHN: Dance! Dance! Dance!
    I've got to dance with you.
    You just must, just because I want
        you to.
    Please dance
    Will you-oo-oo-oo,
    Dance with me
    And I'll dance with you.

REFRAIN 2

GIRLS: I won't dance, don't ask me.
    I won't dance, don't ask me.
    I won't dance, don't ask me to.
    I'm fond of dancing, but I won't dance
        with you.
BOYS: Try just one dance.
    Just for fun,
    Dance one
    Because I ask you to.
    Dance with me
    And I'll dance with you.
GIRLS: When your arms enfold me,
    With your arms you hold me,
    You hold me so close and tight,
    I sort of like it, but it gives me a fright.
BOYS: If my arms should hold you tight
    It's just a dance, and quite all right.
    What is there to give you a fright?
GIRLS: It's never harmed me but
    Who knows when it might?
    Dancing as an exercise may do good,
    I've no doubt it's doing quite a few good.
    Though I know your partners all call you
        good,
    For me you're too good,
    Too good to do good.
    So that's why
    I won't dance, don't ask me.
    I won't dance, don't tempt me.

I won't dance, don't urge me to.
I've got good reason why I won't dance
    with you.
I'm fond of dancing, but I won't dance
    with you.

BOYS: I've done no harm,
What makes you think that I might?
Dancing as an exercise may do good.
So . . .
Do good.
I'll do you good,
I can't be too good,
Too good to do good.
So that's why I say
Try just one dance,
Just for fun, dance one,
Because I want you to,
I will take my chances with you.
I'm fond of dancing,
And I must dance with you.

"Armful of Flame" variation

The Kern Collection at the Library of Congress contains another variation of the lyric, with a specific connection to *Roberta*. On the manuscript Kern has written: "If 'Armful of Flame' is the title of one of Stephanie's dress creations, it should also be the title of this number."

VERSE

SHE: When I seek the pleasure
    To tread a little measure with you, my
      dear,
    A little one-step or two, my dear,
    Your only answer is no.
HE: Though my feet are more than ready
    My brain is strong and far more
      steady,
    My answer, therefore, is a definite no!
SHE: Please don't answer with a definite
    no!
QUARTET: Try just one dance
    Just for fun dance.

REFRAIN

HE: I won't dance, don't ask me.
I won't dance, don't ask me.
I won't dance, thanks just the same.
But I'm not gonna hold an armful of
    flame.
You got charms, you show them.
And what charms, I know them.
I got eyes, but I have learned
What moths that dance with dancing
    flames all have learned.

It's when you dance with dancing
    flames you get burned.
SHE: I'm as safe as you are,
    That is, as far as you are concerned.
HE: Dancing as an exercise may do good.
    And I know your partners all call you
      good.
    But for me you're altogether too
      good.
    For heaven rest us—
    I'm not asbestos.
    So that's why
    I won't dance, don't ask me.
    I won't dance, don't tempt me.
    I won't dance, thanks just the same.
    I know that dancing with a washout is
      tame.
    But I'm not gonna hold an armful of
      flame.
SHE: Dance, dance, dance.
    I've got to dance with you.
    I want you to be game,
    I'll be the same,
    And I'll promise to be tame.
    But I'm not gonna hold an armful of
      flame.

GAIETY CHORUS GIRLS

Alternate title: "Pony Ballet." Not published. Introduced by Albert Burdon (George), Desmond Knight (Gypsy), Stanley Holloway (Eustace), and male ensemble (soldiers). This song is part of a show that the servicemen are performing for each other.

VERSE

MEN: As you were, I remember you.
    As you were, as you used to be,
    I remember you.
    I remember my dreams.
    Dreams are always dreams of
      you.
    And when I'm sentimental,
    All my sentiment centers on you.
    You were not a girl at school
    And you were not the one and
      only
    Girl in all the world for me.
    There were twenty-four of you—
    The chorus of the Gaiety.
    To the twenty-four of you
    I swore that I would always be
      true.

No one else could take your
    places.

REFRAIN

GYPSY, GEORGE,
AND EUSTACE: You were a row of girls,
    And I loved you all.
    When you shook your heads as
      one,
    You seem'd to think it fun.
    You kicked your heels in proper
      style,
    And oh, your smile was beautiful.
    I knew your dances, too,
    Your back kicks and whirls.
    No wonder I recall the day
    I fell in love
    With all the Gaiety chorus girls.

CUT AND UNUSED SONGS

COMICAL SONGS AND A COMICAL DANCE

Not published. Not listed in the program. It is not clear whether this motif was used in the production. Early scripts use it to introduce Gypsy and George at the top of Act One, with a reprise during the World War I scene, and another planned for the Act Three finale, when a small child would join Gypsy, George, and Mary for a quartet version.

Comical songs and a comical dance
By that comical duet,
Purvis and Hood.
Always make their acts good
And your money's worth you'll get.
Comical jokes for respectable folks
For the mothers and the dads.
Sallies of wit, an occasional hit
At the very latest fads.
The short one's Purvis
And the tall one's Hood.
Those West End lads.

DORRIE DESCRIBES

Not published. Not used; replaced by "Lonely Feet." David Glainley is a young aristocrat, a friend to John Marsden, who flirts with Dorrie.

As Dorrie imagines the party in the manor house, various characters enter upstage. In the second half of the number, David explains that the people at the party are younger and less stiff. The characters Dorrie has conjured fade, and his characters take the stage.

Then stage directions explain that she "suggests that they have a little dance together [far downstage] and she can pretend that they are in the ballroom on the hill. She then leads the number with David, singing and dancing it with the chorus behind her. In effect, it is a typical musical comedy dance number, but all those on the stage, except Dorrie and David, are supposed to be imaginary figures."

DORRIE: I imagine a ballroom of marble
And a large flight of stairs;
There is plush on the chairs
And the curtains are made of
plush.
I expect there's a full dozen
flunkies,
Ev'ry one very big,
With a white powdered wig,
And with knee-breeches made
of plush.
Lady Marsden welcomes her
guests
And, oh, she does look
gorgeous.

DAVID: You mean Jack's mother?

DORRIE: Yes, Lady Marsden.
I can see her in her emeralds.
What a sight!

LADY MARSDEN: Are the guests here?

1ST FLUNKY: Yes, my lady.

LADY MARSDEN: Well, why don't you announce
them, you big oaf?

1ST FLUNKY: Lord 'Arry Cricklewood,
And Lady Ticklewood.

2ND FLUNKY: The Duke of Upper Mittledorf
Hoffenstein.

DORRIE: All the blueblood people in
society!

1ST FLUNKY: Mister Robey of *Variety*.

2ND FLUNKY: Commander Wigan of the
Navy himself.

DORRIE: Famous beauties from all
nations
Wearing frocks that cause
sensations.

1ST FLUNKY: Ma'm'selle Cayenne.

DORRIE: She's a Parisienne.

2ND FLUNKY: The ambassador of
Montenegro.

DORRIE: Statesmen and ambassadors,
Even from Montenegro.
He's very black, of course.

DAVID: He's not a negro.

DORRIE: Not a negro?
Of course I knew that.

DAVID: What happens after they all get
there?

DORRIE: Well, the last one to come in
Is the guest of honor.

GUEST OF HONOR: Sorry to be so late, Lady
Marsden.

LADY MARSDEN: So you finally got here.
Now we can start to dance.

DORRIE: Then the music'll start.

LADY MARSDEN: Where's that blue Hungarian
fiddler
Whom I engaged at such great
expense?

[*Fiddler plays.*]

DORRIE: They all start to dance.
I can imagine how beautiful
and graceful
And stately they must be.

DANCERS: Were you at Epsom this
afternoon, my dear?
I had ten quid on your horse.

DORRIE: Their conversation is brilliant.

DANCERS: There is the duchess.
She looks a delight,
Just after her fright—
Fully trying divorce.

DORRIE: I'd like to dance in that house
upon the hill,
With the Belgravia belles.

DANCERS: Isn't it lovely to dance on the
hill?
Aren't we the lucky swells!

DAVID: It's not at all like that, my dear.

[*Dancers stop.*]

You've made a slight mistake, I
fear.

DORRIE: But I know just how Mayfair
looks.
I've read about it all in books.

DAVID: The books you read are quite
misleading,
That is not how Mayfair looks.

[*The party guests recede.*]

DORRIE: All my dreams are fading away;
But tell me, what's the real
thing?

DAVID: Well, the real Lady Marsden is
charming,
But she seldom wears her
emeralds.

DORRIE: Oh!

[*Party guests return, more relaxed. The next several lines are spoken.*]

DAVID: And the young people who
dance aren't quite so stiff
and dignified.

DORRIE: Are they undignified?

DAVID: Not exactly, but they're quite
jolly.

DORRIE: Show me how they dance up
there.

DAVID: I don't have to show you.

DORRIE: Do I dance as well as they do?

DAVID: Rather!

DORRIE: Let's make believe we're up
there with them.

DAVID: Then we are up there! Isn't the
floor crowded?

DORRIE: Scarcely room to do a step.
They're playing a song from
that new show in the West
End, aren't they?

DAVID: Some of them will be singing
the words while they dance.

[DANCERS *sing softly.*]

DORRIE: Do they sing while they dance?

DAVID: Oh, very often.

DORRIE: So will I.
[*sung*] A sweet young thing
Just fresh from school,
All innocence and charm.

DAVID: A bright young thing
Of filmy tulle
That melts into your arm.

BOTH: You'll learn that she
Insistently
Demands to see
A ring.

DORRIE: But by the time you learn it,
you're
In Harrod's buying furniture.

DAVID: To please a sweet young thing.

HERE IT COMES

Not listed in the London program, but melody published in the piano selection. A piano-vocal score is in the Kern Collection in the Music Division of the Library of Congress. Sir John Marsden (Jack) is the man Dorrie marries.

VERSE

JACK: I thought that love was meant
For poets to idealize.
TINY: But now that you are here
It seems a part of life.
GEORGE: I have a feeling that we both
Have dreams to realize.
ALL THREE: That soon our arms will twine.
Your lips and mine
Will be allies.

REFRAIN

JACK, GEORGE,
AND TINY: Here it comes.
The spell at last is on us,
Creeping fast upon us.
Soon we will fall in love.
Here it comes.
The moment it starts
The beat of our hearts
Will rattle like drums.
Soon we'll fall in love.
One little look,
A quick desire
Will set the world on fire.

ROUND (IF A GENTLEMAN MUST WED)

Not published. Not listed in the program. A piano-vocal score is in the Kern Collection in the Music Division of the Library of Congress. The setting is a pub, the night before the wedding.

MEN'S CHORUS: If a gentleman must wed,
Heaven knows where he's headed.
Who knows where he's headed
When he's wedded to a maid?
TENORS: If a gentleman must blunder
Then another man may wonder.
But the very man who'll wonder
Is the very next to blunder,
Little knowing where he's headed,
When he's wedded to a maid!
BASSES: Some gentlemen may wonder,
May wonder why other men
blunder.
Then they are, by thunder,
The next to be wedded
To some sweet young maid.
TENORS: If a gentleman must wed,
Heaven knows where he's headed.
Who knows where he's headed,
When he's wedded to a maid?
BASSES: If a gentleman must wed,
Heaven knows where he's headed.
Who knows when he's wedded to
a maid?

OVERLEAF *The faces of* May Wine *as drawn by Al Hirschfeld. Clockwise from upper left, Walter Slezak, Walter Woolf King, Nancy McCord, Robert C. Fischer, Vera Van, and specialty dancers Jack Cole and Alice Dudley*

Songs of 1935

THE NIGHT IS YOUNG (1935)

A film produced by Harry Rapf for Metro-Goldwyn-Mayer, released January 11, 1935. Directed by Dudley Murphy. Screenplay by Franz Schulz and Edgar Allan Woolf (and Oscar Hammerstein II, uncredited), based on a story by Vicki Baum. Lyrics by Oscar Hammerstein II. Music by Sigmund Romberg. Cinematography by James Wong Howe. Film editing by Conrad A. Nervig. Costume design by Dolly Tree. Orchestra directed by Herbert Stothart. Orchestrations (uncredited) by Wayne Allen, R. H. Bassett, Paul Marquardt, Charles Maxwell, Leonid Raab, and Jack Virgil.

Cast: Ramon Novarro (Archduke Paul "Gustl" Gustave), Evelyn Laye (Elizabeth Katherine Anne "Lisl" Gluck), Charles Butterworth (Willy Fitch), Una Merkel (Fanni Kerner), Edward Everett Horton (Baron Szereny), Donald Cook (Toni Berngruber), Henry Stephenson (Emperor Franz Josef), Rosalind Russell (Countess Zarika Rafay), Herman Bing (Nepomuk), and Mitzi (the horse).

The handsome young archduke Paul Gustave is having an affair with Countess Rafay, who is not approved of by Emperor Franz Josef. As a cover, he claims to be dallying with a ballet girl. He chooses Lisl Gluck and invites her to move into his residence on a strictly platonic basis. However he is charmed by her and is soon frequenting cafés with Lisl and her friends Fanni (a dancer) and Willy (who drives a horsecar). The romance deepens until Paul Gustave's minder Szereny reminds Lisl that the archduke's official responsibilities include an arranged marriage. Sadly but bravely, Lisl says goodbye.

Two songs were published as individual sheets. The Hammerstein Collection in the Music Division of the Library of Congress has a full screenplay dated September 7, 1934, as well as a piano-conductor score for the entire film, including dialogue, descriptions of the camera work, and so on (filed under "T," for the earlier title of *Tiptoes*). There are also handwritten and typed story notes. The Cinema and Television Library at the University of Southern California has a set of typed lyric sheets dated September 4, 1934, some prose story treatments from June and July of that year, and an undated music department memo listing each musical moment and its orchestrator.

Hammerstein spent the summer of 1934 as a producer-in-training. As he explained in a letter to his ex-wife: "A 'producer' guides a production from its inception, chooses a story, casts it, confers with the writers and director and supervises their work. He is regarded as much more important than a writer. The money I'm getting now is very nearly the maximum for a writer, but if I make good as a producer I can command more. Of course I won't attempt the responsibility of producing a picture until I learn more about them." In November 1934, while waiting to see a rough cut, Hammerstein predicted, "The picture will be distinguished for the manner in which the music is introduced, and for excellent character and comedy performances by Charlie Butterworth and others." Viewed today, *The Night Is Young* is a charming film reminiscent of Rodgers and Hart's *Love Me Tonight* (Paramount, 1932, directed by Rouben Mamoulian), with its rhythmic dialogue, changes of locale within a song, and use of "found" sounds, including a music box, a car horn, and clip-clopping hooves.

DANCING MASTER'S DRILL

Not published. These rhythmic instructions are given by Charles Judels (Riccardi) to the opera's ballet chorus. Fraulein Gluck is our heroine.

One, two, three,
One, two, three,
One, two, three,
On your toes.
Up on your
Toes and a
One, two, three,
One, two, three.

Fraulein Gluck,
Fraulein Gluck—
Didn't I
Tell you to
Point out your
Toes?
Lift up your
Stocking, O
Corpo di Bacco.

[*After an interruption.*]

One, two, three,
One, two, three,
Up on your
Toes.
Give me the
Teeth.*
Up on your
Toes.

---

* *Meaning the dancers should smile.*

Give me expression,*
Give me some
Style.
One and a
Two and a . . .

[*He is interrupted again.*]

MY OLD MARE

Not published. Introduced by Charles Butterworth (Willy) with interjections from Una Merkel (his girlfriend, Fanni). The song is punctuated with toots from the horse-drawn streetcar's horn.

VERSE 1

WILLY: I'm proud as can be.
The luckiest thing
Has happened to me.
I've captured a prize,
A beautiful thing
With beautiful eyes.

REFRAIN 1

WILLY: Look her over,
Is she a sweet thing?
Look her over,
Is she a neat thing?
Ev'ry sunrise
We two as one rise,
And in the gloaming
She gets her curry combing.
That's my Mitzi,
My pretty Mitzi,
My old mare.

VERSE 2

WILLY: Her withers are fine,
Her hocks are divine.
FANNI: Well, how about mine?
WILLY: Her tail has a curl,
Her tail has a curl.
FANNI: Go marry the girl!

---

* *The screenplay and piano-vocal score in the Oscar Hammerstein II Collection at the Music Division of the Library of Congress have this line instead: "Take the lead out of your feet."*

REFRAIN 2

WILLY: Look her over,
　　　　Is she a sweet thing?
　　　　Look her over,
　　　　Is she a neat thing?
　　　　What refined legs,
　　　　What hooves and hind legs.
　　　　A mane of jet locks,
　　　　I love her little fetlocks.
　　　　That's my Mitzi,
　　　　My pretty Mitzi,
　　　　My old mare.

THOUGH I AM A NOBLE DUCHESS

Not published. Introduced by Evelyn Laye (Lisl) and Una Merkel (Fanni), who are clowning through a snippet of an operetta called *The Bandit's Bride*.

LISL: Though I am a noble duchess,
　　　You must know I feel as much as you.
　　　I have a heart that beats like yours.
FANNI: [*spoken, as the* BANDIT] I have no heart at all. Your sister is in my power, and I will not let her go until she is mine.
LISL: Oh, won't you spare
　　　My sister dear?
　　　Don't bring disgrace on her poor little head.
　　　Oh, won't you spare
　　　My sister dear?
　　　And if you want to, you may kidnap me instead!

[*The* BANDIT *reveals he is an archduke in disguise.*]

LISL: Though I am a noble duchess
　　　You must know I feel as much as you.
　　　I have a heart that beats like yours.

VIENNA WILL SING

Not published. Sung by Ramon Novarro (Paul Gustave), Evelyn Laye (Lisl), Una Merkel (Fanni), Charles Butterworth (Willy), and an unnamed male singer with the Schrammels Orchestra.

Lift your glass
And drink your new wine,
Then we'll drink some more.
Lift your glass
And clink it with mine
As we've done before.
The new wine will bring
A glow of romance,
Vienna will sing,
Vienna will dance.
So lift your glass
And drink your new wine.
Lift your glass
And clink it with mine.

Unused "getting dressed" version

This early sequence would have introduced the characters of the young archduke (known in early drafts as Franz Otto), his valet, and his aide-de-camp. A music box is playing in the room, and the men sing along and improvise conversation to the tune for the length of three refrains.

NEPOMUK: [*sung while attending to clothes*] Lift your glass and drink your new wine.
　　　　Lift your glass and clink it with mine.
　　　　Doo, duh-lee, duh-loo,
　　　　The new wine will bring
　　　　The glow of romance,
　　　　Vienna will sing
　　　　Vienna will—
FRANZ OTTO: [*sung in the bathtub*] Lift your feet and warm up my bath.
　　　　I am nearly freezing.
NEPOMUK: [*spoken*] Yes, Your Highness.
FRANZ OTTO: Lift your glass and drink your new wine.
SZERENY: [*unconsciously speaking in rhythm*] Just taking your bath?
　　　　Your Highness is late.
　　　　It's seven o'clock.
FRANZ OTTO: [*sung*] The opera can wait.
SZERENY: [*in rhythm*] The emp'ror said "Eight."
　　　　He's as prompt as a bell.
FRANZ OTTO: [*sung*] Szereny, take a pill. You're not well.

WIENER SCHNITZEL

Not published. Introduced by Christian Rub (Café Proprietor), the principals, and restaurant staff. Hammerstein specified, "The following dialogue is to be read in meter with the music that the orchestra is playing, but the speakers are not to seem conscious of performing a musical number."

PROPRIETOR: Will you have goulash or Sausage with sauerkraut?
FANNI: I want my favorite dish.
PAUL GUSTAVE: What do you wish?

REFRAIN 1

FANNI: Wiener schnitzel.
WILLY: With buttered noodles.
PAUL GUSTAVE: [*to* LISL] Wiener schnitzel? With apple strudels?
PROPRIETOR: Wiener schnitzel with buttered noodles.
WILLY: And apple strudels.
PROPRIETOR: [*to* WAITER] They all want apple strudels.
PRINCIPALS: Wiener schnitzel with buttered noodles,*
　　　　I love you.

REFRAIN 2

[*In the kitchen.*]

WAITER: Wiener schnitzel with buttered noodles.
CHEF: Wiener schnitzel.
WAITER: And apple strudels.
CHEF: Wiener schnitzel and buttered noodles.
BAKER: And apple strudels? I'll show them apple strudels.

[*In the dining room.*]

PRINCIPALS: Wiener schnitzel with buttered noodles.
WILLY: My old mare.

* *Hammerstein instructed the cast to deliver this line "as if singing a beautiful sentiment."*

WHEN I GROW TOO OLD TO DREAM

Published as an individual sheet. Introduced by an unidentified Schrammels Orchestra vocalist, Evelyn Laye (Lisl), and Ramon Novarro (Paul Gustave).

Hammerstein wrote at length about the refrain in the introduction to his anthology *Lyrics*.

I was collaborating with Sigmund Romberg. He wrote a beautiful, simple waltz. I fell in love with it. I was certain that everybody would, if I could match the even simplicity of the melody with words of the same quality. The refrain lyrically consists of eight lines. It took me three weeks to write them. One of the lines is repeated twice, so that what I wrote came to only six lines. I had a terrific tussle with this song. The first or second day I was working on it, the music suggested the title, "When I Grow Too Old to Dream." I was delighted with it when I first thought of it. It was so easy to sing. It was so smooth. It was so much in mood with the music. The music was born for it. The next line came very naturally. I sang to myself: "When I grow too old to dream, I'll have you to remember." This was going to be easy to write. I would knock this off in an hour or two.

Then I stopped suddenly. What did it mean? "When I grow too old to dream"—when are you too old to dream? Too old for what kind of dreams? As a matter of fact, when you are old, aren't you likely to dream more than at any other time in your life? Don't you look back and dream about the past? How did this silly line ever come into my head? I threw it aside and worked on another title, then another and another. I finished several refrains based on other titles. I didn't like any of them. In the intervals between each of these efforts, I would go back to the title "When I Grow Too Old to Dream" and try to convince myself that it did mean something. Then I would reject it again, but regretfully, because it had some quality which appealed to me as a songwriter, and I loved to sing it to myself alone in my study. It became so insistent that I began to wonder whether my instinct wasn't truer than my reason. If this line didn't mean anything, why was it so attractive to me? I reanalyzed it and asked myself why my brain had created it, and why I had loved it as soon as I had invented it. I concluded that I must be giving the word "dream" a special meaning, that I was thinking of it in the sense of a lover dreaming only about the present and the future. In saying "When I grow too old to dream," I was really saying, "When I grow too old to love you and to dream about loving you, I'll have you to remember, I will be remembering our love in the past."

The film's hero, Archduke Paul Gustave, initially dismisses the song as a "sentimental old thing." But its sentiment was widely appreciated offscreen: by March 1935, the song had sold 50,000 copies. The leading recording in 1935 was by Glen Gray and the Casa Loma Orchestra, with vocal by Kenny Sargent. Other artists who covered the song include Nelson Eddy and, in 1951, Nat "King" Cole.

VERSE 1

We have been gay,
Going our way.
Life has been beautiful,
We have been young.
After you've gone,
Life will go on,
Like an old song
We have sung.

VERSE 2

After you've gone,
Life will go on.
Time will be tenderly
Melting our tears.
Yet will I find
You in my mind,
Beckoning over the years.

REFRAIN

When I grow too old to dream
I'll have you to remember.
When I grow too old to dream
Your love will live in my heart.
So kiss me, my sweet,
And so let us part,
And when I grow too old to dream
That kiss will live in my heart.

REPEAT REFRAIN

THERE'S A RIOT IN HAVANA

Not published. Introduced by Ramon Novarro (Paul Gustave), who is noodling at the piano while Evelyn Laye (Lisl) reads the newspaper. When Edward Everett Horton (Baron Szereny) enters, he is drawn into their improvised song.

There's a riot in Havana
And a famine in Tibet.
There's a drought in Indiana.
It won't get wet.
There is fighting in the Balkans
And the diplomats are blue,
But I'm spending my time and thought
And all my worry on you.
A kingdom tumbles.
Volcanoes brew.
Vesuvius rumbles.
Popocatepetl too.
There's a quake in Yokahama
And a flood in Tennessee,
But my only concern in life
Is what you're thinking of me.

SZERENY REFRAIN

PAUL GUSTAVE: There's a riot in Havana
And a famine in Tibet.

[*Dialogue covers the next eight measures.*]

Dear Szereny, my only care,
My only worry is you.

[*Dialogue about sending flowers.*]

Where should I send them?
SZERENY: To the Pri-in-cess Mathilde.

[*Dialogue covers the last eight measures.*]

THE NIGHT IS YOUNG

Published as an individual sheet. Introduced by Ramon Novarro (Paul Gustave) and Evelyn Laye (Lisl). The verse is not heard in the film.

VERSE

The failing light
Of falling sun
Melts into a deep'ning blue.
And here is night
And I'm the one
Favored to be here with you.
I thank all the stars that shine
That these happy hours are mine.

REFRAIN

The night is young and the moon is riding high.
The night is young and so am I.
A cricket sighs and I hear you sighing too.
The night is young and so are you.
And through it all I can hear your beauty call,
Like a shy persuading whisper in the sweet stillness.
My heart is yours just as yours belongs to me.
The night is young and so are we.

Early version

Not published and not used. It would have been sung by a fairground puppeteer and his girl as they pack up for the night, then reprised by Paul Gustave and Lisl.

REFRAIN

There's a lark in the meadow,
In the meadow
His song is sung.
And the lark sweetly singing
Tells the meadow
The night is young.
Night is young, the stars above are tying
Silver blossoms on a field of blue.
Right among the stars my heart is flying
When I'm close to you.
Let us stay here together,
Close together
As night goes on
Till the lark in the meadow
Tells the meadow
The night has gone.

CUT AND UNUSED SONGS

GOSSIP RECITATIVE

Not published. Not used in this form. According to Hammerstein's stage directions the lyric was to be "whispered in countermeter to the waltz, starting on the ninth bar." In the film, it was reduced to a brief voiceover.

YOUNG LADY: He called him "His
    Highness."
HER MOTHER: I think he's an archduke!
SEVERAL WHISPERED
    VOICES: An archduke!

STOUT MAN: I think it's Franz Otto.*
1ST OFFICER: And who's the girl with him?
    That can't be the countess.
2ND OFFICER: Some girl from the ballet.
SEVERAL VOICES: A girl from the ballet.
WOMAN: Franz Otto's in love with a
    girl from the ballet.
MAN: A girl from the ballet's in
    love with Franz Otto.

LENA, I LOVE YOU

Not published and not used. Intended to be sung in a puppet show.

MAN: Lena, I love you,
    How I love you, Lena.
    I have never seen a
    Girl I'd rather see.
    I'm full of envy
    Ev'ry time I see you,
    I would like to be you
    And be loved by me.
GIRL: Though you charm and please my eye,
    My ideals are higher.
    I like a man,
    I like a man,
    I like a man who can play a drum.
    With his drumsticks in his hand
    Drowning out the whole darn band.
    Some like 'em dumb,
    Some like 'em numb,
    Some like a man who can play a drum.
    Bass drum, snare drum, kettle too,
    Any little drum will do.

[*Repeat with* MAN *and* GIRL *singing their stanzas simultaneously.*]

RECKLESS (1935)

RECKLESS

Written for the 1935 MGM film *Reckless*. Registered for copyright on February 13, 1934. Music by Jerome Kern.

* *In early scripts, the Ramon Novarro character is named "Franz Otto."*

Verse and refrain published as an individual sheet. Introduced by Jean Harlow* (Mona), girls, and Nina Mae McKinney (Café Singer).

The song is heard in a musical sequence that begins with Harlow declaring her philosophy to other girls in a dormitory,† then shifts to an ocean liner, and ends in a South American café. In the café scene, Carl Randall dances with Harlow, and Allan Jones serenades patrons with the song "Asi Se Besa" (music by Kern, lyric in Spanish by Rafael Storm). Some of the dormitory segment is excerpted in *That's Entertainment* (MGM, 1974).

There has been speculation that Kern and Hammerstein wrote additional musical numbers. *Reckless* materials at the Academy of Motion Picture Arts and Sciences' Margaret Herrick Library and at the University of Southern California's Cinema and Television Library do not identify any other Kern-Hammerstein songs. The *Reckless* file in the Music Division of the Library of Congress includes copyist manuscripts for "Rehearsal Number," Song #1350, December 21, 1934, and "Dormitory Seq.," Song #1350-Rev., January 7, 1935; they have the same musical content and both are credited to Kern, but neither has a lyric or a credited lyricist. However, the source that might be most useful, lyric sheets submitted to the Production Code Administration has not been located.

INTRODUCTION

MONA: What'll you ever be?
    What'll you ever do?
    How will you ever know
    If you don't take a chance?
GIRLS: You have got to gamble with fate.
MONA: I want to live, love, learn a lot.
    I'll light my candle and I'll burn a lot.
GIRLS: You'll have some bad shocks, hard knocks.
MONA: I'm on my own if I bruise.
GIRLS: And there'll be smiles here, shouts,
    cheers.
MONA: And I can take it on the chin if I lose,
    Because I'm reckless.
GIRLS: She's simply reckless.
MONA: Reckless!
GIRLS: She's simply reckless.
MONA: I'm gonna go places and look life in the
    face.

* *Most sources credit Virginia Verrill for Harlow's singing voice, but the laser disc release of* That's Entertainment *names Shirley Ross as the voice double.*

† *The gigantic set does not look like a typical dorm, but a January 1935 scenario by P. J. Wolfson starts the number in a "circular dormitory" where various girls are preparing for bed.*

REFRAIN

MONA: When I'm in love, I'm reckless.
Each time in love, I'm more reckless.
I waste no weeping on lost romances,
I pay my losses and I take new chances.
I'm reckless and I don't want advice.
I'll keep on seeking my fool's paradise.
I waste no weeping, I just keep hoping
For one who's hoping for me.

[Dance.]

MONA: I've made my mind up
That here I'll wind up.
I'll take what's coming to me.

VERSE

MONA: I've been around
It's been well advertised.
I have lived and I've loved.
What is life without love?
Keep your feet on the ground
All my friends have advised.
If you fly, you will fall
So I fly and I fall.
Ev'ry time my heartbeats call me
I waste no weeping
I just keep hoping
For one who's hoping for me.

MAY WINE (1935)

Tryouts: Playhouse, Wilmington, Delaware, November 22–24, 1935; Ford's Theatre, Baltimore, November 25–30, 1935. New York run: St. James Theatre; opened December 5, 1935; closed June 6, 1936; 213 performances. A New Musical Play. Presented by Laurence Schwab. Music by Sigmund Romberg. Lyrics by Oscar Hammerstein II. Book by Frank Mandel based on *The Happy Alienist*, by Wallace Smith and Erich Von Stroheim. Staged by Jose Ruben. Musical direction by Robert Emmett Dolan. Orchestrations by Donald Walker and Robert Russell Bennett. Settings by Raymond Sovey. Costumes designed by Kay Morrison.

Cast: Walter Slezak (Professor Johann Volk), Robert Sloane (Willi Zimmerkopf, a sculptor), Walter Woolf King (Baron Kuno Adelhorst), Nancy McCord (Marie, Baroness Von Schlewitz), Patricia Calvert (Vera, Professor Volk's assistant), Robert C. Fischer (Josef, a clarinet player), Leo G. Carroll (Uncle Pishka), Vera Van (Friedl, Willi's model), and dancers Jack Cole and Alice

Dudley, with Roy Gordon (Inspector Schnorrheim), Tomes Chapman (Sergeant/Stroller), Edward Galloway (Policeman), Leonard Berry (Policeman), Chester Herman (Policeman), Carlo Conte (Herr Schmidt/Dr. Karpis), Victor Casmore (Hans, Pawnbroker), Marie Louise Quevli (Gypsy), Bela Loblov (Musician), Charles Palloy (Musician), Mitchell Harris (a Father), Inga Hill (a Mother/Kathi), Radley Collins (a Son/Pageboy), Marian Huntley (a Daughter), Maury Tuckerman (a Waiter), Earle R. MacVeigh and Betty Kerr (the Lovers), Devona Doxie (a Boxholder), Lee Childs (a Boxholder), Flora Laney, (a Stroller), Leonard Berry (a Stroller), Clifford Menz (a Stroller), Earle R. MacVeigh (Mr. Runtschli of "Die Wochende"), Jessie Graham and Leonard Berry (Old Couple), Mitchell Harris (Dr. Von Schlager), and Leonard Berry (Dr. Herbst).

Professor Johann Volk is a mild and lonely Viennese psychiatrist. His absentminded generosity one afternoon in a barber shop draws the interest of Baron Kuno Adelhorst. Kuno never has much money, but always has a plan to get someone else's. Kuno asks his girlfriend, the equally broke Baroness Marie, to charm the professor. Marie marries Volk by the end of the act, ensuring a handsome lifestyle for herself, Kuno, and Uncle Pishka, another jovial hanger-on. In Act Two, Marie comes to love Volk, but now he is suspicious of her motives. Needing someone to talk to, he commissions a life-size model of Marie from his sculptor friend Willi. (Meanwhile, Willi's neglected girlfriend, Frieda, is finding a willing listener in Kuno.) One night, goaded to extreme jealousy, Volk shoots Marie. After a therapeutic confession—the entire show is a flashback—he is glad to learn that he has only shot the doll.

The main source for this chapter is a holograph piano-vocal score (possibly the rehearsal version) in the Sigmund Romberg Collection in the Music Division of the Library of Congress. Five songs were published as individual sheets. Early scripts are preserved in the New York Public Library for the Performing Arts and in the Frank Mandel Collection at UCLA. It appears from program listings of scenes and characters that several cuts were made before the New York opening, but no complete musical numbers were lost or added.

Although set in Vienna, *May Wine* was not an operetta. There were no overture and no formal ensemble. *Variety*'s review of the Baltimore tryout noted "songs and music [are] secondary to the plot. In fact, the tunes and trilling are chiefly used to motivate and indicate action of the play." In 1935 that was a criticism; in 1945 it would be praise, but Hammerstein and his collaborators still had some kinks to work out. As Romberg scholar William A. Everett points out, most of the songs were soliloquies, which made singing and dancing ensembles unnecessary. The exigencies of the plot even forestalled a big waltz duet for the central couple.

Hammerstein's own report from Baltimore was characteristically upbeat: "We have a good but rather slow first act, devoid of high spots. The second act is a beaut, entertaining and continuing the unusually strong story pull that the first act also has. The finish, when the 'murdered woman' appears and for the first time is embraced by her husband, never fails to evoke a burst of applause."

SOMETHING IN THE AIR OF MAY

Not published. Introduced by various townsfolk (street musicians, policemen, young lovers, drunks).

REFRAIN

Something in the air of May
Can make a fellow romantic.
When he's walking
He is flying
Through the magic air of May.
Girls all seem so fair in May
They make a fellow go frantic.
When they're talking
They are sighing
With the ecstasy of May.
Sighing and replying
To the call that comes in May.

CODA

Lads like eager doves
Hearts aflutter fly
To their lady loves.
Ev'ry butterfly
Wants to get his share
Of some honeydew.
Don't you feel aware
You want something too?
Isn't there some butterfly in you?

Dropped passages from the opening number

In an early version of the script, this number was heard prior to Volk's confession, with the curtain rising on a police station where several springtime revelers explained their offenses in rhyming dialogue. Each admission led into a refrain (or partial) of "Something in the Air of May."

1.

POLICEMAN: [about FRIEDL] Half
undressed and in
the park
And sitting right in a
fountain.
SERGEANT: [to FRIEDL] Were you
drinking?
FRIEDL: I was stinking.
SERGEANT: [to POLICEMAN] Have her
sit right over there.

REPEAT REFRAIN

2.

SERGEANT: [about two men and two
women]: Charge?
2ND POLICEMAN: Parking!
SERGEANT: Parking. What else?
2ND POLICEMAN: Necking!
SERGEANT: Necking?
What have you to say?
1ST MAN: Well, you see, it's
May . . .

REPEAT REFRAIN

3.

SERGEANT: [about a DRUNK] Same
thing?
3RD POLICEMAN: Drunk again!
SERGEANT: Drunk again?
3RD POLICEMAN: Drunk again.
SERGEANT: What have you to say?
DRUNK: It's a lovely day.

REPEAT REFRAIN

SERGEANT: Shut up!

4.

DRUNK: I was feeling fine,
Someone offered wine.
I accepted wine.
Need I tell you more?
FRIEDL: I was known as nice,
I took bad advice.
Now I'm twice as nice
As I was before.
INSPECTOR SCHNORRHEIM: Fraulein Korngold and
Fraulein Rainer,
Herren Meyerhof and
Baum.

TWO MEN: In the spring a young
man's fancy
Finds in love a joy
profound.
FRIEDL AND TWO WOMEN: In the spring a young
man wants
What girls want all year
round.

REPEAT CODA

INTERLUDE IN A BARBER SHOP

Not published. Street musicians outside are playing "an air, supposedly well known to all Viennese." Walter Woolf King (Kuno) sings along from his seat, with rhythmic shaving and stropping motions and recitative by Victor Casmore (the barber's assistant).

KUNO: I met her at the opera,
I met her at the zoo,
Then I walked boldly up to her
And asked her if she—
[spoken] Gustl! a bit of hair here.
GUSTL: Oh, pardon, Baron.
KUNO: [sung] She looked so sweet,
And so completely off her guard,
So petite—

[The song is interrupted.]

SWEET WILHELMINA

Not published. Introduced by a Schrammels orchestra, and those enjoying the afternoon at a café.

REFRAIN

Sweet Wilhelmina,
Will you marry me?
There is no other
Girl that I can see.
Sweet Wilhelmina,
Happy we'll be
If you only will,
Wilhelmina,
Marry me.

VERSE

If you can cook Wiener Schnitzel,
If your house is big enough for two,
You can address me as "Fritzl,"
And I'll move right in with you!

REPEAT REFRAIN

A CHANSON IN THE PRATER (I'M ONLY ME)

Not published. Introduced by Walter Slezak (Volk) and Nancy McCord (Marie). Volk had heard the song on a recent trip to Paris, and tells Kuno that it's an interesting "study of frustration through a sense of inferiority."

VOLK: If I were anybody else but myself,
If you were anyone but you,
I might aspire to tell you all I desire,
As any other man might do.
But in the presence of your beauty
I am as shy as I can be,
For you are you
And you are wonderful,
And who am I?
I'm only me.

CODA

MARIE: When I am with you I am tongue-tied.
And just as shy as I can be.
For you are you
And you are wonderful,
And who am I?
I'm only me!

A DOLL FANTASY

Not published. Introduced by Nancy McCord (Marie).
Marie is performing in a benefit. Kuno explains: "She appears as a doll, and her song makes you feel that if only the secret could be learnt, one could make of that divine creature an obedient doll." Stage directions instruct Marie to begin "with toneless staccato inflection."

MARIE: I know,
I know
Why you like to love a doll like me.
You can,
You can
Love and leave me so conveniently . . .
That's why you love me!

Celluloid eyes of blue
Longingly look at you.
Two little feet made of wood
Stay where they're stood.
I do what you decide I do.
Celluloid eyes can't see,
Loving me, you're still free;
You can control me forever
With the twist of a lever.
For what am I?
A pretty image.
Wax!
You can relax with me . . .

[*During an interlude she loosens up.*]

Ah, me.
If I were only real.
Ah, me.
I know just how I'd feel.

[*Now freely, with great feeling.*]

With my head held high, I'd fly to love.
If you called me, I'd reply to love.
If I only thought you wanted me, I'd want
   you.
I would let you hold me in your arms.
I would be so proud to win your arms.
If I only thought you wanted me, I'd want
   you.
If the joy in my heart were certain,
The doubt in my heart all gone,
We could kiss and ring up the curtain,
And the play would go on!
With my head held high I'd go to love,
Gladly giving all I owe to love.
If I only thought you wanted me, I'd want
   you.

YOU WAIT AND WAIT AND WAIT

Title during the tryout: "When You've Waited for Your True Love." Not published. Introduced by Walter Woolf

King (Kuno) and Nancy McCord (Marie). Kuno has rejected Marie's sexual advances, because he wants her to marry Volk for his money. Kuno sings with a "soothing, comforting attitude."

VERSE

KUNO: Always wait for love.
Don't rush the date for love,
Joy will be sweeter for the waiting.
Don't inflate your love
Or satiate your love
By prematurely celebrating.
MARIE: Heigh-ho,
I want you so.
What's to do when I want you so?
KUNO: Why, oh,
Why can't you see
How happy we will someday be?

REFRAIN 1

KUNO: After saving all our kisses
We'll enjoy the kisses we have saved.
Darling, you will find that this is
How the road to happiness is paved.
In a week, a month or two, dear,
We will be in heaven.
Heaven waits for you, dear.
MARIE: But I don't want to wait for heaven.
KUNO: When you've waited for your true love
And the joy you sought is yours at last,
Then the least that you can do, love,
Is to wait till you can hold it fast.
For you must not hurry life,
You can't flurry life.
You find your mate
And then you wait for fate.
MARIE: And then you wait and wait and wait.

REFRAIN 2

KUNO: After saving all our kisses
We'll enjoy the kisses we have saved.
Darling, you will find that this is
How the road to happiness is paved.
Though I know as well as you know
MARIE: [*spoken*] Kuno.
KUNO: You're no marble Juno.
MARIE: [*spoken*] Kuno.
[*sung*] Treat me less like Juno
And treat me more like Venus, you know.
What's the use of saving kisses
When the more you give
The more you get?
KUNO: You find your mate
And then you wait for fate.
MARIE: And then you wait,

And wait,
And wait.

I BUILT A DREAM ONE DAY

Published as an individual sheet. Introduced by Walter Slezak (Volk), who has written this love song for Marie. He demonstrates the refrain for Josef (Robert C. Fischer), Kuno (Walter Woolf King), and Willi (Robert Sloane), who each show how they would sing it. Stage directions instruct: "Without being conscious of how funny they all look, each continues with the refrain according to his own conception. It becomes a quartet which is harmonious musically but highly divergent in delivery, with each of the four in a different part of the stage, lost in the sweep of his own emotion, every man for himself."

The hit ballad of the show, "I Built a Dream One Day" reached number 19 on the 1936 pop charts with a recording by Ray Noble and His Orchestra, with vocal by Al Bowly.

VERSE

On the day we met I set a dream apart,
Fed it with my imagination,
Kept it as a prize
To live forever in my heart.
Now it's all I own,
All my consolation.

REFRAIN

Out of a smile that I found in your eye,
I built a dream one day.
Out of a song and a half-whispered sigh,
I built a dream one day.
Out of a breeze that blew in your hair,
I built a dream that vanished in air.
Out of a love that was lost on the way,
I built a dream one day.

DANCE, MY DARLINGS

Published as an individual sheet. Introduced by Nancy McCord (Marie) and various couples dancing beneath her hotel window.

VERSE

Happy little lovers,
You have found a little orchestra to dance to.
This is your moment,
Hold each other closely,
And believe in beauty while you have the chance
     to.
This is your moment.
Such moments soon are* gone,
So let the band play on.

REFRAIN

Dance, my darlings,
Dance through the night
While your hearts beat light rhythms of love.
Dance, my darlings,
Dance with your dreams
While the starlight beams down from above.
You are having romance, my darlings,
Joy that may fade
As the starlight fades out of the blue.
So dance, my darlings,
Dance with your dreams,
While your dreams are still dancing with you.

ALWAYS BE A GENTLEMAN

Not published. Introduced by Walter Woolf King (Kuno)
and Nancy McCord (Marie).

REFRAIN 1

KUNO: Always be a gentleman,
         No matter how it hurts.
         Ancient rules of etiquette beset me.
         I would like to have my fun,
         But my family crest won't let me.
MARIE: Always be a gentleman,
         No matter how it hurts.
KUNO: Father taught me that when I was a boy.
         In my secret heart
         I'm longing to be a cad.
MARIE: But each time you start,
         You think of your dear old dad.
KUNO: So I am a gentleman
         With manners that are swell,
         And life is dull as hell!

* Some versions say: "are soon gone."

REFRAIN 2

MARIE: Always be a gentleman,
         No matter how it hurts.
         Bite your lip and curb your inclinations.
         You're supposed to be beyond
         Vulgar folk who sense sensations.

[MARIE hums as she walks to the bed.]

KUNO: If I had the spunk
         To shake ev'ry shackle free,
MARIE: I bet that you'd dunk
         Napoleons in your tea.

REFRAIN 3

MARIE: Always be a gentleman,
         No matter how it hurts.
         In colloquial idiom: "Keep your shirt
            on."
         You must worship from afar
         Anything that has a skirt on.
         Always be a gentleman
         And when someday you meet
         The wench who will eventually be yours,
         Be kind and polite
         Considerate and gallant
         And see her at night
         But never without her aunt!
         Always be a gentleman,
         And see what you will get.
         See what you will get!

Reprise refrain

Introduced by Walter Woolf King (Kuno) and Leo G.
Carroll (Uncle Pischka) in Act Two, Scene 4.

KUNO: When you're born a gentleman
           Some things just aren't done.
PISCHKA: Father taught me that when I was a boy.
KUNO: With so much to see
           And so much to be enjoyed
PISCHKA: A blueblood should be
           Eternally unemployed.
BOTH: Always be a gentleman,
           And set the styles and fads.
           Work is meant for cads!

DEAREST LITTLE WIFE
(VOLK'S LETTER TO MARIE)

Not published. Introduced by Nancy McCord (Marie).

Dearest little wife,
I thought it best to part.
Will it be for long?
That's up to you, love.
Do not call me back
Unless you want me in your heart.
If you never do
Still I'll be your true love.

SOMEBODY OUGHT TO BE
TOLD

Published as an individual sheet. Introduced by Vera
Van (Friedl).
    In one draft of the script Volk says this song has two
interesting elements: "A. The romantic. B. The sex urge.
The melody punctuates the words. It has a pseudo-
African rhythm which creates an emotional glow, a
warmth."

VERSE

I am young and plastic,
I'm enthusiastic,
I'm a bud that's nearly fully blown.
Life is gay and thrilling,
I'm awake and willing,
Yet I am neglected and alone.

REFRAIN 1

Somebody ought to be told
That I've arrived.
Nobody seems to know I'm here.
Somebody ought to be told
That I'm deprived
Of something that my heart holds dear.
I am sentimental.
I want someone to be
Pleasure bent and sweetly sentimental
     over me.
Somebody ought to be told
That I've arrived.
I'm free and fair and twenty-one.
I guess I ought to tell someone.

REFRAIN 2

Somebody ought to be told
That I've arrived.
Nobody seems to know I'm here.
Somebody ought to be told
That I'm deprived
Of something that my heart holds dear.
Both my arms are empty*
And my lips unkissed;
I'm a girl who wants a whirl at all the
    things she's missed.
Somebody ought to be told
That I've arrived.
I'm free and fair and twenty-one.
I guess I ought to tell someone.

Reprise refrain

FRIEDL: Somebody ought to be told
That I've arrived.
Nobody seems to know I'm here.
Somebody's got to be told
That I'm deprived
Of something that my heart holds dear.
Maybe I'm romantic
And maybe I'm a fool.
But I've got looks and I've read books
    that aren't read in school.
KUNO: Somebody's glad to be told
That you've arrived.
You can't be more than twenty-one.
FRIEDL: I'm not.
KUNO: I think I'm going to have some fun!

SOMETHING NEW IS IN MY HEART

Published as an individual sheet. Introduced by Nancy McCord (Marie).

Stage directions instruct: "As if mumbling her thoughts to herself, she starts the verse of the following lyric, keeping it broken, casual and conversational. Not singing until the line 'I know romance.'" Recorded in 2004 by Emily Skinner for *The Broadway Musicals of 1935* (Bayview).

---

* *Additional lyric for lines 7–9:*
I'm a lonely blossom
That wants a honeybee.
I'm a ship without a sail, a sky without a sea.

VERSE

Once I used to laugh,
I used to sneer
At lovers' fancies.
Once I felt so sane and free.
Now I never laugh,
I never sneer.
I know romance is
Real as it can be.
It's come to me.

REFRAIN

Now that you are in my life
I want to live forever.
Something new has come into my heart.
Something in the sun
Makes the day
Brighter than before.
Something in the moon
Makes the night
Thrill me more and more.
Now that you are in my life
I want to live forever.
Hope anew awaits a cue to start.
Dreams that have been sleeping
Are waking.
The dawn of love is breaking.
Now that you are in my life
Something new is in my heart.
Now that you are in my life
And love is in my heart!

JUST ONCE AROUND THE CLOCK

Published as an individual sheet. Introduced by Walter Woolf King (Kuno) and Vera Van (Friedl). Reprised almost immediately by Van and Leo G. Carroll (Uncle Pischka).

Recorded in 2004 by Todd Murray for *The Broadway Musicals of 1935* (Bayview).

VERSE

KUNO: Nothing to regret tomorrow.
FRIEDL: Nothing to regret.
You'll find me making
No demand or claim upon you.
Kiss me and forget.
KUNO: Kiss me and forget.
FRIEDL: Kiss me while you may,
Tomorrow is another day.

KUNO: So while you're glowing
With a sweet warm flame upon
    you,
Let it burn away.
FRIEDL: Let its life be short and gay.

REFRAIN

FRIEDL: Just once around the clock
And then goodbye, dear.
Love likes to fly by night,
So let it fly, dear.
KUNO: Love likes to fly by night,
So let it fly, dear.
And when it's over
Bid me goodbye, dear.
Just as we met with the coming
    of the moonlight
We'll part with the rising of
    the sun.
FRIEDL: Just once around the clock
As happy strangers,
Who seek the joys of life*
Without its dangers.
KUNO: Just once around the clock
Let beauty lead you
And when it's over, darling,
Godspeed you.
FRIEDL AND KUNO: Just as we met with the coming
    of the moonlight
We'll part with the rising of
    the sun.

CHAMPAGNE AND ORCHIDS (1935)

In 1935, Kern and Hammerstein wrote four songs for an MGM project known as *Champagne and Orchids* and as *Summer Breeze*. The songs were registered for copyright on April 30, 1935, but the film, conceived as a vehicle for Jeanette MacDonald and Nelson Eddy, was never made. Hammerstein's scenario for *Summer Breeze* survives in the Hammerstein Collection in the Music Division of the Library of Congress. Piano-vocal scores are in the Music Division of the Library of Congress.

An MGM interoffice memo notes that Kern's additional submission, "Prelude," was an instrumental. A Kern manuscript labeled "Broad Western Prairie" is sometimes associated with *Champagne and Orchids*; no lyric is known to survive.

---

* *In some versions the last word of this line is "love."*

BANJO SONG (WHEN I'VE GOT THE MOON)

Music by Jerome Kern. Not published. Hammerstein included it in his anthology *Lyrics*.

What's my future?
Where am I goin'?
Don't ask me,
Don't ask me.
When I've got the moon
I am wishin' for the sun.
When I'm sittin' in the sun
I am wishin' for the moon.
When I've got no job
I'm as blue as I can be.
When I've got some work to do
I am longing to be free.
I'm a discontented, good-for-nothin' sort of ne'er-
do-well,
Sit around an' mope all day until I hear the dinner
bell,
Sit around an' mope all day an' dream of what can
never be.
(It takes so much to satisfy a shiftless* guy like
me.)
When I've got the moon
I am wishin' for the sun.
When I'm sittin' in the sun
I am wishin' for the moon.
When I've got five bucks,
I am wishin' it was ten,
But if I had you to love
Then I'd never wish again.
What's my future?
Where am I goin'?
You tell me,
You tell me.

CHAMPAGNE AND ORCHIDS

Music by Jerome Kern. Not published.

We've laughed,
We've danced,
We've flirted long enough.

* *A copyist piano-vocal score, dated April 22, 1935, has
the word "crazy."*

We've both advanced,
We know each other's stuff.
The overture to love is under way.
It's time we raised the curtain on our play.
I'll set the stage and keep the background bright
and gay.
You'll have champagne and orchids,
And with champagne and orchids
We'll start the prologue
To a new romance,
To a new romance.
We'll drink and wish the best,
And leave the rest to chance.
And as the hour of midnight
Draws me close to you,
And stars that flow'r at midnight
Blossom in the blue,
You won't believe me,
But you'll make believe you do.

DANCE LIKE A FOOL

Music by Jerome Kern. Not published.

VERSE

So you want to learn to dance
And kick your heel and toe.
You want to give up all that's
Good in life and go
For applause,
That unkind applause.
So you'll stretch your arms and legs
And make your muscles grow.
Neglect your brain and
Break your heart, but always go
For applause,
All you'll get is applause.

REFRAIN

Dance like a fool,
Your public's calling.
Dance like a fool
To keep from falling.
Smile for your patrons,
They pay for your smile.
Hand-painted matrons and play girls, and stray
girls,
And men who admire
Your one or two tricks
Till they desire
A girl with new tricks.
That's all that they want,

If that's all you want,
Fool, go on and dance.

SINGING A SONG IN YOUR ARMS

Music by Jerome Kern. Not published.

VERSE

When I'm with you,
My common sense
Is all but wrecked, dear.
A strange effect, dear,
You have on me.
I seldom talk,
I always sigh.
And when I walk I want to fly.
I want to fly with ev'ry meadowlark I see.
I want to sing most ev'ry song I ever knew—
That's how I feel when I'm with you.

REFRAIN

When I'm in your arms I want to sing, dear.
For your tender arms I've waited long.
Now that you are in my heart,
My heart is in my song.
Now that love has found me,
Life has found new charms.
I'm content to lie beneath a moonlit sky
Singing a song in your arms.

MISCELLANEOUS SONGS

TO ALICE ON HER BIRTHDAY

Music by Alice Hammerstein. In the spring of 1935, Hammerstein was working in Hollywood and his daughter Alice was in New York. His May 15 letter enclosed "my present to you—a poem set to your Christmas present to me."

Her eyes are brown
And she's just fourteen
(This is the seventeenth day of May)

She looks her best
When her face is clean
(Women are funny that way)
She's just too short to be tall
And she's just too big to be small
She's just fourteen
And she's "in between"
But quite serene with it all
Her eyes are brown
And she's just fourteen
(This is the seventeenth day of May)
I'd love her eyes
Were they blue or green
(Fathers are funny that way)

A KISS TO BUILD A DREAM ON

Words and music by Bert Kalmar, Harry Ruby, and Oscar Hammerstein II. Published as an individual sheet.

"A Kiss to Build a Dream On" was intended for the 1935 film *A Night at the Opera* but not used. In 1949, publishing executive Abe Olman came across the song "on the dust-covered shelves of MGM's music department." Soon after, it was placed in the 1951 film *The Strip*, where it was introduced by William Demarest and Mickey Rooney, reprised by Kay Brown, and reiterated by Louis Armstrong. "Kiss" was nominated for the Academy Award for Best Song, but lost to "In the Cool, Cool, Cool of the Evening" by Hoagy Carmichael and Johnny Mercer.

Louis Armstrong's recording for Decca reached sales of 500,000 by the end of January 1952, outperforming all of his previous hits. It was also recorded by Kay Brown, the Hugo Winterhalter Orchestra and Chorus with vocal by Johnny Parker, Jimmy Dorsey, Bob Eberly, Monica Lewis, and Jack Haskell, prompting the *New York Enquirer* to dub it "the sleeper hit of 1951–52." The song reached a new audience in the twenty-first century with a 2004 rendition by Rod Stewart and a 2002 duet by Tony Bennett and k.d.lang.

VERSE

How am I to bear this separation?
Give me just a little hope to cling to,
Fan the flame of my imagination
So I can dream till we meet again.*

REFRAIN

Give me
A kiss to build a dream on,
And my imagination will thrive upon that kiss.
Sweetheart, I ask no more than this—
A kiss to build a dream on.
Give me
A kiss before you leave me,
And my imagination will feed my hungry heart.
Leave me one thing before we part,
A kiss to build a dream on.
When I'm alone with my fancies
I'll be with you,
Weaving romances,
Making believe they're true.
Give me
Your lips for just a moment,
And my imagination will make that moment live.
Give me what you alone can give,
A kiss to build a dream on.

THE MIST WAS ON THE MEADOW

Words and music by Bert Kalmar, Harry Ruby, and Oscar Hammerstein II. Not published. This lyric was an earlier 1935 effort to the tune that became known as "A Kiss to Build a Dream On."

VERSE

I remember when I stood before you
In the meadow with the night descending.
Tremblingly I whispered, "I adore you,"
And felt the thrill of your tender kiss.
I recall the night in all its splendor,

---

* *Prior to publication the verse continued with these lines:*
  Life would simply be beyond endurance
  With a love song but no one to sing to.
  Leave me with a tender reassurance
  That I have not sung my song in vain.

When we vowed our love would be unending,
When I gave my lips in sweet surrender,
It was exactly a night like this.

REFRAIN

Softly
A nightingale was calling,
A summer sun was falling,
And melting in the blue.
Gaily
I walked along with you,
The mist was on the meadow.
Swiftly
My eager heart was beating,
My eager lips repeating,
Their tribute to your charms.
Gently
I held you in my arms,
The mist was on the meadow.
The magic spell of the nighttime*
Whispered to me,
This is the right time
To sing love's melody.
Softly
A nightingale is calling,
A summer sun is falling,
And we're alone again.
Dreaming†
The dreams we cherished when
The mist was on the meadow.

---

* *A second typed lyric sheet gives these words for lines 15–18:*
  The dream was too precious to last, dear,
  Too good to stay true.
  Now that the dream's past, dear,
  What is there left to do?

† *The second typed lyric sheet has this variant ending:*
  Lonely,
  I grow more lonely when
  The mist is on the meadow.

OVERLEAF Left: *Gladys Swarthout and Jan Kiepura as Juliet and Romeo in* Give Us This Night
Right: *Irene Dunne and Randolph Scott in* High, Wide, and Handsome

Songs of 1936–1937

GIVE US THIS NIGHT (1936)

A film produced by William LeBaron for Paramount Pictures. Released on April 4, 1936. Directed by Alexander Hall. Screenplay by Edwin Justus Mayer and Lynn Starling (and Hammerstein, uncredited).* Based on a story by Jacques Bachrach. Music by Erich Wolfgang Korngold. Lyrics by Oscar Hammerstein II. Music conducted by Erich Wolfgang Korngold.

Cast: Jan Kiepura (Antonio), Gladys Swarthout (Maria), Philip Merivale (Marcello Bonelli), Benny Baker (Tomasso), Alan Mowbray (Forcellini), Allen Rogers (the uncredited singing voice of Forcellini), John Miltern (Vincenti), Michelette Burani (Francesca), Sidney Toler (Carabiniere), William Collier Sr. (Priest), Mattie Edwards (Elena), Chloe Douglas (Lucrezia), Charles Judels (Second Carabiniere), Maurice Cass (Guido), Franklin Pangborn (Forcellini's Secretary), Monte Carter (Fisherman), Nick Thompson (Fisherman), Robert Milasch (Fisherman), Constantine Romanoff (Fisherman), Sam Appel (Fisherman), Jack Raymond (Fisherman), Roger Joseph (Fisherman), Charles Stevens (Fisherman), Hank Mann (Fisherman), John Picorri (Fisherman), Jerry Mandy (Old Man), Pedro Regas (Old Man), and Alfred P. James (Old Man).

Four songs were published by Famous Music as individual sheets. The Music Division of the Library of Congress has Hammerstein's June 1935 screenplay titled *Song in the Night* (Hammerstein Collection) and a holograph piano-vocal score (Korngold Collection). The Academy of Motion Picture Arts and Science's Margaret Herrick Library has three subsequent screenplays. The Production Code Administration files in the Herrick Library's Motion Picture Association of America Collection contain correspondence about the songs but not the actual lyrics. The Music Department at Paramount Pictures kindly made cue sheets and song lists available, as well as copies of typed lyric sheets Hammerstein had approved and initialed.

The film does not include a title song. Although it seems likely that Hammerstein and Korngold would have written one, none is registered in the Paramount Music Department. However, a title song credited to Tot Seymour (lyrics) and to Korngold and Phil Bautelje (music) was released "for exploitation purposes."

Give Us This Night is the story of a composer, his

---

* *In November 1935 Hammerstein's agent wrote: "It looks as if you will wind up with someone getting a co-credit. I am assured that it is definitely no reflection on you, as they are in love with your final script, and would have loved to shoot it exactly word for word as you turned it in."*

soprano protégé, and two tenors preparing the premiere of a *Romeo and Juliet* opera. The arias and scenes are seen in rehearsal and performance throughout the film, and they do not correspond with the order of events in Shakespeare's *Romeo and Juliet*.

SORRENTO SONG

Not published. Introduced by Jan Kiepura (Antonio). In *Hollywood Song*, historian Ken Bloom points out that the melody was used a second time during the film as "Morning Song in Naples," lyric by Harry Tobias.

When I am home in Sorrento,
Then I am where I belong.
Girls are all gay in Sorrento,
And ev'ry man can sing a song.
Tra la la la la la la

[*Extended obbligato and whistling.*]

When I am back in Sorrento,
Then I am where I belong,
Garlic is good in Sorrento,*
The girls you kiss will make you strong.
Tra la la la la la la
La, la, lah!

FISHERMAN SONG

Music based on a theme from Offenbach. Prepared for publication, but apparently not released. Introduced by Jan Kiepura (Antonio) and ensemble (Sorrento fishermen and villagers).

Slowly the sun is falling,
Fisherman, raise your sail!
Home and the shore are calling,
Fisherman, raise your sail.
Roll on, roll on, roll on!
Ere day is gone
Roll on, roll on!
Ah!
Roll on, roll on,
Go back across the blue
To those who wait for you.

---

* *This line and the next are not heard in the film.*

SOFTLY THROUGH THE HEART OF NIGHT

Alternate titles: "Opera, Part III" and "Garden Scene." Not published. Incompletely introduced by Gladys Swarthout (Maria, rehearsing the role of Juliet) and Alan Mowbray (Forcellini, rehearsing the role of Romeo). Heard at greater length at the end of the film, with Jan Kiepura singing the part of Romeo.

JULIET: Nearer comes my Romeo and faster beats
    my heart,
    Soon in the moonlight I shall see his
      godlike form.
    Softly, through the heart of night,
    On wings of love he'll fly.
    Softly, through a dreamy mist that dims a
      starry sky.
    So will my Romeo come to me.
ROMEO: So will thy Romeo come to thee.
JULIET: 'Tis he!
ROMEO: To thy waiting arms.
JULIET: O come!
ROMEO: I fly!
JULIET: My sweet!
ROMEO: I fly. I am near, so near.
JULIET: Is it thee I hear?
ROMEO: Breathless with the sweet desire that
      flowers feel in spring,
    Humbler than a slave am I and prouder
      than a king.
    So will thy Romeo come to thee.
JULIET: To thee I would give the world.
ROMEO: To me thou art earth and sky above.
BOTH: To thy arms I fly, my love!

HYMN

Alternate title: "Processional." Not published. Introduced by Gladys Swarthout (Maria), Jan Kiepura (Antonio), and ensemble (churchgoers).

Onward, onward, onward to the highest throne.
Onward, onward, onward to the highest throne.
Heaven lends her light to guide thy way.
Lift up thy voices,
March on and sing!
March on and sing!
Lift up thy voices
March on and sing!
March to thy king!

Blessed, blessed the day,
Hallowed and glorious,
Triumphant and victorious!
Sing! March to thy king! Sing!
Lift up thy voices,
The Lord God is king!
On to the king!
Onward on and on!
On to the king!
Onward to the king!
On and on!

SWEET MELODY OF NIGHT

Published as an individual sheet. Introduced by Jan Kiepura (Antonio). Though temporarily in jail, Antonio sightreads this aria from the new opera *Romeo and Juliet* so well, he is hired for the part of Romeo. A recording by Kiepura is included in the Pearl CD set *Oscar Hammerstein—The Legacy*.

Sweet melody of night,
Sweet song of my delight,
Soft whispers in a windblown tree
And your dear heart whisp'ring to me.
Not a note of music, not a word of rhyme,
Just the breathless echo of a love sublime.
My melody of night,
My moment of delight,
No voices under heaven's wide blue,
But my young heart calling to you!
Like a rose whispering to a vine,*
So I hear your dear heart beating on mine.
Sweet melody of night,
My moment of delight,
No voices under heaven's wide blue,
But my young heart calling to you!

MY LOVE AND I

Alternate title: "Love Scene." Published as an individual sheet. Introduced by Jan Kiepura (Antonio, rehearsing as Romeo) and Gladys Swarthout (Maria, rehearsing as Juliet). Reprised during the performance sequence that ends the film.

———

* *The last six lines are not heard in the film.*

ROMEO: My love and I stand alone in sight of
          heaven,
       The love that I call my own in sight of
          heaven.
       Her eyes look into mine,
       Her eyes are tender,
       Her heart akin to mine in sweet
          surrender.
       And when the dawn lights the sky,
       A star in heaven
       Will tell the sun,
       Will tell the sun:
       My love and I are one.
JULIET: My bounty is as boundless as the sea*
       The more I give, the more I have for thee.
       Thou are the world to me and so will thou
          ever be
       As sure as the moonlight glows above.
       To your arms I fly, my love!
       Ah!
ROMEO: My love and I stand alone in sight of
          heaven,
       The love that I call my own in sight of
          heaven.
       Her eyes look into mine,
       Her eyes are tender,
       Her heart akin to mine in sweet
          surrender.
       And when the dawn lights the sky,
       A star in heaven
       Will tell the sun,
       Will tell the sun:
       My love and I are one!

I MEAN TO SAY "I LOVE YOU"

Published as an individual sheet. Introduced by Jan Kiepura (Antonio), with an immediate reprise by Gladys Swarthout (Maria). The sheet music includes a middle stanza that is not heard in the film.

The composer of *Romeo and Juliet* is Maria's guardian. He has written this song to express his true feelings for her.

———

A star kissed the sky
And I held your hand,

———

* *These words are from Shakespeare, albeit abridged. In the published sheet the language was modernized to:*
     My bounty is as boundless as the blue,
     The more I give the more I have for you.

Too awkward and shy
To make you understand.
I meant to say "I love you."
The moon kissed the sea,
The sea kissed the shore,
And I said that we
Should see each other more.
I meant to say "I love you."
A star kissed the sky,
And I felt that I
Had met love
And let love go by.
Tonight I'll be brave
And rewrite the scene.
Tonight I'll be brave
And say just what I mean.
I mean to say "I love you."

I'll hold you
With all the joy I feel.
Darling, let me hold you,
Let me know you're real.
Press your heart
Close to mine,
Let me feel it beat
A frantic, sweet,
Romantic melody.

Tonight
I want what I have missed,
Arms that never held me,
Lips I've never kissed.
Tonight
I want to be with you—
I don't want any dream,
Unless that dream is true!
Tonight I'll be brave
And rewrite the scene.
Tonight I'll be brave
And say just what I mean.
I mean to say "I love you."

MUSIC IN THE NIGHT (AND LAUGHTER IN THE AIR)

Alternate titles: "Opera, Part I," "Juliet's Entrance," and "Opening Ballroom." Published as an individual sheet. Introduced by Gladys Swarthout (Maria, in the role of Juliet) and the ensemble (members of the opera chorus, as party guests at the Capulet home).

———

ENSEMBLE: Play on, play on, a song of May,
          A dream of youth is on the way.

A dream may come and soon be gone,
Be young, be gay, play on!

JULIET: Eager as a bird that greets the early
dawn,
Blushing like a rose that smiles upon a
lawn.
Thus a gentle maiden, when her heart
is laden,
Brimming with romance will look for
love
And find him at a dance.
Ah! [cadenza]
Music in the night and laughter in the
air,
Eyes that are alight with dreams and
visions fair.
If thou art a maiden and thy heart is
laden,*
Hie thee to a dance and thou wilt find
love there.
Ah! [cadenza]
Music in the night and laughter in the
air,
Eyes that are alight with dreams and
visions fair.
If thou art a maiden and thy heart is
laden,
Hie thee to a dance and thou will find,
Thou will find love there.

CUT AND UNUSED SONGS

ROMEO'S ENTRANCE

Not published and not used. Intended to follow "Music in the Night."

JULIET: Good nurse, sweet nurse, tell me, pray,
Who are they that come this way?

[ROMEO enters.]

NURSE: I know not.
JULIET: O heaven,
O heaven!

---

* The sheet music modernizes these lines:
If you are a maiden and your heart is laden,
Hie thee to a dance and you will find,
You will find love there.

Thy beauty's before me!

NURSE: Braver than brave, stronger than strong
are his arms.
Younger than youth, fairer than fair are
his charms.

WAS THERE EVER A VOICE

Alternate titles: "Metronome Melody," "Romeo's Entrance," and "Opera, Part I (As Romeo sees Juliet for the first time)". Not published and not used. In Hammerstein's screenplay, this aria for Romeo is introduced in a rehearsal scene where Antonio is forced to match tempo with a metronome.

Was there ever a voice
So silver-sweet and tender?
Were there ever two arms,
So soft, so white and slender?
The faintest sound of her voice,
The merest touch of her arms,
Would make my heart rejoice,
Would make my heart rejoice.
If thou wouldst touch me,
My arms would be thine.
If thou wouldst love me,
Thy joy would be mine.

BALCONY SPEECH

Not published and not used. An abridged version of Shakespeare's text.

JULIET: O Romeo,
Wherefore art thou, Romeo?
What's in a name?
That which we call a rose
By any other name would smell as sweet.
O Romeo,
Doff that name,
And for this name which is no part of
thee,
Take all myself!

[There's trouble backstage. FORCELLINI (playing ROMEO) is late for his cue.]

JULIET: I know that gentle voice,
That voice that falls upon my ear,

Faint echo like a shower of rose leaves
falling on a field of dew.

ROMEO: [bellowing from offstage]
[illegible]

JULIET: O my Romeo.
How dare thee sing!
If my kinsmen hear thee, they will
murder thee!

[FORCELLINI bellows from his dressing room.]

JULIET: [stranded onstage alone] Like a rose
whispering to a vine.
O Romeo, Romeo call to me [illegible]
Let me know thou art [near?]
Call to me!
Call to me!

HIGH, WIDE, AND HANDSOME (1937)

A film produced by Arthur Hornblow Jr. for Paramount Pictures. Released on July 21, 1937. Directed by Rouben Mamoulian. Original story, screenplay, and lyrics by Oscar Hammerstein II. Additional dialogue by George O'Neill. Music by Jerome Kern. Choreography by LeRoy Prinz. Orchestrations by Robert Russell Bennett. Music direction by Boris Morros. Additional music by Bernhard Kaun. Edited by Archie Marshek. Costumes designed by Travis Banton. Photographed by Victor Milner and Theodor Sparkuhl. Special photographic effects by Gordon Jennings. Art direction by Hans Dreier and John Goodman. Sound recording by Charles Hisserich and Don Johnson.

Cast: Irene Dunne (Sally Watterson), Randolph Scott (Peter Cortlandt), Dorothy Lamour (Molly Fuller), Elizabeth Patterson (Grandma Cortlandt), Raymond Walburn (Doc Watterson), Charles Bickford (Red Scanlon), Akim Tamiroff (Joe Varese), Ben Blue (Zeke), William Frawley (Mac), Alan Hale (Walt Brennan), Irving Pichel (Mr. Stark), Stanley Andrews (Lem Moulton), James Burke (Stackpole), Roger Imhof (Pop Bowers), Lucien Littlefield (Mr. Lippincott), Edward Gargan (Foreman), and Purnell Pratt (Colonel Blake).

Doc Watterson runs a medicine show. When his rig burns up in a small Pennsylvania town, Doc and his daughter Sally are put up by Peter Cortlandt and his grandmother. Although their backgrounds are very different, a romance develops between Sally and Peter, and he promises to build her a house on the hill where they sometimes meet. But soon after they marry, Peter becomes preoccupied by business. Several local landholders have oil in their lots, but the high cost of transportation eats up their profits. Peter persuades them that a pipeline could break the railway syndicate's monopoly. He is consumed by the job, even allowing them to build on *the* hill. Lonely and bored, Sally takes an interest in Molly, a saloon singer. Peter finds them both singing in a bar and is furious. Sally decides she's had enough and leaves town with a passing circus. But when she gets word that the capitalists have hired a vicious crew to break the line, she returns with members of the circus who fight them off and finish the job.

Six songs were published individually. The Oscar Hammerstein II Collection in the Music Division of the Library of Congress contains a screenplay dated December 21, 1936. The Warner-Chappell Collection there includes copyist piano-vocal scores and a letter with additional lyrics in Hammerstein's hand. The Margaret Herrick Library in Los Angeles has a screenplay from October 1936 and Production Code Administration files showing that six songs were submitted for approval in November and December 1936. Four additional songs were submitted between January and March 1937.

In December 1936, Hammerstein notified Paramount's music department that the song "Go Choose Your East" was a folk tune. A piano-vocal score dated March 19, 1937, credits the lyric of "Workmen's Chorus" to orchestrator Robert Russell Bennett.* A piano-vocal sheet titled "The Fields" consists of the words "High, wide, and handsome" and some square-dance calls. The October 1936 screenplay refers to songs called "Settin' by Myself" and "Drifting" but provides no lyrics.

HIGH, WIDE, AND HANDSOME

Published as an individual sheet; the verse is not heard in the film. Introduced by Irene Dunne (Sally).

VERSE

I wonder if she's lookin' out the window
A-hopin' that I'll soon be there.
Or maybe she is standin' in the garden
With starlight shinin' in her hair.
I wonder if she's half as glad as I am
That Saturday is here once more.
I wonder if she knows I'm gonna kiss her
As soon as we get inside her door.

---

* *"Workmen's Chorus" does not appear in the cue sheet and does not seem to have been used.*

REFRAIN

High, wide, and handsome,
I'm ridin' wide and high.
Run, little horsie, run.
Wish you was a bird
Jest so you could fly!
I'm ridin' high, wide, and handsome,
A yaller moon above.
Why am I ridin' high?
'Cause I'm ridin' to my love.

TO FOOL A SIMPLE MAIDEN (OPERETTA FRAGMENT)

Alternate title: "Water Pitcher Episode." Not published. Introduced by Irene Dunne (Sally), who acts out this scene while doing barnyard chores.

SALLY: To fool a simple maiden
    Whose heart, whose heart with love, alas,
        was laden.
    [*recitative*] You told me you were only a
        miller boy.
    And now I find you are a prince.

[*Pig grunts.*]

    Why did you come to the well every
        morning,
    If not to laugh at me?

[*Pig grunts.*]

    [*spoken*] Don't deny it.
    [*singing basso for the hero's voice*] Ah, no,
        Suzette! I would not laugh at you.
    [*as* SUZETTE] But laugh you did—
    Ha-ha-ha-ha!
    How you laughed to see how easy 'twas
    To fool a simple maiden,
    Whose heart with love was laden.
    To fool a simple maiden,
    Whose heart, whose heart, alas,
    With love was laden.

CAN I FORGET YOU?

Published as an individual sheet, and in Hammerstein's anthology *Lyrics* (refrain only). Introduced by Irene Dunne (Sally).

The verse was written well after the refrain and is not heard in the film.

VERSE

Soon you leave me.
This last night is flying.
Pale stars are weeping,
Sad breezes sigh.
When you leave me,
Can love end with trying?
Can love, so living,
So quickly die?

REFRAIN

Can I forget you?
Or will my heart remind me
That once we walked in a moonlit dream?
Can I forget you?
Or will my heart remind me
How sweet you made the moonlight seem?
Will the glory of your nearness fade,
As moonlight fades in a veil of rain?
Can I forget you?*
When ev'ry night reminds me
How much I want you back again?

WILL YOU MARRY ME TOMORROW, MARIA?

Alternate Title: "Wedding Song." One section is titled "Grandma's Polka." Published as an individual sheet. Introduced by William Frawley (Mac). The December 21, 1936, screenplay explains that "a delighted crowd gathers around Mac. Knowing the old song well, several groups are spontaneously formed for barber-shop harmony. One or two couples start to dance a polka."

---

* *Not heard in the film is a repeat of the refrain, which would end with Sally and Peter dueting. Peter had these words to sing against Sally's last three lines:*
    I'll try to forget you,
    But all in vain, darling,
    For, right or wrong,
    My heart will long for you
    Till you come back again.

Hammerstein submitted the interlude lyric in a February 1937 letter to his music publisher, but it is not heard in the film.

MAC: Will you marry me to-morrow, Maria?*
Will you marry me to-morrow, Maria?
Your ma thinks I'm unsightly,
Your pa insults me nightly,
But tell them both, politely,
To jump in the lake!
I will have no dilly-dallyin', Maria.
I will have no shilly-shallyin', Maria!
Don't wait until to-morrow, Maria,
But get dressed up in your bombazine
And go to the church on the village green.
Maria, I can't wait to marry you.
MEN: Will you make my apple brandy?
Will you take my socks to darn?
GIRLS: Don't fergit that you're a handy
Man around a barn.

INTERLUDE

You will be a right bewitchin' bride
When you're standin' by my side
With a ring upon your finger
To tell the world you're mine.
I will be as nervous as a fool,
Like a new boy at a school.
Like as not you'll squeeze my hand
Then I'll be fine!

ALL: I will have no dilly-dallyin', Maria.
I will have no shilly-shallyin', Maria!
Don't wait until to-morrow, Maria,
But get dressed up in your bombazine
And go to the church on the village green.
Maria, I can't wait to marry you.

THE FOLKS WHO LIVE ON THE HILL

Published as an individual sheet and included in Hammerstein's anthology *Lyrics*. Introduced by Irene Dunne (Sally).

Twice in the 1950s, Hammerstein cited this ballad as a favorite neglected song.

---

* *The name rhymes with "pariah."*

VERSE*

Many men with lofty aims
Strive for lofty goals.
Others play at smaller games
(Being simpler souls).
I am of the latter brand,
All I want to do
Is to find a spot of land,
And live there with you.

REFRAIN

Someday,
We'll build a home on a hilltop high, you and I,
Shiny and new, a cottage that two can fill.
And we'll be pleased to be called,
"The folks who live on the hill."
Someday,
We may be adding a thing or two, a wing or two,
We will make changes as any family will,
But we will always be called,
"The folks who live on the hill."
Our veranda will command a view of meadows
    green,
The sort of view that seems to want to be seen.
And when the kids grow up and leave us,
We'll sit and look at the same old view, just we
    two,
Darby and Joan, who used to be Jack and Jill,
The folks who like to be called
What they have always been called,
"The folks who live on the hill."

JENNY DEAR

Alternate title (from cue sheet): "Titusville Square and Shanty Boat." Not published. Introduced by carousers in a saloon called the Shanty Boat.

I'm going far away,
Jenny dear, Jenny dear.
But I'll come back some day,
Jenny dear, Jenny dear.
The lock of hair you gave me,
A tender token true,
I'll keep it near my heart,
Jenny for you, you, you.

---

* *The verse, which is clearly to be sung by a man, is not heard in the film.*

THE THINGS I WANT

Published as an individual sheet. Introduced by Dorothy Lamour (Molly).

In February 1937, Hammerstein wrote to his music publisher about this song: "Are you not publishing this? I think you should. I spoke to Arthur Hornblow on the 'phone the other day before I sailed and he said this song was one of the high spots of the picture. It is a very good song too."

VERSE

What a world this would be
If I made my wishes come true.
But the world offers me
Only long-shot chances
And vague romances
To see, and pursue,
And to learn they never come true.
All the things that I would choose,
All the prizes I could use,
Are the prizes I'm fated to lose.

REFRAIN

The things I get are what I never seem to want.
The things I want are what I never seem to get.
I'm just a discontented dreamer with a discon-
    tented heart,
I'm just a gambler who can never win a bet.
The kind of man I always find
Is one with fun upon his mind—
And not much time to spare.
And then I find another kind
Who wants to put me on a pedestal
Because I'm fair,
And then he leaves me there
For someone else who's fair.
The things I get are what I never seem to want.
The things I want are what I never hope to see.
And so it isn't any wonder,
Now that I'm in love with you,
That I'm afraid to ask if you're in love with me.

ALLEGHENY AL

Published as an individual sheet. Introduced by Irene Dunne (Sally), and reprised by Dunne and Dorothy Lamour (Molly). Sally has offered to teach Molly a lively song.

VERSE

Steamboat round the bend,
Round the river bend
Brings a scandalous gamblin' man
With lots of money to spend.
He's a howlin' swell,
Rarin', tearin' swell.
High-fallutin' an' hard to please
An' rough on women as well.

REFRAIN

Who's that rascal there?
Who's that steamboat dandy?
Allegheny Al,
Allegheny Al!
Bear grease on his hair
Makes him shine like candy,
Allegheny Al,
Allegheny Al!
With a white di'mond, a white di'mond,*
A-blinkin' on his throat,
An' a sunflower, a sunflower,
A-stinkin' up his coat.
As a quick kisser, a slick kisser,
He gets the ladies' vote.
Don't you let your gal
Meet that steamboat dandy,
Allegheny Al,
Allegheny Al.

---

* Alternate lines 9–14 for second refrain:
　He's a Beau Brummel, a Beau Brummel,
　He wears a beaver hat.
　An' a boiled dickey, a boiled dickey,
　Beneath his silk cravat.
　With his slick manners, his quick manners,
　He knocks the ladies flat.

DOCTOR WATTERSON'S INDIAN WIZARD OIL

Not published, and not used in the final cut. Introduced by Irene Dunne (Sally) and Raymond Walburn (Doc Watterson).

There ain't no need for pain an' aches.
All mis'ry you can foil,
If you keep usin'
Doctor Watterson's Indian Wizard Oil.
It's good for you, it's good for me,
It's good for princes royal.
Two bits is all you pay
For Doctor Watterson's Indian Oil.
If your baby's got the rickets,
Whooping cough, or boil,
That's the time for
Doctor Watterson's Indian Oil.

I'LL TAKE ROMANCE

I'LL TAKE ROMANCE

Music by Ben Oakland. Published as an individual sheet. Introduced by Grace Moore in the 1937 Columbia motion picture of the same title.

Hammerstein had a long-standing business relationship and friendship with music publishers Max and Louis Dreyfus of Chappell and Co., but songs from Columbia's films were usually published by Irving Berlin. Writing to Berlin's partner Saul Bornstein, Hammerstein suggested that the waltz "I'll Take Romance" go to Berlin's firm because:

> You were slated to publish the music of the picture and I just happened to write the lyric as a favor to Everett Riskin and Benny Oakland . . . I would like to know what your company will undertake to do for us in the way of exploiting these two* songs. I am not an unreasonable author who believes that a publisher should spend all his profits in plugging one of my duds, but these two songs (both the music and lyrics of which have already been written) look as promising to me as any that I have written for a long time. You can hear them, make up your own mind about them, and tell us how far you are willing to go with them on the basis of your own judgement.

I'll take romance,
While my heart is young and eager to fly,
I'll give my heart a try,
I'll take romance.
I'll take romance,
While my arms are strong and eager for you,
I'll give my arms their cue,
I'll take romance.
So, my lover, when you want me, call me
In the hush of the evening.
When you call me
In the hush of the evening, I'll rush to my
First real romance
While my heart is young and eager and gay,
I'll give my heart away,
I'll take romance.
I'll take my own romance.

---

* The second song was "A Mist Is Over the Moon."

The Great Waltz. Above: *Luise Rainer*
Below: *Miliza Korjus*

GENTLEMEN UNAFRAID (1938)

Municipal Open Air Theatre ("The Muny"), St. Louis, June 3–12, 1938. No New York production. Presented by the Municipal Theatre Association of St. Louis, under the direction of Richard Berger. Book and lyrics by Otto Harbach and Oscar Hammerstein II. Original story by Edward Boykin. Music by Jerome Kern. Staged by Zeke Colvan. Orchestra directed by George Hirst. Choreography by Theodor Adolphus and Al White Jr. Orchestrations (uncredited) by Robert Russell Bennett, Conrad Salinger, and Charles Miller. Settings by Raymond Sovey. Costumes by Brooks Costume Company, New York, from designs by Billi Livingston. Assistant to the authors: Leighton K. Brill.

Cast: Ronald Graham (Bob Vance), Hope Manning (Linda Mason), Richard "Red" Skelton (Bud Hutchins), Vicki Cummings (Betsy Havens), Kay Picture (Polly Evans), Minto Cato (Liza), Kirk Alyn (Don Mason), Ralph Riggs (Pignatelli), Marcella Uhl (Miss Murdock), Barry Sullivan (Jim Allen), Roland Drew (John Carter), Fred Persson (Benny Havens), Carroll Ashburn (Commandant Reynolds), Avon Long (Joe), Annamary Dickey (Mrs. Mason), George E. Mack (Mr. Mason), Al Downing (Senator Vance), Victor Thorley (Abraham Lincoln), Jerry Sloane (John Wilkes Booth), Lori Trivers (Maizie La Tour), and ensemble.

Gentlemen Unafraid begins at West Point in the spring of 1860. There are many traditions for the graduating class to experience, but instead of celebrating as a group, most Southern cadets are returning to their home states, planning for secession. Although it means going against his father and his girlfriend Linda, Bob Vance feels he owes the Union his allegiance.

Hayfoot, Strawfoot, a revised and simplified version for amateur groups, premiered at Yale University on October 21, 1942, presented by the Yale Dramatic Society in collaboration with the Yale Glee Club. The southern premiere was staged on January 7–8, 1943, at Duke University, under the auspices of Theta Alpha Phi (the National Honorary Dramatic Society), the Hoof and Horn Club, the Duke Players, and the Duke Glee Club.

The Oscar Hammerstein II Collection in the Music Division of the Library of Congress houses several drafts of the script. The Otto Harbach Collection in the Billy Rose Theatre Collection of the New York Public Library for the Performing Arts has drafts from 1938 to 1942 (plus numerous drafts written after Hammerstein and Kern withdrew from the project). The Warner-Chappell Collection and the Kern Collection, both in the Music Division of the Library of Congress, have piano-vocal scores from *Gentlemen Unafraid* and *Hayfoot, Strawfoot*. Two songs were published upon reuse in different circumstances.

This chapter does not include "When You Hear That Humming," "It's Gayer Whistling As You Go," "What's Become of the Night," "Perfect Symphony," and "When a New Star," because the lyrics are by Otto Harbach alone. The songs "Army Blue" and "Bonnie Blue Flag" are authentic West Point and Confederate songs, respectively. A musical manuscript titled "Cantabile" was found with the *Gentlemen Unafraid* materials. The melody was reused the following year in *Very Warm for May* as "All the Things You Are," but no *Gentlemen Unafraid* lyric has been found.

In March 1938, Hammerstein wrote to producer Max Gordon, "This is a play where the numbers are very much a part of the story, giving it a great deal of its strength and emphasis." A few weeks later Hammerstein outlined the musical demands for Dick Berger, production manager for the St. Louis Muny: "This show is so constructed that there is an economy of dialogue and the story is mainly told in musical sequences. The continuous musical accompaniment that lasts throughout Act 1 Scene 1, the tremendous buildup of 'The Land of Good Times' with dance following, and the whole war montage in Act 2, built around 'I Wish Dat Dere Wasn' No War' are gigantic orchestral efforts, far more ambitious than anything Jerry had anticipated."

Although it never made it to Broadway, *Gentlemen Unafraid* is noteworthy because of surviving letters that give a rare glimpse at Harbach and Hammerstein's working relationship. Some extracts:

- Harbach to Kern, undated: "I'd like to see any further scenes that Oscar has written so I may be sure I'm catching the spirit of the characters as he has started them."
- Hammerstein (in Beverly Hills) to Harbach (in Mamaroneck, New York) January 5, 1938: "My chief feeling is that the core of the [Act 2] montage should be a big number, introduced at the beginning of it and serving as the motive for the war. I have already written the lyric to this number and it is to the melody which we had chosen for 'The Road to Glory.' It is really too good to spoil by just mailing the lyric to you. We will have to sing it and explain how it is to be sung when you get here. Now when it is hot off the press, it seems to us both like a terrific thing . . . Send me 'Gentlemen Unafraid' as soon as you can. I have had to do some rewriting in the first scene and I am a little at a loss to just how to cue the number in without the lyric. What are the other two lyrics you say you have finished, and when do we get them? Are you pushing ahead with the dialogue to the last scenes in the first act? I am confident that I will have all my part written when you get here and if you have yours, we'll have our first version of a complete first act, which is a big part of the play."
- Hammerstein to Harbach, April 1, 1938: "Don't worry about the Lincoln number. As long as the music is out here and it is such an easy thing to toss off (none of the words will be very distinguished, I'm afraid), I will attend to it."
- Hammerstein to Harbach, April 11, 1938: "[I] have managed to work out a rather neat refrain for Linda's number in Scene 2, Act 2.* When I write the verse I will send it to you and you can let me know if you think it is an improvement on yours or not."
- Hammerstein to Harbach, April 14, 1938: "I am sending Dick [Berger] a new script containing all of Boykin's corrections and the two cuts that I sent you. I have not put in the enclosed lyric, awaiting your approval, but if you approve, then you can perhaps have it inserted before it goes to the typists. The new script will contain everything except the new Lincoln lyric which I am expecting to have in a few days . . . I am certainly looking forward to seeing you and pitching in with you in earnest. I have an idea we are going to be able to do some great work when we are together in St. Louis."

Work continued immediately after the St. Louis production. Hammerstein spent most of the train journey back to Beverly Hills "dialoguing the new first act." But later that summer, even in the midst of rewrites, he warned Harbach, "Without feeling the possibility of having a smash it is foolish to go ahead and put words down on paper and try to persuade anyone to put money into it." Harbach continued working on the show, including its 1942 adaptation for college performances, but by the fall of 1943, Hammerstein had decided not to continue with the project. On November 19, 1943, during the Boston tryout of *Carmen Jones*, he wrote:

Dear Otto,

Again it seems to me that you have improved the play. But with each new, improved version I become more convinced that I have no interest in the basic subject matter or characters . . . You *do* like these people and their problems and somehow or other you'll get them on the stage and they'll come to life under your hand—but not under mine. I haven't your faith in them nor your affection for them. It has become your play by every right. I have no business sharing either its success or failure—whatever its future may be. I am being very definite about this because I think you are being unfair to yourself and the play, dragging two anchors along with you—Jerry and me. I think you should cut away from us, get another composer to set the lyrics and really go after getting it produced. I think it should be produced and I think it has a fine chance, if you can cast it with fresh, young people. God knows, no one

---

* *Possibly this is "Mister Man."*

could wish you more luck with it than I. You have poured so much good thought and effort into it that there is no limit to the success it deserves . . .

I am so anxious, Otto, that you understand my attitude about this play. I know I've left no doubt about my feeling for it, but I want it to be equally clear to you how unwelcome this decision is, how grateful I am for all the work you've done, carrying my name on it all along, and being willing to share royalties I never could deserve. Please understand this and be assured of my gratitude, for this and lots of other things, for instance, the foundation of a career, which I owe to you more than anyone else.

You know I stand ready to give any help in this venture that you ask of me, and, of course, it goes without saying that the few lines of mine that remain in the script are yours for keeps.

I'll be coming back to town next week, for a few days. I'll phone you then.

Love to Ella, the family and yourself.

As ever,

Oscar

ACT ONE OPENING: SWEET YOUNG CANDIDATE

Lyric by Otto Harbach and Oscar Hammerstein II. Not published. Introduced by the ensemble.

CADETS:	Sweet young candidate,
	Here is my arm.
	May I serve you
	In proving your charm?
SOME GIRLS:	I'm delighted to dance with you.
	I know I've got a chance with you.
OTHER GIRLS:	I'd be blighting my chance with you,
	The polka's not the dance for you.
CADETS WITHOUT PARTNERS:	Sweet young candidate,
	Here is my arm.
	May I serve you
	In proving your charm?
GIRLS WITHOUT PARTNERS:	Though I'm only your second choice,
	My gratitude I gladly voice.

ALL:	Now we are off in the polka's whirl,
	Now let the contest begin.
	Ev'ry cadet has a hopeful girl,
	Now may the best lady win.

VIRGINIA HOEDOWN

Lyric by Otto Harbach and Oscar Hammerstein II. Not published. Introduced by Kay Picture (Polly), Kirk Alyn (Don), and ensemble.

POLLY AND DON:	I call you all who love the South!
ALL SOUTHERNERS:	The folks who live in the land of good times.
SOUTHERN MEN:	Pick out your beau,
	Go into the hoedown.
SOUTHERN GIRLS:	Into the hoedown you go,
	A-slappin' your toe down.
ALL SOUTHERNERS:	Slappin' your toe down so hard
	The floor begs for mercy.
	Show it no mercy;
	Slap it some more!
SOUTHERN MEN:	An' if your beau
	Refuses to hoedown.
SOUTHERN GIRLS:	Don't let him slow down on you,
	But give him the throw down.
ALL SOUTHERNERS:	Pick out a partner that's new
	An' slap the floor some more.
DON:	Just you go down
	To that hoedown,
	'N' do like you done before.

[*Dance.*]

SINGING GIRLS:	Pick out a beau
	To hoedown with you.
	Slap down your toe
	An' do like you do.
	Kick up your heels
	Slap your toe some more.
	When you go down
	To that hoedown
	Do like you done before.
SINGING MEN:	Hay foot, straw foot,
	Hay foot, straw foot,
	Hay foot, straw foot,
	Hay foot, straw foot,

	Hay foot, straw,
	Then hay once more.
	Hoedown,
	Hoedown,
	Keep slappin' the floor.
ALL:	I call you all who love the South!

OUR LAST DANCE

Alternate title: "The Last Dance." Lyric by Otto Harbach and Oscar Hammerstein II. Not published.* Introduced by Hope Manning (Linda) and the ensemble.

LINDA:	In our last dance
	I remember you.
	It was our last dance
	And my heart well knew
	That the music so softly playing
	Was only saying adieu.
	When the last star
	In the morning sky
	Timidly faded
	From the morning sky
	It was over,†
	Our dance was over
	And we were saying goodbye.
MEN:	Once more, once more,
	Let us dance.
	Once more look for
	Lost romance.
GIRLS:	And hold me near you,
	And let me hear you,
GIRLS AND MEN:	Whisper how you've missed me and romance.
	All that's gone is all I own
	Must I go on alone, alone?

[LINDA *and ensemble repeat refrain.*]

---

* *Harbach subsequently reset this melody as "When a New Star," which was published as an individual sheet with a* Hayfoot, Strawfoot *cover.*

† *Variant of her last three lines:*
  It is over
  Our dance is over
  And we are saying goodbye.

GENTLEMEN UNAFRAID

Lyric by Otto Harbach and Oscar Hammerstein II. Not published. Introduced by Kirk Alyn (Don), Ronald Graham (Bob), Hope Manning (Linda), and male ensemble.

Correspondence suggests that Otto Harbach wrote the first draft of this motto song, and it was revised heavily by Hammerstein and Kern. In a *Hayfoot, Strawfoot* draft of the script, Abraham Lincoln recites the second refrain over music.

VERSE

Young man,
To be an officer you must command respect.
Otherwise you can't command your men.
Young man,
It isn't quite enough to hold your head erect.
If you would command good men,
You must be braver than the brave,
You must be duty's humblest slave.
La, la, la, la.*

REFRAIN

When you are Army gentlemen,
Officers and gentlemen
Wearing Army braid,
To the trust that is placed in you
Ever be true.
And remember that you are known as
Gentlemen unafraid.
And those you love,
You must cherish and defend.
On your courage they depend
When they call for aid.
That is why you're allowed to be,
Proud to be known as,
Army gentlemen,
Gentlemen unafraid.

Abraham Lincoln's version

[*Recited over music.*]

When you have seen the thing to do
And have dared to see it through,
Honor unbetrayed,
Win or lose—it is all the same.
Praises and blame
Are the same if you've played the game of

Gentlemen unafraid.
Then undismayed
You can face the years that wait
Off'ring crowns of love or hate,
Glory's cavalcade
Or the frowns of the fates that toss
Fortune or loss,
For you are gentlemen,
Gentlemen unafraid.

WHAT KIND OF SOLDIER ARE YOU?

Lyric by Otto Harbach and Oscar Hammerstein II. Not published. Introduced by Vicki Cummings (Betsy), Richard "Red" Skelton (Bud), and male ensemble.

Later in Act One the song is reprised as a dream ballet. Bud has been knocked unconscious, and he dreams of girls mocking him and passing him around in a dance. At the start of Act Three. the song is sung again by Ronald Graham (Bob), Barry Sullivan (Jim), and male ensemble

VERSE

BETSY: Any time I walk with you
Upon Flirtation Walk
All we ever do is walk!
Never do your arms
Steal around my waist.
I can feel secure,
Everything is pure,
Everything is chaste.
Ugh!

REFRAIN

BETSY: What kind of soldier are you
If you're afraid of a girl?
What kind of soldier are you
If you are close to beauty
And hear a call to duty
And you don't know what to do?
You're not an ornament to the infantry,
You're not an ornament to the cavalry,
When you're neglectful of a girl like me,
Who wants to be
Loved!
If you're afraid of a girl
If you don't know what to do
If you don't even obey
The Army regulations
For tender situations,

What kind of soldier are you?
What kind of soldier are you?

[BETSY *dances with several different boys, who gladly demonstrate how a soldier should hug and kiss a girl.* BUD *sulks, then gathers his courage. But he's a terrible dancer.* BUD *and* BETSY *end up on the floor.*]

Fantasy version

SOPRANOS: [*whispering*] If you're afraid of a girl
ALTOS: [*whispering*] What kind of soldier are you?
SOPRANOS: [*whispering*] If you're afraid of a girl
ALTOS: [*whispering*] What kind of soldier are you?
SOPRANOS: [*whispering*] The girl has done all she can,
ALTOS: [*whispering*] Are you a man or a mouse?
SOPRANOS AND ALTOS: Are you a mouse or a man?
SOPRANOS: You're acting more like a mouse.
SOPRANOS AND ALTOS: [*more sympathetic now*] What you're missing by being so shy!
All the kissing you're letting go by!
SOLOIST: Shy boy,
You run away from what you seek.
Shy boy,
Our lips are yours if you'd but speak.
The quick desire of spring excites you.
The sweet allure of love invites you.
Why, boy, should your response be overdue?
Shy boy.
DREAM BETSY: What kind of soldier are you?
GIRLS: If you're afraid of a girl
What kind of soldier are you?
If you're afraid of a girl
Why don't you take your cue?

[*Four girls seize* BUD *and lift him high in a dance.*]

---

* *The cadet who begins the song doesn't know the text well and is unable to complete the verse. No complete copy has been found.*

Act Three reprise

JIM AND MEN: [*to* BUD] What kind of soldier
are you?

BOB: You can't hold on to your girl.

MEN: What kind of soldier are you?

JIM: Allowing Pignatelli,

BOB: That piece of vermicelli,
To step right into your shoe.

MEN: You're not an ornament to the
infantry,
You're not an ornament to the
cavalry,

BOB: To let a mere Zouave turn out
to be
The man that she

BOB, JIM, AND MEN: Loves!

YOUR DREAM IS THE SAME
AS MY DREAM

Lyric by Otto Harbach and Oscar Hammerstein II. Published as an individual sheet when it was reused in the Universal Pictures film *One Night in the Tropics* (1940); the sheet music cover says lyric by Dorothy Fields, but inside Harbach and Hammerstein are credited. Introduced by Ronald Graham (Bob).

Writing from New York to Hammerstein and Kern in Los Angeles, Harbach said, "I think Oscar's lyric on 'Your dream etc' is swell and makes a lovely development of the first part."

Your dream is the same as my dream,
Your future is mine when I dream.
I want heaven with you
And you want heaven with me.
We each want half of the same romance.
I'm longing for the things that you long for too,
We'll make the most impossible things come true.
Two dreamers, you and I.
There's no height too high
For hearts like ours to fly to.
Your way is the same as my way,
We travel along love's highway.
Your dream is the same as my dream,
Both part of the same romance.

DE LAND O' GOOD TIMES

Lyric by Otto Harbach and Oscar Hammerstein II. Not published. Introduced by Minto Cato (Liza), Hope Manning (Linda), Ronald Graham (Bob), Kay Picture (Polly), and ensemble.

LIZA: Ah call yo' all who love de
South,
De folks who live in de land o'
good times.

BOB: De folks who live in de land o'
good times
Don't hafter holler for dollars
or dimes.
Don't hafter git any gold f'um
no one
'Cause dey got plenty o' gold in
de sun!

LINDA: Dey got persimmons an'
possums
An' magnolia blossoms in de
trees.

LIZA: Dey got a sweet-smellin' rose
An' watermelon dat grows up
to deir knees!

MEN: De folks who live in de land o'
good times
Don't hafter holler for dollars
or dimes.
Don't hafter git any gold f'um
no one
'Cause dey got plenty o' gold in
de sun!

GIRLS: Dey like to sing when dey
work.
De work ain't hard ef yo'
sing.
Ef yo' kin sing, yo' kin work de
whole day long.

LINDA AND POLLY: When plantin' starts in de
spring
'N' planters start in to sing,
Dey got some mighty good
reasons fo' de song.

ALL: Dey got persimmons an'
possums
An' magnolia blossoms in de
trees.

LIZA: An' sumpin' sweet in de roses
Dat's a treat to de noses of de
bees!

ALL: De folks who live in de land o'
good times
Don't hafter holler for dollars
or dimes.

Don't hafter git any gold f'um
no one
'Cause dey got plenty o' gold in
de sun!

LINDA: De southern moonlight is what
you miss most
When yo' have left yo' home
behind yo'.
De southern moonlight is what
you miss most
When dere's a sweetheart to
remind yo'.

BOB: When yo' have left yo' gal
behind yo'
An' in de lonely world yo'
wander,
Yo' keep on wishin' dat yo' was
back dere
Wid all de lucky folks down
yonder.

ALL: Dey got persimmons an'
possums
An' magnolia blossoms in de
trees.

LIZA: Dey got de whiff o' de roses
Floatin' up to deir noses on de
breeze!

ALL: De folks who live in de land o'
good times
Don't hafter holler for dollars
or dimes.
Don't hafter git any gold f'um
no one
'Cause dey got plenty o' gold in
de sun.

LIZA: It fills yo' heart wid delight
To watch de young 'uns at
night.
To watch 'em dance in de moon
While someone fiddles a tune.

BOB AND LINDA: An' dey don't need any music
f'um bands.
Dey make deir music by
clappin' deir hands!

BOB: Dey do a dance wid such feelin'
At deir rockin' and reelin'
jubilees.

LINDA: Dey even wake up de possums
An' dey shake down de
blossoms f'um de trees!

ALL: De folks who live in de land o'
good times
Don't hafter holler for dollars
or dimes.
Don't hafter git any gold f'um
no one
'Cause dey got plenty o' gold in
de sun!

LIZA: Ah call yo' all who love de
South.
ALL: De folks who live in de land o'
good times!

ABE LINCOLN HAS JUST ONE COUNTRY

Lyric by Otto Harbach and Oscar Hammerstein II. Published in 1941 as "Abe Lincoln Had Just One Country."* Introduced by the male ensemble.

Abe Lincoln has just one country,
And one banner to wave.
One Union of brave brothers,
Where no brothers enslave others.
We're all marching along with Lincoln,[†]
With one banner to wave.
This Union was born in freedom,
And this Union must live in freedom,
And this freedom is worth saving
And worth fighting to save!

VERSE

Take a lesson from old Abe Lincoln
In times of stormy weather.
Take a lesson from old Abe Lincoln
And face the storm together.

---

* *The sheet music cover says "Written at the request of Henry Morgenthau, Jr., Secretary of the Treasury, on behalf of United States Defense Bonds and Stamps." A 1942 Lincoln's Birthday broadcast of the Bell Telephone Hour also described this as a new song written specially for the Treasury Department. That is not strictly true, but the published version included a verse not seen in the* Gentlemen Unafraid *material.*

The published sheet for "When a New Star" from Hayfoot, Strawfoot *advertises "Abe Lincoln Had Just One Country," but the editor has not seen a copy with the* Hayfoot *cover.*

[†] *Revised in the published sheet to:*
We're still marching along with Lincoln,

MISTER MAN

Lyric by Otto Harbach and Oscar Hammerstein II. Not published. Introduced by Hope Manning (Linda).

VERSE

LINDA: Many a lofty mountain
Looks far too steep to climb
Standing against a cold gray sky.
But if you get up closer,
You find, most ev'ry time,
Summits are reached by those who try.
Many an unkissed lady
Keeping a man at bay
Wishes that he would come up closer too.
Even though she's a lady,*
She need not shrink away.
She knows a thing or two to do,
So she says.

REFRAIN

LINDA: Mister man,
I've gone about as far as I can go,
With all my never-failing female wiles
And roguish smiles,
I've let you know.
Mister man,
It should be clear to you
That with the slightest persistence,
You'd break my less than faint resistance.
Why not try?
You really haven't very much to lose.
The foolish lover who decides to wait
Must often wait in vain.
Mister man,
You really haven't very much to lose.
Only think of all that you might gain,
All you might gain!

---

* *Lyric variant for the end of the verse:*
Fated to be a lady
I have to act this way,
Hoping the thought may dawn on you
To woo me.

Another variation, from a men's glee club arrangement:
Pity the unkissed lady
Brought up to act this way,
Hoping that she'll be overcome by you.

I WISH DAT DERE WASN' NO WAR

Lyric by Otto Harbach and Oscar Hammerstein II. Not published. "Bonnie Blue Flag" lyric by Harry Macarthy; traditional Hibernian melody. Introduced by Minto Cato (Liza) and colored women, male ensemble, Hope Manning (Linda), and female ensemble.

In an April 1938 letter to Harbach, Hammerstein wrote: "In the lyric 'I Wish Dat Dere Wasn' No War,' when I say 'wasn'' I mean the same sound that Boykin means when he says 'wuzzin,' and I prefer my spelling because it at least indicates what word is intended . . ."

LIZA: How would I know
'Bout de reason for de
fightin'?
How would I know what it's
for?
All dat I know
Is I wish dat dere wasn' no
war.
How would I know
Why dey made my man a
soldier?
How would I know what it's
for?
All dat I know
Is I wish dat dere wasn' no
war.
Dere's a green field
Turnin' white wid cotton
An' a cornfield growin' high.
An' de good Lord is
providin' plenty
An it seems a shame to die.
How would I know
'Bout de battle cry of
freedom
When my man ain't here no
more?
All dat I know
Is I wish dat dere wasn' no
war!

COLORED WOMEN
AND LIZA: Ax de boss
An' he don' know.
Ax de preacher
An' he don' know.
An' de Lord Hisself don'
even know
Why men want war . . .

Dey got enough sunshine.
Dey got enough fish to fry.

Why couldn't dey share it?
No one knows why,
So how would I?

How would I know 'bout de
reason for de fightin'?
How would I know what it's
for?

SOUTHERN SOLDIERS: [offstage] Hurrah! Hurrah!
For southern rights, hurrah!
Hurray for the bonnie blue
flag
That bears a single star!

LIZA: How would I know why
Dey made my man a soldier?
How would I know what it's
for?

SOUTHERN SOLDIERS: [marching onstage] Hurrah!
Hurrah!
For southern rights, hurrah!
Hurray for the bonnie blue
flag
That bears a single star!

COLORED WOMEN: Dere's a green field
Turnin' white wid cotton
An' a cornfield growin' high.
An' de good Lord is
providin' plenty
An' it seems a shame to die.

[White women start to follow soldiers off. But they
stop in horror and scream. A courier runs on.]

WHITE WOMEN: Is it over?
Is he spared?
Has the battle been won at
last?
Say he may be
Coming home to me.

[Some wounded soldiers stagger back onto the stage,
cross, and exit.]

WHITE WOMEN: Home, come home to your
mothers.
Come home to the girls you
love.
Our shoulders are waiting
For weary heads
To rest on.

MORE SOLDIERS: [marching on] We are a band
of brothers
And native to the soil.
We're fighting for the
property
We gained by honest toil.
And when our rights were
threatened

The cry rose near and far,
Hurrah for the bonnie blue
flag that bears a single
star.
Hurrah! Hurrah!
For southern rights,
hurrah!
Hurrah for the bonnie blue
flag that bears a single
star.

WHITE WOMEN: How would I know
Why dey made my man a
soldier?
How would I know what it's
for?
All dat I know
Is I wish dat dere wasn' no
war.

[More wounded soldiers return.]

WHITE WOMEN: Dere's a green field
Turnin' white wid cotton
An' a cornfield growin'
high.
An' de good Lord is
providin' plenty
An' it seems a shame to die.
[with increasing protest]
How would I know
'Bout de battle cry of freedom
When my man ain't here no
more?
All dat I know
Is I wish dat dere wasn' no
war.

[Cannon and rifle fire are heard over a stormy
instrumental arrangement of "Your Dream Is the
Same as My Dream." Flashing spotlights pick out the
principals. LINDA is waiting. BOB is in a Union
uniform. As soldiers fall, women claim them and walk
downstage. Bodies in blue and gray uniforms
lie everywhere. The women kneel in a single row
downstage. All lights go out except one spot, into
which walks ABRAHAM LINCOLN, delivering a portion
of the Gettysburg address.]

ALL WOMEN: Dere's a green field turnin'
white wid cotton
An' a cornfield growin' high
An' de good Lord is
providin' plenty
An' it seems a shame to die.
[growing quite forceful]
How would I know
'Bout de battle cry of
freedom

When my man ain't here no
more—
All dat I know
Is I wish dat dere wasn' no
war.

LITTLE ZOUAVE

Lyric by Otto Harbach and Oscar Hammerstein II. Not
published. Introduced by Vicki Cummings (Betsy) and
male ensemble. Red Skelton (Bud) and Ralph Riggs
(Pignatelli) are part of the number but don't have solo
vocal lines.

In the spring of 1938, Hammerstein wrote enthusias-
tically to St. Louis Muny producer Dick Berger regarding a proposed addition of dancing girls in Zouave
costumes: "Geary's restaurant was in fact adjoining the
back of a theatre, and a musical extravaganza playing
there during the Civil War might easily have had a chorus of Zouaves. They would have been suckers if they
didn't. And that's how the girls come in in Zouave costume, and if they don't like it they can sue us."

In March 1939, Hammerstein worked on a "Little
Cadet" lyric to this melody for a revised scenario with
that title. A version called "Boy With a Drum" was written in 1941 and used in the 1942–1943 *Hayfoot, Strawfoot* productions. The middle section was:

Sounds of your drum
That have become
More than a drum
Marring my dreams;
Somehow it seems
A voice that's saying,
Better that I
Wake you too soon
Than that you lie
Dreaming till noon,
Battles unwon,
Victory undone!

BETSY: Little Zouave,
Why have you come,
Tooting your fife,
Beating your drum,
Catching my eye,*
Capturing my heart?
Little Zouave,

_____

* Variant:
How could you try
Fooling with my heart?

Couldn't we play*
Ever like this,
Happy and gay?
Couldn't we stay
Ever like this,
Never to part?
Since I've heard the
Beat of your drum,
Sound of your fife,
Something has come
Into my life,
Giddy and glad†
Merry and yet mad,
Like a wild alarming rhapsody,
Little Zouave,
What have you done to me?

MEN: Little Zouave,
Why have you come,
Tooting your fife,
Beating your drum,
Causing a stir,
Capturing her heart?
Little Zouave,
Why do you play
Ever like this,
Happy and gay?
Never to stay
Ever like this,
Certain to part?
Since she heard the
Beat of your drum,
Sound of your fife,
Something has come
Into her life,
Giddy and glad
Merry and yet mad!
Like a wild alarming rhapsody,
Little Zouave,
What'll the answer be?

[*All march off.* BETSY *comes back to tell* BUD *she was only fooling.*]

BETSY: Didn't you know
I wouldn't go far?
I've had my fling,
I've had my fun,
Now I am sure

---

* *Variant:*

It would be bliss
Ever, if we
could play like this.
What will I do
When you are through
And we must part?

† *Variant:*

Gleeful and gay

You are the one.
Won't you forgive?
Won't you forget?
Won't you come home
To your Betsy!

CUT AND UNUSED SONG

SWEET AS A ROSE

Lyric by Otto Harbach and Oscar Hammerstein II. Not published. Not used. Introduced by Hope Manning (Linda).

LINDA: Sweet as a rose in the moonlight
So is the dream in my heart.
Gay as a robin in springtime
So is the dream in my heart.
Sweet as a rose in the moonlight,
Bright as a star in the blue
So is the dream in my heart for you.

ADDED SONGS

LITTLE WILY MISS

Alternate title: "The Wily Miss." Two music manuscripts credit both Hammerstein and Harbach; one credits Harbach only. Not published. Introduced in *Hayfoot, Strawfoot* by Betty Jones (Linda), Doris Lavington (Susan), and the ensemble.

SOLO: Once a little wily miss
Thought she'd love to have a kiss.
So she singled out a man
Just as any girl can.
But this man was very good
And he'd never understood
And he'd never learned to act
As a gentleman should.

SOPRANO AND ALTO: It's a terrible impasse
When a little wily lass
Meets a man who seems so nice,
Just to find he's made of ice.

SOLO: For she noticed with dismay
That his eyes were turned away,
And his folded arms at rest
On his masculine chest.
But this little wily miss
Wasn't stumped at all by this,
For she'd seen the summer sun
Make a frozen stream run.

WOMEN AND MEN: Summer sun melts the chilly ice and snow.
When it smiles the frozen river has to flow.
Summer sun makes a frozen river run.

SOPRANO: Said the wily miss,
"If the sun can do this

ALTO: With a smile or two,
That's the thing that I'll do."

SOPRANO AND ALTO: Then she saw she'd caught his eye.
She pretended to be shy,
Was about to go away,
But she managed to stay.
Then she took a pretty pose,
Turned her lips into a rose,
And she let it bloom a while
Till it turned to a smile!

ALL: And then?

SOPRANO AND ALTO: He wanted to thaw.

ALL: And then?

TENORS: He started to thaw.

ALL: And then?

BASSES: He did what he could

ALL: Just to show he'd learned to act
As a gentleman should.

THE KISSING ROCK

Lyric by Otto Harbach and Oscar Hammerstein II. Not published. Apparently written for *Hayfoot, Strawfoot*, but not listed in the program from Duke University's January 1943 performances.

REFRAIN

Near that magic rock
They call "kissing rock,"
There the Kaydets love to stroll.
There no chaperones patrol.
Here girls when they're kissed
Won't struggle or frown.

If they did, the kissing rock
Would come tumbling down!
All along Flirtation Walk
Young lovers walk
And gaily laugh and talk
While strolling.
But around the kissing rock
A silence seems to grow.
Till somewhere
A bugle thrills
The list'ning hills
With echoes rolling.
Or maybe a whis'pring tree
Recalls some love of long ago.
That's why lovers flock
Round the kissing rock.
There, someday, you'll go with me.
I'll be worried as can be!
For I'll kiss you there.
Then, dear, if you frown,
All my world
With the kissing rock
Will come tumbling down!

THE LADY OBJECTS (1938)

During Jerome Kern's convalescence after a serious heart attack, Hammerstein worked for Columbia Pictures as a writer-producer. The Hammerstein Collection at the Library of Congress preserves two screenplays by Hammerstein for *Paris on Broadway:* a first draft dated June 17, 1937, and a final screenplay dated August 27. Ben Oakland provided melodies for at least four songs. Hammerstein had planned other numbers, including a title song, but no additional lyrics have been found. The film itself was never made.

In 1938, Hammerstein's four songs were inserted into *The Lady Objects*, produced by William Perlberg for Columbia Pictures, released on October 12, 1938. It was directed by Erle C. Kenton, written by Charles Kenyon and Gladys Lehman, featuring Lanny Ross (Bill Hayward), Gloria Stuart (Ann Adams), Joan Marsh (June Lane), and Roy Benson (George Martin). Additional songs in the film were written by Milton Drake and Ben Oakland.

WHEN YOU'RE IN THE ROOM

Music by Ben Oakland. Published as an individual sheet. Introduced by Lanny Ross (Bill).

VERSE

When you're not here
What have I got here?
What have I to do?
Wait and sigh,
Time drags by.
When you've got here
Things that were not here
Seem to come with you
And my dull, old world looks new.

REFRAIN

When you're in the room,
The room takes on a glow.
It just seems to know
You are there.
The wallflowers bloom,
The firelight grows bold
And throws a kiss of gold
Into your hair.
Then I look at you and think of lovely things,
Wishing that you would stay.
And the canary sings:
"Don't go away."
When you're in the room
A dream's about to start.
When you're in the room
Heaven's in my heart.

A MIST IS OVER THE MOON

Music by Ben Oakland. Published as an individual sheet. Introduced by Lanny Ross (Bill) (refrain only).

Since the song could be done as a ballad or as a rhythmic foxtrot, Hammerstein had high hopes for its commercial prospects. It was nominated for the Academy Award for Best Song.

VERSE

There are certain moments
When all the world is suddenly sweet,
When hearts are thrilled
And the very air is filled

With a newborn joy.
This is such a moment,
And you are here to make it complete,
To share with me
All the silent ecstasy
Of a newborn joy.

REFRAIN

The sea is calm tonight,
A mist is over the moon.
The stars have lost their light,
A mist is over the moon.
Gently you rest your head upon my shoulder.
The evening grows older,
A bird in the sky flies by
And like the aimless bird
Our boat is drifting along.
And though no sound is heard,
Our hearts are singing a song.
Life is a dream,
But love is real and clearly in sight.
A mist is over the moon tonight.

THAT WEEK IN PARIS

Music by Ben Oakland. Published as an individual sheet. Introduced by Lanny Ross (Bill).

VERSE

Paris was a sweet enchanted city,
Sunshine on the street and you so pretty.
So proud was I to have you walk beside me.
I held my head up high,
Life was fair,
And we owned the earth and air.

REFRAIN

That week in Paris,
The town was ours,
For we happened to be falling in love,
And Paris takes you to her heart when you're in love.
The parks of Paris
Were gay with flow'rs,
For we happened to be falling in love,
And Paris takes you to her heart when you're in love.
Out of her heart she sent those nights,
She allowed us seven.
And we spent those nights
In a seventh heaven.

That week in Paris
The world was ours,
For we happened to be falling in love,
And now it's over and we live our lives apart,
Rememb'ring Paris, when she took us to her
    heart.

HOME IN YOUR ARMS

Music by Ben Oakland. Published as an individual
sheet. Introduced by Lanny Ross (Bill) (refrain only).

VERSE

To a castle on a hill,
To a cottage that smiles on the sea,
You may take me if you will,
And I'll stay there while you stay with me.
For I can live upon a hill
And I can live beside the sea
And be content as very few are,
For I can feel at home wherever you are.

REFRAIN

Home in your arms,
I am home in your arms.
When you were far from me,
I was alone like a ship at sea.
Now I am back where I ought to be,
Back home, back home in your arms.
Here, in my dwelling place,
Here I can look on your lovely face.
Here, in the heaven of your embrace,
I'm home, I'm home in your arms.

THE GREAT WALTZ (1938)

A film produced by Bernard H. Hyman for Metro-
Goldwyn-Mayer. Released on November 4, 1938. Lyrics
by Oscar Hammerstein II. Directed by Julien Duvivier
(with uncredited work by Victor Fleming and Josef von
Sternberg). Screenplay by Samuel Hoffenstein and Wal-
ter Reisch, from a story by Gottfried Reinhardt.
(Uncredited story contributor: Vicki Baum.) Music by
Johann Strauss II, adapted and arranged by Dimitri
Tiomkin. Choreography by Albertina Rasch. Orchestra-
tions by Paul Marquardt. Music directed by Arthur

Gutmann. Cinematography by Joseph Ruttenberg. Film
editing by Tom Held. Art direction by Cedric Gibbons.
Costumes designed by Adrian.

Cast: Luise Rainer (Poldi Vogelhuber Strauss), Fernand Gravey* (Johann "Schani" Strauss II), Miliza Kor-
jus (Carla Donner), Hugh Herbert (Julius Hofbauer,
music publisher), Lionel Atwill (Count Anton "Tony"
Hohenfried), Curt Bois (Kienzl, the violinist), Leonid
Kinskey (Dudelman, the bass player), Al Shean (Cel-
list), Minna Gombell (Mrs. Hofbauer), George Houston
(Fritz Schiller, a tenor), Bert Roach (Vogelhuber), Greta
Meyer (Mrs. Vogelhuber), Herman Bing (Otto Dom-
mayer), Alma Kruger (Mrs. Strauss), Henry Hull
(Emperor Franz Josef), Sig Rumann (Wertheimer the
Banker), and Christian Rub (Coachman).

In this highly fictional biography of the composer
Johann Strauss II, ambitious young "Schani" starts with
an orchestra of friends in a local beer garden, and winds
up at the opera house, and, in an epilogue, is honored
by the emperor. Although married to the quietly sup-
portive Poldi, Strauss's relationship with the famous
singer Carla Donner benefits him professionally and
personally.

Five songs were published by Leo Feist Inc. in a sou-
venir album. Further lyrics are located in the MPAA
Collection at the Academy of Motion Picture Arts and
Sciences' Margaret Herrick Library and in the Dimitri
Tiomkin Collection at the Cinema-Television Library of
the University of Southern California. The Billy Rose
Theatre (and Film) Collection at the New York Public
Library for the Performing Arts has a "cutting continu-
ity" screenplay.

No lyric has been found for "The Artist's Life,"
which may only have been used as an instrumental. The
film's finale uses reprises of the big tunes plus an instrumental of the "Blue Danube" waltz. One of the best-
remembered musical moments in the film is the
lyric-less "Birth of the Vienna Woods," in which the
sounds of birds and rustling trees, the rhythm of coach
wheels, and a coachman's horn inspire Strauss's beloved
composition.

POLKA

Not published. Introduced by Curt Bois (Kienzl, the
violinist), Leonid Kinskey (Dudelman, the bass player),
and other members of Johann Strauss's orchestra.

---

* Earl Covert and Ralph Leon supplied Strauss's
  singing voice.

VERSE

KIENZL: Each man must have his
    hobby*
MAN WITH MUSTACHE: His own kind of hobby.
DUDELMAN: I am fond of beer and
    girls!
MAN WITH MUSTACHE: I am fond of girls and
    beer!
KIENZL: But me, I like to stay up
    And keep my spirits
    way up!
MAN WITH MUSTACHE: With a gay, nice crowd,
CYMBAL PLAYER: And a song that's loud,
MAN WITH HIGH VOICE: Sung by everyone to hear!
KIENZL: Ev'ry night in the week,
    Ev'ry week in ev'ry year.

REFRAIN

ALL: With friends you like to
    drink with,
    The night will quickly
    pass.
ANOTHER MAN: Fill another little,
DUDELMAN: Fill another little,
KIENZL: Fill another little glass!
KIENZL: With friends you like to
    sing with,
    The night is never long.
MAN WITH MUSTACHE: So sing another little,
A THIRD MAN: Sing another little,
PICCOLO PLAYER: Sing another little song!

I'M IN LOVE WITH VIENNA

Published in the vocal selection. Introduced by George
Houston (Schiller, a tenor) and ensemble.

VERSE

Ev'ry tree in the park,
Ev'ry leaf on a tree
Waves a welcome to me
When I walk in Vienna.
Ev'ry tree in the park,
Ev'ry leaf on a tree,

---

* A version dated May 7, 1938, begins:
    When I retire early,
    I'm sullen and surly.
    It's much more fun to stay up
    And wake a newborn day up.

Ev'ry star in the sky
Knows that I am in love!

REFRAIN

I'm in love with Vienna,
I'm in love with Vienna.
Ev'ry sight, ev'ry sound on the street
Is sweet and dear to me.
I was born in Vienna,
I was born in Vienna
With a waltz in my heart,
And with a heart that had to sing.
Sing about Vienna,
Sing about her sights,
And sing about her sounds,
And sing about her nights.
To her and to her life
I ever will belong,
For I'm a part of her song!

THERE'LL COME A TIME

Published in the vocal selection. Introduced by Miliza
Korjus (Carla).

VERSE

Looking at you and wanting you so,
Knowing that you want me,
Certain am I our moment will come,
Certain as I can be.
Ah—[*cadenza*]

REFRAIN

There'll come a time,
There'll come a time
When you and I will be alone.
There'll come a time
When you will hear
The beat of my heart next to your heart.
There'll be a place,
A lovely place,
Where we will meet as lovers do.
And ev'ry kiss you've kept for me
Will find a kiss I've kept for you.
Ah—[*cadenza*]
There'll come a time,
There'll be a place,
Where you will meet
Our great adventure.
Ah—[*cadenza*]
There'll come a time,
A time for love.

REVOLUTIONARY MARCH

Not published. Introduced by the ensemble. This lyric
was submitted to the MPAA Production Code Administration office on June 7, 1938.

REVOLUTIONARIES: Ev'ry man has a right that he
lives for,
That he fights for, that he gives
for—
We are ready to fight and we're
marching,
For the time to march is now.
The march goes on,
It must go on
Till more men and more men
Come by and have gone—
There is work to do
That must be done,
We'll stay in the fight till the
fight is done.

TALES FROM THE VIENNA WOODS

Published in the vocal selection. Introduced by Miliza
Korjus (Carla).

Was it a shepherd's horn
Piercing the morning air?
Was it an angel singing,
Heralding what the day was bringing?
Were you a dream of mine,
Lying beside me there,
Stolen from another world
Making this world fair?

The sun came up and blessed the sky.
The song of birds caressed the sky,
A golden song that seemed to be
A serenade for you and me.
And so they sang the dawn away
And soon the dawn had gone away.
The sun climbed high and higher,
Waking up a sleeping world.
Petals on a rose unfurled,
And the sun climbed high and higher.

Then the touch of your hand made you real to me.
And you looked at me, ah, so tenderly.
Ah, so tenderly did you look at me,

And the sun riding high
Seemed to say, "What a day, what a sky!"
But the day hurried on,
And the sun found a hill and was gone.

Night is flying fast.
Time is dancing past.
But still I look at you
And still you look at me,
And still we seem to be enchanted by each other.
I wonder how a night can fly so fast?
I wonder if a joy like ours can last?

We can laugh and we'll dance
And the music will play.
And we'll take the romance
And be glad that we may.
Ah—[*cadenza*]
We can look at a star
And a dream can go far.
And we'll talk and we'll flirt
And we'll drink to the night.
And we'll drink to our love
And our hearts will be light.
Ah—[*cadenza*]

Our love is ours alone,
No one else's paradise,
Only our own.

ONE DAY WHEN WE WERE YOUNG

Published in the vocal selection. Introduced by Fernand
Gravey (Johann Strauss). Later reprised by Miliza
Korjus.

One day when we were young,*
One wonderful morning in May,
You told me you loved me,
When we were young one day.
Sweet songs of spring were sung
And music was never so gay.
You told me you loved me,
When we were young one day.
You told me you loved me
And held me close to your heart,

---

*A lyric sheet submitted for MPAA approval begins
with these additional lines:
When I grow old I'll think of you
Beside me one morning in May
Just as you were one day . . .

We laughed then, we cried then,
Then came the time to part.
When songs of spring are sung
Remember that morning in May,
Remember,
You loved me
When we were young one day.

YOU AND YOU

A selection from *Die Fledermaus.* Alternate titles: "Du und Du" and "Only You." Published in the vocal selection. Submitted to the MPAA on April 26, 1938, as "Only You," Song #6042. Introduced by Miliza Korjus (Carla), George Houston (Schiller, the tenor), and ensemble.

ENSEMBLE: Here are lovers,
Ha, ha, ha!
Silly lovers,
Ha, ha, ha!
With a secret,
Ha, ha, ha!
With a secret known to ev'rybody.
When the prize is once in reach,
Then the bloom is off the peach—
CARLA: [*to ensemble*] No, you are wrong.
My lover's eyes tell me you are wrong.
[*to* SCHILLER]
What can they know—
Only you and I can know of all our
happiness together
Ah—[*cadenza*]
CARLA: I can tell by the merest look at you
If you're happy or sad,
Excited or blue.
You can tell too.
Hmmmm.
SCHILLER: I can tell by the merest look at you
If you're happy or sad or blue,
Any little word you say
Or a half-uttered sigh
Gives your thoughts away.
BOTH: I'm so close to you,
You're so close to me.
We are just the way two lovers
should be.
No one else fits in my arms

As you always do.
No one else fits in my dreams,
No one like you.
Dreams you make seem true.

Only you,
Only you
Know how to thrill my heart.
Only you
Say and do
Things that can fill my heart.
Only two
Lips divine
Seem to be-
Long on mine.
Only two
Lips divine
Seem to be
Meant for mine.
Perfectly mated
And mated forever we'll be—
Only one you for me.

THE BAT

Another selection from *Die Fledermaus.* Not published. This lyric was submitted to the MPAA on August 26, 1938, as song #6034.

ENSEMBLE: You are the queen of the dance
tonight.
Here for a scene of romance tonight.
You are a star with a shining light,
Stay as you are,
As you are tonight.

How did she get here?
Wonder who she is!
Wonder who she is!
Is she his?
Or his?
CARLA: I'm just a girl who's on her own,
I don't belong to anyone.
And if you want to know the truth,
I'm here to have some fun!
ENSEMBLE: Here's a chance,
A royal chance for ev'ryone now.
For here's a girl

Who wants to have her fun with us
now!
Lady, take whom you please!
Choose your partner.
Lady, take whom you please!
CARLA: The way that I feel I want you all,
Want you all, ev'ry one;
That's how I feel about you all,
But I will belong to none!
ENSEMBLE: The way that you feel you want us all,
Want us all, ev'ry one.
The way you feel you want a million
lovers,
But you'll never belong to one.

VOICES OF SPRING

Not published. Not performed in the film, although a sheet with this title is seen in a music-shop window. Stage directions describe Strauss accompanying a singer, who takes liberties with his song. This song was probably a precursor to "There'll Come a Time."

When a singer's looking for a
Gay and tender little song to sing,
The waltz is best of all.
(Ha, ha!)
When a lover's looking for the
Kind of song a lover longs to sing,
The waltz is best of all.
(Ha, ha!)
And whenever young and happy
People gather in a throng to sing,
You hear the waltz's call.
Ah—[*cadenza*]
Calling sweetly to the dancers
Like a voice from the stars.
Calling sweetly to romancers
Comes the melody of the waltz.
Tra-la-la, tra-la-la, tra-la-la, tra-la-la
Ah—[*cadenza*]
(Ha, ha!)

Three scenes from Very Warm for May. *Top left: Frances Mercer, Jack Whiting, and Grace McDonald. Top right: Hiram Sherman, Grace McDonald, and Eve Arden. Bottom: The troupe performs a surreal ballet.*

VERY WARM FOR MAY
and Other Songs of 1939

VERY WARM FOR MAY (1939)

Tryouts: Playhouse, Wilmington, Delaware, October 21–22, 1939; National Theatre, Washington, D.C., October 23–28, 1939; Forrest Theatre, Philadelphia, October 30–November 4, 1939; Shubert Theatre, Boston, November 6–11, 1939. New York run: Alvin Theatre, opened on November 17, 1939; closed on January 6, 1940; fifty-nine performances. A New Musical Comedy. Presented by Max Gordon. Book and lyrics by Oscar Hammerstein II. Music by Jerome Kern. Production staged and designed by Vincente Minnelli. (Director Hassard Short was brought in during out-of-town tryouts.) Book directed by Oscar Hammerstein II. Dances staged by Albertina Rasch and Harry Losee. Music direction by Robert Emmett Dolan. Orchestrations by Robert Russell Bennet. Special vocal arrangements by Hugh Martin.

Cast: Grace McDonald (May Graham), Jack Whiting (Johnny Graham), Robert Shackleton (Raymond Sibley), Richard Quine (Sonny Spofford), Frances Mercer (Liz Spofford), Hiram Sherman (Ogdon Quiler), Eve Arden (Winnie Spofford), Donald Brian (William Graham), Avon Long (Jackson), Ray Mayer (Kenny), Max Showalter (Lowell Pennyfeather), William Torpey (Jethro Hancock), Len Mence (Beamish), Seldon Bennett (Schlesinger), and Bruce Evans (Electrician). And as members of the Ogdon Quiler Progressive Workshop: Hollace Shaw (Carol), Ralph Stuart (Charles), Peter Chambers (Mr. Magee), Virginia Card (Miss Wasserman), Kay Picture (Miss Hyde), Frank Egan (Mr. Pratt), Vera Ellen (Susan), Don Loper (Smoothy Watson), Maxine Barrat (Honey), Evelyn Thawl (Jane), Kate Friedlich (Sylvia), Walter Long (Walter), Pamela Randell (Pam), Marie Louise Quevli (Alice), Helen Bliss (Helen), Dolores Anderson (Dolores), Beulah Blake (Beulah), Andre Charise (Andre), Louis Hightower (Louis), Sally Craven (Sally), Jack Seymour (Jack), Webb Tilton (Webb), Jack Wilson (Peter), William Collins (Bill), Eleanor Eberle (Eleanor), Helen Donovan (Helen), Rudy Miller (Rudy), Ethel Lynn (Ethel), June Allyson (June), Claire Harvey (Claire), Billie Wirth (Billie), and Miriam Franklyn (Miriam). Matty Malneck's Orchestra: Matt Malneck, violin (Alvin); Milton DeLugg, accordion (O'Cedar); Charles Marlowe, trumpet (Homer); Marshal Fisher, guitar (Marshal); Ralph Hansell, drums (Ralph); Joseph Quintile, harp (Joseph); Jean Plummer, piano (Jean); and Russ Morhoff, bass (Russ).

The film rights to *Very Warm for May* were sold to MGM, which used some of the material for their release *Broadway Rhythm* in 1944. Directed by Roy Del Ruth, produced by Jack Cummings, starring George Murphy, Ginny Sims, Charles Winninger, Gloria DeHaven, Nancy Walker, Ben Blue, and Lena Horne, with Eddie

"Rochester" Anderson and Tommy Dorsey appearing as themselves. The story is different from either stage version. "All the Things You Are" was featured, but most of the score was written by Don Raye and Gene de Paul, with two more songs by Hugh Martin and Ralph Blane. Brief excerpts of "All in Fun," "That Lucky Fellow," and "In Other Words, Seventeen" are heard in one scene.

A 1939 radio broadcast by the original Broadway cast was released on CD (AEI).

Five songs were published. The Rodgers & Hammerstein Organization has an undated three-act script with the gangster plot and song descriptions, and a January 15, 1940, script marked "Playing Version from Max Gordon's Office." The Hammerstein Collection in the Music Division of the Library of Congress has a typescript prepared at MGM of the "altered version played in New York"; Hammerstein's unused July 1941 screenplay; and a handwritten "Thematic Musical Layout" for three acts. The Kern Collection in the Music Division of the Library of Congress has full scores and parts for most songs, ballets, and scene changes, as well as many piano-vocal scores and a few choral arrangements. The MGM/Turner Collection in the Margaret Herrick Library has cleanly retyped scripts for the original and revised stage versions and a copy of the July 1941 screenplay. The MGM Collection in the Cinema-Television Library at the University of Southern California also has two versions of the stage script and Hammerstein's 1941 screenplay, plus draft screenplays by various writers. The MGM Collection also has a detailed report on the October 20, 1939, world premiere in Wilmington.

This chapter does not include "The Strange Case of Adam Standish" (also known as the "Brain Ballet"), which is mostly a monologue over music, with a soloist singing "In the Heart of the Dark." No lyrics have been found for the "Schottische Scene" or the dances titled "The Deer and the Park Avenue Lady" and "Danse Da Da." Music for an unused ballad called "Connecticut" survives, but no lyric has been found. Theater historian Steve Suskin associates a song called "Oh, My Dear" with the screen version of *Very Warm for May* (later known as *Broadway Rhythm*), but no lyric has been found.

Very Warm for May was another 1930s flop for Hammerstein. Jerome Kern blamed the show's failure on extensive plot changes that producer Max Gordon forced them to make during the out-of-town tryout.

In the original version of the plot, young Patsy Jarman runs away from home to elude the gangsters who are blackmailing her father and want to use her as bait to kidnap a young millionaire. She winds up, by chance, at the Spofford estate, and makes herself useful to their summer theater endeavor in exchange for a place to stay. The show's composer, Raymond, takes an immediate interest in her. But she is more interested in the Spoffords' son. The Spoffords'

daughter, Cutie, is the singing star of a preposterous show "under the personal direction" of Ogdon Quiler, who is her boyfriend. Raymond invites Johnny Graham, a Broadway actor-singer-dancer-librettist-director, to doctor the show. Johnny agrees to do it because he's attracted to Cutie. After an all-night rehearsal, the show opens—but it appears that one of the young men from the show has been kidnapped. Various people have tricks up their sleeves, and it all works out fine in the end.

In the version that played on Broadway, May Graham is a member of a show-business family that doesn't support her association with an arty "little theater" group. Although her brother, Johnny, looks down on writer-director Ogdon Quiler's methods and manner, he is romantically inclined toward Liz Spofford, whose mother has given Quiler's troupe housing and a barn to perform in on her Connecticut estate. Johnny is also friendly with the show's composer, and ultimately transforms the show from an exploration of theoretical concepts into viable entertainment.

Hammerstein and Kern tried to find the right tone for Ogdon, and to clarify the objections a show-business professional might have against arty experiments. Some of the ballets were pruned, but additional music was added—specialty arrangements of the "William Tell Overture" and "Swing Low, Sweet Chariot," performed by Matty Malneck's orchestra.

IN OTHER WORDS, SEVENTEEN

Published as an individual sheet (first verse and refrain only). Introduced by Grace McDonald (May) and Donald Brian (Will).

Stage directions in an early script explain that the duet to be written "depicts the tragedy of being too young for some things, too old for others, too dumb, too smart, in fact the victim of great emotional upheavals and stark crises piling up on another. 'In other words,' sings her father, 'seventeen.' "

Kern liked this melody so much, he wanted it to be the title song.

VERSE 1

MAY: When I was just a slip
Of a girl of sweet sixteen
All the grief and woes of the world
Were on my poor young head.
All through the night I tossed in bed.
I used to go to a dance in dark despair,
Hating the dress I had to wear,

Hating the way I wore my hair,
Wishing that I were dead.

REFRAIN 1

MAY: I played with life
And lost the game,
Till years became my guide.
And only now
I'm learning how
To take it in my stride.
My love affairs are well in hand,
I'm confident and serene.
I've reached an age when nothing fazes me.

WILL: In other words, seventeen.

VERSE 2

MAY: There isn't any need to be
So superior.
You belong to your generation,
I belong to mine.

WILL: Darling, I think that yours is fine.
I'm only laughing because in you I see
Just what my father saw in me.
You're just the way I used to be,
Way back in Nineteen Nine.

REFRAIN 2

WILL: The world was small,
And I was big.
I needed room to spread.
I hoped to be like Roosevelt,
The one that we called "Ted."
My Sunday tie was very grand,
Geranium and pale green.
I'd reached that age, that age of impudence.

BOTH: In other words, seventeen.

CODA

MAY: You must have been the goof of the world
When you were young.
You would never find any boy or girl
Like that today.
You fuddy-duddies like to say
That there is nothing we do that's new to
you.
And no parent knows just what we do.
I'm reading Karl Marx and Steinbeck too,
Sprinkled with Hemingway.
My love affairs are well in hand.
I'm confident and serene.
I've reached the age when nothing fazes
me.
In other words, seventeen.

CHARACTERIZATION

Alternate Title: "Ogdon's Characterization." Not published. Introduced by Hiram Sherman (Ogdon) and ensemble (members of the Ogdon Quiler Progressive Workshop).

An early script calls for a "recitation song" in which Ogdon, an avant-garde writer-director, explains a scene he has written to establish a garden location, with dialogue for the garden's inhabitants: a willow tree, a musket, a babbling brook, and a picket fence. A later script instructs: "Music starts in the orchestra, he begins to talk to himself, then addresses his observations to the company, slipping into the pattern of meter and rhyme without crossing any definite line from dialogue to lyric."

OGDON: I want dimension,
I want method!
Each line must be
dissected,
You must be thoroughly
directed in your parts.
You have to feel—
Be authentic and real.
To play for me
You have to be like
tempered steel!
When Quiler directs you,
Your part must live.
You have to give!

THE TROUPE: We'll give and give!

OGDON: When Quiler directs you,
No scene is flat.
I must have this!

[He gestures.]

THE TROUPE: We'll give you that!

[Repeats gesture.]

OGDON: When Quiler directs you,
You'll play your role
With the intensity of
burning coal.

[He focuses on one actor.]

Mr. McGee, you are a tree,
Drooping with pain,
Dripping with rain.
Weep, for you are a
willow.
Mr. McGee, you are a sad
tree.

THE TROUPE: Mr. McGee,
You are a tree.
Drooping with pain,
Dripping with rain.
Weep, for you are a
willow.
Mr. McGee, you are a sad
tree.

OGDON: The world has got you
down.
You are perplexed.

[MCGEE assumes perplexed expression.]

You're under-sexed.

[MCGEE freezes.]

Use your imagination!
Mr. McGee,
Please try to be
More like a tree, Mr.
McGee.

THE TROUPE: Weep, for you are a
willow.

OGDON: Mr. McGee,
You are a sad tree!

[Suddenly transferring his attention to MISS WASSERMAN.]

There is something
about a musket.
A conservative scout, a
musket.
There is never a doubt a
musket is old,
So you mustn't look
bright or new
Like a Remington
"twenty-two."
You're rather smug,
And your friends in
Connecticut are few.

THE TROUPE: There is something
about a musket.
A conservative scout, a
musket.
There is never a doubt a
musket is old.

OGDON: You just sit back upon
your butt
And superciliously
sneer.
That's the character of a
musket, my dear.

[*Addressing* MISS HYDE.]

You are a babbling
    brook,
Merry as a berry,
And busy as a bee.
You're on your way to
    meet the sea!
You're in a hurry,
You've picked out your
    spot.
Don't have to worry if
    school keeps or not.
Pink-cheeked children
    wade in you,
But you haven't the time
    to stop and play.
Little fish are made in
    you,
But you ripple along
    your way.

THE TROUPE: Haven't time to stop and
    play.
Upon your way!
You're a babbling brook,
Merry as a berry
And busy as a bee.

OGDON: You're never in a jam.
You're always on the lam.

OGDON AND THE TROUPE: You're on your way to
    meet the sea.

ALL THE THINGS YOU ARE

Published as an individual sheet.* Introduced by Hiram Sherman (Ogdon, playing the role of Adam Standish), Frances Mercer (Liz, playing the role of Hester), Hollace Shaw (Carol, playing the voice of Hester's heart), and Ralph Stuart (Charles, playing the voice of Adam's heart).

In the script Ogdon explains, "In this scene the two lovers are too shy to express their real feelings, so this duet is sung by their heart voices . . . People in love don't sing into each other's faces, do they? They look at each other in silence, don't they? But somebody's got to sing, so . . . This gentleman plays the voice of my heart. He sings what I feel. This lady plays the voice of the girl's

---

* *Actually, two versions were published. The first edition had the extended "Never can be at ease" verse from the show. The later (and more familiar) one starts: "Time and again I've longed for adventure . . ." Both verses begin with the same melody, but the show version lasts sixteen bars longer.*

heart. Their song expresses our emotions as we look at each other in silence."

While the show lasted only eight weeks on Broadway, this song spent eleven weeks on *Your Hit Parade*, twice in the number 1 position. Tommy Dorsey and Artie Shaw both had best-selling records. Over the years, several songwriters cited "All The Things You Are" as a favorite, and in a list of the 100 most recorded songs from 1890 to 1954, discographer Joel Whitburn ranked it number 9.

In his anthology, *Lyrics*, Hammerstein used the final lines of the refrain to make two points about songwriting.

One of the best examples of good singing endings in this book is the last line of "All the Things You Are." . . . The singer opens his mouth wide to sing the word "are," and it is still open and he can give still more when he sings the second "are" right after it. It is true that the very last word ends in a consonant, but it is a soft consonant. Furthermore, the two notes that are hit by the repetition of the word "are" constitute the climax of the line, and the word "mine" becomes a sort of denouement.

He was less satisfied with the penultimate line, writing:

Some words, for instance, have lost their value through overuse. "Divine" is such a word. It occurs in "All the Things You Are." I didn't like this word when I submitted the song to Jerry Kern and, as I had anticipated, he didn't like it either. For many days I worked, trying to find a substitute. I just couldn't. I was trapped. "All the things you are," referred to poetically and romantically throughout the song, are certainly what I wish to be "mine." I could not surrender this finish. But it demands an "ine" rhyme. "Some day I'll know that moment . . ." What? Sign, line, fine, shine? Nothing served as well as the unwanted "divine," I never could find a way out. The song written in 1937 shows signs of being a long-lived standard ballad—but I shall never be happy with that word!

Show version

VERSE

HESTER: Never can be at ease when I meet
    him,
Never say what I please when I
    meet him,
Only become unbearably dumb
    and coy.

ADAM: Never can press my suit when
    I'm with her.

Timorous, shy, and mute when
    I'm with her,
I am an inarticulate, bashful boy.

HESTER: Ah, me.
If my heart could only find a
    voice.

ADAM: Ah, me.
If my heart could only find a
    voice.

BOTH: He'd [She'd] hear something
    new and thrilling,
Would he [she] but bestow a
    willing ear.
Ah, ah, ah—.

REFRAIN

HESTER'S HEART: You are the promised kiss of
    springtime
That makes the lonely winter
    seem long.
You are the breathless hush of
    evening
That trembles on the brink of a
    lovely song.
You are the angel glow that
    lights a star,
The dearest things I know are
    what you are.
Someday my happy arms will
    hold you,
And someday I'll know that
    moment divine
When all the things you are are
    mine.

ADAM'S HEART: [*countermelody*] You know you
    are my all in all,
All my springtime.
You know you are the gentle
    echo
Of a lovely song, afar and
    strange.
You light the star of night,
You are what you are.
I want that day when my warm
    arms will hold you closely.
I want you.
When will I know when you are
    all mine?

Sheet music version

VERSE

Time and again I've longed for adventure,
Something to make my heart beat the faster.
What did I long for?

I never really knew.
Finding your love, I've found my adventure.
Touching your hand, my heart beats the faster.
All that I want in all of this world is you.

REFRAIN

You are the promised kiss of springtime
That makes the lonely winter seem long.
You are the breathless hush of evening
That trembles on the brink of a lovely song.
You are the angel glow that lights a star,
The dearest things I know are what you are.
Someday my happy arms will hold you,
And someday I'll know that moment divine
When all the things you are are mine.

MAY TELLS ALL

Not published. Introduced by Grace McDonald (May), extemporizing a reason for her turning up suddenly on the Spofford estate, with Eve Arden (Winnie), Richard Quine (Sonny), and ensemble.

MAY: I saw him,
 He was tall and slim,
 He was sleek and trim and mature.
 He saw me
 Near an apple tree,
 Looking dewy-eyed and dimpled and
  demure.
 He was strong and persuasive.
 I took a leap in the dark,
 All aflame with the world-famous
  spark.
 And late that night
 In the dim, warm light
 Of a moon all misty and gray,
 I suppose it was mad
 But I climbed down a ladder
 And away we ran.
 We ran all night and then we ran all
  day.
 I admit it was mad,
 But he brought me the ladder,
 So we ran away!
 He was sweet
 And a treat to have
 In a suite on Avenue "A."
 All day long,
 Singing love's old song . . .
WINNIE: [*interjecting*] Singing polly wolly
 doodle all the day!

MAY: I, alas, was the victim
 Of a perfidious squirt.
 He had wives in Duluth and Detrert!
SONNY: Detrert?
THE TROUPE: The wicked floit!
MAY: When I found out what a cad he
  was,
 What was left for me then to do?
 Well, I fled from the cad
 And I climbed down a ladder
 And I ran and ran, ran and ran,
 Ran and ran, ran and ran,
 Ran and ran, ran and ran,
 Ran and ran, ran and ran,
 Ran and ran, ran and ran.
 I ran like hell!
 Then I came to the barn,
 That's the end of the yarn,
 There's nothing more to tell.

HEAVEN IN MY ARMS (MUSIC IN MY HEART)

Published as an individual sheet. According to the Broadway program, the song was introduced by Jack Whiting (Johnny), Frances Mercer (May), and Hollace Shaw (Carol). The sheet music, however, assigns some of the second verse to the character Raymond, who was dropped from the number during the pre-Broadway tryouts.

VERSE 1

I like it here.
The atmosphere,
The music and lighting
Are gay and exciting.
And look who's here in my arms!
I'm feeling swell,
I want to tell
The trumpet to blow on,
The fiddlers to bow on.
Hope to tell you, I hope to go on.

REFRAIN

On through the night,
Till the night is through.
Let's keep right on dancing
Now that I've met you.
Do I like dancing?
Confidentially, I do.
If this is love,

What a way to start:
Heaven in my arms,
Music in my heart.
A melody
Especially
Contrived for my heart.

VERSE 2

A melody,
Especially
For lovers to dance to.
A tune a gal chants to
Her fav'rite partner of all.
A melody,
Especially
For stags to cut in on,
For stags to butt in on,
It's a melody girls get thin on.

REPEAT REFRAIN

FINALETTO, ACT ONE, SCENE 2: IN OTHER WORDS, SEVENTEEN (REPRISE)

Introduced by Eve Arden (Winnie) and Grace McDonald (May). Stage directions explain that Winnie half talks and half sings.

VERSE

WINNIE: I feel about the same as I did at
 seventeen.
 I have known no mental improvement
  since I reached that age.
 Somehow, I never turned that page.
 You know, "a girl to a woman
  overnight"?
 Not me.
 I suppose I'm not too bright.
 I note no change.
 My heart is light, and so is my head,
 And the same things continue to amuse
  and excite me.
 For instance,

REFRAIN

WINNIE: [*recites against melody*] At seventeen I
 loved the silent pictures,

No screen-struck lunatic could have been
    loonier.
I would have died for Douglas Fairbanks,
    Senior.
And now, now I'm nuts for Douglas
    Fairbanks, Junior.
I note no change.
And life is grand.
I'm gullible and serene.
I've kept that age of blissful
    brainlessness.
MAY: In other words?
WINNIE: Seventeen.

VERSE 2

WINNIE: [*half spoken, half sung*] Darling, the thing
    that happened to you today, whatever it
    is, it won't beat you. It might if you were
    older and intelligent and hopeless about
    things. But when you're young . . .
    [*spoken in meter*] And you are down on
      your luck,
    And things look black.
    You stick out your chin
    And take the smack,
    And land on your ear
    And bounce right back,
    Too dumb to know you're through.

REFRAIN

WINNIE: [*sung*] The reins of life are in your
      hand,
    You're confident and serene
    You can't be licked,
    For nothing fazes you
    While you remain seventeen.

THAT LUCKY FELLOW (THAT LUCKY LADY)

Published as an individual sheet. Introduced by Robert Shackleton (Raymond). Soon after Raymond has sung this to May, she sings it, as "That Lucky Lady," to Sonny.

That Lucky Fellow

VERSE

Your sweethearts, how do you rate them?
No wonder they stand in line—
All hoping you'll nominate them.

For life will be just ducky
For the nominee.

REFRAIN

That lucky fellow
Who gets you,
And knows you love him,
And lets you.
Oh, how he'll laugh when you play the clown!
Oh, how he'll mope while he works in town.
But with each long day behind him
The failing sunlight will find him
Back in your arms, where he wants to be.
How I'd want those arms,
If I were he.

REPEAT REFRAIN*

That Lucky Lady

VERSE

Your women, how do you rate them?
No wonder they stand in line—
All hoping you'll nominate them.
For life will be just ducky
For the nominee.

REFRAIN

That lucky lady
Who gets you,
And knows you love her,
And lets you.
Oh, how she'll laugh when you play the clown!
Oh, how she'll mope while you work in town.
But with each long day behind her
The failing sunlight will find her

---

* *While Raymond repeats the refrain, the kids in the troupe sing this obbligato:*
    Yoo-hoo,
    He's kiddin' you.
    Don't you believe him.
    Be smart and leave him.
    Where he wants to be
    If you'd let him
    And so would we.

In an earlier draft (when "May" was called "Patsy"), the kids sang:
    Don't let him fool you, Pat,
    With his romance an' stuff.
    He writes it by the yard,
    He writes it on the cuff.
    Ain't love grand. Oh gee.
    Give them arms to me.

Back in your arms, where she wants to be.
How I'd want those arms,
If I were she.

L'HISTOIRE DE MADAME DE LA TOUR (GAVOTTE)

Not published. Introduced by Hollace Shaw (Carol, a member of the troupe), Virginia Card (Miss Wasserman, another member of the troupe), and the boys and girls.

The song is introduced during a rehearsal scene where the performers wear only the essential bits of period costume. A late draft of the script comments: "The 18th century flavor contributed by the wigs and shoes is grotesquely diluted in the 20th century bathing suits they wear. But the whole number is sung and danced in a serious 'dead pan' manner."

CAROL: Mademoiselle had dignity in the
    gavotte.
    (As who has not, in the gavotte?)
    Mademoiselle was virtuous.
    Nary a blot marred her perfect
      score.
    Still, she wanted many things.
    You think not?
    A small ring, a big yacht.
    So she met the wealthy Marquis
      de la Tour,
    And she sighed, "This must be
      l'amour."
MISS WASSERMAN: Sweet and shy,
    She overwhelmed him by
    Her innocence and youth.
CAROL: And a teensy-weensy dash of gin
    And French vermouth.
BOTH: Mademoiselle was in a mood.
    The gavotte was not what she
      thought hot.
    And when he suggested she see
      his ancestral château,
    She agreed to go.
MISS WASSERMAN: He provided her a happy ending
    to a happy day.
CAROL: She provided some contributory
    negligee.
MEN: Sweet and shy
    And winning him by her mien
      and youth.
    A teensy-weensy,
    A teensy dash of gin, in truth,
    Will help vermouth.

CAROL AND
MISS WASSERMAN: Then she told her father all,
The poor lamb.
MEN: The cute kid!
GIRLS: The poor lamb!
CAROL AND
MISS WASSERMAN: Father took his blunderbuss,
Called on the scoundrel,
And that's how Mademoiselle
became Madame.

IN THE HEART OF THE DARK

Published as an individual sheet. Introduced by Hollace
Shaw (Carol, in the role of Hester's heart.)

VERSE

Silent evening
Falls in a mist on a distant hill,
The voices of day are still
And I'm alone.
Silent waiting,
While the romances of fancy fill
The world that I own,
When I am alone.

REFRAIN

In the heart of the dark,
I know a dream's on its way
To bring me you.
And soon you arrive,
The moon in your hair.
The night is alive
While you are there.
In the heart of the dark,
I know the sun's on its way
To steal my dream.
I know that you
Will fade in the light,
And all I can do
Is wait for the night.

ALL IN FUN

Published as an individual sheet. Introduced by Frances
Mercer (Liz).

VERSE

We are seen around New York,
"El Morocco" and the "Stork"—
And all the other stay-up-late cafés.
I am on the town with you these days,
That's the way it stands.
Just a fellow and a girl,
We have had a little whirl.
And our feet have left the ground a bit.
We've played around a bit,
That's the way it stands.
For we are strictly good-time Charlies
Who like to drink and dance around
And maybe kick romance around,
And that's the way it stands.

REFRAIN

All in fun,
This thing is all in fun.
When all is said and done
How far can it go?
Some cocktails,
Some orchids,
A show or two.
A line in a column that links me with you.
Just for laughs
I'm with you night and day.
And so the dopes all say
That I'm that way 'bout you.
Here's the laugh—
And when I tell you,
This'll kill you:
What they say is true.

CUT AND UNUSED SONGS

ME AND THE ROLL AND YOU

Not published. Dropped during out-of-town tryouts.

An early draft of the script has May's father at the
piano, trying to decipher a song his daughter has sent to
him. He and his servants can make out only a word or
two of the latest slang. When she arrives, she interprets
it for them and sings it through.

VERSE

You are a fabulous boyfriend,
Your language is vivid and gay.
Now that you've taught me your double-talk,
Never a dull or a drab or uncolorful word do we
say.

REFRAIN

When you're chasing the egg
And I make with the mega
We're the happiest pair in town.
So you goes and you mows 'em down
Just for me and the gold and brown.
We neglect our econ,
But we go for astrona
When the night is a navy blue.
And when you get in the dough
We always know just what to do!
On a Saturday night we go out to a boobtrap,
Me and the roll and you.

QUARTET

Not published. Dropped during out-of-town tryouts.
Introduced by Virginia Card (Miss Wasserman, in the
role of the musket), Kay Picture (Miss Hyde, in the role
of the brook), Frank Egan (Mr. Pratt, in the role of the
picket fence), and Peter Chambers (Mr. McGee, in the
role of the willow tree). All four sing simultaneously.

MUSKET: Though my barrel's caked with
rust,
I'm a good republican.
A mother of the revolution
Used me to nab a minuteman.
I used to own a powder horn,
Now it's all filled up with corn,
In the home of some Greeks
Who are buying up ye old
antiques.
Normally a gun might sigh,
"What good am I without a horn?"
But I'm happy in my garden where
their love was born.
I am happy and content in the old
rose garden
Where love was born!
BROOK: Oh, I babble all the time.
How can I babble all the day?
Babble, babble, babble, babble,
Why am I that way?

How do I find so many things to
say?
In the early morn I start to babble,
Though I speak no word.
All my tributary creeks are just
like me.
Babbling, babbling, babbling,
Even when I pass a garden where
their love was born.
Babble, babble, babble, babble,
I pass a garden where love was
born!

PICKET FENCE: I am just a picket fence.
She's a big republican.
A mother of the revolution used
her to nab a minuteman.
I wish ev'ry morning for a coat of
paint,
But I guess the painter ain't home.
Oh, I am growing gray and old.
But, after all, I'm pretty happy.
Happy, happy I'm living in a
garden where their love was
born.
I am happy and content in the old
rose garden
Where love was born!

WILLOW TREE: Droop, droop, droop, droop.
I droop in my pain.
I droop ev'ry time I drip with rain.
I can't stop drooping.
I go on drooping.
In the breezes of the morn I swish
and swish.
I wish I wouldn't swish.
But though I may droop
From night to morn,
I'm fairly glad I'm living where
their love was born.
Droop, drip, swish,
Droop, drip, swish.
Droop, drip,
In the garden where love was born!

HIGH UP IN HARLEM

Not published. Lyric dropped during the out-of-town
tryout. Introduced by Jack Whiting (Johnny), Grace
McDonald (May), and Frances Mercer (Liz). Specialty
vocal arrangement by Hugh Martin.

According to Miles Kreuger's liner notes for John
McGlinn's *Jerome Kern Treasury*, this vocal trio from
Act Two became a wordless Act One dance called

"Harlem Boogie-Woogie," which was not listed in the
New York program.

VERSE

Tired of de South.
Tired of de sun.
Waffles and yams
Don't please me none.
Tired of de sun
Shinin' all day,
I want an evenin'
Wid Cab Calloway.

REFRAIN

I want to be back in my homeland,
High up in Harlem,
Where I was born.
Sweet saxophones play in de moonlight
High up in Harlem,
Where I was born.
My folks on Seventh Avenue
Walk wid dat Seventh Avenue pep.
When de dancers have a new step
Dey jus' dance deir legs off!
Oh, carry me back to my homeland.
I don't want cotton,
I don't like corn,
I want to be low-down an' happy
High up in Harlem,
Where I was born.

ARM OF THE LAW

Not published. Dropped from Act Two during the out-of-town tryouts.

An early draft of the script gave the following
description:

The opening [of Act Three] is played against a
black velvet drop, in "one-and-a-half." The characters appear on various levees and are picked up
by shifting spots (as in the opening of *The Band
Wagon*). Here is a musical portrayal of the Connecticut State Police, tracking down a reported
kidnapping. In one spot, Patsy at headquarters, is
brought before the Sergeant for speeding, and
then sputters out her assertion that Sonny Spofford has been kidnapped. Immediately the alarm
is sent out, spots picking up police in the seats of
radio-cars, at lamp-post phones, etc, receiving
reports and instructions. This is all done in verse

set to music, and covers the progress of the search
for Sonny and his kidnappers . . . The repetition
of reports and instructions from headquarters to
the searchers and back to headquarters might fit
into the pattern of a musical fugue.

VERSE

Though we're baffled by the Sonny Spofford case
In the end we'll solve the snatch.
When we doggedly continue with a chase,
Ev'ry snatcher meets his match.
We always catch the snatcher!

REFRAIN 1

The Nutmeg State police are great police.
The state can boast
Of a strong, long arm of the law.
The state can track a crook
And back a crook clear off the coast
With a strong, long arm of the law.

INTERLUDE 1

If you presume to park on our parkway,
Then be sedate and circumspect.
We do not chose to have on our parkway
The girls of fair Connecticut necked!

REFRAIN 2

We are a troop of men,
A group of men who menace you
With a strong, long, prominent jaw!
We have the inescapable charm
Of the arm of the law.

INTERLUDE 2

We love our white immaculate houses
With all the shutters painted green.
We think that all New Yorkers are louses
Who paint their houses aquamarine.

Alternate lines

When there's a toll to take on the parkway
You'll find us standing at the gate,
Because the roll we make on the parkway
Enriches old Connecticut State.
So we collect a cut for beautiful Connecticut
And our manners haven't a flaw.
We have the inescapable charm of the
Arm of the law.

WHERE THE WEEPING WILLOWS HIDE THE BROOK

This partial lyric was found in the *Very Warm for May* material in the Jerome Kern Collection in the Music Division of the Library of Congress. A music manuscript, with vocal lines for soloist and ensemble, is labeled "Sally Dance Interlude" and also "Sally Dance Interlude (Segue Harlem)." Inside, the solo line is marked "Addie" (but these words do not appear in the known texts for *Sweet Adeline*).

Where the weeping willows hide the brook,
We would sit beside the brook,
Over and over again.
Soon you'd let me hold your hand in mine,
And your hand felt grand in mine.
Over and over again.
Out in the meadow the daisies would bow to us,
Bells in the distance repeated our vow to us.
Ev'ry bird and butterfly would say
Ev'rything that I would say
Over and over again.

Softly
In a whispering chorus
Ev'ry leaf on a tree
Ev'ry cricket and bee
Had been whispering before us.
"I love you, you love me."

CONTRARY MARY

Not published. Offered for a screen version of *Very Warm for May* but not used. Lyric submitted to the Production Code Administration on June 3, 1942, as song #3990.

When Kern and Hammerstein sold Metro the movie rights to *Very Warm to May* they contracted to write two new songs for $5,000 each. Later documents identify the songs as "Contrary Mary" and "Good Girl." (For "Good Girl," see *Music in the Air*.) On April 10, 1942, Kern wrote to Hammerstein about a meeting with MGM producer Jack Cummings—at which a cast including Kathryn Grayson (May), Gene Kelly (the brother), and Eleanor Powell (a new character) were discussed, and at which Kern sold Cummings on a "hot coloratura number" for Grayson that they already had in the trunk.

No music has been located, which prevents us from knowing if this was the "hot coloratura" number Kern mentioned in his letter.

Tell us a tale of the long lonely trail
Where the throaty coyote calls up to the moon . . .
Sing a refrain of the broad purple plain
Where the geetars, though sweet, are so far out of tune . . .
Upon a ranch in Oklahoma, where the logie dogies
Roam around the ranges all day,
They tell a story of a very frisky filly known as Mary
Who was branded O.K.—Here's what they say:
Contrary Mary was pow'ful sweet,
But she was pow'ful mean . . .
Though all the cowhands were at her feet
An' treat her like a queen,
She paid them no mind . . . she paid them no mind!
The boys would whisper in Mary's ear
Of love an' stuff an' things,
Contrary Mary would take their beer
An' give 'em back their rings.
She paid them no mind when they paid a call.
She paid them no heed!
Didn' pay 'em at all!
A boy named Jimmy Maloney
Has jus' took a job on the place,
But Jim jus' sticks to his pony
An' don't look a gal in the face . . .
It bothers Mary like nothin' can, to be ignored by him,
She's so contrary, the only man that Mary wants is Jim.
Nine times out o' ten yo're goin' to find
They'll go for the men what pay them no mind!
Contrary Mary was pow'ful sweet,
But she was pow'ful mean,
Though all the cowhands were at her feet
An' treat her like a queen,
She paid them no mind, she paid them no mind!
She wouldn't be kind! No, no, no, no.
Contrary Jimmy is Mary's man, she won him fa'r and squar' . . .
Ah, ah . . . that's how they are.

OTHER SONGS OF 1939

HAVANA FOR A NIGHT (VEREDA TROPICAL)

Music and original Spanish lyric by Mexican composer Gonzalo Curiel and Juan Peso published in 1936. American version published in July 1939. The Oscar Hammerstein II Collection in the Music Division at the Library of Congress includes the Spanish sheet music for "Vereda Tropical (Cancion-Bolero)" and an English lyric for the song by Abe Tuvim, titled "Beneath a Tropic Moon." The Tuvim lyric has various annotations in Hammerstein's hand, including a possible first line: "Moon, upon the Caribbean sea."

You were in Havana for a night,
Your boat was anchored in the bay
In old Havana for a night.
Time was hanging heavy on your hands,
It is the custom to be gay
When in Havana for a night.
And so we met
Beneath a sky of tropic stars,
And went around
To all the most attractive bars.
And then we found
A little place to dance
Where we could face romance,
And hear the whisper of guitars.
You were in Havana for a night
And I was happy in your arms
And it was heaven for a night.
Then dawn brought the day,
Your boat left the bay.
And now I dream.
I lie beside the sea,
And I pretend to be
Within your arms once more,
And you are close to me
Till the stars lose their light.
Havana for a night.

SOUR PUSS

Not published. This lyric fragment hastily written by Hammerstein on a carbon of a January 31, 1939, letter to Edwin Lester of the Los Angeles Civic Light Opera.

Nothing is known of the song's purpose or the music it would use.

Sour puss,
You've been pouting all the day.
Aren't you afraid your little
Face'll be frozen that way?
How's about a teeny-weeny
Smile, what d'ye say?
What d'ye say? Sour puss?
Sour puss,
Lift your chin from off your feet.
Wrinkle up your little nose [*illegible*],
You could be sweet.
Be a sweet
Sour puss.

THE SWEETEST SIGHT THAT I HAVE SEEN

Music by Jerome Kern. Published as an individual sheet in 1945 and selected by Hammerstein for his anthology *Lyrics*. Hammerstein detailed the evolution of this stand-alone song in liner notes for the LP *Jerome Kern Songs Personally Selected for George Byron*.

In the spring of 1939, Jerry Kern and I were working on a musical play which we intended to put into production the following autumn (the ill-fated *Very Warm for May*). To be near Jerry I had come with my wife to California . . . One evening, while I was pacing up and down on the beach side of the house, trying to get an idea for a song that would fit into our story, my attention was diverted by a pair of lovers on the beach . . . They both had white hair. His arm lay gently around her shoulder, and they gazed out at the silver Pacific, peace and contentment in their eyes. I tried to get back to work on my lyric, but nothing I had intended to write seemed as important or as interesting as the old couple . . .

After they had gone, I knew . . . I wanted to write about them, but I had no old couple in the cast of characters of *Very Warm for May*. I had no scene on a moonlit beach, and I knew that the tribute I wished to pay these old strangers would not fit into my play in any possible way . . . Nevertheless, under a strange and impractical compulsion I immediately set out to write the lyric to this song, "The Sweetest Sight That I Have Seen." I set it to a melody which Jerry had written several years before . . . The next day I went to Jerry's house, apologized for not having a new song for *Very Warm for May*, confessed my crime and produced the evidence—an unusable lyric. He fell in love with it. He remembered his old melody, but his memory was better than mine. I had not set it with metric accuracy. So there was still some work for us both to do in conforming lyric to music, and vice versa . . .

The verse of the song was written several years later. In the fall of 1944, Hammerstein alerted Kern that he would soon start work. On November 5, Kern advised Hammerstein by telegram of some adjustments. "When I first got it it didn't fit but now it does and it's a lulu. Hope you won't mind elimination of first 'The' in last line. It now reads 'I pause to recall the sweetest of all sights I've seen on the way.' Love Jerry." The next day, in a postcript to a letter, Kern asked "in addition to elimination of that 'the' (per my wire) may I change 'memory' to 'mem'ry'?"

VERSE

My room grows dim in the dying light
Of a fire on the hearth that once was bright.
The house is quiet and I'm alone,
And the dreams that I dream are all my own.
I'm looking back on the flying years,
And skipping the parts that were marked with
   tears.
But over the parts that were brave and gay,
Lovingly letting my mem'ry stray,
I pause to recall the sweetest
Of all sights I've seen on the way.

REFRAIN

I have seen a line of snow-white birds
Drawn across an evening sky.
I have seen divine, unspoken words
Shining in a lover's eye.
I have seen moonlight on a mountaintop,
Silver and cool and still.
I have heard church bells faintly echoing
Over a distant hill.
Close enough to beauty I have been
And, in all the whole wide land,
Here's the sweetest sight that I have seen—
One old couple walking hand in hand.

Top: *The finale of* American Jubilee, *performed outdoors at the New York World's Fair.*
Bottom: *Original sheet music for "The Last Time I Saw Paris"*

AMERICAN JUBILEE | 1940 and War Songs of 1940–1945

AMERICAN JUBILEE (1940)

Specially written for the second half of the 1939 World's Fair. No out-of-town tryout. New York: New York World's Fair Grounds, Flushing Meadows, Queens; previews May 1–11, 1940; opened on May 12, 1940; closed on October 2, 1940; with shows at 3:30 p.m., 5:30 p.m., 8:30 p.m., and 10:45 p.m. Presented by the New York World's Fair Corporation. Produced by Albert Johnson. Lyrics and dialogue by Oscar Hammerstein II. Music by Arthur Schwartz. Directed by Leon Leonidoff. Choreography by Catherine Littlefield. Orchestrations by Hans Spialek. Music direction by Don Voorhees. Choral direction by Ken Christie. Scenic design by Albert Johnson. Costumes by Lucinda Ballard.

Cast: Lucy Monroe, Ray Middleton, Wynn Murray, Paul Haakon, Margret Adams, Gene Marvey, Harry Meehan, Joe Jackson, the Lime Trio, and an ensemble of 350.

Four songs were published. The Billy Rose Theatre Collection at the New York Public Library for the Performing Arts has a script and a souvenir program. In the Music Division of the Library of Congress, the Oscar Hammerstein II Collection has a script and some promotional material; the Warner-Chappell Collection contains several piano-vocal manuscripts in the hands of Arthur Schwartz and Chappell music editor Albert Sirmay.

The show's program lists several musical numbers that were danced but not sung. These include "Flag Drill," following Washington's inauguration; "Lime Trio Specialty," in the P. T. Barnum sequence; "Waltz," in the civil war sequence; "Teddy Roosevelt and His Rough Riders," "Struggle Buggy Days," and "Cakewalk." "The Star-Spangled Banner" was used as the show's finale.

Promotional materials described *American Jubilee* as "A panorama of American history with emphasis not on the winning of battles or the passing of laws, but on the lusty gaity which has always pervaded our nation . . . episodes and famous characters not always found in history books, but nonetheless an essential part of our development and an important ingredient of the state of mind that is America." The cast performed "upon the largest revolving stage ever constructed—a gigantic circular platform, two hundred and seventy feet in diameter and built upon rollers. The magic of Albert Johnson's sets transforms this vast expanse into scene after scene out of the history of our country—authentic and complete to such minute detail as real flowers growing in real earth in the gardens adjacent to Federal Hall in the scene of the inauguration of Washington as President."

ANOTHER NEW DAY

Not published. Introduced by Margret Adams (Teacher) and Lloyd Warren, Walter Kelly, Jeri Anne Raphael, Joan Flicker, Carol Renee, and Gerry McMillan (Children).

Another new day, another new day,
Another new morning to start.
Another new chance to do your best
And do it with all of your heart.
So greet the new day
And hope it may be
A very good morning for you and for me.

WE LIKE IT OVER HERE

Published as an individual sheet. Used during the "Inauguration of George Washington, 1789" sequence. Introduced by Ray Middleton (Captain) and the ensemble (tradesmen, foot and horse guards, guests on the balcony, civilians).

VERSE

This is not the one place in the world
Where the sun lights the trees.
This is not the only flag unfurled,
High and brave in the breeze.
But this is the one place in the world
Where men think what they please.
That's why we're here.
That's why we stay.
We like to live that way.

REFRAIN

We like it over here.
Over here is a good place to be.
We like it over here.
Life is grand in a land that is free.
No man to think for us,
No man to fear—
Thank heaven and the God we trust
It's just as we like it over here.

REPEAT REFRAIN

Unpublished interlude

CAPTAIN: First we had to fight,
　　　　Fight for what we wanted most.
　　　　What we wanted most

Was to make Americans free!
MEN: And we got what we fought for.
CAPTAIN: Then we had to work,
　　　　Work to build a ship of state.
　　　　Build a ship of state
　　　　Strong enough to ride a rough sea!
MEN: And we got what we worked for.
CAPTAIN: For the things we got
　　　　We had to pay.
ENSEMBLE: For what we got we were glad to pay.
CAPTAIN: Now the job is done.
ENSEMBLE: Now the job is done.
　　　　Let's keep what we've won!

JENNY LIND

Alternate titles: "Serenade" and "Firemen's Serenade." Not published. Used during the 1860s sequence. Introduced by Harry Meehan (Fire Chief) and the male singing ensemble.

VERSE 1

CHIEF: We stand beneath your window tonight,
　　　　Jenny,
　　　　Blunt but honest firemen, 'tis true.
　　　　The twinkling stars in heaven are bright,
　　　　But they can't hold a candle to you.
　　　　There's not a man in all this brave brigade
　　　　That wouldn't say what I'm about to tell.
　　　　My darling Swedish Nightingale,
　　　　For you I'd spend a night in jail
　　　　And probably lay down my life as well.

REFRAIN

MEN: Jenny Lind! Jenny Lind!
CHIEF: To you my fondest hopes and dreams are
　　　　pinned.
　　　　You're as pretty as can be,
　　　　And the only girl for me
　　　　Is J-E-double-N-Y
　　　　L-I-N-D.

VERSE 2

CHIEF: The creatures of the forest are thrilled
　　　　Whenever they can hear your golden note.
　　　　The meadowlarks and thrushes are stilled,
　　　　For none of them can cope with your
　　　　throat!

REPEAT REFRAIN

HOW CAN I EVER BE ALONE?

Published as an individual sheet. Introduced by Lucy Monroe (Jenny Lind), Gene Marvey (a soldier who is leaving for battle), and the women's singing ensemble, then danced by Paul Haakon and the Littlefield Ballet.

VERSE

JENNY: When you're far away,
Ev'ry lonely day that I spend,
I'll pretend you are near.
I will hear your voice
And the things you'd say,
Just as if I had you here,
Whisp'ring in my ear.

REFRAIN

How can I ever be alone
When you never leave my heart?
How can I call a dream my own
When you always share a part?
All that's mine is yours, and yours forever.
All the things I feel and say and do.
How can I ever be alone
When the world I live in is you?

BY THE PEOPLE

Not published. Introduced by the male ensemble in a torchlight parade.

American Jubilee's 1860s sequence concludes with scenes titled "Of the People," "By the People," and "For the People." Only "By the People" was sung. It seems to use the same music as the interlude portion of "We Like It Over Here."

Vote for Honest Abe,
Reelect the president.
Vote for Honest Abe,
Reelect a leader we love!
And the Union forever.
Lincoln is the man,
Enemy of slavery.
Lincoln is the man
Fighting for the freedom we love.
And the Union forever!
He will speed the day
That ends the war;

When North and South will be friends once more.
Brothers once again,
Brothers once again,
As we were before.

[*Into refrain of "We Like It Over Here."*]

MY BICYCLE GIRL

Published as an individual sheet. Introduced by Gene Marvey.

Part of an 1890s sequence titled "The Day Before Yesterday." *Variety*'s Ibee noted: "After Marvey sings 'My Bicycle Girl,' routine by Miss Littlefield's ballet rather surprises and highly pleases the audience. There are 48 girls on wheels and they prove they know how to ride. Same goes for boys who do tricks in formation during a sort of road race that gets laughs."

VERSE

As a particular friend of yours,
I wonder if I dare.
Wonder if I dare
Ask a particular favor.
When the Saturdays are fair.
Wonder if you'd care,
Care to join me?

REFRAIN

Will you be my bicycle girl?
Be my Daisy Bell?
If you'll be my bicycle girl,
Life will be perfectly swell.
When we take an afternoon off,
Up the road we'll fly,
Feeling happy-go-lucky and fancy-free.
I'll sing to you,
You'll sing to me.
Wherever we are we will want to be,
While the world rolls by.

TENNESSEE FISH FRY

Published as an individual sheet. Introduced in the 1890s sequence by Wynn Murray (as entertainer May Irwin) and ensemble.

Popular recordings were made by Kay Kyser and His Orchestra with vocal by Sully Mason, Mildred Bailey,

and the Jimmy Dorsey Orchestra with vocal by Helen O'Connell.

VERSE

Hot diggity!
Hot diggity!
Dat ol' sun is climbin' high.
Hot diggity!
Hot diggity!
Time to catch de catfish fo' de fry.
Poor li'l you,*
You never been to a fry?
Well ain't dat a shame,
Ain't dat a shame!
Ain't dat scand'lus!!

REFRAIN

Ain't you never been to a Tennessee fish fry?
Ain't you never fished fo' your dinner down
     south?
If you never been to a Tennessee fish fry,
Den you never had a chunk o' heaven right in your
     mouth!
You ain't tasted cornbread when it's drowned
In a pound of butter!
You ain't swung your sweetest gal around
In a do-see-do!
If you never been to a Tennessee fish fry,
Dere's an awful lot about a picnic dat you don't
     know.

Unpublished patter

[*whistle*]
Got no work to do today
Left it all behind me.
[*whistle*]
Got no grief or misery,
Nuthin' on my mind
But fishin'
An' cookin' de fish
An' smackin' my lips
All over de dish,
An' wishin'
It never would end.
Sweet world, you's my friend!
[*whistle*]
Don't I sing
Like a bird?

---

* *Alternate lyric for lines 7 and 8 from the handwritten piano-vocal score in the Warner-Chappell Collection:*
     What do you do?
     I never been to a fry.

Ain't it spring?
Ain't you heard?

REPEAT REFRAIN

ONE IN A MILLION

Not published. Introduced by Wynn Murray (Advocate for Candidate X) and Harry Meehan (Advocate for Candidate Y), Ray Middleton (the President), and ensemble.

"One in a Million" takes the form of a campaign rally. Shortly before *American Jubilee*'s premiere, a newspaper reported that the finale would be "the inauguration of the President of the U.S. in 1941. The Fair is carefully avoiding, however, any hint of who that gentleman might be." A few months after the opening, the *Herald Tribune* reported that a new scene would be added, with actors impersonating Wendell Willkie and President Roosevelt, but it has not been located.

X'S ADVOCATE: My candidate
    Stands on his merit, he
    Offers you prosperity.
LISTENERS: Blah, blah, blah, blah, blah, blah, blah.
X'S ADVOCATE: My candidate
    Puts chickens in your pot,
    Puts a house upon your lot,
    Cars in your garage.
LISTENERS: Blah, blah, blah, blah, blah!
Y'S ADVOCATE: My candidate!
    His life is free from taint.
    He is what the other ain't!
LISTENERS: Blah, blah, blah, blah, blah, blah, blah.
Y'S ADVOCATE: My candidate
    Calls his opponent's bluff.
    Calls his pot-and-chicken stuff
    Only a mirage!
LISTENERS: Blah, blah, blah, blah, blah.
Y'S ADVOCATE: Vote for Mr. Y!
LISTENERS: Blah, blah, blah, blah, blah.
X'S ADVOCATE: X's public adore him.
    Mr. Y is a cheese.
    X's record speaks for him.
    Folks, let me tell you that he's
    the—

REFRAIN

X'S ADVOCATE: One in a million, a man among
    men.
    Candidate X, the people's choice!

Leads the good life,
Never led another.
Good to his wife,
And devoted to his mother.
One in a million, a man among
    men,
Promises anything you say.
Candidate X will shake your hand
    and kiss your babies
Up to election day!
Y'S ADVOCATE: One a million, a man among men.
    Candidate Y, the people's choice!
    Leads the good life,
    Never led another.
    Good to his wife,
    And devoted to his mother.
    One in a million, a man among
    men,
    Promises anything you say.
    Candidate Y will shake your hand
    and kiss your babies
    Up to election day!
MAN: The president has been elected!
    The president has been elected!
    His name is [*drowned out by horns and bells*].
PRESIDENT: [*spoken over "We Like It Here" melody*]
    I may have been a Republican . . .
    I may have been a Democrat . . .
    But whatever my party may be,
    I am an American. I glory in the
    knowledge that a president of
    our country is chosen not to tell
    Americans what to do, but to do
    what Americans want!
    [*sung*] No man to think for us
    No man to fear.
COMPANY: Thank heaven and the God we
    trust—
    It's just as we like it over here!

[*Soloist begins "Star-Spangled Banner." Teacher and schoolchildren sing with the principals.*]

Unused passage

X'S ADVOCATE: [*affectionately to* Y'S ADVOCATE]
    Now the campaign is over,
    Don't be angry with me.
    I don't care who's elected,
    Honey, as long as you'll be my—

REFRAIN

X'S ADVOCATE: One in a million, a man among
    men.
    One in a million, and he's mine!

When he makes love,
What an inspiration!
When he makes love,
He makes more than conversation.
One in a million, a man among
    men.
Look at him, girls. Is he divine?
Leave him alone!
Those six feet three are all for me,
That beautiful man is mine!

[*The advocates exit together.*]

Another unused passage.

Probably uses the interlude melody from "We Like It Over Here."

ENSEMBLE: President elect,
    We are here to welcome you.
    President elect,
    We are here to welcome you now.
    You're the man that we wanted.
    Never mind your name,
    Never mind your party's name
    It is all the same.
    You're the chief executive now.
    You're the man that we wanted.
    Try to do the things you said you'd do,
    So we can go right ahead with you!
MAN: [*shouting*] Here he comes!
ENSEMBLE: Do the best you can,
    Do the best you can.
GIRL: [*shouting*] Here he comes!
ENSEMBLE: You are our head man!

CUT AND UNUSED SONGS

GATHERED IN THE SQUARE

Not published and not used. This passage would have preceded Washington's inauguration. It seems to fit the interlude melody from "We Like It Over Here."

TEACHER: Gathered in the square
    Waiting for the president,
    One could feel the air
    Rumble with the hum of the throng.
ENSEMBLE: What a day to remember!

TEACHER: Everyone was there
Waiting for the president.
Gathered in the square,
Lifting up their voices in song.
ENSEMBLE: What a day to remember!
MAN: Here he comes!
TEACHER: Then, from down the street,
A cry and a shout!
WOMAN: Here he comes!
TEACHER: Just as the sun in the sky came out.
Then they rang the bells,
How they rang those bells!

ALL THE SONGS IN THE WORLD

Not published. Apparently intended for the character of Jenny Lind. It could have been written for *American Jubilee* and not used; or may have been one of the songs the *New York Herald Tribune* reported Hammerstein and Schwartz were writing for a proposed road tour. On a piano-vocal manuscript, now in the Warner-Chappell Collection at the Library of Congress, the composer wrote, "Words by Oscar Hammerstein IInd. Music by Arthur Schwartz I."

All the songs in the world
Were born to be sung tonight.
A dream that is old as time
Is suddenly young tonight.
Ah—[*cadenza*]
All the songs in my heart
I send out on the air now,
Making room in my heart
For the lover who's there now.
Here's a song from my heart:
Ah—[*cadenza*]
All the bells in the world,
How they long to be rung tonight!
Ah—[*cadenza*]
All the hopes of romance
Fly to heaven above,
Lead the stars in a dance,
To the spell-weaving music of love.
Ah—[*cadenza*]
All the songs in the world
That were born to be sung tonight
Ah—[*cadenza*]*

* *A typed lyric sheet had these words instead of the cadenza:*
Are a part of an olden dream
That is suddenly young tonight.

Here's a song from my heart
Here's a song from my heart:
Ah—[*climactic cadenza*]

WAR SONGS OF 1940–1945

Hammerstein believed a great war song would have immeasurable value. He spent many Monday nights chairing the Music War Committee of the American Theatre Wing, which fielded requests for special patriotic or military songs, tried to match subjects to songwriters, and worked to publish and promote the results. His own first effort was inspired by the fall of Paris and though he worked with several composers in the early 1940s, he never wrote a second war song that meant as much as "Paris" did to its listeners. In March 1942, Hammerstein recapped his efforts in a letter to Laurence Schwab:

My own [war] work has been sporadic. I have raised some money for Bucks County Emergency Hospitals (in case we have to take care of evacuees from an air-raided Philadelphia or New York.) I also went well over my quota in getting donations for the American Theatre Wing War Service. Incidentally, the Canteen we just opened for servicemen has turned out to be a big success. It is situated in the old "Little Club" under the 44th Street Theatre. The boys get food there and entertainment—by performers from current shows—and dancing with girls from the various choruses. Dorothy goes down there twice a week and works behind the counter and in the kitchen and gets tired but has a hell of a time as the special confidante of all the Anzacs who drop in there.

With George Kaufman, Bob Alton, Harold Rome and about twenty other fellows who might be described as top-flight authors and song writers, I am working on a show which will be a war revue designed to come into New York for a run. All material contributed free and all profit to be donated to various war reliefs.*

My chief aim, however, has been to write a great song, and this I have so far failed to do, although I have devoted nearly all my time to it for the past three months. I don't mean a song like "Goodbye Mamma, I'm Going to Yokohama." I mean an important song. The difficulty of writing an expression of what Americans feel today is a very distressing thing because I find as I

* *The show did not happen.*

try to write it that there is something wrong with the script. We don't all feel the same. We don't all have the same understanding of what are the aims of this war, and the spontaneous emotional unity which was achieved by the sudden blow at Pearl Harbor has now been dissipated into something like the bickering period which existed just before. . . . Roger DeLisle did not write the Marsailles and thereby exhort France to revolt against the King. The spirit of the revolution was there and, after years of irritation, had been deeply imbedded in the hearts of all Frenchmen. And all he did as a poet was to crystallize this unified purpose. I, as a minor poet of Tin Pan Alley, feel the need for such whole-hearted unity and clarity of aims—and even then I might not do as good a job as DeLisle. I would like, however, to go into the ring with him sometime as equal weights.

THE LAST TIME I SAW PARIS

Music by Jerome Kern. Published as an individual sheet.
When Hitler's army entered Paris on June 14, 1940, Hammerstein was so disturbed he couldn't work. In 1951, preparing for an appearance on Ed Sullivan's *Toast of the Town*, he recalled:

I kept thinking of the silly and frivolous side of Paris. Revues at the Casino de Paris. Chevalier's straw hat slanting down over one eye. Mistinguette and her famous legs. All these things seemed ridiculous and pathetic and touching when you realized that at this moment the heavy boots of the enemy were stamping down those streets. Then my mind switched from the night life of Paris to the less advertised but much more important day life. The beauty of her buildings. The trees and lawns in her parks. The stimulating confusion of her happy streets. Pretty soon I found myself writing a song about these things. I didn't know if I'd ever see Paris again—at the time I was afraid that I wouldn't—and I tried to sketch a little picture of the city as I had known it, so I could preserve the memory for myself and for anyone else who cared about it as I did.

Kate Smith and Hildegarde both recorded "The Last Time I Saw Paris" on October 16, 1940, for Columbia and Decca respectively. The song was officially introduced by Kate Smith on the *Kate Smith Hour* (CBS Radio) on October 18 and taken up by performers as varied as Noël Coward and Sophie Tucker. Ann Sothern sang it in the 1941 MGM film *Lady Be Good*, and in February 1942 the song won an Academy Award.

Hammerstein received suggestions for such musical follow-ups as "The Next Time I See Paris," but had no interest. Interviewed for an August 1943 article about war songs, he said, "Our feelings have changed. We weren't in the war then, and many Americans felt strongly that we shouldn't go in. That note of sad resignation won't do today. Our objective is not to mourn for Paris, but to fight, and put her back where she was."

VERSE 1

A lady known as Paris,
Romantic and charming,
Has left her old companions and faded from view.
Lonely men with lonely eyes are seeking her in
vain.
Her streets are where they were,
But there's no sign of her—
She has left the Seine.

REFRAIN

The last time I saw Paris,
Her heart was warm and gay.
I heard the laughter of her heart in ev'ry street
café.
The last time I saw Paris,
Her trees were dressed for spring
And lovers walked beneath those trees
And birds found songs to sing.
I dodged the same old taxicabs that I had dodged
for years;
The chorus of their squeaky horns was music to
my ears.
The last time I saw Paris,
Her heart was warm and gay—
No matter how they change her,
I'll remember her that way.

VERSE 2

I'll think of happy hours
And people who shared them:
Old women selling flowers in markets at dawn,
Children who applauded Punch and Judy in the
park,
And those who danced at night
And kept their Paris bright
Till the town went dark.

REPEAT REFRAIN

THIS IS LONDON

Music by Lewis E. Gensler. Not published. Probably written in the winter of 1940–41.

A file at the Rodgers & Hammerstein Organization yielded a scenario by Hammerstein and Gensler for a film about a British woman who lost her husband in the First World War and urges her estranged son to stand up for the country's ideals as a second war begins. The project was pitched to RKO, MGM, and Warner Bros. in the spring and fall of 1941. A piano-vocal score in the file seems to match the first part of the refrain, but lacks the concluding pages.

Opening version

[It is 1911. A friendly cabby gives a newcomer "his own warm affectionate conception of London."]

CABMAN: First visit here?
Well, there's plenty to see.
Not much about London that I don't
know.
Me? I've been drivin' a cab all my life in
this town.
Know it inside and out,
Back and forth,
Up and down!
It frightens you first—
A bit noisy and wild.
But later it's gentle
And sweet as a child,
Is London.
There's a beautiful river that clings to
its side,
Like the town was the groom and the
river his bride . . .
Hear that?
Those are Bow Bells.
If you're born anywhere in the sound of
their voice
You're a Cockney.
I think, if the thing was a matter of
choice,
That's what I'd choose to be,
Is a Cockney.
That means you belong to the town.
It's a lively old town to belong to—
The cries in the street
And the rustle o' feet
And the rollin' o' wheels
And the crackin' o' whips
And a feller that yells
That he sells fish and chips—
It's a tune you could make up a song to!
I expect that you're thinking I'm daft,

To be so much in love with a place.
But drive on, as you do now, with me,
And look full in the fog-colored face
Of London,
And see if you don't get a feeling
Of something that's solid and good.
That's its character—
See what I mean?
It can never be misunderstood.
It's just as you see it today . . .
May God always keep it that way.

REFRAIN

["This is the musical theme of the picture, but the words are spoken here, with a line or two half sung. It is recited in synchronization but not in strict meter."]

This is London,
Bless its name.
Always changing,
Still the same.
A house may fall
And new buildings arise,
But the soul of England remains,
Like the gray mist in the skies.
This is London.
This is ours.
Not the steeples,
Not the tow'rs,
But the men and women
Who work for the town,
And are glad to play their parts—
They are London.
Bless their hearts!

Finale version

[A montage of newsreel footage: Hitler, Mussolini, Chamberlain, retreat from Dunkirk, German bombers, and London blitzed. Then the face of broadcaster Edward R. Murrow is superimposed over the chaos. "The refrain of the theme song, 'This Is London,' is played beneath and Murrow speaks dramatically into the mike, his lines synchronized to the melody but spoken instead of sung." Murrow fades as we see Londoners putting out fires, pulling away debris, cleaning up the remains of their homes.]

MURROW: This is London
Red with flame!
Bruised and battered—
Still the same.
The houses fall
But new buildings arise
And the soul of England remains
Like the gray mist in the skies.

WOMAN: This is London.
[*shouting to the skies*] This is ours!
MURROW: Not the steeples,
Not the tow'rs
But the men and women
Who work for the town
And are glad to play their parts.
They are London.
Bless their hearts.

FOREVER AND A DAY

Music by Jerome Kern. Published as an individual sheet "for sale only in the British Empire (except Canada and Newfoundland) and the Continent of Europe." Registered for copyright as an unpublished song August 19, 1941. Recorded in 1941 by Turner Layton (English Columbia) and by Doreen Stephens (HMV).

Special thanks are due to Kern scholar Stephen Banfield, Stanley Hugh Badock Professor of Music at the University of Bristol, for bringing this song back into circulation.

VERSE

Time has a way of flying,
While the world is standing still;
Time is a flowing river,
Beside a water mill.
Things that are false keep dying,
For a vogue is quickly gone;
Things that are true keep living,
Things that are real go on.

REFRAIN

The morning sun will rise
Forever and a day,
And a golden light will glow in the skies
And melt the night away.
The seas will bring the land
A gift of silver spray,
And the ships of men will sail that sea
Forever and a day.
And an island we call England
Will be bright and green and fair.
And when freedom needs defenders
Freedom will find them there!
And men who love the world
Will work and fight and pray,
So that she may live forever,
Forever and a day!

BUDDY ON THE NIGHTSHIFT

Music by Kurt Weill. Published in the 1982 folio *The Unknown Kurt Weill.*

In 1942, Oscar Hammerstein wrote to Mrs. Carly Wharton at the Authors' League of America's Writers' War Board Committee of Lunch Hour Follies:

Dear Mrs. Wharton:

It is about time I answered your letter of August 12 in which you asked for material to be used in *The Lunch Hour Follies.* Kurt Weill and I wrote a song called "Hello There, Buddy, On the Night Shift" which I think might be developed into a very good number for this purpose. If you would be interested in hearing it, let me know and I will get ahold of Kurt and we will play and sing the number. If it sounds good when we play and sing it, it will have met the acid test of all time.
Kindest regards.
Sincerely,
Oscar Hammerstein, 2nd

In recent years, the song was recorded by Teresa Stratas, Anne Sofie Von Otter, and Andrea Marcovicci. In the spring of 2007, the song was heard on Broadway in the Harold Prince–directed *LoveMusik.*

Hello there, buddy on the nightshift—
I hope you slept all day
Until the moon came out
And woke you up
And sent you on your way.
Hello there, buddy on the nightshift—
I hope you're feeling fine.
I left a lot of work
For you to do
On a long assembly line.
I wish I knew you better
But you never go my way,
For when one of us goes on the job
The other hits the hay!
Goodbye now, buddy on the nightshift—
And push those planes along,
And when the sun comes out
I'll take your place,
All wide awake and strong.
I'll follow you, you'll follow me,
And how can we go wrong?

THE GOOD EARTH

Music by Kurt Weill. Published in the 2002 folio *Unsung Weill.*

In a letter to Lotte Lenya dated February 25, 1942, Weill wrote, "Tomorrow I'll work all day on a song I am writing with Hammerstein for which I had a good idea, a song about China with the title: 'The Good Earth.'" On April 16 he informed her, "I met Hammerstein and we finished the song 'The Good Earth' which is definitely a hit. We'll try to sell it to the movies." Weill eventually did sell it to the movies: with a new lyric by Ira Gershwin, it was heard as "All At Once," in the 1945 film *Where Do We Go from Here?*

The good earth
Is bearing grain in China
And her cherry trees are blooming in Japan.
The good earth
Bestows her simple blessings
With a kind of blind belief in man.
She has seen her fields aflame and bleeding
Where the torch of war has come to mar her plan,
But the good patient earth
Keeps on feeding and forgiving us,
For she can't help believing in man.

NAVY DAY POEM

Recited by Melvyn Douglas at the Navy League Dinner in Washington, DC, on October 27, 1942, while a musical background composed by Sigmund Romberg was played by the Navy orchestra. Published in the December 1942 issue of *Sea Power* magazine.

In October and November letters to Laurence Schwab, Hammerstein described this as his first tribute to the Navy, "unless in the past I have by some accident written some song in some musical comedy which I forget and which had to do with the Navy." He credited Ensign John Driscoll for condensing "what seemed to be the entire history of the Navy in a few pages for me."

In times of peace, our Navy is
A thing of clean and graceful ships,
Riding their anchors in the sun,
And men in solid ranks of blue,
Standing beneath bright-colored flags.
Ruffles and flourishes, gun salutes,
And dances on a moonlit deck—
These are the things we know and love,
In times of peace.

In times of peace we read in books
Of John Paul Jones and Farragut,
Porter, Decatur, and the rest.
We think of them as gods, remote,
Frowning at us from museum walls,
Or gazing across our city parks,
Aloof on marble pedestals—
Heroes are hard to get to know,
In times of peace.

But now we're a Navy at war!
Our ships, not concerned with their beauty,
Ride forward, undraped, into battle,
Gray warriors, naked and angry.

Our heroes, no longer aloof,
Have stepped down from statues and portraits
And taken their places beside us,
As comrades and teachers and fathers.

We know they are with us tonight,
And somehow we feel we can hear them
Quite simply and honestly, asking:
"D'you think you could use an old sailor?"

We can use you, old sailors! We're using you now.
Your strength is the reason we're strong.
The tactics you taught us, the tricks of the
        trade—
All you learned has been passed right along,
Handed down from old Hopkins to Preble to Hull,
Then to Perry to Dewey to Sims.
From father to son and to grandson we pass
Our customs, our rules, and our hymns.
But there's more to our kinship than tangible
        things,
Like armor, maneuvers, and guns.
A heritage far more important than that
Has passed to your fortunate sons,
For in some way, the spirit that beat in your hearts
And led you to victory's height,
Is beating in *our* hearts, all over the world,
And giving us courage tonight.

Stephen Decatur, we know you were there
When Bulkeley's torpedo boats harassed the foe,
Darting through Philippine harbors at night
(That is the kind of a job you would like).
A hundred and thirty-eight years have gone by
Since you and a ketch-full of strong-hearted men
Stole through a Tripoli port after dark,
Boarded a frigate and set her ablaze—
Commodore Preble commanded the fleet.
You and your comrades were called "Preble's
        Boys,"
Somers and Stewart and Bainbridge were there,
Hull and young Wadsworth and Israel, too.
Now you are living all over again,

All of you, fighting the fight as before!
Didn't you cheer the "expendables" on,
Helping their hazardous ventures succeed?

Weren't you there when they made their escape
Dodging the glare of the enemy's lights,
Zigzagging back to their home in Bataan?
. . . Didn't their exploits remind you of yours?

"Bulkeley's Boys" are, after all,
Very much like "Preble's Boys."
Different times and different foes,
Different ships and different guns.
Same alertness, same attack,
Same determined jaws are shut,
Same sea-searching eyes are set
Straight ahead, one goal in view,
Freedom! That's the thing we want.
That's the wish that makes us one,
Somers, Hobson, and O'Hare—
Different names in different years,
Not related in their blood,
No connection anywhere
Saving one important bond,
Something part of all of us
And of which we're all a part,
Something that is part of God,
Something that He gave to man—
Liberty to live his life
As his honest thought dictates,
Not afraid to speak his faith
In the things which he believes,
Asking only what is fair
For himself and fellow men.
That is not so much to ask.

This should not be hard to get.
Ours is but a simple wish
Till we see that wish opposed.
Then a conflagration starts
Burning madly in our hearts.
Freedom is our hot desire!
We must have it, and we will.
We'll protect it with our lives,
Caring not how much we lose.
Just so long as we can win
Freedom, freedom for us all!
While we have a ship to sail,
While we have a plane to fly,
While we have a gun to fire,
We will fight from sea to sea,
Island to island, shore to shore,
Steel to steel and hand to hand—
That is how our fathers fought.
That's our Navy's heritage.
That is how we've won before.
That is how we'll win today.

THE PT BOAT SONG (STEADY AS YOU GO)

Music by Richard Rodgers. Published as an individual sheet. Registered for copyright on March 29, 1943, two days before *Oklahoma!* opened on Broadway. Dedicated to "the officers and men of the motor torpedo boats." Patrol torpedo—"PT"—boats were small and swift wooden vessels that carried substantial firepower.

VERSE

We found some hunks of plywood
And we made them fit,
And we stuck them all together
With some tacks and spit.
First thing you know, we are burning up the seas
In a flock of flying splinters that we call PTs!
(And we love those flying splinters that we call
        PTs.)

REFRAIN

Steady as you go! Steady!
Wind her up and give her the gun,
Pour the soup and make her rattle!
Make that eggshell run!
Steady as you go! Steady!
There's a puff of smoke in the sky.
Got a date to meet a battle—
Make that eggshell fly!
The PTs are peewees, the midgets of the fleet,
But the biggest one the enemy's got
Is the one we run to meet.
So keep the little rough-and-ready
Steady as you go!

A THREE-DAY PASS

Music by George W. Meyer (composer of "For Me and My Gal"). Not published. A typed lyric and a leadsheet for the refrain were found in the Hammerstein collection at the Library of Congress. Written in July 1943 for a Music War Committee effort to provide material for a "Soldier Package Show" called *A Three-Day Pass*. Hammerstein's assignment was: "Ballad: I Live My Life on a Three-Day Pass."

VERSE

I left the camp with a three-day pass in my hand,
I was going to hit ev'ry spot that I wanted to see.

I'm back in camp and my leave turned out to be grand,
But it wasn't a bit like I thought it was going to be.

REFRAIN

A three-day pass—
Long time no see no high-heeled shoes,
And I was in the mood to use
A three-day pass.
Arranged my plans
For what to do and who to see,
But when good luck brought you to me,
I changed my plans.
Had a little list—
Names and numbers too.
Threw the little list away!
Felt that I'd been kissed
By the morning dew,
Hugged by a breeze in May!
The three days passed,
We clung to time as time flew by,
The last night's moonlight left the sky—
The three days passed,
But the dream will last.

DEAR FRIEND

Music by Richard Rodgers. Published as an individual sheet. Written in 1944 for the Fifth War Loan Drive.

Dear friend,
Dear friend, this is a touch.
We won't go into explanations,
But when boys need help so much,
They always call on their relations, dear friend.
Traveling on foreign shores,
Is expensive as can be.
It isn't our fault or yours
It's the high cost of living free, dear friend.
To know that we can count on you
Is all we need to know.
Just say that you'll see us through,
And we'll finish up the show, dear friend.
We still need aeroplanes and guns,
So dig down in your jeans
And please oblige your loving sons,
Your Army, your Navy, your Marines—
Dear friend.

WE'RE ON OUR WAY (INFANTRY SONG)

Music by Richard Rodgers. Published as an individual sheet.

An official request for an infantry song was sent to the Music War Committee of the American Theatre Wing, which Hammerstein chaired. "For our purpose," wrote Major E. H. Coffey, "the words must have an emotional lift to them: that is, while they may say as much as the lyricist likes about the dangers and hardships of Infantry life, they must get over the idea that it is the Infantry that wins every war, or that the rest of the army knows the Infantry will finish up the job, or that the foot-soldier can take it and come up smiling and asking for more." Rodgers and Hammerstein wrote the song in the spring of 1944 and it was featured on the *March of Time* radio broadcast two days after D-day.

Step by step,
Foot by foot,
Yard by yard,
Mile by mile.
The infantry's movin' up,
The infantry's movin' in,
The infantry's movin' on and on and on!
Yea, brother! Verily, yea!
Hallelujah! We're on our way!

Wadin' through the water,
Climbin' up a beach,
Sloggin' through the mud,
Chokin' in the dust.
The infantry's movin' up,
The infantry's movin' in,
The infantry's movin' on and on and on!
Yea, brother! Verily, yea!
Hallelujah! We're on our way!

There's a good time comin' when we all get home,
But you can't get home by givin' in!
So take all you're takin' and give all you got.
There's a good time comin' when we win!
There's a good time comin' when we win!

Step by step
(Wadin' through the water),
Foot by foot
(Climbin' up a beach),
Yard by yard
(Sloggin' through the mud),
Mile by mile
(Chokin' in the dust),
The infantry's movin' up.
The infantry's movin' in.

The infantry's movin' on and on and on!
Yea, brother! Verily, yea!
Hallelujah! We're on our way!
On our way,
On our way,
On our way,
On our way!
Yea!

OL' MAN AUTHOR

Privately circulated. Music by Jerome Kern. New lyric by Oscar Hammerstein II.

Hammerstein was an active member of the Writers' War Board. For a January 1945 presentation, which he described in a letter to his son Bill, Hammerstein prepared a parody of "Ol' Man River":

[The meeting] is for writers and advertising men and radio producers, etc—people who have to do in general with "communication." Its purpose is to vividly point out the harm they are doing by perpetuating the stereotyped comic figures in fiction and entertainment—the drunken, pugnacious Irishman; the lazy, ignorant, crap-shooting Negro; the gangster Italian; the avaricious Jew. This lazy way of getting laughs and making quick ready-made characterization does more harm than hate-mongers and rabble-rousers. The writers, whose intent is not anti-racial, supply a terrific momentum for prejudice without meaning to. We want them to know this. There will be only six hundred people, but they are important key people, and I believe the small meeting may be far-reaching in its final result.

The "Ol' Man Author" lyric was later made available to interested parties, with the following caveat and stage directions. (Two additional pages of recommendations for preparing the performance, and preparing the audience for a discussion of such stereotypes, were also found in Hammerstein's files.)

To be sung by a quartet, consisting of an Irishman, a Negro, an Italian and a Jew.

Four dreary and embarrassed young men wander in. The Negro shakes dice in a bored manner. The Irish boy looks uncomfortable in his bright red wig and green tie. The Jew wears his oversized derby as if it weighed two tons. The Italian has his well-fitted coat wrinkled up by a belt which holds a gun and a stiletto.

It is important to remember that these satirical lyrics were written by Oscar Hammerstein II to be sung before a special audience of *writers* in

New York City. We are enclosing them for your enjoyment. The use of them before groups who might not recognize the satire should be very carefully considered. It is entirely possible that they might do more harm than good.

QUARTET: We are as old as the Mississippi,
Stereotyped as inferior men.
We are condemned to be dumb
and dippy:
ITALIAN: Angelo.
IRISHMAN: Mike.
NEGRO: Eb'nezer.
JEW: And Ben.
IRISHMAN: I'm a harp,
I love to fight!
No one will admit I can read or
write.
I get drunk
And I throw bricks—
When it comes to intellect the
Micks have nix!
QUARTET: We are the men of amusing races,
Fated to be eternal jokes.
Dialect men with amusing faces,
Never are we like other folks.

Ol' man author,
Dat ol' man author,
He may know somethin',
He may know nothin',
But he keeps writin',
He keeps on writin' along.
He don't plant taters,
He don't plant cotton,
He just keeps writin'

And writin' rotten!*
His harmful foolin'
It keeps on droolin' along.
ITALIAN: Rob dat bank and tote dat gat!
(Gangsters are Italians—you all
know that.)
I eat garlic and spaghet'—
OTHER THREE: No one ever let him eat a lamb
chop yet.
QUARTET: We are weary and sick of tryin',
We need a corner to go and die in,
But ol' man author,
He keeps on writin' us wrong!

We are as stale as a vote for Hoover.
Put us away with the high-wheeled
bike.
Put us away with a pest remover—
ITALIAN: Angelo.
JEW: Ben.
NEGRO: Eb'nezer.
IRISHMAN: And Mike.
JEW: I'm a Jew,
And I like money.

---

* In a February 1945 letter to Margaret Leech at the Writers' War Board, Hammerstein complained that on page 2 of the Writers' War Board report:
I found the same misquote from my lyric that I found in Variety. Why in hell have they substituted a "g" for the apostrophe in the word "writin' "? "Writin' rotten" is funny and "writing rotten" is dull. I hope they haven't made these kind of improvements in copying off the entire manuscript. If they are going to go this far, they had better be consistent and change "taters" to "potatoes."
I know I am irrational and hysterical about such things as this but what can I do about it? When you are irrational and hysterical you just can't do nothin'—I mean anything.

Wealthy Christians think that's
funny.
I'm a comic, scheming scamp—
Comic as a Nazi concentration
camp!
QUARTET: We are the men of amusing races,
Fated to be eternal jokes.
Dialect men with amusing faces,
Never are we like other folks.

Ol' man author,
Dat ol' man author,
He may know somethin',
He may know nothin',
But he keeps writin',
He keeps on writin' along!
IRISHMAN: I like taters.
NEGRO: And Ah loves cotton.
JEW: And I like blintzes.
ITALIAN: I don't like nottin'.
QUARTET: The worn-out bromides,
They just keep rollin' along.
NEGRO: Ah shoot crap
And Ah steal fowl.
When you hear me laffin', it'll
make you howl!
Yah, yah, yah!
Yack, yack, yack!
OTHER THREE: Kick him, and he laughs right
back!

[As they sing the last lines, they throw off their hats, wigs, dice, and other paraphernalia, as if they were freed of chains.]

QUARTET: We keep tryin'.
We're in there flyin'.
We're in there fightin'.
We're in there dyin'.
But ol' man author,
He keeps on writin' us wrong!

Two publicity shots from Sunny River
Left: Ethel Levey and Muriel Angelus
Right: Tom Ewell and Joan Roberts

SUNNY RIVER | 1941
and Other Songs of the Early 1940s

SUNNY RIVER (1941)

Tryout as *New Orleans*: Municipal Open Air Theatre (The Muny), St. Louis, June 5–10, 1941. Book and lyrics by Oscar Hammerstein II. Music by Sigmund Romberg. Book staged by Robert Ross; ensemble numbers directed by Jack Donohue. Choreography by Theodor Adolphus and Al White Jr. Cast: James Newill (John Claiborne), Ethel Levey (Lolita), Muriel Angelus (Marie), Tom Ewell (Dominique), Helen Claire (Cecilie), Joan Roberts (Madeleine), William O'Neal (Achille), Dorothy Lee (Emma), Leroy Busch (Jean), Emil Wachter (Emil), Bob Lawrence (Georges), Dudley Harder (Jacques), and ensemble.

Tryout as *Sunny River*: Shubert Theatre, New Haven, November 27–29, 1941. New York run: St. James Theatre, opened on December 4, 1941; closed on January 3, 1942; thirty-six performances. A new musical. Presented by Max Gordon. Book and lyrics by Oscar Hammerstein II. Music by Sigmund Romberg. Production supervised by John Murray Anderson.* Book staged by Oscar Hammerstein II. Dances staged by Carl Randall. Orchestrations by Don Walker.† Music direction by Jacob Schwartzdorf (Blackton). Settings by Stewart Chaney. Costumes by Irene Sharaff.

Cast: Bob Lawrence (Jean Gervais), Muriel Angelus (Marie Sauvinet), Ethel Levey (Lolita), Helen Claire (Cecilie Marshall), Tom Ewell (Daniel Marshall), Vicki Charles (Emma), Joan Roberts (Madeleine Caresse), William O'Neal (Achille Caresse), Donald Clark (Jim), George Holmes (Harry), Gordon Dilworth (Emil), Dudley Clements (George Marshall), Frederic Persson (Judge Pepe Martineau), Richard Huey (Old Henry), Oscar Polk (Aristide), Ainsworth Arnold (Gabriel Gervais), Ivy Scott (Mother Gervais), Byron Milligan (Watchman), Peggy Alexander (Martha), Jack Riano (Harlequin), Miriam LaVelle (Columbine), Howard Freeman (The Drunk), Kenneth Tobey (Doctor), and Carol Renee, Joan Shepherd, and Andrew Bruce Moldow (children).

Although Cecilie Marshall is a nonsinging role with comparatively little stage time, her desires and machinations drive the plot of *Sunny River*. For it is she who comes between the promising young lawyer Jean Gervais and the singer he loves, Marie. Cecilie's marriage to Jean brings him into the best society, but when Marie returns five years later, Jean realizes that he still loves her. He is

---

* *Anderson thanked Hammerstein for this "particularly gracious gesture—and one to which I am not really entitled; since your mastery and sensitive direction is written all over the show."*

† *In the St. Louis program, Romberg thanked Emil Gerstenberger and David Raksin for assisting him with the orchestration.*

on his way to a tryst with Marie when Cecilie is found in a dead faint, and he stays to care for her. In an epilogue after Jean has died in battle, Cecilie and Marie meet one more time, and Cecilie offers her former rival a memento of the man they both loved. Cecilie's brother Daniel has a much lighter story line. Like many young men before him, he learns the birds and the bees from Emma, one of Lolita's girls at the Café des Oleandres. He is a happy hellraiser until he meets Madeleine, whose brother Achille, the champion duellist, enforces her wish to marry Daniel.

London production: Following tryouts in Coventry and Manchester, Emile Littler presented *Sunny River* at London's Piccadilly Theatre, August 18–October 23, 1943. It was directed by Maxwell Wray and starred Dennis Noble (Jean Gervais), Edith Day (Lolita), Evelyn Laye (Marie Sauvinet), Ena Burrill (Cecilie), Don Avory (Daniel), and Marion Wilson (Emma).

Six songs from *Sunny River* were published. Most of the other lyrics in this chapter are from the Romberg holograph piano-vocal score in the Music Division of the Library of Congress. Supplementing the score were a half-dozen drafts of the script from the Hammerstein Collection in the Music Division of the Library of Congress, and a script in the Lord Chamberlain's Plays Collection in the British Library. Two additional songs, dated 1946, were found in the unprocessed Romberg papers at the Library of Congress, possibly written for a movie version that was in discussion.

The many drafts preserved in Hammerstein's papers show the effort he put into this project. After a week of performances at the St. Louis Muny in June, Hammerstein changed its three acts to two, shifted the setting from 1852–66 to 1806–15, fine-tuned the reason for the lovers' separation, adjusted what happened to Marie afterward, dropped a subplot about Jean helping the common folk, and replaced several songs. In October 1941 he informed his uncle Arthur, "The changes I have made are equivalent to whatever rewriting I might have done if I had had the show on the road three weeks . . . In fact, this is an understatement, because I have done much more complete and careful work than I could have done under the circumstances."

Playwright and director George S. Kaufman attended a New Haven tryout performance on Thanksgiving Day. His daughter Anne accompanied him and recalled complaining about the cold train and that they'd get no turkey. Known for his one-liners as well as his ability to doctor a show, Kaufman turned to her and said: "Wait." The New York critics were not kind, and *Sunny River* closed within a month. Soon after the closing, Hammerstein wrote to Max Gordon: "I feel sure that you did everything that was humanly possible to give the show its chance to find a public, and it didn't. I don't believe there is one—certainly not in New York. Operetta is a dead pigeon and if it ever is revived it won't be by me."

A note about character names: Several of the charac-

ters were renamed after the St. Louis production. The leading man, John Claiborne, became Jean Gervais. Dominique, the young man who learns about women, became Daniel. The featured quartet of upstanding citizens called Jean, Emil, Georges, and Jacques became Harry, Emil, George, and Jim. For simplicity in this chapter, the New York character names are used, even when discussing material performed only in St. Louis.

MY GIRL AND I

Not published. Introduced by Bob Lawrence (Jean).

VERSE

Please pardon me if I seem incoherent,
And my talk doesn't sound very sane.
How can a man be concise and coherent
When a man's got a girl on his brain?

REFRAIN

My girl and I
Are in a world our own.
A patch of earth and sky
Put by for us alone.
My girl and I,
A very vain, conceited pair are we.
And we know why,
For I have her and she has me.

Discarded verse from St. Louis

In the St. Louis running order, "My Girl and I" was Jean and Marie's big Act Two love duet, and it began with this verse.

JEAN: The night we met
We were shy,
And then we talked
She and I.
MARIE: And we found we laughed at the same jokes.
We knew the same songs.
JEAN: We liked the same folks.
MARIE: And pretty soon we had planned
To travel on hand in hand.
BOTH: Here we are, all smug and contented,
Walking through wonderland.

CALL IT A DREAM

Refrain published as an individual sheet. Introduced by Muriel Angelus (Marie), the featured male quartet (Donald Clark, George Holmes, Gordon Dilworth, and Dudley Clements), and male ensemble. Lolita and the café girls are present, but don't have individual singing parts.

MARIE: [*entertaining the clients at Café des Oleandres*] She was a Creole belle, Her name was Mad'moiselle Louema Lou Lou, Lou Lou. She came from Martinique, She hadn't learned to speak The way we do, we do.

[*Because* MARIE *is distracted, she's not singing well.* LOLITA *suggests* CLEMENTINA *take over.*]

JIM: We don't care what you sing. You're a charming little thing.

JIM AND OTHER MEN: And your face and your figure are new.

HARRY: Sing your song off the key, It won't matter much to me, For your face and your figure are new.

MEN: And we adore you, adore you!

MARIE: You're all too late, My heart has been given to one.

MEN: With due respect to your fidelity, With us you'll have more fun.

MARIE: I'm glad that you admire me, I'm proud that you desire me, You all could inspire me, [*spoken*] But I'm so much in love with one man, that I hardly know you're alive.

REFRAIN

MARIE: Call it a dream, Say I'm a fool, Feather-brained lady Who should go back to school. I'm crazy, But I'm giving romance One more chance. Say that my heart Rides for a fall. I'll only smile and tell you Love conquers all. I'm crazy, Too far gone to redeem. Say I am And call it a dream.

INTERLUDE

MARIE: You may be satirical And laugh, if you will.

HARRY: Love is highly thought of by us all.

MARIE: Have you felt the lyrical Delight of its thrill?

JIM: We know the thrill.

MARIE: Say what you will.

[*Repeat refrain.*]

IT CAN HAPPEN TO ANYONE

Not published. Introduced by Donald Clark (Jim), George Holmes (Harry), Gordon Dilworth (Emil), Dudley Clements (George), Muriel Angelus (Marie), and ensemble immediately following "Call It a Dream." A reprise by the character of Daniel is part of the Act One, Scene 1 Finaletto.

JIM: What you have said We've heard before In similar words.

HARRY: Or diff'rent words Upon a similar theme.

MARIE: The story of romance Is in the song of the birds.

JIM: An overrated tale!

GEORGE: A yarn that's growing stale.

EMIL: A boy, a girl, and heaven above!

MEN: With all the things to take from life

MARIE: What would you take but love?

EMIL: Men can enjoy gambling.

GEORGE: Men can enjoy drinking.

JIM: Men can enjoy smoking.

HARRY: Men can enjoy thinking.

MEN: Men can do these things without you.

MARIE: [*pointing offstage*] You can gamble in there. Enjoy yourselves.

GIRLS: There you can all enjoy yourselves. Good old gambling, Good old drinking, Good old smoking, Good old thinking. You are not tied up to our skirts.

ALL MEN: Men can enjoy gambling, Men can enjoy drinking, Men can enjoy smoking, Men can enjoy thinking. We are not tied up to your skirts.

MARIE: Till you're hit where it hurts you.

REFRAIN

MARIE: Some night When you're not on your guard, Someone Passes by. Somehow You're aware of your pulse, Rising surprisingly high. Some say It's a chemical thing. Some say It's from moonbeams. Some say They're too clever to fall But it can happen to anyone at all!

[*Ensemble repeats refrain while* MARIE *sings an obbligato.*]

THE BUTTERFLIES AND BEES

Alternate title: "Observe the Bee." Introduced by Tom Ewell (Daniel Marshall, a naive student), Vicki Charles (Emma, one of Lolita's girls), Ethel Levey (Lolita), Dudley Clements (George Marshall, Daniel's father), and Frederic Persson (Judge).

VERSE 1

JUDGE: Now, to you, the oldest thing that's known is new.

LOLITA: It's a thing that Venus and Adonis knew.

MARSHALL: Don't be afraid. You'll stand the test.

EMMA: You have the same start as all the rest.

REFRAIN 1

JUDGE: The flow'rs, the trees,
MARSHALL: The butterflies and bees,
LOLITA: The birds that fill the
forest,
EMMA: The fish that fill the seas,
EMMA, LOLITA,
MARSHALL, AND JUDGE: In doubt about
What they're supposed to
do,
They almost always do all
right
And somehow so will you.

VERSE 2

JUDGE: When you learn that love
is no phenomenon,
LOLITA: You'll be graced with poise
and more aplomb,
anon.
MARSHALL: Don't be dismayed
If you are slow—
LOLITA,
MARSHALL, AND JUDGE: Study and study until you
know.

REFRAIN 2

EMMA: Observe the bee
And see the way that he
Persuades a lovely flower
To give him honey free.
If you want me
To do the same for you,
You just imagine you're a
bee
And do what he would do.

[EMMA *waits with pursed lips.* DANIEL *pantomimes
picking a flower. There is a buzzing sound in orchestra,
and then his eyes light up and he kisses her.*]

REFRAIN 3

EMMA: Observe the bee
And see the way that he
Persuades a lovely flower
To give him honey free.
If you want me
To do the same for you,
DANIEL: I just imagine I'm a bee
And do what he would do!
LOLITA, MARSHALL,
AND JUDGE: Ah me!

Act Two reprise

Daniel begins teaching Madeleine what he'd learned
from Emma years before. The love lesson is interrupted
before the song gets very far.

The flow'rs, the trees,
The butterflies and bees,
The birds that fill the forest,
The fish that fill the seas,
Increase each year
And spread across the map.
If you knew why they multiply,
You'd get right off my lap.

ALONG THE WINDING ROAD

Published as an individual sheet. Introduced by Muriel
Angelus (Marie) and Bob Lawrence (Jean). This was the
big love song in Act One.

VERSE

JEAN: From now and forever my work and play
Are bound and blended with you.
And you'll be a part of my ev'ry day,
And all the things that I do.
MARIE: No load will be too heavy to bear,
No hill too high to climb
As long as you walk by my side and share
The stars and clouds of time.

REFRAIN

JEAN: Along the winding road
I'll travel forever with you,
Along the winding road
Till the wonderful journey is through.
MARIE: Your shoulder next to mine,
We'll travel forever as one.
Along the winding road,
Going over the hill to the sun.
JEAN: Your shoulder next to mine,
We will walk through the wind and the
weather,
And thank the fate divine
That has brought us and kept us together.
MARIE: Along the winding road,
If ever we travel apart,
BOTH: You may be far from view,
But you'll never be far from my heart.

FINALETTO

Not published. Introduced by Dudley Clements
(George), Donald Clark (Jim), George Holmes (Harry),
Gordon Dilworth (Emil), Muriel Angelus (Marie), Ethel
Levey (Lolita), and ensemble. The program shows that
Tom Ewell (Daniel) and Vicki Charles (Emma) are also
in this number.

GEORGE: Special meeting of the Lawyers
Club!
JIM: Special meeting for a special
reason.
JIM AND HARRY: Come into the garden for a
special meeting,
And without delay!
GEORGE AND EMIL: All hurry along!
JIM AND HARRY: All hurry along!
TENORS: All hurry along!
GEORGE, EMIL,
AND BASSES: Now, where is our protégé?
MALE QUARTET
AND SOPRANOS: Now, where is Marie?
MALE QUARTET,
ALL GIRLS,
AND TENORS: Now, where can she be?
ALL: Here, here is Marie!
Here, here is La Sauvinet!
Special meeting of the Lawyers
Club!
Special meeting for a special
reason.
Funnily enough, the reason
seems to be
To see Marie, Marie!
HARRY: How would you like a big
surprise?
One that'll bring you gold?
JIM: One that'll open wide your eyes
When you can hear it told.
GEORGE: A gift, a boon, a blessing!
MALE QUARTET: But it is much too soon to
speak.
ALL: We keep a lady guessing
Before we give away a secret.
MARIE: Ah, tell me!
If you tell your secret
Maybe I'll tell you one.
ALL: We already know.
MARIE: Not this one—
This one is a new one.
JIM: Well, shall we tell her?
GEORGE: Tell mad'moiselle her fate.
EMIL: [*to* JUDGE] Will you tell her?
[*announcing*] Judge Martineau!

[JUDGE *formally offers to send her to Paris immediately for musical training.*]

MARIE: Once in a lifetime,
Once in a lifetime,
A golden chance will come
your way.
HARRY: What is your answer?
We want your answer.
ALL: I think I know what she will
say.
LOLITA: [*aside to* MARIE] Don't say yes
or no.
MARIE: [*cautiously*] Generous and
sensitive
And sweet as you are,
You can all imagine how I feel.
I am like a lark about to fly to
a star.
LOLITA: She wants to sing.
GEORGE: She will go far.
MARIE: [*thinking of* JEAN, *not her
career*]
Call it a dream,
Straight from the sky.
Find me a lady half as happy
as I.
My future light beginning to
gleam.
GEORGE: Your light starts in to gleam.
HARRY: It's the right beginning
and—
ALL: From this night
You're starting a dream.
MARIE: I'm starting a dream.
ALL: From this night
You're starting a dream.

IT CAN HAPPEN TO ANYONE (REPRISE)

Not published. Introduced by Tom Ewell (Daniel), Donald Clark (Jim), George Holmes (Harry), Gordon Dilworth (Emil), Dudley Clements (George), and ensemble.

EMIL: Daniel looks quite diff'rent.
GEORGE: Daniel seems much older.
HARRY: Daniel seems much stronger.
JIM: Daniel seems much bolder.
ALL MEN: [*to* MARSHALL] What's come over this
young man, sir?
MARSHALL: Ask the boy himself,

He ought to know the answer.
EMIL: You haven't been gambling?
JIM: You haven't been drinking?
HARRY: You haven't been smoking?
ALL MEN: You haven't been thinking?
Don't make us go on with the quiz.
DANIEL: Well, you know how it is, boys . . .

REFRAIN 1

DANIEL: Some night
When you're not on your guard,
Someone
Passes by.
Somehow
You're aware of your pulse,
Rising surprisingly high.
One case
May be just like the rest.
Your case
May be diff'rent.
My case
Is peculiar to me,
Somebody told me to imitate a bee!

REFRAIN 2

ALL: Some night
When you're not on your guard,
Someone
Passes by.
Somehow
You're aware of your pulse,
Rising surprisingly high,
One case
May be just like the rest.
Your case
May be diff'rent.
His case
Is peculiar, you see,
Somebody told him to imitate a bee.
His case is peculiar, you see.
We blame it all on the bee!

BUNDLING

Not published. Introduced by Tom Ewell (Daniel), Joan Roberts (Madeleine), and female ensemble.

Daniel is "seated, surrounded by girls, like grandpa telling a bedtime story, and that is the mood in which the lyric should be read."

DANIEL: In the states up north,
When a lad goes forth

To see a girl he thinks nice,
They remain indoors
But the walls and floors
Are caked with frost and ice.
But they're both of sturdy New
England stock
And not discouraged a bit,
So they climb right into the lady's
bed
And make the best of it.
FOUR GIRLS: Her bed?
DANIEL: Her bed.
THERESE: And pray what happens then?
MADELEINE: Are they the same as Louisiana men?
HELEN: How can a girl restrain an eager
swain?
DANIEL: They don't get eager in Vermont and
Maine.
FOUR GIRLS: But please explain.
DANIEL: They are prudent girls
And respectful boys
Who, without a gesture of guilt,
Sit and talk all night
In the candlelight,
Counting up the squares on the quilt.
MADELEINE: Will you tell us how they can be so
close
And yet behave so well?
DANIEL: Do you want to know what my theory
is?
I think they lie like hell!

CAN YOU SING?

Not published. Introduced by Muriel Angelus (Marie, now known as Madame Bravigny) and girls.

MARIE: I have sung for monarchs under
flags of many tints.
All I do, I do with grand éclat.
While resting at Bath, I met
the regent, who's a prince,
And I have pleased the Persian
shah.
People mobbed my droshky
out in Moscow last July.
Then I went to gay Paree.
You know the czar and
Bonaparte do not see eye to
eye,
But both of them speak very
well of me.

[*The girls ask what it's like to be a glamorous prima donna.*]

MARIE: Can you sing tra-la-la-la?
GIRLS: [*amateurishly*] Do re mi so fa, so fa.
MARIE: So far so good.
Keep on the key
And an opera star you'll be.
Then you'll wail:
MARIE AND GIRLS: Tra la la la.
MARIE: Same old scale.
MARIE AND GIRLS: Tra la la la.
MARIE: Winter and spring, summer and fall,
And you'll be sorry you can sing at all.

MAKING CONVERSATION

Not published. Introduced by Muriel Angelus (Marie), Helen Claire (Cecilie), and ensemble.

Hammerstein described this musical scene in an August 1941 draft of the script: "The ladies in the ensemble are not cordial to Marie. Singers were not welcomed in genteel drawing rooms in those days. The gentlemen are attracted to her, and one group recognizes her as the girl who used to sing in the Oleander Café. Cecilie then makes an impressive entrance on the stairs, comes down, greets Marie, and the two women carry off the situation in grand style."

MARIE: 'Twas sweet of you to ask me.
I'm quite surprised to be here.
CECILIE: A famous prima donna
We very seldom see here.
MARIE: I think your house is charming.
So like Monsieur Gervais.
MEN: What did she say?
WOMEN: Let's make a little conversation.
Cover up the situation.
Talk!
Keep talking!
GEORGE: Let us look the other way.
MEN: Treat this affair with tact.
Show that we can act
As gentlemen ought to act.
That's the way to act!
MARIE: I should be
Proud to own
Such a house as this one.
WOMEN: What would you ever do
With a house like this one?

Gay and free,
All alone,
You should never miss one.
MARIE: I am free
And alone,
That is why I miss one.
MEN: We have to make believe
That we believe that Jean
Never was the man
Her heart was set upon.
ENSEMBLE: Let's keep on making conversation.
There's an implication
Of an awkward situation here.

St. Louis version

Stage directions in an earlier draft explain: "This is a musical patter designed to depict a scene of general embarrassment. The lyrics shift nimbly from one group to another. The music has a quick, pulsating, nervous movement underneath."

MARIE: 'Twas sweet of you to ask us.
We're very proud to be here.
CECILIE: A famous prima donna
We very seldom see here.
MARIE: [*to* JEAN] Do you enjoy the opera?
JEAN: [*to* MARIE] Tonight I stayed away!
MARIE: [*to* JEAN] What did you say?
GIRLS: [*to each other*] Now, did she say
"he never stays awake"
Or that "he never stays away."
A-K-E?
JEAN: [*awkwardly*] I was just about to say—
MEN: [*to each other*] A-W-A-Y.
(It could never be A-W-A-K-E!
That could never be.)
JEAN: We're very fond of opera
Throughout Louisiana.
MARIE: They also like their opera
In Paris and Havana.
[*to* JEAN] Especially New Orleans.
CECILIE: [*to* MARIE] You like Louisiana,
Our New Orleans?
MEN: [*to each other*] We have seen that girl before.
GIRLS: [*to* MARIE] You'd feel at home in any other city, too.
New Orleans, or any place at all.
MEN: [*to each other*] Bravigny used to be down in the café,
Employed to sing and play!
We called her Marie.

JEAN: [*to* MARIE] Where do you travel to,
When you leave tomorrow?
CECILIE: [*to* MARIE] Must you go?
TRIO OF GIRLS: [*to* MARIE] Must you go?
CECILIE: [*to* MARIE] Must you leave tomorrow?
MARIE: Florida—Mexico—then across the ocean.
Then Barcelona.
TRIO OF GIRLS: Think of Barcelona!
JEAN: [*vehement, sarcastic*] Rome and Copenhagen!
Think of Copenhagen!
MARIE AND GIRLS: Budapest,
Napoli,
Rio de Janeiro,
Petersburg—
Often we
Shiver under zero.
Singing lead
Baritone
Heroine and hero.
MEN: We have to seem to be
Keeping up a conversation
In an awkward situation.
We have to seem to be
Keeping up a conversation
In an awkward situation.
We have to make believe
That we believe that she
Never was a singer
Whom we called Marie!

[MARIE *and* CECILIE *leave the stage arm in arm.*]

GIRLS: See!
ENSEMBLE: Something in the conversation
Bears an implication
Of an awkward situation here!
A GOSSIPY MAN: With just a little backing,
She didn't do so badly.
JEAN: [*resenting the innuendo*] I do not understand you.
Will you explain it?
GOSSIPY MAN: Gladly!
The senator and others financed her to New York.
JEAN: I begin to see.

[JEAN *exits.*]

MEN: [*amused*] Seems as if he never knew
What happened to Marie!

POEM

Not published. Introduced by Helen Claire. Cecilie, a nonsinging role, recites these lines, which accompany the gift of a clock that belonged to Jean's parents.

The prizes that we seek and win
Are soon forgot as time goes by.
But dreams of what we never get,
These are the things that never die.
These are the things that warm our hearts
When life is like a stream gone dry.
Dreams of what you've never had—
These are the things that never die.

LET ME LIVE TODAY

Alternate titles: "I Can Dream Tomorrow" and Act One Finale. Introduced by Muriel Angelus (Marie), Bob Lawrence (Jean), and ensemble.

In an early draft of the script, when this scene ended the second of three acts, Hammerstein specified: "There will be a set encore for this number—if it is unearned, the number fails in its object." In a spring 1941 letter, Romberg said: " 'Let Me Live To-day' is the only high spot in singing in the show. Nothing can be done unless they are absolutely letter-perfect in their music. I expect even more from this number [than] I got from 'Serenade' in the *Student Prince.*"

REFRAIN

MARIE: I can dream tomorrow,
Let me live today.
If love is mine to take,
Then let me take my love now,
Before its flying beauty fades
away.
JEAN: While my heart is singing,
Let me thrill to its song
And keep the echo ringing high!
MARIE: I can dream tomorrow,
Let me live today!

INTERLUDE

JEAN: Who can be sure?
Who can decide which way of
life is true?
MARIE: No one can know.
None can be sure,
None can decide but you.

JEAN AND GIRLS: One moment comes to all men,
One moment supreme.
One choice is given all men
To live
Or dream.

REPEAT REFRAIN

BOW-LEGGED SAL

London title: "Bow-Legged Gal." Not published. Introduced by the ensemble.

Stage directions warn: "The director of dances should try to avoid the conventional and stilted feeling of forced gayety which usually characterizes such openings. The picture should be a crazy quilt of unmatched groups each doing something different, and soon converging on one central group of negro dancers who are brought in from the street. They must have among them at least one novelty solo dancer who will achieve a solid hand. The dancing is accompanied by banjos and unison singing."

Dancin' wid my bow-legged gal,
I'm dancin' wid my bow-legged gal,
I'm dancin' wid my bow-legged gal named Sal.
No one kin dance like bow-legged Sal,
No one kin dance like bow-legged Sal,
Dat shif'less, feckless, bow-legged gal named
Sal!
She got dat way fum goin' to school,*
She got dat way fum goin' to school,
Dat shif'less, feckless, bow-legged gal named
Sal.
She got two knees dat never kin meet,
Got two knees dat never kin meet,
But as sure as sugar is sweet,
I'm her man an' she is my gal,
Cause I'm in love wid bow-legged Sal,
Cause I'm in love wid bow-legged Sal.
Dat shif'less, feckless, bow-legged gal named
Sal.
Fixin' fo' to marry de gal,
I'm fixin' fo' to marry de gal,
Dat shif'less, reckless, bow-legged gal named
Sal.

---

* *When a drunk reprises this ditty later in the act, there is an additional line here:*
  She rode to school on top of a mule,

SUNNY RIVER

Published as an individual sheet. Introduced by Ethel Levey (Lolita) and ensemble. Added to the show after the St. Louis production.

VERSE

I sit and watch the river,
And see the sunlight quiver
Like diamonds dancin' on the blue.
And then I ask the river,
"Hey! What's your hurry, river?
Where do you take that sunlight to?"

REFRAIN

Sunny river,
Where you goin'?
Are you flowin' down to the sea?
If you're goin'
By the delta,
Sunny river,
I want to be with you.
After Memphis,
After Natchez,
Just before you get to the sea,
You will come to a bend—
That's where you lose your friend.
That's New Orleans,
Sunny river,
Say goodbye to me!

THE DUELLO

Not published. Introduced by William O'Neal (Achille Caresse, a fencing master) and Tom Ewell (Daniel).

An early draft of the script explains: "The lyric, not yet written, will rhapsodize on the joy of feeling your arm made three feet longer by a shaft of finely tempered steel, the music of your blade ringing against the blade of your adversary, the grace of those sharp little points floating and dancing in the air until they are thrust to their mark . . . The music, which has been written, is a most exciting melody."

VERSE

ACHILLE: When you're master of the foil
And a fellow wants to spoil
For a fight,
You will fight!
You will tear his card with grace,

Throw the pieces in his face,
And at dawn . . .

DANIEL: I'll be gone!

ACHILLE: When your arm is three feet longer,
By just one yard of steel—
How you feel,
How you feel!

DANIEL: [*spoken*] Terrible!

ACHILLE: With a parry and a thrust
Knock his blade into the dust.
With a twist
Of the wrist.

REFRAIN

ACHILLE: When you know the duello,
The romantic art of the duello,
Like a bow to a cello
Is a fellow's sword to ev'ry fellow.
And its point lightly dances
In a dance of death the point advances
To its mark
After dark,
Just as sunrise lights up the park.
[*poetically*] Skies have a golden hue,
Trees are decked with dew.
[*shouting*] Lunge!
For the kill!
Meadowlarks are gay
As they greet the day—
Ah, what a thrill.
Then someday the duello
Puts you up against a clever fellow,
And you fall,
And you lie.
On the field of honor you die!

SHE GOT HIM

Not published. Introduced by Joan Roberts (Madeleine, sister to Achille), Vicki Charles (Emma), William O'Neal (Achille), Tom Ewell (Daniel), and ensemble.

Stage directions tell Madeleine to sing "in the manner of a prima donna in an operetta finaletto."

VERSE 1

MADELEINE: Achille, mon frere,
Be kind and spare
The man I stand beside.

ACHILLE: Are you implying that you actually
love this man?

MADELEINE: The thing is factual, I actually love
this man.

And he, in turn,
Is said to yearn
For me to be his bride.

EMMA: You wouldn't kill a man who wants
to marry Madeleine.

DANIEL: You can't imagine how I want to
marry Madeleine.

ALL: He wants to marry Madeleine!

MADELEINE: Step up and kiss the bride.

REFRAIN 1

EMMA: She got him.

LOLITA: She got him.

MADELEINE: I got him.

DANIEL: She got me.

ACHILLE: Give him a hoop to jump through.

TENORS: She got him.

BASSES: She got him.

SOPRANOS: She got him.

ALL: She got him.
Give him a hoop to jump through.

EMMA: She'll kiss him,
And fool him,
And boss him,
And rule him.

ACHILLE: Nothing can pull the chump
through.

ALL: Upsadaisy,
That's the waysee.
Give him a hoop to jump through!

VERSE 2

EMMA: The night is grand.
She holds his hand.

ACHILLE: His heart is light and gay.

MADELEINE: And all the while she has insidious
designs on him.

ALL: She has perfidious, insidious designs
on him.

EMMA: They take a walk.
She lets him talk,
But leads him all the way—

MADELEINE: And soon the family felicitate the
happy groom.

EMMA: And he is standing like a trophy in
the living room.

ACHILLE: And all her beaming relatives are
more than pleased to say:

REFRAIN 2

ALL: She got him,
She got him,
She got him,
She got him.
Give him a hoop to jump through.

She got him,
She got him,
She got him,
She got him.
Give him a hoop to jump through!

GIRLS: No matter
What he meant,
He made an
Agreement.

MEN: Nothing can pull the chump
through!

ALL: Upsadaisy,
That's the waysee!
Give him a hoop to jump through!

TIME IS STANDING STILL

Not published. Introduced by Muriel Angelus (Marie) and Bob Lawrence (Jean). Appears to have been written after the St. Louis production.

VERSE

MARIE: Do you feel as I
That the wasted years gone by
Have been only an illusion in your mind?

JEAN: I see you standing there
And the world seems just as fair
As it ever used to be.

MARIE: It is just the same with me.
And I doubt if I've ever been away,
And my heart keeps wanting to say:

REFRAIN

MARIE: It isn't tonight at all,
It's five years ago.
The same leaves are on the trees
As far as I know.

JEAN: The same moon is smiling,
It never left the sky.

BOTH: Our calendars have told us a lie, dear.

MARIE: The same lazy clouds are drifting
Hither and yon.

JEAN: And nothing is added here,
And nothing is gone.

BOTH: For we are together,
And time is standing still,
While you and I and love go on.

CUT AND UNUSED SONGS

ELEVEN LEVEE STREET

Published as an individual sheet. Dropped after the New Haven tryout. It had been sung by Bob Lawrence (Jean) and Muriel Angelus (Marie) immediately after the Symphonic Pantomime that starts Act One.

Got a home by the shore,
Got a key to a door,
Down on Levee Street,
Eleven Levee Street.
Got a heart full of news,
For the one person who's
Going to make it sweet
To live on Levee Street.
I'm going to show her those rooms,
All so spotless and white,
And that chair that we'll share
When we sit there at night,
All alone and aloof,
'Neath our own little roof,
Down on Levee Street,
Eleven Levee Street.

Unpublished interlude

According to stage directions, "they sing with voices as light as their hearts."

MARIE: Your wife!
JEAN: They will call you Madame Gervais.
MARIE: They will call me Madame,
    And I'll insist on ev'ryone
    Addressing me that way.
    "Madame" from the man in the shops.
JEAN: Madame, may I sell you some chops?
MARIE: My husband's getting tired of chops.
    My "husband." What a word to say!

[*Dialogue.*]

JEAN: Madame,
    You are no longer free.
    Madame,
    You are tied up to me!
MARIE: I seem to be a hopeless case.
JEAN: [*pleased*] A situation you must face,
    Madame.
MARIE: Are you tied up to me?
JEAN: I am, madame, I am.

LORDY

Published as individual sheet, but dropped from Act One after the New Haven tryout. Introduced by Jean (Bob Lawrence).

Before the St. Louis production, Romberg described this as Jean's big number in the show, and "one of my favorites."

De night is friendly,
De stars are winkin',
My sleepy-headed baby's eyes are blinkin'.
I hold him in my arms and set here thinkin',
Lordy, what a sweet world.
De night is friendly,
Wid voices croonin'
An' gals an' fellers in de shadows, spoonin',
An' clouds dat open up to let de moon in.
Lordy, what a sweet world!
Now I ain't callin' dis life perfec',
But I am thankin' my Maker above,
Because fo' ev'rything dat I don' like
Dere's a million things I love!
A bell is chimin'
To toll de hour.
De sky is drippin' light on ev'ry flower,
It like to drown us in a silver shower—
Lordy, what a sweet world!
I'm so happy!
(Yes, sir!)
Happy to be livin',
(Yes, sir!)
Livin'
On a friendly night,
On a friendly night,
In a friendly world,
In a friendly world.
My heart is happy
Thanks to de Lord!

WHEN A LARK LEARNS TO FLY

Not published. An Act One duet for Ethel Levey (Lolita) and Muriel Angelus (Marie), dropped from the show after the New Haven tryout.

LOLITA: When a lark learns to fly
    She goes flying to a star.
    But the star flies too high
    And the journey seems too far.

So she comes home to sing
And to tell us in her song
To love the earth
Where we belong,
And let the stars remain in the sky—
Where they are.
MARIE: Can't we stay in heaven for a while?
    Have our way in heaven?
LOLITA: For a while.
    But your day in heaven
    Has to end.
MARIE: Must it end?
LOLITA: Yes, my friend—

[MARIE *repeats the song.*]

INDUCTION INTO THE LOUISIANA LAWYERS CLUB

Not published. Dropped from the show after the New Haven tryout. Introduced by Dudley Clements (George Marshall), George Holmes (Harry), Donald Clark (Jim), Gordon Dilworth (Emil), Frederic Persson (Judge), and the male ensemble.

GEORGE: Here's a candidate for you to
    see,
    He's a lawyer of Louisiana.
    Better look him over,
    But he doesn't look so good
    to me.
MEN: Who suggested him?
    Who suggested him?
HARRY: How could he have won a law
    degree?
    What can law be like in
    Louisiana?
    Better look him over,
    But he doesn't look so good
    to me!
MEN: Who suggested him?
    Who suggested him?
QUARTET: Fellow members of the Union
    Club
    Give the candidate a close
    inspection,
    Carefully reporting any
    imperfection
    That you may see.
HARRY: Too long in the leg.
JUDGE: [*spoken*] Black ball.
JIM: Too blue in the eye.

JUDGE: [spoken] Black ball.
GEORGE: Too short in the neck.
JUDGE: [spoken] Black ball.
EMIL: You will never qualify!
QUARTET AND MEN: Too thick in the chest!
ALL: Too thin in the thigh,
Too flat in the feet,
You will never qualify!
Take a vote and we will signify
In the manner that is
customary.
JUDGE: Anyone in favor of him,
signify
By saying aye!
ALL: Aye! Aye!
ALL: Unanimously
Elected is he!

[Shouts of approval.]

Earlier version, "Doctors of Law"

HARRY: We are here once again,
Staid and sober legal men.
GEORGE: Not so sober or legal tonight.
JIM: We are here once again
At our yearly meeting when
We feel "non compos mentis"
EMIL: But bright!
HARRY, JIM,
AND GEORGE: You can drink with a judge,
You can give the judge a nudge,
And he won't even give you a fine!
ALL MEN: With the night on the wane
You will find the legal brain
Growing mellow, benumbed, and
benign.
GEORGE
AND EMIL: Doctors of law,
Learned attorneys,
HARRY: Fighters for justice are we.
JIM: All day we argue and rebut
GEORGE: Like any good LLD—but
ALL: When courts adjourn,
When lights are burning,
Frozen legal hearts can thaw.
Give us a case of champagne to
adjudicate
And a lady's affection to alienate
Through the night we'll be gay.
But the light of day will always
find us
Back in the courtroom, doctors
of law.

THE MEN ARE IN THE DINING ROOM

Not published. Dropped after the St. Louis production, where it was used to open Act Two of a three-act structure. Introduced by the female ensemble.

ALL GIRLS: The men are in the dining
room,
The men are dawdling in the
dining room.
TRIO OF GIRLS: As they pass around the
port,
They speculate on sport,
And quote the current jest
or witty retort.
ALL GIRLS: And we are here in the
sitting room,
The girls are sitting in the
sitting room.
GIRLS STANDING
AT SPINET: All our conversations spent
Pretending we're contented
With a sentimental ballad.
ALL GIRLS: The kind of ballad that
makes you sick!
YOUNG MATRON: [to CECILIE] How I adored
your salad.
MME. FONTAINE: I've been ailing for a week.
MME. MARTINEAU: The judge and I don't speak!
MADELEINE: My hair has lost its waves.
TENNESSEE MATRON: Ah've had such trouble with
mah slaves!
ALL GIRLS: The men are in the dining
room,
The men are dawdling in the
dining room!
TRIO: When they push their chairs
away
And "join the ladies," as
they say,
ALL: They'll find the ladies bright
and gay!
Ha!
OFFSTAGE MEN: Ha, ha!
ALL GIRLS: Ha!
OFFSTAGE MEN: Ha, ha!
ALL GIRLS: Ha!
And we'll make them think
they're in the way,
In the way,
In the sitting room.

THIS NIGHT WILL SEEM LONG AGO

Not published. Dropped after the St. Louis production, where it was introduced by Muriel Angelus (Marie) and James Newill (Jean) late in Act One.

INTRODUCTION

JEAN: Very small, very white,
Glaring at me in the sun.
MARIE: Balcony, you said, above the door?
JEAN: Would hold one cat and nothing more!
MARIE: And did you go inside,
And what did you find?
JEAN: I took one look.
Then the lease was signed.
MARIE: I know you're only joking,
But you fill my heart with fear.
JEAN: I took the house, my darling.
It is rented for a year!
And since you are the tenant,
You must have a key.
BOTH: A home, beyond believing,
Awaiting you and me.
MARIE: And we will hide in heaven,
And no one will know.
JEAN: After we are married,
All the world can know.
Marie,
"My wife."
Tell me, how does it sound, love?
MARIE: In all
My life!
I could never have found love,
Had not your heart come beating next to
mine.
JEAN: A clever heart, that!
Shrewd and designing . . .

[Dialogue about packing their things and meeting
there tonight.]

MARIE: Jean!
I know I'm not the wife for you,
Don't make me spoil your life for you—
JEAN: I have no life but you!
MARIE: When a man's a lawyer,
He will argue black is white!
JEAN: Only trust your lawyer,
It will all come right.
MARIE: If I trust my lawyer,
He'll make wrong seem right.

JEAN: [*spoken*] I won't talk like a lawyer. I'll just
ask you one question. Suppose I walked
through that gate now, never to return.
Do you think I *could* stay away from you?

MARIE: No, no, no, no!

VERSE

JEAN: [*sung*] Stay here in my arms,
Here is your home.
I am your love,
You are my bride.
So may you be, and be mine forever,
And never leave my side.

MARIE: As we are tonight,
We'll go on,
We'll go on.

JEAN: Watching time in flight,
We'll go on,
We'll go on.

MARIE: Heaven's aflame and flooded with light,
See how the clouds are spreading.

JEAN: So may the sun of morning be bright
Shining on our wedding.

BOTH: Raise your hand to a star,
Swear by the star:
We will go on
Just as we are.
To be bound and blended
As lovers to the end.

REFRAIN

JEAN: When we look back and sigh
Over the years gone by
This night will seem long ago,
This night will seem long ago.

MARIE: And all our friends will say,
There's a charmingly gay old couple they
know
Who are in love today,
Just as they were,
Long ago.

LET'S PLAY WE'RE HAVING FUN

Not published. Dropped after the St. Louis production.
An Act Two (of three) comedy number for Tom Ewell
(Daniel), Dorothy Lee (Emma), and ensemble. Reprised
by Ethel Levey (Lolita).

In stage directions, Hammerstein explained that
Daniel is wary of Emma's charms (and of her husband's

sword craft). "She keeps pulling the unwilling Dominique
[Daniel] around, and trying unsuccessfully to inculcate
him into her own joie de vivre. His attitude really creates
a satirical comment on all 'whoopee' numbers."

During the rehearsal period, Romberg noted, "I have
a special orchestration made of this number and I
expect a great deal from it. Ethel Levey's reprise in the
beginning of the Third Act of a verse and chorus of this
number will be a 'show stopper.' She did it for me and
she is dynamite."

VERSE

EMMA: I'm feeling wild and restive,
And you feel gay and festive.
So why not let down our reserves?
And we'll ignite a party
And be so bright and hearty
We'll get on ev'rybody's nerves!

REFRAIN

EMMA: Let's play we're having fun!
Hurray! We're having fun!
Oh-ho! What a night!
Bring on the dynamite!
Let's play we paint the town,
And then we tear it down.
I'm high as a kite,
Got to go out tonight!
Got to go to noisy places,
Dance around on people's toes.
Put aside the social graces—
Let's be loud and rough and rowdy.
Let's play we're having fun!
Hooray! We're having fun!
I'm high as a kite!
Got to go out tonight!

[*Ensemble repeats refrain.*]

EMMA: Let's throw bread balls at the dancers.
Let's pour wine down people's necks!
If they squawk, we'll give 'em answers
That are loud . . .

ALL: [*joining in*] . . . and rough and rowdy.
Let's play we're having fun!
Hooray! We're having fun!
I'm high as a kite!
Got to go out tonight!

Verse for Lolita's reprise

He's feeling wild and restive
And she feels gay and festive,
Tonight's a night to feel that way.
Tonight's a night to break loose,

If you've got feet to shake loose,
Then shake 'em loose is what I say:

US IS GOING TO HAVE US A TIME

Not published. An unused Act Two comedy number for
Emma and Daniel. Probably written before the St. Louis
production.

VERSE

EMMA: Tonight ah got dat feelin',
Dat got-to-get-out feelin'.
Ah feel it in mah funny bones.
Tonight ah got to break loose,
Ef you got feet to shake loose
Let's us git goin', Mr. Jones.

REFRAIN

DANIEL: Us is goin' to,
Us is goin' to,
Us is goin' to have us a time.

EMMA: Goin' to have a,
Goin' to have a,
Goin' to have a wonderful time, honey.

DANIEL: Go git dressed up,
Show de rest up.

EMMA: Throw yo' chest up,
Way out o' sight!

DANIEL: Us is out on de town.

EMMA: Us is tearin' it down!

BOTH: Us is goin' to,
Goin' to have a,
Have a time tonight!

WHAT MAKES YOU THE BEST?

Not published. Another unused Act Two comedy number for Emma and Daniel. Found in the Romberg holograph piano-vocal score, but not mentioned in any
scripts or programs seen by the editor.

DANIEL: What made you stand apart from all
the rest?
What made you the best of them all?

EMMA: By what peculiar charm were you
possessed?
What made you the best of them all?
Though not much older than a babe,
you,
When you made your debut,
You showed a lot of promise for your
age!
DANIEL: You only had to ask,
I acquiesed,
Knowing I was destined to fall.
BOTH: What made you stand apart from all
the rest?
What made you the best of them all?
EMMA: What makes you stand apart from all
the rest?
What makes you the best of them
all?
By what peculiar charm are you
possessed?
What makes you the best of them
all?
You're not spectacularly virile, like
Henry or Cyril.
In savoir faire you don't compare to
Paul.
And when it comes to grace in all he
does
I must put my husband the first.
What makes you stand apart from all
the rest?
DANIEL: Maybe it's because I'm the worst.
EMMA: You aren't strong or handsome or very
long on wit.
Your minuet could stand some
improvement, you'll admit.
A GIRL: Analysis will never explain the reason
why
A gal is his forever when once he gets
her eye.
GIRLS: What makes you stand apart from all
the rest?
What makes you the best of them all?
By what peculiar charm are you
possessed?
What makes you the best of them all?
1ST GIRL: Is it the fascinating way you make love
on a bayou?
2ND GIRL: The way you comb your hair?
3RD GIRL: The way you stand?
4TH GIRL: The way you pinch your snuff?
5TH GIRL: The way you pinch anything in reach
of your hand?
ALL GIRLS: What makes you stand apart from all
the rest,
What makes you so much better than
grand?

NATURE STUDIES

Not published. Dropped before the St. Louis production. Would have been sung by the judge in an Act Two,
Scene 3, Mardi Gras sequence. After this single refrain,
the script says "similar illuminating verses may be written about starfish, weasels, etc."

Of all things, beast or bird,
Penguins are the most absurd.
From their lives I infer
They have not much character.
For instance:
Penguins never like to fly.
Penguins aren't very bold.
Only now and then they fly
When sitting down becomes too cold.

HER NAME WAS MAY

Not published. Dropped before the St. Louis production. Sung early in Act One by the judge, who has known
this ditty since his youth.

I dream of her yet,
Her name was May.
She walked in the meadow with me one day,
A kerchief of scarlet on her head,
The coat that she wore was flaming red.
A bull in the pasture passed our way—
Though that was in March, 'twas the end of May.

FOR ME

Not published. Dropped during rehearsals for the St.
Louis production. An Act Two comedy number for
Daniel, Madeleine, and ensemble. Hammerstein
intended to write a reprise or a response for Act Three
titled "For You," where the men would chaff Daniel
about married life.

DANIEL: For me the pleasure of waking and
rising
And dressing and shaving alone!
For me the joy of promiscuous
kissing
And calling my evenings my own.

For some who are the Benedict type,
It's good to take a wife.
For me, the careless career of a
bachelor
Seems a much natcheler life.
MEN: At the day's end, when you tire,
You'll be feeling that desire
For your slippers
By an armchair,
And your armchair
By a fire.
MADELEINE: In the sunset's failing light
I'll be waiting ev'ry night
With your slippers
In my left hand,
And your armchair
In my right!
MEN: You're bound to propose when you
feel her caress,
On marriage you'll quickly agree.
GIRLS: You will!
DANIEL: I'll never propose, for the girl might
say "yes,"
And what would ensue
Would be all right for you
But
For me, the pleasure of knowing I'm
going
To go where I go when I please.
For me, the freedom to romp in
impromptu
Shenanigans, shindigs, and sprees!
When once I find the girl of my
dreams
I'll know that she's the one.
Until I find her
I'll have to try all of the others,
And that'll be fun.

I DON'T THINK OF YOU AS AN ANGEL

Not published. Dropped before the St. Louis production. It is the anniversary of Jean and Cecilie's marriage.
He admits that in his youth he had a blinding love for
another woman, but tells Cecilie his current feelings.

REFRAIN

JEAN: I don't think of you as an angel
Who belongs in a world above.
You're a down-to-earth kind of angel
And in your arms are peace and love.

When my luck is bad,
On your heart I call,
And a look in your eye sees me through.
When my news is good,
It's no good at all
Till I bring it home to you.

INTERLUDE

CECILIE: Can the man be in love with me?
JEAN: There's a strong possibility.
CECILIE: Then, perhaps, it's time I told him
That I feel just as he.
JEAN: You feel just as he.
And how would that be?
His interest you awake.
CECILIE: Suppose what I said
Should go to his head?
JEAN: A chance that you must take.
CECILIE: Do you want to know how I love you?
JEAN: I do.

REFRAIN 2

CECILIE: I don't think of you as an angel.
You'd look funny if you had wings.
So I think of you as a partner,
With whom I share what fortune brings.
JEAN: There are things we lose
CECILIE: But the loss is small—
BOTH: For a look in your eye sees me through.
CECILIE: Anything I gain
Isn't mine at all
BOTH: Till I give it all to you.

PART OF ME

Not published. A song idea for Marie in Act Three. In an
early script, Hammerstein noted: "Rommy, the following poem is designed only to give you the spirit of the
lyric I will eventually set to whatever music you write."
No music was found.

A part of me will never change,
The part of me that belongs to you.
The love that was yours through all the years
Will be yours till the years are through.
A part of me will never change,
Though hopes may fade that once were new.
The dream that was mine when our hearts were
young
Will always belong to you.

Y' BETTER NOT

Not published. An additional song for Lolita and ensemble. Appears to have been prepared in 1946, possibly for
a film adaptation of *Sunny River* that was never made.

VERSE

LOLITA: When the evening breeze is gentle
And the air is soft and sweet,
It is easy to be sentimental—
It is difficult to be discreet.
When my lover's arms are ready
And the moon provokes romance,
Something tells me to be strong and
steady—
Something tells me I should take a
chance!

REFRAIN

LOLITA: My heartbeats advise me to love while
I may,
No matter what,
No matter what!
ENSEMBLE: No matter what?
LOLITA: No matter what!
But off in the thickets the crickets all
say:
"Y' better not,
Y' better not,
Y' better not."
ENSEMBLE: Y' better not?
LOLITA: "Don't let night fly by," say the stars
in the sky.
"Give him all the kisses you have got."
But off in the thickets, the crickets all
sigh:
ENSEMBLE: "Y' better not,
Y' better not,
Y' better not,
Y' better not!"
LOLITA: The crickets tell me what I should not
do,
But I am list'ning to my heartbeats
too.
"It's night and it's spring," say the
birds on the wing.
"Give him all the kisses you have got."
ENSEMBLE: But off in the thickets the crickets all
sing:
"Y' better not,
Y' better not,
Y' better not,
Y' better not!"
LOLITA: But I am trembling in the glow of love,

And after all, what does a cricket
know of love?
ENSEMBLE: "Y' better not,
Y' better not,
Y' better not,
Y' better not!"

I'M IN LOVE WITH YOU

Not published. Appears to have been prepared in 1946,
possibly for a film adaptation of *Sunny River* that was
never made.

VERSE

Independently I faced the world,
Free was I to go my way.
Now my world revolves around your arms,
They call and I obey.

REFRAIN

I'm in love with you,
I'm in love with you,
Love ev'ry dream I dream about you.
Love the things you say,
Love the things you do.
Hate ev'ry day when I'm without you.
I love tonight because I have you near me,
And, oh, you are sweet when you are near me.
You look so happy when you hear me saying,
I'm in love with you.

OTHER SONGS OF THE EARLY 1940S

SERENADE TO A PULLMAN PORTER

Music by Harry Ruby. Published as an individual sheet
by Mills Music, copyright date July 16, 1941. The editor
has not been able to learn anything about the song's purpose or the circumstances of its creation. No commercial recordings are known.

Chief, don't be late!
Super Chief, don't be late!
Fly through de moon an' de rain.
Fly, Super Chief,
Bring me my sweet relief.
You got my man on your train.
He's a feller by de name of Jim.
My heart is beating for Jim now.
I'm sure for certain he longs for me,
De way I long for him now.
All day an' night,
In a coat snowy white,
He's workin' hard for his pay.
Best porter on de Santa Fe!
Ring de bell!
Where's de porter?
Night and day,
Dey want service on de Santa Fe.
Here's de porter!
Comin' up on de fly
Wid dat ice an' dat Canada Dry!
Dat's my porter, dat's my man,
Givin' service on de Santa Fe.
Ev'ry quarter, ev'ry dime, ev'ry buck
He brings home to his mamma for luck!
Chief, don't be late!
Super Chief, don't be late!
Fly through de dark an' de light.
Fly, Super Chief,
Bring me my sweet relief
Dressed in a coat snowy white.
Lord, make dat train on time tonight!

SONGS WITH WILLIAM HAMMERSTEIN

Hammerstein's elder son had a serious interest in music and had begun composing in the mid-1930s, including these three songs with lyrics by his father. When America joined the Second World War, William Hammerstein served in the United States Navy, mostly in the South Pacific. He seems to have given up songwriting after his discharge, but enjoyed a long career in show business as a stage manager, and as a producer and director for stage and television. For many years he was the family spokesman for his father's work.

FASCINATING PEOPLE

Music by William Hammerstein. Registered for copyright as an unpublished song on March 27, 1940. The song was offered to the singer-pianist Hildegarde, but she probably never performed it.

VERSE

By men of fame I'm never flustered.
For men of wit who try their best,
I have a deadpan look that leaves them all
    appalled.
But, darling, you say, "Pass the mustard,"
And I'm tremendously impressed.
And when you ask me what the time is, I'm
    enthralled.
And I've the same effect on you.
We find us a most amusing couple.

REFRAIN

You and I
Are fascinating people;
At least it seems so to you and me.
You and I
Can talk away an evening
And the talk is always of you and me.
I keep asking, "Do you love me?"
And you keep saying you do.
Then I deftly change the subject
By saying, "I love you."
You and I
Are fascinating people,
And to you and me
We will always be.

A TREE OUTSIDE MY WINDOW

Music by William Hammerstein. Registered for copyright as an unpublished song on February 5, 1941.

VERSE

I have some work to do,
But I don't feel like doing work today.
The sky is far too blue,
And spring is calling me to come and play.
My conscience tells me I must ignore it
And if I'm strong and firm
I'll feel the better for it.

And then a breeze comes up
And blows my good intentions all away.

REFRAIN

A tree outside my window
Is waving its leaves at me
As if to say,
"It's a lovely day,
Come out, come out and see."
A bird outside my window
Is singing upon the tree.
His songs all say:
"It's a lovely day,
Come out, come out and see.
You can pass up work and worry
For more important things,
You can throw a stone in the middle of a brook
And watch the water make rings!
There's sunlight on the meadow,
You can see it right through the tree.
The world is gay,
It's a lovely day,
Come out, come out and see for yourself,
Come out, come out and see!"

FRIENDLY LITTLE FARM

Music by William Hammerstein. Published as an individual sheet. In January 1942, Oscar Hammerstein informed music publisher J. J. "Jack" Bregman of Bregman, Vocco, and Conn, Inc., that "Billy and I have signed our contracts and they should be back in your office by now. He got a terrific kick out of it." Another version of the song was found in William Hammerstein's files.

VERSE

I thought the grass was greener
And the sky a fairer blue
In every other valley but my own;
But now that I have roamed the world
In search of something new,
I'm longing for the oldest dream I've known.

REFRAIN

There's a friendly little farm down in Arkansaw,
Where a lazy river flows beside a mill,
And an old familiar chime gently beckons you,
To a friendly little chapel on the hill.
Ev'ry Sunday how I long to be there.
In my dreams I see you standing with me there.

And when church is letting out down in Arkansaw
I can see us walking homeward arm in arm,
Walking homeward to that friendly little farm.

Unpublished version

VERSE

I won't be back until
I've done a job I came to do.
I'll follow any course my fate must chart.
But on this Sunday morning,
When I'm writing home to you,
I'm writing with a picture in my heart.

REFRAIN

On a friendly little farm down in Arkansaw
There's a river running by a lazy mill
And the sound of gentle bells faintly echoing
From a little church that's just beyond the hill.
All the family get dressed up for Sunday
For they aim to look their best on that one day.
And when church is letting out, I can see them all,
Walking homeward, hand in hand and arm in arm
Walking homeward to our friendly little farm.

OVERLEAF *The original cast performing the title song*
Top: *Celeste Holm and Lee Dixon*
Bottom: *Alfred Drake and Joan Roberts*

OKLAHOMA! | 1943

Top: *Dance hall girls in Agnes de Mille's dream ballet. Left to right, Joan McCracken, Kate Friedlich, Margit DeKova, Bobby Barrentine, and Vivian Smith*
Bottom: *Dancers Marc Platt and Katharine Sergava as Dream Curly and Dream Laurey*

OKLAHOMA! (1943)

Tryouts (as *Away We Go!*): Shubert Theatre, New Haven, March 11–13, 1943; Colonial Theatre, Boston, March 15–27, 1943. New York run: St. James Theatre; opened on March 31, 1943; 2,212 performances. A musical play based on *Green Grow the Lilacs* by Lynn Riggs. Music by Richard Rodgers. Book and lyrics by Oscar Hammerstein II. Presented by the Theatre Guild under the supervision of Theresa Helburn and Lawrence Langner. Directed by Rouben Mamoulian. Dances by Agnes de Mille. Settings by Lemuel Ayers. Costumes by Miles White. Orchestrations by [Robert] Russell Bennett. Orchestra directed by Jacob Schwartzdorf [Jay Blackton].

Cast: Betty Garde (Aunt Eller Murphy), Alfred Drake (Curly McLain), Joseph Buloff (Ali Hakim), Joan Roberts (Laurey Williams), Lee Dixon (Will Parker), Howard Da Silva (Jud Fry), Celeste Holm (Ado Annie Carnes), Ralph Riggs (Andrew Carnes), George Church (Dream Jud/Jess), Marc Platt (Dream Curly/Chalmers), Katharine Sergava (Dream Laurey/Ellen), with Barry Kelley (Ike Skidmore), Edwin Clay (Fred), Herbert Rissman (Slim), Jane Lawrence (Gertie Cummings), Ellen Love (Kate), Joan McCracken (Sylvie/featured dancer), Kate Friedlich (Armina/featured dancer), Bambi Linn (Aggie/Dream Child), Owen Martin (Cord Elam), Paul Shiers (Mike), George Irving (Joe), Hayes Gordon (Sam), and ensemble of singers and dancers.

In the Oklahoma Territory in the first years of the twentieth century, a sunny cowboy (Curly) and a menacing farmhand (Jud) vie to take a farm girl named Laurey to a box social. Laurey's fears and yearnings are portrayed in a lengthy dream ballet. Meanwhile, Ado Annie juggles her feelings for local boy Will Parker with her attraction to traveling salesman Ali Hakim. The night of Laurey and Curly's wedding, Jud returns. He pulls a knife on Curly and in the struggle Jud is killed. Andrew Carnes, the local judge, is among the wedding guests and he assists Curly in pleading self-defense. The rest of the guests declare him not guilty.

Awards: Special Pulitzer Prize for Drama, 1944. Special Tony Award in 1993 (fiftieth anniversary).

A national tour began on October 15, 1943, at the Shubert Theatre in New Haven and played, with occasional layoffs during the summer months, until May 1, 1954. A special company toured Army bases in the Pacific from February to October, 1945.

A London production opened on April 29, 1947, at the Theatre Royal, Drury Lane. In the late 1940s and early 1950s *Oklahoma* was also presented in Johannesburg, Melbourne, Copenhagen, and Oslo. *Oklahoma!* was performed in Paris at the Théâtre des Champs-Elysées during the Salute to France in the summer of 1955. A notable revival by London's Royal National Theatre—directed by Trevor Nunn with choreography by Susan Stroman, starring Hugh Jackman (Curly), Josefina Gabrielle (Laurey), and Shuler Hensley (Jud)—opened at the Olivier Theatre on July 15, 1998, and is commercially available on DVD.

A film version produced by Arthur Hornblow Jr. was released October 11, 1955. Directed by Fred Zinnemann. Screenplay by Sonya Levien and William Ludwig. Choreography by Agnes de Mille. Music direction by Jay Blackton. Orchestrations by Robert Russell Bennett. Starring Gordon MacRae (Curly), Shirley Jones (Laurey), Rod Steiger (Jud), Gloria Grahame (Ado Annie), Gene Nelson (Will Parker), Eddie Albert (Ali Hakim).

Broadway revivals: A production directed by William Hammerstein, with de Mille's choreography, opened on December 13, 1979. It starred Christine Andreas (Laurey), Laurence Guittard (Curly), Bruce Adler (Ali Hakim), Christine Ebersole (Ado Annie), Harry Groener (Will Parker), and Martin Vidnovic (Jud Fry). Trevor Nunn's Royal National Theatre production came to Broadway in 2003, opening on March 21; Patrick Wilson played Curly, with Josefina Gabrielle and Shuler Hensley repeating their London roles.

Recordings: There are more than twenty-five cast albums for *Oklahoma!* and countless versions of individual songs. The original Broadway cast album was followed by, among others, the original London cast (1947); the movie soundtrack (1955); the studio cast of John Raitt, Florence Henderson, and Phyllis Newman (1964); the 1979 Broadway revival cast; the 1998 Royal National Theatre (London) cast. The original Broadway cast album is notable for being the first time in the United States that the score of a musical was recorded in full by the original cast and orchestra. In 1992, the soundtrack album from the film of *Oklahoma!* was awarded Double Platinum status (sales of two million units) by the recording Industry Association of America (RIAA).

The primary sources for this chapter are the published vocal score and the published script. Several of the songs were published as individual sheets. Early drafts of the script are preserved at the New York Public Library for the Performing Arts and in the Oscar Hammerstein Collection in the music division of the Library of Congress, where there are also lyric worksheets. The Richard Rodgers Collection at the Library of Congress includes piano-vocal scores and sketches. Tim Carter's *Oklahoma! The Making of an American Musical* is a scholarly account of the show's development; Max Wilk's *OK! The Story of Oklahoma!* is a popular history.

OH, WHAT A BEAUTIFUL MORNIN'

Published as an individual sheet. Introduced by Alfred Drake (Curly).

"Oh, What a Beautiful Mornin' " was the first lyric written for the show. The following is an excerpt from the lengthy account Hammerstein gave in the introduction to his anthology *Lyrics:*

We had agreed that we should start the play outside a farmhouse. The only character on the stage would be a middle-aged woman sitting at a butter churn. The voice of Curly, a cowboy, would be heard off-stage, singing. Searching for a subject for Curly to sing about, I recalled how deeply I had been impressed by Lynn Riggs' description at the start of his play.

"It is a radiant summer morning several years ago, the kind of morning which, enveloping the shapes of earth—men, cattle in the meadow, blades of the young corn, streams—makes them seem to exist now for the first time, their images giving off a visible golden emanation that is partly true and partly a trick of imagination, focusing to keep alive a loveliness that may pass away."

On first reading these words, I had thought what a pity it was to waste them on stage directions. Only readers could enjoy them. An audience would never hear them. Yet, if they did, how quickly they would slip into the mood of the story. Remembering this reaction, I reread the description and determined to put it into song. "Oh, What a Beautiful Mornin' " opens the play and creates an atmosphere of relaxation and peace and tenderness. It introduces the light-hearted young man who is the center of the story. My indebtedness to Mr. Riggs' description is obvious. The cattle and the corn and the golden haze on the meadow are all there. I added some observations of my own based on my experience with beautiful mornings, and I brought the words down to the more primitive poetic level of Curly's character. He is, after all, just a cowboy and not a playwright.

In 1956 Hammerstein told children's author Elizabeth Rider Montgomery: "Although it is true that I am very slow in my lyric writing . . . this is one of the few songs that I wrote quickly. I would say that I finished it in about three days."

Discographer Edward Foote Gardner ranks "Oh, What a Beautiful Mornin' " as the seventeenth most popular song of 1943. Theatre Guild records show sheet music sales at four thousand copies a day in the fall of

1943. Supplementing the original cast album were popular 1940s recordings by Bing Crosby and Frank Sinatra.

VERSE 1

There's a bright, golden haze on the meadow,
There's a bright, golden haze on the meadow.
The corn is as high as a elephant's eye,
An' it looks like it's climbin' clear up to the sky.

REFRAIN

Oh, what a beautiful mornin'!
Oh, what a beautiful day!
I got a beautiful feelin'
Ev'rythin's goin' my way.

VERSE 2

All the cattle are standin' like statues,
All the cattle are standin' like statues.
They don't turn their heads as they see me ride by,
But a little brown mav'rick is winkin' her eye.

REFRAIN

Oh, what a beautiful mornin'!
Oh, what a beautiful day!
I got a beautiful feelin'
Ev'rythin's goin' my way.

VERSE 3

All the sounds of the earth are like music—
All the sounds of the earth are like music.
The breeze is so busy it don't miss a tree,
And a ol' weepin' willer is laughin' at me.

REFRAIN

Oh, what a beautiful mornin'!
Oh, what a beautiful day!
I got a beautiful feelin'
Ev'rythin's goin' my way . . .
Oh, what a beautiful day!

THE SURREY WITH THE FRINGE ON TOP

Published as an individual sheet. Introduced by Alfred Drake (Curly), Joan Roberts (Laurey), and Betty Garde (Aunt Eller).

Hammerstein would sometimes cite "Surrey" as a favorite song, "because of the sweetness and honesty in the music and the quality of pathetic innocence in the lyric." Rodgers reported, "Oscar was so moved by this song that just listening to it made him cry. He once explained that he never cried at sadness in the theatre, only at naïve happiness, and the idea of two bone-headed young people looking forward to nothing more than a ride in a surrey struck an emotional chord that affected him deeply."

VERSE 1

CURLY: When I take you out tonight with me,
Honey, here's the way it's goin' to be:
You will set behind a team of snow-white horses
In the slickest gig you ever see!

REFRAIN 1

CURLY: Chicks and ducks and geese better scurry
When I take you out in the surrey,
When I take you out in the surrey with the fringe on top.
Watch thet fringe and see how it flutters
When I drive them high-steppin' strutters—
Nosey-pokes'll peek through their shutters and their eyes will pop!
The wheels are yeller, the upholstery's brown,
The dashboard's genuine leather,
With isinglass curtains y' c'n roll right down
In case there's a change in the weather;
Two bright side lights winkin' and blinkin',
Ain't no finer rig, I'm a-thinkin';
You c'n keep yer rig if you're thinkin' 'at I'd keer to swap
Fer that shiny little surrey with the fringe on the top.

VERSE 2

AUNT ELLER: Would y' say the fringe was made of silk?
CURLY: Wouldn't have no other kind but silk.
LAUREY: Has it really got a team of snow-white horses?
CURLY: One's like snow—the other's more like milk.

REFRAIN 2

CURLY: All the world'll fly in a flurry
When I take you out in the surrey,
When I take you out in the surrey with the fringe on top.
When we hit that road, hell fer leather,
Cats and dogs'll dance in the heather,
Birds and frogs'll sing all together, and the toads will hop!
The wind'll whistle as we rattle along,
The cows'll moo in the clover,
The river will ripple out a whispered song,
And whisper it over and over:
Don't you wisht y'd go on ferever?
Don't you wisht y'd go on ferever?
Don't you wisht y'd go on ferever and ud never stop
In that shiny little surrey with the fringe on the top?

[*Dialogue.*]

REFRAIN 3

CURLY: I can see the stars gittin' blurry
When we ride back home in the surrey,
Ridin' slowly home in the surrey with the fringe on top.
I can feel the day gittin' older,
Feel a sleepy head near my shoulder,
Noddin', droopin' close to my shoulder till it falls, kerplop!
The sun is swimmin' on the rim of a hill,
The moon is takin' a header,
And jist as I'm thinkin' all the earth is still,
A lark'll wake up in the medder . . .
Hush! You bird, my baby's a-sleepin'—
Maybe got a dream worth a-keepin'.
Whoa! You team, and jist keep a-creepin' at a slow clip-clop;
Don't you hurry with the surrey with the fringe on the top.

KANSAS CITY

Published as an individual sheet. Introduced by Lee Dixon (Will Parker), Betty Garde (Aunt Eller), and dancing men.

VERSE

WILL: I got to Kansas City on a Frid'y.
By Sattidy I l'arned a thing or two.
For up to then I didn't have an idy
Of whut the modren world was comin' to.
I counted twenty gas buggies goin' by theirsel's
Almost ev'ry time I tuck a walk.
Nen I put my ear to a Bell telephone,
And a strange womern started in to talk!

AUNT ELLER: Whut next!
BOYS: Yeah, what?
WILL: Whut next?

REFRAIN 1

WILL: Ev'rythin's up to date in Kansas City.
They've gone about as fur as they c'n go!
They went and built a skyscraper seven stories high—
About as high as a buildin' orta grow.
Ev'rythin's like a dream in Kansas City.
It's better than a magic-lantern show.
Y' c'n turn the radiator on whenever you want some heat,
With ev'ry kind o' comfort ev'ry house is all complete,
You c'n walk to privies in the rain an' never wet yer feet—
They've gone about as fur as they c'n go!

AUNT ELLER: Yes, sir!
ALL: They've gone about as fur as they c'n go!

REFRAIN 2

WILL: Ev'rythin's up to date in Kansas City.
They've gone about as fur as they c'n go!
They got a big theayter they call a burleekew.

Fer fifty cents you c'n see a dandy show.
One of the gals was fat and pink and pretty,
As round above as she was round below.
I could swear that she was padded from her shoulder to her heel,
But later in the second act, when she began to peel,
She proved that ev'rythin' she had was absolutely real—
She went about as fur as she could go!

ALL: Yes, sir!
She went about as fur as she could go!

I CAIN'T SAY NO

Published as an individual sheet. Introduced by Celeste Holm (Ado Annie).

VERSE

It ain't so much a question of not knowin' whut to do,
I knowed whut's right and wrong since I been ten.
I heared a lot of stories—and I reckon they are true—
About how girls're put upon by men.
I know I mustn't fall into the pit,
But when I'm with a feller—I fergit!

REFRAIN 1

I'm jist a girl who cain't say no,
I'm in a turrible fix.
I always say "Come on, le's go!"
Jist when I orta say nix!
When a person tries to kiss a girl
I know she orta give his face a smack.
But as soon as someone kisses me
I somehow sorta wanta kiss him back.
I'm jist a fool when lights are low.
I cain't be prissy and quaint—
I ain't the type thet c'n faint—
How c'n I be whut I ain't?
I cain't say no!

INTERLUDE

Whut you goin' to do when a feller gets flirty
And starts to talk purty?
Whut you goin' to do?
S'posin' 'at he says 'at yer lips're like cherries,
Er roses, er berries?
Whut you goin' to do?
S'posin' 'at he says 'at you're sweeter'n cream
And he's gotta have cream er die?
Whut you goin' to do when he talks thet way?
Spit in his eye?

REFRAIN 2

I'm jist a girl who cain't say no,
Cain't seem to say it at all.
I hate to disserpoint a beau
When he is payin' a call.
Fer a while I ack refined and cool,
A-settin' on the velveteen settee—
Nen I think of thet ol' golden rule,
And do fer him whut he would do fer me.
I cain't resist a Romeo
In a sombrero and chaps.
Soon as I sit on their laps
Somethin' inside of me snaps—
I cain't say no!

ENCORE REFRAIN

I'm jist a girl who cain't say no.
Kissin's my favorite food.
With er without the mistletoe
I'm in a holiday mood.
Other girls are coy and hard to catch,
But other girls ain't havin' any fun.
Ev'ry time I lose a wrestlin' match
I have a funny feelin' that I won.
Though I c'n feel the undertow,
I never make a complaint
Till it's too late fer restraint,
Then when I want to I cain't—
I cain't say no!

REPRISE

WILL: S'posin' 'at I say 'at yer lips're like cherries,
Er roses er berries?
Whut you gonna do?
Cain't you feel my heart palpitatin' an' bumpin',
A waitin' fer sumpin',
Sumpin' nice from you?

I gotta git a kiss an' it's gotta be quick
Er I'll jump in a crick an' die.

ANNIE: What's a girl to say when you talk that-a-
way?

[*They embrace.*]

MANY A NEW DAY

Published as an individual sheet. Introduced by Joan Roberts (Laurey) and singing and dancing girls.

VERSE

Why should a womern who is healthy and strong
Blubber like a baby if her man goes away?
A-weepin' an' a-wailin' how he's done her
    wrong—
That's one thing you'll never hear me say!
Never gonna think that the man I lose
Is the only man among men.
I'll snap my fingers to show I don't care.
I'll buy me a brand-new dress to wear.
I'll scrub my neck and I'll bresh my hair,
And start all over again!

REFRAIN 1

Many a new face will please my eye,
Many a new love will find me.
Never've I once looked back to sigh
Over the romance behind me.
Many a new day will dawn before I do!
Many a light lad may kiss and fly,
A kiss gone by is bygone;
Never've I asked an August sky,
"Where has last July gone?"
Never've I wandered through the rye,
Wonderin' where has some guy gone—
Many a new day will dawn before I do!

REFRAIN 2

Many a new face will please my eye,
Many a new love will find me.
Never've I once looked back to sigh
Over the romance behind me.
Many a new day will dawn before I do!
Never've I chased the honeybee
Who carelessly cajoled me;
Somebody else just as sweet as he
Cheered me and consoled me.
Never've I wept into my tea
Over the deal someone doled me—

Many a new day will dawn,
Many a red sun will set,
Many a blue moon will shine, before I do!

IT'S A SCANDAL! IT'S A OUTRAGE!

Published in the vocal score. Introduced by Joseph Buloff (Ali Hakim) with the boys and girls.

In an early lyric sheet, where the title is "A Scandal fer the Jaybirds," Hammerstein describes how Ali Hakim will pace up and down while the orchestra vamps, and instructs: "Throughout this entire number, the peddler must be burning, and he transmits his indignation to the men who sing in a spirit of angry protest by the time the refrain is reached."

ALI HAKIM: [*spoken*] Trapped! Tricked!
    Hoodblinked! Hambushed!
      MEN: [*sung*] Friend,
        Whut's on yer mind?
        Why do you walk
        Around and around,
        With yer hands
        Folded behind,
        And yer chin
        Scrapin' the ground?
ALI HAKIM: [*spoken freely*] Twenty minutes ago I
      am free like a breeze,
        Free like a bird in the woodland wild,
        Free like a gypsy, free like a child,
        I'm unattached.
        Twenty minutes ago I can do what I
          please,
        Flick my cigar ashes on a rug,
        Dunk with a doughnut, drink from a
          jug—
        I'm a happy man!
        I'm minding my own business like I
          oughter
        Ain't meanin' any harm to anyone.
        I'm talking to a certain farmer's
          daughter—
        Then I'm looking in the muzzle of a
          gun!
      MEN: [*sung*] It's gittin' so you cain't have
          any fun!
        Ev'ry daughter has a father with a
          gun!

REFRAIN 1

      MEN: It's a scandal, it's a outrage!
        How a gal gits a husband today!
ALI HAKIM: If you make one mistake when the
          moon is bright,
        Then they tie you to a contract,
        So you make it ev'ry night!
      MEN: It's a scandal, it's a outrage!
        When her fambly surround you and
          say:
        "You gotta take an' make an honest
          womern outa Nell!"
ALI HAKIM: To make you make her honest, she
          will lie like hell!
      MEN: It's a scandal, it's a outrage!
        On our manhood it's a blot!
        Where is the leader who will save us
        And be the first man to be shot?
ALI HAKIM: Me?
      MEN: Yes, you!

REFRAIN 2

      MEN: It's a scandal, it's a outrage!
        Jist a wink and a kiss and you're
          through!
ALI HAKIM: You're a mess, and in less than a year,
          by heck!
        There's a baby on your shoulder
          making bubbles on your neck!
      MEN: It's a scandal, it's a outrage!
        Any farmer will tell you it's true.
ALI HAKIM: A rooster in a chicken coop is better
          off'n men.
        He ain't the special property of just
          one hen!
      MEN: It's a scandal, it's a outrage!
        It's a problem we must solve
        We gotta start a revolution!
      GIRLS: All right, boys! Revolve!

PEOPLE WILL SAY WE'RE IN LOVE

Published as an individual sheet. The two refrains appear in *Lyrics*. Introduced by Alfred Drake (Curly) and Joan Roberts (Laurey).

In the introduction to his anthology, *Lyrics*, Hammerstein wrote:

The problem of a duet for the lovers in *Oklahoma!* seemed insurmountable. While it is obvious almost from the rise of the curtain that Curly and Laurey are in love with each other, there is also a violent antagonism between them, caused mainly by Laurey's youthful shyness, which she disguises by pretending not to care for Curly. This does not go down very well with him, and he fights back. Since this mood was to dominate their scenes down into the second act, it seemed impossible for us to write a song that said "I love you," and remain consistent with the attitude they had adopted toward each other. After talking this over for a long time, Dick and I hit upon the idea of having the lovers warn each other against any show of tenderness lest other people think they were in love, of course, while they say all those things, they are obliquely confessing their mutual affection. Hence the title, "People Will Say We're in Love."

This song became extremely popular, spending thirty weeks on the Hit Parade. Discographer Edward Foote Gardner ranks it as the number two song of 1943; according to Theater Guild records, in the fall of 1943 the sheet music was selling at the rate of nine thousand copies a day.

The song was also popular with American soldiers and sailors overseas. Naval Lieutenant (JG) Tom Ewell, who had played Daniel in *Sunny River* (1941), wrote to Hammerstein from "somewhere in Italy" about how homesick he and the men were after twenty months. They'd been given a day off to swim and relax. "Someone on the veranda put on 'People Will Say We're in Love' on the gramophone. Everyone took up the refrain. When it finished we all felt, well—it's kinda hard to explain—but somehow we all felt that home had been a little closer."

VERSE 1

LAUREY: Why do they think up stories that link
   my name with yours?
CURLY: Why do the neighbors gossip all day
   behind their doors?
LAUREY: I know a way to prove what they say is
   quite untrue.
   Here is the gist, a practical list of
   "don'ts" for you:

REFRAIN 1

LAUREY: Don't throw bouquets at me,
   Don't please my folks too much,
   Don't laugh at my jokes too much—
   People will say we're in love!
   Don't sigh and gaze at me
   (Your sighs are so like mine),
   Your eyes mustn't glow like mine—
   People will say we're in love!
   Don't start collecting things

   (Give me my rose and my glove);
   Sweetheart, they're suspecting things—
   People will say we're in love!

VERSE 2

CURLY: Some people claim that you are to blame
   as much as I.
   Why do you take the trouble to bake my
   fav'rit pie?
   Grantin' your wish, I carved our initials
   on that tree.
   Jist keep a slice of all the advice you give
   so free!

REFRAIN 2

CURLY: Don't praise my charm too much,
   Don't look so vain with me,
   Don't stand in the rain with me—
   People will say we're in love!
   Don't take my arm too much,
   Don't keep your hand in mine.
   Your hand feels so grand in mine,
   People will say we're in love!
   Don't dance all night with me,
   Till the stars fade from above.
   They'll see it's alright with me,
   People will say we're in love!

ACT TWO REPRISE

CURLY: Let people say we're in love.
   Who keers whut happens now!
LAUREY: Jist keep your hand in mine.
   Your hand feels so grand in mine.
BOTH: Let people say we're in love!
   Starlight looks well on us,
   Let the stars beam from above.
   Who cares if they tell on us?
   Let people say we're in love!

PORE JUD IS DAID

Published in the vocal score. Included in *Lyrics*. Introduced by Alfred Drake (Curly) and Howard Da Silva (Jud).

In the introduction to *Lyrics*, Hammerstein wrote:

Jud Fry worried us. A sulky farmhand, a "bullet-colored, growly man," a collector of dirty pictures, he frightened Laurey by walking in the shadow of a tree beneath her window every night. He was heavy fare for a musical play. Yet his elimination was not to be considered because the

drama he provided was the element that prevented this light lyric idyll from being so lyric and idyllic that a modern theater audience might have been made sleepy, if not nauseous, by it . . . The question was how to make him acceptable, not too much a deep-dyed villain, a scenery chewer, an unmotivated purveyor of arbitrary evil. We didn't want to resort to the boring device of having two other characters discuss him and give the audience a psychological analysis. Even if this were dramatically desirable, there are no characters in this story who are bright enough or well-educated enough to do this. So we solved the problem with two songs, "Pore Jud" and "Lonely Room." . . . [In "Pore Jud"] Jud becomes then, for a while, not just wicked, but a comic figure flattered by the attentions he might receive if he were dead. He becomes also a pathetic figure, pathetically lonely for attentions he has never received while alive. The audience begins to feel some sympathy for him, some understanding of him as a man.

CURLY: Pore Jud is daid,
   Pore Jud Fry is daid,
   All gether round his cawfin now and cry.
   He had a heart of gold
   And he wasn't very old—
   Oh, why did sich a feller have to die?
   Pore Jud is daid,
   Pore Jud Fry is daid.
   He's lookin', oh, so peaceful and serene—
JUD: And serene!
CURLY: He's all laid out to rest
   With his hands acrost his chest.
   His fingernails have never b'en so clean.
CURLY: But the folks 'at really knowed him,
   Knowed 'at beneath them two dirty shirts
    he alw'ys wore,
   There beat a heart as big as all outdoors.
JUD: As big as all outdoors.
CURLY: Jud Fry loved his fellow man.
JUD: He loved his fellow man.

CURLY: Pore Jud is daid,
   Pore Jud Fry is daid,
   His friends'll weep and wail fer miles
    around—
JUD: Miles around.
CURLY: The daisies in the dell
   Will give out a diff'runt smell
   Becuz pore Jud is underneath the ground.
JUD: Pore Jud is daid,
   A candle lights his haid,
   He's layin' in a cawfin made of wood—
CURLY: Wood.
JUD: And folks are feelin' sad

Cuz they useter treat him bad,
And now they know their friend has gone
    fer good—
CURLY: Good.
 BOTH: Pore Jud is daid,
    A candle lights his haid—
CURLY: He's lookin', oh, so purty and so nice!
    He looks like he's asleep.
    It's a shame that he won't keep,
    But it's summer and we're runnin' out of
      ice . . .
 BOTH: Pore Jud—pore Jud!

LONELY ROOM

Published in the vocal score. The lyric appears in *Lyrics*, except for the last five lines. Introduced by Howard Da Silva (Jud).

Hammerstein wrote: "When Lynn Riggs attended a rehearsal of *Oklahoma!* for the first time, I asked him if he approved of this number. He said, 'I certainly do. It will scare the hell out of the audience.' That is exactly what it was designed to do."

The floor creaks,
The door squeaks,
There's a field mouse a-nibblin' on a broom,
And I set by myself
Like a cobweb on a shelf,
By myself in a lonely room.

But when there's a moon in my winder
And it slants down a beam 'crost my bed,
Then the shadder of a tree starts a-dancin' on the
    wall
And a dream starts a-dancin' in my head.
And all the things that I wish fer
Turn out like I want them to be,
And I'm better'n that smart-aleck cowhand
Who thinks he is better'n me,
And the girl that I want
Ain't afraid of my arms,
And her own soft arms keep me warm.
And her long, yeller hair
Falls acrost my face
Jist like the rain in a storm . . .

The floor creaks,
The door squeaks,
And the mouse starts a-nibblin' on the broom.
And the sun flicks my eyes—
It was all a pack o' lies!
I'm awake in a lonely room.

I ain't gonna dream 'bout her arms no more!
I ain't gonna leave her alone!
Goin' outside,
Git myself a bride,
Git me a womern to call my own.

Lyrics from an early draft, "Lonely Little Room"

But last night the moon passed my winder
And a beam slanted down 'crost my bed,
And the shadder of a tree
Got to dancin' on the wall,
And a dream got to dancin' in my head!
I bust that door from its hinges.
Then I walked with a five-mile stride
Till I stood on the shoulder of a mountain
And picked out a star I cud ride!
When I pulled down a star
And I called to a girl
And she hopped right up by my side.
In the flash of an eye
We was whizzin' through the sky—
Me on my star—with my bride . . .

OUT OF MY DREAMS

Published as an individual sheet. Laurey's refrain appears in *Lyrics*. Introduced by Joan Roberts (Laurey) and singing and dancing girls.

REFRAIN

1ST GIRL: Out of your dreams and into his arms
    you long to fly.
2ND GIRL: You don't need Egyptian smellin' salts
    to tell you why.
1ST GIRL: Out of your dreams and into the hush
    of falling shadows—
3RD GIRL: When the mist is low, and stars are
    breaking through—
4TH GIRL: Then out of your dreams you'll go—
ALL GIRLS: Into a dream come true.

VERSE

GIRLS: Make up your mind, make up your
    mind, Laurey, Laurey dear.
    Make up your own, make up your own
    story, Laurey dear.
    Ol' Pharaoh's daughter won't tell you
    what to do.
    Ask your heart—whatever it tells you
    will be true.

REFRAIN

LAUREY: Out of my dreams and into your arms
    I long to fly.
    I will come as evening comes to woo a
    waiting sky.
    Out of my dreams and into the hush
    of falling shadows,
    When the mist is low, and stars are
    breaking through,
    Then out of my dreams I'll go
    Into a dream with you.

VERSE FROM PUBLISHED SHEET

Won't have to make up any more
    stories. You'll be there!
Think of the bright midsummer-night
    glories we can share.
Won't have to go on kissing a
    daydream, I'll have you
You'll be real, real as the white moon
    lighting the blue.

THE FARMER AND THE COWMAN

Published in the vocal score. Introduced by Ralph Riggs (Andrew Carnes), Betty Garde (Aunt Eller), and company.

In a 1953 comment about the importance of the book of a musical, Hammerstein explained:

At the opening of the second act of *Oklahoma!* is a number called "The Farmer and the Cowman Should Be Friends." Agnes de Mille created the gayest, most energetic, most engaging kind of country dance, and the music by Dick Rodgers seems to lift the dancers into the air, taking a good part of the audience with it. It doesn't look much as if this is a book writer's moment, does it? Music, lyrics, choreography, dancing, principals, and ensemble are holding the stage. But how did they all get there on the stage? How did this thing happen? The author did some research on the period of the story. He learned of the crisis that hit the southwest when the farmers moved in and started to build fences. The cattlemen hated the orderliness that the farmers were bringing into the land. The farmers hated the cowman's easy-going ways, and they forbade their daughters to have truck with them. This seemed promising dramatic and comic material. A good deal of time and writing went into the effort of making this a part of the musical adaptation of *Green Grow the Lilacs*, but there was little room for this added element, and so eventually it became whittled down until it found its final form in a song. Now the dancing and the music are undoubtedly the heroes of the occasion, but they owe their existence to book writing.

CARNES: The farmer and the cowman
should be friends,
Oh, the farmer and the cowman
should be friends.
One man likes to push a plough,
The other likes to chase a cow,
But that's no reason why they
cain't be friends.

Territory folks should stick
together,
Territory folks should all be pals.
Cowboys dance with farmers'
daughters,
Farmers dance with the ranchers'
gals.

ALL: Territory folks should stick
together,
Territory folks should all be pals.
Cowboys dance with farmers'
daughters,
Farmers dance with the ranchers'
gals.

CARNES: I'd like to say a word fer the
farmer.

AUNT ELLER: [*spoken*]: Well, say it!

CARNES: He come out west and made a lot
of changes.

WILL PARKER: He come out west and built a lot
of fences.

CURLY: And built 'em right acrost our
cattle ranges!

[*Spoken insults are exchanged.*]

CARNES: [*trying to make peace*]: The
farmer is a good and thrifty
citizen.
No matter whut the cowman says
or thinks.
You seldom see 'im drinkin' in a
bar room—

CURLY: Unless somebody else is buyin'
drinks!

CARNES: But the farmer and the cowman
should be friends,
Oh, the farmer and the cowman
should be friends.

The cowman ropes a cow with
ease,
The farmer steals her butter and
cheese,
That's no reason why they cain't
be friends.

ALL: Territory folks should stick
together,
Territory folks should all be pals.
Cowboys dance with farmers'
daughters!
Farmers dance with the ranchers'
gals!

AUNT ELLER: I'd like to say a word for the
cowboy.
The road he treads is difficult and
stony.
He rides fer days on end,
With jist a pony fer a friend.

ADO ANNIE: I shore am feelin' sorry fer the
pony!

AUNT ELLER: The farmer should be sociable
with the cowboy.
If he rides by an' asks fer food an'
water,
Don't treat him like a louse,
Make him welcome in yer house.

CARNES: But be shore that you lock up yer
wife an' daughter.

[*More insults bring the men close to blows.* AUNT
ELLER *stops the fracas by firing a gun. She points it at*
CARNES *to start him singing again.*]

CARNES: The farmer and the cowman
should be friends.

A FEW MEN: Oh, the farmer and the cowman
should be friends.

ALL: One man likes to push a plough,
The other likes to chase a cow,
But that's no reason why they
cain't be friends.

IKE SKIDMORE: And when this territory is a state,
An' jines the Union jist like all the
others,
The farmer and cowman and the
merchant
Must all behave theirsel's and act
like brothers.

AUNT ELLER: I'd like to teach you all a little
sayin',
And learn the words by heart the
way you should.
"I don't say I'm no better than
anybody else,
But I'll be damned if I ain't jist as
good!"

ALL: I don't say I'm no better than
anybody else,
But I'll be damned if I ain't jist as
good!

Territory folks should stick
together,
Territory folks should all be pals.
Cowboys dance with farmers'
daughters!
Farmers dance with the ranchers'
gals!

ALL ER NUTHIN'

Published in the vocal score. Introduced by Lee Dixon (Will Parker) and Celeste Holm (Ado Annie).

WILL: You'll have to be a little more
standoffish,
When fellers offer you a buggy ride.

ADO ANNIE: I'll give a imitation of a crawfish,
And dig myself a hole where I c'n
hide.

WILL: I heared how you was kickin' up some
capers
When I was off in Kansas City, Mo.
I heared some things you couldn't
print in papers,
From fellers who been talkin' like
they know!

ADO ANNIE: [*spoken*] Foot!
[*sung*] I only did the kind of things I
orta—sorta,
To you I was as faithful as c'n be,
fer me.
Them stories 'bout the way I lost my
bloomers—Rumors!
A lot of tempest in a pot o' tea!

WILL: The whole thing don't sound very
good to me.

ADO ANNIE: Well, y' see.

WILL: [*spoken in rhythm*] I go and sow my
last wild oat!
I cut out all shenanigans!
I save my money—don't gamble er
drink,
In the backroom down at Flannigan's!
I give up lotsa other things,
A gentleman never mentions—
But before I give up any more,
I wanta know your intentions!

REFRAIN 1

WILL: With me it's all er nuthin'!
Is it all er nuthin' with you?
It cain't be "in between"
It cain't be "now and then"
No half-and-half romance will do!
I'm a one-woman man,
Home-lovin' type,
All complete with slippers and pipe.
Take me like I am er leave me be!
If you cain't give me all, give me
nuthin'—
And nuthin's whut you'll git from
me!

ADO ANNIE: Not even sump'n?
WILL: Nuthin's whut you'll git from me!
ADO ANNIE: It cain't be "in between"?
WILL: Uh-uh.
ADO ANNIE: It cain't be "now and then"?
WILL: No half-and-half romance will do!
ADO ANNIE: Would you build me a house,
All painted white,
Cute and clean and purty and bright?
WILL: Big enough fer two but not fer three!
ADO ANNIE: Supposin' 'at we should have a third
one?
WILL: He better look a lot like me!
ADO ANNIE: The spit an' image!
WILL: He better look a lot like me!

[*Dance.*]

REFRAIN 2

ADO ANNIE: With you it's all er nuthin'—
All fer you and nuthin' fer me!
But if a wife is wise,
She's gotta realize,
That men like you are wild and free.
So I ain't gonna fuss,
Ain't gonna frown,
Have your fun, go out on the town,
Stay up late and don't come home till
three,
And go right off to sleep if you're
sleepy—
There's no use waitin' up fer me!
WILL: Oh, Ado Annie!
ADO ANNIE: No use waitin' up fer me!

OKLAHOMA

Published as an individual sheet. Appears in *Lyrics.* Introduced by Betty Garde (Aunt Eller), Barry Kelley (Ike Skidmore), Alfred Drake (Curly), Joan Roberts (Laurey), Edwin Clay (Fred), Owen Martin (Cord Elam), Ralph Riggs (Andrew Carnes), and the ensemble.

In a 1959 eulogy to Theresa Helburn, Hammerstein recalled:

We were in a taxi going up to [a backers' audition], and Terry said to me: "I wish you and Dick would write a song about the earth." Coming out of a clear sky, the suggestion shocked me. I had no idea what she meant. I said: "What do you mean, Terry?" And she said: "Oh, I don't know, just a song about the earth—the land."... Two days later, I had written a lyric which I had never intended to write. I described "a brand new state" that was going to provide barley, carrots, and potatoes, pasture for the cattle, flowers on the prairie. I spoke of wind sweeping down the plain and how sweet the waving wheat smelled when the wind came right behind the rain. I introduced a couple who expressed happiness that they belonged to the land and that the land they belonged to was grand. A song about the earth!

The song was initially assigned to Curly and Laurey, with a tap dance by Jess (George Church). The dancing was cut after the New Haven tryout and the singing ensemble added. Robert Russell Bennett devised the vocal harmonies while on the train from New York to Boston. Agnes de Mille added to the number's impact by having the whole ensemble move in a "flying wedge" toward the footlights. Soon after, the show was renamed *Oklahoma;* and during the second week in Boston, it became *Oklahoma!*

INTRODUCTION

AUNT ELLER: They couldn't pick a better time
to start in life—
IKE SKIDMORE: It ain't too early and it ain't too
late.
CURLY: Startin' as a farmer with a
brand-new wife—
LAUREY: Soon be livin' in a brand-new
state!

VERSE

ALL: Brand-new state
Gonna treat you great!
FRED: Gonna give you barley,
Carrots and pertaters—
CORD ELAM: Pasture fer the cattle—

ANDREW CARNES: Spinach and termayters!
AUNT ELLER: Flowers on the prairie where the
June bugs zoom—
IKE SKIDMORE: Plen'y of air and plen'y of
room—
FRED: Plen'y of room to swing a
rope—
AUNT ELLER: Plen'y of heart and plen'y of
hope.

REFRAIN

CURLY: Oklahoma,
Where the wind comes sweepin'
down the plain
And the wavin' wheat
Can sure smell sweet
When the wind comes right
behind the rain.
Oklahoma!
Every night my honey lamb
and I
Sit alone and talk
And watch a hawk
Makin' lazy circles in the sky.
We know we belong to the land,
And the land we belong to is
grand.
And when we say:
Yee-ow! A-yip-i-o-ee-ay!
We're only sayin',
You're doin' fine, Oklahoma!
Oklahoma, O.K.!

REPEAT REFRAIN

CODA

O-K-L-A-H-O-M-A
Oklahoma!
Yee-ow!

CUT AND UNUSED SONGS

BOYS AND GIRLS LIKE YOU AND ME

Published with an *Away We Go!* cover, but dropped during out-of-town tryouts. Included in *Lyrics.* More recently published in the folio "Rodgers and Hammerstein Rediscovered." This Act Two duet for Curly and

Laurey was superseded by a reprise of "People Will Say We're in Love."

The song was subsequently recorded by Judy Garland for the film *Meet Me in St. Louis* (1944) but not used; permission was then granted for use in MGM's *Take Me Out to the Ball Game* (1949), but it was not used there, either. Rodgers used the melody as underscore in the second broadcast of *Cinderella* (1965), and the song finally found a home in the 1996 stage version of *State Fair*.

VERSE

They walk on every village street,
They walk in lanes where branches meet,
And stars send down their blessings from the
  blue.
They go through storms of doubt and fear,
And so they go from year to year,
Believing in each other as we do,
Bravely marching forward two by two.

REFRAIN

Boys and girls like you and me
Walk beneath the skies.
They love just as we love
With the same dream in their eyes.
Songs and kings and many things
Have their day and are gone
But boys and girls like you and me
We go on and on.

SOMEONE WILL TEACH YOU

One of the first lyrics written for *Oklahoma!*, this duet for Laurey and Curly was superseded by "People Will Say We're in Love." No music is known to have been written. Tim Carter's *Oklahoma! The Making of an American Musical* includes another draft of this lyric.

VERSE 1

LAUREY: [*in a superior and motherly tone*] You're
      shy and you got no confidence.
      You hide in a hole like a crawfish.
      Folks cain't account for the way you act
      And they say you act stand-offish.
      I understand how you feel.
      Onct I was jist like you.
      Nen love come along and cured me,
      And 'at's whut'll cure you, too.

REFRAIN 1

LAUREY: Someone will teach you and clearly
      explain
      Why you are the cream of the crowd.
      Someone will teach you to walk down a
        lane
      As if you were ridin' a cloud.
      Someone will kiss you and tell you you're
        wonderful,
      You'll think you're wonderful, too.
      Fer somehow the right one can make you
        believe
      They's no one on earth like you.

VERSE 2

CURLY: I think I git whut yer drivin' at.
      You're jist feelin' great.
      But air you sartin yer arrivin' at
      Yer last and final fate?
      I don't know how to put it in words—
      Mebbe I oughter write a letter—
      But jist don't take the first feller that
        comes . . .
      Mebbe some day you'll do better.

REFRAIN 2

CURLY: Someone will teach you and clearly
      explain
      How really important you are.
      Someone will teach you to stand in the
        rain
      As if you were under a star.
      Someone will kiss you and tell you you're
        wonderful,
      You'll think you're wonderful, too.
      Fer somehow the right one can make you
        believe
      They's no one on earth like you.

CODA AFTER CURLY'S EXIT

LAUREY: Wisht I c'd kiss you and tell you you're
      wonderful.
      You'd think you're wonderful, too.
      And somehow—oh, somehow I'd make
        you believe
      They's no one on earth like you!

WE WILL BE TOGETHER

This Act Two duet for Ado Annie and Will Parker was superseded by "All er Nothin'." A year later Rodgers and Hammerstein tried to reuse it in *State Fair* as a song for Emily and Marty (her singing partner). An early screenplay explains: "That's a cute idea for a duet, Marty. When the lyric is about being together, the two voices are in a close harmony. When it says they may drift apart, the notes separate!"

We will be together,
Singing in the sun.
You'll be close to me as *b* to *a*.
Two contented voices
Blended into one,
We'll go harmonizing on our way.
When we drift apart as people do,
I'll come harmonizing back to you.
Doesn't matter whether
We have rain or sun,
We'll have sun if we can sing together!

WHEN AH GO OUT WALKIN' WITH MAH BABY

Recently published in the folio "Rodgers and Hammerstein Rediscovered" and performed in the 1996 stage version of *State Fair*. Dropped before *Away We Go* rehearsals began. In the earliest drafts of the script, Ali Hakim's wares include sheet music, and he demonstrates this song.

Hammerstein provided this description of the lyric to be written: "The Peddler, who has seen these gems performed in St. Louis, gives a rendition of a song like 'Bill Bailey,' cakewalk and all, imitating Marie Cahill or whatever artist he had seen. Then a group of girls, with a sheet of music to read from, sing a popular, sentimental ballad of the period in soft, 'close' harmony. One of them is probably the grandmother of the Andrews Sisters, and very likely started all this kind of vocal trouble."

When ah go out walkin' with mah baby,
Stars are dancin' in mah baby's eyes!
When ah do the cakewalk with mah baby,
Me an' mah baby always wins de prize!
When ah take her home we start in spoonin',
Spoonin' suits mah baby to a T.
Pretty soon you're goin' to see some honeymoonin'
'Cause if I don't marry her, she'll marry me!

WHY, OH WHY

From lyric worksheets in the Hammerstein Collection in the Music Division of the Library of Congress. Tim Carter identifies this as an early attempt to lead into the dream ballet. No music is known to have been written.

I hear a breeze in a tree, sighing
Why, oh why, oh why . . .
Seems like an echo of me sighing
Softly sighing why, oh why, oh why
Must I be all alone?
I dream, but my dream's my own.
I know a boy who must be sighing,
Why, oh why, oh why?
Lonely and wistful are we, sighing,
Gazing at the sky and sighing, why
Can't we combine our dreaming—
Only the breeze and the boy and I?

YOU ARE A GIRL

Not published. No music is known to have been written. This precursor to "Out of My Dreams" was found in Hammerstein's lyric worksheets, headed "Prelude to Ballet."

GIRLS: You are a girl who knows what she
wants
And you can choose
Flowers for your Easter hat
And buckles for your shoes.
You are a girl who knows what she
wants,
And when you find him,
You will know the man
Your heart has waited for,
And when you are in his arms
You will want no more.
ALTOS: What do you want?
SOPRANOS: Is it Curly?
LAUREY: Maybe so.
ALTOS: Or—
SOPRANOS: Ha-ha-ha!
ALTOS: Is it Jud?
LAUREY: Oh, no.
GIRLS: No?
LAUREY: No!
GIRLS: Laurey! Make your mind up—by
yourself.
Don't ask Aunt Eller,
Don't ask the stars,
Don't ask the peddler—he only
guesses.
Don't ask elixirs or 'Gyptian
princesses.
You are a girl who knows what she
wants.

[*Fading away.*]

You are a girl who knows what she
wants . . .
LAUREY: I am a girl who knows what she wants
And I can choose
Flowers for my Easter hat,
And buckles for my shoes.
I am a girl who knows what she wants,
And I have found him,
I have found the man
My heart has waited for,
And once I am in his arms
I will want no more. *

---

* *Hammerstein's stage directions explain that Laurey will speak a few additional lines as the music continues. Next, a wispy figure of a bride would glide in from the shadows. And then he wrote: "Take it, Agnes!"*

Left: *Dorothy Dandridge and Harry Belafonte in the 1954 film*
Right: *Luther Saxon and Muriel Smith in the original Broadway production*

CARMEN JONES | 1943

CARMEN JONES (1943)

Tryouts: Erlanger Theatre, Philadelphia, October 19–November 7, 1943; Opera House, Boston, November 9–28, 1943. New York run: Broadway Theatre; opened December 2, 1943; closed February 10, 1945; 503 performances. Presented by Billy Rose. Music by Georges Bizet. Adaptation and English lyrics by Oscar Hammerstein II, based on Henri Meilhac and Ludovic Halévy's adaptation of Prosper Mérimée's *Carmen*. Staging, lighting, and color schemes of entire production by Hassard Short. Libretto directed by Charles Friedman. Choreography by Eugene Loring. Settings designed by Howard Bay. Costumes designed by Raoul Pène Du Bois. New orchestral arrangements by Robert Russell Bennett. Orchestra conducted by David Mordecai. Choral direction by Robert Shaw.

Cast: Muriel Smith and Muriel Rahn (Carmen alternates), Luther Saxon (Joe alternate), Napoleon Reed (Corporal Morrell alternate/Joe alternate), Carlotta Franzell and Elton J. Warren (Cindy Lou alternates), Glenn Bryant (Husky Miller), June Hawkins (Frankie), Jessica Russell (Myrt),* Edward Lee Tyler (Rum), Dick Montgomery (Dink), Robert Clarke (Foreman alternate/Corporal Morrell alternate/soldier), George Willis (Foreman alternate/soldier), Jack Carr (Sergeant Brown), Sibol Cain (Sally/Card Player), Edward Roche (T-Bone), William Jones (Tough Kid), Cozy Cole (Drummer), Melvin Howard (Bartender/Bullett Head), Edward Christopher (Waiter), Randall Steplight (Soldier), Elijah Hodges (Soldier), P. Jay Sidney (Mr. Higgins), Fredye Marshall (Miss Higgins), Alford Pierre (Photographer), Urylee Leonardos (Card Player), Ethel White (Card Player), Ruth Crumpton (Dancing Girl), William Dillard (Poncho), Sheldon B. Hoskins (Dancing Boxer), Randolph Sawyer (Dancing Boxer), Tony Fleming Jr. (Referee), and ensemble.

Hammerstein considered *Carmen* "a perfect wedding of story and music" and challenged himself to make it come alive for an English-speaking audience. He set the action in the present (early 1940s) and changed the opera's Spanish and Gypsy characters to African-Americans, but made few changes to the plot. Joe, a soldier with a hometown sweetheart, falls in love with Carmen, a temptress. After helping her to escape from jail, he goes AWOL to follow her to Chicago. But Carmen has already moved on to a new lover, Husky Miller, a boxer. Cindy Lou, Joe's sweetheart, tracks him down in order to tell him that his mother is dying. Carmen tells Joe to go—and stay away. He leaves, warning Carmen

---

* *Some sources, including the cast album, say that June Hawkins played Myrt and Jessica Russell played Frankie.*

that if he can't have her, no one will. The night of Husky's big fight, Joe returns. Carmen rejects him again and he kills her.

A national tour began on May 2, 1945, at New York's City Center and ended there on May 4, 1946, having visited twenty-six cities over its twelve-month duration.

A film version was produced and directed by Otto Preminger for 20th Century–Fox and released in October 1954, starring Dorothy Dandridge (Carmen; sung by Marilyn Horne), Harry Belafonte (Joe; sung by LeVern Hutcherson), Olga James (Cindy Lou), Pearl Bailey (Frankie), Diahann Carroll (Myrt; sung by Bernice Peterson), Roy Glenn (Rum; sung by Brock Peters), Nick Stewart (Dink; sung by Marvin Hayes); Joe Adams (Husky Miller; sung by Marvin Hayes), and Brock Peters (Sergeant Brown). The film uses only a portion of the show's score.

Notable revivals include two in London: at the Old Vic in 1991, directed by Simon Callow and starring Wilhelmenia Fernandez or Sharon Benson, Damon Evans, Michael Austin, and Gregg Baker; and at the Royal Festival Hall in the summer of 2007, directed by Jude Kelly, with the London Philharmonic and Philharmonia orchestras alternating for the five-week run. A concert version was performed at the Kennedy Center in Washington, D.C., in November 2002, starring Vanessa Williams, Tom Randle, Harolyn Blackwell, and Gregg Baker, with Plácido Domingo conducting the National Symphony Orchestra.

Recordings include the original Broadway cast, featuring Muriel Smith, Luther Saxon, and Carlotta Franzell; a 1947 radio cast featuring Smith, Saxon, and Elton J. Warren; the 1954 film soundtrack; a 1962 studio cast featuring Grace Bumbry; and the 1991 Old Vic cast.

The primary source for this chapter is the published libretto (Knopf, 1945). Seven of the songs were published, and some lyrics were reprinted in the show's souvenir program and in Hammerstein's anthology, *Lyrics*. A new vocal selection was published in 1991. The Billy Rose Theatre Collection at the New York Public Library for the Performing Arts has chorus parts from the original production and a script. The Hammerstein Collection in the Music Division of the Library of Congress has an undated draft of the script where the Escamillo character is a bandleader named Hepcat Miller; a transitional draft of the script; and page proofs for the published libretto. All references to the opera in this chapter are based on the Dover edition of the vocal score.

No lyric has been found to match the sextet and chorus that open the opera's third act (corresponds to "Écoute, compagnon, écoute!" and "Notre métier est bon," Dover score of *Carmen*, page 239). During a 1957 speech at Swarthmore College, Hammerstein said, "Even so good an opera as *Carmen*, [with] such a tightly constructed libretto fitting the music so perfectly, I believe is overblown. In the second [sic] act you have smugglers hiding in the hills. But it's hard to give the

impression that the smugglers are hiding in the hills when a whole convention of smugglers comes on from all sides, and they start to bellow as loud as they can. They don't care whether the cops catch them or not."

In the introduction to the published libretto, Hammerstein pointed out that operas "written by distinguished dramatic poets, are translated [into English] by scholarly but untalented gentlemen who know nearly nothing about the science of writing phonetic, singable lyrics. They are not poets, nor dramatists, nor showmen. A good adaptation of an opera requires a librettist who is all of these." Thinking as a poet, dramatist, and showman, Hammerstein set his adaptation in the 1940s American South. The dialect spellings were intended to reflect a very real world.

The show's success gave him great satisfaction. Soon after the first tryout performance in Philadelphia, he wrote to his son Bill:

> It has turned out as I had hoped—and I had great hopes, as you know. This is the first time I ever sat down and wrote a play without first arranging for a production with a manager in advance. It is also the first time I've opened a play out of town and not had one bit of rewriting to do! It will open on Broadway just as it opened in Philadelphia—except for some polishing in the direction of the scenes and numbers. It is a dream show . . .
>
> The production is one of the most beautiful I've ever seen (Hassard Short, Raoul Pène Du Bois, Howard Bay). The girl playing Carmen is probably the best in several generations. The tenor is fair. Ditto the toreador. Cindy Lou (Micaela) sings her aria in the second act and gets not applause, but an earthquake. The show itself seems to surprise people, then sort of tickle them (plenty of laughs), then it winds up by sweeping them off their feet and leaving them limp. I am not exaggerating—just reporting.

SEND ALONG ANUDDER LOAD

Corresponds with "Sur la place, chacun passe" (Dover score of *Carmen*, page 6). Introduced by the male ensemble (soldiers and workers).

Send along anudder load
An' win dat war, win dat war!
One more to go an' den one more,
One more to go an' den one more,
One more to go,
One more to go.

Send 'em along an' win dat war!
Send 'em along! Send 'em along!
Send 'em along! Send 'em along!

An earlier version

Git along, you ingineers,
An' build dat road, build dat road.
Hang it across de mountainside,
Hang it across de mountainside.
Hang it across,
Hang it across,
Hang it across de mountainside.

CAIN' LET YOU GO

Corresponds with "Il y sera" (Dover score, page 13). Introduced by Napoleon Reed and Robert Clarke (Corporal Morrell alternates) and Carlotta Franzell and Elton J. Warren (Cindy Lou alternates).

MORRELL: Cain' let you go!
Before we let you go, we
Would like a slice o' sumpin' nice
Yore savin' up for Joey,
Oh, we—
MEN: Cain' let you go!
Before we let you go, we
Would like a slice o' sumpin' dat
belongs to Joe!
CINDY LOU: I'm a chick dat likes one rooster,*
Never mess aroun' wid two.
Dat is why I mus' refuse ter
Be more den jus' perlite to you!

I LIKE YOUR EYES

Corresponds to "Je reviendrai" (Dover score, page 16). Introduced by Carlotta Franzell and Elton J. Warren (Cindy Lou alternates) and male ensemble.

---

* Corresponds with "Mais en attendant qu'il vienne" (Dover score, page 14), which is sung by the character Moralès. An early draft had these lines for Morrell:
  Lemme walk beside you, sugar.
  I don' mean you any harm.
  Lemme walk beside you, sugar—
  Yo' shoulder sure could use my arm.

CINDY LOU: I like your eyes,
Your teeth are white an' snowy—
But when it comes to teeth an' eyes,*
Dere ain' no flies on Joey—oey!
MEN: She likes your eyes,
Your teeth are white an' snowy,
You's awful nice but not as nice as
good ol' Joe!

LIFT 'EM UP AND PUT 'EM DOWN

Corresponds to "Avec la garde montante" (Dover score, page 23). Introduced by the children and the female ensemble.

CHILDREN AND
ADULT SOPRANOS: Lift 'em up an' put 'em down,
Lift 'em up an' put 'em down.
Mark time an' lift your tootsies
Six inches off de groun'!
Lift em' up an' put 'em down,
Marchin' all aroun' de town,
Comp'ny! Squads right!
Dat means turn aroun'!
Wish dat I was twen'y-one,†
Ol' enough to tote a gun,
I'd go an' be a soldier—
Dere de ones dat have de fun!
Wisht I was a bugler man,
Playin' in de army ban'.
I'd blow it till I busted,
Playin' in de army ban'—
Ta ta ta ta ta ta
Ta ta ta ta ta ta ta, [etc]

---

* Variant for lines 3 and 4:
  You's awful nice but not as nice
  As Joey-oey-oey-oey.

† An early version of the last ten lines:
  Paw wuz drafted months ago
  Now he is de bugle man.
  You oughter hear him blow it!
  No one blows it like he can.
  Gonna go an' tell my maw
  Gonna go away wid Paw.
  I wanna blow dat bugle—
  Ta ta ta ta ta ta
  Ta ta ta ta ta ta ta [etc.]

HONEY GAL O' MINE

Corresponds to "La cloche a sonné" (Dover score, page 34). Introduced by the male ensemble.

MEN: Middle of de day,
People gettin' hungry.
Poor folks eat dere lunch,
Rich folks wine an' dine.
I don't wan' no lunch,
I ain' feelin' hungry.
I jus' wanna see dat honey gal o' mine—
Honey gal o' mine,
Honey gal o' mine.

GOOD LUCK, MISTER FLYIN' MAN

Corresponds to "Dans l'air nous suivons des yeux" (Dover score, page 36). Introduced by the female ensemble. In Act One of Bizet's opera, the ensemble women work in a cigarette factory. Hammerstein used that setting in his first draft but rewrote the lyric after deciding to change it to a parachute factory.

Good luck, Mister Flyin' Man,
When you bail out,
When you bail out.
Jus' pull dat string—
Like a bird on de wing you will sail out.
Good luck while yore fallin' down
From above,
From above.
You'll reach de groun'—
It's as easy as fallin' in love.
Goodbye to silk stockin's an' silk underwear!
We gotta have silk dat kin float in de air.
Our paratroop fellers
Need yeller umbrellers,
De kind we know will get dem dere!
Good luck, Mister Flyin' Man,
Flyin' Man, floatin' down,
Floatin' through the blue—
Happy landin' to you,
Happy landin' to you,
Happy landin' to you!
Flyin' Man . . . Flyin' Man.

First-draft version

We make all de cigarettes
Dey can sell you, dey can sell you.
Good fo' yo' voice—
As de radio program'll tell you.
Mister man, ef you smoke our bran'
You'll be clever, you'll be wealthy
An' smoke all you can,
It's de onliest way to git healthy!
Our cigarette puts you to sleep in de night.
Our cigarette makes you wake up feelin' right.
Our cigarette fattens you,
Our cigarette flattens you,
It's smooth, it's fresh, it's mild, it's light!
We make de bes' cigarettes,
Dere de bes' fo' yo' ches'—
Dere de bes' of all!
You kin try all de res',
But you'll git a terrible cough in de ches'!
Dere de bes'
Fo yo' ches'!

DAT'S LOVE

Published as an individual sheet. Lyric appears in Hammerstein's anthology, *Lyrics*. Corresponds to the Habanera (Dover score, page 43). Introduced by Muriel Smith and Muriel Rahn (Carmen alternates) and ensemble.

INTRODUCTION

CARMEN: I won' pick out de man—
An' he won' pick out me!
It don' go dat way.
You cain' ever know
Where your crazy heart
wants to go!

VERSE 1

CARMEN: Love's a baby dat grows
up wild
An' he don' do what you
want him to,
Love ain' nobody's angel
child
An' he won' pay any
mind to you.
One man gives me his
diamon' stud
An' I won' give him a
cigarette.

One man treats me like I
was mud—
An' what I got dat man
c'n get.
Dat's love . . . dat's love!
Dat's love . . . dat's love!
ENSEMBLE: Love's a baby dat grows
up wild
An' he don' do what you
want him to.
Love ain' nobody's angel
child
An' he won' pay any
mind to you.

REFRAIN

CARMEN: You go for me an' I'm
taboo,
But if yore hard to get I
go for you,
An' if I do, den you are
through, boy,
My baby, dat's de end of
you.
ENSEMBLE: De end of you!
CARMEN: So take your cue, boy,
Don' say I didn' tell you
true.
ENSEMBLE: She tol' you true!
CARMEN: I tol' you truly,
If I love you dat's de end
of you!
ENSEMBLE: You go for me an' I'm
taboo,
But if yore hard to get I
go for you,
An' if I do, den you are
through, boy,
My baby, dat's de end of
you, de end of you.
CARMEN: So take your cue, boy,
Don' say I didn' tell you
true.
ENSEMBLE: She tol' you true!
CARMEN: I tol' you truly,
If I love you dat's de end
of you!

VERSE 2

CARMEN: When your lovebird
decides to fly
Dere ain' no door dat you
c'n close.
She jus' pecks you a
quick goodbye

An' flicks de salt from
her tail, an' goes!
If you listen den you'll
get taught,
An' here's your lesson
for today:
If I chase you den you'll
get caught,
But once I got you I go
my way!
Dat's love . . . dat's love!
Dat's love . . . dat's love!
ENSEMBLE: When your lovebird
decides to fly
Dere ain' no door dat you
c'n close.
She jus' pecks you a
quick goodbye
An' flicks de salt from
her tail, an' goes!

REFRAIN 2

CARMEN AND ENSEMBLE: You go for me an' I'm
taboo,
But if yore hard to get I
go for you,
An' if I do, den you are
through, boy.
My baby, dat's de end of
you.
ENSEMBLE: De end of you!
CARMEN: So take your cue, boy,
Don' say I didn' tell
you true.
ENSEMBLE: She tol' you true.
CARMEN: I tol' you truly,
If I love you dat's de end
of you!

CODA

MEN: Hey, Joe! Don' let her
git her hooks into
you!*
Say, Joe! Don' do
anythin' I wouldn' do!
GIRLS: You go for me an' I'm
taboo,
But if yore hard to get I
go for you.
An' if I do, den you are
through, boy,
My baby, dat's de end of
you!

* Corresponds to "Carmen! sur tes pas nous nous pressons tous!" (Dover score, page 55).

Introduction (early version)

How kin I choose a man?
'N' how kin he choose me?
It don' go dat way,
It ain' quite so set—
'Tain' what you choose dat you get!

LEAD-IN TO YOU TALK JUS' LIKE MY MAW

Corresponds with "Votre mère avec moi sortait de la chapelle" (Dover score, page 62). Introduced by Carlotta Franzell and Elton J. Warren (Cindy Lou alternates).

I tol' your maw she's crazy to be frettin'—
But jus' de same
I up an' came.
I hopped a bus dis mornin',
Your maw loan me carfare,
An' what she didn' say
To sen' me on my way!
A t'ousand millyun messages she give me for
    you!
I cain' remimber all—'cepin' jus' one or two.
Joe, your maw say she awful lonesome,
But outside o' dat, she feelin' fine.
She say your cat is gittin' kittens—
It look like eight, an' maybe nine.
Den de nex' t'ing is hard to tell you—
I'se inbarrassed as I kin be.
She—she say: "When you see my Joey,
Give my Joey a kiss for me."

YOU TALK JUS' LIKE MY MAW

Lyric published in the show's souvenir program and in Hammerstein's anthology, *Lyrics*. Corresponds with "Ma mère je la vois!" (Dover score, page 64). Introduced by Luther Saxon and Napoleon Reed (Joe alternates) and Carlotta Franzell and Elton J. Warren (Cindy Lou alternates).

JOE: You talk jus' like my maw,
    You even walk jus' like my maw,
    An' I know why I'm stuck on you—
    It's 'cause I'm jus' like my paw!

CINDY LOU: I talk jus' like yo' maw,
    I even walk jus' like yo' maw,
    An' I kin see why you like me—
    'Cause you is like yo' paw,
    You's awful like yo' paw.
BOTH: Lemme tell you what de Lawd did:
    He made you [me] live nex' door,
    So we could fall in love
    De way my [yo'] paw an' maw did.
JOE: Is you my Cindy Lou?
CINDY LOU: I is yo' Cindy Lou,
    An' I belong to you.
JOE: An' I belong to you.
    I am yo' Joe, my Cindy Lou,
    An' I belong to you.
CINDY LOU: You is my Joe, I'se Cindy Lou
    An' I belong to you.

MURDER, MURDER

Corresponds to "Au secours! au secours!" (Dover score, page 77). Introduced by the female ensemble.

GIRLS: Murder! Murder!
    Golly, what a gal!
    Carmen! Carmen
    Got ahold of Sal.
    She got her by de throat,
    She tearin' out her eyeballs!
    Sal yellin' like a goat,
    Don' wanna lose her eyeballs.
    Wid Carmen tearin' out her hair
    An' Carmen startin' in to bite,
    Sal losin' all her clo'es,
    Look like a holy sight!
    Sal got a bloody nose!
    Oh, baby! What a fight!
    What a fight!
    What a fight!
    What a fight!

Early version

1ST GROUP: Hurry up! Hurry up!
    Git a man in here!
    Hurry up! Hurry up!
    Git an ingineer!
    Carmen is not to blame!
2ND GROUP: Who else to blame but Carmen?
1ST GROUP: She in de right jus' de same.
    Dat Sally done call her a name!
2ND GROUP: Don' pay no min' to dem.
1ST GROUP: Don' pay no min' to *dem*.

2ND GROUP: Dey's lyin' by de clock!
1ST GROUP: *Dey* tell a pack o' lies!

YOU AIN'T A POLICE'M

Alternate title: Finale of Scene 1. Corresponds to "Tra la-la-la-la . . . Coupe-moi, brûle-moi" (Dover score, page 89). Introduced by Muriel Smith and Muriel Rahn (Carmen alternates).

You ain' a police'm,
You ain' a police'm,
An' you c'n do nothin' to me.
You ain' a police'm,
You ain' a police'm,
Dee dum de di dee dum di dee!

You ain' a police'm,
You ain' a police'm,
An' you c'n do nothin' to me.
You ain' a police'm,
You ain' a police'm,
Dee dum de di dee dum di dee!

CARMEN JONES IS GOIN' TO JAIL

Uses the same melody as "Lift 'Em Up and Put 'Em Down." Covers the change from Scene 1 to Scene 2. Introduced by offstage ensemble.

Carmen Jones is goin' to jail,
Carmen Jones is goin' to jail,
Carmen's gotta stay in jail
Sit all day upon her tail.
Carmen Jones in goin' to jail,
Is goin' to jail, is goin' to jail,
Hooray!

DERE'S A CAFÉ ON DE CORNER

Published in the vocal selection. Lyric published in the show's souvenir program. The first three stanzas appear in Hammerstein's anthology, *Lyrics*. Corresponds to the Seguidilla, "Près des remparts de Séville" (Dover score, page 95). Introduced by Muriel Smith and Muriel Rahn (Carmen alternates) and Luther Saxon and Napoleon Reed (Joe alternates).

CARMEN: Dere's a café on de corner,
　　　　Run by my frien' Billy Pastor,
　　　　A spot where a man takes a
　　　　Lady when he wants to move faster!
　　　　Guess I'll go an' say hello to Pastor.
　　　　How kin a lady drink alone?
　　　　How kin a lady dance alone?
　　　　No lady kin romance alone—
　　　　I oughta have a sweetie pie!
　　　　De one I had, I give de air to—
　　　　I threw his toothbrush out de door!
　　　　Now dat I'm free, my heart is sighin'.
　　　　I'm off de hook an' lookin' for more!
　　　　Dozens o' fellers telephone me,
　　　　All axin' me to make a date.
　　　　I'm holdin' out for sumpin' special,
　　　　But I don' know how long I'll wait!

　　　　Where will I wind up?
　　　　Who'll I be true to?
　　　　Ain' made my mind up—
　　　　Waitin' for you to!
　　　　Whatcher say, brudder?
　　　　Whatcher say, boy?
　　　　Ain' it time dat we got away?

　　　　Dere's a café on de corner,
　　　　Run by my frien' Billy Pastor.
　　　　Dere's no way to know jus' how
　　　　Far I will go if I has ter!
　　　　Maybe dat's a promise,
　　　　Maybe it's a threat!

INTERLUDE*

JOE: [*spoken*] Go away! Don' you know you
　　　　don' dass talk to me?
CARMEN: Who say I talk to you?
　　　　I'm singin' to myself—
　　　　Jus' singin' to myself.
　　　　An' I'm thinkin' . . .
　　　　To think a little ain' 'gin' de law.
　　　　I'm thinkin' I oughta be wise
　　　　An' look in dat young sargint's eyes.
　　　　So dreamy,
　　　　So sweet an' dreamy,
　　　　He'll wanta free me—
　　　　An' see me later on!

───────────

* Corresponds to recitative "Je ne te parle pas" (Dover score, page 100).

But I don' wan' no sargint ef I kin have
　　　　you,
　　　　Your arms are stronger den his.
　　　　Ef you take me out,
　　　　Dere ain' nuffin' dat's nice I won' do.
　　　　I'll show you what a woman is!
JOE: Look here, is you tryin' to fool me?
　　　　Swear to Gawd you wouldn' fool me!
　　　　'Cause I'd free you,
　　　　If I could see you.
　　　　Say kin I see you,
　　　　An' out on de town we'll go?
CARMEN: Yes.
JOE: [*untying her*] We got a date den?
CARMEN: See you at ten!
JOE: Where do we meet?
CARMEN: At Billy Pastor's.
JOE: Okay!
CARMEN: Don' keep me waitin' at Pastor's.
JOE: I won' be late!
CARMEN: At ten o'clock sharp on de corner!
　　　　See dat you're right in dere pitchin'—
　　　　'Cause I ain' de kin' of a mare
　　　　Dat'll stan' widout hitchin'!
　　　　Tra-la-la-la-la-la-la-la-a.

───────────

BEAT OUT DAT RHYTHM ON A DRUM

Lyric published in Hammerstein's anthology, *Lyrics*. Corresponds to the Chanson bohème (Dover score, page 113). Introduced by June Hawkins (Frankie)* and ensemble. Early scripts instruct:

> Those who are not dancing keep time by humming a drumlike accompaniment. Those who don't hum, hit their glasses with forks or the table with their hands, or the floor with their feet. The dice are shaken in time and the peculiar click of the pinball machine is also *a tempo* . . . It takes the place of the castanets in the original *Carmen* and occurs wherever they were clicked in the orchestration of this song.

In the Broadway production, this number featured spectacular drumming by Cozy Cole.

───────────

VERSE 1

FRANKIE: I'll tell you why I wanna dance—
　　　　It ain' de sweetness in de music.

───────────

* *Sources vary whether the song was led by the character Frankie or Myrt, and whether the singer was June Hawkins or Jessica Russell.*

I like de sweetness in de music,
　　　　But dat ain' why I wanna dance!
　　　　It's sumpin' thumpin' in de bass,
　　　　A bumpin' underneath de music.
　　　　Dat bum-bum-bumpin' under music
　　　　Is all I need
　　　　To start me off.
　　　　I don' need nuthin' else to start me
　　　　off!

REFRAIN 1

FRANKIE: Beat out dat rhythm on a drum,
　　　　Beat out dat rhythm on a drum,
　　　　Beat out dat rhythm on a drum,
　　　　An' I don' need no tune at all.
ENSEMBLE: Beat me dat rhythm on a drum,
　　　　Beat me dat rhythm on a drum,
　　　　Beat me dat rhythm on a drum,
　　　　An' I don' need no tune at all!

VERSE 2

FRANKIE: I feel it beatin' in my bones,
　　　　It feel like twen'y millyun tomtoms.
　　　　I know dere's twen'y millyun
　　　　tomtoms
　　　　Beatin' way down deep inside my
　　　　bones!
　　　　I feel it beatin' in my heart,
　　　　An' den I get a kin' o' dream
　　　　An' in my dream it kin' o' seem
　　　　Dere's jus' one heart
　　　　In all de worl'—
　　　　Dere ain't but one big heart for all de
　　　　worl'!

REFRAIN 2

FRANKIE: Beat out dat rhythm on a drum,
　　　　Beat out dat rhythm on a drum,
　　　　Beat out dat rhythm on a drum,
　　　　Dere's one big heart for all de worl'!
ENSEMBLE: Beat me dat rhythm on a drum,
　　　　Beat me dat rhythm on a drum,
　　　　Beat me dat rhythm on a drum,
　　　　Dere's one big heart for all de worl'!

VERSE 3

FRANKIE: An' now dat heart is beatin' fast,
　　　　An' dat's a rhythm I kin dance to,
　　　　I'm mighty glad I got a chance to,
　　　　Wid dat one big heart dat's beatin'
　　　　fast!
　　　　Tomorrow mornin' let it rain,
　　　　Tomorrow mornin' let it pour,
　　　　Tonight we's in de groove together.

Ain' gonna worry 'bout stormy
    weather—
Gonna kick ol' trouble out de door!

REFRAIN 3

FRANKIE: Beat out ol' trouble on a drum,
Beat out ol' trouble on a drum,
Beat out ol' trouble on a drum,
An' kick his carcass through de
    door!

ENSEMBLE: Beat out dat rhythm on a drum,
Beat out dat rhythm on a drum,
Beat out dat rhythm on a drum,
An' kick ol' trouble out de door.
Kick 'im out de door!
Kick 'im out de door!
Kick 'im out de door!

STAN' UP AN' FIGHT

Published in the vocal selection. Lyric was published in the show's souvenir program and appears in Hammerstein's anthology, *Lyrics*. Corresponds with the Toreador Song, "Votre toast, je peaux vous le rendre" (Dover score, page 133.) Introduced by Glenn Bryant (Husky Miller) and ensemble.

VERSE 1

HUSKY: Thanks a lot!
I'm sure glad to be,
To be where I c'n see
So many frien's o' mine.
How've I been doin'?
How've I been doin'?
If you really wanta know
    de truth,
I'm doin' fine!
Seventeen
Decisions in a row,
An' only five on points—
De res' was all KO.
Jackson an' Johnson,
Murphy an' Bronson,
One by one dey come,
An' one by one, to
    dreamland dey go!
How's it done?
You ask me, how's it
    done?
I got a trainer man
Who taught me all I know.

Sure feels good to have
    him in my corner,
Hear his voice a-whisp'rin'
    low:
"Big boy, remember,
You mus' remember—

REFRAIN

HUSKY: Stan' up an' fight until
    you hear de bell,
Stan' toe to toe,
Trade blow fer blow!
Keep punchin' till you
    make yer punches
    tell—
Show dat crowd watcher
    know!
Until you hear dat bell,
Dat final bell,
Stan' up an' fight like
    hell!"

[Ensemble repeats refrain.]

VERSE 2

HUSKY: When you fight
Out in de open air
In a patch o' light
De ring looks small an'
    white.
Out in de blackness,
Out in de blackness,
You c'n feel a hun'erd
    thousan' eyes fillin' de
    night!
Cigarettes
Are blinkin' in de dark,
An' makin' polka dots
Aroun' de baseball park,
People are quiet—
Den dere's a riot!
Someone t'rows a punch
An' plants it right smack
    on de mark!
Somebody's hurt!
You kinda think it's you.
You hang across de
    ropes—
Da's all you want to do!
Den you look aroun' an'
    see your trainer's eyes,
Beggin' you to see it
    through,
Dey say, "Remember,
Big boy, remember—

REFRAIN

HUSKY AND ENSEMBLE: Stan' up an' fight until
    you hear de bell,
Stan' toe to toe,
Trade blow fer blow!
Keep punchin' till you
    make yer punches
    tell—
Show dat crowd watcher
    know!
Until you hear dat bell,
Dat final bell,
Stan' up an' fight like
    hell!"

WHIZZIN' AWAY ALONG DE TRACK

Corresponds to the Quintet, "Nous avons en tête une affaire" (Dover score, page 155). Introduced by Edward Lee Tyler (Rum), Dick Montgomery (Dink), Jessica Russell (Myrt), June Hawkins (Frankie), and Muriel Smith and Muriel Rahn (Carmen alternates).

RUM: Wanna make a trip on de
    crack Chicago train?
FRANKIE: Now dat's a trip you oughta
    make—
MYRT: It won' be hard for you to
    take!
RUM: Trab'l 'bout as fast as a
    Kansas hurricane!
DINK: It only takes a half a day
To be a thousand miles away!
CARMEN: Away!
DINK: Come on!
FRANKIE: Away.
RUM: Come on!
MYRT: Away.
RUM, DINK,
FRANKIE, AND MYRT: Come on away!
Dat streamline injine won'
    delay!
CARMEN: Away!
DINK: Come on!
RUM: Come on!
MYRT: Away!
RUM: Come on!
FRANKIE, MYRT,
AND CARMEN: Away!
RUM, DINK: Come on!

Dat streamline injine jus'
    cain' wait,
Dat streamline injine ain' no
    freight,
Dat streamline injine won'
    be late!

Whizzin' away along de
    track,
Clickety clack, clickety
    clack,
Leavin' de wind away in
    back,
Clickety clack, clickety
    clack,
Up a hill an' down a hill
An' out upon de plains
    again—

FRANKIE AND MYRT: Through a storm an' outa de
    storm
An' pretty soon it rains agin!

RUM AND DINK: You hit a curve an' sway
    aroun'—

CARMEN: An' den you pass anudder
    town!

RUM AND DINK: You curve de udder way
    aroun'—

FRANKIE AND MYRT: An' den you pass anudder
    town!

ALL FIVE: But you don' stop, 'cause
    yore Chicago boun'!
You keep on roarin' down de
    road
An' keep on,
Leavin' de wind away in
    back,
Clickety clack, clickety
    clack,
Up a hill an' down a hill
An' out upon de plains agin,
Through a storm an' outa de
    storm
An' pretty soon it rains agin!
Only takes half a day
To be a thousand miles away.
It only takes a half a day
To be a thousand miles away,
Away.

MYRT: Come on away!
THE OTHER FOUR: Chicago!
Chicago!
MYRT: Come on away,
Away, away.
THE OTHER FOUR: Come on away,
Come on away.
Hey!
MYRT: On a Chicago train!

THE OTHER FOUR: On a Chicago train!
RUM: Go pack your duds—
Ain't got much time.
MYRT: Carmen'll come.
FRANKIE: I knowed she would.
DINK: Well, let's git goin'.
CARMEN: Wait! Lemme say my say . . .
If you bustin' to go, den go,
But jus' count me out of de
    party.
Jus' count me out.
'Cause I ain' in!

RUM AND DINK: Oh, Carmen, honey, have a
    heart.
Carmen, you cain' run out
    on us.
Don' waste our time wid all
    dis fuss!

CARMEN: Don' wan' no part of it,
Don' wan' no part of it,
Don' wan' no part!

FRANKIE AND MYRT: Oh, Carmen, honey, have a
    heart.

CARMEN: Don' wan' no part of it,
Don' wan' no part of it,
Don' wan' no part!

DINK: What you got dat you like so
    much better den dis?
MYRT: Whaddye got?
MYRT AND RUM: Whaddye got?
MYRT, RUM, AND
FRANKIE: Whaddye got?
MYRT, DINK,
FRANKIE, AND RUM: Whaddye got?
CARMEN: If I tol' you you'd only
    laugh.
MYRT: Oh, no.
DINK: Not me.
FRANKIE: Go on.
RUM: Give out.
CARMEN: You got to promise not to
    laugh—
DINK AND MYRT: Okay.
FRANKIE AND RUM: Okay.
CARMEN: Dere's a man I'm crazy for!

[*The others laugh.*]

CARMEN: I'm in love—an' dat ain' no
    laugh.
DINK: Well, shut my mouf an' call
    me dumb!
RUM: An' beat me! I'm a kettle
    drum!
RUM AND DINK: De birdies in de trees are
    hummin',
"Carmen's in love,
Carmen's in love!"

Still we ask: Won' you come?
An' break your date, give de
    gate to your chum?
CARMEN: Anudder night I might've
    come
To raise some
    pandemomium,
But now de mockin' birds
    are hummin',
"Carmen's in love,
Carmen's in love!"
Leave me here wid my Joe,
An' take your train to
    Chicago an' go.
RUM: We gotta git you on dat train!
CARMEN: Some udder time.
RUM: What makes you think
    dere'll be anudder time?

RUM, DINK, FRANKIE
AND MYRT: What makes you think
    dere'll be anudder time?
RUM AND DINK: To git a trip—
FRANKIE AND MYRT: To git a trip—
RUM AND DINK: To Illinois—
FRANKIE AND MYRT: To Illinois—
RUM AND DINK: An' git it free?
FRANKIE AND MYRT: An' git it free?
CARMEN: Dat is a place dat I'd sure
    like to see . . .
ALL FIVE: Whizzin' away along de
    track,
Clickety clack, clickety
    clack,
Leavin' de wind away in
    back,
Clickety clack, clickety
    clack.
Up a hill an' down a hill
An' out upon de plains agin,
Through a storm an' outa de
    storm
An' pretty soon it rains agin!
Only takes a half a day
To be a thousand miles away.
It only takes a half a day
To be a thousand miles away,
Away.
MYRT: Come on away!
THE OTHER FOUR: Chicago!
Chicago!
MYRT: Come on away,
Away, away.
THE OTHER FOUR: Come on away,
Come on away.
Hey!
ALL: Whizzin' away along de track
Off to Chicago, Illinois!

SCENE FOR CARMEN AND JOE

Corresponds to "La, la, la" (Dover score, page 190). Introduced by Muriel Smith and Muriel Rahn (Carmen alternates) and Luther Saxon and Napoleon Reed (Joe alternates).

CARMEN: [*spoken in rhythm, countermetrically to the music*] Thinkin' 'bout you all de time
While you was away from me.
I been dreamin' 'bout tonight,
Wonderin' if you would be
Feelin' half as lovin'
As your Carmen feels for you!

[JOE *tells* CARMEN *it took an hour to get there.*]

CARMEN: [*improvising a little chant, spoken, not sung, to the melody*] Poor chile! Never mind—
Carmen take him home wid her,
Carmen will unlace his shoes
An' send him off to sleep.

[JOE *tells* CARMEN *he must leave right away.*]

CARMEN: Boy! Ef dis ain' one on Carmen!*
Boy! Ain' dis a joke on Carmen!
I t'row myse'f about
An' dislocate a hip
An' wear my girdle out
To in'ertain a drip!
I wuz gay! I wuz bright!
An' oh, what pretty plans
I cooked up fo' tonight!
Go on an' git your bus!
But dat's de end of us!

DIS FLOWER

Published in the vocal selection. Lyric published in the show's souvenir program and also in Hammerstein's anthology, *Lyrics.* Corresponds to the Flower Song, "La fleur que tu m'avais jetée" (Dover score, page 200). Introduced by Luther Saxon and Napoleon Reed (Joe alternates).

----

* *Corresponds to "Ah! j'étais vraiment trop bête," (Dover score, page 194).*

Dis flower dat you threw my way
Has been my frien' by night an' day.
I saw it fade an' lose its bloom,
But still it kept a sweet perfume.
In my cell, through ev'ry darkened hour,
On my lonely eyes lay dis flower,
An' so I'd sleep de whole night through
An' dream of you, an' dream of you!
Den I'd wake up, wid no one near me,
An' talk fo' de jail walls to hear me—
"She ain' de bes',
Dere all de same!
Like all de res'
She jus' a dame!"
Den I tol' myse'f I wuz ravin',
Dere wuz jes' one t'ing I wuz cravin'—
It wuzn' food,
It wuzn' dough!
I guess you know
Dat it wuz you!
I only saw you once—
Once wouldn' do!
I don' know anythin' about you;
I don' know much about a shinin' star.
Jus' know de worl' is dark widout you—
Das all I know.
I only wan' you as you are . . .
Das how I love you.

IF YOU WOULD ONLY COME AWAY

Corresponds to "Là-bas, là-bas dans la montagne" (Dover score, page 205). Introduced by Muriel Smith and Muriel Rahn (Carmen alternates).

CARMEN: If you would only come away,
If you would hide away wid me,
You would be where you wanna be,
Wrapped in your Carmen's arms from day to day—
Come away, Joey. Hide away . . .

[*Dialogue.*]

CARMEN: I don' wan' you bustin' yore arm,
Totin' a army rifle, an' dat is a fac'!
Yore arm musn' come to no harm—
Pore little Carmen needs it to hold up her back.
Couldn' we have oursel's a time?
Nobody dere but you an' me—

You an' me, honey, would dat be bad?
All alone like Romeo an' Venus!

ACT ONE FINALE

Corresponds with "Le ciel ouvert, la vie errante" (Dover score, page 228). Introduced by Muriel Smith and Muriel Rahn (Carmen alternates) and ensemble.

CARMEN: Joey, it's time for you to go.
THE GANG AT PASTOR'S: Goodbye, now!
Lots o' good luck,
Lootenant Joe!
JOE: Goodbye, now!
THE GANG AT PASTOR'S: When you are flyin' far away,
All o' your friends'll hope an' pray,
By night an' day we'll pray!
So go an' do de bes' you can,
'Cause da's as good as any man can do!
Jus' go an' do de bes' you know,
An' we'll be proud, proud of our Joe!

DE CARDS DON' LIE and DAT OL' BOY

Corresponds to the Card Scene, "Mêlons! Coupons!" (Dover score, page 262). Introduced by June Hawkins (Frankie), Jessica Russell (Myrt), Muriel Smith and Muriel Rahn (Carmen alternates), and members of the female ensemble.

De Cards Don' Lie

MYRT: Cut dem.
GROUP OF GIRLS AND FRANKIE: Cut dem!
GIRL: Seven!
FRANKIE: Seven!
MYRT: Da's quite a card!
FRANKIE: Da's quite a card.
GIRL: D'you mean good or bad?

OTHER GIRLS: Is that good or bad?
MYRT: Quiet, please!
GIRLS AND FRANKIE: Quiet, please!
FRANKIE AND MYRT: Will dis gal see
A bright an' happy
fewcher?
Or will she be
A good-f'-nuffin'
moocher?
MYRT: Come on, you
cards, an' tell
her true!
GIRL: Come on, you
cards, and tell
me true!
FRANKIE: An' tell her how
she gonna do!
GIRL: An' tell me how
I'm going to do!
FRANKIE AND MYRT: F'good or bad!
F'high or low!
Come on, you
cards, an' let 'er
know
Whatever way de
win' will blow!
MYRT: All set?
GIRL: All set!
FRANKIE: F'sho?
THREE GIRLS, MYRT, AND
FRANKIE: Let's go!

Dat Ol' Boy

CARMEN: Le's see what dey say about me.*
De nine o' spades!
De nine!
Dere he is—de ol' boy!
Plain as kin be!
Death got his han' on me . . .

It ain' no use to run away f'um dat ol'
boy
Ef he is chasin' you.
It's bes' to stan' right up an' look him in
de face
When he is facin' you.
Y'gotta be puhpared to go wid dat ol'
boy,
No matter what de time.
So I won' fill my pretty eyes wid salty
tears—
Cuz I ain' got de time!
I'm gonna run out ev'ry secon' I got lef'

---

* Lyric published in Hammerstein's anthology, Lyrics.
Corresponds to "Voyons, que j'essaie à mon tour"
(Dover score, page 271).

Before he t'rows me down.
I'm gonna laugh an' sing an' use up all
my bref
Before he mows me down!
While I kin fly aroun' I'll do my flyin'
high!
I'm gonna keep on livin'
Up to de day I die.
De nine! . . . Hello! Ol' boy—hello!

De Cards Don' Lie continues

MYRT AND FRANKIE: De cards kin see
De lady's got a fewcher,
And she won't be
A good-f'-nuffin'
moocher.
FRANKIE: De cards'll never lie to
you.
CARMEN: De nine.
MYRT: De cards'll never lie to
you.
FRANKIE: Dey tell you how you
gonna do!
CARMEN: Hello!
ALL THREE: Dey tell you how you
gonna do!
De cards don' lie.
MYRT AND FRANKIE: De cards don' lie!
De cards'll tell a
fortune
That'll fit a lady like a
glove.
CARMEN: De cards don' lie,
De cards don' lie.
FRANKIE: Here's money!
MYRT: An' love!
CARMEN: De cards don' lie.
FRANKIE: More money!
MYRT: More love!
CARMEN: De cards don' lie!
FRANKIE: Da's money!
FRANKIE AND MYRT: Da's love!
FRANKIE, MYRT, CARMEN,
AND GIRLS: The cards don't lie!

PONCHO DE PANTHER
FROM BRAZIL

Corresponds with "Morceau d'ensemble" (Dover score,
page 281). Introduced by June Hawkins (Frankie), Jessica Russell (Myrt), Glenn Bryant (Husky Miller),
Edward Lee Tyler (Rum), and ensemble.

GIRLS AND MEN: Poncho, de panther from Brazil!
What a man!
A man would be a fool to fool wid
Poncho, de punchin' cavalero,
De champ o' Rio de Janeiro!
MEN: [indicating HUSKY] He's from de
north—
GIRLS: An' his name is Husky Miller!
MEN: [indicating PONCHO] He's from de
south—
GIRLS: He's a Latin killer-diller!
ALL: Dere shakin' han's,
An' dey wan' de worl' to know
Dere shakin' han's
'Cross de Gulf o' Mexico!
HUSKY AND ALL: Poncho, you panther from
Brazil,
Welcome here!
Come here an' have yourself a
party!
Poncho, yo're welcome in
Chicago—
You can unpack your brush an'
comb,
Make yourself at home!
Come an' make Chicago your
home!

MY JOE

Lyric published in the show's souvenir program and
in Hammerstein's anthology, Lyrics. Corresponds to
"C'est des contrebandiers le refuge ordinaire . . . Je dis,
que rien ne m'épouvante" (Dover score, page 299).
Introduced by Carlotta Franzell and Elton J. Warren
(Cindy Lou alternates).

How kin I love a man when I know he don' wan'
me?
He ain' been good. He ain' been kind.
He gimme up for a ol' roadside woman—
But I cain' drive him from my mind!

My Joe,
He wuz always my Joe.
Dere wuz no one but me—
Joe said dere never could be.
We wuz in love
An' I reckon we showed it—
F'um de way people talked,
Reckon ev'ryone knowed it.
Kids on de street where we'd go,
Useter yell at us:
"Cindy Lou belongs to Joe!"
Lawd! Oh, Lawd, y'know dat dat wuz true,
An' Joey belonged to Cindy Lou.

I is skeered.
Oh, Lawd! I is skeered!
I'se like a leaf dat los' her tree.
I'se alone.
Oh, Lawd! I'se alone!
He got hisse'f anudder woman.
Now she got his arms all aroun' her—
No, Lawd! I cain' believe it's so.
No! No! Don' yer let her keep my Joe.
Make him t'row her back where he foun' her!
Joe! Y'said dat both your arms wuz mine—
Remember? Y'said your arms wuz mine.

I'se yo' gal,
I wuz always yo' gal,
Dere wuz no one but me—
You said dere never could be.
We wuz in love
An' I reckon we showed it—
F'um de way people talked,
Reckon ev'ryone knowed it.
Kids on de street where we'd go,
Useter yell at us:
"Cindy Lou belongs to Joe!"
Lawd! Oh, Lawd, look down an' try to see
How you kin make Joe come home to me.

Oh, Lawd, look down.
Lead my Joe
Off de road
Where he strayin'.
Oh, tell my man
Where to go—
Oh, Lawd, I'se callin' on you!

ACT TWO, SCENE 1 FINALE

Corresponds to "Là bas est la chaumière" (Dover score, page 323). Introduced by Carlotta Franzell and Elton J. Warren (Cindy Lou alternates), Muriel Smith and Muriel Rahn (Carmen alternates), Luther Saxon and Napoleon Reed (Joe alternates), June Hawkins (Frankie), Jessica Russell (Myrt), and Edward Lee Tyler (Rum).

CINDY LOU: Your maw is lonesome
an' worried
Cuz you stay away so
long—
She cain' sleep in de
night now
An' she don' feel none
too strong.

So she tol' me to come
an' find you
An' to say she is sick an'
blue.
She tol' me to remind
you
Dat you's all she got—
All she got in de world
is you!

CARMEN: You oughta go an' see
your maw,
You better go an' see
your maw.

JOE: You would like dat, I
reckon!

CARMEN: Go wid de lady now!

JOE: You would like dat, I
reckon!
You would like to git me
away—
Dat'd leave you free to
play!
No! No you don't!
Y'know you are tied to
me,
An' y'know you'll never
git away.
Yore de shore an' I'm
de sea,
By my side yore tied to
stay!
Where you go I'm goin'
too,
An' when you die I'm
gonna die wid you!

FRANKIE, MYRT, AND RUM: Leave de gal an' go
away—
She got a life of her
own.
Leave de gal an' go
away!
Go away! Leave her
alone!

CINDY LOU: Oh, lissen, Joe, lemme
say
A word for yore ear
alone—
Cuz I gotta say what I
come to say,
An' it must be known!

[CINDY LOU *tells them* JOE's *mother is dying.* CARMEN *tells* JOE *to go and not to return.*]

JOE: [*to* CARMEN]* No!

—————
*Corresponds to "Ah! je te tiens" (Dover Score,
page 329).

Where I go you go wid
me,
An' you know dat's de
way it's gotta be,
Down to hell or up to
heav'n—
Down rivers an' 'cross
de sea—
Where you go I'm goin'
too,
An' when you die I'm
gonna die wid you!

—————

GIT YER PROGRAM FOR DE BIG FIGHT

Corresponds to the opening of Act Four, "À deux cuartos!" (Dover score, page 338). Introduced by the ensemble.

—————

BASSES: Git a program for de big
fight!

BASSES AND TENORS: Git yer program for de big
fight!

ALL: Git a weenie on a roll, a
Glass of ice-col' Coca-Cola!

HIGH SCHOOL GIRLS: Oh, baby! What a dreamy
night!
Gonna see Husky Miller
fight!
What it cost to come to de
fight?

BOYS: Four bucks!

GIRLS: Four bucks!

BOYS: Da's what dey rolled me!

MEN: I bet dem little debutants
Got dere name on dere
underpants!

OTHER MEN: Some o' dem don' wear
underpants!

DEAF OLD MAN: What's dat?

MEN: Dat's what a feller told me!

TENORS: Git a cushion for de lady!
Git a cushion for de lady!
She will see more of de
fight,
She won' be sore when de
fight's over!

TENORS AND SOPRANOS: Who wants to buy a
pretty fan?
Got a dime for a pretty fan?
Gittin' pow'ful hot in de
stan'!

MEN: What's dat?

GIRLS: Dat's what a feller sold me!

[*Dialogue as* PONCHO *passes through the crowd*.]

ALL: Wait'll Husky Miller hits
  him!
  Wait'll Husky Miller hits
  him!
  He'll knock dat big rhumba
  man
  Clear back to Rio de
  Jan-ei-ro!

POLICE: Move along, dere!
  Move along, dere!
  Move along, dere!
  Git on your way!

DAT'S OUR MAN

Corresponds to "Les voici!" (Dover score, page 347).
Introduced by the ensemble.

CHILDREN: Lemme see! Lemme see!
  I wanna see Husky!

ALL: Husky! Husky!

BASSES: Dere he is!

TENORS: Dere he is!

SOPRANOS: Dere he is!

SOPRANOS AND TENORS: De kid himself!
  Well, looka dat Husky!

ALL: Dat's our man, de man
  wid de wallop,
  Hotter dan a firecracker!
  When he land dat ol'
  belly whacker—
  Kayo! Kayo! Kayo!
  Attaboy, Husky, make
  wid de wallop!
  Win dat dough an' den
  you can doll up,
  Wid a di'mon big as a
  scallop!
  Attaboy!
  Attaboy!
  Attaboy!

CHILDREN: When I'm big an' strong
  as Husky,
  I'll go home an' lick my
  pa!
  I will make a million
  dollars
  An' I'll give it all to Ma!

POLICE: Move on, move on!
  Move on, move on!

ALL: Cheese it, kids, here
  come de cops!

POLICE: Move on, move on!
  Move on, move on!

ALL: [*derisively*] Yah, yah, yah,
  yah!
  Yah, yah, yah, yah!

[*Police exit. Dancing girls primp.*]

MEN: Git a load of all dem
  tomayters!
  Linin' up so dey can
  ketch his eye!
  No hope! No soap!
  He's got a woman—
  Bait yer hook fer fish you
  can fry!

GIRLS: Go 'way! Go 'way f'um
  me, go 'way!
  I gotta have a man wid
  shoulders!
  Go 'way, go 'way, go 'way!
  Give me de man de
  people come to see—
  You's only ticket holders!

MEN: Okay! Okay!

CHILDREN: Go 'way!

GIRLS: When he comes by
  I'm gonna try!
  When he comes by
  I'm gonna try!

MEN: Go fish fer fish
  Dat you can fry!

SOPRANOS: Dere jus' gittin' outa de
  taxi!
  Dere jus' gittin' outa de
  taxi!

TENORS: Dere headin' right dis way!

SOPRANOS: Dere headin' right dis way!

BASSES: Dere headin' right dis way!

SOPRANOS: He's got a gal!
  He's de only man I would
  die for—
  But, of course, he *would*
  have a gal!

BASSES: Come on, now!

SOPRANOS: Come on, now!

TENORS: Togedder!

SOPRANOS: Togedder!

[HUSKY *and* CARMEN *enter, followed by* RUM, DINK,
MYRT, *and* FRANKIE.]

SOPRANOS: Husky Miller!

ALL: Husky Miller!

Stan' up an' fight until
  you hear de bell,
Stan' toe to toe,
Trade blow for blow!
Keep punchin' till you
  make yer punches
  tell,
Show dat crowd whatcher
  know!
Until you hear dat bell,
Dat final bell,
Stan' up an—

Dat's our man, de man
  wid de wallop,
Hotter dan a firecracker!
When y' lan' dat ol' belly
  whacker—
Kayo! Kayo! Kayo!
Attaboy, Husky, make
  wid de wallop!
Win dat dough an' den
  you can doll up,
Wid a di'mon big as a
  scallop!

SOPRANOS: Attababy!

BASSES: Attababy!

TENORS: Attababy!

ALL: Hey!
  Husky Miller!
  Husky Miller!

BASSES: Husky—

TENORS AND SOPRANOS: Miller!

BASSES: Husky—

TENORS AND SOPRANOS: Miller!

BASSES: Husky—

TENORS AND SOPRANOS: Husky—

ALL: Miller!

SCENE FOR JOE AND CARMEN

Corresponds to "Je ne menace pas" (Dover score, page
374). Introduced by Luther Saxon and Napoleon Reed
(Joe alternates) and Muriel Smith and Muriel Rahn (Carmen alternates).

JOE: But all I want to do is love
  you like I useter,
  To hol' your han' in my
  han'
  An' feel your heart nex' to
  my heart.

Cain' we begin again?
Couldn' we start all over?
Couldn' we begin again?

CARMEN: If you wanna start a fire
where a fire was before,
De coal you burn mus' be
new coal!
Our flame is out—cold as de
snow!
We had oursel's some fun,
didn' we?
An' now it's done!

JOE: But where can I put my
mem'ries?
Dey got no sea to drown in.
De little things
Dat useter make us laugh
When we was clownin',
An' all de things we'd say
or do
Are all part of me an' you . . .

CARMEN: Joe, you is makin' it tough
now,
Fer y'self, de same as fer me.
Joe! Ain' you heard me say
enough, now?
No! No! NO!
What useter be ain' no
mo'!

JOE: But where kin y'put your
mem'ries?
Dey got no sea to drown
in.
De little t'ings
Dat useter make us laugh
When we was clownin',
An' all de things we'd say
or do
Are all part of me an' you!
Do you fergit
How I useter love you?
No one but Joe
Ever loved y'so good.
Le's go away an' begin our
life all over,
Carmen all alone wid Joe.

CARMEN: Oh, why mus' you keep on
poun'in',
Poun'in out de same ol'
tune?
Why should I say
I love yer,
When I don' no mo'?
No, I don' no mo'!
Don' be dat way!
Give up what you don' own
no mo'!

JOE: Don' y't'ink dere's a chance?
Only say dat y'do!

CARMEN: No . . . dat wouldn't be true!
Ain' gonna lie! Ain' gonna
lie!
I look at life straight in de
eye!

OFFSTAGE ENSEMBLE: Dat's our man, de man wid
de wallop,
Hotter dan a firecracker!
When he lands dat ol' belly
whacker—
Kayo! Kayo! Kayo!
Attaboy, Husky, make wid
de wallop!
Win dat dough an' den you
can doll up,
Wid a di'mon' big as a
scallop!
Kayo! Kayo! Kayo!
Let's go!

[CARMEN *starts to leave.* JOE *grabs her.*]

CARMEN: I love him!
Why cain' you get dat
through yer head?
Dat's de man I want.
I love him!

OFFSTAGE ENSEMBLE: Dat's our man, de man wid
de wallop,
Hotter dan a firecracker!
When he lands dat ol' belly
whacker—
Kayo! Kayo! Kayo!
Attaboy, Husky, make wid
de wallop!
Win dat dough!
Come on, let 'er go!

[JOE *stabs* CARMEN.]

OFFSTAGE ENSEMBLE: Stan' up an' fight until you
hear de bell.
Stan' toe to toe,
Trade blow for blow!
Keep punchin' till you make
yer punches tell,
Show dat crowd what cher
know!
Until you hear dat bell,
Dat final bell,
Jus' fight
Like hell!

JOE: String me high on a tree
So dat I soon will be
Wid my darlin', my baby—
My Carmen!

CUT AND UNUSED SONGS

Early drafts of *Carmen Jones* contain quite a few lyrics that were cut from the final production script. Certain big songs got new lyrics because of a shift in characterization. When the show began rehearsals in September 1943, the opera's toreador Escamillo had been updated to Husky Miller the boxer. But as late as May 1943, Hammerstein had planned for the character to be a Cab Calloway–style bandleader called Hepcat Miller. The Hepcat lyrics appear in this section, along with lyrics for several dropped musical passages and recitatives. It appears that Hammerstein devised words for almost the entire opera, but decided that some moments were better served by dialogue than by singing.

OH BOY, OH BOY, OH BOY

Not used. Corresponds to the Act One opening sequence "Regardez donc cette petite" (Dover score, page 10).

MORRELL: Oh boy, oh boy, oh boy, oh boy!
It look like a package of love.
I'se right.
[*To men*] Eyes right.
Fo' de honor ob de army!

MEN: Give her dat stuff dere's plenty of.

MORRELL: Sweetheart, you's lookin' lonesome.

CINDY LOU: Me? I wan' a ingineer.

MORRELL: Ingineer? Dat's me!

CINDY LOU: You ain' de ingineer I'm lookin fo'.
You ain' Joe.
Does you know my Joe?

MORRELL: Does we know a ingineer called Joe?

CINDY LOU: He's tall an' good-lookin' as he kin be.

MORRELL: Dere ain' no Joe like dat in dis yere
company!

CINDY LOU: Am I in de wrong place?

MORRELL: No. You's in de right place,
Right in the right place!
Yo' Joe will come—
Jus' stick aroun',
Don' make no fuss.
Ef he ain' foun',
Den you got us!

UH-UN, MN-HMN

Not used. Corresponds to "Chez vous? Chez nous!" (Dover score, page 15).

CINDY LOU: [nodding no] Uh-un.
MORRELL AND MEN: [nodding yes] Mn-hmn!
CINDY LOU: Uh-un.
MORRELL AND MEN: Mn-hmn!
CINDY LOU: I tol' you no!
I mus' go.
I mus' look fo' Joe!
MORRELL: I got ten good women,
sugar—
Got 'em piled up in a heap.
You would make eleven,
sugar—
But yore de only one I'd keep.
CINDY LOU: I's got one man
All my own.
An' you got ten good gals,
So you won' be alone!

WHAT A NERVE!

Not used. Corresponds to "Quels regards! Quelle effronteire!" (Dover score, page 58).

JOE: What a nerve! Who she think dat she is?
Throwin' a rose right at my heart.
I suppose she think she is smart.
Nuttin' wrong wid de rose.
It don' mean any harm.
But dat Carmen—
Dat's a red-hot bundle.
Dey don' grow like dat on a farm!

YO' MAW'S OKAY

Not used. Corresponds with "J'apporte de sa part" (Dover score, page 60).

CINDY LOU: Yo' maw's okay, an here's
A letter dat she writ you.
I ain't read it.
JOE: Thanks a million!

CINDY LOU: Yo' maw is in a stew—
She skeered some bad luck gonna fall
on you.
She say—
JOE: She say?
CINDY LOU: She say—
It's kin' o' spooky
De way yo' maw kin always smell
De mis'ry comin' befo' it comes!
Last Satiddy she foun'
Two buzzard fedders on de groun'!
JOE: Ol' superstishun!
Make me sorer den a pup.
CINDY LOU: She look in de cup
Fo' what de tea leaves say—
An' dey say sumpin' up!

SALLY TOOK A CIGARETTE

Not used. Corresponds with "La Manuelita disait" (Dover score, page 79).

1ST GROUP OF GIRLS: Sally took a cigarette
An' threw it right in her eye!
Cross my heart an' hope to
die,
Cross my heart an' hope to
die!
2ND GROUP: Carmen got ahold o' Sal
An' wid a aim dat wuz fine
Kick her right in her behin',
Kick her right in her behin!
1ST GROUP: Sally comin' back fo' more
An' say Carmen is a trollop!
Carmen give her such a
wallop
She lan' Sally on de floor!
2ND GROUP: Den dey started in fo' fair,
Tearin' out each udder's
hair,
Ev'rybody jinin' in—
Sargin' Brown, it wuz a sin!
ALL: It wuz a shame an' a sin—
Ev'rybody jinin' in!

IS DAT TRUE?

Not used. Corresponds to "Non, rien! j'obéis à mes chefs" (Dover score, page 93). In the "Hepcat" draft,

Hammerstein noted: "Following lines are written in meter to indicated music, but may or may not be sung."

JOE: Is dat true? Well, ain' dat jus' too bad!
CARMEN: Lissen, Joe. Be a sport.
Ef you put me inside o' de jail,
How kin I be nice to you?
An' I could be awful nice, Joe.
JOE: Quit it, now!
CARMEN: Yes, I could.
Dat flower I threw at yo' heart . . . dat's
me.
I see you kep' de flower.
Li'l Carmen inside o' yo' coat!
You's in her power.
JOE: Lay off o' me, now!
Dis kin' o' stuff
Ain' gonna git you anywheres.

GIT HEP, GIT HEP WID DE HEPCAT

Not used. Corresponds to "Vivat! vivat le Toréro!" (Dover score, page 128.).

MEN: [from offstage] Git hep, git hep
wid de Hepcat,
Fo' he's a killer diller.
Git hep, git hep wid de Hepcat,
Git hep wid Hepcat Miller!
Hep, hep, hep!
Hep, hep!
Hep, hep!
SERGEANT BROWN: [to BILLY PASTOR] You cain'
close yo' place up right
now—
You gotta keep it open fo' de
Hepcat,
Hepcat Miller an' all his ban'
Now ain' dat sumpin'—
He got de whole blame ban',
He got de whole blame ban'!
ALL: Hooray fo' Hepcat Miller,
Fo' he's a killer diller.
Git hep wid Hepcat Miller,
Hep, hep fo' Hepcat Miller!
Hooray! Hooray! Hooray!
Hooray!

OPEN DE DOOR, DE BAN' IS GETTIN' HOT

Not used. Hammerstein's "Hepcat" draft contains this earlier lyric for Bizet's "Toreador Song." It was replaced by "Stand Up and Fight."

VERSE 1

HEPCAT: T'anks a lot!
I'm sure glad to be
Back in Carolin',
Back home in Carolin'.
I been to Utah,
I been to Texas—
Ain' no state dat kin tetch
Dis ol' state o' mine!
I play
In ev'ry clip cafe
Where white folks pay
Dere money down.
Ermines an' sables
Choke up de tables
When de big news gits aroun'
Dat Hep is back in de town!
On de openin' night,
De gala openin' night,
De town is dere—
Dere ain' a chair to spare!
Firs' we play a sweet an' quiet teaser.
Den we start warmin' up de air,
An' den we burn 'em!
An how! An' how!

REFRAIN 1

Open de door, de ban' is gettin' hot!
Open de door, open de door!
When I give out wid ev'ryt'ing I got,
You know what music's for!
I swing yo' sweetie's feet
Right off de floor,
An' make her cry fo' more!

[HEPCAT conducts as ensemble repeats refrain.]

VERSE 2

HEPCAT: When I play
De fellers bring dere gals.
You see all kin's o' gals
Sashayin' roun de hall . . .
Cuties an' grannies
Wavin' dere fannies
Like a lot o' apples on a bough—
Waitin' to fall!

Lights are low,
De songs we sing are low,
An' ev'ryt'ing is low—
Excep' de cover charge.
Fo' bucks fo' chicken!
Oh, what a lickin'
You mus' take to get a break wid Rose,
Betty, or Marge!
But what's de odds?
What diff'runce what you pay,
Ef I has got a way to make yo' mama
warm?
What's de odds,
Ef I kin make de music
Dat kin make yo' mama warm?
I make de music
Dat makes her warm!

REFRAIN 2

Open de door, de ban' is gettin' hot!
Open de door, open de door!
When I give out wid ev'ryt'ing I got,
You know what music's for!
Yo' sweetie kisses you
Out on dat floor,
An' den she cries fo' more!

C'M YERE TOOTS

Not used. Corresponds to "La belle, un mot" (Dover score, page 151).

HEPCAT: C'm yere, Toots! Don't go,
We gotta git acquainted.
I'd like to know yo' name—
An' o' course you know mine.
CARMEN: Miss Jones—Miss Carmen Jones . . .
My frien's all call me Carmen.
HEPCAT: My heartbeat f'um now on is Carmen!
CARMEN: Hepcat, you is got de cornies' line!
HEPCAT: I'll bide my time, my chickabiddy,
An' maybe bye 'm bye
You an' I
Kin go stiddy.
CARMEN: You may get sick o' waitin',
I is all dated up.
HEPCAT: I met lots o' chicks in my time who acted
hard to git.
CARMEN: I ain' actin' at all!
HEPCAT: Babe, I never failed yet.

YOU GIT YOUR CUT NO MATTER WHAT

Not used. Hammerstein's "Hepcat" draft contains this earlier setting of the "Gypsy Quintet." In that version, Dink—then called Dinky—and Rum were bootleggers. It was replaced by "Whizzing Away Along the Track."

DINKY: Would you like to
make you some
dough-re-mi?
FRANKIE: I need some dough
an' nuthin' but!
MYRT: I need some mo' an'
nuthin' but!
DINKY: Gonna be as easy as
A-B-C—
Come in with us an'
git yo' cut.
RUM: Ef you come in, you
git a cut!
CARMEN: A cut?
DINKY: A cut!
FRANKIE: A cut?
RUM: A cut!
MYRT: A cut?
RUM AND DINKY: A cut!
CARMEN, FRANKIE, AND MYRT: A cut?
Of all you make
RUM AND DINKY: Of all we make
You take a cut!
You git yo' share no
matter what.
We need yo' help a
awful lot!
'Cause what we need
Is what you got!

How d'ye work a
shady deal?
Bring in a dame,
bring in a dame!
How d'ye trim a
stingy heel?
Bring in a dame,
bring in a dame!
When yo' scheme is
on de beam
An' needs a push to
put it t'rough—
CARMEN, FRANKIE, AND MYRT: Git a fluff wid
plen'y o' stuff
An' she will put it
t'rough for you!

RUM AND DINKY: Do what you do the
way you do—

CARMEN, FRANKIE, AND MYRT: We do the way you
say to do—

RUM AND DINKY: We'll tell you how to
do it, too.

CARMEN, FRANKIE, AND MYRT: I wish I knew, I wish
I knew!

RUM AND DINKY: We'll soon tell you
Just how you do it
too.

CARMEN, FRANKIE, AND MYRT: We wish we knew
Just how to do it
too.

[*Hammerstein's early draft says: "They go into a second refrain here, the vocal parts of which are too complicated and long to include in this script."*]

DINKY: [*after refrain*] Is dat
a deal? Is we all
set?

FRANKIE: When do we start?

MYRT: You name de time.

DINKY: Now is de time,
kids!

CARMEN: Wait! Lemme say
my say!
Ef you bustin' to
go, den go—
But jus' count me
out of de party,
Jus' count me out,
Cuz I ain' in!

RUM AND DINKY: Oh, Carmen, honey,
have a heart!
Carmen, it ain' like
you to fuss!
Carmen, you cain'
run out on us!

CARMEN: Don' wan' no part!
Don' wan' no part!
Don' wan' no part!
Don' wan' no part!

FRANKIE AND MYRT: Oh, Carmen, honey,
have a heart!

CARMEN: Don' wan' no part!
Don' wan' no part!
Don' wan' no part!

DINKY: What you got to git
off yo' ches'?
What's on yo' ches'?

MYRT: Git it off!

MYRT AND RUM: Git it off!

MYRT, RUM, AND FRANKIE: Git it off!

MYRT, RUM, FRANKIE AND
DINKY: Git it off!

CARMEN: But ef I tol' you
what, you'd
laugh!

DINKY: Oh, no.

RUM: Not me.

FRANKIE: Go on.

MYRT: Give out!

CARMEN: You gotta promise
not to laugh!

DINKY AND RUM: Okay.

FRANKIE, AND MYRT: Okay.

CARMEN: Dere's a man I's
crazy for!

[FRANKIE, MYRT, RUM, *and* DINKY *laugh for four measures.*]

FRANKIE AND MYRT: She got a man she
crazy fo'!

FRANKIE, MYRT, RUM, AND
DINKY: What a gal! What a
laugh!

FRANKIE: What a laugh!

DINKY: Come on, baby. Be
yo'se'f!

CARMEN: I'se in love—an' dat
ain' no laugh!

RUM AND DINKY: Well shut my mouf
an' call me
dumb!
Our little frien' has
foun' a chum!
De birdies in de
trees are
hummin',
"Carmen's in love,
Carmen's in
love!"
Still we ask:
Won' you come?
An' break yo' date,
Give de gate
To yo' chum!

CARMEN: Anudder night I
might've come
To raise some
pandemomium.
But now de
mockin'birds 'r
hummin',
"Carmen's in love,
Carmen's in
love."
Ef I go
Out to slum,
I might be late
Fo' my date

Wid' my chum!

DINKY: You say it like it
really so!

CARMEN: I'll say it's so!

FRANKIE, MYRT, RUM, AND
DINKY: You passin' up a
hefty wad o'
dough!
You passin' up a
hefty wad o'
dough!

RUM AND DINKY: You gotta go,
Carmen. You
gotta go.
We got no chance.

FRANKIE AND MYRT: You passin' up—

RUM AND DINKY: A hefty wad—

FRANKIE AND MYRT: O' heaby dough—

RUM AND DINKY: Unless yo go.

FRANKIE AND MYRT: Y'gotta go!

CARMEN: But why an' how yo'
gotta use me
now?

[*"From here go into final refrain."*]

WHO DAT? WHO DERE?

Not used. Corresponds to "Halte-là! Qui va là? Dragon d'Alcala" (Dover score, page 186).

JOE: [*offstage*] Who dat? Who dere?
Is yer frien' or foe?
Gimme de coun'ersign
So es I kin know.
I's a frien' an' I is on my way to see my
baby,
Gotta see my baby!
Oh, ef dat's de case, pass across de line.
Ef yer love yo' baby, dat's de bes'
coun'ersign!
Pass across de line,
Pass across de line!

FRANKIE: Carmen, dat's a man!

MYRT: Dat's a hunk o' man!

DINKY: How 'bout bringin' him up into de hills?

RUM: Reckon we kin use him.

CARMEN: What he know 'bout stills?

DINKY: You could teach him good.

CARMEN: Yeah, I guess I could.

IS DAT YOU, JOE?

Not used. Corresponds to "Enfin c'est toi!" (Dover score, page 187).

CARMEN: Is dat you, Joe?
JOE: Dat's me!
CARMEN: I'se glad dey let you out.
JOE: I ain't so sad myse'f.
CARMEN: Is you sore?
JOE: Sore at who?
    I got put in fo' you,
    I'd git put in again, too!

[He gives her a package.]

CARMEN: Marshmeller fudge!
JOE: Yes! All fo' Carmen.
CARMEN: Mos' o' de army wuz down here dis
    evenin'.
    Dey sure did like to dance.
JOE: Did you dance?
CARMEN: You is jealous! I see it in yo' face!
JOE: Okay. What if I is?
CARMEN: Go easy, ol' boy. Go easy!

I'LL DO A DANCE

Not used. Corresponds to "Je vais danser en votre honneur" (Dover score, page 189).

CARMEN: I'll do a dance, special fo' you.
    Dat's what I'se gonna do!
    Fo' you an' no one else—
    I'll give you a private floor show.
    Jus' take a seat, sonny boy.
    Dis is yore show!

[She does a sultry dance. A bugle is heard far away.]

JOE: Hey, wait a minute! What's dat?
    You hear dem blow dat bugle?
CARMEN: An' so what? Let 'em blow.
JOE: Hear it blowin' de blues!
    Oh, dat's terribul news!
    It means I gotta go.
    It means I gotta go!
CARMEN: Ain' dat sumpin'? Now ain' dat sumpin'?
    I like to dance my pants off
    Jus' to please Mister Joe,
    An' he jus' wanna prance off

When dat ol bugle blow!
JOE: It sayin': "All de men on leave come
    back fo' roll call!"
    Dere's sumpin' up!
    I jus' mus' go back to de camp.
CARMEN: To de camp?
    Is you kiddin'?

BEAT OUT DAT RHYTHM (REPRISE)

Not used. The rehearsal draft of the Act One finale included this reprise of "Beat Out Dat Rhythm on a Drum," celebrating Joe's acceptance to flying school. There is no corresponding passage in the opera.

VERSE

FRANKIE: He's gonna fly 'em high an' low!
DINK: He's gonna set de sky on fire!
CARMEN: When Joey gits to be a flyer
    He's gonna knock 'em for a row!
SOLDIER: Le's ev'rybody drink to Joe
    An' give de man a little send off!
RUM: You gotta give de man a send off!
    Go give dat band a shot of rum—
CARMEN: An' tell dat drummer man to slug dat
    drum!

REFRAIN

CARMEN: Beat out dat rhythm on a drum,
    Beat out dat rhythm on a drum,
    Beat out dat rhythm on a drum
    An' show 'em how to win de war!
ALL: Beat out dat rhythm on a drum,
    Beat out dat rhythm on a drum,
    Beat out dat rhythm on a drum,
    An' kick ol' Hitler out de door!
    Kick 'im out de door,
    Kick 'im out de door,
    Kick 'im out de door!
    Yeeow!

HIGH ON A HILL WE'D HIDE AWAY

Not used. Hammerstein's early version of "If You Would Only Come Away."

CARMEN: High on a hill we'd hide away,
    Hidin' away f'um all de crowd,
    Livin' above a cotton cloud.
    Dizzy wid love, we'd live f'um day to day,
    In our own hillside hideaway.
    I know a perfec' place to stay,
    We c'd be safe an' snug an' free—
    Fergit dat bugle an' come wid me.
    I don' wan' you bustin' yo' arm,
    Totin' a army rifle, an' dat is a fac'!
    Dat arm musn' come to no harm—
    Po' li'l Carmen need it to hol' up her back!
    Couldn' we have oursel's a time?
    Nobody dere but you an' me,
    You an' me,
    Baby, would dat be bad?
    All alone . . . upon dat happy mountain,
    Jus' you an' me—
    Would dat be bad?
JOE: Oh, Gawd!
CARMEN: High on a hill we'd hide away—
JOE: Aw, Carmen!
CARMEN: Hidin' away f'um all de crowd—
JOE: Aw, Carmen!
CARMEN: Livin' above a cotton cloud,
    Dizzy wid love, above a cloud—
JOE: What you wanna try to tan'alize me fo'?
CARMEN: Oh, come away an' you kin hide
    An' live upon de mountainside wid
    Carmen!
JOE: Please lemme be!
    You'll drive me nuts!
CARMEN: Oh, come away an' live fo' love—an' me!
    How would dat be? How would dat be,
    Wid no one dere but you an' me!
JOE: Lay off me!
    Won' you lay off me?
CARMEN: Hidin' away f'um all de crowd,
    Hidin' away f'um all de crowd,
    Livin' above a cotton cloud,
    High on a hill we'll hide away.
JOE: Won' you go away?

OH, SARGIN' BROWN

Not used. Corresponds to "Bel officier" (Dover score, page 216).

CARMEN: Oh, Sargin' Brown,
    Oh, Sargin' Brown,
    When you come bustin' down my do'
    you put yo' foot in it!
    You's out o' luck tonight!

You wuz a cluck tonight!
Instid o' staying home in bed
You come aroun' to fin' romance—
An' nearly foun' a poun' o' lead in yo'
    pants!
DINKY: Oh, Sargin' Brown—
RUM: Oh, Sargin' Brown—
DINKY: Oh, Sargin' Brown—
RUM: Oh, Sargin' Brown—
DINKY: Down in de cellar dere's a room, an'
    you'll be put in it!
We got a room fo' you—
RUM: We got a room fo' you!
DINKY: Done up in peacock blue!
RUM: Done up in peacock blue!
CARMEN: We hope it ain' too gay!
DINKY: Jus' follow us!
RUM: Jus' follow us an' we will show you de way.
DINKY: An' we will show you de way.
BROWN: [to JOE] Ef you go back to de camp,
Den I'll make de charge
Dat firs' y'tried to murder, den
    y'kidnapped me!
An' ef you don' go back to camp,
You's a deserter!
DINKY: An' so what?
Make yo' charges.
We's gonna help Joe git away.
You gonna stay while we all git away.
ALL: You gonna stay while we all git away.
JOE: Git away? Where'll I git to? What 'm I
    gonna do?
CARMEN: Do like I said, honey. Come up in de
    hills wid Carmen.
De army police neber fin' yer dere.
[to the others] Folks, dis is Joe. He's
    joinin' de gang.
Joe, we gonna take you in! You's elected!
We's all in a jam,
But who gives a dam?

DERE'S MY HOME DOWN BELOW

Not used. Corresponds to "Je me dis que là bas" (Dover score, page 259).

JOE: Dere's my home down below,
    An' it seem long ago
    I lef' a trustin' ol' lady
    Who believed me an loved me . . .
    She oughter see me now!

I IS HEPCAT MILLER

Not used. Corresponds to "Je suis Escamillo, toréro de Grenade!" (Dover score, page 307).

HEPCAT: I is Hepcat Miller. I'se de man wid de
    dance ban'.
JOE: I's Joe Louis . . .
    Now c'mon! Give yo' name!
    Don' try no lousy joke,
    Or de las' t'ing you see
    Will be a puff o' smoke!
HEPCAT: Look at me! Ain' you seen my puss in all
    de papers?
    I stan' like dis, an' pose,
    Dressed up in ev'nin' clo'es—
    Why, boy, you must o' seen my pitcher in
    de papers!
JOE: What you doin' up here ef it's you?
HEPCAT: What I do? I come to see a frien' o' mine.
JOE: Meanin' who?
HEPCAT: Miss Jones.
JOE: Fer true?
HEPCAT: Dat's who! Carmen Jones . . .
    Dis hill is high to climb,
    But I made record time
    When she sen' down a message to come
    up an' see her!
JOE: Dat so?
HEPCAT: She had a man, but da's washed up, she
    say.
    He don' know dat he's goin' but he's on
    his way!
JOE: An' you'll step in his shoes.
HEPCAT: D'ye blame me?
JOE: An' you'll step in his shoes!
HEPCAT: I's singin' you de news out loud, boy!
    I is proud fo' to tell yo'!
JOE: Go back home to yo' saxophome!
    Dat gal is off yo'.
    Go on back home
    Befo' I boff yo'!
HEPCAT: You an' who else?
    You an' who else?
JOE: I'll give yo' one mo' chance to go back
    down de hill.
HEPCAT: I jus' come up de hill!
JOE: You got a gun?
HEPCAT: [takes off coat] Who in hell needs a gun?
    I git it now.
    You mus' be Carmen's boyfrien'.
    Or you wuz her boyfrien'.
    Is I right?
JOE: Shut up an' fight.
HEPCAT: He wan's to fight! Well, well!

JOE: You'll see.
HEPCAT: Le's see.
JOE: You'll see.
HEPCAT: Come on.
JOE: You c'mon!
HEPCAT: Show what yer got.
JOE: Okay.
HEPCAT: Give all y'got!
JOE: Here's all I got!

[CARMEN's arrival stops JOE from choking HEPCAT.]

ALL DE SWELLS IN TOWN ARE DERE, KIDS

Not used. Hammerstein's "Hepcat" draft contains this earlier lyric for the scene that opens Act Four of the opera. A crowd is gathered outside the Hoity Toity Club. The number was rewritten as "Git Yer Program for de Big Fight."

ALL: All de swells in town are dere,
    kids!
    Glamour gals an' millyunair
    kids,
    Sassy dames an' classy mobsters,
    Cuttin' rugs an' chewin'
    lobsters.
    An' dain'y liddle debutantes
    Wid dere names on dere
    unnerpants!
1ST GIRL: Some o' dem don' wear
    unnerpants!
2ND GIRL: Sez you!
1ST GIRL: Sez me!
GROUP OF GIRLS: You's on'y guessin'!
GROUP OF MEN: Dey all come here to hear de
    ban'.
    Hep'll make mo' den twen'y
    gran!
    Hep'll make a cool twen'y gran'!
GROUP OF GIRLS: Sez you!
GROUP OF MEN: Sez us!
ALL: He won' make less'n!
    Sassy dames an' classy mobsters,
    Cuttin' rugs and chewin'
    lobsters!
    Oh, boy! Ef we wuz inside,
    We'd show dem dopes how to
    glide!
    We c'd show dem how to glide
    Ef we wuz ever allowed inside!

[*Lighting effect turns large poster of* HEPCAT *into a window through which he is seen silhouetted on the bandstand.*]

ALL: Lookit dat,
Lookit him!
De shadder o' Hepcat!
Attaboy! Attakid! Atta Hep!
Go wave dat stick,
You shadder o' Hepcat!

WAVE DAT STICK

Not used. In the "Hepcat" draft this is sung by fans waiting outside the club's back door. It was rewritten as "Dat's Our Man."

ALL: Wave dat stick an' do lak
y'do, boy!
Wave dat stick an' make
'em foller!
Make 'em slap dat bass fo'
you, boy!
An' blow
An' blow
An' blow
Until dem horns start in
ter holler!
Wave dat stick an' do lak
y'do, boy,
Give 'em hell an'
hullabaloo, boy—
Lak y'do, lak y'do, lak
y'do.

[*Dance.*]

Make dat crumpit play on
de trumpit,
Make him hit it loud an'
hard.
Make dat hobo blow on de
oboe
So we hear out here in de
yard!

C'mon, c'mon, c'mon,
c'mon—
Bang dat brass an' bang it
hard!
C'mon, c'mon, c'mon,
c'mon
C'mon! C'mon! C'mon!

[*Dance.*]

THREE GIRLS WHO
PEEKED INSIDE: Y'oughter git a load ob de
white folks—
It's a caution how dey
dance in dere!
MEN: Show us, show us how is
dey dancin'!
Show us what goes in dere.
SOPRANOS: Le's see ef dey kin swing
an' sway!
Do dey git gay like you an'
me do?
ALL: Le's see, le's see, le's see!
SOPRANOS: Le's see y'give a imitation
Ob de way dey do what
we do!
ALL: Le's see, le's see, le's see!
C'mon an' show us how
dey do,
C'mon an' show us how
dey do.

[*Some dance. Some cheer them on. Some report the doings inside.*]

SOPRANOS: De crowd is applaudin' fo'
Hep,
Dey shoutin' an clappin'
fo' Hep!
TENORS: He's gonna make a
speech!
SOPRANOS AND TENORS: He's gonna talk.
Hep is gonna talk!
BASSES AND SOPRANOS: In de microphome he is
talkin'
SOPRANOS: We cain't hear a word he
say!
TENORS AND BASSES: We cain't hear him! We
cain't hear him!
We cain't hear a word de
Hepcat say.
SOPRANOS AND TENORS: In de microphome
What he say?
MEN: He's comin'!
ALL: He's comin'! De Hepcat is
comin'!
Atta Hepcat! Atta Hepcat!
Atta Hepcat!
Open de door, de ban' is
gettin' hot.
Open de door, open de door.
When ol' Hep gives dem
dancers eb'ryt'ing he's
got,
Den dey know what dere
feet is for!

[HEPCAT *and* CARMEN *appear on the club's back steps.*]

You is de king o' swing!
You is a hot shot!
You's a darb!

Wave dat stick' an' do lak
y'do, boy!
Wave dat stick an' make
'em foller!
Make 'em slap dat bass fo'
you, boy!
An' blow
An' blow
An' blow
Until dem horns start in
ter holler.
Wave dat stick an' do lak
y'do, boy!
Give 'em hell an'
hullabaloo, boy—
'Ray f'de Hepcat!
'Ray f'de Hepcat
Hooray fer Hepcat!
Hepcat! Hepcat! Hepcat!

WON'T YOU SAY DAT YOU LOVE ME?

Not used. Corresponds to "Si tu m'aimes, Carmen" (Dover score, page 367).

HEPCAT: Won' you say dat you love
me?
Won' you whisper you love
me?
In my heart lives a star,
But it won' rise or shine
Till I hear you say
You is mine, all mine.
CARMEN: Don' y' know dat I love yer?
Mus' I tell yer I love yer?
Ain' my eyes been flashin'
light
Jus' like a bright 'lec'ric sign?
HEPCAT AND CARMEN: I is yours, all yours.
You is mine, all mine.
BASSES: [*heard from offstage*] Hepcat,
Hepcat!
Where in the hell is Hepcat?

[HEPCAT *exits into the club.*]

HEY, CARMEN, LOOK OVER DERE

Not used. Corresponds to "Carmen, un bon conseil" (Dover score, page 369).

FRANKIE: Hey, Carmen,
Look over dere.
Do you see what I see?
CARMEN: What you mean?
Over where?
MYRT: It's his nibs.
CARMEN: Whose nibs?
MYRT: Joe!
Cain't y'see?
Over dere by de Buick.
He's hidin'.
CARMEN: Yep.
You is right.
FRANKIE: Don't go dere!
CARMEN: Who's a-skeered o' him?
What kin he do to me?
Let him come.
Git it ober wid now.
MYRT: He's nuts.
Suppose he kills yer?
CARMEN: Den I'll be dead.
FRANKIE: You's wacky!

[FRANKIE *and* MYRT *exit into the club.*]

Top: Jan Clayton and John Raitt
Bottom: The graduation finale: "You'll Never Walk Alone"

Carousel | 1945

CAROUSEL (1945)

Tryouts: Shubert Theatre, New Haven, March 22–24, 1945; Colonial Theatre, Boston, March 27–April 15, 1945. New York run: Majestic Theatre; opened on April 19, 1945; 890 performances. A New Musical Play. Based on Ferenc Molnar's *Liliom* as adapted by Benjamin F. Glazer. Music by Richard Rodgers. Book and Lyrics by Oscar Hammerstein II. Presented by the Theatre Guild under the supervision of Lawrence Langner and Theresa Helburn. Directed by Rouben Mamoulian. Dances by Agnes de Mille. Orchestrations by Don Walker. Musical direction by Joseph Littau. Settings by Jo Mielziner. Costumes by Miles White.

Cast: John Raitt (Billy Bigelow), Jan Clayton (Julie Jordan), Jean Darling (Carrie Pipperidge), Eric Mattson (Enoch Snow), Christine Johnson (Nettie Fowler), Jean Castro (Mrs. Mullin), Murvyn Vye (Jigger Craigin), Bambi Linn (Louise), Peter Birch (Boatswain), Annabelle Lyon (Hannah), Robert Pagent (Carnival Boy), Mimi Strongin (Bessie), Jimsey Somers (Jessie), Walter Hull (Juggler), Robert Byrn (1st Policeman), Franklyn Fox (David Bascombe), Pearl Lang (June Girl), Connie Baxter (Arminy), Marilyn Merkt (Penny), Joan Keenan (Jennie), Ginna Moise (Virginia), Suzanne Tafel (Susan), Louis Freed (Jonathan), Lawrence Evers (2nd Policeman), Blake Ritter (Captain), Jay Velie (1st Heavenly Friend—Brother Joshua), Russell Collins (Starkeeper), Ralph Linn (Enoch Snow Jr.), Lester Freedman (Principal).

The setting is a coastal New England town between 1873 and 1888. Julie, a young millworker, is powerfully attracted to Billy, a carousel barker. He is vain and weak and not likely to be a good provider, but she marries him. (By contrast, her feisty friend Carrie is courted by Enoch Snow, a comically stuffy fisherman.) Only weeks into their marriage, Billy hits Julie; he also considers a return to the carousel and the woman who runs it. When Julie tells him she is pregnant, he vows to make a proper life for his family, but the best opportunity that presents itself is an armed robbery masterminded by Jigger Craigin. When it is bungled, Billy kills himself. He goes to the gates of Heaven, and before the final judgment, Billy gets a chance to return to Earth to help his daughter, Louise, now fifteen and unhappy. Although Billy flubs his first attempt, at the end of the story he silently urges Louise to believe in herself and tells Julie that he did love her.

Awards: New York Drama Critics Circle Award, Best Musical, 1944–45. Donaldson Awards 1944–45: Best Musical; Best Performance in a Musical (male): John Raitt; Best Direction: Rouben Mamoulian; Best Dancer (male): Peter Birch; Best Dance Direction: Agnes de Mille; Best Book: Oscar Hammerstein II; Best Lyrics: Oscar Hammerstein II; Best Score: Richard Rodgers.

A national tour began on May 29, 1947, at the Shubert Theatre, Chicago, and visited fifty-four cities before ending at the Majestic Theatre, New York, March 5, 1949.

London: Theatre Royal, Drury Lane, June 7, 1950 (566 performances).

A film version, produced by Henry Ephron for Twentieth Century–Fox, was released on February 16, 1956. Screenplay by Henry and Phoebe Ephron. Directed by Henry King. Choreography by Rod Alexander; Louise's ballet from the original by Agnes de Mille. Music Director: Alfred Newman. Cast: Gordon MacRae (Billy Bigelow), Shirley Jones (Julie Jordan), Cameron Mitchell (Jigger Craigin), Barbara Ruick (Carrie Pipperidge), Claramae Turner (Nettie Fowler), Robert Rounseville (Enoch Snow), Susan Luckey (Louise), Jacques d'Amboise (Louise's dancing partner).

Notable revivals: Music Theatre of Lincoln Center at the New York State Theatre (1965); Royal National Theatre (London), directed by Nicholas Hytner (1992). Hytner's production was transferred to Lincoln Center Theatre's Vivian Beaumont Theatre in 1994 and won Tony Awards for Best Revival of a Musical, Best Direction of a Musical, Best Choreography (Sir Kenneth MacMillan), Best Featured Actress in a Musical (Audra McDonald), and Best Scenic Design (Bob Crowley).

Recordings: There are nearly twenty cast albums of *Carousel*. The original Broadway cast album was followed by the film soundtrack (1956), the Music Theatre of Lincoln Center cast (1965), the Royal National Theatre production (1992) and its Broadway transfer (1994), and several studio albums.

The primary sources for this chapter are the published vocal score and the published libretto. Several songs were published individually. Early drafts of the script and lyric worksheets were studied at the Rodgers & Hammerstein Organization in New York City and in the music division of the Library of Congress. Rodgers's holograph piano-vocal scores are also at the Library of Congress.

YOU'RE A QUEER ONE, JULIE JORDAN

Published in the vocal score. Included in *Lyrics*. In the revised vocal score, this is the first part of "No. 4 Mister Snow (Julie and Carrie sequence)." Introduced by Jean Darling (Carrie) and Jan Clayton (Julie).

CARRIE: You're a queer one, Julie Jordan!
You are quieter and deeper than a well,
And you never tell me nothin'—
JULIE: There's nothin' that I keer t'choose tell!
CARRIE: You been actin' most peculiar;
Ev'ry mornin' you're awake ahead of me,
Alw'ys settin' by the winder—
JULIE: I like to watch the river meet the sea.
CARRIE: When we work in the mill, weavin' at the loom,
Y'gaze absentminded at the roof,
And half the time yer shuttle gets twisted in the threads
Till y'can't tell the warp from the woof!
JULIE: 'Tain't so!
CARRIE: You're a queer one, Julie Jordan!
You won't ever tell a body what you think.
You're as tight-lipped as an oyster,
And as silent as an old Sahaira spink!
JULIE: Spinx.

MISTER SNOW

Published as an individual sheet. Introduced by Jean Darling (Carrie Pipperidge).

His name is Mister Snow,
And an upstandin' man is he.
He comes home ev'ry night in his round-bottomed boat
With a net full of herring from the sea.
An almost perfect beau,
As refined as a girl could wish,
But he spends so much time in his round-bottomed boat
That he can't seem to lose the smell of fish.

The fust time he kissed me, the whiff of his clo'es
Knocked me flat on the floor of the room;
But now that I love him, my heart's in my nose,
And fish is my fav'rite perfume.
Last night he spoke quite low,
And a fair-spoken man is he,
And he said, "Miss Pipperidge, I'd like it fine
If I could be wed with a wife.
And, indeed, Miss Pipperidge, if you'll be mine,
I'll be yours fer the rest of my life."
Next moment we were promised
And now my mind's in a maze,
Fer all I ken do is look forward to
That wonderful day of days . . .

REFRAIN

When I marry Mister Snow,
The flowers'll be buzzin' with the hum of bees,

The birds'll make a racket in the churchyard trees,
When I marry Mister Snow.
Then it's off to home we'll go,
And both of us'll look a little dreamy eyed,
A-drivin' to a cottage by the oceanside
Where the salty breezes blow.
He'll carry me 'cross the threshold,
And I'll be as meek as a lamb.
Then he'll set me on my feet,
And I'll say, kinda sweet:
[spoken] "Well, Mister Snow, here I am!"
[sung] Then I'll kiss him so he'll know
That ev'rythin'll be as right as right ken be
A-livin' in a cottage by the sea with me,
For I love that Mister Snow—
That young, seafarin', bold and darin',
Big, bewhiskered, overbearin' darlin', Mister
    Snow!

THE BENCH SCENE, including IF I LOVED YOU

"If I Loved You" verse and refrain published as an individual sheet. The "If I Loved You" segment and two additional stanzas were included in *Lyrics*. Introduced by John Raitt (Billy) and Jan Clayton (Julie).

In 1951, Hammerstein answered a fan's query: "In the case of 'If I Loved You' the melody—the entire melody—was written first, and I set the lyric to it."

Discographer Edward Foote Gardner ranks "If I Loved You" as number seven for the year 1945. Frank Sinatra, Bing Crosby, and Perry Como had best-selling versions. Robert Lissauer's *Encyclopedia of Popular Music in America* also mentions recordings by Roy Hamilton in 1954 and by Chad and Jeremy in 1965.

BILLY: [spoken] That your name? Julie? Julie
    somethin'?
JULIE: [sung] Julie Jordan.
BILLY: You're a queer one, Julie Jordan.
    Ain't you sorry that you didn't run away?
    You can still go, if you wanta—
JULIE: I reckon that I keer t'choose t'stay.
    You couldn't take my money
    If I didn't hev any,
    And I don't hev a penny, that's true!
    And if I did hev money
    You couldn't take any
    'Cause you'd ask, and I'd give it to you!
BILLY: You're a queer one, Julie Jordan.
    Have y'ever had a feller you give money to?
JULIE: No.
BILLY: Ain't y'ever had a feller at all?

JULIE: No.
BILLY: Well y'musta had a feller you went walkin'
    with—
JULIE: Yes.
BILLY: Where'd you walk?
JULIE: Nowhere special I recall.
BILLY: In the woods?
JULIE: No.
BILLY: On the beach?
JULIE: No.
BILLY: Did you love him?
JULIE: [spoken] No! Never loved no one—I told
    you that!*
BILLY: [spoken] Say, you're a funny kid. Want to
    go into town and dance maybe? Or—
JULIE: [spoken] No. I have to be keerful.
BILLY: [spoken] Of what?
JULIE: [spoken] My character. Y'see, I'm never
    goin' to marry.
    [sung] I'm never goin' to marry.
    If I was goin' to marry,
    I wouldn't hev t'be sech a stickler.
    But I'm never goin' to marry,
    And a girl who don't marry
    Has got to be much more pertickler!

[Following lines spoken.]

BILLY: Suppose I was to say to you that I'd marry
    you?
JULIE: You?
BILLY: That scares you, don't it? You're thinkin'
    what that cop said.
JULIE: No, I ain't. I never paid no mind to what
    he said.
BILLY: But you wouldn't marry anyone like me,
    would you?
JULIE: Yes, I would, if I loved you. It wouldn't
    make any difference what you—even if
    I died fer it.
BILLY: How do you know what you'd do if you
    loved me? Or how you'd feel—or any
    thin'?
JULIE: I dunno how I know.
BILLY: Ah—
JULIE: Jest the same, I know how I—how it'd
    be—if I loved you.
    [sung] When I worked in the mill, weavin'
    at the loom
    I'd gaze absentminded at the roof,

---

* These lines were dropped:
BILLY: Do you love me, Julie Jordan?
JULIE: No!
BILLY: Then explain just what you're doin' here
    with me.
    Why'd you stay here in the first place?
JULIE: I like to watch the moon upon the sea.

And half the time the shuttle'd tangle in
    the threads,
And the warp'd get mixed with the woof . . .
If I loved you—
BILLY: [spoken] But you don't.
JULIE: [spoken] No, I don't . . .
    [sung] But somehow I ken see
    Jest exackly how I'd be . . .

If I loved you,
Time and again I would try to say
All I'd want you to know.
If I loved you,
Words wouldn't come in an easy way—
Round in circles I'd go!
Longin' to tell you, but afraid and shy,
I'd let my golden chances pass me by.
Soon you'd leave me,
Off you would go in the mist of day,
Never, never to know
How I loved you—
If I loved you.

[Pause.]

BILLY: [spoken] Well, anyway—you don't love me.
    That's what you said.
JULIE: [spoken] Yes . . . I can smell them, can you?
    The blossoms. The wind brings them down.
BILLY: [spoken] Ain't *much* wind tonight. Hardly
    any.
    [sung] You can't hear a sound—not the
    turn of a leaf,
    Nor the fall of a wave, hittin' the sand.
    The tide's creepin' up on the beach like a
    thief,
    Afraid to be caught stealin' the land.
    On a night like this I start to wonder what
    life is all about.
JULIE: [sung] And I always say two heads are
    better than one, to figger it out.
BILLY: [spoken] I don't need you or anyone to help
    me. I got it figgered out for myself. We
    ain't important. What are we? A couple
    of specks of nothin'. Look up there.
    [sung] There's a helluva lot o' stars in the
    sky,
    And the sky's so big the sea looks small,
    And two little people—
    You and I—
    We don't count at all.*

---

* The published libretto but not the vocal score has
these additional lines:
JULIE: There's a feathery little cloud floatin' by
    Like a lonely leaf on a big blue stream.
BILLY: And two little people—you and I—
    Who cares what we dream?

[*spoken*] You're a funny kid. Don't
  remember ever meetin' a girl like you.
  You—are you tryin' t'get me to marry
  you?

JULIE: [*spoken*] No.

BILLY: [*spoken*] Then what's puttin' it into my
  head? You're different all right. Don't
  know what it is. You look up at me with
  that little kid face like—like you
  trusted me. I wonder what it'd be like.

JULIE: [*spoken*] What?

BILLY: [*spoken*] Nothin'. I know what it'd be like.
  It'd be awful. I can just see myself—
  [*sung*] Kinda scrawny and pale, pickin' at
    my food,
  And lovesick like any other guy—
  I'd throw away my sweater and dress up
    like a dude
  In a dickey and a collar and a tie . . .
  If I loved you—

JULIE: [*spoken*] But you don't.

BILLY: [*spoken*] No I don't.
  [*sung*] But somehow I can see*
  Just exactly how I'd be.

  If I loved you,
  Time and again I would try to say
  All I'd want you to know.
  If I loved you,
  Words wouldn't come in an easy way—
  Round in circles I'd go!
  Longin' to tell you, but afraid and shy,
  I'd let my golden chances pass me by.
  Soon you'd leave me,
  Off you would go in the mist of day,
  Never, never to know
  How I loved you—
  If I loved you.

BILLY: [*spoken*] I'm not a feller to marry anybody.
  Even if a girl was foolish enough to
  want me to, I wouldn't.

JULIE: [*spoken*] Don't worry about it—Billy.

BILLY: [*spoken*] Who's worried!

JULIE: [*spoken*] You're right about there bein' no
  wind. The blossoms are jest comin' down
  by theirselves. Jest their time to, I reckon.

[*They embrace.*]

Act Two reprise

BILLY: Longing to tell you,
  But afraid and shy,
  I let my golden chances pass me by.

---

* *In the published sheet, these lines are:*
  I know I would be
  Like you said you'd be with me.

Now I've lost you;
Soon I will go in the mist of day,
And you never will know
How I loved you,
How I loved you.

GIVE IT TO 'EM GOOD, CARRIE

Published in the vocal score. Introduced by Jean Darling (Carrie) with girls and men.

GIRLS: [*spoken in rhythm*] Give it to 'em good,
  Carrie,
  Give it to 'em good!

CARRIE: [*sung*] Get away, you no-account
    nothin's
  With yer silly jokes and prattle!
  If y'packed all yer brains in a
    butterfly's head
  They'd still hev room to rattle.

GIRLS: [*spoken in rhythm*] Give it to 'em good,
  Carrie,
  Give it to 'em good!
  Tell 'em somethin' that'll l'arn 'em!

CARRIE: [*sung*] Get away, you roustabout
    riff-raff,
  With yer bellies full of grog.
  If y'packed all yer brains in a
    pollywog's head,
  He'd never even grow to be a frog!

GIRLS: The polywog'd never be a frog!
  [*spoken*] That'll l'arn 'em, darn 'em!

ALL MEN: [*sung*] Now jest a minute, ladies,
  You got no call to fret.
  We only asked perlitely
  If you was ready yet.
  We'd kinda like this clambake
  To get an early start,
  And wanted fer to tell you
  We went and done our part.

BASSES: Look at them clams!

BARITONES: Been diggin' 'em since sunup!

BASSES: Look at them clams!

TENORS: All ready fer the boats.

ALL MEN: Diggin' them clams—

TENORS: We're all wore out and done up—

ALL MEN: And what's more we're hungry as
    goats!

GIRLS: You'll get no drinks er vittles
  Till we get across the bay,
  So pull in yer belts
  And load them boats

And let's get under way.
The sooner we sail,
The sooner we start
The clambake cross the bay!

JUNE IS BUSTIN' OUT ALL OVER

Published as an individual sheet. Included in *Lyrics*. Introduced by Christine Johnson (Nettie Fowler), Jean Darling (Carrie), and the ensemble.

In February 1945, financier G. M. Loeb attended a presentation of songs from *Carousel* for potential investors, and he then wrote to Hammerstein regarding the mating habits of sheep. "I do not think rams mate with ewes in June as they do in your lyrics but I am not really certain. We have been told to keep our rams separate at all times except when the ewes are in heat but we did not follow this precaution and in several years all mating seemed confined to September–October—no mounting whatsoever in June, or if so no results." Hammerstein responded: "I was delighted with the parts of your letter praising my work and thrown into consternation by the unwelcome news about the eccentricly frigid behavior of ewes in June. I have since checked your statement and found it to be true. It looks very much as if in the interest of scientific honesty I shall have to abandon the verse dealing with sheep."

In the end, Hammerstein retained the "ewe sheep"/ "new sheep" stanza. But when the film was made, certain lines were not acceptable to the Production Code Administration. To replace the "lusty"/"Augusty" stanza he supplied the following:

  June is bustin' out all over,
  The moonlight is shinin' on the shore,
  And the girls who were contrary
  With the boys in January
  Aren't nearly so contrary any more.

VERSE

NETTIE: March went out like a lion,
  A-whippin' up the water in the bay.
  Then April cried
  And stepped aside,
  And along come pretty little May!
  May was full of promises,
  But she didn't keep 'em quick enough
    fer some,
  And a crowd of Doubtin' Thomases
  Was predictin' that the summer'd
    never come.

MEN: But it's comin', by gum!

Y'ken feel it come,
Y'ken feel it in yer heart,
Y'ken see it in the ground!
GIRLS: Y'ken hear it in the trees,
Y'ken smell it in the breeze—
ALL: Look around, look around, look
around!

REFRAIN 1

NETTIE: June is bustin' out all over!
All over the meadow and the hill,
Buds're bustin' outa bushes,
And the rompin' river pushes
Ev'ry little wheel that wheels beside a
mill.
ALL: June is bustin' out all over!
NETTIE: The feelin' is gettin' so intense
That the young Virginia creepers
Hev been huggin' the bejeepers
Outa all the mornin'-glories on the fence.
Because it's June!
MEN: June—June—June—
ALL: Jest because it's June—June—June!
NETTIE: Fresh and alive and gay and young,
June is a love song, sweetly sung.

REFRAIN 2

ALL: June is bustin' out all over!
1ST MAN: The saplin's are bustin' out with sap!
1ST GIRL: Love he's found my brother, Junior!
2ND MAN: And my sister's even lunier!
2ND GIRL: And my ma is gettin' kittenish with
Pap!
ALL: June is bustin' out all over!
NETTIE: To ladies the men are payin' court.
Lotsa ships are kept at anchor
Jest because the captains hanker
Fer a comfort they ken only get in
port!
ALL: Because it's June!
June—June—June—
Jest because it's June—June—June!
NETTIE: June makes the bay look bright and
new,
Sails gleamin' white on sunlit blue.

REFRAIN 3

CARRIE: June is bustin' out all over!
The ocean is full of Jacks and Jills.
With her little tail a-swishin'
Ev'ry lady fish is wishin'
That a male would come and grab her
by the gills!
ALL: June is bustin' out all over!
NETTIE: The sheep aren't sleepin' any more.

All the rams that chase the ewe sheep
Are determined there'll be new sheep,
And the ewe sheep aren't even keepin'
score!
ALL: On accounta it's June!
June—June—June—
Jest because it's June—June—June!

ENCORE

NETTIE: June is bustin' out all over,
The beaches are crowded ev'ry night.
From Penobscot to Augusty
All the boys are feelin' lusty,
And the girls ain't even puttin' up a
fight.
ALL: Because it's June!
June—June—June—
Jest because it's June—June—June!

Act One, Scene 3 reprise

NETTIE: June is bustin' out all over!
ALL: The flowers are bustin' from their
seed!
NETTIE: And the pleasant life of Riley
That is spoken of so highly
Is the life that ev'rybody wants to
lead!
ALL: Because it's June!
June—June—June—
Jest because it's June—June—June!

MISTER SNOW (REPRISE)

Published in the vocal score. Introduced by Jean Darling (Carrie Pipperidge) and Eric Mattson (Enoch Snow) and girls.

GIRLS: When you walk down the aisle
All the heads will turn.
What a rustlin' of bonnets there'll be!
And you'll try to smile,
But your cheeks will burn,
And your eyes'll get so dim you ken
hardly see!

With your orange blossoms quiverin' in
your hand,
You will stumble to the spot where the
parson is.
Then your finger will be ringed with a
golden band,

And you'll know the feller's yours—and
you are his.
CARRIE: When I marry Mister Snow—
GIRLS: What a day!
What a day!
CARRIE: The flowers'll be buzzin' with the hum of
bees—
GIRLS: The birds'll make a racket in the
churchyard trees—
CARRIE: When I marry Mister Snow.
GIRLS: Heigh-ho!
CARRIE: Then it's off to home we'll go—
GIRLS: Spillin' rice
On the way!
CARRIE: And both of us'll look a little dreamy
eyed,
A-drivin' to a cottage by the oceanside
Where the salty breezes blow—

[SNOW enters unseen.]

GIRLS: You and Mister Snow!
CARRIE: He'll carry me 'cross the threshold,
And I'll be as meek as a lamb.
Then he'll set me on my feet
And I'll say, kinda sweet:
"Well, Mister Snow, here I am!"
SNOW: Then I'll kiss her so she'll know—
CARRIE: Mister Snow!
GIRLS: Mister Snow!
SNOW: That everything'll be as right as right ken
be,
A-livin' in a cottage by the sea with me,
Where the salty breezes blow!
I love Miss Pipp'ridge and I aim to
Make Miss Pipp'ridge change her
name to
Missus Enoch Snow!

WHEN THE CHILDREN ARE ASLEEP

Published as an individual sheet. Introduced by Jean Darling (Carrie Pipperidge) and Eric Mattson (Enoch Snow). Anticipating the Boston tryout, in a January 1945 draft of the script Hammerstein wrote, "There will probably be an encore. If not, the author and composer will probably jump in the Charles River."

INTRODUCTION

SNOW: I own a little house,
And I sail a little boat,

And the fish I ketch I sell—
And, in a manner of speakin',
I'm doin' very well.
I love a little girl
And she's in love with me,
And soon she'll be my bride
And, in a manner of speakin',
I should be satisfied.

CARRIE: [*spoken*] Well, ain't you?

SNOW: If I told you my plans, and the things I
    intend,
It'd make ev'ry curl on yer head stand on
    end!
When I make enough money outa one
    little boat,
I'll put all my money in another little
    boat.
I'll make twic't as much outa two little
    boats,
And the fust thing you know I'll hev four
    little boats!
Then eight little boats,
Then a fleet of little boats!
Then a great big fleet of great big boats!
All ketchin' herring,
Bringing it to shore,
Sailin' out again
And bringin' in more,
And more, and more,
And more!

[*Dialogue.*]

SNOW: [*spoken*] . . . Carrie, I'm goin' to get rich
    on sardines. I mean we're goin' t'get
    rich—you and me. I mean you and
    me—and—all of us.
[*sung*] The fust year we're married we'll
    hev one little kid,
The second year we'll go and hev another
    little kid,
You'll soon be darnin' socks fer eight
    little feet—

CARRIE: Are you buildin' up to another fleet?

SNOW: We'll build a lot more rooms,
Our dear little house'll get bigger,
Our dear little house'll get bigger.

CARRIE: And so will my figger!

SNOW: [*spoken*] Carrie, ken y'imagine how it'll
    be when all the kids are upstairs in
    bed, and you and me sit alone in the
    firelight—me in my armchair, you on
    my knee—mebbe?

REFRAIN 1

SNOW: [*sung*] When the children are asleep, we'll
    sit and dream

The things that ev'ry other dad and
    mother dream.
When the children are asleep and lights
    are low,
If I still love you the way I love you today,
You'll pardon my saying "I told you so!"
When the children are asleep, I'll dream
    with you.
We'll think: "What fun we have had!"
And be glad that it all came true.

CARRIE: When children are awake,
A-rompin' through the rooms
Or runnin' on the stairs,
Then, in a manner of speakin',
The house is really theirs.
But once they close their eyes
And we are left alone
And free from all their fuss,
Then, in a manner of speakin',
We ken be really us . . .

REFRAIN 2

CARRIE: When the children are asleep
We'll sit and dream—

SNOW: Dream all alone—

CARRIE: The things that ev'ry other dad and
    mother dream—

SNOW: Dreams that won't be interrupted.
When the children are asleep and lights
    are low,

CARRIE: Lo and behold!
If I still love you the way I love you
    today,
You'll pardon my saying, "I told you
    so!"

When the children are asleep,
I'll dream with you.

SNOW: You'll dream with me.

CARRIE: We'll think: "What fun we hev had!"
And be glad that it all came true.

SNOW: When today
Is a long time ago—

BOTH: You'll still hear me say
That the best dream I know
Is—

SNOW: You!

CARRIE: When the children are asleep
I'll dream with you.

Sheet music verse

When we've tucked the kids
In their downy beds,
And listened to each one pray,
We'll kiss the tops
Of their tousled heads

And tiptoe quietly away.
We'll tiptoe into our sittin' room,
Where we love to be by ourselves,
Where the flickrin' glow of the firelight
Makes the books wink down from their shelves.
And there ev'ry evenin' we'll always be,
Me in my armchair, you on my knee.

BLOW HIGH, BLOW LOW

Published in the vocal score. Included in *Lyrics*. Introduced by Murvyn Vye (Jigger Craigin), John Raitt (Billy), and male ensemble.

MEN: Blow high, blow low!
A-whalin' we will go!
We'll go a-whalin', a-sailin' away.
Away we'll go,
Blow me high and low!
For many and many a long, long day!
For many and many a long, long day!

JIGGER: The people who live on land
Are hard to understand—
When you're lookin' for fun they clap
    you into jail!
So I'm shippin' off to sea,
Where life is gay and free,
And a feller can flip
A hook in the hip of a whale.

ALL: Blow high, blow low!
A-whalin' we will go!
We'll go a-whalin', a-sailin' away.
Away we'll go,
Blow me high and low!
For many and many a long, long day.
For many and many a long, long day!

BILLY: It's wonderful just to feel
Your hands upon a wheel
And to listen to wind a-whistlin' in a sail,
Or to climb aloft and be
The very first to see
A chrysanthemum spout come out o' the
    snout of a whale!

ALL: Blow high, blow low!
A-whalin' we will go!
We'll go a-whalin', a-sailin' away,
Away we'll go,
Blow me high and low!
For many and many a long, long day!
For many and many a long, long day!

JIGGER: A-rockin' upon the sea,
Your boat will seem to be
Like a dear little baby in her bassinet,

For she hasn't learned to walk,
And she hasn't learned to talk,
And her little behind
Is kind of inclined to be wet!
MEN: Blow high, blow low!
A-whalin' we will go!
We'll go a-whalin', a-sailin' away,
Away we'll go,
Blow me high and low!
For many and many a long, long day!
For many and many a long, long day!

SOLILOQUY

Published as an individual sheet. Included in *Lyrics*. Introduced by John Raitt (Billy).

According to notes from a January 1944 meeting with Theresa Helburn and Lawrence Langner, "Mr. Rodgers suggested a fine musical number for the end of the scene where Liliom discovers he is to be a father, in which he sings first with pride of the growth of a boy, and then suddenly realizes it might be a girl, and changes completely with that thought. It was felt this might be the end of the first act."

Hammerstein told interviewer Arnold Michaelis that "without it I don't think you could have a play. If you didn't show Billy Bigelow, the inside of Billy Bigelow, the soft side, the human side, he would just be a lout for whom you'd have no sympathy whatever."

I wonder what he'll think of me!
I guess he'll call me
"The old man."
I guess he'll think I can lick
Ev'ry other feller's father—
Well, I can!
I bet that he'll turn out to be
The spit an' image
Of his dad,
But he'll have more common sense
Than his puddin'-headed father
Ever had.
I'll teach him to wrassle,
And dive through a wave,
When we go in the mornin's for our swim.
His mother can teach him
The way to behave,
But she won't make a sissy out o' him—
Not him!
Not my boy!
Not Bill . . .

[*spoken*] Bill.

[*sung*] My boy, Bill!
I will see
That he's named
After me,
I will!
My boy, Bill—
He'll be tall
And as tough
As a tree,
Will Bill.
Like a tree he'll grow,
With his head held high
And his feet planted firm on the ground,
And you won't see no-
body dare to try
To boss him or toss him around!
No pot-bellied, baggy-eyed bully'll boss him
around!

I don't give a damn* what he does,
As long as he does what he likes.
He can sit on his tail
Or work on a rail
With a hammer, a-hammerin' spikes.
He can ferry a boat on the river
Or peddle a pack on his back
Or work up and down
The streets of a town
With a whip and a horse and a hack.
He can haul a scow along a canal,
Run a cow around a corral,
Or maybe bark for a carousel
Of course it takes talent to do *that* well.
He might be a champ of the heavyweights
Or a feller that sells you glue,
Or President of the United States—
That'd be all right too.
[*spoken*] His mother'd like that. But he wouldn't
be President unless he wanted to be!
[*sung*] Not Bill!
My boy, Bill—
He'll be tall
And as tough
As a tree,
Will Bill!
Like a tree he'll grow,
With his head held high,
And his feet planted firm on the ground,
And you won't see no-
body dare to try
To boss him or toss him around!
No fat-bottomed, flabby-face, pot-bellied, baggy-
eyed bastard'll boss him around!

---

* *This word was changed to "darn" for the original cast recording and the 1955 film, which also expurgated "hell," "virgin," "bastard," and "God."*

And I'm damned if he'll marry his boss's
daughter,
A skinny-lipped virgin with blood like water,
Who'll give him a peck and call it a kiss
And look in his eyes through a lorgnette . . .

[*spoken*] Say! Why am I takin' on like this? My kid
ain't even been born yet!

[*sung*] I can see him
When he's seventeen or so
And startin' in to go
With a girl.
I can give him
Lots o' pointers, very sound,
On the way to get round
Any girl.
I can tell him—

[*spoken*] Wait a minute! Could it be? What the
hell! What if he is a girl? Bill! Oh, Bill! What
would I do with her? What could I do *for* her?
A bum—with no money!
[*sung*] You can have fun with a son,
But you got to be a father
To a girl!
She mightn't be so bad at that—
A kid with ribbons
In her hair,
A kind o' sweet and petite
Little tintype of her mother—
What a pair!
[*spoken*] I can just hear myself braggin' about
her!*
[*sung*] My little girl,
Pink and white
As peaches and cream is she.
My little girl
Is half again as bright
As girls are meant to be!
Dozens of boys pursue her,
Many a likely lad
Does what he can to woo her
From her faithful dad.
She has a few
Pink and white young fellers of two or three—

---

* *On the original cast recording of "Soliloquy" an additional stanza is heard here. It was cut soon after the New York opening.*

When I have a daughter,
I'll stand around in barrooms,
Oh, how I'll boast and blow!
Friends'll see me comin'
And empty all the barrooms,
Through ev'ry door they'll go,
Weary of hearin' day after day
The same old things that I always say.

But my little girl
Gets hungry ev'ry night
And she comes home to me . . .
[spoken] My little girl! My little girl!
[sung] I got to get ready before she comes,
I got to make certain that she
Won't be dragged up in slums
With a lot o' bums—
Like me!
She's got to be sheltered and fed, and dressed
In the best that money can buy!
I never knew how to get money,
But I'll try—
By God! I'll try!
I'll go out and make it
Or steal it or take it
Or die!

A REAL NICE CLAMBAKE

Published as an individual sheet. Included in *Lyrics*.
Introduced by Jean Darling (Carrie), Christine John-
son (Nettie), Jan Clayton (Julie), Eric Mattson (Enoch
Snow), and ensemble.

ALL: This was a real nice clambake,
We're mighty glad we came.
The vittles we et
Were good, you bet!
The company was the same.
Our hearts are warm,
Our bellies are full,
And we are feelin' prime.
This was a real nice clambake
And we all had a real good time!
NETTIE: Fust come codfish chowder,
Cooked in iron kettles,
Onions floatin' on the top,
Curlin' up in petals!
JULIE: Throwed in ribbons of salted pork—
ALL: An old New England trick—
JULIE: And lapped it all up with a clamshell,
Tied on to a bayberry stick!
ALL: Oh-h-h—
This was a real nice clambake,
We're mighty glad we came.
The vittles we et
Were good, you bet!
The company was the same.
Our hearts are warm,
Our bellies are full,
And we are feelin' prime.
This was a real nice clambake

And we all had a real good time!
SNOW: Remember when we raked
Them red-hot lobsters
Out of the driftwood fire?
They sizzled and crackled
And sputtered a song
Fitten fer an angels' choir.
GIRLS: Fitten fer an angels',
Fitten fer an angels',
Fitten fer an angels' choir!
NETTIE: We slit 'em down the back
And peppered 'em good,
And doused 'em in melted butter—
CARRIE: Then we tore away the claws
And cracked 'em with our teeth
'Cause we weren't in the mood to putter!
GIRLS: Fitten fer an angels',
Fitten fer an angels',
Fitten fer an angels' choir!
A MAN: Then at last come the clams—
MEN: Steamed under rockweed
An' poppin' from their shells—
ALL: Jest how many of 'em
Galloped down our gullets—
We couldn't say oursel's!
Oh-h-h—
This was a real nice clambake,
We're mighty glad we came.
The vittles we et
Were good, you bet!
The company was the same.
Our hearts are warm,
Our bellies are full,
And we are feelin' prime.
This was a real nice clambake
And we all had a real good time!
We said it afore—
And we'll say it agen—
We all had a real good time!

GERANIUMS IN THE WINDER and STONECUTTERS CUT IT ON STONE

Published in the vocal score. Introduced by Eric Mattson (Enoch Snow), Murvyn Vye (Jigger Craigin), Connie
Baxter (Arminy), and the ensemble.

Geraniums in the Winder

SNOW: Geraniums in the winder,
Hydrangeas on the lawn,

And breakfast in the kitchen
In the timid pink of dawn,
And you to blow me kisses
When I headed fer the sea—
We might hev been
A happy pair
Of lovers—
Mightn't hev we?
And comin' home at twilight,
It might hev been so sweet
To take my ketch of herring
And lay them at your feet!
I might hev hed a baby
To dandle on my knee,
But all these things
That might hev been
Are never,
Never to be!

Stonecutters Cut It on Stone

JIGGER: I never see it yet to fail,
I never see it fail!
A girl who's in love with a
virtuous man
Is doomed to weep and wail.
Stonecutters cut it on stone,
Woodpeckers peck it on wood:
There's nothin' so bad fer a
woman
As a man who thinks he's good!
My mother used to say to me:
"When you grow up, my son,
I hope you're a bum like yer
father was,
'Cause a good man ain't no fun."
JIGGER
AND ENSEMBLE: Stonecutters cut it on stone,
Woodpeckers peck it on wood:
There's nothin' so bad fer a
woman
As a man who thinks he's good!
SNOW: 'Tain't so!
JIGGER: 'Tis too!

[From here on, the ensemble takes sides.]

SNOW'S GROUP: 'Tain't so!
JIGGER'S GROUP: 'Tis too!

[Dialogue.]

A GIRL: I never see it yet to fail.
GIRLS: I never see it fail.
A girl who's in love with any man
Is doomed to weep and wail.
1ST GIRL: [spoken] And it's even worse after
they marry you.

2ND GIRL: [*spoken*] You ought to give him
 back that ring, Carrie. You'd
 be better off.

3RD GIRL: [*spoken*] Here's Arminy—been
 married a year. She'll tell you.

ARMINY: [*sung*] The clock jest ticks yer life
 away,
 There's no relief in sight.
 It's cookin' and scrubbin' and
 sewin' all day
 And Gawd-knows-whatin' all
 night!*

ALL WOMEN: Stonecutters cut it on stone,
 Woodpeckers peck it on wood;
 There's nothing so bad fer a
 woman
 As a man who's bad or good!

WHAT'S THE USE OF WOND'RIN'?

Published as an individual sheet. Included in *Lyrics*. Introduced by Jan Clayton (Julie) and female ensemble.

In the introduction to *Lyrics*, Hammerstein mentioned that this song was not a big seller of sheet music or recordings. "I believe 'What's the Use of Wond'rin'?' was severely handicapped because of the final word, 'talk.' The trouble with this word is the hard 'k' sound at the end of it. The last two lines of the refrain are, 'You're his girl and he's your feller, And all the rest is talk.' This is exactly what I wanted the character to say. . . . I realized that I was defying convention in ending with the word 'talk,' but I had a perverse desire to try it anyway."

GIRLS: Tell it to her good, Julie,
 Tell it to her good!

JULIE: What's the use of wond'rin'
 If he's good or if he's bad,
 Or if you like the way he wears his hat?
 Oh, what's the use of wond'rin'
 If he's good or if he's bad?
 He's your feller and you love him—
 That's all there is to that.
 Common sense may tell you
 That the endin' will be sad
 And now's the time to break and run away.
 But what's the use of wond'rin'
 If the endin' will be sad?
 He's your feller and you love him—

---

* *Changed for the film to "And not much sleepin' at night."*

There's nothin' more to say.
Somethin' made him the way that he is,
Whether he's false or true.
And somethin' gave him the things that
 are his—
One of those things is you.
So, when he wants your kisses
You will give them to the lad,
And anywhere he leads you, you will walk.
And anytime he needs you,
You'll go runnin' there like mad.
You're his girl and he's your feller—
And all the rest is talk.

YOU'LL NEVER WALK ALONE

Published as an individual sheet. Included in *Lyrics*. Introduced by Christine Johnson (Nettie).

Recordings by Frank Sinatra and Judy Garland sold well in 1945 and 1946. Since then it has been covered by performers of every type of music, including Plácido Domingo, Elvis Presley, Patti LaBelle, Ray Charles, Aretha Franklin, and Tammy Wynette.

The song's message of inspiration and consolation has led to its inclusion in some contemporary hymnals and has made it a favorite with charities. In the United States, the song is especially associated with the Jerry Lewis Muscular Dystrophy telethons and with AIDS Walk New York.

In the United Kingdom, after a very popular recording by Gerry and the Pacemakers (1965), the song became an anthem for the Liverpool Football Club, and now can be heard at many stadiums. A 1985 rendition by a group of British pop and rock stars was used to raise funds for victims of the Bradford stadium fire and reached number one on the British charts.

When you walk through a storm
Keep your chin up high*
And don't be afraid of the dark.
At the end of the storm
Is a golden sky

---

* *The original sheet music gives this line as "Hold your head up high." It may be that Hammerstein authorized the change. A tantalizing clue is a March 1952 letter from Albert Sirmay, music editor at Chappell & Co: "Dear Oscar, for the sake of security, please just glance at the first page of 'You'll Never Walk Alone' on which you changed two words." The letter's attachment has been lost.*

And the sweet, silver song of a lark.*
Walk on through the wind,
Walk on through the rain,
Though your dreams be tossed and blown.
Walk on, walk on, with hope in your heart,
And you'll never walk alone!
You'll never walk alone.

THE HIGHEST JUDGE OF ALL

Published in the vocal score. Introduced by John Raitt (Billy).

Take me beyond the pearly gates,
Through a beautiful marble hall,
Take me before the highest throne
And let me be judged by the highest Judge of all!
Let the Lord shout and yell,
And His eyes flash flame,
I promise not to quiver when He calls my name;
Let Him send me to hell,
But before I go,
I feel that I'm entitled to a hell of a show!
Want pink-faced angels on a purple cloud,
Twangin' on their harps till their fingers get red,
Want organ music—let it roll out loud,
Rollin' like a wave, washin' over my head.
Want ev'ry star in heaven
Hangin' in the room,
Shinin' in my eyes
When I hear my doom!
Reckon my sins are good big sins,
And the punishment won't be small;
So take me before the highest throne
And let me be judged by the highest Judge of all.

---

* *Ted Chapin points out another discrepancy: When the song is introduced immediately following Billy's death, Nettie sings "of a lark." But when the song is reprised for the finale of Act Two, Dr. Seldon and the townsfolk sing "of the lark." As Chapin wrote in the Fall 2000 issue of* Happy Talk, *the Rodgers & Hammerstein Organization's newsletter: "Does he [Dr. Seldon] remember it wrong? Did the sampler that Julie gave Nettie get it wrong? Did Julie get the sampler from Dr. Seldon in the first place? Are the townsfolk sloppy? Is this just a mistake that neither Hammerstein nor Rodgers ever caught? Most productions just assume it is a mistake and sing 'a lark' both times. But is that the right decision?"*

CARRIE'S INCIDENTAL

Published in the vocal score. Introduced by Jean Darling (Carrie). Carrie sings part of "an awful ketchy song" she heard in a show in New York.

I'm a tomboy,
Jest a tomboy!
I'm a madcap maiden from Broadway!
I'm a tomboy,
A merry tomboy!
I'm a madcap maiden from Broadway!

Left to right, Dick Haymes, Charles Winninger, Fay Bainter, and Jeanne Crain in the 1945 film version of State Fair

STATE FAIR | 1945
and Songs of 1946

STATE FAIR (1945)

A film produced by William Perlberg for Twentieth Century–Fox, released August 29, 1945. Music by Richard Rodgers. Lyrics by Oscar Hammerstein II. Screenplay by Oscar Hammerstein II, adaptation by Sonya Levien and Paul Green, based on the novel by Philip Stong. Directed by Walter Lang. Dances directed by Hermes Pan. Photographed by Leon Shamroy. Film editing by J. Watson Webb. Music direction by Alfred Newman and Charles Henderson. Orchestrations by Edward Powell. Art direction by Lyle R. Wheeler and Lewis Creber. Cast: Jeanne Crain (Margy Frake, sung by Louanne Hogan), Dana Andrews (Pat Gilbert), Dick Haymes (Wayne Frake), Vivian Blaine (Emily Edwards), Charles Winninger (Abel Frake), Fay Bainter (Melissa Frake), Donald Meek (Hippenstahl), Frank McHugh (McGee), Percy Kilbride (Dave Miller), Henry Morgan (Barker), Jane Nigh (Eleanor), William Marshall (Marty), and Phil Brown (Harry Ware).

A second *State Fair* film, produced by Charles Brackett for Twentieth Century–Fox, was released on March 15, 1962, with the original score supplemented by five new songs by Rodgers (both words and music). (The film's setting was Texas, so the song "All I Owe Ioway" was dropped.) Screenplay by Richard Breen. Directed by José Ferrer. Choreography by Nick Castle. Music direction by Alfred Newman. Associate music direction by Ken Darby. Orchestrations by Edward B. Powell. Photographed by William C. Mellor. Film editing by David Bretherton. Art direction by Jack Martin Smith and Walter M. Simonds. Costumes by Marjorie Best. Cast: Pat Boone (Wayne Frake), Bobby Darin (Jerry Dundee), Pamela Tiffin (Margy Frake; sung by Anita Gordon), Ann-Margret (Emily Porter), Tom Ewell (Abel Frake), Alice Faye (Melissa Frake), Wally Cox (Hipplewaite), David Brandon (Harry), Clem Harvey (Doc Cramer), Robert Foulk (Squat Judge), Linda Heinrich (Betty Jean), Edward "Tap" Canutt (Red Hoerter), and Margaret Deramee (Lilya).

There have been two stage versions of *State Fair*. Ozzie Nelson and Harriet Nelson headlined a production adapted by Lucille Kallen at the St. Louis Municipal Opera in June 1960. A second adaptation, by Tom Briggs and Louis Mattioli, opened at the Music Box Theatre in New York City on March 27, 1996, after an extensive national tour and ran there for 110 performances. A Theatre Guild Production presented by David Merrick, Inc., with Philip Langner, Robert Franz, Natalie Lloyd, Matt Garfield, Meredith Blair, Gordon Smith, Norma Langworthy, and Sonny Everett in association with Mark N. Sirangelo and the PGI Entertainment Company. Directed by James Hammerstein and Randy Skinner. Choreography by Randy Skinner. Orchestrations by Bruce Pomahac. Vocal arrangements by Kay Cameron. Dance arrangements by Scot Woolley. Music direction by Kay Cameron. Scenic design by James Leonard Joy. Costume design by Michael Bottari and Ronald Case. Lighting design by Natasha Katz. Cast: Kathryn Crosby (Melissa Frake), John Davidson (Abel Frake), Andrea McArdle (Margy Frake), Donna McKechnie (Emily Arden), Scott Wise (Pat Gilbert), Ben Wright (Wayne Frake), and ensemble.

Recordings: Individual songs from *State Fair* were recorded by a full panoply of 1940s vocalists. Soundtrack recordings were released in 1945 and 1962. There is also a cast album from the 1996 Broadway staging.

Most of the songs from *State Fair* were published. The Rodgers & Hammerstein Organization has some early drafts of the screenplay. A folder of handwritten notes for the screenplay is in the music division of the Library of Congress. The New York Public Library for the Performing Arts has a copy of the revised final shooting script, dated December 8, 1944. Both films are available on VHS and DVD.

This chapter does not include the 1962 additions—"It's the Little Things in Texas," "More Than Just a Friend," "Never Say No to a Man," "This Isn't Heaven," and "Willing and Eager"—because the lyrics were by Richard Rodgers. See the *Oklahoma!* chapter for the dropped song "We Will Be Together," and for two interpolations used in both stage versions, "When Ah Go Out Walking With Mah Baby" and "Boys and Girls Like You and Me." For other Rodgers and Hammerstein songs interpolated into the 1996 stage production, see: *Me and Juliet* ("You Never Had It So Good" and "That's the Way It Happens"); *Allegro* ("So Far"), *Pipe Dream* ("The Man I Used to Be" and "Next Time It Happens"). The stage song "Driving at Night," used to cover a scene change, is a posthumous creation by James Hammerstein. The melody comes from "Two Short Years," a song dropped from *Allegro*; the lyric is based on lines from the original *State Fair* novel.

OUR STATE FAIR

Published in the vocal selection. Introduced by Percy Kilbride (Dave Miller), Charles Winninger (Abel Frake), and Fay Bainter (Melissa Frake).

Our state fair is a great state fair,
Don't miss it, don't even be late!
It's dollars to doughnuts that our state fair
Is the best state fair in our state!

IT MIGHT AS WELL BE SPRING

Published as an individual sheet. Refrain appears in *Lyrics*. Winner of the 1945 Academy Award for Best Song. Introduced by Jeanne Crain (Margy Frake) and Louanne Hogan (singing voice for Jeanne Crain).

In a live April 1956 interview for *Youth Wants to Know*, Hammerstein explained:

> The leading girl in the story was restless and acts like, well, it is spring fever, at the beginning of the story and I started to write a song about a girl having spring fever. And then, with a terrible shock, I realized no state fairs are held except in the autumn. Then I thought, well, maybe she just feels this way, although it is fall, and that gave me an even better theme, "It Might As Well Be Spring." Then I wasn't quite sure about it and I told Dick the title and he said, "That's great," and that gave me the courage to go ahead with it.

Discographer Edward Foote Gardner rates this song as number sixteen for 1945. Best-selling recordings include versions by Margaret Whiting with Paul Weston's Orchestra, Dick Haymes, and Sammy Kaye.

VERSE

The things I used to like
I don't like anymore.
I want a lot of other things
I've never had before.
It's just like mother says—
I sit around and mope,
Pretending I am wonderful—
And knowing I'm a dope!

REFRAIN

I'm as restless as a willow in
    a windstorm,
I'm as jumpy as a puppet on
    a string!
I'd say that I had spring fever,
But I know it isn't spring.
I am starry-eyed and vaguely
    discontented,
Like a nightingale without a
    song to sing.
Oh, why should I have spring
    fever
When it isn't even spring?
I keep wishing I were
    somewhere else,

Walking down a strange new
street,
Hearing words that I have never
heard
From a man I've yet to meet.
I'm as busy as a spider, spinning
daydreams,
I'm as giddy as a baby on a swing.
I haven't seen a crocus or a
rosebud
Or a robin on the wing,
But I feel so gay—in a
melancholy way—
That it might as well be
spring . . .
It might as well be spring.

PARTIAL REPRISE

MARGY: [*daydreaming*] I keep wishing I
were somewhere else,
Walking down a strange new
street,
Hearing words that I have never
heard
From a man I've yet to meet.
He would be a kind of
handsome combination
Of Ronald Colman, Charles
Boyer, and Bing!

VOICE OF
RONALD COLMAN: [*spoken*] Margy . . . my dear little
Margy. I'd make the world a
ruby for your little finger, and
say, "I love you, I love you, I
love you."

VOICE OF
CHARLES BOYER: [*spoken*] Ah, Margy. You are
beautiful. You are so very
beautiful.

VOICE OF
BING CROSBY: [*sung*] And we feel so gay
In a melancholy way
That it might as well be spring,
Boo-boo boo-boo boo-boo
Ya-da da-dee.
[*whistles*]

Mocking reprise

MARGY: In our air-conditioned,
patent-leather farmhouse
On our ultra-modern, scientific
farm,
We'll live in a streamlined
heaven
And we'll waste no time on
charm.

No geraniums to clutter our
veranda,
Nor a single little sentimental
thing.
No Virginia Creepers—nothing
useless—
HARRY: But September isn't spring!

THAT'S FOR ME

Published as an individual sheet. Refrain appears in
Lyrics. Introduced by Vivian Blaine (Emily Edwards).
Discographer Edward Foote Gardner ranks this as the
twentieth most popular song of 1945. Popular record-
ings include versions by Jo Stafford, Dick Haymes, and
Kay Kyser.

VERSE

Right between the eyes!
Quite a belt, that blow I felt this morning!
Fate gave me no warning,
Great was my surprise!

REFRAIN

I saw you standing in the sun,
And you were something to see.
I know what I like, and I liked what I saw,
And I said to myself,
"That's for me!"
"A lovely morning," I remarked,
And you were quick to agree.
You wanted to walk and I nodded my head
As I breathlessly said,
"That's for me!"
I left you standing under stars—
The day's adventures are through.
There's nothing for me but the dream in my
heart,
And the dream in my heart—
That's for you!
Oh, my darling,
That's for you!

IT'S A GRAND NIGHT FOR SINGING

Published as an individual sheet. Refrain appears in
Lyrics. Introduced by William Marshall (Marty), Dick
Haymes (Wayne), and ensemble.

REFRAIN

It's a grand night for singing,
The moon is flying high,
And somewhere a bird who is bound he'll be
heard,
Is throwing his heart at the sky.
It's a grand night for singing,
The stars are bright above,
The earth is aglow, and, to add to the show,
I think I am falling in love,
Falling, falling in love!

INTERLUDE

Maybe it's more than the moon,
Maybe it's more than the birds,
Maybe it's more than the sight of the night
In a light too lovely for words.

Maybe it's more than the earth,
Shiny in silvery blue.
Maybe the reason I'm feeling this way
Has something to do with you.

REPEAT REFRAIN

ISN'T IT KINDA FUN?

Published as an individual sheet. Introduced by Dick
Haymes (Wayne) and Vivian Blaine (Emily).

REFRAIN

WAYNE: Maybe you'll never be the love of my life,
Maybe I'm not the boy of your dreams,
But isn't it kinda fun to look in each
other's eyes,
Swapping romantic gleams?
Maybe you're not a girl to have and to
hold,
Maybe I'm not a boy who would stay,
But isn't it kinda fun carousing around
the town,
Dancing the night away?

Isn't it kinda fun holding hands,
According to a sweet and corny custom?
Isn't it kinda fun making vows,
Admitting that we both intend to
    bust 'em!
Maybe we're out for laughs, a girl and
    a boy,
Kidding across a table for two,
But haven't you got a hunch that this is
    the real McCoy
And all the things we tell each other are
    true?

INTERLUDE

EMILY: I'm not a girl for sentimental tripe,
    I never go for the Romeo type.
WAYNE: Over a dewy eyed Juliet
    No one has seen me drool yet.
EMILY: I don't say our hearts are tied
    By love's eternal tether.
WAYNE: But using words less dignified,
    Isn't it kinda fun to be together?

[*Both repeat refrain.*]

ALL I OWE IOWAY

Published as an individual sheet. Introduced by William Marshall (Marty), unidentified male quartet (entertainers), Vivian Blaine (Emily), Charles Winninger (Abel Frake), Fay Bainter (Melissa Frake), Donald Meek (Hippenstahl), and the ensemble.

VERSE

MARTY: I can hear them callin' hogs
    In the clear Ioway air.
    I can sniff the fragrant whiff
    Of an Ioway rose.
QUARTET: You've got Ioway in your
    heart!
MARTY: I've got Ioway in my hair,
    I've got Ioway in my ears
    And eyes and nose!

REFRAIN

MARTY: Oh, I know
    All I owe
    I owe Ioway.
    I owe Ioway all I owe and I
    know why.
    I am Ioway born and bred

And on Ioway corn I'm fed,
Not to mention her barley,
    wheat, and rye.
MARTY AND QUARTET: I owe Ioway for her ham
    And her beef and her lamb
    And her strawberry jam
    And her pie.
MARTY: I owe Ioway more than I can
    ever pay
    So I think I'll move to
    Californ-i-ay!
EMILY AND QUARTET: What a shame!
    What a shame!
    You'll be good and
    gosh-darn sorry when
    you go!
MARTY: Don't I know!
EMILY
AND QUARTET: When you leave your native
    state
    You'll be feelin' far from
    great—
    You'll be good and gosh-
    darn sorry when you go!

INTERLUDE

MARTY: I'm a seed—of Ioway grain.
EMILY: You're a breeze—that Ioway
    blew.
MARTY: I'm a drop—of Ioway rain.
EMILY
AND QUARTET: You're a drip—of Ioway
    dew!

REFRAIN 2

EMILY: Oh, I know
    All I owe
    I owe Ioway.
    I owe Ioway all I owe and I
    know why.
    I am Ioway born and bred
    And on Ioway corn I'm fed,
    Not to mention her barley,
    wheat, and rye.
    I owe Ioway for her ham
    And her beef and her
    lamb—
ABEL FRAKE: And her strawberry jam—
MELISSA FRAKE: And her pie.
ABEL FRAKE: I owe Ioway more than
    anyone should owe,
    So I think I'll start in owin'
    Idaho!
EMILY, ABEL,
AND ENSEMBLE: What a shame!
    What a shame!

You'll be cryin' like a baby
    when you go!
ABEL FRAKE: Don't I know!
    When I leave my native
    heath
    With my lip between my
    teeth,
    I'll be bawlin' like a baby
    when I go!

INTERLUDE

EMILY: You're a seed—of Ioway
    grain.
    You're a breeze—that Ioway
    blew.
HIPPENSTAHL: I'm a drop—of Ioway rain.
MRS. HIPPENSTAHL: You're a drip—of Ioway
    dew!

REFRAIN 3

MARTY,
EMILY, QUARTET,
AND ENSEMBLE: Oh, I know
    All I owe
    I owe Ioway.
    I owe Ioway all I owe and I
    know why.
    I am Ioway born and bred
    And on Ioway corn I'm fed,
    Not to mention her barley,
    wheat, and rye.
    I owe Ioway for her ham
    And her beef and her lamb
    And her strawberry jam
    And her pie.
    I owe Ioway more than
    anyone should owe,
    So I think I'll start in owin'
    Idaho!
    Better stay!
    Better stay!
    You'll be good and
    gosh-darn sorry if
    you go!
MARTY: Don't I know!
ALL: When you leave your native
    state
    You'll be feelin' far from
    great—
    You'll be good and
    gosh-darn sorry when
    you go!

I owe Ioway for her ham
And her beef and her lamb
And her strawberry jam

And her pie.
I owe Ioway more than I can
ever pay
So I think I'll move to
Californ-i-ay!

I-O-W,
I-O-W,
I-O-W,
I-O-W,
A
Hooray!
Ioway!

Additional lines from sheet music

I owe Ioway for her ham
And her beef and her lamb
And her strawberry jam
And her pie.
Though I'm owin' her more
than I can ever pay,
If she'll keep me on the
cuff, I'd like to stay.
Better stay, better stay
You'll be good and gosh-darn
happy if you do.
If Ioway is your home
You're a fool to want to roam
'Cause there can't be any
better home for you!

CUT AND UNUSED SONG

KISS ME AND GO YOUR WAY

Not used. No music is known to have been written. Little is known about this fragment, apparently linked to *State Fair*.

Kiss me and go your way
But never say goodbye.
Go like a star,
Just as a star fades in a morning sky.

Leave me without farewell,
Don't try to tell me why.
Kiss me for love
While we're in love,
While both our hearts beat high.
Don't ever kiss me goodbye.

SONGS OF 1946

ALL THROUGH THE DAY

From the Twentieth Century Fox film *Centennial Summer* (1946). Music by Jerome Kern. Published as an individual sheet. Introduced in the film by Larry Stevens (Richard Lewis Esq.,) Cornel Wilde (Philippe Lascalles), and Jeanne Crain (Julia Rogers). Jeanne Crain's songs were dubbed by Louanne Hogan.

"All Through the Day" was one of the top songs of 1946, spending months on the Lucky Strike Hit Parade, and was nominated for the Academy Award for Best Song in 1947. Popular recordings were made by Frank Sinatra (Columbia), Perry Como (RCA Victor), and Margaret Whiting (Capitol).

"All Through the Day" is sometimes identified as Kern's last song, but was probably written prior to "Nobody Else But Me."

VERSE

I sit alone in the golden daylight,
But all I see is a silver sky;
For in my fancy I sweep away light,
And keep my image of the sky,
Just the way we like it, you and I.

REFRAIN

All through the day I dream about the night,
I dream about the night here with you.
All through the day I wish away the time,
Until the time when I'm here with you.
Down falls the sun,
I run to meet you,
The evening mist melts away;
Down smiles the moon, and soon your lips recall
The kiss I dreamed of all through the day.

REPEAT REFRAIN

I HAVEN'T GOT A WORRY IN THE WORLD

Music by Richard Rodgers. Published as an individual sheet. Introduced by Helen Hayes in *Happy Birthday* (opened October 31, 1946, at the Broadhurst Theatre; written by Anita Loos, directed by Joshua Logan, and produced by Rodgers and Hammerstein). *Happy Birthday* was not a musical, and Hayes was not a singer, but the story called for her character to lose her inhibitions after an evening at a bar. Bernadette Peters revived the song in 2002 with a swinging arrangement by Jonathan Tunick.

VERSE

Sentimental music, sweet and low,
Lamps upon the tables wink and glow.
All the smiling waiters seem to know
Exactly how I feel.

REFRAIN

I'm dancing with my honey,
My honey's close to me,
And I haven't got a worry in the world.
I'm happy as a bluebird.
How happy can you be?
I haven't got a worry in the world.
I'm floating and flying
Above the cares of day.
My honey's arms are sighing:
"Enjoy us while you may!"
I'm dreamy as a lovebird,
How dreamy can you be?
My heart is in a flurry,
My pulse is in a hurry,
But I haven't got a worry,
I haven't got a worry in the world.

OVERLEAF Top: *Richard Rodgers, Agnes de Mille, and Oscar Hammerstein during rehearsals*
Bottom: *Roberta Jonay (center) and dancers*

323

ALLEGRO (1947)

Tryouts: Shubert Theatre, New Haven, September 1–6, 1947; Colonial Theatre, Boston, September 8–October 4, 1947. New York run: Majestic Theatre; opened on October 10, 1947; closed on July 10, 1948; 315 performances. A New Musical Play. Presented by the Theatre Guild under the supervision of Lawrence Langner and Theresa Helburn. Book and lyrics by Oscar Hammerstein II. Music by Richard Rodgers. Direction and choreography by Agnes de Mille. Orchestrations by [Robert] Russell Bennett. Dance arrangements by Trude Rittmann. Orchestra directed by Salvatore Dell'Isola. Chorus directed by Crane Calder. Settings and lighting by Joe Mielziner. Costumes by Lucinda Ballard.

Cast: Annamary Dickey (Marjorie Taylor), William Ching (Dr. Joseph Taylor Sr.), Muriel O'Malley (Grandma Taylor), John Battles (Joseph Taylor Jr.), Roberta Jonay (Jennie Brinker), John Conte (Charlie Townsend), Kathryn Lee (Hazel), Gloria Wills (Beulah), Lisa Kirk (Emily), Edward Platt (Mayor/Minister), Ray Harrison (Friend of Joey/Bertram Woolhaven), Frank Westbrook (Friend of Joey), Robert Byrn (Principal/Philosophy Professor), Evelyn Taylor (Mabel), Stanley Simmons (Bicycle Boy), Harrison Muller (Georgie), Susan Svetlik (Miss Lipscomb/Shakespeare Student), Sam Steen (Cheerleader), Charles Tate (Cheerleader), Wilson Smith (Coach/Buckley), Paul Parks (Ned Brinker), David Collyer (English Professor), William McCully (Chemistry Professor), Raymond Keast (Greek Professor), Blake Ritter (Singer), Katrina Van Oss (Molly), Julie Humphries (Millie), Sylvia Karlton (Dot), Patricia Bybell (Addie), Lawrence Fletcher (Dr. Bigby Denby), Frances Rainer (Mrs. Mulhouse), Lily Paget (Mrs. Lansdale), Bill Bradley (Jarman), Jean Houloose (Maid), and Stephen Chase (Brook Lansdale), with ensemble of singers and dancers.

Hammerstein sketched the plot as follows: "The story starts in 1905 on the day Joseph Taylor Jr. is born and follows his life to his thirty-fifth year. The three major locations of action are in his home town, his college town, and a large city, all in the same Midwestern state. . . . The singing chorus is used frequently to interpret the mental and emotional reactions of the principal characters, after the manner of a Greek chorus." Joe is a doctor's son who aspires to be a doctor himself. His other great desire is to marry his childhood sweetheart, Jenny Brinker. He achieves both but Jenny's social and material ambitions bring them to the city, where he services a wealthy clientele and she begins an affair. In addition to Joe's parents and grandmother, other major characters are Charlie Townsend (Joe's college roommate and best man) and Emily (Joe's nurse and assistant).

Awards: Donaldson Awards for Best Book, Best Lyrics, Best Score.

A national tour was launched at the Shubert Theatre, Philadelphia, on November 5, 1948, and visited 16 cities, ending at the Great Northern Theatre, Chicago, June 11, 1949.

An original cast recording was made by RCA. A new complete recording was issued by Sony in 2008 featuring Laura Benanti (Jenny), Norbert Leo Butz (Charlie), Liz Callaway (Emily), Nathan Gunn (Dr. Joseph Taylor Sr.), Judy Kuhn (Beulah), Audra McDonald (Marjorie Taylor), Marni Nixon (Grandma), and Patrick Wilson (Joe).

The primary sources for this chapter are the published vocal score and the published libretto. Also consulted were drafts of the script and rehearsal material at the Rodgers & Hammerstein Organization and piano-vocal scores in the Richard Rodgers Collection in the music division of the Library of Congress.

Legend has it that the *South Pacific* ballad "Younger than Springtime" was originally a song cut from *Allegro*; but no trace of it has been found.

In a March 1958 interview with Mike Wallace, Hammerstein said:

> There were many things in the story of *Allegro* which reflected reactions I'd had to life as I grew up.
>
> . . . The discovery that after you're successful, whether you be a doctor or a lawyer or a librettist, there is a conspiracy that goes on in which you join, a conspiracy of the world to render you less effective by bestowing honors on you and taking you away from the job of curing people, or of pleading cases, or writing libretti, and putting you on committees. If you're a doctor, you're suddenly running a hospital instead of tending to the sick directly. You're better off if you remain a doctor.
>
> I'm a fine one to talk, because since I wrote *Allegro*, I think I'm on more committees than I was then, and I get drawn into these things and can't help myself.

OPENING (JOSEPH TAYLOR, JUNIOR)

Published in the vocal score. Introduced by the ensemble and William Ching (Dr. Joseph Taylor Sr).

ALL: The lady in bed is Marjorie Taylor,
Doctor Joseph Taylor's wife.
A SOPRANO: Except for the day when she married Joe,
This is the happiest day of her life!
ALL: Except for the day when she married Joe,
This is the happiest day of her life!
BOYS: His hair is fuzzy,
His eyes are blue.
His eyes may change—
They often do.
He weighs eight pounds
And an ounce or two—
Joseph Taylor, Junior!
GIRLS: When he wakes up
He wants to eat,
And when he sleeps he wets his seat,
But you'd forgive anyone as sweet
As Joseph Taylor, Junior!
DRUNKS: His hair is fuzzy
His eyes are blue
His eyes may change—
They often do.
He weighs eight pounds
And an ounce or two—
Joseph Taylor—*hic*—Junior!
CHOIR: Ring out, ring out,
Oh bells of joy,
And all the ships at sea, ahoy!
The doctor's wife
Has a bouncing boy,
Joseph Taylor, Junior!
CHILDREN: See what Mrs. Taylor's done!
Had herself an eight-pound son!
Hail him! Hail him, ev'ryone!
Joseph Taylor, Junior!
ENSEMBLE: Joseph Taylor, Junior!
Ring, oh bells of joy
For Joseph Taylor, Junior,
Marjorie's eight-pound boy!
DR. JOSEPH TAYLOR: Joseph Taylor, Junior,
Marjorie's eight-pound boy!

REPRISE

[JOE JR. *is at college.*]

You must forgive him
If he looks new.
He may grow older—
They often do.
He weighs one hundred and fifty-two,
Joseph Taylor, Junior.

I KNOW IT CAN HAPPEN AGAIN

Published in the vocal score. Included in *Lyrics*. Introduced by Muriel O'Malley (Grandma Taylor).

Starting out, so foolishly small,
It's hard to believe you will grow at all.
It's hard to believe that things like you
Can ever turn out to be men,
But I've seen it happen before,
So I know it can happen again.
Food and sleep and plenty of soap,
Molasses and sulphur, and love, and hope—
The winters go by, the summers fly,
And all of a sudden you're men!
I have seen it happen before,
And I know it can happen again.

ONE FOOT, OTHER FOOT

Published in the vocal score. Included in *Lyrics*. Introduced by the singing and dancing ensembles.

Pudgy legs begin to grow long
And one sunny day, when you're feeling strong,
You straighten a knee and suddenly
You're struck with a daring idea!

One foot, other foot,
One foot, other foot,
One foot, other foot,
One foot, other foot.

Now you can go
Wherever you want,
Wherever you want to go,
One foot out
And the other foot out—
That's all you need to know!

Now you can do
Whatever you want,
Whatever you want to do.
Here you are
In a wonderful world
Especially made for you,
Especially made for you!

Now you can march around the yard,
Shout to all the neighborhood,

Tell the folks you're feeling good
(Folks ought to know when boys feel good).

Now you can imitate a dog,
Chase a bird around a tree,
You can chase a bumblebee
(Once is enough to chase a bee).

Now you can play among the flow'rs,
Grab yourself a hunk o' dirt,
Smudge it on your mother's skirt
(That little dirt won't hurt a skirt).

One foot, other foot,
One foot, other foot,
Now you can do
Whatever you want,
Whatever you want to do.
Here you are in a wonderful world,
Especially made for you,
Especially made for you,
Especially made for you.

To walk in, to run in,
To play in the sun in,
Especially made for you.
For now you can walk,
You taught yourself to walk,
You puzzled it out yourself,
And now you can walk.

[*spoken*] One foot, other foot, one foot, other foot,
    one foot, other foot, one foot, other foot.

[*sung*] Now you can go
Wherever you want,
Wherever you want to go.
One foot out
And the other foot out,
One foot out
And the other foot out,
One foot out
And the other foot out,
And the world belongs to Joe,
And the world belongs to Joe!

WINTERS GO BY

Published in the vocal score. Included in *Lyrics*. Introduced by the ensemble.

The winters go by,
The summers fly,

And soon you're a student in "high"!
And now your clothes are spotlessly clean,
Your head is anointed with brilliantine!
You're brimming with hope
But can't quite cope
With problems that vex and perplex,
For you don't quite know how to treat
The bewild'ringly opposite sex!

POOR JOE

Published in the vocal score. Included in *Lyrics*. Introduced by the ensemble.

Poor Joe!
The older you grow,
The harder it is to know
What to think,
What to do,
Where to go!

DIPLOMA

Published in the vocal score. Introduced by the ensemble and Robert Byrn (high school Principal).

ENSEMBLE: Your love for Jennie
        Becomes more keen,
        Your arms get long,
        Your legs get lean,
        And all at once you are seventeen!
PRINCIPAL: Joseph Taylor, Junior!

A FELLOW NEEDS A GIRL

Published as an individual sheet. Included in *Lyrics*. Introduced by William Ching (Dr. Joseph Taylor Sr.) and Annamary Dickey (Mrs. Marjorie Taylor). The song was a hit for both Frank Sinatra and Perry Como.

DR. TAYLOR: A fellow needs a girl
        To sit by his side
        At the end of a weary day,
        To sit by his side

And listen to him talk
And agree with the things he'll say.
A fellow needs a girl
To hold in his arms
When the rest of his world goes wrong,
To hold in his arms
And know that she believes
That her fellow is wise and strong.
When things go right
And his job's well done,
He wants to share
The prize he's won.
If no one shares,
And no one cares,
Where's the fun
Of a job well done
Or a prize you've won?
A fellow needs a home
His own kind of home,
But to make his dream come true,
A fellow needs a girl,
His own kind of girl—
My kind of girl is you.

MARJORIE: My fellow needs a girl
To sit by his side
At the end of a weary day,
So I sit by his side
And listen to him talk
And agree with the things he'll say.
My fellow needs a girl
To hold in his arms
When the rest of the world goes wrong,
To hold in his arms
And know that she believes
That her fellow is wise and strong.
When things go right
And his job's well done,
He wants to share
The prize he's won,
If no one shares,
And no one cares,
Where's the fun
Of a job well done?
DR. TAYLOR: Or a prize you've won?
MARJORIE: My fellow needs a home,
His own kind of home,
But to make his dreams come true—
DR. TAYLOR: A fellow needs to love—
MARJORIE: His one only love—
BOTH: My only love is you.*

_____

*The published sheet has this alternate version of the
final three lines for a female singer:
A fellow needs a girl,
His own kind of girl—
Am I the girl for you?*

A DARN NICE CAMPUS

Published in the vocal score. Included in *Lyrics*. Introduced by John Battles (Joseph Taylor Jr.).

_____

It's a darn nice campus,
With ivy on the walls,
Friendly maples
Outside the lecture halls,
A new gymnasium,
A chapel with a dome—
It's a darn nice campus . . .
And I wish I were home.

It's a darn nice campus,
I'm going to like it fine!
Darn cute coeds,
They have a snappy line;
Darn nice fellers,
As far as I can tell—
It's a darn nice campus . . .
And I'm lonely as hell!

REPRISE

[JENNIE *is reading* JOE's *letter.*]

"It's a darn nice campus,
With ivy on the walls,
Friendly maples
Outside the lecture halls.
I like my roommate,
And you would like him too—
It's a darn nice campus . . .
But I'm lonely for you."

WILDCATS

Published in the vocal score. Introduced by the ensemble (College Freshmen), Sam Steen and Charles Tate (Cheerleaders), and John Battles (Joseph Taylor Jr.)

_____

The Wildcats are on a rampage!
Hear those Wildcats yell—Yow!
The Wildcats are out to beat you,
To beat you to a fare-thee-well—Wow!
Wow! Wow! Wow! Go the Wildcats
And another team goes down—
It's another day of victory
For the purple and brown!

SO FAR

Out-of-town-tryout programs use the title "We Have Nothing to Remember." Published as an individual sheet. Introduced by Gloria Wills (Beulah). Frank Sinatra and Perry Como both had hit recordings.

The following anecdote was prepared by Hammerstein for the introduction to *Lyrics* but was not used:

Songwriters fall in love with the songs they write and try to put them into shows where they don't belong. I have done it myself now and then, even though I know it is a dangerous rule to break. Each time, of course, I invented some rationalization and told myself why, in this particular case, it was all right and the song fit the story after all. A case, the most recent one I remember, was in *Allegro*. Dick and I had written a number for a movie called "So Far."* The movie was never done. We liked the song very much, persuaded the studio to give it back to us, and we put it into *Allegro*. It was not suitable for any of the leading characters, and we wrote in a small part for a girl who could sing it to one of our leading characters.

VERSE

No keepsakes have we
For days that are gone,
No fond recollections to look back upon,
No songs that we love,
No scene to recall
We have no traditions at all.

REFRAIN

We have nothing to remember so far, so far.
So far, we haven't walked by night
And shared the light of a star.
So far, your heart has never fluttered so near, so near,
That my own heart alone could hear it.
We haven't gone beyond the very beginning,
We've just begun to know how lucky we are,
So we have nothing to remember so far, so far—

_____

* *Musical-theater historian Miles Kreuger identifies the movie as* Jenny Was a Lady, *explaining that in exchange for releasing actress Jan Clayton for thirteen weeks of live performances in* Show Boat *in 1946, Jerome Kern had promised MGM producer Samuel Marx that he and Hammerstein would write a song for her next film at no charge. After Kern's death, Richard Rodgers adopted the responsibility of supplying the song. A lyric sheet is dated May 6, 1946.*

But now I'm face to face with you,
And now at last we've met
And now we can look forward to
The things we'll never forget.

REPEAT REFRAIN

YOU ARE NEVER AWAY

Published as an individual sheet. Included in *Lyrics*.
Introduced by John Battles (Joseph Taylor Jr.) and the
singing ensemble. A popular recording was made by
Buddy Clark.

You are never away
From your home in my heart;
There is never a day
When you don't play a part
In a word that I say
Or a sight that I see—
You are never away,
And I'll never be free.
You're the smile on my face,
Or a song that I sing,
You're a rainbow I chase
On a morning in spring;
You're a star in the lace
Of a wild willow tree—
In the green, leafy lace
Of a wild willow tree.
But tonight you're no star,
Nor a song that I sing;
In my arms, where you are,
You are sweeter than spring;
In my arms, where you are,
Clinging closely to me,
You are lovelier, by far,
Than I dreamed you could be—
You are lovelier, my darling,
Than I dreamed you could be!

WHAT A LOVELY DAY FOR A WEDDING

Published in the vocal score. A fragment appears in
Lyrics. Introduced by Paul Parks (Ned Brinker), John
Conte (Charlie Townsend), and the singing ensemble.

In a preface to the published libretto of *Allegro*,

Hammerstein addressed various complaints about the
show, including one that all the townfolk were virtuous
and all the city folks wicked, pointing out: "The wedding guests in the country church are as catty a crowd of
gossips as can be found."

GUESTS: What a lovely day for a
wedding!
Not a cloud to darken the
sky.
It's a treat to meet at a
wedding,
To laugh and to gossip and
to cry.
What a lovely day for a
wedding!
What a day for two to be
tied!
It's a lovely day for a
wedding—
NED: But not for the father of the
bride.
What I'm about to get
I don't exactly need—
A doctor for a son-in-law,
Another mouth to feed!
GUESTS: What he's about to get
He doesn't really need—
A doctor for a son-in-law,
Another mouth to feed.
What a lovely day for a
wedding!
There's a lively tang in the
air.
It's a treat to meet at a
wedding
When fam'lies are letting
down their hair.
What a lovely day for a
wedding!
We have come by motor and
shay.
It's a treat to meet at a
wedding
And say what we usually
say.
THE TAYLOR GROUP: What can he see in her?
THE BRINKER GROUP: What can she see in him?
THE TAYLOR GROUP: The Brinkers all are
stinkers!
THE BRINKER GROUP: All the Taylor crowd is grim!
What can she see in him?
THE TAYLOR GROUP: What can he see in her?
ALL: In many ways we differ
But in one thing we concur:
It's a lovely day for a
wedding!

What a day for two to be
tied!
It's a lovely day for a
wedding—
NED: But not for the father of the
bride.
BRIDESMAIDS: It's a lovely day for a
wedding,
Not a cloud to darken the
sky,
It's a lovely day for a
wedding—
CHARLIE TOWNSEND: As long as the bridegroom
isn't I.
BRIDESMAIDS: Why?

IT MAY BE A GOOD IDEA

Published in the vocal score. Included in *Lyrics*. Introduced by John Conte (Charlie Townsend).

It may be a good idea for Joe,
But it wouldn't be good for me
To sit in a mortgaged bungalow
With my little ones on my knee.
I'd much rather go and blow my dough
On a casual chickadee.
I don't want a mark that I'll have to toe;
My toe can go where it wants to go;
It wants to go where the wild girls grow
In extravagant quantity.
To bask in the warm and peaceful glow
Of connubial constancy
May be awfully good for good old Joe
But it wouldn't be good for me.*

—————————
* *Discarded verse:*
Possibly I'm cynical,
Material and clinical,
And possibly I lack the lofty aim
Of many who
Stay shackled to
One dame.
Truthfully, a nuptial tie
I look upon with glassy eye,
And truthfully, I do not think my life
Is incomplete
Without a sweet
Young wife.
Hymen, god of marriage
Doesn't spell for me romance.
Hyman's just a man I know
Who presses all my pants!

ACT ONE FINALE

Published in the vocal score. The first stanza is included in *Lyrics*. Introduced by the ensemble and Muriel O'Malley (Grandma Taylor).

ENSEMBLE: Let the church light up with the glory
That belongs to ev'ry bride and groom,
May the first bright day of their story
Be a flower that will ever bloom.

GRANDMA TAYLOR: Starting out, so foolishly small,
It's hard to believe they will grow at all.
But winters go by and summers fly,
And all of a sudden they're men!

ENSEMBLE: To have and to hold
From this day forward
For better, for worse,
For richer, for poorer,
In sickness and in health,
To love and to cherish,
Till death do us part,
Till death do us part.

WISH THEM WELL

Published in the vocal score. Included in *Lyrics*. Introduced by the ensemble.

Two more lovers
Were married today.
Wish them well! Wish them well! Wish them well!
Brave and happy,
They start on their way,
Wish them well! Wish them well! Wish them well!
They have faith in the future
And joy in their hearts,
If you look in their eyes
You can tell
How brave and happy
And hopeful are they.
Wish them well, wish them well, wish them well.
Wish them well, wish them well, wish them well . . .

MONEY ISN'T EVERYTHING

Published as an individual sheet. Included in *Lyrics*. Introduced by Roberta Jonay (Jennie Brinker Taylor), Kathryn Lee (Hazel), Patricia Bybell (Addie), Julie Humphries (Millie), and Sylvia Karlton (Dot).

REFRAIN 1

MILLIE: "Money isn't ev'rything!
What can money buy?"
ADDIE AND DOT: An automobile, so you won't get wet—
Champagne, so you won't get dry!
MILLIE: "Money isn't ev'rything!
What have rich folks got?"
ADDIE AND DOT: A Florida home, so you won't get cold—
A yacht so you won't get hot!
DOT: An orchid or two
So you won't feel blue
If you have to go out at night.
ADDIE: And maybe a jar
Of caviar,
So your appetite won't be light!
MILLIE: "Oil tycoon and cattle king,
Radio troubadour,
Belittle the fun that their fortunes bring,
And tell you that they are sure
Money isn't ev'rything!"
MILLIE, ADDIE, DOT: Money isn't ev'rything,
Money isn't ev'rything—
JENNIE AND HAZEL: Unless you're very poor!

INTERLUDE

MILLIE: "Can money make you honest?
Can it teach you right from wrong?
Can money keep you healthy?
Can it make your muscles strong?"
ADDIE: Can money make your eyes get red,
The way they do from sewing?
Can money make your back get sore,
The way it gets from mowing?
DOT: Can money make your hands get rough,
As washing dishes does?
JENNIE AND HAZEL: Can money make you smell the way
That cooking fishes does?
MILLIE: "It buys you gems and fancy clothes
And juicy steaks to carve,
But it cannot build your character—"
JENNIE, HAZEL, ADDIE, DOT: Or teach you how to starve!

REFRAIN 2

MILLIE: "Money isn't ev'rything!
If you're rich, you pay—"
ADDIE AND DOT: Elizabeth Arden to do your face
The night you attend a play!
ADDIE, DOT, MILLIE: Feeling like the bloom of spring,
Down the aisle you float!
A Tiffany ring and a Cartier string
Of pearls to adorn your throat!
Your Carnegie dress
Will be more or less
Of a handkerchief round your hip,
Sewed on to you so
That your slip won't show—
JENNIE AND HAZEL: And whatever you show won't slip!
ADDIE, DOT, MILLIE: To your creamy shoulders cling
Ermines white as snow.
Then on to cafés where they sway and swing
You go with your wealthy beau.
There you'll hear a crooner sing:
"Money isn't ev'rything!"
ALL: Money isn't ev'rything,
As long as you have dough!

YATATA, YATATA, YATATA

Published in the vocal score. Introduced by John Conte (Charlie Townsend) and the ensemble (party guests).

ALL: [*chanted*] Yatata, yatata, yatata, yatata
Yatata, yatata, yatata, yatata . . .
1ST GIRL: Broccoli!
1ST MAN: Hogwash!

2ND MAN: Balderdash!

3RD MAN: Phoney baloney!

2ND GIRL: Tripe and trash!

ALL: [*chanted*] Yatata, yatata, yatata, yatata
Yatata, yatata, yatata, yatata
Yatata, yatata, yatata, yatata
Yatata, yatata, yatata, yatata . . .

3RD GIRL: Busy!
Busy!
I'm busy as a bee!
I start the day at half past one!
When I am finished phoning
It's time to dress for tea.

ALL THREE GIRLS: Nothing we have to do gets done!

CHARLIE: [*to himself*] The deep-thinking gentlemen and ladies
Who keep a metropolis alive
Drink cocktails
And knock tails
Ev'ry afternoon at five.

ALL: [*chanted*] Yatata, yatata, yatata, yatata
Yatata, yatata, yatata, yatata . . .

4TH MAN: There goes Doctor Denby!

5TH MAN: Doctor Bigby Denby!

ALL: Bigby Denby Bigby Denby Bigby Denby Bigby Denby!

GROUP OF LADIES: Doctor!
Doctor!
I need another shot!

A SECOND GROUP: The shots he gives are too divine!
He fills a little needle and he gives you all it's got!
Your fanny hurts, but you feel fine!

HALF OF THE ENSEMBLE: [*chanted*] Yatata, yatata, yatata, yatata
Yatata, yatata, yatata, yatata
Yatata, yatata, yatata, yatata
Yatata, yatata, yatata, yatata . . .

THE OTHER HALF: Broccoli, hogwash, balderdash
Phoney baloney, tripe and trash!
Goodness knows where the day has gone!

ALL: The days come fast and are quickly gone,
But the talk talk talk goes on and on
And on and on and on!

MEN: Lansdale!
Lansdale!
The multimillionaire!
He manufactures Lansdale soap!

CHARLIE: So when he tells a story
His listeners declare
He's twice as comical as Bob Hope!

ALL: [*chanted*] Yatata, yatata, yatata, yatata
Yatata, yatata, yatata, yatata . . .

[*Chant continues under dialogue.*]

CHARLIE: The deep-thinking gentlemen and ladies
Who keep a metropolis alive
Drink cocktails
And knock tails
Ev'ry afternoon at five!

ALL: Broccoli, hogwash, balderdash
Phoney baloney, tripe and trash!

DENBY: Goodness knows where the years have gone!

ALL: The years of a life are quickly gone,
But the talk talk talk goes on and on,
Goes on and on and on.
The prattle and the tattle,
The gab and the gush,
The chatter and the patter
And the twaddle and the tush
Go on and on and on and on and on!
Yatata, yatata, yatata . . .

[*The chant continues as the scene fades.*]

Stanzas cut during tryouts

WOMAN: Darling!

WOMAN WITH TINY POODLE: Angel!

WOMAN: Where did you get that pup?
Is oo your mama's precious boy?

WOMAN WITH TINY POODLE: This little man is fully grown—
They're breeding them that way.
He's a miniature-miniature pygmy toy!

JENNIE: [*to* DR. BIGBY DENBY] Doctor!

CHARLIE: [*to* DR. BIGBY DENBY] Uncle!

JENNIE: How sweet of you to come!

DR. BIGBY DENBY: How sweet of you to ask me, dear!

CHARLIE: How was it down in Florida?

DR. BIGBY DENBY: Filled with parvenus!
I don't know where I'll go next year!

1ST HOUSEWIFE: Servants!

2ND HOUSEWIFE: Servants!

1ST HOUSEWIFE: They all want Sunday off!

2ND HOUSEWIFE: And ev'ry other Thursday too!

1ST HOUSEWIFE: In the employment agencies,
The questions that they ask!

FOUR WOMEN NEARBY: You'd think that they were hiring you!

THE GENTLEMAN IS A DOPE

Published as an individual sheet. Included in *Lyrics*. Introduced by Lisa Kirk (Emily). Singer Jo Stafford had a popular recording.

VERSE

The boss gets on my nerves;
I've got a good mind to quit.
I've taken all I can;
It's time to get up and git
And move to another job
Or maybe another town.
The gentleman burns me up,
The gentleman gets me down.

REFRAIN

The gentleman is a dope,
A man of many faults,

A clumsy Joe
Who wouldn't know
A rhumba from a waltz.
The gentleman is a dope,
And not my cup of tea.
Why do I get in a dither?
He doesn't belong to me.
The gentleman isn't bright,
He doesn't know the score;
A cake will come,
He'll take a crumb
And never ask for more.
The gentleman's eyes are blue,
But little do they see.
Why am I beating my brains out?
He doesn't belong to me.
He's somebody else's problem;
She's welcome to the guy!
She'll never understand him
Half as well as I.
The gentleman is a dope,
He isn't very smart.
He's just a lug
You'd like to hug
And hold against your heart.
The gentleman doesn't know
How happy he could be.
Look at me crying my eyes out
As if he belonged to me—
He'll never belong to me.

ALLEGRO

Published in the vocal score. Included in *Lyrics*. Introduced by John Conte (Charlie Townsend), John Battles (Joseph Taylor Jr.), Lisa Kirk (Emily), and the ensemble.

CHARLIE: Our world is for the
forceful
And not for sentimental
folk,
But brilliant and
resourceful
And paranoiac gentle folk!
JOE: Not soft and sentimental
folk!
CHARLIE: "Allegro," a musician
Would so describe the
speed of it,
The clash and competition
Of counterpoint—
EMILY: The need of it?

CHARLIE: We cannot prove the need
of it!
We know no other way
Of living out a day.
Our music must be
galloping and gay!
JOE: We muffle all the
undertones,
The minor blood-and-
thunder tones,
The overtones are all we
care to play!
ALL THREE: Hysterically frantic,
We are stubbornly
romantic
And doggedly determined
to be gay!
EMILY: Brisk, lively,
Merry and bright!
Allegro!
Same tempo
Morning and night!
Allegro!
Don't stop whatever
you do,
Do something dizzy and
new,
Keep up the hullabaloo!
EMILY AND ENSEMBLE: Allegro! Allegro!
Allegro! Allegro!
Allegro! Allegro!
JOE: We spin and we spin and we
spin and we spin,
Playing a game no one can
win,
The men who corner
wheat,
The men who corner gin,
The men who rule the
airwaves,
The denizens of din—
ENSEMBLE: They spin and they spin,
They spin and they spin.
CHARLIE: The girls who dig for gold
And won't give in for tin,
The lilies of the field,
So femininely thin,
They toil not, they spoil
not,
But oh, how they spin!
ENSEMBLE: Oh, how they spin!
Oh, how they spin!
JOE: May's in love with Kay's
husband,
He's in love with Sue!
Sue's in love with May's
husband,
What are they to do?

Tom's in love with Tim's
wife,
She's in love with Sam!
Sam's in love with Tom's
wife,
So they're in a jam!
CHARLIE: They are smart little sheep
Who have lost their way,
CHARLIE, JOE, EMILY: Blah! Blah! Blah!
CHARLIE, JOE, EMILY,
AND ENSEMBLE: Brisk, lively,
Merry and bright!
Allegro!
Same tempo
Morning and night!
Allegro!
Don't stop whatever
you do,
Do something dizzy and
new,
Keep up the hullabaloo!
Allegro! Allegro!
Allegro! Allegro!
Allegro! Allegro!

COME HOME

Published as an individual sheet (refrain only). Introduced by William Ching (Dr. Joseph Taylor Sr.), Annamary Dickey (Marjorie Taylor), and ensemble.

ENSEMBLE: We are the friends that you left
behind.
DR. TAYLOR: You need us, Joe.
ENSEMBLE: And we need you,
We can bring happiness and peace to
your mind.
DR. TAYLOR: We want you, Joe.
ENSEMBLE: We want you
To come,
Come home.

REFRAIN

MARJORIE: Come home, come home,
Where the brown birds fly
Through a pale blue sky
To a tall green tree,
There is no finer sight for a man to
see—
Come home, Joe, come home!
Come home and lie
By a laughing spring,
Where the breezes sing

And caress your ear.
There is no sweeter sound for a man
    to hear—
Come home, Joe, come home.
You will find a world of honest
    friends who miss you,
You will shake the hands of men
    whose hands are strong,
And when all their wives and kids
    run up and kiss you,
You will know that you are back
    where you belong.
You'll know you're back
Where there's work to do,
Where there's love for you
For the love you give,
There is no better life for a man to
    live—
Come home, Joe, come home.
Come home, son, come home.

FINALE ULTIMO

Published in the vocal score. Introduced by the ensemble.

The scene is the dedication of a new wing of the hospital. Dr. Bigby Denby surprises Joe by announcing his promotion to physician-in-chief. Joe begins an acceptance speech, then surprises himself by declining the appointment. The ensemble's mini-reprises are sung between, and sometimes over, the ceremonial remarks.

ENSEMBLE: Broccoli, hogwash,
    balderdash,
Phoney baloney, tripe,
    and trash!
No one knows where his
    youth has gone,
No one knows where his
    heart has gone,
But the talk, talk, talk
Goes on and on and on
    and on and on.
Yatata, yatata, yatata,
    yatata.
Yatata, yatata, yatata,
    yatata.

[DENBY *begins his remarks.*]

ENSEMBLE: The prattle and tattle,
The gab and the gush,
The chatter and the
    patter,

And the twaddle and the
    tush
Go on and on and on
    and on and on!

[DENBY *introduces* JOE. *The ensemble utters some of* JOE's *internal thoughts about whether to stay or go, then* JOE *begins to address the gathering.* GRANDMA *and* MARJORIE *enter.* JOE *announces he will go into practice with his father.*]

HALF OF THE ENSEMBLE: One foot, other foot,
One foot, other foot,
One foot, other foot,
One foot, other foot.
One foot, other foot,
One foot, other foot,
One foot, other foot,
One foot, other foot.
THE OTHER HALF: Come home, come
    home,
Where the brown birds
    fly
Through a pale blue sky
To a tall green tree.
There is no finer sight
For a man to see!
Come home, Joe, come
    home!

[DENBY *and* LANSDALE *protest.* JOE *starts to leave.*]

HALF OF THE ENSEMBLE: One foot, other foot,
One foot, other foot,
One foot, other foot,
One foot, other foot.
THE OTHER HALF: One foot, other foot,
Now you can do
Whatever you want,
Whatever you want to
    do.

[EMILY *asks if* JOE *will need a nurse.*]

HALF OF THE ENSEMBLE: One foot, other foot,
One foot, other foot,
One foot, other foot,
One foot, other foot.
THE OTHER HALF: Here you are in a
    wonderful world
Especially made for
    you!

[CHARLIE *joins* JOE *and* EMILY.]

EMILY AND FULL ENSEMBLE: One foot, other foot,
One foot, other foot.

ALL: One foot, other foot,
One foot, other foot.
Now you can do
Whatever you want,
Whatever you want to
    do.
One foot out and the
    other foot out,
One foot out and the
    other foot out,
One foot out and the
    other foot out—
And the world belongs
    to you!

CUT AND UNUSED SONGS

SITTING ON THE PORCH IN THE MOONLIGHT

Dropped during the Boston tryout. This text comes from a May 5, 1947, typescript. The ensemble had performed this number between "You Are Never Away" and Marjorie's argument with Jennie. The porch sitters are Dr. and Mrs. Taylor, Joe and Jennie, and Jennie's father. Lines of the song intersperse the characters' attempts at casual conversation.

ENSEMBLE: Sitting on the porch in the moonlight,
With a glass of lemonade in your
    hand,
You let your fancies wander
To a private fairyland.
Far away you fly in the moonlight
From the folly of a world full of men
Then someone shoots his mouth off
And you're back on earth again,
You're back on earth again.

WHAT A LOVELY DAY FOR A WEDDING (PANTOUM VERSION)

Written for the wedding that ends Act One, but replaced during the out-of-town tryouts. Introduced by the ensemble. In an article about *Allegro* for the spring 1994 issue of Lincoln Center Theater's *New Theater Review*, Stephen Sondheim wrote of the many ways the production was experimental—it was an epic, it used a Greek chorus, it used unconventional scenic effects. "Oscar also experimented with lyrics. He was fascinated with certain forms that had never been used. He wrote a song . . . in an Indian form of lyric called 'pantoum.' . . . The idea of a pantoum is that you don't just do ABAB rhymes or ABAC rhymes. You actually repeat the whole line instead of rhyming it."

BRIDE'S SIDE: What a lovely day for a wedding.
GROOM'S SIDE: It is beautiful and bright and clear.
ALL: What a lovely day for a wedding.
BRIDE'S SIDE: Only relatives and friends are here.

ALL: It is beautiful and bright and clear.
GROOM'S SIDE: He will have his hands full with
Jennie.
ALL: Only relatives and friends are here.
BRIDE'S SIDE: Doctor Taylor hasn't a penny.

GROOM'S SIDE: He will have his hands full with
Jennie.
BRIDE'S SIDE: Joey isn't what I'd call a catch.
Doctor Taylor hasn't a penny.
GROOM'S SIDE: Mrs. Taylor didn't want this match.

BRIDE'S SIDE: Joey isn't what I'd call a catch.
ALL: What a lovely day for a wedding.
GROOM'S SIDE: Mrs. Taylor didn't want this match.
ALL: What a lovely day for a wedding.

I HAVE LET THE TIME RUN ON

A dropped portion of the wedding sequence. It is not specifically listed in the New Haven program, but an orchestration survives.

DR. JOSEPH
TAYLOR SR.: I have let the time run on,
And I gave him no advice.
When he asked me what I thought
I just said that she was "nice."
But a father seldom says

What he really ought to say.
I'm a coward, I suppose,
Or I'd tell the boy today.
GUESTS: Not today!
Not today!
Keep it rosy, keep it pretty, keep it
gay!
OLD LADY: Let us have no harsh intrusion
Of reality's confusion
In the organized illusion
Of this happy wedding day.
HAZEL: I know Jennie like a book,
I'm her very closest friend.
I was in this from the start
And I know how it will end.
Should've told her what I think,
But I couldn't figure how.
If I only had the nerve
I'd go in and tell her now.
GUESTS: Not today!
Not today!
Keep it rosy, keep it pretty, keep it
gay!
Let us have no harsh intrusion
Of reality's confusion
In the organized illusion
Of this happy wedding   day!

TWO SHORT YEARS

Lyric dropped after the New Haven tryout, where it opened act two. The music remains in the score. Sung by the ensemble.

REFRAIN 1

Two short years
Are not much time
In the age of an infinite world.
Two short years
Are two quick trips
That a small, dizzy planet has twirled.
But the days on a planet
Can be filled with strife
And joy and love and tears,
And a girl on a planet
Lives a lot of life
In two short years.

REFRAIN 2

Thrills and cheers
And chills and fears
Overlap in a flying montage,
Crowd each day
Then melt away
In the wake of a waning mirage.
But a dream often lingers,
Like a lovely chime
That echoes in your ears;
For a dream on a planet
Lives a long, long time
After two short years.

REPRISE

These lines were intended for the "Yatata" sequence.

Four short years
Are not much time
In the age of an infinite world.
A young, ambitious,
And attractive wife
Who plans and perseveres
Can create many changes
In a doctor's life
In four short years.

JOSEPH TAYLOR, JUNIOR (PARODY)

Theatre historian Steven Suskin found the following parody, presumably about Theresa Helburn, in the papers of Agnes de Mille. Along with Lawrence Langer, Helburn ran the Theatre Guild, which produced *Allegro*, *Carousel*, and *Oklahoma!*

Her brain is fuzzy,
Her hair is blue.
She'll change her mind—
She often do.
She's all of that
And looney too—
But Lawrence Langner's loonier.

OVERLEAF *Two scenes from the original Broadway production of* South Pacific
Top: *Mary Martin and Ezio Pinza*
Bottom: *"There is nothin' like a dame."*

SOUTH PACIFIC | 1949

SOUTH PACIFIC (1949)

Tryouts: Shubert Theatre, New Haven, March 7–12, 1949; Shubert Theatre, Boston, March 15–April 2, 1949. New York run: Majestic Theatre; opened on April 7, 1949; closed on May 16, 1953, and reopened at the Broadway Theatre on June 29, 1953, closed on January 16, 1954; 1,925 performances. A New Musical Play. Music by Richard Rodgers. Lyrics by Oscar Hammerstein II. Book by Oscar Hammerstein II and Joshua Logan, adapted from *Tales of the South Pacific* by James A. Michener. Presented by Richard Rodgers and Oscar Hammerstein II in association with Leland Hayward and Joshua Logan. Book and musical numbers staged by Joshua Logan. Orchestrations by Robert Russell Bennett. Orchestra under the direction of Salvatore Dell'Isola. Settings and lighting by Jo Mielziner. Costumes by Motley.

Cast: Mary Martin (Ensign Nellie Forbush), Ezio Pinza (Emile de Becque), Myron McCormick (Luther Billis), Juanita Hall (Bloody Mary), William Tabbert (Lt. Joseph Cable), Betta St. John (Liat), Martin Wolfson (Capt. George Brackett), Harvey Stephens (Cmdr. William Harbison), Henry Slate (Stewpot), Archie Savage (Abner), Fred Sadoff (Professor), Don Fellows (Lt. Buzz Adams), Barbara Luna (Ngana), Michael De Leon and Noel De Leon (alternating as Jerome), Richard Silvera (Henry), Musa Williams (Bloody Mary's assistant), Alan Gilbert (Yeoman Herbert Quale), Thomas Gleason (Sgt. Kenneth Johnson), Dickinson Eastham (Seabee Richard West), Henry Michel (Seabee Morton Wise), Bill Dwyer (Seaman Tom O'Brien), Biff McGuire (Radio Operator Bob McCaffrey), Jim Hawthorne (Cpl. Hamilton Steeves), Jack Fontan (Staff Sgt. Thomas Hassinger), Beau Tilden (Seaman James Hayes), Jacqueline Fisher (Lt. Genevieve Marshall), Roslyn Lowe (Ensign Dinah Murphy), Sandra Deel (Ensign Janet MacGregor), Bernice Saunders (Ensign Cora MacRae), Pat Northrop (Ensign Sue Yaeger), Gloria Meli (Ensign Lisa Minelli), Mardi Bayne (Ensign Connie Walewska), Evelyn Colby (Ensign Pamela Whitmore), Helena Schurgot (Ensign Bessie Noonan), Richard Loo (Marcel), Mary Ann Reeve, Chin Yu, and Alex Nico, Eugene Smith, and William Ferguson (ensemble).

During World War II, on a small U.S.-occupied island in the South Pacific, Nellie Forbush, a cheerful Arkansas nurse, falls in love with the French planter Emile de Becque. They discuss marriage but when she learns that he has two children by a Polynesian woman she rejects him. At the same time Princeton-educated Lieutenant Joe Cable has an affair with Liat, a young Tonkinese woman, but knows his family and friends would never accept her. Thwarted in love, de Becque joins Cable for a very dangerous mission. Only Emile

survives, but he returns to find that Nellie has changed her mind and befriended his children. Comedy is provided by Luter Billis, an entrepreneurial Seabee, and by Bloody Mary, Liat's entrepreneurial mother.

South Pacific was awarded the Pulitzer Prize for Drama in 1950. The show was deemed Best Musical by the Tony Awards, the Donaldson Awards, and the New York Drama Critics Circle. Additional honors were given to Ezio Pinza (Tony and Donaldson awards for Best Male Performance in a Musical; Donaldson Award for Best Male Debut), Mary Martin (Tony and Donaldson awards for Best Female Performance in a Musical), Myron McCormick (Tony and Donaldson awards for Best Male Supporting Performance in a Musical), Juanita Hall (Tony and Donaldson awards for Best Female Supporting Performance in a Musical), Joshua Logan (Tony and Donaldson awards for Best Direction), Oscar Hammerstein II (Donaldson Award for Best Lyrics), Oscar Hammerstein II and Joshua Logan (Tony and Donaldson awards for Best Book) and Richard Rodgers (Tony and Donaldson awards for Best Score).

A five-year national tour of 118 cities began at Cleveland's Hanna Theatre on April 24, 1950, led by Janet Blair and Richard Eastham.

A London production, starring Mary Martin and Wilbur Evans, opened at the Theatre Royal Drury Lane, on November 1, 1951; 802 performances. The musical was also staged in Melbourne (1952), Stockholm (1952), Madrid (1955), Istanbul (1962), Tokyo (1966), and Cape Town (1968).

A film version was produced by Buddy Adler for Magna Theatre Corp and released by Twentieth Century–Fox on March 19, 1958. Screenplay by Paul Osborn. Directed by Joshua Logan. Choreography by LeRoy Prinz. Music direction by Alfred Newman. Associate music direction by Ken Darby. Orchestrations by Edward B. Powell, Pete King, Bernard Mayers, Robert Russell Bennett. Cast: Rossano Brazzi (Emile; sung by Giorgio Tozzi), Mitzi Gaynor (Nellie), John Kerr (Cable; sung by Bill Lee), Ray Walston (Billis), Juanita Hall (Bloody Mary; sung by Muriel Smith), and France Nuyen (Liat). A television adaptation featuring Glenn Close (Nellie), Rade Serbedzija (Emile), and Harry Connick Jr. (Cable) aired on ABC in 2001. In 2006, PBS/*Great Performances* broadcast a Carnegie Hall concert version of the show featuring Reba McEntire (Nellie), Brian Stokes Mitchell (Emile), Alec Baldwin (Billis), Jason Danieley (Cable), and Paul Gemignani conducting the Orchestra of St. Luke's. The first Broadway revival opened on April 3, 2008, at the Vivian Beaumont Theatre, produced by Lincoln Center Theater and directed by Bartlett Sher, with Kelli O'Hara (Nellie), Paulo Szot (Emile), Loretta Ables Sayre (Bloody Mary), Matthew Morrison (Cable), Li Jun Li (Liat), and Danny Burstein (Billis).

The songs from *South Pacific* were extremely popular. A week before the show's Broadway opening, Rodgers's secretary prepared a list of forty-nine com-

mercial recordings, by the likes of Perry Como, Frank Sinatra, Bing Crosby, Jo Stafford, Peggy Lee, Dinah Shore, and Margaret Whiting, which, Rodgers bragged, was "an all-time vulgarity." Likewise, four months into the run, music publisher Max Dreyfus exulted: "As of today, 10th August, 4:30pm the total sales of the *South Pacific* numbers has reached 1,000,853 copies. I am safe in saying there hasn't been anything like it since *Oklahoma!*" In addition to the singles, *South Pacific* inspired such recordings as *Les Brown's Dance to South Pacific*, and *George Wright Goes South Pacific on the Mighty Wurlitzer Pipe Organ* and an album by Frank Sinatra and his Rat Pack friends.

The original cast album (Columbia) and the 1958 film soundtrack (RCA Victor) each sold more than one million units. More than twenty other cast albums followed, including the 1967 Music Theater of Lincoln Center cast (Florence Henderson, Giorgio Tozzi), a 1986 studio "crossover" cast (Kiri Te Kanawa, José Carreras), a 1996 London studio cast (Paige O'Hara, Justino Díaz; the complete musical score on two CDs), the 2001 television cast, the 2001 Royal National Theatre cast, the 2006 Carnegie Hall concert cast, and the 2008 Lincoln Center Theater cast.

The main sources for this chapter are the published vocal score and the published libretto. A dozen of the songs were also published as individual sheets. Early drafts of the script are preserved at the Rodgers & Hammerstein Organization in New York City; Rodgers's manuscripts and files of Hammerstein's lyrics-in-progress are in the Music Division of the Library of Congress. Mary Martin and Joshua Logan recorded their *South Pacific* memories in their respective memoirs. James A. Lovensheimer's master's thesis, "The Musico-Dramatic Evolution of Rodgers and Hammerstein's *South Pacific*" (Ohio State Univerity, 2003), provided another useful source. *The South Pacific Companion* by Laurence Maslon was published in 2008.

Some of *South Pacific*'s lyrics were changed for radio and the film. This chapter uses the Broadway wording and acknowledges the most notable of subsequent changes.

On July 6, 1949, Hammerstein sent this report to Josh Logan:

Last night, the audience behaved like a large group of people who had all met somewhere else and said, "Let's all go over to the Majestic Theatre and get drunk." Their behavior was irrational . . . They jumped at every joke and every note of the music like fish to bait they loved and didn't care whether they got hooked or not. . . .

When Mary sang "Wonderful Guy," she did not quite get out the last note before they burst in with applause. Then she walked over to the hat like a barefoot boy with feet of vanilla and the applause grew in volume and intensity. At the end of the song when all the girls join her, the applause was deafening and a couple of whistles could be heard. This, of course, lasted and carried over into the entrance of the girls with some more to spare. When Mary reappeared and started to do the turns across the stage, there were definite whistles and it sounded more like a football game than a show. I am not sure but what, in some way, we have combined all man's emotions into that play so that the reactions are somewhat like the combination of a big football game and a bull fight and grand opera and tragedy and comedy, the thrills of first love, fireworks on the Fourth of July and a soupçon of that exaltation which the Wright Brothers must have felt when their first mechanical kite left the ground. Now *I'm* drunk!

DITES-MOI

Published as an individual sheet. Introduced by Barbara Luna (Ngana) and Michael De Leon or Noel De Leon (alternating as Jerome).

The English version was prepared for popular recordings of the song. Hammerstein sent the lyric to Rodgers on May 4, 1949, writing: "I found it impossible to make a close translation that didn't sound silly, and so this is a free adaptation. Do you think this will do?"

Dites-moi
Pourquoi
La vie est belle?
Dites-moi
Pourquoi
La vie est gai?
Dites-moi
Pourquoi,
Chère mad'moiselle,
Est-ce que
Parce que
Vous m'aimez?

English adaptation

Tell me why
The sky
Is filled with music.
Tell me why
We fly
On clouds above.
Can it be
That we
Can fly to music
Just because,

Just because
We're in love?

A COCKEYED OPTIMIST

Published as an individual sheet and included in *Lyrics*. Introduced by Mary Martin (Nellie).

When the sky is a bright canary yellow
I forget ev'ry cloud I've ever seen—
So they call me a cockeyed optimist,
Immature and incurably green!

I have heard people rant and rave and bellow
That we're done and we might as well be dead—
But I'm only a cockeyed optimist,
And I can't get it into my head.

I hear the human race
Is falling on its face
And hasn't very far to go,
But ev'ry whip-poor-will
Is selling me a bill
And telling me it just ain't so!

I could say life is just a bowl of Jell-O
And appear more intelligent and smart,
But I'm stuck like a dope
With a thing called hope,
And I can't get it out of my heart!
Not this heart!

TWIN SOLILOQUIES

Published only in the vocal score. Introduced by Mary Martin (Nellie) and Ezio Pinza (Emile).

The form of this song and its content were directly inspired by lines in James Michener's story "Our Heroine" that describe the characters' inner thoughts in alternating paragraphs.

NELLIE: Wonder how I'd feel,
  Living on a hillside,
  Looking on an ocean,
  Beautiful and still.
EMILE: This is what I need,
  This is what I've longed for,
  Someone young and smiling
  Climbing up my hill!

NELLIE: We are not alike;
  Probably I'd bore him.
  He's a cultured Frenchman—
  I'm a little hick.
EMILE: Younger men than I,
  Officers and doctors,
  Probably pursue her—
  She could have her pick.
NELLIE: Wonder why I feel
  Jittery and jumpy!
  I am like a schoolgirl,
  Waiting for a dance.
EMILE: Can I ask her now?
  I am like a schoolboy!
  What will be her answer?
  Do I have a chance?

Reprise (Act One, Scene 12)

NELLIE: This is how it feels
  Living on a hillside . . .
EMILE: This is what I need,
  This is what I've longed for,
  Someone young and smiling
  Here upon my hill!

SOME ENCHANTED EVENING

Published as an individual sheet and included in *Lyrics*. Introduced by Ezio Pinza (Emile).

According to discographer Edward Foote Gardner, this was the number one song of 1949, with best-selling recordings by Frank Sinatra, Bing Crosby, Perry Como, and Jo Stafford. Later it became a hit for Jay and the Americans (1965) and Jane Olivor (1977).

Some enchanted evening
You may see a stranger,
You may see a stranger
Across a crowded room.
And somehow you know,
You know even then,
That somewhere you'll see her again and again.
Some enchanted evening
Someone may be laughing,
You may hear her laughing
Across a crowded room—
And night after night,
As strange as it seems,
The sound of her laughter will sing in your dreams.
Who can explain it?
Who can tell you why?

Fools give you reasons—
Wise men never try.
Some enchanted evening,
When you find your true love,
When you feel her call you
Across a crowded room—
Then fly to her side
And make her your own,
Or all through your life you may dream all alone.
Once you have found her,
Never let her go.
Once you have found her,
Never let her go!

Reprise

The following lines introduce the reprise of "Some Enchanted Evening" in Act One, Scene 7.

NELLIE: Born on the opposite sides of a sea,
We are as different as people can be.
EMILE: It's true.
NELLIE: And yet you want to marry me.
EMILE: I do.
NELLIE: I've know you a few short weeks and yet
Somehow you've made my heart forget
All other men I have ever met
But you, but you.

[EMILE and NELLIE repeat refrain.]

Reprise (Act Two)

NELLIE: Some enchanted evening,
When you find your true love,
When you feel him call you
Across a crowded room—
Then fly to his side
And make him your own,
Or all through your life you may dream
all alone.

BLOODY MARY

Published in the vocal score. Introduced by the male ensemble (Sailors, Seabees, Marines).

Bloody Mary is the girl I love,
Bloody Mary is the girl I love,
Bloody Mary is the girl I love—
Now ain't that too damn bad!

Her skin is tender as DiMaggio's glove,
Her skin is tender as DiMaggio's glove,
Her skin is tender as DiMaggio's glove—
Now ain't that too damn bad!
Bloody Mary's chewin' Betel nuts,
Bloody Mary's chewin' Betel nuts,
Bloody Mary's chewin' Betel nuts—
And she don't use Pepsodent.
Now ain't that too damn bad!

THERE IS NOTHIN' LIKE A DAME

Published as an individual sheet. Included in *Lyrics*. Introduced by Myron McCormick (Billis), Henry Slate (Stewpot), Fred Sadoff (Professor), and the male ensemble.

VERSE 1

SAILOR: We got sunlight on the sand,
We got moonlight on the sea—
SEABEE: We got mangoes and bananas
You can pick right off a tree—
SAILOR: We got volleyball and Ping-Pong
And a lot of dandy games—
BILLIS: What ain't we got?
ALL: *We ain't got dames!*
MARINE: We get packages from home,
SAILOR: We get movies, we get shows—
STEWPOT: We get speeches from our skipper—
SOLDIER: And advice from Tokyo Rose—
SEABEE: We get letters doused wit' poifume—
SAILOR: We get dizzy from the smell—
BILLIS: What don't we get?
ALL: *You know damn well!*
BILLIS: We have nothin' to put on a clean
white suit for.
What we need is what there ain't no
substitute for.*

REFRAIN

ALL: There is nothin' like a dame—
Nothin' in the world!
There is nothin' you can name
That is anythin' like a dame.

---

* *When necessary, this line was changed to:*
We got nothin' to look masculine and cute for.

VERSE 2

MARINE: We feel restless, we feel blue,*
SEABEE: We feel lonely, and in brief,
We feel every kind of feelin'—
PROFESSOR: But the feelin' of relief.
SAILOR: We feel hungry as the wolf felt
When he met Red Riding Hood—
ALL: What don't we feel?
STEWPOT: *We don't feel good!*
BILLIS: Lots of things in life are beautiful,
but, brother,
There is one particular thing that is
nothin' whatsoever in any way,
shape, or form like any other.

REFRAIN 2

ALL: There is nothin' like a dame—
Nothin' in the world!
There is nothin' you can name
That is anythin' like a dame.
Nothin' else is built the same!
Nothin' in the world—
A TENOR: Has a soft and wavy frame
Like the silhouette of a dame.
A BASS: There is absolutely nothin' like the
frame of a dame!

VERSE 3

MARINE: So suppose a dame ain't bright
Or completely free from flaws—
SAILOR: Or as faithful as a bird dog—
SEABEE: Or as kind as Santa Claus—
SOLDIER: It's a waste of time to worry†
Over things that they have not—
SAILOR: Be thankful for—
ALL: *The things they got!*

REFRAIN

ALL: There is nothin' like a dame—
Nothin' in the world!

---

* *When necessary, the first four lines of verse 2 were
changed to:*
We get lonely and we long
For the fair and gentle sex—
We would like to feel the feelin'
Of some arms around our necks.

† *When necessary, the final four lines of verse 3 were
changed to:*
It's a waste of time to worry
When you haven't got a date
When you're alone
They all look great.

There is nothin' you can name
That is anythin' like a dame.

CODA

ALL: There are no books like a dame
And nothin' looks like a dame.
There are no drinks like a dame
And nothin' thinks like a dame.
Nothin' acts like a dame
Or attracts like a dame.
There ain't a thing that's wrong with
any man here
That can't be cured by puttin' him
near
A girly, womanly, female, feminine
dame!

BALI HA'I

Published as an individual sheet. Included in *Lyrics* (where the words are spelled in standard English rather than dialect). Introduced by Juanita Hall (Bloody Mary).

Hammerstein's writing process always took longer than Rodgers's, and the difference was regularly mentioned in articles about them. In the most dramatic example, Hammerstein brought the lyric for "Bali Ha'i" to a lunch meeting at Joshua Logan's apartment. Rodgers pushed the silverware aside, turned the lyric sheet over, and started notating the melody. Rodgers was sensitive about his work seeming effortless. He "defended" himself by listing the details he'd been thinking about for months: he had the song title, he knew it should "evoke the exotic mystical qualities of a South Seas island," and that it would be sung by a contralto. "Therefore, as soon as I read the words I could hear the music to go with them. If you know your trade, the actual writing should never take long."

Discographer Edward Foote Gardner ranks "Bali Ha'i" as the number 22 song of 1949. Popular recordings were made by Perry Como, Paul Weston, Bing Crosby, Peggy Lee, and Frank Sinatra.

VERSE

Mos' people live on a lonely island
Lost in de middle of a foggy sea.
Mos' people long fo' another island,
One where dey know dey would lak to be.

REFRAIN

Bali Ha'i
May call you,

Any night,
Any day.
In your heart
You'll hear it call you:
"Come away,
Come away."
Bali Ha'i
Will whisper
On de wind
Of de sea:
"Here am I,
Your special island!
Come to me,
Come to me!"
Your own special hopes,
Your own special dreams,
Bloom on de hillside
And shine in de streams.

If you try,
You'll find me
Where de sky
Meets de sea;
"Here am I,
Your special island!
Come to me,
Come to me!"
Bali Ha'i,
Bali Ha'i,
Bali Ha'i.

Someday you'll see me,
Floatin' in de sunshine,
My head stickin' out
F'um a low-flyin' cloud;
You'll hear me call you,
Singin' t'rough de sunshine,
Sweet and clear as can be:
"Come to me,
Here am I,
Come to me!"
If you try,
You'll find me
Where de sky
Meets de sea;
"Here am I,
Your special island!
Come to me,
Come to me!"
Bali Ha'i,
Bali Ha'i,
Bali Ha'i.

Reprise (Act One, Scene 9)

Sung by female ensemble (native and French girls) as Cable and Billis land at Bali Ha'i.

Bali ha'i
T'appelle
Dans le jour,
Dans la nuit.
Dans ton coeur,
Toujours resonne,
"Par ici,
Me voici."
Si tu veux,
Tu me trouveras
Où le ciel
Trouve la mer.
"Me voici,
Laisse moi te prendre
Par ici,
Me voici!"
Bali ha'i,
Bali ha'i,
Bali ha'i!

I'M GONNA WASH THAT MAN RIGHT OUTA MY HAIR

Published as an individual sheet. Introduced by Mary Martin (Nellie) and female ensemble (nurses).

NELLIE: I'm gonna wash that man
right outa my hair,
I'm gonna wash that man
right outa my hair,
I'm gonna wash that man
right outa my hair,
And send him on his way!
I'm gonna wave that man
right outa my arms,
I'm gonna wave that man
right outa my arms,
I'm gonna wave that man
right outa my arms,
And send him on his way!
Don't try to patch it up—
NURSES: Tear it up, tear it up!
NELLIE: Wash him out, dry him out—
NURSES: Push him out, fly him out!
NELLIE: Cancel him and let him go—
NURSES: Yea, sister!
I'm gonna wash that man
right outa my hair,
I'm gonna wash that man
right outa my hair,
I'm gonna wash that man
right outa my hair,
And send him on his way!

NELLIE: If the man don't understand
you,
If you fly on separate beams,
Waste no time!
Make a change!
Ride that man right off your
range!
Rub him outa the roll call
And drum him outa your
dreams!
NURSES: Oh-ho!
DINAH: If you laugh at different
comics—
2ND NURSE: If you root for different
teams—
NELLIE, DINAH, AND
2ND NURSE: Waste no time!
Weep no more!
Show him what the door is for!
NURSES: Rub him outa the roll call
And drum him outa your
dreams!
NELLIE: You can't light a fire when the
wood's all wet—
NURSES: No!
NELLIE: You can't make a butterfly
strong—
NURSES: Uh-uh!
NELLIE: You can't fix an egg when it
ain't quite good—
NURSES: And you can't fix a man when
he's wrong!
NELLIE: You can't put back a petal
When it falls from a flower
Or sweeten up a feller
When he starts turning
sour.
NURSES: Oh no, oh no!

[NELLIE *shampoos*.]

NURSES: If his eyes get dull and fishy
When you look for glints and
gleams,
Waste no time!
Make a switch!
Drop him in the nearest
ditch!
Rub him outa the roll call
And drum him outa your
dreams!
Oh-ho! Oh-ho!
NELLIE: I went and washed that man
right outa my hair,
I went and washed that man
right outa my hair,
I went and washed that man
right outa my hair,

And sent him on his way!
NURSES: She went and washed that
man right outa her hair,
She went and washed that
man right outa her hair,
She went and washed that
man right outa her hair,
ALL: And sent him on his way!

A WONDERFUL GUY

Published as an individual sheet. Included in *Lyrics*. Introduced by Mary Martin (Nellie) and female ensemble (nurses). Discographer Edward Foote Gardner ranks this the thirty-fourth most popular song of 1949. Best-selling recordings were made by Margaret Whiting, Dinah Shore, and Fran Warren.

In his introduction to *Lyrics*, Hammerstein points out the song's "interior rhymes, undemanded rhymes and lighthearted similes. The emotion expressed in this song is so simple that it can afford to wear the decorations and embroidery of more ingenious rhyming. There is no subtle philosophy involved. A girl is in love and her heart is sailing. She is sentimental and exuberant and triumphant in the discovery. The job of the lyric is to capture her spirit. I think it does."

VERSE

I expect every one
Of my crowd to make fun
Of my proud protestations of faith in romance,
And they'll say I'm naive
As a babe to believe
Any fable I hear from a person in pants.
Fearlessly I'll face them and argue their doubts
away.
Loudly I'll sing about flowers and spring.
Flatly I'll stand on my little flat feet and say,
Love is a grand and a beautiful thing!
I'm not ashamed to reveal
The world-famous feeling I feel.

REFRAIN

I'm as corny as Kansas in August
I'm as normal as blueberry pie.
No more a smart
Little girl with no heart,
I have found me a wonderful guy.
I am in a conventional dither
With a conventional star in my eye,
And you will note
There's a lump in my throat

When I speak of that wonderful guy.*
I'm as trite and as gay
As a daisy in May,
A cliché coming true!
I'm bromidic and bright
As a moon-happy night
Pouring light on the dew.
I'm as corny as Kansas in August,
High as a flag on the Fourth of July!
If you'll excuse
An expression I use,
I'm in love,†
I'm in love,
I'm in love,
I'm in love
I'm in love with a wonderful guy!

REPEAT REFRAIN

VERSE 2 (FROM PUBLISHED SHEET)

I expect every one
Of my crowd to make fun
Of my proud protestations of faith in romance.
And they'll say I'm naive
As a babe to believe
Any fable I hear from a person in pants.
I've been known to share your satirical attitude,
Thinking that love could be kept in its place,
Till all of a sudden that lyrical platitude
Bounced up and hit me smack in the face!
That's how I turned out to be
The happy young woman you see.

Cut stanza

This interlude was dropped during out-of-town tryouts.

NURSES: She's as normal as school in September
Or an unattached leaf in November
Or a snowflake that falls in December
Or an ostrich's tail on a fan!
She's a sweet and as dumb as a
bumpkin—
Any girl who is that kind of chump kin
Get as plump as a Halloween pumpkin
Sitting home ev'ry night with a man.
NELLIE: Sitting home will be all right with me
If my home's on a hill by the sea.

---

* *In a reprise, the line is changed to:*
When I speak to that wonderful guy.

† *In the reprise, Emile finishes the song, with the last lines changed to:*
I'm in love, I'm in love,
And the girl that I love,
She thinks I'm a wonderful guy!

YOUNGER THAN SPRINGTIME

Published as an individual sheet. Included in *Lyrics*. Introduced by William Tabbert (Cable).

"Younger Than Springtime" was written during rehearsals. Joshua Logan recalled that it was Rodgers and Hammerstein's third attempt at Cable's love song. Hammerstein wrote it to a Rodgers melody that had been waiting since *Allegro* for the right use.

Both earlier attempts appear with the cut songs at the end of this chapter.

VERSE

I touch your hand,
And my arms grow strong,
Like a pair of birds
That burst with song.
My eyes look down
At your lovely face,
And I hold the world
In my embrace.

REFRAIN

Younger than springtime are you,
Softer than starlight are you;
Warmer than winds of June are the gentle lips you
    gave me.
Gayer than laughter are you,
Sweeter than music are you;
Angel and lover, heaven and earth
Are you to me.
And when your youth and joy invade my arms
And fill my heart, as now they do,
Then younger than springtime am I,
Gayer than laughter am I,
Angel and lover, heaven and earth,
Am I with you.

REPRISE

Younger than springtime were you,
Softer than starlight were you.
Angel and lover, heaven and earth
Were you to me.

HAPPY TALK

Published as an individual sheet. Included in *Lyrics*. Introduced by Juanita Hall (Bloody Mary).

REFRAIN

Happy talk,
Keep talkin' happy talk,
Talk about things you'd like to do.
You gotta have a dream;
If you don't have a dream,
How you gonna have a dream come true?

VERSE 1

Talk about a moon
Floatin' in de sky,
Lookin' like a lily on a lake;
Talk about a bird
Learnin' how to fly,
Makin' all de music he can make.

REPEAT REFRAIN

VERSE 2

Talk about a star
Lookin' like a toy,
Peekin' t'rough de branches of a tree;
Talk about a girl,
Talk about a boy,
Countin' all de ripples on de sea

REPEAT REFRAIN

VERSE 3

Talk about a boy
Sayin' to a girl:
"Golly, baby! I'm a lucky cuss!"
Talk about de girl
Sayin' to de boy:
"You an' me is lucky to be us!"

FINAL REFRAIN

Happy talk,
Keep talkin' happy talk,
Talk about things you'd like to do.
You gotta have a dream;
If you don't have a dream,
How you gonna have a dream come true?
If you don't talk happy
An' you never have a dream,
Den you'll never have a dream come true.

HONEY BUN

Published as an individual sheet. Introduced by Mary Martin (Nellie). The occasion is a "Thanksgiving Follies" to entertain the troops. Nellie is dressed as a sailor, and her "doll" is Luther Billis wearing a coconut bra and grass skirt. Mary Martin wrote in her memoir, "I will never forget the half-embarrassed, half-pleased look on Oscar's face when he first sang me the lyrics. Never in his life had he written such corny words, but I shrieked with joy."

VERSE

My doll is as dainty as a sparrow,
Her figure is something to applaud.
Where she's narrow, she's narrow as an
    arrow,
And she's broad where a broad should be
    broad!

REFRAIN

A hundred and one
Pounds of fun—
That's my little Honey Bun!
Get a load of Honey Bun tonight!
I'm speakin' of my
Sweetie pie,
Only sixty inches high—
Ev'ry inch is packed with dynamite!
Her hair is blonde and curly,
Her curls are hurly-burly.
Her lips are pips!
I call her hips
"Twirly" and "Whirly."
She's my baby,
I'm her pap!
I'm her booby,
She's my trap!
I am caught and I don't wanta run
'Cause I'm havin' so much fun with
    Honey Bun!

CODA

She's my baby,
I'm her pap!
I'm her booby,
She's my trap!
I am caught and I don't wanta run
'Cause I'm havin' so much fun with
    Honey Bun
Believe me, sonny!
She's a cookie who can cook you till
    you're done
Ain't bein' funny!

Sonny,
Put your money
On my Honey Bun!

ENCORE REFRAIN

NURSES: A hundred and one
Pounds of fun—
That's my little Honey Bun!
Get a load of Honey Bun tonight!
I'm speakin' of my
Sweetie pie—
BILLIS: Only sixty inches high—
ALL: Ev'ry inch is packed with dynamite!
Her hair is blonde and curly,
Her curls are hurly-burly.
Her lips are pips!
I call her hips
"Twirly" and "Whirly."
She's my baby,
I'm her pap!
I'm her booby,
She's my trap!
BILLIS: I am caught and I don't wanta run—
ALL: 'Cause I'm havin' so much fun with
Honey Bun!
And that's the finish,
And it's time to go, for now the show is
done.
We hope you liked us,
And we hope that when you leave your
seat and run
Down to the mess hall
You'll enjoy your dinner each and every
one.
NELLIE: Enjoy your turkey!
ALL: And put some chestnut dressing on our
Honey Bun!

YOU'VE GOT TO BE CAREFULLY TAUGHT

Published as an individual sheet. Introduced by William Tabbert (Cable).

During the show's out-of-town tryouts, some theater professionals warned that this song was too preachy, but Rodgers and Hammerstein refused to cut it. In a 1952 letter Hammerstein explained: "In the second act, when two stories converged—Emile de Becque having been rejected by the Navy nurse because he has two Polynesian children; and Cable, having rejected Liat, the Tonkinese girl, because of her race, and being disgusted with himself for doing so—a song was called for, some

expression of the cruelty and the fallacy of this kind of prejudice."

Officially, Rodgers and Hammerstein defended the song on dramatic grounds, but Hammerstein was privately proud of its message, writing to his publisher in 1955: "We may not make much money on this song, but we certainly have a wide circulation, haven't we? I am very gratified by this and very glad that it is doing as much good as it seems to be doing." As late as 1957, he was getting one or two requests each week from people who wanted to quote the lyric in an article, book, or public meeting.

Curiously, he did not include "You've Got to Be Carefully Taught" in his own anthology, *Lyrics*. Addressing Hammerstein biographer Stephen Citron in 1988, Hammerstein's son William wrote, "I think (THINK!—he never discussed this with me) that . . . when he compiled these lyrics he might still have been over-sensitive to the criticism from some Great Americans who thought the subject shouldn't be brought up in a musical—or, indeed, at all."

The song and its critics got national publicity in February 1953, when *South Pacific*'s national tour played Atlanta, Georgia. State Representative David C. Jones and State Senator John D. Shepard were so distressed by the song's justification of intermarriage that they announced they would "offer appropriate legislature to prevent the showing of movies, plays, musicals or other theatricals which have an underlying philosophy inspired by Moscow." Hammerstein told reporters that it was indeed a song against racial prejudice and that he was surprised by the idea that "anything kind and humane" must have originated in Moscow.

CABLE: You've got to be taught to hate and fear,
You've got to be taught from year to year,
It's got to be drummed in your dear little
ear—
You've got to be carefully taught!

You've got to be taught to be afraid
Of people whose eyes are oddly made,
And people whose skin is a different
shade—
You've got to be carefully taught.

You've got to be taught before it's too late,
Before you are six or seven or eight,
To hate all the people your relatives
hate—
You've got to be carefully taught!
You've got to be carefully taught!

YOU'VE GOT TO BE CAREFULLY TAUGHT (CONTINUED)

Published in the vocal score. Introduced by Ezio Pinza (Emile de Becque).

This passage was added after the Broadway opening. It is not in the first edition of the vocal score, but was certainly part of the show by April 1950 when the national tour began, and appears in the subsequent editions of the script and score.

I was cheated before
And I'm cheated again
By a mean little world
Of mean little men.
And the one chance for me
Is the life I know best.
To be on an island
And to hell with the rest.
I will cling to this island
Like a tree or a stone,
I will cling to this island
And be free—and alone.

Earlier lyric

The rehearsal draft of the script had these words for Emile:

Love is quite different.
It grows by itself.
It will grow like a weed
On a mountain of stones;
You don't have to feed
Or put fat on its bones;
It can live on a smile
Or a note of a song:
It may starve for a while,
But it stumbles along,
Stumbles along with its banner unfurled,
The joy and the beauty, the hope of the world.

THIS NEARLY WAS MINE

Published as an individual sheet. Introduced by Ezio Pinza (Emile). Written during rehearsals.

REFRAIN

One dream in my heart,
One love to be living for,
One love to be living for—
This nearly was mine.
One girl for my dreams,
One partner in Paradise,
This promise of Paradise—
This nearly was mine.
Close to my heart she came,
Only to fly away,
Only to fly as day
Flies from moonlight!
Now, now I'm alone,
Still dreaming of Paradise,
Still saying that Paradise
Once nearly was mine.

INTERLUDE

So clear and deep are my fancies
Of things I wish were true,
I'll keep remembering evenings
I wish I'd spent with you.
I'll keep remembering kisses
From lips I'll never own
And all the lovely adventures
That we have never known.

REPEAT REFRAIN

Cut verse

The world's a lousy dish—
You may quote me if you wish—
But in this same world I was very glad to be
Where the soft eyes of beauty nearly smiled
    on me.

CUT AND UNUSED SONGS

BRIGHT CANARY YELLOW

Included in *Lyrics*. As Ted Chapin explained in the introduction to the song folio *Rodgers and Hammerstein Rediscovered*, "Bright Canary Yellow" and "Loneliness of Evening" share a melody. "Bright Canary Yellow" appears in early drafts of Act One, Scene 1, where it leads almost directly into "A Cockeyed Optimist."

NELLIE: [*dreamily*] The sky is a bright canary
        yellow,
        The sea is a robin's-egg blue.
        It makes you wish,
        When you fall asleep,
        You will dream about the view.
EMILE: Bizarre and improbable and pretty
        As a page from the fairy-tale books,
        It makes you wish
        That the world could be
        As lovely as it looks.

LONELINESS OF EVENING

Published as a stand-alone song. Included in *Lyrics*. Most recently published in the song folio *Rodgers and Hammerstein Rediscovered*. Performed during the out-of-town tryouts under the title "Will My Love Come Home to Me?" but dropped before Broadway. Introduced by Mary Martin (Nellie Forbush) and Ezio Pinza (Emile de Becque). Emile has written these lines to accompany a bouquet for Nellie, who has not spoken to him since she met his children. (The film of *South Pacific* shows the text of the second stanza in a close-up.) Rodgers later inserted this song in the 1965 remake of *Cinderella*, where it was introduced by Stuart Damon (Prince) with the final line changed to "Will my love appear to me?".

NELLIE: [*She sings the text of* EMILE'*s note.*]
        I wake in the loneliness of sunrise
        When the deep purple heaven turns blue,
        And start to pray,
        As I pray each day,
        That I'll hear some word from you.
EMILE: I lie* in the loneliness of evening,
        Looking out on a silver-flaked sea,
        And ask the moon:
        Oh, how soon, how soon,
        Will my love come home to me?

MY GIRL BACK HOME

Published as an individual sheet. Cut from the stage version, but restored for the film. Introduced by John Kerr (Lt. Cable), with the singing voice of Bill Lee, and Mitzi Gaynor (Nellie).

_____

* *Hammerstein used the word "walk" in* Lyrics.

Hammerstein prepared the following comment for the film's soundtrack album:

Those of you who are familiar with the show score of *South Pacific* will discover a new musical number in this collection. It is called "My Girl Back Home." Strictly speaking it is not new because it was written for the original production. The necessity of cutting the show down to a reasonable playing time forced us to eliminate this song before it ever was tried on an audience. We have always been a little wistful about this and wondered whether it was a wise decision.

CABLE: My girl back home—
        I'd almost forgot!
        A blue-eyed kid—
        I liked her a lot.
        We got engaged—
        Both families were glad;
        And I was told
        By my uncle and Dad
        That if I were clever and able
        They'd make me a part of a partnership
        Cable, Cable—and Cable!

        How far away!
        Philadelphia, PA—
        Princeton, NJ—
        How far are they
        From coconut palms
        And banyan trees
        And coral sands
        And Tonkinese!
NELLIE: How far away!
        Little Rock, Ark.—
CABLE: Princeton, NJ—
        How far are they—
NELLIE: How far are they—
BOTH: From coconut palms
        And banyan trees
        And coral sands
        And—

[*They are interrupted.*]

NOW IS THE TIME

Dropped after the New Haven opening. Included in *Lyrics*. Most recently published in *Rodgers and Hammerstein Rediscovered*. Introduced by Ezio Pinza (Emile de Becque) in act one between "I'm Gonna Wash That Man Right Outa My Hair" and "I'm in Love With a Wonderful Guy." Nellie has asked him about the future.

"All one can do about the future is to hope," he answers. "My hope comes from the happiness I feel now."

A reprise planned for act two, when Emile agrees to join Cable's mission, was replaced during rehearsals by "This Nearly Was Mine." Emile would have sung the first stanza and Cable the third, with one lyric change.

Now is the time,
The time to live,
No other time is real.
Yesterday has gone,
Tomorrow is a guess,
Today you can see and feel.
You can feel the wind from the fresh green sea.
You can smell the salt in the spray.
Now is the time,
The time of your life,
The time of your life is today!

With heav'nly wine
From an earth-born vine
To caress your lips when you're dry,
With food to eat
From a field made sweet
By the sun and the rain from the sky,
Why flee in fear
Of a future year
And accept defeat with a bow?
While your limbs are sound,
While your pulses bound,
You can conquer the future now!

Now!
Now is the time,
The time to act,
No other time will do.
Live and play your part
And give away your heart
And take what the world gives you.
Let your arms get rich on the gold of love,*
When the gold of love comes your way.
Now is the time,
The time of your life,
The time of your life is today!

---

* *Alternate lyric for this and the following line in the reprise:*
   For you just can't wait to be served by fate
   On a silver plate or a tray.

SUDDENLY LUCKY

Not used or published. This lyric for Joe Cable appears in a rehearsal draft of the script, in the place later filled by "Younger than Springtime." Music for the verse has not been identified. The refrain uses the tune later known as "Getting to Know You."

VERSE

We've had a break,
A very good break.
Let's just take
This very good break,
Enjoy it while we may
And be glad it came our way . . .

REFRAIN

Suddenly lucky,
Suddenly our arms are lucky;
Suddenly lucky,
Suddenly our lips have kissed,
Suddenly dreamy,
Suddenly our eyes are dreamy
Seeing the world
In rosy mist.
Suddenly lucky,
Suddenly to be together,
Suddenly owning
Happiness no gold can buy.
Suddenly grateful,
Little do we worry whether
Some people may be wealthier than we
We are luckier to be
You and I.

SUDDENLY LOVELY

This precursor to a precursor was rediscovered in Hammerstein's papers at the Library of Congress in 1994, and given its "Broadway premiere" at a Hammerstein Centennial event at the Gershwin Theatre July 12, 1995.

Suddenly lovely,
Suddenly my life is lovely.
Suddenly living
Certainly looks good to me.
Suddenly happy,
Suddenly my heart is happy—
Is it a girl?
Could be, could be.

Suddenly lovely,
Suddenly to be together,
Suddenly sharing
Ev'rything we hear and see.
Suddenly wond'ring,
Suddenly I wonder whether
Are we in love for ever and for good?
Are we happy as we could be?
Could be!

MY FRIEND

Not used or published. The first attempt at Cable's love song to Liat. A musical sketch is in the Richard Rodgers Collection in the music division of the Library of Congress.

Lost for decades, but described in Joshua Logan's book *Josh*, the lyric to "My Friend" was found by Ted Chapin during preparations for the 2008 Broadway revival of *South Pacific*. In this particular draft of Act One, Liat fumbles for English words to tell Cable what her mother had said about him: "She like you . . . and you good man. I mus' be . . . your friend."

VERSE

CABLE: The sun is falling low
        And fading in the sky.
        Before the rush of night
        The sun and I must fly.
        Unhappy is the sun
        To leave his lovely sky—
        Unhappier am I
        To bid my girl goodbye.

REFRAIN

CABLE: Well, my friend,
        Our day is at an end.
        Our next kiss will have to be our last.
        Soon, my friend,
        I'll be around the bend,
        Alone with a dream already past.
        Up to now,
        I've made no solemn vow
        Forever and ever to be true.
        But tell me how,
        Oh, darling, tell me how
        I'd want any other girl but you.
        My friend,
        What else will I ever want but you?

INTERLUDE

CABLE: Funny little thing,
You stand there silently blinking.
Funny little girl,
I'd like to know what you're thinking.
LIAT: Je t'aime
CABLE: You don't understand
A single world I've been saying.
You have no idea
How much I wish I were staying.
LIAT: Je t'aime.
CABLE: Je t'aime.
I love you!
LIAT: I love you!

[*They embrace.*]

CABLE: Up to now,
I've made no solemn vow
Forever and ever to be true.
But tell me how,
Oh, darling, tell me how
I'd want any other girl but you.
My friend,
What else will I ever want but you?

BRIGHT YOUNG EXECUTIVE OF TODAY

Not published. No music was composed for this lyric. This lyric was found in the earliest known version of Act One, Scene 1—but neither the title nor text appears in subsequent drafts.

The context: When the play starts, Emile has already been briefing Cable for months. Cmdr. William Harbison is just being told about their special mission. The audience soon learns that Harbison had been "making pretty good time" with Nellie "until some blabber-mouth told her I was married." Bill Harbison's character is further revealed when he says: "I'm always leery of these European bozos. This whole mess we're in is their fault. They're always making a botch of their own affairs, and then calling us in to straighten them out." Harbison thinks the war will be won by the American executive type—not the generals, but the men who run the big industrial firms. He himself was known as the "troubleshooter" of his firm.

BILL: When I get out of a uniform,
Will I be happy again,
Working under the watchful eye
Of good old W.N.!

[*The following six lines are spoken.*]

JOE: Who dat?
BILL: That's my boss, Woodcock
Nordlinger. We call him W.N.
JOE: Oh.
BILL: Where was I?
JOE: Under his watchful eye.
BILL: Oh, yes.

[*He resumes singing.*]

His hearty voice and his piercing
look
I still can hear and see,
The day that he gave me
extravagant praise
And followed it up with a
nominal raise,
And said these unforgettable
words to me:

"The hope of the world
Is the well-trained, wide-awake,
Bright young executive of today,
The cream of the crop
Is the clean-cut, confident,
Bright young executive of today.
No feather-brained romancer,
Before he'll give an answer,
The facts and all the figures he'll
survey!"—

[*EMILE enters. JOE exchanges a look with him and they listen to BILL together.*]

"So bet all you can borrow
On the man of tomorrow—
The bright young executive of
today!"
JOE: [*explaining to EMILE*] We have
other important men.
BILL: But nobody counts as much
As the modern executive type
With the organizational touch!
EMILE: Of course you have the artist—
JOE: [*to BILL*] How do you rate the
artist?
BILL: A screwball and a bohemian.
He's an unreliable type.
JOE: Well, what about the writer?
EMILE: How do you rate the writer?
BILL: He goes for walks in the country,
Plays with dogs and smokes a
pipe.
JOE: The farmer?
BILL: Just a rube.

EMILE: The actor?
BILL: He's a cad.
JOE: The teacher?
BILL: He's a boob.
JOE: The laborer?
BILL: Money-mad.
EMILE: Money-mad?
BILL: Money-mad!
EMILE: [*to JOE*] The laborer, too?
BILL: [*broadminded*] I admit we need
all kinds of men—
JOE: [*jumping in with the eagerness
of a substitute half-back*] But
not one tenth as much
As the peppy executive type
With the organizational touch!

[*JOE now sings the refrain as earnestly as BILL, and BILL is completely carried away and unaware of any satirical intent.*]

The hope of the world
Is the heads-up, on-your-toes,
Bright young executive of today.
You meet him at lunch
In the high-flown Rainbow Room,
Along on the roof of the RCA!
His luncheon conversation
Is filled with information:
"The Ford Coupe," he'll say, "is
here to stay!"
BILL: [*carried away*] I'll say!
JOE: [*very, very vigorously*] Click your
heels and salute, you're
With the man of the future—
The bright young executive of
today!

[*EMILE comes to an involuntary salute.*]

BILL: [*transported*] He's solid and he's
sound,
With both feet on the ground—
EMILE: He's not the type to stand
around
With one foot off the ground!

[*He stands on one foot.*]

JOE: It's never hard to tell
The man who's rung the bell—
He wears a white carnation
In his tailor-made lapel!
BILL: He doesn't go off half-cocked!
His eye is on the ball!
JOE: And now and then, like mortal
men,
He doesn't go off at all!

[*Before* BILL *has time to analyze this one,* JOE *has barged into the refrain* con spirito, *as before.*]

But—
The hope of the world
Is the drive-hard—
EMILE: Crack-the-whip—
JOE AND EMILE: Bright young executive of
today!
BILL: They all wait to hear
What the sane and sensible
Bright young executive has to
say!
JOE: He'll tell you that inflation
Will never hurt the nation,
Unless, of course, it comes and
then it may!
EMILE: Hooray!
JOE, BILL, EMILE: Click your heels and salute,
you're
With the man of the future—
JOE: The clear-eyed, clean-limbed,
BILL: Hard-headed—
EMILE: [*proud to have suddenly thought of
the word*] Spark-plug!

[*They all take a deep breath and let it out.*]

EMILE, JOE, BILL: The bright young executive of
today!

IN A SLENDER BEAM

Not published. Not used. This text appears in an early draft of Act One, after "Twin Soliloquies."

NELLIE: In a slender beam
Of a single star
We cling together, you and I.
EMILE: We need no more light
Of the lavish night
Than enough to see each other by.
NELLIE: And as time goes on,
From year to year
We'll stay together as we are.
EMILE: Living out our dream
In a slender beam—
BOTH: Of one bright star.

THE KING AND I | 1951 and
Other Songs of the Early 1950s

THE KING AND I (1951)

Tryouts: Shubert Theatre, New Haven, February 26–March 3, 1951; Shubert Theatre, Boston, March 5–24, 1951. New York run: St. James Theatre; opened on March 29, 1951; closed on March 20, 1954; 1,246 performances. A musical play based on the novel *Anna and the King of Siam* by Margaret Landon. Book and lyrics by Oscar Hammerstein II. Music by Richard Rodgers. Presented by Rodgers and Hammerstein. Directed by John van Druten. Choreography by Jerome Robbins. Settings and lighting by Jo Mielziner. Costumes by Irene Sharaff. Orchestrations by Robert Russell Bennett. Dance arrangements by Trude Rittmann. Music direction by Frederick Dvonch.

Cast: Gertrude Lawrence (Anna Leonowens), Yul Brynner (the King), Dorothy Sarnoff (Lady Thiang), Doretta Morrow (Tuptim), Larry Douglas (Lun Tha), Johnny Stewart (Prince Chulalongkorn), Charles Francis (Captain Orton), Sandy Kennedy (Louis Leonowens), Leonard Graves (Interpreter), John Juliano (the Kralahome), Len Mence (Phra Alack), Baayork Lee (Princess Ying Yaowalak), Robin Craven (Sir Edward Ramsay), and ensemble (royal children, royal dancers, wives, amazons, priests, slaves, musicians).

Hoping to modernize his court, the autocratic King of Siam hires an English widow, Anna Leonowens, to tutor his children and wives. The Western ideals she brings along with the English language lead to conflicts humorous and serious. Romance is provided by Tuptim and Lun Tha, a Burmese concubine and the young man who loves her. Lady Thiang is first among the King's wives and a friend to Mrs. Anna; the Kralahome is the King's emissary.

The King and I won the 1952 Tony Award for Best Musical and for Best Actress in a Musical (Gertrude Lawrence). Yul Brynner was given both the Tony and the Donaldson award, as were scenic designer Jo Mielziner and costume designer Irene Sharaff. Donaldson Awards were also presented to Doretta Morrow and Jerome Robbins.

A London production, starring Valerie Hobson (Anna) and Herbert Lom (the King), opened at the Theatre Royal, Drury Lane, on October 8, 1953; 926 performances. Other productions were staged in Melbourne (1962), Dublin (1965), Tokyo (1965 and 1968), Munich (1966), and Tel Aviv (1966).

A film version, produced by Charles Brackett for Twentieth Century Fox, was released in June 1956. Directed by Walter Lang. Screenplay by Ernest Lehman. Choreography by Jerome Robbins. Cast: Deborah Kerr (Anna, sung by Marni Nixon), Yul Brynner (the King), Terry Saunders (Lady Thiang), Rita Moreno (Tuptim, dubbed by Leona Gordon), Martin Benson (the Kralahome), Rex Thompson (Louis Leonowens), Carlos Rivas (Lun Tha, dubbed by Reuben Fuentes), Patrick Adiarte (Prince Chulalongkorn), and Yuriko (Eliza). The film won an Academy Award for Brynner as Best Male Actor, along with Oscars for Best Scoring of a Musical Film, Best Set Decoration (color), Best Art Direction (color), Best Costume Design (color) and Best Sound Recording. In *Film Daily*'s poll *The King and I* was voted the best film of 1956. An animated adaption of the musical was released by Morgan Creek Productions in 1999.

There were major New York revivals in 1964 (Music Theatre of Lincoln Center), with Risë Stevens and Darren McGavin; 1977, with Constance Towers and Yul Brynner; 1985, with Mary Beth Peil and Brynner; 1996, with Donna Murphy and Lou Diamond Phillips.

There have been more than twenty *King and I* cast albums, including versions in Hebrew, German, Japanese, and Dutch. The original Broadway cast album was followed by, among others, the 1953 London cast; the 1956 movie soundtrack; the 1964 Lincoln Center cast; a 1964 studio cast, with Barbara Cook and Theodore Bikel; the 1977 Broadway cast; a 1992 Hollywood studio cast, with Julie Andrews and Ben Kingsley; and the 1996 Broadway cast. Jay Records' two-CD 1998 London studio recording, with Valerie Masterson and Christopher Lee, includes the entire score of the musical, including the complete "Small House of Uncle Thomas" ballet.

Many of the songs became popular outside of the show. Bing Crosby, Frank Sinatra, Dinah Shore, Johnny Mathis, Perry Como, Sammy Davis Jr., Bobby Darin, Lena Horne, Matt Monro, Margaret Whiting, and Andy Williams each recorded two or more songs from *The King and I*.

The main sources for this chapter are the published vocal score and the published libretto. Sheet music was also issued for several songs. Early drafts of the script, with prose descriptions of the lyrics to be written, are preserved at the Rodgers & Hammerstein Organization in New York.

Hammerstein sent this report on June 5, 1951, to the show's director, John van Druten, who had returned to California:

Last week I sat through the performance in row 4, and had a wonderful time. In every way I think the play has improved. The characterizations have been enriched. No changes have been made, but the actors just seemed to have eased into their roles better, and I couldn't find any places where we had lost ground. I did make some notes, but they were superficial. Gertrude is magnificent. None of the nonsense that we were warned [of] has shown up in her performance so far. She seems very deeply aware of the character of Anna, and the danger of Gertrude Lawrence introducing herself into it.

The advance sale is making all the boys around the box office very happy indeed, and they tell me that we are the hottest ticket in town. I do not find this hard to believe because I have never had such enthusiastic reactions for any play with which I have been connected. Friends, and people I have never seen before, or heard of, come up to me and drool.

I WHISTLE A HAPPY TUNE

Published as an individual sheet. Introduced by Gertrude Lawrence (Anna) and Sandy Kennedy (Louis).

Whenever I feel afraid,
I hold my head erect
And whistle a happy tune,
So no one will suspect
I'm afraid.
While shivering in my shoes,
I strike a careless pose
And whistle a happy tune
And no one ever knows
I'm afraid.
The result of this deception
Is very strange to tell,
For when I fool the people I fear,
I fool myself as well!
I whistle a happy tune,
And ev'ry single time
The happiness in the tune
Convinces me that I'm
Not afraid!
Make believe you're brave
And the trick will take you far;
You may be as brave
As you make believe you are.
[*whistling*]
You may be as brave
As you make believe you are.

MY LORD AND MASTER

Published as an individual sheet. Introduced by Doretta Morrow (Tuptim).

He is pleased with me!
My lord and master
Declares he's pleased with me—
What does he mean?
What does he know of me,
This lord and master?

When he has looked at me,
What has he seen?
Something young,
Soft and slim,
Painted cheek,
Tap'ring limb,
Smiling lips
All for him,
Eyes that shine
Just for him—
So he thinks . . .
Just for him!
Though the man may be
My lord and master,
Though he may study me
As hard as he can,
The smile beneath my smile
He'll never see.
He'll never know I love
Another man,
He'll never know
I love another man!

HELLO, YOUNG LOVERS

Published as an individual sheet. Introduced by Gertrude Lawrence (Anna). Perry Como made a best-selling recording in 1951. The song had a revival in 1960, when a recording by Paul Anka spent twelve weeks on *Billboard*'s Hot 100.

Various sources report that Hammerstein wrote "Hello, Young Lovers" in forty-eight hours, after spending a month on several unsuccessful attempts. In 1957, Hammerstein told interviewer Arnold Michaelis: "I wrote five songs. Not all to that melody. I wrote some lyrics to another melody Dick wrote, and then we cast aside both the lyric and the melody. And then I wrote, finally, 'Hello Young Lovers.' " Those early efforts have not been found.

Hammerstein had definite ideas about how the song should be performed. A February 1953 letter to the stage manager of *The King and I* included a "suggestion to Connie [Carpenter, then playing Anna] that instead of imagining the young lovers being down at about where the horn section is . . . I think the lovers ought to be somewhere on the first balcony. They are all the young lovers in the world. . . . She makes it small by singing down to the orchestra pit to her left."

VERSE

When I think of Tom,
I think about a night
When the earth smelled of summer
And the sky was streaked with white,
And the soft mist of England
Was sleeping on a hill—
I remember this,
And I always will. . .
There are new lovers now on the same silent hill,
Looking on the same blue sea,
And I know Tom and I are a part of them all,
And they're all a part of Tom and me.

REFRAIN

Hello, young lovers, whoever you are,
I hope your troubles are few.
All my good wishes go with you tonight—
I've been in love like you.
Be brave, young lovers, and follow your star,
Be brave and faithful and true;
Cling very close to each other tonight—
I've been in love like you.
I know how it feels to have wings on your heels,
And to fly down a street in a trance.
You fly down a street on the chance that you'll
    meet,
And you meet—not really by chance.
Don't cry, young lovers, whatever you do,
Don't cry because I'm alone;
All of my mem'ries are happy tonight,
I've had a love of my own,
I've had a love of my own, like yours—
I've had a love of my own.

A PUZZLEMENT

Published in the vocal score. Introduced by Yul Brynner (the King). During the out-of-town tryouts, several patter stanzas were cut from the song.

VERSE

When I was a boy,
World was better spot.
What was so was so,
What was not was not.
Now I am a man—
World have change a lot:
Some things *nearly* so,
Others *nearly* not.

REFRAIN 1

There are times I almost think
I am not sure of what I absolutely know.
Very often find confusion
In conclusion I concluded long ago.
In my head are many facts
That, as a student, I have studied to procure.
In my head are many facts
Of which I wish I was more certain I was sure!
[*spoken*] Is a puzzlement. What to tell a growing
    son?*
[*sung*] What, for instance, shall I say to him of
    women?
Shall I educate him on the ancient lines?
Shall I tell the boy, as far as he is able,
To respect his wives and love his concubines?†
Shall I tell him every one is like the other,
And the better one of two is really neither?
If I tell him this, I think he won't believe it—
And I nearly think I don't believe it either!

REFRAIN 2

When my father was a king,
He was a king who knew exactly what he knew,
And his brain was not a thing
Forever swinging to and fro and fro and to.
Shall I then be like my father
And be willfully unmovable and strong?
Or is better to be right?
Or am I right when I believe I may be wrong?‡
Shall I join with other nations in alliance?
If allies are weak, am I not best alone?

---

* *That spoken line replaced the following stanza out of town:*
    In the doing of endeavor
    I am reasonably clever
    And intelligent as almost anyone,
    But today I seem to never
    Know a single truth whatever
    I can confidently tell a growing son.

† *These lines originally followed but were cut out of town:*
    Never talk to them of governmental problems—
    And especially in moment of embrace.
    Never think of them except in groups of twenty—
    Never favor any single pretty face!

‡ *These lines originally followed but were cut out of town:*
    I deliberate and worry,
    In the fear that if I hurry,
    By my hurry some disaster may befall.
    But perhaps I ought to hurry,
    For if all I do is worry
    I will end by doing nothing much at all!

If allies are strong with power to protect me,
Might they not protect me out of all I own?*
Is a danger to be trusting one another,
One will seldom want to do what other wishes . . .
But unless someday somebody trust somebody,
There'll be nothing left on earth excepting fishes!

REFRAIN 3

There are times I almost think
Nobody sure of what he absolutely know.
Ev'rybody find confusion
In conclusion he concluded long ago,
And it puzzle me to learn
That though a man may be in doubt of what he
    know,
Very quickly will he fight,
He'll fight to prove that what he does not know is
    so!
Oh-h-h, oh-h-h!
Sometimes I think that people going mad!
Ah-h-h, ah-h-h!
Sometimes I think that people not so bad!
But no matter what I think
I must go on living life.
As leader of my kingdom I must go forth,
Be father to my children,
And husband to each wife—
Et cetera, et cetera, and so forth.

If my Lord in Heaven, Buddha, show the way,
Ev'ry day I try to live another day.
If my Lord in Heaven, Buddha, show the way,
Ev'ry day I do my best—for one more day!
[spoken] But . . . is a puzzlement!

Boys' reprise

Introduced by Johnny Stewart (Prince Chulalongkorn)
and Sandy Kennedy (Louis) in Act One, Scene 4.

CHULALONGKORN: There are times I almost think
                They are not sure of what they
                    absolutely know.
       LOUIS: I believe they are confused
                About conclusions they
                    concluded long ago.
CHULALONGKORN: If my father and your mother
                are not sure of what they
                    absolutely know,

---

* These lines originally followed but were cut out of
    town:
    Is it best then to be free and unentangled,
    Independent, isolated, and aloof?
    Or is country at a loss when disconnected,
    As a warp is at a loss without a woof?

                Can you tell me why they fight?
       LOUIS: They fight to prove that what
                they do not know is so!
CHULALONGKORN: Oh-h-h, oh-h-h!
                Sometimes I think that people
                    going mad.
       LOUIS: Ah-h-h, ah-h-h!
                Sometimes I think that people
                    not so bad.
CHULALONGKORN: But no matter what I think,
                I must go on living life,
                And someday as a leader I
                    must go forth,
                Be father to my children
                And husband to each wife.
                Et cetera, etc etera, and so
                    forth.
                If my Lord in Heaven, Buddha,
                    show the way,
                Ev'ry day I try to live another
                    day,
                If my Lord in Heaven, Buddha,
                    show the way,
                Ev'ry day I do my best—for
                    one more day.
                [spoken] But—
       LOUIS: Is a puzzlement.

ROYAL BANGKOK ACADEMY

Published in the vocal score. Introduced by the children
and wives.

We work and work
From week to week
At the Royal Bangkok Academy.
And English words
Are all we speak
At the Royal Bangkok Academy.
If we pay
Attention to our teacher
And obey her every rule,
We'll be grateful for
These golden years
At our dear old school.
The Royal Bangkok Academy,
Our dear old school.

GETTING TO KNOW YOU

Published as an individual sheet. Introduced by
Gertrude Lawrence (Anna) and ensemble (children and
wives).

In January 1951, Rodgers and Hammerstein pre-
viewed the show's score for Josh Logan, who wrote in a
letter afterward:

I am also a little bit worried to hear that there is
going to be no mass singing in the first act, and no
dancing except for a tiny bit at the opening. May I
make a suggestion? Is it possible that in the
schoolroom scene when the children are learning
that they could be given a dancing song with a lot
of kids singing with her? If this could be inserted
[it would] give some chance for a little more fun in
this act. It would be nice to have something quite
Western, as for instance a polka or gallop or whatever could be done in that period.

In her memoir, Mary Martin recalled that after the
first show in New Haven she made a similar suggestion
to Rodgers and Hammerstein, specifically recommend-
ing a melody that had gone unused in the score of *South
Pacific* ("Suddenly Lovely"/"Suddenly Lucky"). The
song was was added in Boston.

When questioned by Arnold Michaelis about the
lines that begin the verse, Hammerstein admitted, "As
far as I know it is not a very ancient saying, I just said it
was."

VERSE

[spoken] It's a very ancient saying,
But a true and honest thought,
That "if you become a teacher
By your pupils you'll be taught."
[sung] As a teacher I've been learning
(You'll forgive me if I boast)
And I've now become an expert
On the subject I like most:
[spoken] Getting to know you . . .

REFRAIN

[sung] Getting to know you,
Getting to know all about you,
Getting to like you,
Getting to hope you like me.
Getting to know you—
Putting it my way, but nicely,
You are precisely
My cup of tea!
Getting to know you,
Getting to feel free and easy;
When I am with you,

Getting to know what to say.
Haven't you noticed?
Suddenly I'm bright and breezy
Because of
All the beautiful and new
Things I'm learning about you,
Day by day.

WE KISS IN A SHADOW

Published as an individual sheet. Introduced by Larry
Douglas (Lun Tha) and Doretta Morrow (Tuptim).
"We Kiss in a Shadow" was originally located early in
act two. It was shifted to the first act during the Boston
tryout.

We kiss in a shadow,
We hide from the moon,
Our meetings are few
And over too soon.
We speak in a whisper,
Afraid to be heard—
When people are near,
We speak not a word!
Alone in our secret,
Together we sigh
For one smiling day to be free
To kiss in the sunlight
And say to the sky:
"Behold and believe what you see!
Behold how my lover loves me!"

Interim reprise

Shifting "We Kiss in a Shadow" to act one left a gap in
act two. The following reprise, from a Boston era script,
was probably used until "I Have Dreamed" was written
and orchestrated.

TUPTIM: We'll kiss in the moonlight,
We'll tell every star.
LUN THA: And heaven will know
How happy we are.
TUPTIM: No more will we whisper,
Afraid to be heard.
When people are near,
We'll sing every word.
LUN THA: No longer in secret,
No longer we'll sigh.
Tomorrow at last we'll be free—
BOTH: To kiss in the sunlight,
And say to the sky:

"Behold and believe what you see!
Behold how my lover loves me!"

SHALL I TELL YOU WHAT I THINK OF YOU?

Published in the vocal score. Introduced by Gertrude
Lawrence (Anna).
The July 1950 draft of the script includes Hammer-
stein's intentions for the song:

. . . reveal Anna's character, the well-bred and
genteel Victorian surface, and the inner strength
and haughtiness of this woman, her pride, her
deep love for the royal children, and [for] the
Siamese people, to whom she has become
attached, and her admiration and affection for the
King, however reluctantly she admits it right now.
This number then is designed, not only to give
added dimension to the character, but to afford
the actress an opportunity to loosen up and go
beyond the bounds of propriety within which a
lady had to keep herself in 1862. Here is a chance
for more lusty comedy than she can reveal in
other scenes of the play.

Your servant! Your servant!
Indeed I'm not your servant
(Although you give me less than servant's pay)—
I'm a free and independent employée . . . employee.
Because I'm a woman,
You think, like every woman,
I have to be a slave or concubine—
You conceited, self-indulgent libertine . . .
libertine.
How I wish I'd called him that! Right to his face!
Libertine! And while we're on the subject, sire,
There are certain goings-on around this place
That I wish to tell you I do not admire:
I do not like polygamy
Or even moderate bigamy
I realize
That in your eyes
That clearly makes a prig o' me!
But I am from a civilized land called Wales,
Where men like you are kept in county gaols.
In your pursuit of pleasure, you
Have mistresses who treasure you.
They have no ken
Of other men
Beside whom they can measure you.
A flock of sheep, and you the only ram—
No wonder you're the wonder of Siam!

[spoken] I'm rather glad I didn't say that. Not with
the women right there . . . and the children.
[sung] The children, the children,
I'll not forget the children,
No matter where I go I'll always see
Those little faces looking up at me . . .
At first, when I started to teach,
They were shy and remained out of reach,
But lately I've thought
One or two have been caught
By a word I have said
Or a sentence I've read,
And I've heard an occasional question
That implied, at the least, a suggestion
That the work I was trying to do
Was beginning to show with a few . . .
That Prince Chulalongkorn
Is very like his father,
He's stubborn—but inquisitive and smart . . .
I must leave this place before they break my heart,
I must leave this place before they break my heart!
[spoken] Goodness! I had no idea it was so late.
[sung] Shall I tell you what I think of you?
You're spoiled!
You're a conscientious worker
But you're spoiled.
Giving credit where it's due,
There is much I like in you,
But it's also very true
That you're spoiled!
Everybody's always bowing
To the King.
Everybody has to grovel
To the King.
By your Buddha you are blessed,
By your ladies you're caressed,
But the one who loves you best
Is the King!
All that bowing and kowtowing
To remind you of your royalty
I find a most disgusting exhibition.
I wouldn't ask a Siamese cat
To demonstrate his loyalty
But taking that ridiculous position!
How would you like it if you were a man
Playing the part of a toad?
Crawling around on your elbows and knees,
Eating the dust in the road! . . .
[spoken in rhythm] Toads! Toads! All of your
people are toads!
Yes, Your Majesty—No, Your Majesty—
Tell us how low to go, Your Majesty—
Make some more decrees, Your Majesty—
Don't let us up off our knees, Your Majesty—
Give us a kick, if it please Your Majesty,
Give us a kick, if you would, Your Majesty—
Oh! That was good, Your Majesty!

SOMETHING WONDERFUL

Published as an individual sheet. Introduced by Dorothy Sarnoff (Lady Thiang).

VERSE

This is a man who thinks with his heart.
His heart is not always wise.
This is a man who stumbles and falls,
But this is a man who tries.
This is a man you'll forgive and forgive
And help and protect, as long as you live . . .

REFRAIN 1

He will not always say
What you would have him say,
But now and then he'll say
Something wonderful.
The thoughtless things he'll do
Will hurt and worry you—
Then all at once he'll do
Something wonderful.
He has a thousand dreams
That won't come true.
You know that he believes in them
And that's enough for you.
You'll always go along,
Defend him when he's wrong
And tell him when he's strong
He is wonderful.
He'll always need your love,
And so he'll get your love
A man who needs your love
Can be wonderful!

REFRAIN 2 (AFTER ANNA EXITS)

She'll always go along,
Defend him when he's wrong
And tell him when he's strong
He is wonderful.
He'll always need her love—
And so he'll get her love
A man who needs your love
Can be wonderful!

WESTERN PEOPLE FUNNY

Published in the vocal score. This act-two opener was added during the Boston tryout and introduced by

Dorothy Sarnoff (Lady Thiang) and the women's ensemble (wives and slaves).

LADY THIANG: To prove we're not barbarians
They dress us up like savages!
To prove we're not barbarians
We wear a funny skirt!
Ah . . . !
WOMEN: To prove we're not barbarians
They dress us up like savages!
To prove we're not barbarians
We wear a funny skirt!
LADY THIANG: Western people funny,
Western people funny,
Western people funny,
Of that there is no doubt.
They feel so sentimental
About the Oriental,
They always try to turn us
Inside down and upside out!
WOMEN: Upside out and inside down!
LADY THIANG: To bruise and pinch our little toes
Our feet are cramped in leather
shoes—
They'd break if we had brittle toes,
But now they only hurt!
Ah . . . !
WOMEN: To bruise and pinch our little toes
Our feet are cramped in leather
shoes—
They'd break if we had brittle toes,
But now they only hurt!
Western people funny,
Western people funny,
Western people funny,
Too funny to be true!
LADY THIANG: They think they civilize us
Whenever they advise us
To learn to make the same mistake
That they are making too!
Ah . . . !
WOMEN: They think they civilize us
Whenever they advise us
To learn to make the same mistake
That they are making too!
ALL: They make quite a few!

I HAVE DREAMED

Published as an individual sheet. Added to the score during the Boston tryout. Introduced by Larry Douglas (Lun Tha) and Doretta Morrow (Tuptim). The song has been recorded by dozens of artists; a 1965 version by

Chad & Jeremy reached number 91 on *Billboard*'s Hot 100.

REFRAIN

LUN THA: I have dreamed that your arms are
lovely,
I have dreamed what a joy you'll be.
I have dreamed every word you'll
whisper
When you're close,
Close to me.
How you look in the glow of evening
I have dreamed, and enjoyed the view.
In these dreams I've loved you so
That by now I think I know
What it's like to be loved by you—
I will love being loved by you.

VERSE

TUPTIM: Alone and awake I've looked at the
stars,
The same that smiled on you;
And time and again I've thought all the
things
That you were thinking too.

REFRAIN

TUPTIM: I have dreamed that your arms are
lovely,
I have dreamed what a joy you'll be.
I have dreamed every word you'll
whisper
When you're close,
Close to me.
How you look in the glow of evening
I have dreamed, and enjoyed the view.
In these dreams I've loved you so
That by now I think I know—
BOTH: What it's like to be loved by you—
I will love being loved by you.

THE SMALL HOUSE OF UNCLE THOMAS (BALLET)

Published in the vocal score. Introduced by Doretta Morrow (Tuptim, as the Narrator), Dusty Worrall (Uncle Thomas), Ina Kurland (Topsy), Shellie Farrell (Little Eva), Yuriko (Eliza), Gemze de Lappe (King Simon of Legree), Michiko (Angel), and ensemble (royal dancers, musicians, and drummer).

Rodgers and Hammerstein were the first to link Tuptim, the unhappy Burmese concubine, with the runaway slave Eliza from Harriet Beecher Stowe's novel *Uncle Tom's Cabin*.*

Note: Most of Tuptim's lines are spoken rather than sung, with percussion ringing between each speech. The chorus generally speaks to a rhythm notated in the score. There are several small differences between the text in *Six Plays by Rodgers and Hammerstein* and the text in the complete piano-vocal score. The version below follows the published libretto.

TUPTIM: [*spoken*] Your Majesty, and honorable guests, I beg to put before you "Small House of Uncle Thomas."
CHORUS: Small house of Uncle Thomas! Small house of Uncle Thomas! Written by a woman, Harriet Beecher Sto-wa!
TUPTIM: [*spoken*] House is in Kingdom of Kentucky, ruled by most wicked king in all America, Simon of Legree. Your Majesty, I beg to put before you loving friends . . . Uncle Thomas!
CHORUS: Dear old Uncle Thomas!
TUPTIM: Little Eva!
CHORUS: Blessed Little Eva!
TUPTIM: Little Topsy!
CHORUS: Mischief-maker Topsy!
TUPTIM: Happy people.
CHORUS: Very happy people!

[*They dance.*]

TUPTIM: Happy people, happy people!
[*spoken*] Your Majesty, I beg to put before you one who is not happy—the slave Eliza.
CHORUS: Poor Eliza, poor Eliza, Poor unfortunate slave!

---

* In chapter 23 of Margaret Landon's adaptation of Anna Leonowens's memoirs, an out-of-favor wife of the king is so fascinated by *Uncle Tom's Cabin* that she takes to calling herself "Harriet Beecher Stowa Son Klin." But in Landon's book Tuptim is a slave-holder, and she remains a slaveholder in the 1946 *Twentieth Century Fox film* Anna and the King of Siam.

TUPTIM: Eliza's lord and master King Simon of Legree. She hates her lord and master And fears him. This king has sold her lover To far away province of O-hee-o. Lover's name is George.
CHORUS: George.
TUPTIM: Baby in her arms Also called George.
CHORUS: George.
TUPTIM: Eliza say she run away and look for lover George.
CHORUS: George.
TUPTIM: So she bid goodbye to friends and start on her escape. "The Escape."
CHORUS: Run, Eliza, run, Eliza! Run from Simon!
TUPTIM: Poor Eliza running, And run into a rainstorm.

[*Dancers perform a rainstorm.*]

TUPTIM: Comes a mountain.
CHORUS: Climb, Eliza!
TUPTIM: Hide, Eliza!
CHORUS: Hide, Eliza, hide from Simon! Hide in forest!
TUPTIM: Eliza very tired. [*spoken*] Your Majesty, I regret to put before you King Simon of Legree.

[SIMON *dances.*]

CHORUS: Because one slave has run away Simon beating every slave.
TUPTIM: [*spoken*] Simon clever man. He decide to hunt Eliza, not only with soldiers, but with scientific dogs who sniff and smell, and thereby discover all who run from king.
CHORUS: Run, Eliza, run! Run, Eliza, run! Run Eliza, run, run. Run from Simon, run, run! Eliza run, Eliza run from Simon, run! Eliza run. Eliza run from Simon, run!

Eliza run, Eliza run, Run, run! Simon getting closer. Eliza getting tired. Run, Eliza, Run from Simon, Run, Eliza, run!
TUPTIM: Eliza come to river, Eliza come to river.
CHORUS: Poor Eliza!
TUPTIM: Who can save Eliza?
CHORUS: Only Buddha, Buddha, Buddha, Buddha! Save her, Buddha! Save her, Buddha, save her! What will Buddha do?
TUPTIM: Buddha make a miracle! Buddha send an angel down. Angel make the wind blow cold. Make the river water hard, Hard enough to walk upon.
CHORUS: Buddha make a miracle! Praise to Buddha!
TUPTIM: Angel show her how to walk on frozen water.

[*Ice-skating dance.*]

TUPTIM: Now, as token of his love, Buddha make a new miracle.
CHORUS: Praise to Buddha! Praise to Buddha!
TUPTIM: Send from heaven stars and blossoms, Look like lace upon the sky. So Eliza cross the river, Hidden by this veil of lace. Forgot to tell you name of miracle—snow!
TUPTIM AND CHORUS: Of a sudden she can see Wicked Simon of Legree, Sliding 'cross the river fast, With his bloodhounds and his slaves!
TUPTIM: What has happened to the river?
TUPTIM AND CHORUS: Buddha has called out the sun, Sun has made the water soft. Wicked Simon and his slaves Fall in river and are drowned.
TUPTIM: [*spoken*] On other side of river is pretty city, Canada, where Eliza sees lovely small house— guess who live in house?

Uncle Thomas!

CHORUS: Dear old Uncle Thomas!

TUPTIM: Little Eva!

CHORUS: Blessed Little Eva!

TUPTIM: Little Topsy!

CHORUS: Mischief-maker Topsy!

TUPTIM: Lover George!

CHORUS: Faithful lover George.

TUPTIM: Who is looking like angel to
    Eliza.
They have all escaped from
Wicked king and make
    happy reunion.
Topsy glad that Simon die,
Topsy dance for joy.
I tell you what Harriet
    Beecher Stowe say
That Topsy say:
"I specks I'se de wickedest
    critter
In de world!"

[*She steps forward.*]

But I do not believe
Topsy is wicked critter.
Because I too am glad
For death of king—
Of any king who pursues
Slave who is unhappy and
    tries to join her lover!
And, Your Majesty,
I wish to say to you . . .

[*She collects herself.*]

Your Majesty—
And honorable guests . . .
I will tell you end of story . . .
Is very sad ending.
Buddha has saved Eliza
But with the blessings of
    Buddha
Also comes sacrifice.

CHORUS: Poor Little Eva,
Poor Little Eva,
Poor unfortunate child!

TUPTIM: Is Buddha's wish
That Eva come to him
And thank him personally
For saving of Eliza and
    baby.
And so she die
And go to arms of Buddha.

CHORUS: Praise to Buddha,
Praise to Buddha!

SONG OF THE KING

Published in the complete vocal score. Introduced by Yul Brynner (the King) and Gertrude Lawrence (Anna). The July 1950 draft of the script describes:

a new song which will be Anna's attempt to describe a romantic love totally foreign to the King's idea of relations between man and woman. In his part of the song, which answers hers, his logical Oriental arguments against sentimental monogamy must be difficult for Anna to answer. Indeed, she cannot answer them on the basis of logic, but can fall back only on the fact that in the Western world, this thing which seems so foolish and impossible to him is happening every hour of the day, every day, and a man and a girl are falling in love, believing that they are the only people in the world for each other. At the end of the song, while he does not admit that he is convinced to any degree, it is apparent that Anna has impressed him. It is also apparent that she has impressed him, not so much by her words, but by the fact that he has found her very attractive in her bare-shouldered dress, and somehow can feel this illogical impulse himself, however vaguely.

KING: A woman is a female who is human,
Designed for pleasing man, the human male.
A human male is pleased by many women,
And all the rest you hear is fairy tale.

ANNA: Then tell me how this fairy tale began, sir.
You cannot call it just a poet's trick.
Explain to me why many men are faithful
And true to one wife only—

KING: They are sick!
A girl must be like a blossom
With honey for just one man.
A man must live like honey bee
And gather all he can.
To fly from blossom to blossom
A honey bee must be free,
But blossom must not ever fly
From bee to bee to bee.

SHALL WE DANCE?

Published as an individual sheet. Introduced by Gertrude Lawrence (Anna) and Yul Brynner (the King). This song grows out of Anna's description of European-style romance.

VERSE

ANNA: We've just been introduced,
I do not know you well;
But when the music started,
Something drew me to your side.
So many men and girls
Are in each other's arms—
It made me think we might be
Similarly occupied.

REFRAIN 1

ANNA: Shall we dance?
On a bright cloud of music shall we fly?
Shall we dance?
Shall we then say good night and mean
    goodbye?
Or perchance
When the last little star has left the sky,
Shall we still be together
With our arms around each other
And shall you be my new romance?
On the clear understanding
That this kind of thing can happen,
Shall we dance?
Shall we dance?
Shall we dance?

[ANNA *begins to teach the* KING *the polka. While she sings, he calls out the beats.*]

REFRAIN 2

ANNA: Shall we dance?

KING: One, two, three, *and*—

ANNA: On a bright cloud of music shall we fly?

KING: One, two, three, *and*—

ANNA: Shall we dance?

KING: One, two, three, *and*—

ANNA: Shall we then say good night and mean
    goodbye?

KING: One, two, three, *and*—
[*sung*] Or perchance,
When the last little star has left the sky—

ANNA: Shall we still be together?
With our arms around each other,
And shall you be my new

BOTH: Romance?

ANNA: On the clear understanding
That this kind of thing can happen
Shall we dance?
Shall we dance?
Shall we dance?

REPEAT REFRAIN

CUT AND UNUSED SONGS

WAITING

Not published. Dropped from Act One, Scene 2 after the New Haven world premiere. Introduced by Gertrude Lawrence (Anna), Murvyn Vye (the Kralahome), and Yul Brynner (the King).

ANNA: Over half a year have I been waiting,
  waiting,
  Meekly and obediently waiting,
  waiting,
  Wearily but resolutely waiting,
  waiting,
  Outside that door!
  While you did your New Year
  celebrating, waiting!
  While your royal consort was
  cremating, waiting!
  Waiting, waiting, waiting, waiting,
  waiting, waiting!

[*Referring to* AMAZONS *who have been trying to pull her down.*]

  What's all this for?
KRALAHOME: You bow, you bow—
ANNA: I bow?
KRALAHOME: You bow.
ANNA: [*nodding her head to the* KING] I bow.
KRALAHOME: [*pointing to the "toads" on the floor*]
  Bow low.
ANNA: Bow low?
KRALAHOME: Bow low, like so—
ANNA: Ah, no!
  I bow like so!

[*She curtseys.*]

KRALAHOME: Like so you bow!
ANNA: I don't know how.
KRALAHOME: Bow low!
KING: Bow! Bow!
ANNA: I don't know how!
KRALAHOME: [*spoken*] How long you in Bangkok?
ANNA: [*spoken*] Seven months and fourteen
  days.
KING: [*spoken*] What you do here?
ANNA: [*sung*] Pardon me for recapitulating—
  waiting!

Pardon me, Your Majesty, for hating
  waiting!
Not another minute am I waiting,
  waiting.

[*Pointing her parasol at* KING.]

  And one thing more—
KING: How dare you to
  Do such thing here?
  Who is King here?
  Now you go! You offend me!
  Make her go—she offend me.
KRALAHOME: Now you go!
  Maybe now you learn to be
  discreeter, sweeter!

[*The* AMAZONS *grab* ANNA.]

ANNA: I shall tell the British consul!
KING: Beat her! Beat her!
ANNA: I am British—
KRALAHOME: Take her out and beat her, beat her!
KING: Outside that door!
KRALAHOME: Go!
ANNA: Don't you dare to touch me!
KING AND
KRALAHOME: Go!
ANNA: I shall tell the consul!
KING AND
KRALAHOME: Go!
ANNA: I shall write to Gladstone!
KING AND
KRALAHOME: Go!
ANNA: Let me go, you heathen!
KING AND
KRALAHOME: Go!
ANNA: I'm a British subject!
KING AND
KRALAHOME: Go!
ANNA: Let me down. How dare you?
KING AND
KRALAHOME: Go!

[ANNA *is carried from the room.*]

Early version

Found in the July 1950 draft of the script. No music was composed for this version.

ANNA: I am Mrs. Thomas Louis Leonowens
  And, Your Majesty, I hope you will believe
  me
  When I tell you how sincerely I deplore
  The indecorum of bursting through your
  door.

Behavior so unruly is a thing I deem
  unfortunate
And if I seem unduly and aggressively
  importunate,
To offer my excuses I most earnestly
  desire,
To make an explanation
And plead extenuation
And pray for mitigation . . .
Do you speak English, Sire?

Your Majesty may remember, you invited
  me to Siam
And definite were the duties of my
  mission:
To make my mother tongue
Familiar to your young—
The intricacies of grammar,
The mysteries of our spelling
And, later on, the art of composition.

[*Dialogue about her bowing. The* KING *does not insist on her prostration.*]

When I arrived in Bangkok I was filled
  with proper faith
And a thirst for work that only work could
  quench,
I was filled with high resolve,
I was filled with joie de vivre—
Joie de vivre . . .
Does your Majesty speak French?
[*spoken*] Sorry.
[*sung*] I am trying to imply
That my hopes were gay and high—
I was sanguine, I was buoyant, I was eager.
But my bright anticipation
Has met with stimulation
That I have to say is rather less than
  meager . . .
I have waited seven months—
KING: [*spoken*] Seven months are not so long.
ANNA: Seven months are *very* long
  When you're waiting.
  You've been occupied, you know,
  With a full and steady flow
  Of occasions that required
  Celebrating.
  Celebrating the new year
  Took six weeks of your career!
  While you welcomed the new year
  I was waiting.
  [*spoken*] The fireworks were enchanting.
KING: [*spoken*] Thank you.
ANNA: [*sung*] While the haircut of your son,
  Ceremoniously done
  Was your source of wholesome fun,
  I was waiting.

While you mourned a former queen
Who had left this vale of woe
Only four short years ago,
I was waiting.
And the fires were low and slow
That consumed the noble queen—
While the long-departed Queen
Was cremating . . .
I was waiting.

KING: [*spoken*] Funeral last thirty days. Fireworks
    every night, huh?

ANNA: [*spoken*] Delightful.

KING: [*spoken*] You like the double pinwheel?
    Very good?

ANNA: [*spoken*] *Very* good.

    [*sung*] While you reviewed parades and
      drills, I waited.
    While you were hunting in the hills, I
      waited.

KING: [*spoken*] For white elephants. We find not
    even one!

ANNA: Your Majesty, forgive me for my rudeness
    and irrev'rence,
    I am well aware that sev'rance of our
      contract may ensue.
    I am conscious of my seeming lack of
      sense and sensibility,
    Admitting the humility I know is due to
      you,
    But qualified and willing and as resolute as
      I am
    To embark your royal children on their
      study,
    The way that I've been treated by the
      Siamese of Siam
    Is, to put it bluntly, absolutely shocking!

ANNA AND SON KLIN

Not published. This lead-in to "Hello, Young Lovers" was dropped during rehearsals. The July 1950 script includes this description:

Anna starts to tell [the King's women] of her courtship and marriage with the glamorous and resplendent Major Thomas Louis Leonowens, their life in India, then in Singapore, and the unique and unusual bond between them. This is a song entitled "Tom and I." The verse, or interlude, and possibly the refrain, will be so constructed that there are short interludes, or "in-bits," during which Son Klin [Lady Thiang] interprets to the other girls what Anna is saying. After the first refrain, while the music continues,

Son Klin, either in lyric or dialogue, suggests to Anna that her conception of the Major, who was eleven years her senior, is not unlike their conception of their King husband. She seems to have looked up to him just as much as they do the King. Anna suddenly realizes that this is nearly true and that the only difference was that Tom did not demand such adoration, but he got it! In a second refrain, the girls, who now understand what she has said, join with Son Klin in a beautiful humming arrangement behind Anna's singing . . . [Anna] takes a locket that hangs on a chain from her neck and she opens it to show the picture of her husband. All the women gather around her and form a pretty conversation piece, and as they look at the picture they finish, with Anna, the last eight measures of the refrain. The lights fade out on this tableau.

He was tall, very tall,
And his eyes were clear and blue.
He was slim, very slim
In his coat of scarlet hue.
When he walked across a ballroom floor,
He was like a thing divine;
And all the ladies turned their heads,
And, natur'lly, I turned mine.

Having just arrived in India
From a little town in Wales
And, pathetic'lly susceptible
To tall and handsome males,
I was shy and rather gawky
And a very *young* sixteen.
And quite unequipped for coping
With the Indian social scene.
[*spoken*] And especially this officer from Putney.
[*sung*] I was dazzled by the splendor
Of Calcutta and Bombay,
And the pukka sahibs in Poona
Were like people in a play.
The celebrities were many
And the parties very gay
I recall a curry dinner
And a certain Major Grey
[*spoken*] Who kept plying me with something he
    called "chutney."
[*sung*] I was so much in love
I could scarcely sleep or eat,
And I longed for the day
When he'd sweep me off my feet.
Then at last he seized me in his arms
In a way that frightened me!
I slapped his face, and ran and ran,
But I couldn't run as fast as he.

WHO WOULD REFUSE?

Not published. Dropped during the out-of-town tryouts. The Kralahome sang this after "Something Wonderful."

Who would refuse
A man like him?
Who would leave the side
Of a man like him
Who looks on himself with pride?
Never will he
Retreat from life,
Never will he hide
(For you dare not hide
When you look on yourself with pride).
He will stand alone and ask no help
And show not a sign of fear.
And because he will not ask for help
Help will be always near.
Women and men
Will follow him,
Proud to be allied
To a man like him
Who looks on himself with pride!

WHY? WHY? WHY?

Not published. Dropped before the out-of-town tryouts began.

The July 1950 script explains:

In this number, the King, supported by Son Klin [Lady Thiang] and his wives, demand of Anna why the Western people have adopted certain customs. Pick out some of the less logical and more ridiculous things that European Victorians were doing at the time, and some of the things that we are still doing, and weigh the argument pretty much on the side of the East. Anna, of course, has part of the number—the part of the defender—and she tries to explain why the Western people do and believe certain things.

[After an interruption, the King] goes back into the song "Why Why Why?," making the point that in the East women are kept covered up, whereas in the West, where they have so many rules about respectability and sex regulations, the women are dressed so as to make it very difficult to obey western laws and "rules of man and woman, et cetera, et cetera, et cetera." Anna is irritated by his tone and the lyric argument with the King becomes heated.

KING: Why? Why?
Why? Why? Why?
Why are your people so
    peculiar?
Why can't your people be like
    mine?
Why don't they ever even try?
Why are your people so
    peculiar?
Why? Why? Why?
Rather than live in England I
    would drown!
Politics, et cetera, a most
    depressing thing.
Ev'rything inside out and
    upside down.
English men have woman queen
    and treat her like a king!

SON KLIN: Woman should have babies!

ANNA: Queen Victoria's had nine!

KING: Eighty-one months subtracted
    from her reign!
I keep right on governing while
    I am having mine.
Seventy-seven children I obtain.

ANNA: [spoken] The queen's husband,
    Prince Albert, has never so
    much as looked at another
    woman.

[KING exchanges a glance with his WIVES.]

KING: Why?

THE WIVES: Why? Why?
Why? Why? Why?
Why are your people so peculiar?
Why can't your people be like
    mine?
Why don't they ever even try?
Why are your people so
    peculiar?
Why? Why? Why?

ONE WIFE: Look at the foolish way that we
    are dressed,
Just to make it pleasant for a
    British diplomat!

ANOTHER WIFE: Pulling in waist and pushing
    out of chest
Almost I forget where all the
    things I have are at!

SON KLIN: Swollen skirt is something I can
    never comprehend.

KING: This is a thing I too have
    thought about,
That a woman has no legs is
    useless to pretend.

SON KLIN: Sooner or later man is finding
    out.

KING: She is right!

KING AND WIVES: Why? Why?
Why? Why? Why?
Why are your people so
    peculiar?
Why can't your people be like
    mine?
Why don't they ever even try?
Why are your people so
    peculiar?
Why? Why? Why?

NOW YOU LEAVE

Not published. Dropped during the out-of-town tryouts. Introduced by Dorothy Sarnoff (Lady Thiang) in act two, between "Shall We Dance" and the finale.

In the July 1950 draft of the script, Son Klin (later renamed Lady Thiang) says "accusingly" to Anna: "You start many things and you finish nothing. Now you leave. You start to teach my son what is good. Now you leave. To be half taught in these things is worse than to be taught not at all. You have failed my son, and I shall remember you for this always, every time I shall look at him, as long as I live."

You start in to teach
What is good for learning;
Now you leave.
The hope in our hearts
Like a flame is burning;
Now you leave.
The lessons you taught are wasted
Away on the wind they blow!
You start many things and you finish nothing.
Now you go,
Now you go.

OTHER SONGS OF THE EARLY 1950S

HAPPY CHRISTMAS, LITTLE FRIEND

Music by Richard Rodgers. Published as an individual sheet. The song debuted in the December 29, 1952, issue of *Life* magazine. In 1953, it became the official Christmas Seal Sale song. It was recorded by Rosemary Clooney and Dinah Shore.

VERSE

The soft morning light
Of a pale winter sun
Is tracing the trees on the snow.
Leap up, little friend,
And fly down the stairs,
For Christmas is waiting below.
There's a tree in the room
Running over with stars
That twinkle and sing to your eyes.
And under the tree
There are presents that say,
"Unwrap me and get a surprise!"

REFRAIN

Happy Christmas, little friend,
May your heart be laughing all day.
May your joy be a dream you'll remember,
As the years roll along on their way.
As the years roll along on their way,
You'll be showing your own kid a tree.
Then at last, my friend, you'll know
How happy a Christmas can be,
How happy a Christmas can be.

MERRY CHRISTMAS, TERRY

Hammerstein sent this greeting to Theresa Helburn in December 1952.

Thank you for your verses, Terry.
Now in answer may I say
Two can write in rhythm merry.
Every doggerel has his day.

Love and Merry
Christmas, Terry.

THERE'S MUSIC IN YOU

Music by Richard Rodgers. Published as an individual sheet. Introduced by Mary Martin in the 1953 film *From Main Street to Broadway*.

A project of the Council of the Living Theatre, the film mixed a story about an aspiring playwright and his small-town girlfriend with cameos by theater personalities, including Ethel and Lionel Barrymore, Tallulah Bankhead, Joshua Logan, and John van Druten, in rehearsal and audition scenes. Rodgers and Hammerstein appeared as themselves, writing this very song, then visiting a rehearsal and attending an opening night.

More recently, the song was heard in the 1997 television adaptation of *Cinderella*, where Whitney Houston sang it as Fairy Godmother.

REFRAIN

Someone wants you,
You know who.
Now you're living—
There's music in you.
Now you're hearing
Something new,
Someone playing
The music in you.
Now you're living,
You know why.
Now there's nothing
You won't try—
Move a mountain,
Light the sky,
Make a wish come true—
There is music in you.

INTERLUDE

Robins are chirping,
Church bells are chiming,
Poets are rhyming
The music in you.
Pine trees are whisp'ring,
Children are shouting,
Fountains are spouting
The music in you.

Kittens are purring it,
Breezes are stirring it,
Airplanes are roaring it,
Trains are encoring it,
Glasses are clinking it,
Students are thinking it—
All around you,
The same sweet sound
You can hear in the earth
And down from the sky:
"What a lucky girl,*
What a lucky girl,
Got your guy,
Got your guy!"

REPEAT REFRAIN

* *Alternate lyric for male singer:*
    "You have found your girl,
    You have found your girl,
    What a guy,
    What a guy!"

OVERLEAF *Joan McCracken as Carmen in* Me and Juliet

ME AND JULIET | 1953

ME AND JULIET (1953)

Tryouts: Hanna Theatre, Cleveland, April 20–May 2, 1953; Shubert Theatre, Boston, May 6–23, 1953. New York run: Majestic Theatre; opened May 28, 1953; closed April 3, 1954; 358 performances. A New Musical Comedy. Music by Richard Rodgers. Book and lyrics by Oscar Hammerstein II. Presented by Rodgers and Hammerstein. Directed by George Abbott. Dances and musical numbers staged by Robert Alton. Vocal and orchestral arrangements by Don Walker. Musical direction by Salvatore Dell'Isola. Scenery and lighting by Jo Mielziner. Costumes designed by Irene Sharaff.

Cast: Isabel Bigley (Jeanie, a chorus singer), Bill Hayes (Larry, assistant stage manager), Joan McCracken (Betty/replacement principal dancer, "Carmen"), Ray Walston (Mac, stage manager), Mark Dawson (Bob, electrician), Joe Lautner (Ruby, company manager), Arthur Maxwell (Charlie/featured lead, "Me"), George S. Irving (Dario, conductor), Helena Scott (Lily/singing principal, "Juliet"), Bob Fortier (Jim/principal dancer, "Don Juan"), Svetlana McLee (Susie/principal dancer, "Carmen"), Randy Hall (George, 2nd assistant stage manager), Jackie Kelk (Herbie, candy counter boy), Barbara Carroll (Chris, rehearsal piano player), Herbert Wasserman (Milton, drummer), Joe Schulman (Stu, bass fiddle player), Michael King (Michael, chorus boy), Patty Ann Jackson (Monica, chorus dancer), Henry Hamilton (voice of Mr. Harrison, a producer), Deborah Remsen (voice of Miss Davenport, choreographer), Norma Thornton (Hilda, an aspirant for a dancing part), Thelma Tadlock (Marcia, another aspirant for a dancing part), Buzz Miller (Buzz, principal dancer), Ralph Linn (Ralph, alley dancer), Gwen Harmon (Miss Oxford, a bit player), Francine Bond (Sadie, an usher), Lorraine Havercroft (Mildred, another usher), Barbara Lee Smith and Susan Lovell (theater patrons), singing and dancing ensembles.

Larry, assistant stage manager for a long-running Broadway show, has a crush on Jeanie, a chorus singer who has been dating Bob, one of the show's electricians. After Larry coaches Jeanie for the job of understudy for the role of Juliet, they fall in love, secretly become engaged, and then marry. Meanwhile, stage manager Mac keeps the company and crew in line, and tries to withstand the lures of Betty Loraine, the new dancer playing the role of Carmen. These backstage plotlines, which are partly conveyed in songs, are interspersed with rehearsals and performances of numbers from the show on which they are all employed, "Me & Juliet."

An original cast recording was made by RCA Victor.

The principal sources for this chapter are the published vocal score and the published libretto. Several songs were published as individual sheets. The Oscar Hammerstein II Collection in the Music Division of the Library of Congress has several drafts of the script at different stages. The Richard Rodgers Collection there has piano-vocal scores and sketches.

Hammerstein described the show's setting in a February 1953 letter to his former collaborator Frank Mandel:

> Having finished the book on my new play, *Me and Juliet*, I am now grinding out the lyrics, and it is a tough job, just as tough as all of them seem to be. We go into rehearsal March 19th, and I know I will not be ready with all the songs, but it will not be the first time I have had to write songs during rehearsals. In fact I don't remember any rehearsals during which I didn't have to write songs. Do you?
>
> This is an original story about the theatre. I have tried to avoid all the cliches of backstage stories, and to treat a theatrical troupe like a village community. The play [within a play] is a hit and has been running for five months, and so there is no issue of whether it will be successful, and no issue of whether any individuals will be successful.
>
> So this is a story merely concerning the relationships of the people in the company. All the scenes take place in and around the theatre, on the bare stage and on the stage set for the play that they are doing, and up on the light bridge and in the house manager's office and in the stage door alley.

As Hammerstein explained to Mandel, *Me and Juliet* is about the cast and crew of a Broadway show, also called "Me & Juliet." Sometimes we see the actors and technicians offstage and backstage; at other times we see the actors rehearsing or performing their assigned roles. In the material that follows *Me and Juliet* (in italics) refers to the actual show and its framing story, while "Me & Juliet" (in quotes) refers to the show within a show.

A VERY SPECIAL DAY

Published as an individual sheet. Introduced by Isabel Bigley (Jeanie).

VERSE

Am I building something up
That really isn't there?
Do I make a big romance
Of a small affair?

Should I be more practical
As friends would have me be?
Being practical is very hard for me.

REFRAIN

I wake up each morning
With a feeling in my heart
That today will be a very special day.
I keep right on clinging
To that feeling in my heart
Till the winds of evening blow my dream away.
Later on, at bedtime,
When my world has come apart,
And I'm in my far-from-fancy negligée
With a piece of toast to munch
And a nice hot cup of tea,
I begin to have a hunch
That tomorrow's going to be
A very special day for me.

Earlier draft of verse

Shall I give him up?
Shall I run away?
Could I go on without him?
What'll happen if I stay?
If I run away,
Am I weak or strong?
Could I be right about him
And the others all be wrong?

Additional lines for refrain

In July of 1953, while on the Cunard liner *Queen Elizabeth*, Hammerstein sent Rodgers an additional lyric for the second half of the refrain, prefacing it: "Do you think this is all right? Or am I being lulled already by the slight roll of the boat?" The letter ended: "Do with it what you will, Love Oscar."

Sad and disillusioned
Is the feeling in my heart
So I watch the lights go out across the bay.
Then a birdsong greets my ear
And the moon falls on the sea,
And they make it very clear
That tomorrow's going to be
A very special day for me.

THAT'S THE WAY IT HAPPENS

Published as an individual sheet. Introduced by Isabel Bigley (Jeanie). Reprised later in the scene by Bill Hayes (Larry).

JEANIE: You're a girl from Chicago
On the road with a show—
Not a soul in New Haven
You can say you know.
You wish you were a mile or so from Michigan Lake,
Home with your mother and a T-bone steak.
Then along comes a fellow
With a smile like a kid,
And he gets your attention
With a timely bid.
He says he knows a bistro where they give you a break
With French-fried potatoes and a T-bone steak!
You are shy and uncertain,
But he pleads and you yield,
And you don't have an inkling
That you're signed and sealed
By merely telling someone you'd be glad to partake
Of French-fried potatoes and a T-bone steak.
That's the way it happens,
That's the way it happens,
That's the way it happened to me!

REPRISE

LARRY: You're a guy in New Haven
On the road with a show—
There's a girl in the comp'ny
That you hardly know.
You watch her and you wonder if she'd like to partake
Of French-fried potatoes and a T-bone steak.
Then along comes a fellow
Who is quicker than you,
And he does what you thought that You would like to do—
He takes her to a bistro where they give you a break
With French-fried potatoes and a T-bone steak.
Now you see them together
And you know in your heart

That you lost what you wanted
At the very start,
Because you didn't ask her if she'd like to partake
Of French-fried potatoes and a T-bone steak!
That's the way it happens,
That's the way it happens,
That's the way it happened to me.

OPENING OF "ME & JULIET"

Published in the vocal score. Introduced by Helena Scott (Lily, as Juliet), Bob Fortier (Jim, as Don Juan), Svetlana McLee (Susie, as Carmen), Arthur Maxwell (Charlie, as Me), and ensemble.

This song is the opening of the show within the show. To help the audience quickly learn who is who in "Me & Juliet," Hammerstein made the major characters very familiar types: Juliet, Don Juan, Carmen, and an ordinary guy.

VOICES: Where is this?
JULIET: It doesn't matter.
The scene of the play
Is neither here nor there.
All the things
About to happen
Are things that are always happening everywhere.
VOICES: When is this?
JULIET: It doesn't matter.
The time of the play
Is neither now nor then.
Every year
The world is changing—
But women remain the same, and so do men!

[Spotlights hit CARMEN and DON JUAN.]

VOICES: Who are they?
ME: They are the most important people in my life.
VOICES: Who are you?
ME: [spoken over music] I? I am ME. I am an ordinary character, with an exceptional interest in myself. My own conception of ME—is—er—idealized. The things that happen to ME seem remarkable. The people I know—well, look at them! This man,

here, is my boss. His name is Emil Phlugfelder. But he has so many girls chasing him that I call him Don Juan.

[DON JUAN and girls dance and exit.]

On the mezzanine floor of the place where I work there's a girl—one of the file clerks. I look up from my desk and there she is, on the balcony. I always see her in a kind of glow. To me, she is—Juliet! She's the girl I'm going to marry.

[ME walks toward CARMEN.]

This one is a girl I am *not* going to marry . . . But she *bothers* me. I see her everywhere—in the subway, in the park, on the beach. I call her Carmen.

[CARMEN dances toward ME, *followed by a stampede of men.*]

Now you know them all, the characters who will shape my life. But this one [*indicating* JULIET]—my life didn't really begin till I met her. I'll never forget our first date. We sat on a park bench and fed the pigeons. Ah, Juliet! Look at her! So young, so in need of protection.
As soon as you see a girl like that you want to marry her, so you can protect her from all the men who want to protect her from you! She makes me think of beautiful things: sunlit meadows, the laughter of children—Juliet! When she speaks, it is like the faint echo of far-off bells on a misty morning. Speak to me, Juliet!

MARRIAGE-TYPE LOVE

Published as an individual sheet. Introduced by Arthur Maxwell (Charlie, as Me), Helena Scott (Lily, as Juliet), and ensemble.

VERSE

ME: When first I laid my longing eyes on you,
I saw my future shining in your face,
And when you smiled and murmured "How d'you do?"

The room became a dream-enchanted place.
The chandeliers were shooting stars;
The drums and horns and soft guitars
Were sounding more like nightingales;
The window curtains blew like sails;
And I was floating just above the floor,
Feeling slightly taller than before.

REFRAIN

ME: Out of nowhere
Came the feeling,
Knew the feeling—
Marriage-type love.
We were dancing
And your eyelash
Blinked on my lash—
Marriage-type love!
We made a date, couldn't wait
For my day off.
Now it's a thing with a ring
For the payoff!
I'm your pigeon,
Through with roaming,
I am homing
To marriage-type love and you.

Spoof refrain

Cut before the Broadway opening. In an early draft of
the script, some of the chorus kids tease Charlie with
this parody. Another unused reprise can be found at
the end of this chapter in the dropped sequence from
act two.

When we're necking
Feel neckstatic—
Symptomatic
Of marriage-type love!
Want to love you
Something awful!
Make it lawful—
Marriage-type love!
I'm in a daze, in a glow, in a tizzy.
I'm in a haze, feeling so hers-and-hizzy!
Call a member
Of the clergy—
This is urgy!
Call a justice!
Cast the anchor!
Burn the bridges!
Lock the stable!
Man the lifeboats!
Marriage-type love for me!

KEEP IT GAY

Published as an individual sheet. Introduced by Mark
Dawson (Bob); reprised by Joan McCracken (Betty).*
Perry Como made a popular recording.

In early scripts, where it had the dummy title "Love
Can Be Fun," Hammerstein explained, "This song is an
appeal to keep love in its place, to have fun with it and
don't let it get you down, or drive you into any foolish
vows that you're not going to keep. It is a light-hearted
comment, making fun of the pain that love gives the
romanticists."

VERSE

When a girl would meet Don Juan,
She'd get goofy for the Don.
Like a snake who meets a mongoose,
That young lady was a gone goose.
Any time a girl would say:
"Shall we name a wedding day?"
Juan would try another gambit
(He liked weddings not a damn bit).
He would gaze into the lady's eye,
Strumming his guitar to stall for time;
Then he'd make his usual reply—
That old reliable Andalusian rhyme:

REFRAIN

Keep it gay,
Keep it light,
Keep it fresh,
Keep it fair.
Let it bloom
Ev'ry night,
Give it room,
Give it air!
Keep your love a lovely dream and never wake it.
Make it happy and be happy as you make it!
Let it sing
Like a nightin—
gale in May,
Keep it gay.
Keep it free
Or you'll frighten
It away.
Take it easy and enjoy it while you take it!

_____

* *"Keep It Gay" is another song from "Me & Juliet,"
the show-within-the-show, where it is performed by
Don Juan and ensemble. However, it is first heard in*
Me and Juliet *when Bob, a member of the stage crew,
sings along from his perch on the light bridge. It is
reprised when Betty auditions to take over the role of*
Carmen.

Keep it gay,
Keep it gay,
Keep it gay!

THE BIG BLACK GIANT

Published as an individual sheet. Introduced by Bill
Hayes (Larry); reprised by Joe Lautner (Ruby).

The water in a river is changed every day
As it flows from the hills to the sea.
But to people on the shore the river is the same—
Or at least it appears to be.
The audience in a theater is changed every night
As a show runs along on its way.
But to people on the stage the audience looks the
    same,
Every night, every matinee:

A big black giant
Who looks and listens
With thousands of eyes and ears,
A big black mass
Of love and pity
And troubles and hopes and fears;
And every night
The mixture's different,
Although it may look the same.
To feel his way
With every mixture
Is part of the actor's game.

One night it's a laughing giant,
Another night a weeping giant,
One night it's a coughing giant,
Another night a sleeping giant.
Every night you fight the giant
And maybe, if you win,
You send him out a nicer giant
Than he was when he came in.

But if he doesn't like you, then all you can do
Is to pack up your makeup and go.
For an actor in a flop there isn't any choice
But to look for another show.

That big black giant
Who looks and listens
With thousands of eyes and ears,
That big black mass
Of love and pity
And troubles and hopes and fears,
Will sit out there

And rule your life
For all your living years.

Alternate ending for Ruby's reprise

That big black giant
Who looks and listens
With thousands of eyes and ears,
He claps his hands
And luck is with you,
He frowns and it disappears.
He'll chill your heart
And warm your heart
For all your living years.

NO OTHER LOVE

Published as an individual sheet. Introduced by Isabel
Bigley (Jeanie) and Bill Hayes (Larry).

Rodgers's melody was first heard as an instrumental
motif, "Beneath the Southern Cross," in the 1952 television series *Victory at Sea*. As "No Other Love," the song
was one of the major hits of 1953, spending eighteen
weeks on television's *Your Hit Parade*.

VERSE

How far away are you?
How many lonely sighs, dear?
How many weeping skies, dear?
How far away are you?
How long have I to go?
How many moons to see, dear,
Till you come back to me, dear?
When will I know?
When will I know?

REFRAIN

No other love have I,
Only my love for you,
Only the dream we knew—
No other love.
Watching the night go by,
Wishing that you could be
Watching the night with me,
Into the night I cry:
Hurry home, come home to me!
Set me free,
Free from doubt
And free from longing!
Into your arms I'll fly,
Locked in your arms I'll stay,
Waiting to hear you say:

No other love have I,
No other love!

IT'S ME

Published as an individual sheet. Introduced by Joan
McCracken (Betty) and Isabel Bigley (Jeanie).

VERSE 1

BETTY: I'm colorless and shy,
Inhibited and dull.
My entrance into any room is followed by
a lull.
This droopiness in me
Miraculously melts
When I step on a stage and make believe
I'm someone else.
Quite suddenly I'm mentally and
physically equipped
With most unusual qualities—it says so
in the script!

REFRAIN 1

JEANIE: Who is that delectable dame,
Cool as cream and hotter than flame?
Who? Who could it be?
BETTY: It's me! It's me! It's me!
JEANIE: Who's that queenly gift to the boys—
BETTY: Always keen and lousy with poise?
JEANIE: Who? Who could it be?
BETTY: It's me! It's me! It's me!
When the authors make me say
Words that make me wittier,
I feel just as smart as they—
And what's more, I'm prettier!
JEANIE: Who's that girl who's getting the wows?
Who's that babe who's taking the
bows?
BETTY: In a daze I wonder, who is she?
Imagine my surprise
When once I realize
It's nobody else but wonderful, beautiful
me!

VERSE 2

BETTY: My picture hangs in Sardi's
For all the world to see.
I sit beneath my picture there and no one
looks at me.
I sometimes wear dark glasses,
Concealing who I am,

Then all at once I take them off—and no
one gives a damn!
But when I start to play a part, I play the
part okay;
No longer am I no one when I'm
someone in a play.

REFRAIN 2

JEANIE: Every man is flipping his lid
Over that phenomenal kid—
Who? Who could it be?
BETTY: It's me! It's me! It's me!
JEANIE: Whose hot kiss from passionate lips
Perpetrates a total eclipse?
Who? Who could it be?
BETTY: It's me! It's me! It's me!
Oh, what I can perpetrate
By my osculation!
Just one little kiss and *pouf*—
There goes perpetration!
JEANIE: Who has learned the formula which
Satisfies the seven-year itch?
Who's that dazzling personali-tee?
BOTH: Well, here's the big surprise:
Hot dog, and damn my eyes—
It's nobody else but wonderful, beautiful
me!

INTERMISSION TALK

Alternate title: "Ten Minutes Intermission." Published
in the vocal score. Introduced by Jackie Kelk (Herbie,
the candy-counter boy) and ensemble.

HERBIE: Lemonade,
Freshly made!
A bottle of ice-cold
Coke!
BORED PATRON: I love to go to a theater
lounge
To enjoy a noisy smoke.
HERBIE: Lemonade,
Freshly made!
STARRY-EYED GIRL: I simply adore the show!
BORED PATRON: I wouldn't wait for the
second act
If I had some place to go!
MUSIC LOVER: I like the one that goes:
"Da di da dum,
Da di da dum,
Da di da dum.
Marriage-type love."

WIFE: I don't think it's right
To be sulky all night
Over one little bill from
Saks!

BUSINESSMAN: What do I care if they
balance the budget,
As long as they cut my
tax?

MUSIC LOVER: I like the one that goes:
"No other love have I . . .
Hurry back home tonight!
It's me, it's me, it's me . . ."*

HER COMPANION: That doesn't sound quite
right.

GIRL: The fellow beside me
keeps dropping his
program
And groping around my
feet.

BORED PATRON: The couple behind me had
garlic for dinner.
Would you like to trade
your seat?

FASTIDIOUS PERSON: I think the production is
fine,
The music is simply
divine!
The story is lovely and
gay—
But it just isn't my kind of
play.

HAPPY MOURNERS: They don't write music
anymore
Like the old Vienna valses!
The guy today who writes
a score

* In July 1953, a Brooklyn showgoer wrote to
Hammerstein about a lapse in logic during
"Intermission Talk." The snippet from "It's Me,"
should not have been known to the intermission
crowd, as it was only sung backstage. He responded:

You are quite right in pointing out the error in
Me and Juliet. I wrote the lyric for "Intermission
Talk" during rehearsals and didn't discover the
mistake I had made until we were on the road
working on the show. It was one of those things
that I intended to fix when I got round to it, but
there were so many more important revisions to
make that I never did get round to it, and in fact
never did believe that anyone would be keen
enough to catch me at it, but of course in time
some one does, and we are always learning this
lesson over and over again. I hope you will
confine my secret to a few thousand of your most
intimate friends. This is not the kind of thing I
like to have bruited about.

Doesn't know what
schmaltz is!
The plots are all too
serious,
No longer sweet and gay.
The authors who think
Certainly stink.
The theater is fading away.

The theater is dying,
The theater is dying,
The theater is practically
dead!
Someone ev'ry day writes
"We have no more
playwrights,
The theater is sick in the
head."
Some singer of dirges
Gets earnest and urges
The public to have a good
cry—

HERBIE: But the show still goes
on—
The theater's not gone.

HAPPY MOURNERS: We wish it would lie down
and die,
Why in hell won't it lie
down and die?

STARRY-EYED GIRL: I thought that I'd laugh
myself silly
On the ev'ning I spent
with Bea Lillie.

BUSINESSMAN: I sure had to hassle and
hustle
Buying tickets for
Rosalind Russell!

SATISFIED PATRON: I just had a picnic at
Picnic
And loved everyone in the
cast!

HAPPY MOURNERS: Your talk is absurd!
Why haven't you heard?
The theater's a thing o' the
past,
Tra-la.
The theater's a thing o' the
past!

ROMANTIC PATRON: My love for my husband
grew thinner
The first time I looked at
Yul Brynner,
And back in my bed on
Long Island
I kept dreaming of
Brynner in Thailand.

BUSINESSMAN: I love Shirley Booth and
Tom Ewell.

ENTHUSIASTIC PATRON: *The Crucible*—boy, what a
play!

HAPPY MOURNERS: The poor little schmoes!
Not one of them knows
The theater is passing
away—
Hey! Hey!
The theater is passing
away!
The theater is dying,
The theater is dying,
The theater is practic'lly
dead!
The ones who are
backing it
Take a shellacking
And never get out of the
red.

ALL THE REST: But actors keep acting,
And plays keep attracting,
And seats are not easy to
buy.
And year after year
There is something to
cheer—

HAPPY MOURNERS: We'd much rather have a
good cry!

ALL THE REST: [*spoken*] Why in hell don't
you lie down and die?

HAPPY MOURNERS: The theater is—

ALL THE REST: —living!

HAPPY MOURNERS: The theater is—

ALL THE REST: —living!
Why don't you lie down
and die?

IT FEELS GOOD

Published in the vocal score. Introduced by Mark Dawson (Bob).

VERSE

When you lay off your liquor, you get in a rut
And forget the fun you have missed for years.
Then it touches your lips—and you go off your
nut,
Like a dame who hasn't been kissed for years!
You feel the world go drifting by
As if you're on a boat,
And every time you drink some rye
(To keep the boat afloat),
A small but red-hot butterfly
Flutters down your throat.

REFRAIN

It feels good—
Not good like something sweet,
Not good like something beautiful,
But good like something strong.
It feels right—
Not right like right or left,
But right like in an argument—
The other guy is wrong!
It feels good
To feel high,
High above a world of weasels and their lousy
    weasel talk.
A good drink and you fly
Over all the things that frighten all the little jerks
    who walk.
You feel smart—
Not smart like smarty-pants,
But smart like finding out the truth:
Like someone bangs a gong,
And that gong is a signal that the road's all clear,
With no one and nothing in the world to fear!
The limit for you is the sky,
And you are a hell of a guy!
And if you feel like breaking up a certain place,
Or if you feel like pushing in a certain face,
You are the bozo who can!
You are a hell of a man!
Not a weasel,
Not a louse,
Not a chicken,
Not a mouse,
But a man!

SEQUENCE IN ACT TWO OF "ME & JULIET," including WE DESERVE EACH OTHER

Introduced by Bob Fortier (Jim, as Don Juan), Joan McCracken (Betty, as Carmen), and dancing ensemble.

DON JUAN: Hiya, Carmen.
CARMEN: Hiya, Don.
DON JUAN: How ya feelin'?
CARMEN: Fit.
DON JUAN: Feel like dancin'?
CARMEN: Don, you're on.
DON JUAN: Baby, this is it!
CARMEN: Let's create some chaos.
DON JUAN: This could be the night.

CARMEN: Let us be the first two wrongs that ever
made a right.

We Deserve Each Other

Published in the vocal score. Sung by by Joan McCracken (Betty, as Carmen) and danced by McCracken, Bob Fortier (Jim, as Don Juan), and ensemble. This song was added during the Boston tryout, to replace a much longer sequence.

CARMEN: We deserve each other,
          We deserve each other—
          I'll tell the world that we do.
          You and your miniature sparrow brain,
          I and my tiny IQ.
          We deserve each other—
          Let me tell you, brother,
          I am a difficult girl;
          You're an impossible character—
          Why don't we give it a whirl?
          I don't want to reform you;
          To make your mistakes you are free—
          But I just want to be certain
          That your greatest mistake will be me!
          If you want to wrestle,
          I'm the weaker vessel,
          And I'll be easy to swerve.
          We deserve each other—
          So let us take what we deserve.

[*Dance.*]

I'M YOUR GIRL

Published as an individual sheet. Introduced by Isabel Bigley (Jeanie) and Bill Hayes (Larry).

VERSE

JEANIE: Once and for always
        Let me make it clear
        What I am to you
        And what you are to me.
        I want to tell you while I have you near
        This is how it is
        And how it's going to be.

REFRAIN 1

JEANIE: I'm your girl,
        It's time you knew,
        All I am

Belongs to you.
Any time you're out of luck,
I'm unlucky too.
I'm your partner, your lover, your wife,
    your friend.
I'll be walking beside you till journey's
    end.
With your arms around me,
I'll be yours alone—
I'm the girl you own.

REFRAIN 2

LARRY: Any time I'm out of luck,
       You're unlucky too.
JEANIE: I'm your partner,
LARRY: Your lover,
JEANIE: Your wife,
LARRY: Your friend.
       I'll be walking beside you till journey's
       end.
BOTH: With your arms around me,
      I'll be yours alone—
      I'm the one you own.

CUT AND UNUSED SONGS

MARRIAGE-TYPE LOVE FINALE (REPRISE)

This text does not appear in the published script or score of *Me and Juliet*, but is heard on the cast album at the beginning of the Act Two finale. Another version appears below in the cut "Sequence from Act Two of 'Me & Juliet'."

ENSEMBLE: Out of nowhere
          Came the feeling.
          Knew the feeling—
          Marriage-type love!
ME: Me and Juliet
    Built the dream up,
    Had to team up—
ENSEMBLE: Marriage-type love!
MEN: Caught in the spell of the moon in
     their blue room
GIRLS: They did so well, they will soon need a
       new room.
ME: Ev'ry evening
    Next to my chair

There's a high chair.
It's family-type love for me!

OPENING OF "ME & JULIET" (EARLY VERSION)

Near the end of the Boston tryout, Hammerstein wrote to William F. McDermott of the *Cleveland Plain Dealer* about revisions: "The best change of all is in the first 'Me and Juliet' sequence in which we make it clear to the audience that the play within the play is intended as a human and humorous allegory rather than a big, beautiful, soggy spectacle, as it was when you saw it."

VOICES: Where is this?
JULIET: It doesn't matter.
The scene of the play is
neither here nor there.
All the things
About to happen
Are things that are always
happening everywhere.
VOICES: When is this?
JULIET: It doesn't matter.
The time of the play is neither
now nor then.
Every year
The world is changing—
DON JUAN: But women remain the same—
CARMEN: And so do men!
DON JUAN: I'm Don Juan.
DON JUAN'S GIRLS: Don Juan.
CARMEN: I'm Carmen.
DON JUAN'S GIRLS: [*harmonizing sweetly*] She's
common.
CARMEN: I'm Juliet,
The maiden,
So frail, so fair, so pure,
So young,
Inexperienced,
So shy, so unsure,
So innocent, so trusting, a
prey to passion's whim.
I make a fellow eager to
protect me
From others who are eager to
protect me from him.
The story of our play
(Just like many another play)
Is to show what I—
DON JUAN: And I—
CARMEN: And I—

JULIET, DON JUAN,
AND CARMEN: Can do
To that plain and simple
character,
That complicated character,
That fascinating character—
You.
ME: Me!

[*Lights dim on other characters.*]

Me, who am I?
A far-from-perfect guy—
A jerk who wants to do what's
right
But often does what's wrong,
A drip whose voice is way
off-key
But loves to sing a song,
A dope who dreams like a lion
But wakes up like a lamb—
Me, who am I
But the guy
I am,
The guy
Who'm I?
Juliet!
Say you love me!
JULIET: My bounty is boundless as the
sea,
And like the sea my maiden
love is deep.
The more I give, the more I
have for thee,
And all I own is thine alone to
keep,
And all I own is thine alone to
keep.

SEQUENCE FROM ACT TWO OF "ME & JULIET," including MARRIAGE-TYPE LOVE (REPRISE) and BOSS, MAY I HAVE A RAISE? and THE BABY YOU LOVE and MEAT AND POTATOES

Not published. Dropped out of town. Introduced by Arthur Maxwell (Charlie, as Me), Bob Fortier (Jim, as Don Juan), Helena Scott (Lily, as Juliet), Joan McCracken (Betty, as Carmen), and ensemble.

Marriage-type Love (reprise)

ME: Now I got it,
Got the feeling.
What a feeling—
Marriage-type love!
Me and Juliet
Built the dream up,
Had to team up—
Marriage-type love!
Caught in the spell of the moon in our blue
room,
We did so well that we'll soon need a new
room!
Any minute
Baby'll be here,
We'll be three here—
Family-type love for me!
[*sung to himself*] My boy Bill,
He'll be tall and as tough as a tree . . .
[*spoken*] But wait, what if he is a girl?

Boss, May I Have a Raise?

[DON JUAN, *the boss, enters.*]

MEN AND GIRLS: The boss! The boss! The
boss! The boss!
ME: [*oblivious*] My little girl,
pink and white as
peaches and cream—
DON JUAN: Get to work!
ME: —is she!
DON JUAN: What are you dreaming
about?
ME: I'm going to have a baby!
DON JUAN: A baby!
ME: A baby!
I'm going to have a baby!
So may I have a raise?
May I have a raise, boss?
Just a little raise?
DON JUAN: No!

[DON JUAN *exits.*]

ME: You can have fun with a
son, but you've got to
be a father to a girl.
GIRL WITH TELEPHONE: [*spoken*] The hospital?
GIRLS AND MEN: [*spoken*] Hospital?

[*They bundle* ME *into his hat and coat. They all pace.*]

365

JULIET: [offstage] Ouch!

NURSE: [spoken] A baby daughter—
seven pounds, six ounces.

[ME hands out cigars and then faints. As ME is carried off, DON JUAN is carried in on a barber chair, flanked by manicurists and employees.]

1ST MAN: Boss, may I have a raise?
DON JUAN: No!
2ND MAN: Boss, may I have a raise?
DON JUAN: No!
3RD MAN: Boss, may I have a raise?
DON JUAN: No!
4TH MAN: Boss, may I have a raise?
DON JUAN: No!

[ME approaches DON JUAN, but doesn't even get a chance to ask before he is turned down. JULIET enters, and DON JUAN rises, brushing away all the attendants.]

ME: My wife—my boss.
My boss—my wife.
JULIET: In bringing this request to
your attention,
Believe me, sir, with all my
heart I hope
You will not think my
husband is ungrateful
For what is in his weekly
envelope.
We know you meet a
monumental payroll,
With tears we read your
annual report.
But, sir, we have acquired
a baby daughter,
And milk is five and
twenty cents a quart!
DON JUAN: Milk?
ENSEMBLE: Milk?
DON JUAN: My mother nursed me till
I was three.
Look! You can see what it
did for me!
ENSEMBLE: Look!
JULIET: You're wonderful.
DON JUAN: You think so?
Now let us see what we can
do.

[Looks ME up and down.]

What can we make out of
you?
A salesman!

ME: A salesman!
DON JUAN: A traveling salesman.

[ME is handed a suitcase and exits. DON JUAN sends flowers to JULIET.]

JULIET: [reading the card on the
flowers] "Will you dine
with me tonight?
May I call for you at
eight?"
Shall I dine with him
tonight?
Would my amatory mate
Want his wife to make a
date
With his amatory boss?
Would he have me risk the
loss
Of whatever I might lose?
Shall I leave it to the toss
Of a coin to help me
choose?
If it lands heads or tails,
I will go.
If it lands on its edge,
I'll say no!

[She tosses the coin.]

I have no time to fritter—
I'll change my dress and
phone my babysitter!

[Sung to ME's picture.]

Oh, darling, never let this
make you bitter;
You know without my
having to explain:
I'm not a girl who over
rates the glitter
Of dining out on pheasant
and champagne—
I'd rather be with you
Sipping beer and chewing
stew
Or walking from the
subway in the rain,
And anything I do
I only do for you,
For you, for you, my dear,
For you and your business
career!

The Baby You Love*

[DON JUAN arrives, greets JULIET and they walk into a nightclub, where a samba version of "Keep It Gay" can be heard. JULIET is quiet, and DON JUAN tells her to talk pretty—talk about the most beautiful thing in life. He faces away as she pulls a picture from her purse and sings an old-fashioned ballad-type melody against the samba rhythm.]

JULIET: You're not living till you're living with
your baby—
DON JUAN: [flirtatiously] Don't I know it!
JULIET: Till you've kissed those golden curls
upon her head.
There's no vision like the vision of a
baby
When she's lying half asleep upon
your bed.
DON JUAN: [still not aware of the picture] Juliet!
JULIET: Always hold her in your arms when
she's in trouble—
She's as soft and light and tender as a
dove.
Hold her close and wait till she brings
up her bubble!

[This last line gets DON JUAN's attention, and he turns.]

She's your baby, the baby you love.

[The GIRLS pick up a second refrain and sing it while they do bumps and grinds quite incongruous to the lyric. Toward the end they are all pretty well overcome with emotion, and crying. The scene shifts for a moment to the stage manager's desk. When we return, DON JUAN is seeing JULIET home. The evening is a bust. CARMEN enters from the opposite side.]

Meat and Potatoes

CARMEN: [à la Mae West] Meat and potatoes,
Meat and potatoes,
I'm in the mood for
Meat and potatoes!
Quaint and dainty birds or fish
Ain't the type of dish I wish.
I want a real meal,
Not a genteel meal.
I want a beef
Or mutton or veal meal.

---

* This song is listed in the original Broadway
program, but was dropped soon after the opening. It
does not appear in the published libretto or score, nor
on the cast album.

When I'm hungry I get crude
And what I want is food—
Capital F, capital double O, D!
Pass that plate of meat and potatoes
    to me!
GIRLS: Meat and potatoes,
Meat and potatoes,
I'm in the mood for
Meat and potatoes!
Quaint and dainty birds or fish
Ain't the type of dish I wish.
CARMEN: Leave out the salad—
Salad is pallid!
I want a meal more
Solid than salad.
A slice of cow that's nicely browned
To wrap my map around—
ALL: Capital F, capital double O, D!
Pass that plate of meat and potatoes
    to me!

YOU NEVER HAD IT SO GOOD

It's not clear who would have sung this or when. Published when used in the 1996 stage production of *State Fair*.

You never had it so good,
For once in your life, you're living.
Show your baby you're grateful
For all your baby is giving.
You never had it so good,
You crazy, attractive mug, you!
Show your baby you're grateful
Or baby's going to slug you.
I'll sew, I'll bake,
I'll try to make
Your evenings all enchanted.
My honey cake,
I'm yours to take,
But don't take me for granted!
Just do what anyone would—
Confess you're a lucky feller,

Come to baby and tell her
You've been misunderstood.
Kiss your baby and tell her
You never had it so good.

WAKE UP, LITTLE THEATER

Dropped from act one a week before the Cleveland opening.

This song is a pre-show ritual for Larry and members of the chorus and crew. As the number develops, Bob and Larry slip into a "duet duel," each trying to be the louder.

Julius Baum is sweeping up the stage,
Sweeping up the stage, sweeping up the stage.
Julius Baum is sweeping up the stage,
Curtain time coming soon!

Herbie Fox is talking to a girl,
Talking to a girl, talking to a girl.
Herbie Fox is talking to a girl,
Curtain time coming soon.

Theater, you've been asleep all day—
Time to get up and start your play.
Stars are shining in the skies,
Open up your pretty eyes,
Limber up your legs,
Stretch up on your toes,
Clear your foggy pipes
With a few arpeggios,
Like ah—ah—ah—
And mi—mi—mi—
And silly sounds like those.

Wake up, little theater,
Wake up, wake up!
Curtain time coming soon.
Light up the lights,
Tune up the flutes,
Clean up the canvas moon!

Put paint on your people and make them seem
Shiny and brave and bright.

The public is coming to call on you—
You've got to be good tonight.
You've got to *look* good,
You've got to *sound* good,
You've got to *be* good tonight!

End-of-show reprise

Julius Baum is going home to bed,
Going home to bed, going home to bed.
Julius Baum is going home to bed,
Sleepy time coming soon.
Good night, little theater,
Good night, good night.
Sleepy time coming soon.
Turn out the lights,
Wrap up the flutes,
Roll up the canvas moon!

OVERLEAF *The company at the finale of* Pipe Dream. *Left to right, Mike Kellin (center, in T-shirt), G. D. Wallace (with hat), William Johnson (arm in a sling), Judy Tyler, and Helen Traubel*

PIPE DREAM | 1955

PIPE DREAM (1955)

Tryouts: Shubert Theatre, New Haven, October 22–29, 1955; Shubert Theatre, Boston, November 1–26, 1955. New York run: Shubert Theatre; opened November 30, 1955; closed June 30, 1956; 246 performances. Music by Richard Rodgers. Book and lyrics by Oscar Hammerstein II. Based on the novel *Sweet Thursday* by John Steinbeck. Presented by Rodgers and Hammerstein. Directed by Harold Clurman. Dances and musical numbers staged by Boris Runanin. Orchestrations by Robert Russell Bennett. Dance arrangements by John Morris. Musical direction by Salvatore Dell'Isola. Scenery and lighting by Jo Mielziner. Costumes by Alvin Colt.

Cast: Helen Traubel (Fauna), William Johnson (Doc), Judy Tyler (Suzy), Mike Kellin (Hazel), G. D. Wallace (Mac), Jayne Heller (Millicent Henderson), Rufus Smith (Jim Blaikey), John Call (Ray Busch), Guy Raymond (George Herman), Steve Roland (Bill), Keith Kaldenberg (Red), Hobe Streiford (Whitey), Nicholas Orloff (Dizzy), Warren Kemmerling (Eddie), Warren Brown (Alec), Kenneth Harvey (Joe "the Mexican"), Ruby Braff (Pancho), Temple Texas (Agnes), Jackie McElroy (Mable), Marilyn Bradley (Emma), Mildred Slavin (Beulah), Louise Troy (Marjorie), Pat Creighton (Cho Cho Sen), Sandra Devlin (Sumi), Joseph Leon (Sonny Boy), Jerry LaZarre (Esteban), Kasimir Kokich (Waiter), Patricia Wilson (Harriet), Ruth Kobart (Hilda), Marvin Krauter (Fred), Gene Kevin (Slick), Don Weissmuller (Slim), Sigyn (Basha), Marsha Reynolds (Bubbles), Annabelle Gold (Sonya), Jenny Workman (Kitty), Patti Karkalits (Weirde), Scotty Engel (Johnny Carriagra), Rudolfo Cornejo (Pedro), Calvin Thomas (Dr. Ormandy).

The denizens of Steinbeck's Cannery Row in Monterey, California, "rattle along" without much aspiration, and without much complication, until Suzy arrives out of nowhere, hungry enough to break a plate glass window to get at some doughnuts. Kindly Fauna, the madam of the Bear Flag Café, offers her a job and a place to stay. And Doc, an underemployed but content marine biologist, sews her up. Attracted to each other, Suzy and Doc each feel deficient in the other's eyes. Doc resolves to write a scientific paper, but Mac and Hazel, his amiable pals from the Palace Flophouse, see no writing, just a new irritability. They resolve to cheer up Doc by buying a fancy microscope with the proceeds from a fixed raffle. In favor of the match, Fauna coaches Suzy for a date with Doc and dresses her as a bride for the costume party that is the climax of the raffle. The road to love is not smooth, but after Suzy sets up housekeeping in an empty boiler (the "pipe" of *Pipe Dream*) and Doc is disabled by a broken arm, they find that they are not just needy but have something to offer the other.

Costume designer Alvin Colt received a Tony Award for his body of work, 1955–56.

An original cast recording was made by RCA Victor. This chapter's major sources are the published vocal score and the published libretto. Several of the songs were published as individual sheets. The Hammerstein Collection in the Music Division of the Library of Congress includes four boxes of *Pipe Dream* scenes, lyric worksheets, and scripts. The Richard Rodgers Collection there includes holograph sketches and piano-vocal scores.

ALL KINDS OF PEOPLE

Published in the vocal score. Introduced by William Johnson (Doc) and Mike Kellin (Hazel). Reprised by Rufus Smith (Jim Blaikey, the local cop).

VERSE 1

DOC: The starfish may look unimportant,
Lying limply on his underwater shelf.
He may look unimportant to you,
But he's very interesting to himself.

REFRAIN

DOC: It takes all kinds of people to make up a
world,
All kinds of people and things.
They crawl on the earth,
They swim in the sea,
And they fly through the sky on wings.
All kinds of people and things,
And brother, I'll tell you my hunch:
Whether you like them
Or whether you don't,
You're stuck with the whole damn bunch!

VERSE 2

DOC: I don't think so much of the buzzard,
He is something I would never like to be.
But who knows what goes on in his mind?
He may think he is superior to me!
HAZEL: [*outraged*] Aw now, Doc!

VERSE 3

DOC: You may not admire armadillos,
They're repulsive and they lead peculiar
lives.
They may not look attractive to you
But they're very interesting to their wives.

REPEAT REFRAIN

PARTIAL REFRAIN FOR REPRISE

JIM: One guy will kill you for dough,
And one guy will rob you of lunch.
One guy will help you,
And he makes you fall
In love with the whole darn bunch.

THE TIDE POOL

Published in the vocal score. Introduced by William Johnson (Doc), Mike Kellin (Hazel), G. D. Wallace (Mac), and Judy Tyler (Suzy).

MAC: It's nothin' at all when the
tide is high,
It's just a bunch o' waves.
HAZEL: They whip all around all 'a
rocks
An' chase all 'a fish into
caves.
DOC: But if you get there when
the tide is low
And the pool is clear and
clean,
You can see to the
bottom—
HAZEL: The damndest collection
o' creeps you ever seen!
DOC: Hungry flowers that live on
fish,
Scooping in whatever
comes,
Crabs that grab another
crab
And chew his legs—
SUZY: [*spoken*] The dirty bums!
HAZEL: Starfish, havin' himself a
lunch,
Eats a mussel off a shell.
MAC: Shrimps 'n' limpets 'n'
snails 'n' eels,
What a smelly tale they
tell—
Fightin' each other
'N' eatin' each other
'N' lousin' up the sea!
HAZEL: Stupid sons o' fishes,
If you're askin' me!
DOC: Out on the top of the water
Everything seems all right.
There's a sun on the bay at
daytime

And a moon on the bay at
    night.
MAC: A breeze blows in from offa
    the reef
An' you hear the whistlin'
    buoy—
HAZEL: While Doc an' me are
    chewin' the fat
An' talkin' a lot o' hooey.
DOC AND MAC: Out on the top of the
    water
It's quieter than a well—
DOC, MAC, AND HAZEL: While under the water,
    under the water,
They're raising holy hell!
DOC: Get a load of the octopus!
Looking for a crab to eat,
Oozes out of slimy weeds,
Creeping on his floppy
    feet.
MAC: Crab too busy to see him
    come,
Crab's a cinch to catch
    because
He is chewin' another crab,
Strugglin' in his greedy
    claws—
DOC, MAC, AND HAZEL: Fighting each other
And eating each other
And lousing up the sea,
Fighting and feeding
And mating and breeding
And filling up the sea—
Stupid sons o' fishes!
Stupid sons o' fishes!
Stupid sons o' fishes!
To live in a tide pool!

EVERYBODY'S GOT A HOME BUT ME

Published as an individual sheet. Introduced by Judy Tyler (Suzy). Eddie Fisher made a popular recording.

VERSE

Scooted outa Frisco over Route One-Oh-One,
Bummed a ride as far as San Jose,
Rode aboard a Greyhound till I run outa dough,
Landed on my can in Monterey!
But I see a lotta things along the way
And I did a lotta thinkin' on the way.

REFRAIN

I rode by a house
With the windows lighted up,
Lookin' brighter than a Christmas tree,
And I said to myself
As I rode by myself,
Everybody's got a home but me.
I rode by a house
Where the moon was on the porch
And a girl was on her feller's knee,
And I said to myself
As I rode by myself,
Everybody's got a home but me.
I am free,
And I'm happy to be free,
To be free in the way I want to be—
But once in a while,
When the road is kinda dark
And the end is kinda hard to see,
I look up and I cry
To a cloud goin' by,
Won't there ever be a home for me, somewhere?
Everybody's got a home but me.
I am free,
And I'm happy to be free,
To be free in the way I want to be—
But once in a while,
When I'm talkin' to myself
And there's no one there to disagree,
I look up and I cry
To the big empty sky,
Won't there ever be a home for me, somewhere?
Everybody's got a home but me!

A LOPSIDED BUS

Alternate title: "On a Lopsided Bus." Published in the vocal score. Introduced by G. D. Wallace (Mac), Mike Kellin (Hazel), John Call (Ray), Guy Raymond (George), Steve Roland (Bill), Hobe Streiford (Whitey), Warren Brown (Alec), and the male ensemble (the Flophouse gang).

MAC: What do you do all day, Ray?
    What do you do all day?
RAY: I wake at six
And take my wife
Her breakfast on a tray.
I walk the kids to school,
Then I run to catch a bus—
MAC: That's the life for us, boys!
ALL: That's the life for us!

WHITEY: [spoken] Then what, Ray?
GEORGE: [spoken] Tell the boys, Ray.
RAY: I work all day on an adding machine,
Adding the boss's dough.
At six o'clock I am back on a bus,
Back to my home I go.
My supper I sup,
I feel so beat up
I'm soon asleep in my bed.
MAC: When you grow old and die, Ray,
How will you know you're dead?
ALL: When you grow old and die, Ray,
How will you know you're dead?
ALEC: If you work like a horse till the day
    you're dead,
You're a part of a horse
And it ain't the head!
GEORGE: This is the kind of day I like:
When questions of life are philosophied
By thoughtful companions, sittin'
    around
And gettin' a little bit ossified.
BILL: Life is a bowlful of cherries—
WHITEY: Except when the cherries ain't there.
MAC: Life is a room full o' feathers
That keep gettin' in your hair.
BILL: You said it, Mac!
ALEC: You got it, Mac!
RAY: You hit it right on the button!
GEORGE: We always keep goin', but where do
    we go?
BILL: What do we know?
HAZEL: Nuttin'.
MAC: On a lopsided, ramshackle bus
We ride from day to day.
We bounce and we bump and we rattle
    along.
We rattle along on our way.
Every year it's a hassle for us
To get from June to May,
But somehow or other, by hook or by
    crook,
We rattle along on our way.
Every time that we start to fall all apart
And we're near the end of our rope,
A screwball comes through with a
    gimmick that's new
And our hearts go crazy with hope!
We hop on our lopsided bus
And chase another day,
As happy as candles that shine on a cake,
As gay as the bells on a sleigh!
We rattle along,
Rattle along,
Rattle along on our way.
ALL: On a lopsided, ramshackle bus
We ride from day to day.

MAC: We wobble around on a rock-happy road
And rattle along on our way.
ALL: Every year it's a hassle for us
To get from June to May,
But somehow or other, by hook or by
crook,
We rattle along on our way.
BILL: When the engine won't work 'n it's goin'
berserk
And we're near the end of our rope,
We fix up the thing with an old piece of
string—
HAZEL: And our hearts get lousy with hope!
ALL: We hop on our lopsided bus
And chase another day,
As happy as candles that shine on a cake,
As gay as the bells on a sleigh!
We rattle along,
Rattle along,
Rattle along on our way.
We rattle along,
Rattle along—
And try to find our way.

BUM'S OPERA

Published in the vocal score. Introduced by Keith Harvey (Joe "the Mexican") and the male ensemble (the Flophouse gang), with Ruby Braff (Pancho) on the trumpet.

VERSE 1

JOE: You may be a wise and intelligent man,
A genius type of Joe—
But if a dumb tomato comes after you,
You'll forget whatever you know.

REFRAIN 1

JOE: You can dodge a stick or a stone,
You can duck a punch when it's thrown,
But you can't get away from a dumb tomato
When she wants you for her own.
BOYS: You can dodge a stick or a stone,
You can duck a punch when it's thrown,
But you can't get away from a dumb tomato
When she wants you for her own!

VERSE 2

JOE: You may be a good and respectable man,
No cards, no gin, no rum—
But if a wild tomato comes after you,

She will turn you into a bum.

REFRAIN 2

JOE: You can dodge a bill when it's due,
You can duck a flying lassoo—
But you can't get away from a wild tomato
When she throws herself at you.

VERSE 3

JOE: You may be a young and an innocent boy,
Your chin grows only fuzz—
But if a ripe tomato comes after you,
You won't be as young as you wuz!

REFRAIN 3

BOYS: You can dodge a bill when it's due,
You can duck a flying lassoo—
JOE: But you can't get away from a ripe tomato
When she throws a curve at you.
BOYS: Man, you're through,
There is nothing you can do
When they throws their curves at you!

[*Dance.*]

FAUNA'S SONG

Introduced by Helen Traubel (Fauna). There are two versions of "Fauna's Song." The version in the vocal score serves as a dancing coda to "Bum's Opera." The version in the published libretto (and heard in part on the cast album) is Fauna's refutation of the claims made in "Bum's Opera."

Vocal score version

Babaloo! Babaloo! Babaloo!
I yi, I yi, yi,
I yi, yi, yi, yi, yi, yi, yi.
Oh, oh,
Oh, oh, oh,
Oh, oh,
Oh—
The beguine has begun
And it's driving me crazy.
Ah ooh,
Ah ooh,
Ah ooh!

Libretto and cast album version

Babaloo! Babaloo! Babaloo!

I have heard you say
How tomatoes are the ruin of man,
But I ain't seen the day or the night
When a woman made a pass at a man
And the man put up a fight.

You can't catch a fish without a worm for bait,
You can't catch a worm if you get up too late,
You can't plug a duck unless you sit and wait,
And snarin' a bear is no snap;
The zebra is hard to catch and hard to tame—
Among all the animals we call wild game,
A man is the only one that you can name
Who tries to be caught in a trap!
You hunt him at nightfall;
He's easily thrown.
He's gotta go rovin';
He can't be alone.
He looks out the window when the moon is high;
He looks in the lookin' glass and ties his tie,
Decides he's a fascinatin' type of guy
And goes out and looks for a trap
To be caught in—
He goes out and looks for the trap!

The zebra is hard to catch and hard to tame—
Among all the animals we call wild game,
There ain't any animals that you can name
As wild and as dumb as a man.
You hunt him at nightfall;
He's easy to get.
If you are a female,
He'll fall in your net.
He walks into trouble with a hopeful eye,
A pigeon who wants to be a pigeon pie,
A fish who is feelin' in the mood to fry,
He goes out and looks for a pan
To be fried in!
He goes out and looks for the pan!

THE MAN I USED TO BE

Published as an individual sheet. Introduced by William Johnson (Doc); danced by Don Weissmuller (who "flits about the stage easily and gracefully in contrast with the worried 'self' who sings the song").

Hammerstein worked on this lyric during July and August of 1955, while on location in Arizona for the filming of *Oklahoma!*. He'd sing lines to himself on the fifty-mile drive from his motel to the site of Aunt

Eller's farm and "walk the prairie in search of rhymes" between takes. When the song was performed on television's *Ed Sullivan Show* in 1956, Hammerstein explained that after Doc meets Suzy, "his friends notice a change in him. He's beginning to notice it himself. We've written a song that catches him in the midst of this self-analysis. And the song also gives the audience a glimpse of the kind of man he was before the curtain rose on the play."

VERSE

You've changed, bub,
You've changed a lot—
And the gang you used to go with all concur.
You've changed, bub,
You're not yourself—
If this is yourself, you're not the man you were!

REFRAIN 1

The man I used to be,
A happy man was he,
And aimless as a leaf in a gale.
Whatever has become
Of that lighthearted bum
Who thought he had the world by the tail?
The man I used to be—
His life was gay and free
And aimless as a cloud in the sky.
He thought he knew the game,
Then along came a dame
Who turned him into some other guy.
I've got ambition now,
I've got a mission now;
I aim to reach the top of the tree.
That other fly-by-night,
Who flew so high by night,
Has vanished like a sail on the sea,
And I'll never find that easy-living, easy-taking,
    easy-giving fellow that I used to call me—
You can never find the man you used to be.

REFRAIN 2

The man I used to be
Would go to sleep at three
Or four a.m. or seven or nine,
And when his weary head
Wasn't near any bed,
A table or a chair would be fine!
A man without a goal,
A sort of friendly soul,
He liked to play the role of a host
To any thirsty pal
Or a casual gal
Who'd stay to cook his coffee and toast.
He was a ne'er-do-well

Who wouldn't dare do well;
He never saw the top of a tree.
But kind of sad I was
To see the cad I was
Dissolving like a sail on the sea,
And I'll never find that fatalistic, free-and-easy,
    egotistic optimist who used to be me—
You can never find the man you used to be.

SWEET THURSDAY

Published as an individual sheet. Introduced by Helen Traubel (Fauna). Johnny Mathis made a popular recording in 1962.

REFRAIN

When the sun flew in my window
And crept in bed with me,
I knew that this would be
A sweet Thursday.
When the wind got confidential
And whispered through a tree,
I knew that this would be
A sweet Thursday.
My head was up in the clouds;
My heart was flapping its wings.
I looked at the sky
And wanted to try
To do impossible things.
What a day it's been for dreaming!
My dreams have all come true.
And if one I kept for you*
Turns out to be right,
It's going to be a sweet Thursday night for me!
It's going to be a sweet Thursday night!

VERSE

A good kind of confident feeling
Has followed me all day long.
My luck was in,
I played to win—
I knew I couldn't go wrong.

---

* *Alternate line for repeat of refrain:*
    "And if one for Doc and Sue."

A bright red geranium told me,*
Today was my day for fun.
A katydid
Said: "Take it, kid,
You better take it and run!"
Some shirts hanging up on a clothesline
Kept waving their tails my way—
"Hiya, Fauna? Hiya, babe?
Ain't this a doll of a day?"
Ain't this a doll of a day?

REPEAT REFRAIN

Verse from published sheet

What a jerk of a day was Wednesday!
By the time I got to sleep,
All the interest in life
That I had left
I'd have sold you awful cheap.
But I opened my eyes this morning
And I knew by every sign
That whatever I wanted
To do today
Would be sure to turn out fine.

SUZY IS A GOOD THING

Published as an individual sheet. Introduced by Helen Traubel (Fauna) and Judy Tyler (Suzy). Each line of the introduction and Refrain 1 is first sung by Fauna and then by Suzy.

INTRODUCTION

I got eyes that can see pretty sunsets
And pretty dresses in store winders.
And I got ears that can hear music
And the sound of waves on a beach.
I got a nose that can smell flowers
And food cookin' on a stove.

---

* *Hammerstein revised lines 6–12 of the verse in pencil on a typescript; it is not clear why the revisions did not become part of the official text.*
    A bright red geranium told me:
    "Today is all yours to take!"
    A katydid
    Said: "Take it, kid,
    The dice are ready to shake!"
    A white shirt that hung on a clothesline
    Kept waving his tail my way—

And I got two feet that can take me anywhere I
    want to go,
And I can walk and run and climb and swim in the
    sea.
And if I am somethin' that can do all this,
Why should I
Be ashamed to be me?

REFRAIN 1

Suzy is a good thing;
This I know is true.
Suzy is a good thing.
She may make mistakes,
As other people do—
Everybody makes a few.
Suzy's eyes are searching eyes;
The world they seek is new.
Suzy looks for love
As other people do.
Suzy will find her love, too—
Someone is looking for Sue.

INTERLUDE

FAUNA: Tonight you're goin' out with a man—
SUZY: With a man who asked me to go!
FAUNA: Right!
SUZY: And I ain't scared o' sayin' anythin'
    wrong
    'Cause I won't say only what I know!
FAUNA: Good!
SUZY: I'm goin' out to eat tonight—
    A feller is takin' me there.
    I'll hold my hand on his arm good and
    tight,
    And I'll hold my chin in the air,
    And if anyone tries to make a crack,
    I'll look like I don't care.
    Because I'm Suzy!

[*They repeat refrain.*]

Verse from published sheet

If you walk with your eyes on the ground,
How can you tell where you're going?
Raise your eyes, take a good look around—
There are things to be learning and knowing.
And the best thing to know is yourself:
You are not just a hat in a crowd,
You're a special thing called you—
Be glad, be brave, be proud.

ALL AT ONCE YOU LOVE HER

Published as an individual sheet. Introduced by Jerry LaZarre (Estéban), serenading Doc and Suzy in Spanish, then by William Douglas (Doc) and Judy Tyler (Suzy) singing in English; reprised, preceded by a verse, by Helen Traubel (Fauna). Perry Como had a popular recording.

In a 1955 article about *Pipe Dream*, Hammerstein noted that his folder of notes for this song was "thicker than the manuscript of the whole play. It contains the development of three complete lyrics—the two I discarded and the one I kept."

ESTÉBAN: No bien le has encendido el
    Pitillo ya quieres.
    Apenas la
    Conoces bien,
    Es dueña ya de tu alma.
    Y su mirar
    Te hace soñar.
    Y ella también te quiere.
    Le das el beso de tu amor,
    El que será por siempre.
    Y tu ansiedad
    Del corazón
    Ya sabe donde ir.

Male version

DOC: You start to light
    Her cigarette
    And all at once
    You love her.
    You've scarcely talked,
    You've scarcely met,
    But all at once
    You love her.
    You like her eyes,
    You tell her so;
    She thinks you're wise
    And clever.
    You kiss good night
    And then you know
    You'll kiss good night
    Forever!
    You wonder where
    Your heart can go—
    Then all at once you know.

Female version

SUZY: He starts to light
    Your cigarette

    And all at once
    You love him.
    You've scarcely talked,
    You've scarcely met,
    But all at once
    You love him.
    He likes your eyes,
    He tells you so;
    You think he's wise
    And clever.
    You kiss good night
    And then you know
    You'll kiss good night
    Forever!
    You wonder where
    Your heart can go—
    Then all at once you know.

Fauna's verse for reprise

The romance that you have waited for
Will come when it comes.
Without a word of warning it will start.
With a sudden blare of trumpets
And the rattle of drums
A dream will take possession of your heart.

Three precursors

These precursors to "All at Once You Love Her" were found in the Hammerstein Collection in the Music Division of the Library of Congress.

1

I need no sigh
Of soft guitars
To serenade my lady,
No gleaming sky
Of dreaming stars
To serenade my lady.
I need no rhyme
To praise her grace.
No need have I for music.
For every time
We're face to face,
She fills my heart with music.
And [with my arms?],
My singing arms,
I serenade my love.

2

The moon is low
Upon the sea.
The fading stars are flying.
The winds that blow
Upon the sea

Like soft guitars are sighing.
Stay close, my love,
Stay close to me
While night is caught around us.
Stay close, my love,
And dream with me
The dream we sought has found us.

3

You start to light
Her cigarette.
Are you in love?
You wonder.
You both recite
An old duet.
Are you in love?
You wonder.
Your talk is bright.
The phrases flow.
You've never been so clever.
You kiss goodnight.
And then you know
You'll kiss goodnight
Forever.

THE HAPPIEST HOUSE ON THE BLOCK

Published in the vocal score. Introduced by Helen Traubel (Fauna) and female ensemble. This song was added during the out-of-town tryouts.

VERSE 1

FAUNA: Merry Christmas from me and the
         family—
     Remember if ever you're blue
     This little frame house on the corner
     Will always be open to you.

REFRAIN 1

FAUNA: The happiest house on the block
     Is quietly sleeping all day,
     But after eleven
     Our little blue heaven
     Is friendly and foolish and gay.
     The roses that grow 'round our door
     Will welcome you in when you knock.
     You'll meet everyone in
     The town having fun in
     The happiest house on the block.

VERSE 2

BECKY: What a beautiful holiday greeting!
MABEL: Look at Santa Claus blowin' a kiss!
EMMA: It makes a girl proud to be part of
       An organization like this.

REFRAIN 2

FAUNA: The happiest house on the block,
     Where nothing's too good for a guest.
GIRLS: Our parlor is cheery,
     There's rest for the weary,
     The weary who don't want to rest!
FAUNA: A home for the brave and the free,
     Where nobody punches a clock—
GIRLS: Alone on that basis
     Our own little place is
     The happiest house on the block.

VERSE 3

FAUNA: There's a friend who drops in very often,
     He is kind of mixed up in his life:
     He longs for a home and a woman
     Whenever he's home with his wife.

[Girls repeat refrain 1 while FAUNA sings obbligato.]

THE PARTY THAT WE'RE GONNA HAVE TOMORROW NIGHT

Published in the vocal score. Additional material is sung on the cast album. Introduced by G. D. Wallace (Mac) and the ensemble.

MAC: Party comin' up on Cannery
     Row.
GROWING GROUP: Party comin' up on Cannery
     Row.
GIRLS: Hear the rumble over Cannery
     Row?
GROWING GROUP: Hear the rumble over Cannery
     Row?
MAC: Rumblin', mumblin',
     murmurin' low—
GROWING GROUP: Rumblin', mumblin',
     murmurin' low—
MAC: Like a cyclone ready to blow!
GROWING GROUP: Like a cyclone ready to blow!
ALL: Gettin' ready to pop,
     Gettin' ready to bust,

Gettin' ready to blow!
A NEWCOMER: When do we go?
CROWD: Tomorrer!
NEWCOMER: Tomorrer!
ALL: Tomorrer! Tomorrer! Tomorrer!

REFRAIN 1

MAC: Oh, there never was a party
     Like the party that we're gonna
       have tomorrow night!
     What a sweetheart of a party—
     We'll be rowdy, loud, and hearty
       till the sun gets bright!
     Oh, there never was a clambake
       we recall
     Or a rumpus or a ruckus or a
       ball
     Like the party that we're gonna
       have tomorrow night,
     The best damn party of all!

REFRAIN 2

ALL: Oh, there never was a party
     Like the party that we're gonna
       have tomorrow night!
HAZEL: What a sweetheart of a party,
     We'll be drinking à la carty till
       the stars turn white.
AGNES: Oh, the crowd has never had
       itself a ball
     Like that hist'ry-making,
       record-breaking brawl—
ALL: Like that party that we're gonna
       have tomorrow night,
     The best damn party of all!

REPEAT REFRAIN 1

INTERLUDE

A MAN: You never et such beautiful
       spaghetti!
     The boys have never thrown so
       much confetti!
ANOTHER MAN: The girls have never looked so
       come-and-getty—
ALL MEN: As the girls are gonna look
       tomorrow night!
MAC: Before the party reaches its
       conclusion
     There may be an occasional
       confusion,
     A casual abrasion or contusion.
HAZEL: What?
MAC: There'll be lots of busted heads
       tomorrow night!
HAZEL: Oh!

REFRAIN 3

ALL MEN: Oh, there never was a party
Like the party that we're gonna
have tomorrow night!
Everyone'll tie a bun on
And the games and fun'll run on
till the sun gets bright!
By the time we get to climbin'
up the wall,
Got a feelin' that the ceilin's
going to fall
At the party that we're gonna
have tomorrow night,
The best damn party of all!

Blaikey's reprise

Dropped after the New Haven tryout. Introduced by Rufus Smith (Jim Blaikey).

Oh, there never is a party
Like the party that you're gonna have tomorrow
night.
You may think you are a smarty,
But the way you plan a party never turns out right.
With a little gin the men begin to brawl
And the uninsulted ladies start to bawl—
The party that you're gonna have tomorrow
night
Will never happen at all.

WE'RE A GANG OF WITCHES

Introduced by Helen Traubel (Fauna) and female ensemble.

FAUNA: Come out, all ye witches,
Come out, all ye witches!
FOUR GIRLS: We are a gang of witches,
We are a witch's mob.
We got it in for Snow White,
She's nothin' but a slob.
We'll put her on a broomstick
And take her for a ride.
We'll drop her in a lime pit—
She'll be no prince's bride!
FAUNA: [reciting] I ain't no witch at all!

[Two girls help remove her black hat and cloak.]

I am Snow White's fairy godmother.
Now I make all of you fairy
godmothers.

[Girls remove black masks.]

GIRLS: [sung] Welcome to Snow White,
All hail Snow White—
Snow White, Snow White, Snow
White, Snow White!

[SUZY enters in bridal garb.]

Snow White!

Discarded introduction

Intended as a lead-in to "We Are a Gang of Witches," but cut, this text was prepared by the character Mac. Hammerstein's stage directions say that Fauna "looks over at Mac with a frown that is an unmistakable comment on his lyric writing."

FAUNA: I am a witch,
My mother was a witch—
A witch's witch am I!
I'm makin' a pitch,
It's a witch's pitch—
Because it's the Fourth of July!
Doc's birthday!
May Doc get rich
And never hit a ditch
I'm wishin', which is why
My pitch is a switch
For a witch to wish—
That's a witch's lullaby!

WILL YOU MARRY ME?

Published in the vocal score. Introduced by Judy Tyler (Suzy). Fauna chimes in for a repeat and others join them. When William Johnson (Doc) realizes the song was addressed to him, he begins to sing it, but Suzy storms out.

In an early draft of the script, Hammerstein provided the dummy title "Here Is Your Bride" and noted that the song to be written would not be satirical, although the situation had comic overtones.

Dialogue prior to the party scene establishes "Will You Marry Me?" as a popular song of the day. When the Bear Flag girls ask why Suzy is going to sing it at the party, Fauna explains: "The word 'marry' don't

come natural to a man. You gotta keep throwin' it in front of him to kinda put it in his head."

"Will You Marry Me?" was originally written for *South Pacific*. Folders of music from the 1949 pit orchestra show that it was positioned between "I'm Gonna Wash That Man Right Outa My Hair" and "I'm in Love with a Wonderful Guy" and then replaced before Broadway by a reprise of "Some Enchanted Evening."

Will you marry me?
All I own I want you to share.
This is not to be
Any light, summer-night love affair.
Like a ship at sea,
Vainly I looked for a shore.
Say you'll marry me
And I will look no more!

THINKIN'

Published in the vocal score. Introduced by Mike Kellin (Hazel). Hammerstein was still writing this lyric as rehearsals began.

VERSE 1

I suffer somethin' awful when I think;
Thinkin' puts my brain on the blink.
I feel a kind of tickin'
And a scrapin' in my head
Like a million skaters clickin' round a rink!
And here's the part that always gets me sore—
Thinkin' never changes the score.
By the time you make yer mind up
It's a cinch you're gonna wind up
Behind the eight ball like you was before!

REFRAIN 1

I grit my teeth
An' shut my eyes
An' I screw my eyebrows together
An' I cover my ears so there ain't no chance to
hear.
[spoken] Like this.
[sung] I stay this way fer a minute er two
An' try to think a problem through
To dig and dig and dig fer a big ideer!
Then I open my eyes
An' ungrit my teeth
An' I separate my eyebrows
An' I take my hand off my ear so I can hear.
I pull my thoughts together

An' I tie them in a knot.
Then I look at what I got—
[spoken] Nothin!

VERSE 2

A feller gets in trouble when he thinks;
Thinkin' gets your brain full o' kinks!
Once you let a problem face you
And you try to face it back,
It'll foller you an' chase you like a jinx.
I'm better off to let a problem be—
Half a' time it blows out to sea.
That's the only way to trick it,
See? If I don't try to lick it,
It ain't got any chance o' lickin' me!

REFRAIN 2

It all begun
When he meets a broad
An' he says he's writin' a paper
Which is gonna be full o' that scientific crap—
Then right away it's a federal case!
He won't let no one in his place,
An' Mac says Doc's been caught in a cul-de-sap!
Then the Fourth o' July
Come along last night
An' it falls right on Doc's birthday.
When he sings "Will You Marry Me?" Suzy runs
    away—
Could Suzy be the reason
Why Doc is in a rut
An' goin' off his nut?

[The orchestra rises to great heights and brilliant
chords which describe the complicated process of
HAZEL's thinking and the torture of it all. Then the
music stops. A vacant expression comes into HAZEL's
now open eyes. He speaks.]

What was the problem?

HOW LONG?

Published in the vocal score. Introduced by Helen
Traubel (Fauna), William Johnson (Doc), and ensemble.
Added during the out-of-town tryouts.

FAUNA: Stand up to the girl like a man.
GIRLS: Stand up to the girl like a man!
FAUNA: Just let her know you run the
    show

And she'll go along with the
    plan.
MEN: Stand up to the girl like a guy,
    Stand up to the girl like a guy.
HAZEL: And tell her to behave herself
    Or you'll put a mouse on her
    eye.
FAUNA: If she wants to make you wait,
    Don't get in no big debate.
    Don't beg and plead and pray
    to the girl,
    But stand right up and say to
    the girl—
ALL: And say to the girl,
    And say to the girl—

REFRAIN 1

FAUNA: How long
    Do we gotta talk it over?
    How long
    Do we gotta horse around?
    I tell you to yer face I want you
    and you drive me nuts,
    But all I ever get from you is ifs
    and ands and buts!
    How long
    Do we gotta race the motor
    Before we can really get to go?
    How long
    Do you make a feller guess how
    sweet you are,
    Before you will really let him
    know?

[Now DOC's male friends try to exhort him.]

MEN: The man you used to be
    Would make a fricassee
    Of any chick who tried to get
    tough!
DOC: The man I used to be
    Had an old recipe
    For calling any feminine
    bluff—
    You start in sweet and gentle
    Then you wind up firm and
    rough!
FAUNA AND GIRLS: That's the stuff!
MEN: Stand up to the girl!
ALL: Stand up to the girl!
DOC: I'll say to the girl—
ALL: You'll say to the girl—

REFRAIN 2

DOC: How long—
ALL: —do we gotta talk it over?

DOC: How long
    Do we gotta horse around?
    How long do you believe that
    you can keep me on the
    hook?
    How long do you believe that
    you can play me for a
    schnook?
    How long
    Must I walk alone at evening
    While stars squander silver on
    the sea?
    How long
    Till you open up your arms and
    let me know
    How warm and how lovely they
    can be?
MAC: Toughen it up!
ALL: Toughen it up!
GIRLS: Stand up to the girl like a man!
MEN: Stand up to the girl like a man!
GIRLS: Stand up to the girl like a man!
MEN: Stand up to the girl like a man!
ALL: Good luck to you, Doc—you'll
    need it!
    Good luck to you, Doc—you'll
    need it!
    Good luck to you, Doc.
    Good luck to you, Doc.
    You'll need it when you say to
    her,
    How long? How long? How
    long—
MEN: —do we got to talk it over?
GIRLS: Either we do or either we don't.
    And when am I gonna know?
ALL: How long? How long? How
    long—
MEN: —do we gotta horse around?
GIRLS: Either you will or either you
    won't.
    So make with a yes or no!
ALL: How long do you believe that
    you can keep me on the
    hook?
MEN: Ta da da da.
GIRLS: How long do you believe that
    you can play me for a
    schnook?
MEN: How long do you believe that
    you can play me for a kind
    of—
    How was that?
ALL: How long do we gotta race the
    motor?
    Before we can really get to go?
    How long do you make a feller
    guess how sweet you are?

How long till you really let him
know?

Toughen it up.
Toughen it up.
Toughen it up.
Toughen it up, Doc.
Toughen it up, Doc.
Toughen it up!
Stand up to the girl like a man!
Toughen it up!

THE NEXT TIME IT HAPPENS

Published as an individual sheet. Introduced by Judy Tyler (Suzy) and William Johnson (Doc).

VERSE

SUZY: I leapt before I looked
And I got hooked.
I played with fire and burned—
That's how I learned.
I must admit I owe a lot to you:
From now on I will know what not to do.

REFRAIN

SUZY: The next time it happens
I'll be wise enough to know
Not to trust my eyesight when my eyes
begin to glow.
The next time I'm in love
With anyone like you,
My heart will sing no love song till I know
the words are true.
"The next time it happens"—
What a foolish thing to say!
Who expects a miracle to happen every day?
It isn't in the cards
As far as I can see
That a thing so beautiful and wonderful
Could happen more than once to me.

[DOC *repeats refrain*.]

CUT AND UNUSED SONGS

NOBODY'S FOOL

Not used or published. No music is known to have been written. In early drafts of the script, Suzy sang this to Mac in Act One, Scene 1.

VERSE

I've got nothing special to boast of;
I am not the girl of the year.
I may not be making the most of
What a clown might call my "career."
But I've learned a lesson or two:
I can tell roast beef from baloney,
And I know a dream coming true
Is the fairy tale of a phony.

REFRAIN

I am nobody's fool,
Nobody's fooling me.
My feet are on the ground
Where they're supposed to be,
And all that I believe
Is what my eyes can see—
Nobody's fool am I.
I'm not just out of school;
I've been around enough
To know that love is just
A game of blind man's bluff,
So put that in your pipe
Or write it on your cuff—
Nobody's fool am I.
I really have to laugh
When I think of goofy guys
Telling goofy girls
There are stars in their eyes.
Stars in their eyes—
Boy, is that sad!
Stars in their eyes—
Boy, am I glad
I am nobody's fool!
Nobody thinks it's fine
To kiss me while he's whispering a corny line,
Or hold me so his heart is beating close to mine—
Nobody's fool,
Nobody's fool am I!

HE'S A FUNNY KIND OF GUY

Not used or published. No music is known to have been written. This is another early song idea for Act One, Scene 1. One script says, "Suzy discusses her impressions of Doc, and Mac chimes in and gives his." The lyric below seems to be for Suzy only.

A funny guy to meet—
He looks you in the eye
And knocks you off your feet.
I wonder what he's like
When you really get to know him . . .
He's a funny kind of guy.

I imagine he's the type
Who goes for steak and pie;
He likes to smoke a pipe
And hates to wear a tie—
You know what I would do
If I really got to know him?
I would make him wear a tie.

Will I really get to know him?
Not a chance!
He's the kind I never really get to know.
He's the kind who dances by me at a dance.
He is always someone else's sister's beau.

Just a guy who dances by
Is all he'll ever be.
He'll never waste a sigh
On any dame like me,
Or wonder what she's like
When you really get to know her.
He's a funny kind of guy—
A special kind of guy.

CANNERY ROW

Not used or published. No music is known to have been written. In a very early version of Act One, Scene 2, the local cop, Jim Blaikey, describes the town to some visitors (and to the audience).

BLAIKEY: Cannery Row is a part of the world,
And everything good you can find in the world
You can find in Cannery Row.
It's also a fact, if you want to be fair,

That anything bad you can find any where
You can find in Cannery Row.

You can find in Cannery Row
A burglar and a preacher,
A good-lookin' high-school teacher
Who owes her job to the mayor—
She did some favors for him,
And he kept his promise to pay her.

You can find in Cannery Row
Children playin' hookey,
Dozens of girls called Cookey,
And I hear, because of his feet,
That they call the constable Flatso.

Cannery Row is a part of the world;
The worst and the best in the rest of the
    world
You will find in—

[*Interrupted, then resumes.*]

Cannery Row is my beat, don't you see?
What happens to them always happens
    to me—
I'm the cop on Cannery Row!

[*Recognizing someone down the street.*]

There's a walk I think that I know,
A certain aimless drifter,
A chiseler and a grifter
Who goes by the name of Mac.
He looks like he's feelin' low.

[MAC *enters and they discuss how* DOC *has changed.*]

BLAIKEY: [*sung*] Everything happens in Cannery
        Row.
        If you wait long enough you can bet all
            you owe
        It'll come to Cannery Row!
    MAC: A guy who is classy and decent like Doc
        To turn himself into a laughingstock!
BLAIKEY: It's the talk of Cannery Row.

[*More dialogue.*]

BLAIKEY: [*sung*] Cannery Row is a part of the world,
        And everything good you can find in the
            world
        You can find in Cannery Row.
        Once in a while there's a problem to face,
        But Cannery Row is a hell of a place,

And the cop on Cannery Row
Is in love with Cannery Row,
In love with Cannery Row!

A MAN OF SOME INTELLIGENCE

Not used or published. No music is known to have been
written. This soliloquy for Doc was a precursor to "How
Long?"

A man of some intelligence,
IQ—one-forty-two,
With a master's degree
And a Ph.D.
From Chicago U.

I'm no delinquent juvenile,
My age is fairly ripe,
But I'm making a call—
It's a formal call—
On a girl who lives in a pipe!

What makes me feel so panicky?
I'm not a nervous type.
It appears I'm afraid
Of a forthright maid
I'm about to meet in a pipe—

Afraid that she might tell me
Exactly what to do
With my master's degree
And my Ph.D.
From Chicago U.
[*spoken*] I should have taken a big slug of whiskey,
    but it would have been on my breath and she
    would have known why I had taken it. I wonder
    if she's frightened too. You never know.
    Women can hide things better than men. What
    a fool I am! I'm falling to pieces! That damn
    little—! No, don't do that. Don't build your
    courage by running her down. You're going to
    her, not she to you.

[*He paces.*]

I wish I knew what to do.
[*sung*] I know what I should do:
I should turn around and run,
Run like a thief in the night!
I know my life with her

May be nothing more than one
Long and continuous fight!
[*becoming more emphatic*] Over and over
I'll wish I'd never seen her—
We'll have no peace at all,
No matter how we try.

[*suddenly becoming quieter and earnest*] If I don't
    get her,
I'll dream of her forever,
Long for the girl I lost
Until the day I die.

I can think of many reasons
Why this girl is not for me.
She is not for me—
Any child would know.
But what good are all the reasons
To explain what shouldn't be,
When what shouldn't be
Happens to be so?

Behind the light of reason in the brain,
There is something more than reason,
There's a light that's even brighter
Something
That nothing
Would explain.

Julie Andrews in the title role

CINDERELLA | 1957

CINDERELLA (1957)

A television musical produced by Richard Lewine for CBS-TV and broadcast live "at the stroke of eight" on Sunday, March 31, 1957. Music by Richard Rodgers. Teleplay and lyrics by Oscar Hammerstein II. Directed by Ralph Nelson. Choreographed by Jonathan Lucas. Settings and costumes by William and Jean Eckart. Orchestrations by Robert Russell Bennett. Musical direction by Alfredo Antonini.

Cast: Julie Andrews (Cinderella), Howard Lindsay (King), Dorothy Stickney (Queen), Ilka Chase (Stepmother), Kaye Ballard (Stepsister Portia), Alice Ghostley (Stepsister Joy), Edith (Edie) Adams (Fairy Godmother), Jon Cypher (Prince Christopher), Robert Penn (Town Crier), Alexander Clark (Captain of the Guard), Iggie Wolfington (Chef), David F. Perkins (Court Tailor), and an ensemble of singers and dancers. This broadcast was seen by 107 million viewers, averaging four viewers per television set in America.

A remake, produced and directed by Charles S. Dubin, was first broadcast on CBS-TV on February 22, 1965, and was aired annually through 1974. The revised teleplay was by Joseph Schrank. Orchestrations by Robert Russell Bennett and John Green. Music direction by John Green. Cast: Lesley Ann Warren (Cinderella), Ginger Rogers (Queen), Walter Pidgeon (King), Celeste Holm (Fairy Godmother), Jo Van Fleet (Stepmother), Stuart Damon (Prince) Pat Carroll (Prunella), Barbara Ruick (Esmerelda), and ensemble.

Another television remake was aired on November 2, 1997, on ABC-TV. Directed by Robert Iscove. Choreographed by Rob Marshall. Teleplay revised by Robert L. Freedman. Cast: Brandy Norwood (Cinderella), Bernadette Peters (Stepmother), Veanne Cox (Calliope), Natalie Desselle (Minerva), Paolo Montalban (Prince), Jason Alexander (Lionel), Whoopi Goldberg (Queen Constantina), Victor Garber (King Maximillian), Whitney Houston (Fairy Godmother), and ensemble.

The *Cinderella* songs (plus a few from *Me and Juliet* and one written by Tommy Steele) were used for a "panto" production that opened in London in December 1958 (and was revived in the winter of 1960–61). A stage version adapted by Don Driver was first presented in 1961 at the St. Louis Muny. A 1981 stage version based on the 1957 teleplay is still being used.

Julie Andrews recorded six songs for a special promotional disc sent to TV news editors and radio disc jockeys; there was also a full cast album. All three television productions are available on DVD, the original in a restored black-and-white kinescope of the original color presentation. A film of a dress rehearsal of that 1957 production can be seen at the Paley Center for Media (formerly the Museum of Television and Radio) in New York City.

Six of the songs were published as individual sheets. A vocal score of the Don Driver version was published, but superseded in 1981 by one that went back to the original version.

For "The Loneliness of Evening" (used in the 1965 version), see the *South Pacific* chapter. For "There's Music in You" (used in the 1997 version), see Other Songs of the Early 1950s page 356. "The Sweetest Sounds" (used in the 1997 version) has a lyric by Richard Rodgers; "Falling in Love with Love" (used in the 1997 version) has a lyric by Lorenz Hart.

THE PRINCE IS GIVING A BALL

Published in the vocal score. Introduced by Robert Penn (Town Crier) and ensemble.

TOWN CRIER: The Prince is giving a ball!
SEXTET: The Prince is giving a ball!
CROWD: The Prince is giving a ball!

[*Fanfare.*]

ALL: The Prince is giving a ball!
TOWN CRIER: His Royal Highness
Christopher Rupert
Windemere Vladimir
Karl Alexander François
Reginald Launcelot
Herman—
SMALL BOY: Herman?
TOWN CRIER: —Herman Gregory James
Is giving a ball!
SEXTET: The Prince is giving a ball!
ALL: The Prince is giving a ball!
FATHER: Our daughter's looking
dreamy-eyed.
MOTHER: The Prince is giving a ball.
DAUGHTER: They say he wants to find a
bride;
He may find one at the ball.
GIRL BRUSHING HAIR: If only he'd propose to me!
KNEELING GIRL: I pray that he'll propose to
me!
GIRL WITH MIRROR: Why *shouldn't* he propose
to me?
WOMAN WITH IRON: I wish I hadn't married
Sam.
MOTHER PULLING
CORSET STRINGS: Pull in your little
diaphragm.
BRUNETTE: I'll wear a gown of satin
jade.

BLONDE: And me, I'm in a pink
brocade.
KID SISTER: And me, I'm in the second
grade!
SEXTET: The Prince is giving a ball!
The Prince is giving a ball!
TOWN CRIER: His Royal Highness,
Christopher Rupert, son
of Her Majesty Queen
Constantina Charlotte
Ermintrude Gwinyvere
Maisie—
SMALL GIRL: Maisie?
TOWN CRIER: —Maisie Marguerite Anne
Is giving a ball!
SEXTET: The Prince is giving a ball!
The Prince is giving a ball!
LARGE GIRL: I wish I didn't like to eat.
DIETRICH-TYPE GIRL: I wish I were demure and
sweet.
GIRL WITH GLASSES: I wish I were a bolder girl.
GRANDMA: I wish I were a younger girl.
KID SISTER: I wish I were an older girl!
SEXTET: The Prince is giving a ball!
The Prince is giving a ball!
TOWN CRIER: His Royal Highness,
Christopher Rupert, son
of His Majesty King
Maximillian Godfrey
Ladislaus Leopold
Sidney—
CROWD: Sidney?
TOWN CRIER: —Sidney Frederick John
Is giving a ball.
ALL: The Prince is giving a ball!
The Prince is giving a ball!
The Prince is giving a ball!

IN MY OWN LITTLE CORNER

Published as an individual sheet. Introduced by Julie Andrews (Cinderella).

VERSE

I'm as mild and as meek as a mouse;
When I hear a command I obey.
But I know of a spot in my house
Where no one can stand in my way.

REFRAIN 1

In my own little corner,
In my own little chair,
I can be whatever I want to be.
On the wing of my fancy
I can fly anywhere
And the world will open its arms to me.
I'm a young Norwegian princess or a milkmaid,
I'm the greatest prima donna in Milan,
I'm an heiress who has always had her silk made
By her own flock of silkworms in Japan!
I'm a girl men go mad for;
Love's a game I can play
With a cool and confident kind of air,
Just as long as I stay
In my own little corner,
All alone
In my own
Little chair.

REFRAIN 2

[*She daydreams during the first line of music.*]

I can be whatever I want to be.
I'm a slave in Calcutta,
I'm a queen in Peru,
I'm a mermaid dancing upon the sea.
I'm a huntress on an African safari
(It's a dang'rous type of sport and yet it's fun).
In the night I sally forth to seek my quarry
And I find I forgot to bring my gun!
I am lost in the jungle
All alone and unarmed
When I meet a lioness in her lair!
Then I'm glad to be back
In my own little corner,
All alone
In my own
Little chair.

REPRISE

In my own little corner,
In my own little chair,
I can be whatever I want to be.
On the wing of my fancy
I can fly anywhere
And the world will open its arms to me.
I am in the royal palace, of all places!
I am chatting with the Prince and King and
    Queen,
And the color of my two stepsisters' faces
Is a queer sort of sour-apple green.
I am coy and flirtatious when alone with the
    Prince

[*Imagined conversation over music.*]

I'm the belle of the ball
In my own little corner,
All alone
In my own
Little chair.

Draft ending

I am dancing in a palace, of all places,
And my gown is like a cloud of snowy white.
There is envy on the other ladies' faces
When the Prince leads me out into the night!
I grow faint when he tells me
I'm the girl of his dreams
And the thrill is more than my heart can bear.
He is mine! . . . So it seems
In my own little corner,
All alone
In my own
Little chair.

Reprise fragment for Godmother's entrance

GODMOTHER: I just knew I would find you
        In that same little chair
        In the pale pink mist of a foolish
            dream.

YOUR MAJESTIES (A LIST OF THE BARE NECESSITIES)

Published in the vocal score. Introduced by Iggie Wolfington (Chef), George Hall (Steward), Howard Lindsay (King), and Dorothy Stickney (Queen).

CHEF: Your Majesties.
STEWARD: Your Majesties.
CHEF: A list of the bare necessities.
KING: A list of the bare necessities for what?
QUEEN: For seventeen hundred guests!
KING: [*to* QUEEN] That seems a lot.
QUEEN: Proceed, gentlemen.

[*Brief dialogue.*]

QUEEN: A thousand baby lobsters for the salad.
KING: Wow!
QUEEN: And five hundred pheasant for the pie.
KING: Ai-yai!

QUEEN: A thousand pounds of caviar.
KING: A thousand?
QUEEN: Hush.
KING: It's more than the sturgeon can supply!
CHEF: I told the steward to get us
    Forty acres of lettuce
    And six hundred suckling pigs for
        roasting.
KING: What about the marshmallows?
QUEEN: Who wants marshmallows?
KING: I do.
QUEEN: Why?
KING: For toasting!
STEWARD: Now if it please
    Your Majesties,
    I have a list of wine—
    The best of all
    The vintages
    From every nation's vine.
KING: I want the wine of my country!
QUEEN: Hush! Hush! Hush!
QUEEN: [*reading*] Sherry and port and muscatel,
    Kimmel and eau de vie,
    Dry Champagne and sweet Moselle,
    Burgundy and Chablis,
    Aquavit and Liebfraumilch,
    Hock and chocolate malted milch,
    Brandy, Drambuie, and vodka,
    White and crystal-clear!
KING: I want the wine of my country!
    I want the wine of my country!
    I want the wine of my country!
    The wine of my country is beer!

IMPOSSIBLE/IT'S POSSIBLE

Published as an individual sheet. Introduced by Edith Adams (Fairy Godmother) and Julie Andrews (Cinderella).

INTRODUCTION

GODMOTHER: Fol-de-rol and fiddledy dee,
        Fiddledy faddledy foddle,
        All the wishes in the world
        Are poppycock and twaddle!

        Fol-de-rol and fiddledy dee,
        Fiddledy faddledy foodle,
        All the dreamers in all the world
        Are dizzy in the noodle.

REFRAIN

GODMOTHER: Impossible
For a plain yellow pumpkin
To become a golden carriage!
Impossible
For a plain country bumpkin
And a prince to join in marriage!
And four white mice will never be
    four white horses—
Such fol-de-rol and fiddledy dee of
    course is
Impossible!
But the world is full of zanies and
    fools
Who don't believe in sensible rules
And won't believe what sensible
    people say,
And because these daft and dewy-
    eyed dopes
Keep building up impossible hopes,
Impossible things are happ'ning
    every day!
Impossible!
Impossible!
Impossible!
Impossible!
Impossible!
Impossible!
Impossible!
Impossible!

CINDERELLA: It's possible
For a plain yellow pumpkin
To become a golden carriage!
It's possible
For a plain country bumpkin
And a prince to join in marriage!
GODMOTHER: And four white mice are easily
    turned to horses!
CINDERELLA: Such fol-de-rol and fiddledy dee of
    course is
Quite possible!
BOTH: It's possible!
CINDERELLA: For the world is full of zanies and
    fools—
BOTH: Who don't believe in sensible rules
And won't believe what sensible
    people say.
And because these daft and
    dewy-eyed dopes
Keep building up impossible hopes,
Impossible things are happening
    every day!
It's possible!
It's possible!
It's possible!
It's possible!
It's possible!

It's possible!
It's possible!

TEN MINUTES AGO

Published as an individual sheet. Introduced by Jon Cypher (Prince) and Julie Andrews (Cinderella).

PRINCE: Ten minutes ago, I saw you.
I looked up when you came through
    the door.
My head started reeling;
You gave me the feeling
The room had no ceiling or floor.
Ten minutes ago, I met you,
And we murmured our how-do-you-
    do's.
I wanted to ring out the bells
And fling out my arms
And to sing out the news:
I have found her!
She's an angel,
With the dust of the stars in her
    eyes!
We are dancing,
We are flying,
And she's taking me back to the
    skies.
In the arms of my love I'm flying
Over mountain and meadow and glen,
And I like it so well
That for all I can tell
I may never come down again!
I may never come down to earth
    again!
CINDERELLA: Ten minutes ago I met you,
And we murmured our how-do-you-
    do's.
I wanted to ring out the bells
And fling out my arms
And to sing out the news:
I have found him! I have found him!

[*They dance for a few measures.*]

In the arms of my love I'm flying
Over mountain and meadow and
    glen,
And I like it so well
That for all I can tell
I may never come down again!
BOTH: I may never come down to earth
    again!

STEPSISTERS' LAMENT

Published as an individual sheet. Introduced by Alice Ghostley (Joy) and Kaye Ballard (Portia).

JOY: Why would a fellow want a girl like her,
A frail and fluffy beauty?
Why can't a fellow ever once prefer
A solid girl like me?
PORTIA: She's a frothy little bubble
With a flimsy kind of charm,
And with very little trouble
I could break her little arm!
JOY: Oh, oh, why would a fellow want a girl
    like her,
So obviously unusual?
Why can't a fellow ever once prefer
A usual girl like me?
PORTIA: Her cheeks are a pretty shade of pink,
But not any pinker than a rose is.
JOY: Her skin may be delicate and soft,
But not any softer than a doe's is.
PORTIA: Her neck is no whiter than a swan's.
JOY: She's only as dainty as a daisy.
PORTIA: She's only as graceful as a bird.
BOTH: So why is the fellow going crazy?
Oh, why would a fellow want a girl like
    her,
A girl who's merely lovely?
Why can't a fellow ever once prefer
A girl who's merely me?
What's the matter with the man?
What's the matter with the man?
What's the matter with the man?

DO I LOVE YOU BECAUSE YOU'RE BEAUTIFUL?

Published as an individual sheet. Introduced by Jon Cypher (Prince) and Julie Andrews (Cinderella). Reprised by Cypher and Dorothy Stickney (Queen). Vic Damone and Tony Martin both made hit recordings.

In a 1957 interview, Hammerstein admitted:

[Sometimes I think that] I can't write any more love songs because I have said all there is to say, or all I have to say about it. But when I am pushed into a corner, suddenly I sometimes, if I am lucky, get a new thought about people in love that I haven't had before. Only last year I got an idea and wondered why I hadn't got it long ago. And that is a song I wrote in *Cinderella*, "Do I Love

You Because You're Beautiful or Are You Beautiful Because I Love You?" That's the story of love. I don't know why I or some other lyric writer didn't think of that before.

During the writing of *Cinderella*, Hammerstein made an extended trip to Australia. Correspondence preserves some of the minute details he and Rodgers would typically discuss face-to-face. Hammerstein asked if the words "making believe"—in the lines "Am I making believe I see in you / A girl too lovely to / Be really true"—seemed strong enough to convey the Prince's emotion. Rodgers replied that he had no qualms about "making believe," but wasn't "too lovely to be really true" a split infinitive? Hammerstein explained that he had "tried very hard to dodge 'really,' and couldn't get out of it. I even considered asking you to eliminate the two notes and substitute a long one: thus 'A girl too lovely to be true,' but feared it was less interesting musically." They also exchanged views on how the song could attain a big lift at the finish by changing from a minor key to a major and whether, if the song were introduced earlier in the plot, it could be sung by a girl. In the final letter, Rodgers wrote: "Once you and I sit down in a room and discuss these matters of syllables and notes there isn't the remotest possibility of disagreement. I can change the melody line to conform to what you would like to do quite easily and I know that you have ways of avoiding a split infinitive. In any event, it will be good to have you back and to sit and talk things over."

PRINCE: Do I love you
Because you're beautiful,
Or are you beautiful
Because I love you?
Am I making believe I see in you
A girl too lovely to
Be really true?
Do I want you
Because you're wonderful,
Or are you wonderful
Because I want you?
Are you the sweet invention of a
lover's dream,
Or are you really as beautiful as you
seem?

CINDERELLA: Am I making believe I see in you
A man too perfect to
Be really true?
Do I want you
Because you're wonderful,
Or are you wonderful
Because I want you?

BOTH: Are you the sweet invention of a
lover's dream,

Or are you really as wonderful as you
seem?

WHEN YOU'RE DRIVING THROUGH THE MOONLIGHT

Published in the vocal score. Introduced by Julie Andrews (Cinderella), Kaye Ballard (Portia), Alice Ghostley (Joy), and Ilka Chase (Stepmother).

REFRAIN 1

CINDERELLA: When you're driving through the
moonlight on the highway,
When you're driving through the
moonlight to the dance,
You are breathless with a wild
anticipation
Of adventure and excitement
and romance.
Then at last you see the towers of
the palace
Silhouetted on the sky above the
park,
And below them is a row of
lighted windows,
Like a lovely diamond necklace
in the dark!

PORTIA: It looks that way—

JOY: The way you say.

STEPMOTHER: She talks as if she knows.

CINDERELLA: I do not know
These things are so.
I only just suppose . . .

REFRAIN 2

CINDERELLA: I suppose that when you come
into the ballroom,
And the room itself is floating in
the air,
If you're suddenly confronted
by His Highness
You are frozen like a statue on
the stair!
You're afraid he'll hear the way
your heart is beating
And you know you mustn't make
the first advance.
You are seriously thinking of
retreating—

Then you seem to hear him
asking you to dance!
You make a bow,
A timid bow,
And shyly answer "Yes."

STEPMOTHER: How would you know
That this is so?

CINDERELLA: I do no more than guess.

JOY AND PORTIA: You can guess till you're blue in
the face
But you can't even picture such a
man.

JOY: He is *more* than a prince—

PORTIA: He's an *ace*!

CINDERELLA: But sisters, I really think I can—

STEPMOTHER: [*spoken*] Can what?

CINDERELLA: I think that I can picture such a
man.

JOY AND PORTIA: He is tall—

CINDERELLA: And straight as a lance!

JOY AND PORTIA: And his hair—

CINDERELLA: Is dark and wavy.

JOY AND PORTIA: His eyes—

CINDERELLA: Can melt you with a glance!

JOY AND PORTIA: He can turn a girl into gravy!

[*Dialogue over music.*]

A LOVELY NIGHT

Published as an individual sheet. Introduced by Julie Andrews (Cinderella), Ilka Chase (Stepmother), Kaye Ballard (Portia), and Alice Ghostley (Joy).

REFRAIN

CINDERELLA: A lovely night,
A lovely night,
A finer night you know you'll never
see.
You meet your prince,
A charming prince,
As charming as a prince will ever be!
The stars in a hazy heaven
Tremble above you
While he is whispering,
"Darling, I love you!"
You say goodbye,
Away you fly,
But on your lips you keep a kiss,
All your life you'll dream of this
Lovely, lovely night.

[CINDERELLA *repeats the refrain. Then* PORTIA, JOY, *and* STEPMOTHER *sing it through twice and exit.*]

CODA

CINDERELLA: The stars in a hazy heaven
Trembling above me,
Danced when he promised
Always to love me.
The day came through,
Away I flew,
But on my lips he left a kiss—
All my life I'll dream of this
Lovely, lovely night.

CUT AND UNUSED SONG

IF I WEREN'T KING

Not published. Not used. Written for the King, some henchmen, and the Queen, it would have followed "Ten Minutes Ago," but was dropped during rehearsals.

REFRAIN 1

KING: If I weren't King,
What a drifter I would be!
Like a kite without a string,
Irresponsible and free.
While the King was busy
opening some bazaar,
I'd be nonchalantly
leaning on a bar.
When the monarch made a
speech,
I'd be lying on a beach,
Holding seashells to my ear to
hear them sing.
And when cornerstones were
laid,
They'd be laid without my
aid—
If only I weren't a King!

[*Brief dialogue over music.*]

REFRAIN 2

HENCHMAN: If you weren't King—
CHORUS OF
HENCHMEN: Irresponsible and free—
KING: Not afraid of anything,
How courageous I could be!
Knowing well that my
opinions weren't news,
I'd be recklessly expressing all
my views.
In the taverns of the town
I would drown the others
down.
With a drink or two I'd make
the rafters ring!
I'd condemn the palace rule,
Call His Majesty a fool!—
If only I weren't a King.

[*Brief dialogue over music.*]

REFRAIN 3

KING: Before I was King—
OLDER HENCHMAN: Just a lad of twenty-one—
KING: Like an eagle on the wing
I flew out to find my fun!
OLDER HENCHMAN: What a rascal! What a lover!
What a sport!
Quite a problem to his father
and the court.
KING: How distinctly I recall
At this very kind of ball,
I was in this very garden in the
spring,
With a foolish little wench
Acting foolish on a bench—
Of course long before I was
King!
QUEEN: Not so long before!

[*Brief dialogue over music.*]

REFRAIN 4

QUEEN: If you weren't King,
If you lived like other folks,
With no courtiers in a ring
Laughing loudly at your jokes,
You would miss the joy of
knowing you're the boss.
As a subject you would be a
total loss.
On your birthday you would
miss
All the tiny tots you kiss
And the solemn songs of
praise your people sing,
And no longer could you sigh,
Brushing teardrops from your
eye
And wish that you weren't a
King!
[*spoken*] You'd simply hate it!

[*Brief dialogue over music.*]

REFRAIN 5

KING: If I weren't King—
QUEEN: Don't you really think, my pet,
You would miss like anything,
The attention that you get?
All the curtsies, all the bows,
the bended knees,
And the chorus of gesundheits
when you sneeze!
You'd look sad and some what
bare
With no crown to grace your
hair
And no scepter for your royal
arm to swing.
You look best upon a throne
That is right beside my own.
Your Queen's very glad you're
a King!

Top left: *Jack Soo has Yuriko gliding through his memoree.*
Top right: *Left to right, Keye Luke, Juanita Hall, Miyoshi Umeki, and Conrad Yama*
Bottom: *Dancers at the Celestial Bar*

FLOWER DRUM SONG | 1958

FLOWER DRUM SONG (1958)

Tryout: Shubert Theatre, Boston, October 27–November 29, 1958. New York run: St. James Theatre; opened December 1, 1958; closed May 7, 1960; 600 performances. A New Musical. Music by Richard Rodgers. Lyrics by Oscar Hammerstein II. Book by Oscar Hammerstein II and Joseph Fields, based on the novel by C. Y. Lee. Presented by Rodgers and Hammerstein in association with Joseph Fields. Directed by Gene Kelly. Choreography by Carol Haney. Orchestrations by Robert Russell Bennett. Dance arrangements by Luther Henderson Jr. Musical direction by Salvatore Dell'Isola. Scenic production by Oliver Smith. Costumes designed by Irene Sharaff. Lighting by Peggy Clark.

Cast: Miyoshi Umeki (Mei Li), Larry Blyden (Sammy Fong), Pat Suzuki (Linda Low), Juanita Hall (Madam Liang), Ed Kenney (Wang Ta), Keye Luke (Wang Chi Yang), Arabella Hong (Helen Chao), Jack Soo (Frankie Wing), Patrick Adiarte (Wang San), Conrad Yama (Dr. Li), Rose Quong (Liu Ma), Harry Shaw Lowe (Mr. Lung), Jon Lee (Mr. Huam), Peter Chan (Professor Cheng), George Young (Head Waiter), Anita Ellis (Nightclub Singer), Chao Li (Dr. Lu Fong), Eileen Nakamura (Madam Fong), Yuriko (Dancer/Mei Li in ballet), Baayork Lee (Dancer/Child), Linda Ribuca, Yvonne Ribuca, Susie Lynn Kikuchi, Luis Robert Hernandez (Children), and ensemble.

Set in San Francisco's Chinatown in the 1950s, this story follows three young women and two young men through romances complicated by the generation gap and widely diverging levels of assimilation. Mei Li is a brand-new arrival, imported from China by the family of Sammy Fong to be his bride. Sammy already has a long-time girlfriend, Linda, who is fully Americanized. Since Old Master Wang seeks a traditional type of bride for his son Wang Ta, Sammy tries to reassign the wedding contract to them. But Ta is attracted to Linda and resists his father's attempt to arrange a marriage. Meanwhile, lonely seamstress Helen Chao pines for Ta.

A national tour began May 11, 1960, at the Riviera Theatre in Detroit and played twenty-two cities, closing at the Hanna Theatre, Cleveland, on October 14, 1961.

A London production, presented by Williamson Music Ltd, opened at the Palace Theatre on March 24, 1960, and ran for 464 performances.

A film version, produced by Ross Hunter in association with Joseph Fields for Universal-International Picture, was released on November 9, 1961. Directed by Henry Koster. Screenplay by Joseph Fields. Choreography by Hermes Pan. Music direction by Alfred Newman. Cast: Nancy Kwan (Linda Low, sung by B. J. Baker), Jack Soo (Sammy Fong), James Shigeta (Wang Ta), Miyoshi Umeki (Mei Li), Juanita Hall (Madam Liang), Benson Fong (Wang Chi Yang), Victor Sen Yung (Frankie Wing),

Reiko Sato (Helen Chao, sung by Marilyn Horne), Kam Tong (Dr. Li, sung by John Dodson), Patrick Adiarte (Wang San), and Soo Yong (Madam Fong).

A Broadway revival, with a new book by David Henry Hwang, opened at the Virginia Theatre on October 17, 2002, following an engagement at the Mark Taper Forum in Los Angeles in the fall of 2001. It was directed and choreographed by Robert Longbottom and featured Lea Salonga (Mei Li), Sandra Allen (Linda Low), Alvin Ing (Chin), Randall Duk Kim (Wang), Hoon Lee (Chao), Allen Liu (Harvard), José Llana (Ta), Jodi Long (Madam Liang).

Recordings include the original Broadway cast (Columbia), the 1960 original London cast (EMI Angel), the 1961 film soundtrack (MCA/Decca), and the 2002 Broadway revival (DRG).

The main sources for this chapter are the published vocal score and libretto. Several songs were published as individual sheets. The Rodgers & Hammerstein Organization in New York has a few drafts of the libretto. The Hammerstein Collection in the Music Division of the Library of Congress has lyric worksheets for several songs as well as Dictaphone belts onto which Hammerstein dictated rewrites. The Music Division's Richard Rodgers Collection has holograph piano-vocal scores and sketches.

YOU ARE BEAUTIFUL

Published as an individual sheet. Introduced by Ed Kenney (Wang Ta) and Juanita Hall (Madam Liang). In Boston, the song was titled "She Is Beautiful," with words adjusted so that Ta sang about the girl rather than to her. The lyric is meant to be a traditional Chinese poem, known to both Ta and his aunt.

Hammerstein learned belatedly that in Chinese the word "ho" means "river," and adjusted the first line of the verse. As he explained in a March 1959 letter, "If you said 'Along the Hwang Ho River,' you would really be saying 'Along the Hwang River River.' "

VERSE

MADAM LIANG: Along the Hwang Ho Valley,
Where young men walk and
dream—

MADAM LIANG
AND WANG TA: A flower boat with singing girls
Came drifting down the stream.
WANG TA: I saw the face of only one
Come drifting down the stream.

REFRAIN

WANG TA: You are beautiful,
Small and shy,

You are the girl whose eyes met
mine
Just as your boat sailed by.
This I know of you,
Nothing more.
You are the girl whose eyes met
mine
Passing the river shore.
You are the girl whose laugh I
heard,
Silver and soft and bright,
Soft as the fall of lotus leaves
Brushing the air of night.
While your flower boat
Sailed away,
Gently your eyes looked back on
mine,
Clearly you heard me say:
"You are the girl I will love
someday."

A HUNDRED MILLION MIRACLES

Published as an individual sheet. Introduced by Miyoshi Umeki (Mei Li), Conrad Yama (Dr. Li), Keye Luke (Wang Chi Yang), Juanita Hall (Madam Liang), and Rose Quong (Liu Ma).

MEI LI: My father says
That children keep growing,
Rivers keep flowing, too.
My father says
He doesn't know why
But somehow or other they do.
DR. LI: They do!
Somehow or other they do.
MEI LI: A hundred million miracles,
A hundred million miracles
Are happening every day.
And those who say they don't
agree
Are those who do not hear or see.
A hundred million miracles,
A hundred million miracles—
DR. LI: Are happening every day!
[spoken] The miracle of changing
weather.
MEI LI: When a dark blue curtain
Is pinned by the stars,
Pinned by the stars to the sky,
Every flow'r and tree
Is a treat to see,

The air is very clean and dry.
Then a wind comes blowing
The pins all away.
Night is confused and upset!
The sky falls down
Like a clumsy clown—
The flowers and the trees get wet.

ALL BUT MEI LI: Very wet!
MEI LI: A hundred million miracles—
ALL: A hundred million miracles
Are happening every day.
MEI LI: And when the wind shall turn his
face,
The pins are put right back in
place!
ALL: A hundred million miracles,
A hundred million miracles
Are happening every day!
MADAM LIANG: In every single minute
So much is going on
Along the Yellow River* or the
Tiber or the Don.
ALL: A hundred million miracles!
WANG: A swallow in Tasmania
Is sitting on her eggs,
And suddenly those eggs have
wings
And eyes and beaks and legs!
ALL: A hundred million miracles!
MADAM LIANG: A little girl in Chungking,
Just thirty inches tall,
Decides that she will try to walk
And nearly doesn't fall!
ALL: A hundred million miracles!
A hundred million miracles,
A hundred million miracles,
A hundred million miracles
Are happening every day!
MEI LI: A hundred million miracles,
A hundred million miracles
Are happening every day.
My father says
The sun will keep rising
Over the eastern hill.
My father says
He doesn't know why,
But somehow or other it will.
ALL: It will!
Somehow or other it will.

Additional lines from Hammerstein's worksheets, used in the film

A Swede is getting sunburned.
The sun from overhead

* *Some versions substitute "Yangtse-Kiang" for "Yellow River."*

A hundred million miles away
Will make him brown or red.

A sprig of ivy, very small
Will climb and cover all the wall.

Reprise

Sung by Mei-Li as she beats the back of Master Wang's neck to cure his cough.

MEI LI: A hundred million miracles,
A hundred million miracles
Are happening every day.
I beat your neck behind the ear,
And soon your cough will disappear.
A hundred million miracles,
A hundred million miracles,
Are happening every day.

Draft stanza used in the film and the 2002 revival

DR. LI: [*spoken*] The miracle of making music.
MEI-LI: [*sung*] An idle poet
Makes words on a page,
Writes on a page with his brush.
A musical friend
Makes notes to blend
Suggested by an idle thrush.
Then a young soprano
Who reads what they wrote,
Learns ev'ry note, ev'ry word.
Puts all they wrote
In her lovely throat—
And suddenly a song is heard!
A hundred million miracles,
A hundred million miracles
Are happening every day
A poem, a singer, and a tune
Can sail together to the moon!
A hundred million miracles
Are happening every day!

I ENJOY BEING A GIRL

Published as an individual sheet. Introduced by Pat Suzuki (Linda Low) and dancers. The song was a hit for Suzuki. Doris Day and Peggy Lee also had popular recordings.

I'm a girl and by me that's only great!
I am proud that my silhouette is curvy,
That I walk with a sweet and girlish gait,
With my hips kind of swively and swervy.
I adore being dressed in something frilly
When my date comes to get me at my place.
Out I go with my Joe or John or Billy,
Like a filly who is ready for the race!

REFRAIN 1

When I have a brand-new hairdo,
With my eyelashes all in curl,
I float as the clouds on air do—
I enjoy being a girl!
When men say I'm cute and funny,
And my teeth aren't teeth, but pearl,
I just lap it up like honey—
I enjoy being a girl!
I flip when a fellow sends me flowers,
I drool over dresses made of lace,
I talk on the telephone for hours
With a pound and a half of cream upon my face!
I'm strictly a female female,
And my future, I hope, will be
In the home of a brave and free male
Who'll enjoy being a guy
Having a girl like me!

REFRAIN 2

When men say I'm sweet as candy
As around in a dance we whirl,
It goes to my head like brandy—
I enjoy being a girl.
When someone with eyes that smoulder,
Says he loves every silken curl
That falls on my ivory shoulder—
I enjoy being a girl!
When I hear the compliment'ry whistle
That greets my bikini by the sea,
I turn and I glower and I bristle—
But I'm happy to know the whistle's meant for
me!
I'm strictly a female female,
And my future, I hope, will be
In the home of a brave and free male
Who'll enjoy being a guy
Having a girl like me.

ENCORE

There is some part of every girl in me,
Though I try to be different from the others.
We have all got a tendency to be
Very much like our sisters and our mothers.
We have problems to solve at different ages—

We grow older, and up they come again!
They are always the same at different stages,
And they have to do with how to handle men.

From men we may take an awful beating;
They're pains in our pretty little necks.
But all girls are interested in eating—
And we must have another sex to pay the checks!

I'm strictly a female female,
And my future, I hope, will be
In the home of a brave and free male
Who'll enjoy being a guy
Having a girl like me.

I AM GOING TO LIKE IT HERE

Published in the vocal score. Introduced by Miyoshi Umeki (Mei Li). This song uses a poetic form called "pantoum" in which entire lines are repeated.

I am going to like it here.
There is something about the place,
An encouraging atmosphere,
Like a smile on a friendly face.

There is something about the place,
So caressing and warm it is—
Like a smile on a friendly face,
Like a port in a storm it is!

So caressing and warm it is—
All the people are so sincere,
Like a port in a storm it is,
I am going to like it here!

All the people are so sincere,
There's especially one I like.
I am going to like it here.
It's the father's first son I like!

There's especially one I like,
There is something about his face.
It's the father's first son I like—
He's the reason I love the place.

There is something about his face,
I would follow him anywhere.
If he goes to another place . . .
I am going to like it there!

LIKE A GOD

Published in the vocal score. Introduced by Ed Kenney (Wang Ta).

VERSE

Am I the man that you love?
If that is true, I am more,
Something beyond and above
The man that I was before.

REFRAIN

Like a god
With my head above the trees,
I can walk with a godlike stride.
With a step I can clear the seven seas,
When I know you are by my side.
Like a god
With a mountain in my hand
And my arm thrown around the sky—
All the world
Can be mine at my command,
When you're near and I hear you sigh.
When you're near and I hear you sigh,
There is no sweeter song I know.
With a heart full of hope I fly,
Higher I go,
Stronger I grow!
Like a god
I can tear away the mist
From the sky when you want it blue.
In the wake of the mist
Like a goddess you'll be kissed
By a god in love with you

CHOP SUEY

Published in the vocal score. Introduced by Juanita Hall (Madam Liang), Patrick Adiarte (Wang San), and ensemble.

REFRAIN 1

MADAM LIANG: Chop suey,
Chop suey,
Living here is very much like chop suey:
Hula Hoops and nuclear war,
Doctor Salk and Zsa Zsa Gabor,
Harry Truman, Truman Capote, and Dewey—
Chop Suey!
ENSEMBLE: Chop suey!
MADAM LIANG: Stars are drifting overhead,
Birds and worms have gone to bed.
Men work late in laboratories,
Others read detective stories,
Some are roaming round the country,
Others sit beneath just one tree.
Tonight on TV's late late show,
You can look at Clara Bow!
ENSEMBLE: Who?

REFRAIN 2

ALL: Chop suey!
Chop suey!
Good and bad, intelligent, mad and screwy.
MADAM LIANG: Violins and trumpets and drums—
Take it all the way that it comes.
Sad and funny, sour and honeydewy—
ALL: Chop suey!
MADAM LIANG: Ballpoint pens and filter tips,
Lipsticks and potato chips!
FOUR GIRLS: In the dampest kind of heat wave
You can give your hair a neat wave.
MADAM LIANG: Hear that lovely "La Paloma,"
Lullaby by Perry Coma!
WANG SAN: Dreaming in my Maidenform bra,
Dreamed I danced the cha-cha-cha—
GIRLS: Chop suey,
Chop suey—
BOYS: Cha, cha, cha-cha-cha,
Cha, cha, cha-cha-cha—
ALL: Mixed with all the hokum and ballyhooey—
MADAM LIANG: Something real and glowing and grand
Sheds a light all over the land—
ALL: Boston, Austin, Wichita, and St. Louis—
Chop suey!
Chop suey!
Chop suey!
Chop suey!
Chop suey!

ENCORE REFRAIN

ALL: Weather chilly all through Philly,
Hot and clammy in Miami—
MADAM LIANG: Mississippi River swollen—
Missus Astor's fur is stolen.
ALL: No!
MADAM LIANG: Thinks a juvenile delinquent

Knows exactly where her mink went!
Doctor Norman Vincent Peale
Tells you how to feel—
ALL: Big deal!
ALL: Chop suey,
Chop suey,
Rough and tough and brittle and
    soft and gooey—
Peking duck and Mulligan stew,
Plymouth Rock and Little Rock,
    too.
Milk and beer and Seven-Up and
    Drambuie—
Chop suey!
Chop suey!
Chop suey!
Chop suey!
Chop suey!

YOU BE THE ROCK

Not listed in the program. Published in the vocal score as "Jazz Bit." Introduced by Pat Suzuki (Linda Low) and Patrick Adiarte (Wang San).

LINDA: You be the rock,
    I'll be the roll.
SAN: You be the soup,
    I'll be the bowl.
    You be the furnace
    I'll be the coal.
    Rock, rock, rock!

DON'T MARRY ME

Published as an individual sheet. Introduced by Larry Blyden (Sammy Fong) and Miyoshi Umeki (Mei Li).

When Larry Blyden stepped into the role of Sammy during the Boston tryout, he insisted on an additional song for the character. Hammerstein wrote the lyric in about four days and told *Newsweek:* "It gives us a chance to show a more sympathetic side of the character he plays, and it allows Miyoshi, who joins him in it, to show a humorous side of her character."

VERSE

SAMMY: You are young and beautiful,
    Sweet as the breath of May.

Earnestly I speak to you—
Weigh every word I say:

REFRAIN 1

SAMMY: If you want to have a rosy future
    And be happy as a honey bee
    With a husband who will always love you,
        baby,
    Don't marry me!
    If you want a man you can depend on,
    I can absolutely guarantee
    I will never fail to disappoint you, baby,
    Don't marry me!
    I eat litchi nuts and cookies in bed,
    And I fill the bed with nutshells and
        crumbs.
    I have irritating habits you'll dread,
    Like the way I have of cracking my
        thumbs!
    My grandpa was a big game hunter,
    He met Grandma swinging on a tree—
    If you want to have attractive children,
        baby,
    Don't marry me!

REFRAIN 2

MEI LI: I would like to see my sons and daughters
    Sliding up and down their father's knee.
SAMMY: They'll get splinters in their little fannies,
        cookie,
    Don't marry me!
    I'm devoted to my dear old mama
    And if you and Mama disagree,
    I would always side with her against you,
        schnookie,
    Don't marry me!
MEI LI: I would always like to know where you
        go—
    I don't like a man to keep me in doubt.
SAMMY: Honey, that's a thing that's easy to know:
    You will always know where I am—I'm out!
    I am talking like a Chinese uncle,*
    I'm as serious as I can be,
    I am saying this because I love you,
        darling,
    Don't marry me!
    Marry a dope,
    Innocent and gaga.
    Marry a Khan—
    Ali or the Aga.
    Marry for money
    Or marry for free,
    But don't marry me!

---

* *In a fragmentary act-two reprise, Sammy sings:*
    In the presence of my Chinese uncles,

GRANT AVENUE

Published as an individual sheet. Introduced by Pat Suzuki (Linda Low) and ensemble.

REFRAIN

LINDA: Grant Avenue, San Francisco,
    California, U.S.A.
    Looks down
    From Chinatown
    Over a foggy bay.
    You travel there in a trolley,
    In a trolley up you climb—
    Dong dong!
    You're in Hong Kong,
    Having yourself a time.
    You can eat, if you are in the mood,
    Shark-fin soup, bean-cake fish.
    The girl who serves you all your food
    Is another tasty dish!
    You know you
    Can't have a new way of living
    Till you're living all the way
    On Grant Avenue.
ALL: Where is that?
LINDA: San Francisco,
    That's where's that!
    California,
    U.S.A.

INTERLUDE

LINDA: A Western street with Eastern manners.
    Tall pagodas and golden banners
    Throw their shadows through the lantern
        glow.
    You can shop for precious jade or
    Teakwood tables or silk brocade or
    See a bold and brassy nightclub show,
    On the most exciting thoroughfare I know.

REPEAT REFRAIN

LOVE, LOOK AWAY

Published as an individual sheet. Introduced by Arabella Hong (Helen Chao). The song was a hit for Tony Bennett.

VERSE

I have wished before,
I will wish no more . . .

REFRAIN

Love, look away!
Love, look away from me.
Fly when you pass my door,
Fly and get lost at sea.
Call it a day.
Love, let us say we're through,
No good are you for me,
No good am I for you.
Wanting you so, I try too much.
After you go, I cry too much.
Love, look away.
Lonely though I may be,
Leave me and set me free,
Look away, look away, look away from me.

Verse in published sheet music

They say you make the world go round,
They say you conquer all—
Love, won't you please stop conq'ring me?
Take someone your size,
I'm small.
Too small to fight against the odds,
Too tired to chase romance,
Knowing I need one man alone,
And knowing I have no chance.

FAN TAN FANNIE

Published in the vocal score. Introduced by Anita Ellis (Nightclub Singer) and female ensemble.

Fan Tan Fannie
Was leaving her man,
Fan Tan Fannie
Kept waving her fan,
Said, "Goodbye, Danny,
You two-timing Dan,
Some other man
Loves your little Fannie!
Bye, bye!
In the icebox
You'll find in a can,
Some leftovers
Of moo-goo-gai-pan.
Fan Tan Fannie

Has found a new guy,
His name is Manny,
He's good for Fannie,
So goodbye, Danny,
Goodbye."

GLIDING THROUGH MY MEMOREE

Published in the vocal score. Introduced by Jack Soo (Frankie Wing), who sings to nightclub girls dressed as various types.

VERSE

I am a vagabond sailor,
All my friends call me "sport."
I am a fellow for action,
Any storm in a port.
Now that I'm home and I'm resting,
Home from over the sea,
All of the girls who adored me
Go gliding through my memoree!

REFRAIN

A sweet colleen from Ireland,
Her hair was fiery red,
Her eyes gave out a green light
That said I could go ahead.
I met a girl in Sweden
Of whom I grew quite fond,
A stately Scandinavian type,
A buxom, blue-eyed blonde.
And then, in merry England,
A girl who worshipped me,
Gliding through my memoree—
That's how I see them,
Gliding through my memoree!
In sunny Barcelona,
A dancing chick I picked.
Her castanets were clicking
Like nothing ever clicked!
A very friendly ma'mselle
In oo-la-la Paree
She was a girl who couldn't say
Anything but oui!
'Twas fun to cast an anchor
In lovely Casablanker.
I loved a Grecian doll and
Another doll in Holland,
But of all the girls in every hemisphere,

There is no one like the girl I have right here—
Right here on . . .

[*Leads into reprise of "Grant Avenue."*]

THE OTHER GENERATION

Published in the vocal score. Introduced by Juanita Hall (Madam Liang) and Keye Luke (Wang Chi Yang). Reprised by Patrick Adiarte (Wang San) and children.

VERSE 1

WANG: I am puzzled by the attitude
    Of children over here.
    They are often disobedient,
    They seem to have no fear
    Of the father.
MADAM LIANG: They come home when they are
        tired out
    Or when they want to eat.
    And they act as if their coming
        home
    Were quite a special treat
    For the father.
WANG: My older son, at twenty-one,
    Has just discovered love,
    A complicated subject
    He knows very little of.
MADAM LIANG: Your younger son confuses me,
    The way he uses words,
    He tells me I am "cukey"
    And "something for the birds!"

REFRAIN 1

WANG: What are we going to do about
    The other generation?
MADAM LIANG: How will we ever communicate
    Without communication?
WANG: You don't know where they go or
        what they do—
MADAM LIANG: And what peculiar thoughts they
        think,
    They never reveal to you.
WANG: A very discouraging problem is
    The other generation.
    They want to lead a life that's all
        their own.
MADAM LIANG: Perhaps we ought to let them,
    Forsake them and forget them!
    But then we'd only find ourselves
        alone
BOTH: With one another!

I don't believe we'd like to be
alone!

VERSE 2

WANG: When you speak from your
experience,
You meet with cool disdain.
Every child is born with knowledge
Beyond the puny brain
Of the father.
MADAM LIANG: Every child is born with confidence
A parent can't achieve
And the kind of intuition
That compels him to believe
What he'd rather.
WANG: My older son has chosen a
daughter-in-law for me,
A dancer in a nightclub is my
daughter-in-law to be!
MADAM LIANG: She dances and undresses till she's
naked as a flea,
And everyone can look at—
BOTH: What he alone should see!

REFRAIN 2

BOTH: What are we going to do about
The other generation?
How will we ever communicate
Without communication?
MADAM LIANG: They never take the blame for one
mistake—
WANG: Oh, no!
Their parents are responsible
For every mistake they make!
BOTH: A very discouraging problem is
The other generation—
And soon there'll be another one as
well!
MADAM LIANG: And when our out-of-hand sons
Are bringing up our grandsons,
I hope our grandsons give their
fathers hell!
WANG: Can't wait to see it!
BOTH: I hope our grandsons give their
fathers hell!

Children's reprise

VERSE

SUSIE: Well, the more I see of grown-ups,
The less I want to grow.
ALL: The more I see what they have learned,
The less I want to know.
WANG SAN: And yet we've got to all grow up,
There's no place else to go.

SUSIE: I wonder why we're all so poor
And they've got all the dough!

REFRAIN

ALL: What are we going to do about
The other generation?
LUIS: How will we ever communicate
Without communication?
ALL: When we are using words the modern
way—
WANG SAN: They're much too big to try to dig
The colorful things we say.
SUSIE: If we could take over the training of
The other generation—
ALL: We know we could improve them quite
a lot.
BAAYORK: But they will never let us,
They stay the way they met us,
And so we're simply stuck with what
they've got.
SUSIE: You can't improve them.
ALL: The kids are simply stuck with what
they've got.

REFRAIN 2

ALL: What are we going to do about
The other generation?
BAAYORK: How are we going to stop them when
they
Start an explanation
Of what it used to mean to be a kid!
WANG SAN: The clean and wholesome fun they
had,
The innocent things they did!
SUSIE: They all had a wonderful childhood in
The other generation.
WANG SAN: The games they'd play were bright and
gay and loud.
BAAYORK: They used to shout "Red Rover,
Red Rover, please come over!"
SUSIE: They must've been an awful droopy
crowd
When they were younger.
ALL: They must have been an awful droopy
crowd.

SUNDAY

Published as an individual sheet. Introduced by Pat
Suzuki (Linda Low) and Larry Blyden (Sammy).

VERSE

LINDA: Now that we're going to be married,
I'll keep imagining things,
Things that can happen to people
When they are wearing gold rings.
SAMMY: Being together each morning,
Sharing our coffee and toast—
That's only one of the pictures.
Here's what I picture most:

REFRAIN

SAMMY: Sunday,
Sweet Sunday,
With nothing to do,
Lazy
And lovely,
My one day with you.
Hazy
And happy,
We'll drift through the day,
Dreaming the hours away.
While all the funny papers lie or fly
around the place,
I will try my kisses on your funny face.
Dozing,
Then waking
On Sunday, you'll see
Only
Me!

[LINDA *repeats refrain.*]

CUT AND UNUSED SONGS

MY BEST LOVE

Published as an individual sheet, but dropped before
Broadway. The song was originally intended for Keye
Luke (Wang Chi Yang). In Boston, Rodgers and Hammerstein tried having Juanita Hall (Madam Liang) sing
it instead.

VERSE

How can a young man know where his heart will go?
Only an old man knows what a man should know.
All that was true for me shall be true for you.
You are romantic, I was romantic too.

REFRAIN

A new true love you meet each day.
The girls are fresh and sweet, like buds in May.
Like buds that grow in May,
They bloom and blow away.
Then you meet your young bride-to-be,
Radiant and lovely is she!
When all the gay parade has passed,*
My best love comes last.

VARIANT REFRAIN

A new true love I'd meet each day.
The girls were fresh and sweet, like buds in May.
Like buds that grew in May,
They bloomed and blew away.
Then I met my young bride-to-be,
Radiant and lovely for me.
When all the gay parade had passed,
My best love came last.

---

* *Alternate line:*
    When all the other loves have passed,

MY ARMS ARE NOT BEING USED

Not published. No music is known to have been composed. This song was a precursor to "Love, Look Away."

My arms are not being used
By the man they were meant for—
The truth keeps banging away
Like a door in a gale.
My arms are not being used
By the man they were meant for—
The song keeps grinding along
Like a train on the rail.
The days I've spent on a dream
What on earth were they spent for?
The love that waits in my heart,
Where on earth can it go?
The joy that waits in my arms
For the man they were meant for,
The man they were meant for will never know!
The man they belong to will never know!

THE SOUND OF MUSIC (1959)

Tryouts: Shubert Theatre, New Haven, October 3–10, 1959; Shubert Theatre, Boston, October 13–November 6, 1959. New York run: Lunt-Fontanne Theatre: opened November 16, 1959; closed November 3, 1962; moved to Mark Hellinger Theatre, November 6, 1962; closed June 15, 1963; 1,443 performances total. Music by Richard Rodgers. Lyrics by Oscar Hammerstein II. Book by Howard Lindsay and Russel Crouse, suggested by *The Trapp Family Singers* by Maria Augusta Trapp. Produced by Leland Hayward, Richard Halliday, Richard Rodgers, and Oscar Hammerstein II. Directed by Vincent J. Donehue. Musical numbers staged by Joe Layton. Orchestrations by Robert Russell Bennett. Choral arrangements by Trude Rittman. Musical direction by Frederick Dvonch. Scenic design by Oliver Smith. Costumes by Lucinda Ballard. Mary Martin's clothes by Mainbocher. Lighting by Jean Rosenthal

Cast: Mary Martin (Maria Rainer), Theodore Bikel (Captain Georg von Trapp), Kurt Kasznar (Max Detweiler), Marion Marlowe (Elsa Schraeder), Lauri Peters (Liesl), Brian Davies (Rolf Gruber), Elizabeth Howell (Sister Berthe), Muriel O'Malley (Sister Margaretta), Patricia Neway (Mother Abbess), Karen Shepard (Sister Sophia), John Randolph (Franz), Nan McFarland (Frau Schmidt), Joseph Stewart (Kurt), Kathy Dunn (Louisa), William Snowden (Friedrich), Marilyn Rogers (Brigitta), Mary Susan Locke (Marta), Evanna Lien (Gretl), Luce Ennis (Ursula), Stefan Gierasch (Herr Zeller), Kirby Smith (Baron Elberfeld), Michael Gorrin (Admiral von Schreiber), and ensemble.

In Salzburg, Austria, in 1938, Maria, a postulant nun, becomes governess for the seven children of widower Captain Georg von Trapp. Maria relaxes the household's military discipline and teaches the children music. The Captain is engaged to sophisticated Elsa Schraeder but begins to fall in love with Maria. Maria runs to the Mother Abbess to ask for guidance and gets her blessing. A parallel plot line concerns the impending Anschluss. Even teenage Liesl's boyfriend becomes a Nazi supporter. Elsa and another houseguest, concert promoter Max Detweiler, warn the Captain not to oppose the new regime. His anti-Nazi stance is part of what breaks the engagement. When the Reich calls him for active service, he decides to leave Austria with Maria and the children. With Max's help, singing in a national festival becomes part of the family's escape plan. With the aid of the convent they manage to evade the soldiers and to flee across the mountains to Switzerland.

The production received Tony Awards for Best Musical (tied with *Fiorello!*); Best Leading Actress in a Musical, Mary Martin; Best Supporting Actress in a Musical, Patricia Neway; Best Music Direction, Frederick Dvonch; and Best Scenic Design for a Musical, Oliver Smith.

A national tour led by Florence Henderson began at the Riviera Theatre in Detroit on February 27, 1961, and visited thirty-five cities, ending in Toronto on November 23, 1963.

A London production opened at the Palace Theatre on May 18, 1961, and ran until January 14, 1967 (2,385 performances). That production became the longest-running American musical in the West End, and held the title for five decades. Other 1960s productions were staged in Melbourne, Johannesburg, and Tokyo. The show continues to be popular around the globe. At the beginning of the twenty-first century an American company has toured China and Southeast Asia, and Vienna's Volksoper has a German-language production in its repertory. Andrew Lloyd Webber's 2006 London Palladium production was preceded by a reality-television casting competition on BBC-TV called *How Do You Solve a Problem Like Maria?*

A film version, produced and directed by Robert Wise for Twentieth Century–Fox, was released March 2, 1965. Screenplay by Ernest Lehman. Associate producer: Saul Chaplin. Choreography by Marc Breaux and Dee Dee Wood. Production designed by Boris Leven. Orchestrated and conducted by Irwin Kostal. Photographed by Ted McCord. Edited by William Reynolds. Cast: Julie Andrews (Maria), Christopher Plummer (Captain von Trapp, singing dubbed by Bill Lee), Eleanor Parker (Elsa Schraeder), Richard Haydn (Max Detweiler), Peggy Wood (Mother Abbess, singing dubbed by Margery McKay), Charmian Carr (Liesl), Heather Menzies (Louisa), Nicholas Hammond (Friedrich), Duane Chase (Kurt), Angela Cartwright (Brigitta), Debbie Turner (Marta), Kym Karath (Gretl), Daniel Truhitte (Rolf), Anna Lee (Sister Margaretta), Portia Nelson (Sister Berthe), Marni Nixon (Sister Sophia), Evadne Baker (Sister Bernice). The film won five Academy Awards: for Best Picture; Best Director; Best Film Editing; Best Music, Scoring of Music, Adaptation or Treatment (Irwin Kostal); and Best Sound (James Corcoran and Fred Hynes). It is one of the most successful movie musicals ever.

There have been almost thirty cast recordings, including Dutch, Danish, Spanish, Swedish, Hebrew, and Japanese versions. The Grammy-winning original Broadway cast album was followed by, among others, a 1960 recording of the show's songs by members of the Trapp Family Singers; the film soundtrack (1965), which has sold more than 11 million copies worldwide; a 1988 studio cast led by Frederica von Stade; the 1998 Broadway revival cast, and the 2006 London cast. Individual songs have been covered in a range of styles, from Percy Faith to Benny Goodman, Herb Alpert, John Coltrane, and Gwen Stefani ("Wind It Up," inspired by "The Lonely Goatherd").

Information about the show and the *Sound of Music* phenomenon—which has extended to dress-up sing-along screenings of the film; themed tours in Salzburg, Austria; and performances of the musical by the famed Salzburg Marionettes—can be found in The *"Sound of Music" Companion* by Laurence Maslon; *The Sound of Music: The Making of America's Favorite Movie* by Julia Antopol Hirsch; as well as in memoirs by Richard Rodgers, Mary Martin, Theodore Bikel, and Charmian Carr.

The main sources for this chapter are the published vocal score and the published libretto. Many of the songs were published as individual sheets. The Oscar Hammerstein II Collection in the Music Division of the Library of Congress has lyric worksheets for most songs. The Richard Rodgers Collection has piano-vocal scores.

This chapter does not include "I Have Confidence" and "Something Good," which were written by Rodgers alone, after Hammerstein's death, for use in the film.

THE SOUND OF MUSIC

Published as an individual sheet. Introduced by Mary Martin (Maria).

VERSE

My day in the hills
Has come to an end, I know.
A star has come out
To tell me it's time to go.
But deep in the dark green shadows
Are voices that urge me to stay.
So I pause and I wait and I listen
For one more sound,
For one more lovely thing
That the hills might say . . .

REFRAIN

The hills are alive
With the sound of music,
With songs they have sung
For a thousand years.
The hills fill my heart
With the sound of music—
My heart wants to sing
Ev'ry song it hears.
My heart wants to beat
Like the wings
Of the birds that rise
From the lake to the trees.
My heart wants to sigh
Like a chime that flies
From a church on a breeze,

To laugh like a brook
When it trips and falls
Over stones in its way,*
To sing through the night
Like a lark who is learning to pray—!
I go to the hills
When my heart is lonely;
I know I will hear
What I've heard before—
My heart will be blessed
With the sound of music,
And I'll sing once more.

Draft refrain

Hammerstein's worksheets include a draft labeled "My final version before musical setting required changes." It uses the first eight lines of the refrain as above and then continues:

My heart wants to beat
Like the wings of the birds
That rise from the lake to the trees.
My heart wants to sigh
Like the tones of a chime
That float from a church on a breeze,
To laugh like a brook
When it trips on a stone,
To hum like the leaves on the vines,
To pray in the dark
Like a nightingale,
To sing through a storm like the pines.
The hills give me strength
When my heart is lonely
And lost in the fog
Of a thousand fears.
The hills fill my heart
With the sound of music
And my heart wants to sing,
My heart wants to sing,
My heart wants to sing
Every song it hears.

———

* *In the movie soundtrack, Julie Andrews sings "on its way." On the original cast recording and in the published libretto, the words are "in its way": that is the lyric Hammerstein wrote.*

MARIA

Published as an individual sheet. Introduced by Patricia Neway (Mother Abbess), Muriel O'Malley (Sister Margaretta), Elizabeth Howell (Sister Berthe), and Karen Shepard (Sister Sophia).

    Hammerstein worked on this lyric for seventeen days in late May and early June of 1959 and wrote forty-five pages of lyric ideas, potential rhymes, and early drafts.

VERSE

SISTER BERTHE: She climbs a tree and scrapes her knee,
Her dress has got a tear.
SISTER SOPHIA: She waltzes on her way to Mass
And whistles on the stair.
SISTER BERTHE: And underneath her wimple
She has curlers in her hair.
SISTER SOPHIA: I've even heard her singing in the abbey!
SISTER BERTHE: She's always late for chapel—
SISTER SOPHIA: But her penitence is real.
SISTER BERTHE: She's always late for everything
Except for ev'ry meal.
I hate to have to say it
But I very firmly feel
BERTHE AND SOPHIA: Maria's not an asset to the abbey.
SISTER MARGARETTA: I'd like to say a word in her behalf:
Maria . . . makes me . . . laugh!

REFRAIN

SISTER SOPHIA: How do you solve a problem like Maria?
MOTHER ABBESS: How do you catch a cloud and pin it down?
SISTER MARGARETTA: How do you find a word that means Maria?
SISTER BERTHE: A flibbertigibbet!
SISTER SOPHIA: A will-o'-the-wisp!
SISTER MARGARETTA: A clown!
MOTHER ABBESS: Many a thing you know you'd like to tell her,
Many a thing she ought to understand.
SISTER MARGARETTA: But how do you make her stay
And listen to all you say?
MOTHER ABBESS: How do you keep a wave upon the sand?

SISTER MARGARETTA: Oh, how do you solve a problem like Maria?
MOTHER ABBESS: How do you hold a moon beam in your hand?

INTERLUDE

SISTER MARGARETTA: When I'm with her I'm confused,
Out of focus and bemused,
And I never know exactly where I am.
SISTER BERTHE: Unpredictable as weather,
She's as flighty as a feather.
SISTER MARGARETTA: She's a darling!
SISTER BERTHE: She's a demon!
SISTER MARGARETTA: She's a lamb!
SISTER SOPHIA: She'll outpester any pest,
Drive a hornet from his nest.
SISTER BERTHE: She could throw a whirling dervish out of whirl.
SISTER MARGARETTA: She is gentle,
She is wild—
SISTER SOPHIA: She's a riddle,
She's a child.
SISTER BERTHE: She's a headache!
SISTER MARGARETTA: She's an angel!
MOTHER ABBESS: She's a girl . . .

REFRAIN

ALL FOUR: How do you solve a problem like Maria?
How do you catch a cloud and pin it down?
How do you find a word that means Maria?
SISTER MARGARETTA: A flibbertigibbet!
SISTER SOPHIA: A will-o'-the-wisp!
SISTER BERTHE: A clown!
ALL FOUR: Many a thing you know you'd like to tell her,
Many a thing she ought to understand,
MOTHER ABBESS: But how do you make her stay—
SISTER SOPHIA: And listen to all you say?
SISTER MARGARETTA: How do you keep a wave upon the sand?
ALL FOUR: Oh, how do you solve a problem like Maria?
How do you hold a moon beam in your hand?

MY FAVORITE THINGS

Published as an individual sheet. Introduced by Mary Martin (Maria) and Patricia Neway (Mother Abbess).

Raindrops on roses and whiskers on kittens,
Bright copper kettles and warm woolen mittens,
Brown paper packages tied up with strings—
These are a few of my favorite things.
Cream-colored ponies and crisp apple strudels,
Doorbells and sleigh bells and schnitzel with
    noodles,
Wild geese that fly with the moon on their wings—
These are a few of my favorite things.
Girls in white dresses with blue satin sashes,
Snowflakes that stay on my nose and eyelashes,
Silver-white winters that melt into springs—
These are a few of my favorite things.
When the dog bites,
When the bee stings,
When I'm feeling sad,
I simply remember my favorite things
And then I don't feel so bad!

DO-RE-MI

Published as an individual sheet. Introduced by Mary Martin (Maria), Lauri Peters (Liesl), William Snowden (Friedrich), Kathy Dunn (Louisa), Joseph Stewart (Kurt), Marilyn Rogers (Brigitta), Mary Susan Locke (Marta) and Evanna Lien (Gretl).

VERSE

MARIA: Let's start at the very beginning,
    A very good place to start.
    When you read you begin with A-B-C.
    When you sing you begin with
        do-re-mi.
CHILDREN: Do re mi?
MARIA: Do-re-mi.
    The first three notes just happen to be
    Do-re-mi.
CHILDREN: Do-re-mi!
MARIA: Do-re-mi-fa-so-la-ti.

REFRAIN

MARIA: Doe—a deer, a female deer,
    Ray—a drop of golden sun,
    Me—a name I call myself,
    Far—a long, long way to run,

Sew—a needle pulling thread,
La—a note to follow sew,
Tea—a drink with jam and bread.
That will bring us back to do!
Do-re-mi-fa-so-la-ti-do.
CHILDREN: So-do!

REPEAT REFRAIN WITH COUNTERMELODY

So-do-la-fa-me-do-re.
So-do-la-ti-do-re-do.
When you know the notes to sing,
You can sing most anything.

SIXTEEN GOING ON SEVENTEEN

Published as an individual sheet. Introduced by Brian Davies (Rolf) and Lauri Peters (Liesl); reprised in act two by Mary Martin (Maria) and Peters.

VERSE

ROLF: You wait, little girl, on an empty stage
    For fate to turn the light on.
    Your life, little girl, is an empty page
    That men will want to write on.
LIESL: To write on.

REFRAIN 1

ROLF: You are sixteen going on seventeen,
    Baby, it's time to think.
    Better beware,
    Be canny and careful,
    Baby, you're on the brink.
    You are sixteen going on seventeen,
    Fellows will fall in line,
    Eager young lads
    And roués and cads
    Will offer you food and wine.
    Totally unprepared are you
    To face a world of men.
    Timid and shy and scared are you
    Of things beyond your ken.
    You need someone older and wiser
    Telling you what to do . . .
    I am seventeen going on eighteen,
    I'll take care of you.

REFRAIN 2

LIESL: I am sixteen going on seventeen,
    I know that I'm naïve.

Fellows I meet
May tell me I'm sweet
And willingly I'll believe.
I am sixteen going on seventeen,
Innocent as a rose.
Bachelor dandies,
Drinkers of brandies—
What do I know of those?
Totally unprepared am I
To face a world of men,
Timid and shy and scared am I
Of things beyond my ken.
I need someone older and wiser
Telling me what to do . . .
You are seventeen going on eighteen,
I'll depend on you.

Act Two reprise

INTERLUDE*

MARIA: A bell is no bell till you ring it,
    A song is no song till you sing it,
    And love in your heart
    Wasn't put there to stay—
    Love isn't love
    Till you give it away.

REFRAIN

MARIA: When you're sixteen going on seventeen,
    Waiting for life to start,
    Somebody kind
    Who touches your mind
    Will suddenly touch your heart!
LIESL: When that happens, after it happens,
    Nothing is quite the same.
    Somehow you know
    You'll jump up and go
    If ever he calls your name!
MARIA: Gone are your old ideas of life,
    The old ideas grow dim—
    Lo and behold, you're someone's wife,
    And you belong to him!
    You may think this kind of adventure
    Never may come to you . . .
    Darling sixteen-going-on-seventeen,
    Wait—a year—or two.
LIESL: I'll wait a year
BOTH: Or two.

_____

These six lines were written originally as a prelude to "Climb Ev'ry Mountain," but never were used in that song.

THE LONELY GOATHERD

Published as an individual sheet. Introduced by Mary Martin (Maria), Lauri Peters (Liesl), William Snowden (Friedrich), Kathy Dunn (Louisa), Joseph Stewart (Kurt), Marilyn Rogers (Brigitta), Mary Susan Locke (Marta), and Evanna Lien (Gretl).

In December 2006, Gwen Stefani's song "Wind It Up," which samples "The Lonely Goatherd," entered the Top 10 of *Billboard*'s Hot 100 chart. The song and the music video charted across Europe as well as in India, China, and Latin America.

VERSE 1

High on a hill was a lonely goatherd,
Layee odl, layee odl layee oo,
Loud was the voice of the lonely goatherd,
Layee odl layee odl oo.
Folks in a town that was quite remote heard
Layee odl, layee odl layee oo,
Lusty and clear from the goatherd's throat, heard
Layee odl layee odl oo.

REFRAIN

O ho lay-dee odl lee o
O ho lay-dee odl ay!
O ho lay-dee odl lee o
Hodl odl lee-o-lay!

VERSE 2

A prince on the bridge of a castle moat heard
Layee odl, layee odl layee oo.
Men on a road with a load to tote heard
Layee odl layee odl oo.
Men in the midst of a table d'hôte heard
Layee odl layee odl layee ee oo.
Men drinking beer with a foam afloat heard
Layee odl layee odl oo.

REFRAIN

O ho lay-dee odl lee o
O ho lay-dee odl ay!
O ho lay-dee odl lee o
Hodl odl lee-o-lay!

VERSE 3

One little girl in a pale pink coat heard
Layee odl, layee odl layee oo.
She yodeled back to the lonely goatherd,
Layee odl layee odl oo.
Soon her mama with a gleaming gloat heard
Layee odl layee odl layee oo—

What a duet for a girl and goatherd,
Layee odl layee odl oo!

REFRAIN

O ho lay-dee odl lee o
O ho lay-dee odl ay!
O ho lay-dee odl lee o
Hodl odl lee-o-lay!

CODA

Happy are they—lay dee o ladee lee o,
O lay dee o day dee lay dee o!
Soon the duet will become a trio,
Layee odl layee odl oo!
Hodi lay-ee
Hodi lay-ee
Hodi lay-ee
Hodi lay-ee
Hodi lay-ee
Hodi lay-ee
O-de-layee odl lee-ee odl lay!

HOW CAN LOVE SURVIVE?

Introduced by Marion Marlowe (Elsa Schraeder) and Kurt Kasznar (Max). The song is directed to Captain von Trapp, but he has no singing lines.

VERSE

MAX: In all the famous love affairs
The lovers have to struggle.
In garret rooms away upstairs
The lovers starve and snuggle.
They're famous for misfortune which
They seem to have no fear of,
While lovers who are very rich
You very seldom hear of.

REFRAIN 1

ELSA: No little shack do you share with me,
We do not flee from a mortgagee,
Nary a care in the world have we—
MAX: How can love survive?
ELSA: You're fond of bonds and you own a lot,
I have a plane and a diesel yacht—
MAX: Plenty of nothing you haven't got!
BOTH: How can love survive?
ELSA: No rides for us
On the top of a bus
In the face of the freezing breezes.

MAX: You reach your goals
[*to the* CAPTAIN] In your comfy old Rolls
[*to* ELSA] Or in one of your Mercedeses!
ELSA: Far, very far off the beam are we,
Quaint and bizarre as a team are we,
Two millionaires with a dream are we,
We're keeping romance alive,
Two millionaires with a dream are we—
We'll make our love survive . . .

REFRAIN 2

ELSA: No little cold-water flat have we,
Warmed by the glow of insolvency—
MAX: Up to your necks in security,
How can love survive?
ELSA: How can I show what I feel for you?
I cannot go out and steal for you,
I cannot die like Camille for you—
How can love survive?
MAX: You millionaires
With financial affairs
Are too busy for simple pleasure.
When you are poor
It is *toujours l'amour*—
For *l'amour* all the poor have leisure!
ELSA: Caught in our gold-plated chains are we,
Lost in our wealthy domains are we,
Trapped by our capital gains are we,
But we'll keep romance alive—
MAX: Trapped by your capital gains are we—
ELSA: We'll make our love survive!

Discarded refrain

These lines are from an earlier draft for Elsa and the Captain, whose title had one more word: "How Can Our Love Survive?"

CAPTAIN AND ELSA: All of the clothes that we wear
are new.
CAPTAIN: I own a lake and a mountain,
too.
ELSA: I own a street and an avenue!
BOTH: How can our love survive?
ELSA: I own some soil
That is oozing with oil,
I have emeralds as big as roses.
CAPTAIN: Blue chips have I
That are stacked up as high
As an ostrich up on his toes is!
ELSA: We're fond of golf, and a
course have we.
Every financial resource have
we—
CAPTAIN: Rolls that would choke any
horse have we,

But we'll keep romance alive.
BOTH: Rolls that would choke any
horse have we,
Yet will our love survive.

SO LONG, FAREWELL

Published as an individual sheet. Introduced by Lauri
Peters (Liesl), William Snowden (Friedrich), Kathy
Dunn (Louisa), Joseph Stewart (Kurt), Marilyn Rogers
(Brigitta), Mary Susan Locke (Marta), and Evanna Lien
(Gretl).

THE CHILDREN: There's a sad sort of clanging
From the clock in the hall
And the bells in the steeple, too;
And up in the nurs'ry
An absurd little bird
Is popping out to say "coo-coo."
(Coo-coo, coo-coo.)
Regretfully they tell us
But firmly they compel us
To say goodbye to you . . .
So long, farewell,
Auf Wiedersehen, good night.
MARTA: I hate to go and leave this pretty
sight.
CHILDREN: So long, farewell,
Auf Wiedersehen, adieu.
KURT: *Adieu, adieu*
To yieu and yieu and yieu.
CHILDREN: So long, farewell,
Au'voir, auf Wiedersehen.
LIESL: I'd like to stay and taste my first
Champagne.
[*spoken*] No?
CAPTAIN: [*spoken*] No!
CHILDREN: So long, farewell,
Auf Wiedersehen, goodbye.
FRIEDRICH: I leave and heave a sigh and say
goodbye!
Goodbye!
BRIGITTA: I'm glad to go, I cannot tell a lie.
LOUISA: I flit, I float, I fleetly flee, I fly.
GRETL: The sun has gone to bed and so
must I.
So long, farewell,
Auf Wiedersehen, goodbye.
Goodbye, goodbye, goodbye.

CLIMB EV'RY MOUNTAIN

Published as an individual sheet. Introduced by Patricia
Neway (Mother Abbess). Hammerstein's working title
was "Face Life."

Theater historian Max Wilk, who has written about
Oklahoma! and *The Sound of Music*, notes that the
song's message developed through correspondence with
Sister Gregory, a teacher at Rosary College in River Forest, Illinois. In a February 23, 1958, letter about the
religious vocation, she framed two essential questions—
"What does God want me to do with my life? How does
he wish me to spend my love?"—which Hammerstein
copied out on a lyric sheet dated August 18.

Climb ev'ry mountain,
Search high and low,
Follow ev'ry byway,
Every path you know.
Climb ev'ry mountain,
Ford ev'ry stream,
Follow ev'ry rainbow
Till you find your dream.
A dream that will need all the love you can give
Ev'ry day of your life for as long as you live.
Climb ev'ry mountain,*
Ford ev'ry stream,
Follow ev'ry rainbow
Till you find your dream.

NO WAY TO STOP IT

Published in the vocal score. Introduced by Theodore
Bikel (Captain von Trapp), Kurt Kasznar (Max), and
Marion Marlowe (Elsa).

VERSE

ELSA: You dear, attractive, dewy-eyed
idealist—

---

* *An early version ended with these lines instead:*
Search ev'ry forest,
Dark though it be.
Follow ev'ry valley
To its own blue sea.
Climb ev'ry mountain,
High though it seem—
Never be contented
Till you find your dream . . .
Find your dream!

Today you have to learn to be a realist!
MAX: You may be bent on doing deeds of
derring-do,
But up against a shark what can a
herring do?
ELSA: Be wise, compromise!
CAPTAIN: Compromise and be wise.
ELSA: Let them think you're on their side,
Be noncommital.
CAPTAIN: I will *not* bow my head to the men I
despise.
MAX: You don't have to bow your head,
Just stoop a little!

REFRAIN

ELSA: Why not learn to put your faith and
your reliance
On an obvious and simple fact of
science?
A crazy planet full of crazy people
Is somersaulting all around the sky,
And ev'ry time it turns another
somersault,
Another day goes by!
And there's no way to stop it,
No, there's no way to stop it,
No, you can't stop it even if you try.
So I'm not going to worry,
No, I'm not going to worry,
Ev'ry time I see another day go by.
MAX: While somersaulting at a cockeyed
angle,
We make a cockeyed circle round the
sun.
And when we circle back to where we
started from,
Another year has run.
And there's no way to stop it,
No, there's no way to stop it
If the earth wants to roll around the
sun!
You're a fool if you worry,
You're a fool if you worry
Over anything but little Number One!
CAPTAIN: That's you!
ELSA: That's I.
MAX: And I.
CAPTAIN: And me!
That all-absorbing character—
ELSA: That fascinating creature—
MAX: That super-special feature—
ALL THREE: Me!
CAPTAIN: So ev'ry star and ev'ry whirling
planet,
And ev'ry constellation in the sky
Revolve around the center of the
universe,

A lovely thing called I!

ALL THREE: And there's no way to stop it,
No, there's no way to stop it,
And I know though I cannot tell you
why.
That as long as I'm living,
Just as long as I'm living,
There'll be nothing else as wonderful
as—

ELSA: I!

ALL THREE: I—I—I
Nothing else as wonderful as I!

AN ORDINARY COUPLE

Published in the vocal selection. Introduced by Mary Martin (Maria) and Theodore Bikel (Captain von Trapp).

REFRAIN

An ordinary couple
Is all we'll ever be,
For all I want of living
Is to keep you close to me;
To laugh and weep together
While time goes on its flight,
To kiss you ev'ry morning
And to kiss you ev'ry night.
We'll meet our daily problems,
And rest when day is done,
Our arms around each other
In the fading sun.
An ordinary couple,
Across the years we'll ride,
Our arms around each other,
And our children by our side . . .
Our arms around each other.

Verse from published sheet

This verse appears in the sheet music, but is not used in the play and is not in the vocal score.

If ever we are married
I'll never pretend to any dream of any greater
glory
Than just to be your husband, your lover, your
friend
And live with you an old and simple story.

EDELWEISS

Published as an individual sheet. Introduced by Theodore Bikel (Captain von Trapp), Mary Martin (Maria von Trapp), and the children.

In 1970, Rodgers answered a question about the origin of the song, writing:

I am happy to tell you that the song "Edelweiss" from *The Sound of Music* is not an old tune but one which I wrote when the musical play was being tried out in New Haven. I felt that the Captain in the play needed a song of his own to sing in the little concert given just before the finale. I wanted something that had a "folk" quality and had the tune ready for Oscar Hammerstein II when he was well enough to visit Boston during our run there. He then wrote the words and we put the song in the show.

It was Hammerstein's last complete lyric.

Edelweiss,
Edelweiss,
Every morning you greet me.
Small and white,
Clean and bright,
You look happy to meet me.
Blossom of snow,
May you bloom and grow,
Bloom and grow forever—
Edelweiss,
Edelweiss,
Bless my homeland forever.

CUT AND UNUSED SONGS

LOVE IS NOT BLIND

Not published and not used. No music is known to have been written. A typed lyric sheet says that as the nuns help her dress for the wedding, Maria "explains what it has meant to her to fall in love."

Love is not blind,
I have never seen so clearly.
Love is not a fool,
I have never been so wise.
Every time I see a smile

On the lips I love so dearly,
The truth and the wonder of all the world
Are shining before my eyes.
Love is not blind
I have never seen so clearly.
Love is not a dream,
Though in dreaming love may start.
Every time I feel the touch
Of a hand I love so dearly,
The joy and the glory of all the world
Are dancing around my heart.
I have learned how remarkable a smile can be
When it's meant for me alone.
I have learned how remarkable a hand can be
When it lingers in my own.
I have looked through the blossoms of a moonlit
tree
At a bird or a cloud or a star,
And I know what a miracle a sky can be
When someone is looking at the sky with me—
When you love
You can see so clearly.
When you love
You become so wise
With the truth and the wonder
And joy of the world
Shining before your eyes,
Shining in all their glory,
Shining before your eyes.

I HAVE LOVED AND I'VE LEARNED

Not published and not used. Written in June 1959.

VERSE

I used to lend my heart
To quick romance;
Now I defend my heart,
I take no chance,
No longer play around
With childish hopes—
I know my way around,
I know the ropes.

REFRAIN

I have loved
And I've learned
Not to leap
For the bait,
I have learned

Not to leap before I look.
I have loved
And I've learned
That the bait
That looks great
May be bait
That will land me on a hook.
No more leaping,
I'm worldly wise.
I keep sweeping
Stars out of my eyes.
I have loved
And been burned
By the flame
And I've learned
How to run
When I feel the faintest glow,
But
You can make me forget all I know,
Darling, I'm forgetting all I know.

Hammerstein at his captain's desk in the study at Highland Farm, Doylestown, Pennsylvania. The sampler on the wall behind him has the lyrics of "The Sweetest Sight."

Undated Lyrics

UNDATED LYRICS

AM I TOO OPTIMISTIC, MISS O'DAY?

A neat copy in Hammerstein's hand, with one stage direction, was found among unpublished material in the Hammerstein Collection in the Music Division of the Library of Congress.

When you talk, you are charming,
Miss O'Day, Miss O'Day.
When you talk, you are charming,
Miss O'Day, Miss O'Day.
It is not what you say,
It is just the way
That you say what you say, Miss O'Day.
You are sweet when you're silent,
Miss O'Day, Miss O'Day.
With a look or a sigh
Or a downcast eye
You can say what you say, Miss O'Day.
Now we are at your doorway,
Now we must say good night.
What, Miss O'Day, is your way,
Your way of saying good night?
Am I too optimistic,
Miss O'Day, Miss O'Day?
Or can you say good night
With your lips pressed tight?

[*Take long breath.*]

That's the way, Miss O'Day, that's the way.

AS LOVELY AS YOU SEEM

Music by Sigmund Romberg. A typed lyric sheet was found among unpublished material in the Hammerstein Collection in the Music Division of the Library of Congress. Musical-theater historian Michael Feinstein provided the editor with a copyist piano-vocal score, including a verse that he had discovered in a Warner Bros. archive. Even with the character names as clues, neither the editor nor William A. Everett, author of *Sigmund Romberg* (Yale University Press, 2007), have been able to identify the story for which it was written.

VERSE

PAUL: Oriental star[s] are caught in a cloud,
Spread upon a velvet sky,
Slaves are being bought and sold in a
crowd,
Oriental night is flying.
I am unconcerned with man and his fate,
I've a problem of my own.
LIANE: [*spoken*] What are you doing there, sir!
PAUL: What am I doing here?
LIANE: [*spoken*] Sir!

REFRAIN

PAUL: I'm wondering if you can really be
As lovely as you seem.
Wondering if you can really be
The answer to my dream.
Looking in your eyes, I ask myself,
"Can eyes be so divine?"
Looking at your lips, I ask myself,
"Can they be meant for mine?"
When once I win your arms
I'll find within your arms
The sweet reply to the question I'm asking
all the time,
Wondering if you can really be
As lovely as you seem,
Wondering if you can really be
The answer to my dream.

THE DUTCH TREAT CLUB

Music by Richard Rodgers. Not published. Founded in Manhattan in 1905, the Dutch Treat Club still holds weekly luncheons with entertainment from the worlds of arts and letters. Rodgers's membership began in 1939 and Hammerstein was enrolled in 1947. In the spring of 1957—"fifteen years and ten nights" since the opening of *Oklahoma!*—the club gave the songwriting pair a gold medal for distinction in the arts; but there is no evidence linking this number to that occasion.

VERSE 1

There are baseball clubs and bridge clubs
And clubs for the men who row;
There's the dear old Union League Club
(A branch of the C.I.O.).
There are breakfast clubs and nightclubs
And clubs for picking flow'rs;
And they all may have their virtues—
But you cannot say that about ours!

REFRAIN

Give a cheer for the dear Dutch Treat Club,
A club with no purpose at all.
Our clubhouse is a ballroom
Where we never give a ball.
As a matter of fact we're not Dutch [*clap, clap*]
As a matter of fact we don't treat [*clap, clap*]
As a matter of fact we're not a club,
So why the hell do we meet?

VERSE 2

There are clubs for hunting foxes
And clubs for the men who fish,
There are boxing clubs for he-men
And clubs for the boys who swish.
There are clubs where men meet women,
And if you have the pluck
You may stay with them for dinner
And they'll give you one hell of a duck!

REPEAT REFRAIN

I FOUND YOU IN APRIL

A typed lyric sheet was found among unpublished material in the Hammerstein Collection in the Music Division of the Library of Congress. This may be a verse for a song titled "Autumn Is Here," but no such refrain has been located.

I found you in April,
And having the faith
Of a vine on a wall
That climbs towards the moon,
I hoped for you
And won your kisses
One morning in June.
The green cloak of summer was turned by the sun
To saffron and crimson and gold.
The cloak has fallen and time has run
And I have lost ev'ry kiss I won,
And my arms have nothing to hold.

Autumn is here . . .

I HAVE SEEN THE STARLIGHT

Music by Arthur Hammerstein. A hastily written lyric in Hammerstein's hand was found among unpublished material in the Hammerstein Collection in the Music Division of the Library of Congress. A piano-vocal score in another hand was provided by Alice Hammerstein Mathias. When asked if the song was intended for a particular project, she said songs written with Uncle Arthur were generally written to please Uncle Arthur. Hammerstein biographer Hugh Fordin speculated that it expressed Hammerstein's anguish about being in love with Dorothy Jacobson while they were both married to others.

VERSE

Lying here alone upon the tropic sands,
Gazing at a sky that no one understands,
Gazing at the sky and lying here alone,
I'm wond'ring how and why I lost a world I used
    to own.

REFRAIN

I have seen the starlight in the palm trees,
I have seen the moonlight on the sea,
I've looked at night and I've been happy
Because you looked at night with me.
There are times when starlight leaves the palm trees,
There are times when moonlight leaves the sea.
But they come back to them
When once the clouds have passed—
Dear, why, oh why don't you come back to me?

I'M GLAD I AM YOUNG

This lyric in Hammerstein's hand appears on a leadsheet in Romberg's hand, titled "No. 1 Rosa and Paul," found in the miscellaneous Romberg manuscripts in the Music Division of the Library of Congress.

VERSE

Linnets in a tree are singing away,
Meadowlarks agree with all that they say:
"Here is night, lovely night,
Here's a night in May!"
You are seventeen and I'm twenty-one,
We are both in love and life has begun.
I don't look back on the past

Or await a future day.
I am living
For the present,
For this night in May!

REFRAIN

I'm glad I am young,
I'm glad you are fair,
I'm glad we are both romantic.
I'm glad that the moon is riding the sky
And whip-poor-wills croon a sweet lullaby.
I'm glad I am young,
I'm glad you are fair.
No wonder my dreams can thrive
With you in my arms and spring in the air,
No wonder I'm glad I'm alive!

I'M SO YOUNG

A handwritten lyric sheet was found among unpublished material in the Hammerstein Collection in the Music Division of the Library of Congress. The editor associates Hammerstein's cursive-style handwriting with the 1920s, but there is no firm evidence of the date.

I'm so young,
And you're my big illusion.
I'm so young,
And you're my first confusion.
Ma thinks you're awful
And Pa thinks you're worse.
My friends say it's unlawful,
I should have a nurse!
Maybe you
Are not a big go-getter.
Maybe you
Are just a lukewarm [fretter?]
But I'm so young,
I don't know any better,
And I think you're grand.

IN THE SUMMER

This fragment of a lyric or poem in Hammerstein's hand was found among unpublished material in the Hammerstein Collection in the Music Division of the Library of Congress.

In the summer when the hay was long,
I was happy as the day was long.
Lazily I drowsed,
Drowsily I lay
In the hay when the day was long.
But that's all over.

INERTIA

A lyric typed on lined paper, and some handwritten notes, were found among unpublished material in the Hammerstein Collection in the Music Division of the Library of Congress. The subject suggests a connection to Hammerstein's work in the 1940s and 1950s with the United World Federalists.

Inertia.
How I love that place!
We loll all day in languid grace,
And facts are what we never face
In Inertia, my old home.
Inertia—
If the signs all say
Tomorrow's war is on the way,
We make believe it's yesterday
In Inertia, my old home.
Inertians are a race you cannot reach.
We live behind a wall of patient smiles,
And all the folk with new ideas to teach
We look upon as harmless juveniles.
Inertians knew the steamboat
Was merely Fulton's folly;
Inertians knew the earth could not be round.
Inertians knew that Hitler
Was quaint and rather jolly
And all his threats were nothing more than sound.
Supported by this record of what we've said
    before,
We confidently tell you now
"There always will be war!"

THE STARS IN THE WINDOW

A handwritten lyric was found among unpublished material in the Hammerstein Collection in the Music Division of the Library of Congress.

The stars in the window
Are crystal and cold;
Outside is silver,
Inside is gold.
The glow of the firelight
Caresses your hair
(From the way that it dances
It's glad to be there).
I read you a story,
You knit me a sock.
The cat starts to blink
And we look at the clock.
The flames are now embers
And gone is their gleam—
The end of an evening
Just a part of my dream.
And new dreams are born
As the evening grows old,
Outside is silver,
Inside is gold.

THANK YOU FOR LOVING ME

Music by Jerome Kern. Not published. Date not known; could be 1930s or '40s. Typed and holograph lyric sheets were found at the Rodgers & Hammerstein Organization. A copyist piano-vocal score is in the Kern Collection at the Library of Congress. In an October 6, 1958, letter to Eva Kern (who was then Mrs. George Byron), Hammerstein confirmed: "I did write the lyric to 'Thank You for Loving Me.' I don't remember all of it, but I know that I wrote a setting to this music which originally was incidental music for a song in *Music in the Air* where Karl bandages Sieglinde's leg."

We have walked together
Down a primrose lane.
We have seen a sunrise
Come out of the sea.
The world is thrilling and joyous again—
Thank you for loving me.
I have run to meet you,
Eager for your kiss,
Like a bursting blossom
Awaiting a bee.
I know that heaven is something like this—
Thank you for loving me.
And now, if you no longer feel the flame upon you,
If passion's faint perfume has died away,
I'll make no pitiful appeal, or claim upon you.
I love you far too much to ask you to stay.
If the dance is over,

Let it be the end.
Dance away, my lover,
Be happy and free!
Goodbye and bless you, my sweetheart—my friend.
Thank you for loving me.

A TYPICAL AMERICAN FAMILY

The following fragments are from a sheaf of handwritten worksheets found in Hammerstein's folder of "Song Ideas."

In Maine or Kentucky or Texas
You'll meet us wherever you roam
A typical American family
In a typical American home.

We live in a house
Where the doorknob is loose
And somehow it never gets fixed.
Our clocks and our watches can never agree
And our handkerchiefs always get mixed.

Brother and sis [pick?] out mealtimes
To do all their wrangling and squawking.
Parents are seen but seldom heard,
The children do most of the talking.

To wash your hands in the bathroom
Is not such an easy proceeding.
It's hard to get in when Father's home,
That's where he does all his reading.

WE WERE ONCE LITTLE GIRLS AND BOYS

This lyric fragment handwritten by Hammerstein on an index card, was found in his "Song Ideas" file.

We were once little girls and boys.
GIRLS: We were girls, we made dolls.
MEN: We were boys, we [made?] noise
Silly and simple and healthy
Now we are nervous and wealthy
In a world of confusion and noise.
If you look close underneath our
[neuroses?]

You'll find little girls and boys.
We are still little girls and boys.

WHAT'S A LITTLE KISS? (WALTZ FRAGMENT)

This unidentified typed stanza was found among unpublished material in the Hammerstein Collection in the Music Division of the Library of Congress.

What's a little kiss?
Just a pair of lips that meet another pair.
Was it more than this
When you held me in your arms and found me fair?
Was it more than this
When we said goodbye?
Just a morning star
Weeping, while its light was fading from the sky.

ANOTHER DANCE

This lyric, typed on Oscar Hammerstein II stationery was found among unpublished material in the Hammerstein Collection in the Music Division of the Library of Congress.

Another dance
Before we kiss
And say goodbye,
Another dance
Before the stars
Begin to die.
Hold me and cling to me tight,
Cling to this last lovely night.
Another day
And who can say
Where you may be?
Your ship of gray
Will sail away
Across the sea,
But I'll go on dreaming we're dancing,
And I will dream
Till you come home to me.

Index

This is an alphabetical index of song titles and first lines (including first refrains) of Oscar Hammerstein's lyrics. When the first line of a refrain begins with or is identical to the song title, the first line is not included. Alternate titles are listed except where they duplicate first lines. The index also includes individual song copyright information.

The following copyright information should be added to individual notices according to the corresponding number:

Publishing rights in those songs whose copyright information ends with (1) are currently controlled by Universal Music Publishing Group, 2440 Sepulveda Boulevard, Suite 100, Los Angeles, CA 90064. All songs published by Universal Music Publishing Group have music by Jerome Kern unless otherwise indicated.

Publishing rights in those songs whose copyright information ends with (2) are currently controlled by EMI Music Publishing, 75 Ninth Avenue, 4th Floor, New York, NY 10011.

Publishing rights in all other songs on the list are controlled by Williamson Music Company, 229 West 28th Street, 11th Floor, New York, NY 10001.

Permission to publish any of the songs in any form must be obtained from its indicated publisher prior to publication.

A NOTE ON THE TYPE

The text of this book was set in Bodoni, a typeface named for Giambattista Bodoni, born at Saluzzo, Piedmont, in 1740. The son of a printer, Bodoni went to Rome as a young man to serve as an apprentice at the press of the Propaganda. In 1768 he was put in charge of the Stamperia Reale in Parma by Duke Ferdinand, a position he held until his death in 1813, in spite of many offers by royal patrons to tempt him elsewhere. His earliest types were those imported from the Paris typefoundry of Fournier, but gradually these were superseded by his own designs, which, in the many distinguished books he printed, became famous all over Europe. His later arrangements with the duke allowed him to print for anyone who would employ him, and with the commissions that flowed in he was able to produce books in French, Russian, German, and English, as well as Italian, Greek, and Latin. His *Manuale tipografico*, issued in 1818 by his widow, is one of the finest specimen books issued by a printer/type designer.

Composed by Creative Graphics,
Allentown, Pennsylvania

Printed and bound by R. R. Donnelley,
Shenzhen, China